OLD TESTAMENT THEOLOGY

THE OLD TESTAMENT LIBRARY

Editorial Advisory Board

Horst Dietrich Preuss

OLD TESTAMENT THEOLOGY
Volume II

Westminster John Knox Press
Louisville, Kentucky

Translated by Leo G. Perdue from *Theologie des Alten Testaments,* Band II: *Israel's Weg mit JHWH,* published 1992 by W. Kohlhammer, Stuttgart

© 1992 W. Kohlhammer GmbH

English translation © 1996 Westminster John Knox Press

Book design by Drew Stevens

First published 1996
by Westminster John Knox Press
Louisville, Kentucky

This book is printed on acid-free paper that meets the American National Standards Institute Z39.48 standard. ♾

PRINTED IN THE UNITED STATES OF AMERICA

96 97 98 99 00 01 02 03 04 05 — 10 9 8 7 6 5 4 3 2 1

Library of Congress Cataloging-in-Publication Data

Preuss, Horst Dietrich, 1927–
[Theologie des Alten Testaments. English]
Old Testament Theology / Horst Dietrich Preuss.
p.   cm. — (Old Testament library)
Includes bibliographical references and indexes.
ISBN 0-664-21844-X (v. 1 : alk. paper)
ISBN 0-664-21843-1 (v. 2 : alk. paper)
1. Bible. O.T.—Theology.   I. Title.   II. Series.
BS1192.5.P6913   1995
230—dc20   95-19162

CONTENTS

PREFACE

This second volume of my *Old Testament Theology* was able to appear some six months after the publication of Volume I in the autumn of 1991. For this I am grateful. The manuscript for Volume II was completed in March 1991.

Since both volumes form a unity in my effort to comprehend the world of the Old Testament's witness, there is not in Volume II a new enumeration of main sections and chapters. Rather, those which appear in Volume I are continued.

I am thankful once again for the significant support provided me by the Reverend Doctor Jutta Hausmann and the Reverend Michael Baldeweg. Mrs. Andrea Siebert once more typed the manuscript in its final form.

The conclusion of this work corresponded with my transition to retirement. Thus, at this time I have taken the opportunity to look back at the lengthy number of years of teaching and the many women and men students whom I encountered during this time in Celle, Göttingen, and finally here in Neuendettelsau. In numerous discussions I have learned much from their questions and I have received from them a great deal of encouragement for what is presented here.

I dedicate therefore this book to these men and women students to whom I am grateful and whom I remember with great fondness.

Horst Dietrich Preuss

Neuendettelsau
August 1991

PART THREE. THE CONSEQUENCES OF AND FURTHER THINKING ABOUT PRIMAL ELECTION: ADDITIONAL OBJECTS OF THE HISTORICAL, ELECTING ACTS OF YHWH

Yahweh's historical election and obligation of the nation stand at the center of the Old Testament. According to the Old Testament witness, the people of Israel were constituted by the exodus and Sinai, and thus from their very origins they belonged to YHWH. Nevertheless, on their journey with and under YHWH they encountered phenomena that engaged their faith as something new and different. YHWH, the God of the exodus and of Sinai, guided the group chosen by him into the land of Canaan, an act that led to a new situation with which the nature of their faith had to contend.[1] On the one hand, population groups were encountered here and there that joined with the Moses group, who worshiped YHWH. On the other hand, when this group took up residence in the land of Canaan, they came across other tribes who had already settled there. Through the coalescence of these different groups a society was formed and then a nation. These early inhabitants of Canaan, who eventually merged with the YHWH worshipers who later settled the land, quite naturally possessed their own traditions of faith. These traditions were not at all identical with Yahwistic faith even if in certain areas the two may have been compatible. The so-called "narratives of the ancestors" reflect this situation (see chapter 6). There were conflicts with portions of the early Canaanite inhabitants,[2] and the problems connected with these conflicts were given and continued to receive both a dimension of faith and a theological interpretation. Israel's historical journey continued in the land of Canaan. Charismatic "judges" were successful in securing Israel's possession of the land of Canaan against external enemies. A kingship that was foreign to this point, both to YHWH and to Israel, arose because of the increasing pressure on the "tribes" that had united (see chapter 7). Jerusalem, previously settled by non-Israelites, was integrated into the newly emerging Kingdom of Israel and Judah as its capital city and introduced not only things that were new but also beliefs that were foreign to Yahwistic faith. Even so, these new elements also found their proper place (cf. chapter 8). Jerusalem, the city of God, came to have a temple of YHWH that eventually gained a position of prominence, thus raising the question about the position and function of priests and other cultic personnel within the contours of Yahwistic faith (see chapter 9). Finally, the prophets appeared who placed in question Israel's election and forced the people to engage in a critical, indeed even threatening dialogue with its God and his new activity. The prophets also appeared during the great, radical, political upheavals with their explicative and threatening word (see chapter 10).

Thus the areas have been mentioned that are to be described in this third major section. The intention of these discussions is to demonstrate how Israel both could and had to speak about many new things concerning "election" (and its opposite, "rejection"). Consequently, the dominating basic structure of Israel's faith in YHWH, on the one hand, was able to stay the course and yet, on the other hand, had to learn to employ what was new.

Chapter 6. The Narratives
about the Ancestors[3]

The overview of the statements about election (in Vol. I, Chap. 2) has shown that not only the people of Israel but also the ancestors mentioned prior to YHWH's action on behalf of his people came to be specifically designated within the Old Testament as the "chosen." It is especially the case that already in Genesis the activity of God on behalf of the ancestors is described as an activity of election. It is now time to develop in greater detail what previously was briefly outlined by considering the stories of the ancestors (Genesis 12–36) which are an important component not only of the Book of Genesis but also of the Old Testament overall. Through this investigation an important feature of Old Testament faith will become clear, namely, the process not only of theologizing in the Old Testament but also of giving an Israelite expression to a belief or practice.[4] Understanding this process allows one to recognize much of the particular character of the Old Testament conception of faith.

The Elohist in Exodus 3 and the Priestly document in Exodus 6 associate the first revelation of the name of YHWH with Moses. Indeed, the Elohist probably begins his narrative with the ancestors because of the fact that he does not transmit a primeval history. In Josh. 24:2 the discussion concerns the ancestors having at an earlier time worshiped gods other than YHWH, while in Exod. 3:13 the questioning response of Moses makes no sense if YHWH and the "God of the Ancestors" had been one and the same. The discussion in Gen. 33:20 in fact is still of "El, the God of Israel," so that it should come as no surprise to realize that the theophoric element of the name "Israel" is El, not YHWH (or an abbreviated form of this name).[5] Do the stories of the ancestors allow one to understand this problem in a more precise way?[6]

6.1   Historical Background?

At the outset we must take seriously the fact that we do not possess to this point extrabiblical references that may be associated with the ancestors, with the groups connected to and represented by them, and with events that possibly could be related to them. This is no surprise when one considers that the stories of the ancestors are played out within the framework of clans and families and are nowhere woven together with the larger history of the ancient Near East. The late text of Genesis 14,[7] which unveils an entirely different Abraham from the one in Genesis 12–13 and 15–25, attempts to make such a connection with the larger history. However, this text is not to be evaluated as historical in nature, since, for example, the kings mentioned here are not identifiable. Neither an association of the ancestors with an Aramaic migration (a view now contested) nor a connection with customs that are evidenced in Mesopotamian texts out of Mari or Nuzi,[8] which is difficult to assume because they are traced to various regions and different times, is capable of being fully confirmed and of yielding historically verifiable results. At the same time, this ancient Near Eastern evidence addresses rather general matters (adoption; inheritance laws; etc.). Consequently, the time period for the ancestors cannot be chronologically determined, for it is not possible[9] to find external evidence that would position these figures within a particular period. This leaves only the stories of the ancestors themselves from which to extract a historical background. However, in making this attempt, one encounters serious difficulties because of the character of the text which certainly had a lengthy oral prehistory and the noticeable sparsity of corresponding details.[10] What can be disclosed is the general milieu in which these narratives with their unmistakable coloring move and play themselves out. Accordingly, it may be asked whether the description of this milieu has a certain historical probability and an inner resonance. Whatever the answer may be, the sociological milieu of the stories of the ancestors as well as the period narrated in these stories do not point to the postexilic period. Further, the personal names[11] encountered in the stories of the ancestors are in no way typically Israelite; rather, they occupy and maintain a special place within the Old Testament. Finally, an expression such as the "God of my fathers" (cf. earlier in Vol. I)[12] is certainly present in Israel's ancient Near Eastern environment, but it is not attested in texts that are unambiguously postexilic.

6.2   The Milieu of the Narratives about the Ancestors

In the ancestral stories, the ancestors and their groups are mentioned in connection with the region of Haran (Gen. 11:31; and 12:4b, 5: P). Jacob takes his flight to Haran to escape Esau (Gen. 27:43; 28:10; 29:4). Laban and his family were settled there (Gen. 27:43), and he was related by marriage to Jacob and Isaac (Gen. 25:20 P; Gen. 31:20, 24 J; cf. 25:6; 27:43; 29:1ff.). It was to Haran that Isaac went in search of a wife (Genesis 24). Accordingly, one may conclude that the ancestors and their groups were, so to say, associated with regions outside Palestine and were not characterized as residing exclusively and immediately in Canaan.[13] This could hardly be narrated without some basis in fact or some indication from previous data.

The stories of the ancestors describe the ancestors and the groups or clans associated with or represented by them as seminomadic[14] herders of flocks ("nomads on the edge of civilization": M. Weippert), as in transition from migration to a settled life (Gen. 12:8; 13:3; 20:1; 29:1ff.; 30:25ff., 32ff.; 46:32; and 47:1ff.), and as distinctive from the differently formed city dwellers (Gen. 18:1–3, 20; and 19:1–3). In addition, the narratives to a large extent geographically point to areas that are positioned near the borders of nations (Mamre/Hebron for Abram; Sodom in Genesis 18f.) and to the predominantly sparsely settled strip of land called Canaan, where one contests others for the few broad stretches of territory (Gen. 13:7) or for cisterns and wells where the right of access had to be determined by contract (Gen. 21:25ff.; 26:15ff.). During conflicts, a flight "into the wilderness" comes to mind (Gen. 16:7; 21:14). The division of farmland into modest tracts, which had already been carried out (Gen. 26:12; 27:27ff.), particularly allows the seminomadic manner of life to be recognized. At the same time, "nomadic" does not stand in full opposition to "settled" in these regions. Both ways of life often existed side by side, to be sure, among particular population groups that intermingled. Subsequently, these two ways of life are not simply to be arranged in chronological succession.[15] In any event, tents in the stories of the ancestors are not seldom mentioned (Gen. 12:8; 13:3, 5, 18; 18:1ff.; 24:67; 25:27;[16] 26:17, 25; 31:25, 33; 33:19; and 35:21). The discussion also points to the ancestors being under way and traveling (Gen. 12:1, 4, 6, 8, 10; 13:1, 3, 11ff., 17; 20:1; etc.),[17] taking possessions along (Gen. 12:5), and moving the herds (Gen. 13:5).[18] Also a place for the burial of the dead had to be acquired, and the later Priestly source appropriately complements a narrative like the one found in Genesis 23 with its own theological views.[19]

6.3 Concerning the Problem of the "God of the Ancestors"

The problem of the origins of the religion of these ancestral groups who either did not or at least at the outset did not believe in YHWH is addressed by Josh. 24:2 and Exod. 3:13. This problem is corroborated by the fact that in the narratives of the ancestors appellations or, better, names of God emerge that point to non-Yahwistic spheres.[20] In contradistinction to A. Alt and to the scholars who follow his lead,[21] one shall no longer have to think, in this regard, of a particular "god of the fathers" on the basis of rare passages that are difficult to interpret.[22] This involves the different epithets of the "Fear of Isaac" (hardly "kinsman"; פחד יצחק: *paḥad yiṣḥāq*, Gen. 31:42, 53b) and the "Strong One of Jacob" (אביר יעקב: *'ăbîr ya'ăqōb*, Gen. 49:24; cf. Ps. 132:2, 5; Isa. 1:24; 49:26; and 60:16, to which may be added occasionally also the "Herdsman (or Stone?) of Israel" (Gen. 48:15; 49:24) and the "Shield of Abra(ha)m (or

Patron)" (Gen. 15:1). Alt had concluded on the basis of these names and other matters which he brought into consideration that there was a pre-Palestinian stratum in the ancestral narratives that pointed to a kind of "god of the fathers" who belonged to the religion of the ancestors and who bore these mentioned names among the respective tribes and their ancestors. Alt used parallels from the history of religions in the ancient Near East that were chronologically and geographically far removed from the religion of the ancestors. Nevertheless, according to Alt, this God may have been first worshiped by these mentioned ancestors who were the fathers receiving the revelation and founding the cult. The patron deity "chose" the ancestors, providentially led them, saw to the well-being of their families and clans, was not bound to a specific sanctuary, and stood in a continuing, accompanying relationship to them. The promises of descendants and land were, according to Alt, originally pre-Palestinian in origin and then were brought into and made constitutive for the Palestinian "stratum of ideas."[23]

It can be demonstrated rather quickly that the Old Testament texts themselves do not always allow for such a comprehensive construction.[24] "Herdsman of Israel" and "Strong One of Jacob" are not typical epithets for an ancestral religion. The "Shield of Abra(ha)m" is a name that is developed only from Gen. 15:1, and even there it is not directly stated. It is only with the "Fear of Isaac" that there is not simply a brief mentioning of or allusion to one of these divine epithets.[25] While this epithet cannot alone bear the weight of such a hypothetical reconstruction of ancestral religion, it could nevertheless still point to a pre-Yahwistic stage of religion. Furthermore, since the religiohistorical parallels that Alt drew are too far removed chronologically as well as geographically from the possible period of the ancestors and Palestine, one shall have to be skeptical of the significance of these materials for the reconstruction of an ancestral religion. Perhaps these epithets have to do, rather, with a "surname"[26] of the contemporary ancestral deities.

In the narratives of the ancestors and elsewhere in the Old Testament, the discussion, however, is about "the God of Abraham, the God of Isaac, and the God of Jacob," summarized in the expression "the God of the Ancestors." It is clear, though, that these epithets are not directly and always identified with YHWH.[27] In addition, a "God of my/your/our ancestor" is mentioned[28] especially in the Jacob tradition,[29] an expression that elsewhere in the ancient Near East was certainly not unusual.[30] Moreover, this designation allows one to recognize the close association it has with the expressed themes of the ancestral narratives. These themes include providential care, duration, and the multiplication of the tribe or the promise of a son. Accordingly, the deity of the ancestors at the time would have been perhaps a tribal deity who was also named "El." In addition, many scholars have considered it a certainty that the appellation "God of the fathers or of X" (Exod. 3:6; 15:2), traditio-historically speaking, was older. This view, clearly anchored in Old Testament passages such as Gen. 31:42, 53, also appears to be true, for instance, of the epithet the "Strong One of Jacob." Exodus 3:13 allows one to recognize, in any case, that the identification of YHWH and the "God of the Ancestors" was not obvious.[31] In addition, it is difficult to argue away the fact that Gen. 31:53 provides evidence that each of the parties mentioned here has "his" deity.[32]

V. Maag[33] has attempted to comprehend more precisely and to set forth in religiosociological terms the religious type of the ancestral narratives together with the religion of the ancestors that Alt and his followers had proposed. The religion of the ancestors is characterized by Maag as one of guidance where God's protection of and binding with the ancestral group stand at the center. In this religion, a numinous "cares in a special way for the families and clans."[34] He leads them by each issuance of his word, gives instruction for impending travels, promises new pasturelands, and leads his people to them. Here may be the essence of "faith" which trusts in this divine guidance.[35] In the cornerstone passage of Gen. 12:1ff. Maag finds a promise concerning a migration that goes beyond the changing of pastureland, that is, the so-called transhumance.[36] Since this text has been stamped rather strongly with the theology of the Yahwist,[37] writing in the time of the (Davidic and) Solomonic empire, and since it points to things other than migration, Maag's assessment and view of Gen. 12:1–3 have rightly not found much support.

6.4 Ancestral Religion and El Religion

The primary point that emerges from what has been said up to now is that the ancestral groups cannot clearly be associated with pre-Yahwistic deities such as the "Strong One of Jacob." Only the epithet "Fear of Isaac" could come close to such a connection, although the already small amount of evidence has greatly diminished even further. The references to the "God of my ancestor" and other similar expressions are by contrast more frequent and more typical for the ancestral narratives and the texts that refer to them.

Besides this, the groups of the ancestors were connected with certain epithets of the deity El,[38] and these epithets of El, which usually stand beside the "God of my ancestor," also appear each time to be associated with certain sanctuaries of Canaan. The ancestral groups could have belonged to those clans and tribes that dwelt in the regions in the environs in which these sacred places were located. Alt was of the opinion that he was able to detect the second, however still pre-Yahwistic, stratum at this point.

In this connection, one is primarily to think of the notices about the founding of cults (Gen. 12:7f.; 13:18; 35:1, 7), sayings about the founding of cults, and sanctuary legends (Gen. 28:10ff.; 32:31) that "seek to trace back to the ancestors the Canaanite sanctuaries that then existed."[39] It is to be asked, however, whether the religion of the ancestors is encountered[40] and to be comprehended first or at least as an El religion, especially since the biblical references that mention this religion are clearer than those for a layer situated immediately prior to this one. The appellation "God (El!) of my ancestor" and its variations could have been inserted into this material dealing with an El religion. Then one would have to reckon on the whole only with one stage of religion situated prior to the complete Yahwistic shaping of the religion of the ancestors.[41] If so, this ancestral religion could then be seen as an El religion that is expressed in the form of personal piety.[42]

Also mentioned in the ancestral narratives are an אל בית-אל = 'ēl bēt'ēl (El Bethel) (Gen. 28:16–19;[43] 31:13; and 35:7; cf. Jer. 48:13) in association with Jacob and the sanctuary at Bethel,[44] an אל ראי = 'ēl rō'î (El Roi) localized in the southern Negeb and connected with Ishmael (Gen. 16:13), an אל עולם = 'ēl 'ôlām (El Olam) in Beersheba (Gen. 21:33) in relationship with Abraham (Gen. 17:1), an אל שדי[45] = 'ēl šadday (El Shaddai), an "El, God of Israel" at Shechem (Gen. 33:20), and an אל עליון[46] = 'ēl 'elyôn (El Elyon) in Jerusalem (Gen. 14:18ff.; cf. Num. 24:16; Pss. 46:5; 47:3; and 82:6). In addition, one should also mention Penuel (Gen. 32:31), while outside the ancestral narratives El appears also as אל ברית = 'ēl bĕrît (El Berith) of Shechem (Judg. 9:46; in 9:4 Baal Berith). In all of these combinations, El is used more as a personal name and an epithet and less so as an appellation. What is involved, it seems, are local expressions of the Canaanite high god El,[47] which cannot be simply passed over in silence in and after the taking up of the narratives of the ancestors. Also the names Isra*el* and possibly even Jacob-El clearly remind us of this fact, and Gen. 46:1 is especially significant testimony to the father god El (cf. 46:3; 49:25).

The comprehensive religiohistorical process[48] could perhaps be seen as follows: the worshipers of the deities named in the ancestral narratives already dwelt in Palestine as large families or clans who neither knew nor confessed YHWH as their God. They had already settled there prior to the entrance into Canaan by the Moses group and had become associated with the Canaanite sanctuaries mentioned in these narratives. When the Moses group[49] immigrated to Canaan, they brought with them their Yahwistic faith and shaped later Israelite faith with the character of their own beliefs. Moreover, the name "Israel" was attached to a pre-Yahwistic group in central Palestine that had already settled in the land, a fact to which the Merneptah Stele,[50] for example, provides witness. This latter group also worshiped El (Gen. 33:20)![51] It may have been the case that the Jacob group was associated with this pre-Yahwistic group or even comprised a portion of it and later joined the Moses group and its Yahwistic faith. The ancient kernel[52] contained in Joshua 24 reflects these events. Dwelling for a longer time in the land of Canaan, the Jacob group provided a common bond by passing on its name "Israel" to the later groups that joined with it, groups that included the ancestral families and clans (cf. Jacob as Israel: Gen. 32:28f. J; 35:10 P). They possessed most likely a numerical superiority to the Moses group, even though the Yahwistic faith proved to be the stronger. Thus those who belonged to the groups of the ancestors and who received the Yahwistic faith were accepted by the Moses group. In any case, the portion of ancient Israel that immigrated to Canaan as the Moses group did not regard as foreign Canaanites everyone who had already settled in the land (Joshua 24). In connection with this amalgamation of groups, the uniting of YHWH and El could have resulted, a union that would have been made easier if each of these groups had worshiped only one deity within the bounds of a non-polemical exclusivity (H.-P. Müller)[53] and if each god of the ancestors would have been named the "God of my ancestor."[54] Subsequently, one is not to think of the combination of the ancestral and Moses groups as only a purely literary process.[55]

This would mean, then, that the amalgamation and identification of the statements about El with YHWH probably took place for the first time in the land of Canaan, not before, and also not under Moses. This identification with YHWH was possible because the deity of the groups also was not bound to a sanctuary. Rather, he led his group as a deity who accompanied them on their journeys (Gen. 26:3; 28:15; 31:3; 46:4; etc.). He was worshiped by them as their only God and as the one who, for example, also especially defended the ancestress (Gen. 12:10ff.; 20; 26:1–13). This faith also involved a close relational community between the worshipers and their deity. He was the "personal God" of the ancestor and the group connected with him.[56] Consequently, the "election"[57] of the groups of the ancestors by YHWH was prefigured here. In addition, since the promise of the land in the stories of the early ancestors was clearly contrasted with the one given to the Moses group,[58] this ancestral promise came to typify the deity of the ancestors. The connections of the ancestral God and his promises to the ancestors in an ancestral religion that is incorporated into Yahwistic religion are not to be seen only as a "literary combination of disparate traditions,"[59] since this lack of a unified tradition is a problematic presupposition to later (including even postexilic) writers.

The possibility is not to be excluded that, concealed behind the ancestral groups, there were clans or tribes who had experienced a conquest of the land (from the south?) apart from the one by the Moses group or who had experienced in its own way a different process of settlement. These groups, who had not previously settled in the land,[60] entered into an Israel that was in the process of formation, including the occupation of its sanctuaries by YHWH (Gen. 28:10ff.). Thus Abraham, Isaac, and Jacob become the primogenitors of Israel or of its various parts. Moreover, this "sense of being on the way"[61] was maintained within Israelite religion. By means of the faith of the groups of the ancestors, this religion was augmented to become a religion of guidance. Within the sphere of this religion of guidance, existence is experienced as and believed to be history, that is, a journey with YHWH. "This God leads to a future that is not only a pale repetition and confirmation of the present but rather is the goal of events that are found now to be in process,"[62] and this goal is reached only under the condition of the performance of obedience.[63]

6.5 YHWH Religion and the Promises to the Ancestors

The existing (also theological) placement of the stories of the ancestors continues to show many of these original features. Decisive, however, is their final form which now lies before us, that is, what Israel has made out of these figures and the narratives about them, especially in the writings of the Yahwist,[64] the Elohist,[65] the Priestly source, and the (Deuteronomistic?) redaction(s).

The Yahwist introduced a programmatic text (Gen. 12:1–3), followed by the first expression of the promise of the land (12:7). This theme of the "land" pervades the ensuing Abram-Lot narratives (Genesis 13; 18/19) as their basic component. The Elohist, meanwhile, is clearly observable in Genesis 20–22, although possibly this fragmentary text may already have been introduced in Gen. 15:1* (3–4?). In these narratives of the ancestors, the three fathers are brought together (by JE?) in a linear succession as father, son, and grandson, while the Jacob narrative provided the primary expression of these familial connections as well as their conclusion. Single narratives, as, for example, Genesis 22 or 32:23ff., were brought into service to provide overarching statements of purpose. From the ancestral narratives as a whole, a national history was in the process of preparation. These ancestral narratives, which formed the early stage of the history of Israel along with many of its neighboring nations: Ishmaelites, Moabites, and Ammonites, comprised the history of election in the making and created the period of promise. Promises, which now dominated the ancestral narratives, have taken on and strengthened the function of encompassing history theologically, describing it as possessing providential, purposeful continuity. In association with this, the important elements and themes of Yahwistic faith are expanded: word, faith, way, promise, history, and goal. In this way the ancestral narratives are brought into the service of the proclamation of Yahwistic faith. These narratives now help to interpret Yahwistic faith especially by means of a consciously shaped, overarching structure that reaches from the promise of the land at the beginning of the story to the fulfillment of the gift of the land at the end. The land is seen as a gift of God that has been in preparation for a long time. Through his promise, God had already given this land to the ancestors against every appearance to the contrary ("at that time the Canaanites were in the land": Gen. 12:6; 13:7: J) or merely in return for earnest money (Genesis 23 P). Thus YHWH had already acted in a gracious, electing, and generous manner on Israel's behalf through its ancestors, even before it was fully constituted as a people. This was narrated, not with the help of a prehistorical myth, but rather in the form of stories that encompassed history. Accordingly, the promises embedded in the ancestral narratives become especially important,[66] for Israel lives in the ancestral narratives as a people of promise in the land of promise. Israel lives thereby in hope. In addition, the Yahwistic faith's relation to the future is also strengthened in this way. Through his word, God keeps history in operation and directs it in its course.

In the stories of the ancestors,[67] one should distinguish between the ancient texts, which are genuine to their contexts and first came together through redactional activities, and groups of later texts that were secondarily inserted in the growth of the tradition. To the latter category are to be assigned especially Gen. 15:13–15 and 22:15–18. Belonging entirely to the theological purpose and *kerygma* of the Yahwist are the promises of blessing for other peoples that are issued through the ancestors and then through the Israel that followed.[68] According to the Yahwist, this blessing is not to be an active assignment given only to Israel but rather is to be transmitted through Israel and is to be interpreted as an effect that is taking place (Gen. 12:3; 26:4;[69] 28:14).[70] Further, this blessing became a concept that was historical and that extended into the future because of its combination with a promise.[71] This concept did not take effect immediately; rather, in its action it was incorporated within the ongoing course of history and came to be associated with Israel's own continuing journey. In all probability, the content of blessing served the Yahwist in the theological evaluation of the Davidic dynasty ("blessing, not achievement"), since he probably is to be placed in the period of the Davidic-Solomonic empire.[72] K. Berge has demonstrated that the promises of blessing in the Yahwist are not to be seen as Deuteronomistic.[73] The Deuteronomistic promises of blessing are associated with the mention of obedience, something that is still completely absent in those of the Yahwist.

Among the texts that contain a promise of the land,[74] Gen. 12:7 and 28:13–16 are identifiably ancient.[75] This promise can be issued only to the ancestor alone ("I will give to you . . ."), or it can say, "I will give to you and your descendants . . . ." To maintain here that the expression "your descendants" may in each case be a later elaboration[76] misjudges the contents of this promise. Here the land indeed was not promised to the "ancestor" but rather to his descendants who are immediately mentioned. That the Priestly document later consciously features (Genesis 17) "and your descendants" says, however, nothing at all to suggest that each election of the descendants within the promise of the land has to be secondary. It is striking that not one of the promises of the land can be attributed to the Elohist. As the Elohistic texts within the Sinai pericope especially demonstrate,[77] this source was more interested theologically in the thoughts about the people than about the land. The association of Abram with Jerusalem (Gen. 14:18–20) as well as the significance of the promise of the land in the Yahwist could point to the fact that many characteristics of the Abram/Abraham narratives had legitimating functions in the period of the formation of the monarchy.[78]

The promises of increase[79] and descendants, from which the promise of a son given only to Abraham (Gen. 15:4; 16:11; 18:10, 14; 21:1–3)[80] is to be removed for traditiohistorical reasons, are found rather frequently.[81] The promise of the land, as well as promises of increase, offspring, and a son, was provided with particular elements of tension. The land was promised to the ancestors, although it was occupied by other people (Gen. 12:6; 13:7: J). The father was promised descendants, even though the ancestral mother of the tribe was introduced as barren (Gen. 11:30) or characterized as too old to bear children (Gen. 18:11). Consequently, how these promises were to be fullfilled was not self-evident. However, they were to demonstrate at the same time something of the power of God who will bring his promises to their fruition in spite of these obstacles. These promises of descendants and increase in the Yahwist point in all probability to the background of the Davidic-Solomonic empire.[82]

Finally, the promise of divine presence ("I will be with you!" and similar statements) should be mentioned. This promise is given not to Abraham but to Isaac (Gen. 26:3, 24) and is especially encountered in the Jacob narratives (Gen. 28:15 [20]; 31:3; 32:10; and 46:4; cf. 48:15, 21; 50:24). In Gen. 26:3, 24; 28:15; and 31:3, one encounters this promise in what appears to be its original content: prior to the time the ancestor begins his journey, God promises to accompany and guide him along the way.[83]

For the Elohist,[84] three additional themes carry significance within the ancestral stories. He speaks readily of the fear of God (Gen. 20:11; 22:12), refers to Abraham as already a prophet (Gen. 20:7),[85] and organizes the Jacob narratives around the theme of a vow and its being honored (Gen. 28:10f., 17f., 20–22, 31:7, 11, 13; and 35:1, 3, 7).[86]

Thus, what Yahweh promised to the ancestors is realized in and for the nation. The Deuteronomists therefore extend the ancestral promises until they reach their fulfillment at the end of the conquest, that is, at the conclusion of the Book of Joshua (Josh. 21:44f.; and 23:14). The nation is thought not only to have originated from a family but also to continue to exist in a close relationship like a family. Indeed, the parents and the children have solidarity under both the blessing and the curse,[87] while Deuteronomy is able to unite later generations under its "today" and to point to the acts of YHWH that bind the people together.[88] Through this combination of stories of the ancestors and the later history of the nation, it becomes possible, for example, to consider the exodus as a promise of the God of the ancestors that has been made good (Exod. 3:13ff.), while the "I am YHWH" joins together the stories of the ancestors (Gen. 28:13ff.) and those of the exodus. In order to narrate its prehistory and early history, Israel was not to move over into mythical discourse. On the contrary, YHWH has acted in history to elect the ancestors[89] (Gen. 12:1–3; 25:23; cf. 18:19; 24:7), and this activity bore within itself divine promise (Gen. 24:7). However, this promise could be placed in question (the sacrifice of Isaac, Genesis 22) or the blessing could be lost (Esau-Jacob). This promise could be further shaped in a didactic manner, with the deceiver Jacob becoming the Israel who strives with God[90] (Gen. 27:36; 32:28f.), with the blessing obtained under false pretenses (Genesis 27), and with the blessing that this deception attained (Gen. 32:27). The ancestral father Jacob and the nation of Israel later can appear in identifiably parallel situations.[91] Thus the stories of the ancestors provide the origin of Israel's history,[92] and they contain in their early expressions the themes of becoming a people, promises, the possession of the land, and the relationship between people and land. These stories also provide in all that is narrated not only etiologies for later acts of God but also paradigms for divine action.[93] They allow one to recognize the fundamental structures of Yahwistic faith, of which Gen. 12:1–3; 15:7; and 48:15f. are typical examples with the form and content of their promises.

6.6 The "Ancestors" in Later Texts

The Priestly source[94] adds to these narratives emphases that reinforce what had been said. The promise of increase reappears in this source in the repetition of the command of blessing in Gen. 1:28 (cf. Gen. 8:17; 9:1, 7; 17:2, 6, 20; 28:3; 35:11; and 48:4) and culminates in the formation of the people "in Egypt," often mentioned previously in these narrative texts (Gen. 47:27; and Exod. 1:7; cf. Lev. 26:9). The land becomes for the ancestors the "land of sojourning" (ארץ מגורים = *'eres měgûrim;* Gen. 17:8; 28:4; etc.),[95] which they cannot finally possess but rather must once again leave. P provides a transparent view of the situation of the exilic community. Here the Abrahamic covenant is made especially important (Genesis 17).[96] On the one hand, it is stressed that this "covenant" (ברית = *běrît*) is to be "forever" (Gen. 17:7, 13, 19) and that it is not limited to Abraham himself but rather also extends to "your descendants who come after you" (Gen. 17:7, 19). On the other hand, this Abrahamic covenant is maintained by circumcision as the sign of the covenant (אות = *'ôt,* "sign"; Gen. 17:11) in a way that is analogous to the rainbow in the priestly covenant of Noah. Circumcision and the keeping of the Sabbath (Gen. 2:1–4a P) establish for the exilic and the postexilic communities their signs of membership. While the Priestly source brings into prominent display the Abrahamic covenant, it is remarkably silent about a "covenant" (ברית = *běrît*) within the Sinai event.[97] A number of scholars have sought to discover the basis and meaning of this silence. W. Zimmerli[98] has pointed out in this regard that P addresses the ratification of covenants in the covenant of Noah and especially in the covenant of Abraham. These two covenants stress in a more accentuated way the feature of grace than does the covenant of Sinai which places more emphasis on human obligation. Since Israel has broken the Sinai covenant, a covenant that sets forth the obligations that are based on the will of YHWH, P now reaches back to the covenant of Abraham in order to state in a consoling manner that Israel still stands within the covenant of grace. "When Israel desires to be certain of the unswerving loyalty of its God during the hour of judgment, it looks behind the covenant of Sinai to YHWH's ancient, undefiled covenant of promise with the ancestors." Thus exilic and postexilic Israel harkens back to the covenant of Abraham, which still promises for them as YHWH's "descendants" the possibility of a new future in community with him. Once more the period of Moses lies open anew before those who are addressed. And according to P, the place where the ancestors are buried provides the earnest money for the possession of the land of promise (Genesis 23).

Later on, Israel found its own ideal of piety particularly in Abraham and in Jacob (see them together in Isa. 41:8; and Micah 7:20). This ideal was limited at first to Abraham, especially in texts such as Gen. 12:1–9; 15; 17–18; and 22 which portray him as an exemplary pious person whom at the same time, YHWH has treated in paradigmatic fashion. Jacob's becoming a paradigm of piety was made possible through the changing of his name from "Jacob" to "Israel" (v. 29), a story narrated in the ancient, however, much redacted text in Gen. 32:23ff. that was taken up later by P in Gen. 35:10, and through the fact that he was also regarded as the actual tribal ancestor of the twelve tribes and therefore the nation of Israel (cf. 1 Kings 18:31; Isa. 58:14). The names "Jacob" and "Israel" are encountered together in the Jacob narratives and in the Joseph narrative (cf., e.g., Gen. 37:1f.; 37:3; and 46:1f.). Elsewhere "Jacob" or the "house of Jacob" stands for the nation of Israel or more specifically for the Northern Kingdom of Israel, the Southern Kingdom of Judah, or both, and expresses the singularity of Israel as the people of God[99] (cf. Amos 7:2, 5). These are the same parameters within which later interpreters of this name give expression to their understandings (Amos 3:13; 9:8). Especially for Deutero-Isaiah, the parallel presence of "Jacob" and "Israel" is commonly used to address the people's opposition to God (Isa. 40:27; 41:14, 21; 43:1, 22; and often).

That the "ancestors" are seldom mentioned outside Genesis and that they are largely omitted in the prophets down to the exile is not due to a lack of awareness of these figures and what had been narrated about them. Rather, the call of the ancestors belonged to popular piety which the prophets saw it necessary to challenge (Amos 5:14?; cf. Ps. 47:10 and Matt. 3:9, "We have Abraham for our father"). The few mentionings of the ancestors within prophecy[100] underscore this interpretation, since these references are almost always polemical in nature (Hos. 12:4ff.;[101] Jer. 9:3;[102] Ezek. 2:3; 20:4, 24, 27, 30; 33:24; and Micah 2:7; cf. also Amos 6:8; 8:7 ["pride of Jacob"]; Mal. 1:2f.; 3:6; Isa. 43:22 + 28; and perhaps 43:27[103]).[104] By contrast, a fully positive, comforting reference to the ancestors that seeks to awaken a new feeling of trust is entered alongside the recourse to the smallness of the house of Jacob in the first intercessory prayer of Amos (Amos 7:2, 5) that follows the judgment of the exile.[105] Jacob/Israel are both "elected" by YHWH (Ezek. 20:5). Isaiah 63:16 (cf. 59:20) presupposes this possibility of a consoling relationship in offering up a petition of lament to YHWH. Ezekiel 33:24 shows that one could base a claim to the land by making reference to Abraham.

Nevertheless, of special significance is the recourse to the "ancestors" and to YHWH as the "God of the ancestors" in the literature influenced by the Deuteronomistic School. The final form of Genesis 15 belongs primarily here. In Gen. 15:1, 6, "fearlessness" and "faith" in YHWH's power in spite of every test are presented as paradigmatic virtues in relationship to the "covenant" (v. 18).[106] In the Deuteronomic and Deuteronomistic literature in a proper sense, the oath of YHWH to the ancestors (and their descendants) is especially significant,[107] for it assumes the older promise of the land but moves beyond it in a much more emphatic way.[108] This oath concerning the land is further strengthened by consideration of the covenant (ברית = běrît) that occurs in this context (Deut. 4:31; 7:9, 12; 8:18; and 29:11f.; cf. Gen. 15:18; and Deut. 29:12, 24; cf. 1 Kings 8:21; 2 Kings 13:23; and 17:15 concerning "covenant").[109] It is the salvific gift of the land that is important to the Deuteronomic/Deuteronomistic movement. This movement intentionally shapes the gift of the land into a theological theme to respond to both the perils of the occupation of the land (Deuteronomy) and its loss (Deuteronomistic literature). The Deuteronomic/Deuteronomistic literature knows also, however, of the promises of descendants and increase (Deut. 1:10f.; 4:37; 7:13; 8:1; 10:15, 22; 13:18; 30:16; and Josh. 24:3; cf. Deut. 26:5; in 28:62f. these are used in a negative, contrasting way in the structure of the curses, while in 30:5 they are connected with the exhortation to return) and of the promise of blessing (Deut. 1:11; 14:29; 15:10, 18; 16:15; 23:21; and 24:19; cf. 7:13; and 26:15). These promises allow a positive reference to the ancestors to enter into the prayers that are significant for this literature (Exod. 32:13; Deut. 9:27; 1 Kings 18:36; cf. also 1 Kings 8:21, 34, 48, 53, and 57). The Deuteronomic/Deuteronomistic literature does not have in mind only the ancient ancestors when referring to the "ancestors."[110] Rather, for Deuteronomistic thinking, the "ancestors" are those who are connected to the history held in common by those now being addressed. This present audience shares the experiences of earlier generations that include guilt (Deut. 5:9; 1 Kings 9:9; 14:22; 2 Kings 17:14f., 41; 21:15; 22:13; Jer. 3:25; and 23:27; cf. "to do evil/good . . . as did your father"[111]) as well as redemption (Deut. 26:7), the salvific deed of the exodus from Egypt (Josh. 24:17; Judg. 2:1; 6:13; and 1 Sam. 12:6, 8), the gift of the land (1 Kings 14:15; and 2 Kings 21:8), the gift of the temple (Jer. 7:14), the promises (Deut. 9:5; and 26:3), and the covenant (Deut. 5:3) which has been broken even though it was a covenant with the ancestors (Jer. 11:10f.; and 31:32). Thus the "God of the ancestors" is rather frequently mentioned also in the Deuteronomistic literature, not only in the form of the God of Abraham, Isaac, and Jacob (Deut. 1:11, 21; 6:3; and 10:22; cf. 4:1f.; and 12:1?), but also as the God of those ancestors who existed in the past throughout the entire history of Israel, a God whom they have abandoned but ought not to have abandoned (Deut. 8:3, 16; 31:16; Josh. 18:3; Judg. 2:12, 17, 20, 22; 3:4; 1 King 9:9; and often). The present generation is newly admonished and warned by these historical statements about the past (cf., e.g., 2 Kings 17:41). YHWH has loved and elected the ancestors and their successors (Deut. 4:37; 10:15; cf. 30:5, 9). Other gods, whom the ancestors have not known, Israel ought not to have served and should not serve (Deut. 13:7; 32:17; cf. Josh. 24:14f.; Jer. 19:4; 44:3), else their fate will take the threatened form of punishment (Deut. 28:64; cf. 28:36; 1 Sam. 12:15; Jer. 23:39; 24:10). In its review of Israel's history, the Deuteronomistic literature formulates this punishment, already now experienced in the exile, as the working out of the curse threatened for worshiping false gods. When a new gift of the land is promised to the exiled community, this promise is taken from the gift of the land to the ancestors (Jer. 16:15; 25:5; and 30:3). These many-sided references to the ancestors allow one to recognize both a typical example and an essential, constituent character of Israelite faith and historical thought.[112]

In the Chronicler's work of history,[113] YHWH is called on in prayer as the God of these fathers (1 Chron. 29:18), and the people of Israel are exhorted to turn to him (2 Chron. 30:6). YHWH, the God of the ancestors, commissions prophets to be messengers of warning (2 Chron. 36:15f.; cf. Jer. 7:25). The abandonment of the God of the ancestors is criticized (2 Chron. 7:22; 21:10; 24:18, 24; and 28:6). The community (and this is not limited only to Judah and Jerusalem: 2 Chron. 13:12; and 28:9) is once more and with emphasis designated as the descendants of these ancestors to whom YHWH has given the land (2 Chron. 20:7), while in Neh. 9:7 the ancestors are designated *expressis verbis* as the "chosen" (cf. Ps. 105:6).[114] The psalms especially recognize, however, that the sins of the ancestors are closely connected with Israel's own sinfulness (Pss. 78:7f.; 95:8f.; 106:7; Lam. 5:7; Ezra 9:7; Neh. 9:2; and Dan. 9:16) in the same way that the actions of Yahweh on behalf of the ancestors (Ps. 78:12) and their faithfulness (Ps. 22:5) are related. The reference to the ancestors also serves here both an admonitory function ("not like the ancestors!") and the purpose of strengthening the faith through "memory" (Ps. 105:5–8). "The God of Jacob" is also in the psalms the God of the people of God in whom one takes refuge and from whom one seeks salvation.[115] Since the narratives of the ancestors were oriented differently, the theology of Zion and the Jerusalem temple[116] was characteristically inserted into these texts only as additions that, at the same time, however, had programmatic features (Gen. 14:18–20; 22:2: Moriah, according to 2 Chron. 3:1, in place of Jerusalem).[117] While Abraham could really not have lived close by Jerusalem, the narratives of the ancestors must have had some relationship with this city. Then the princes of the nations[118] could gather together there with the people of the God of Abraham, and there they would recognize, even as Abraham did, YHWH as (their) only God (Ps. 47:10; cf. Josh. 24:2), an act in which the promise of Gen. 12:3 would find its fulfillment.[119] And when in the postexilic period it became necessary to reflect over the question concerning the relationship of divine and human justice (cf. Job), then this problem was attached to the figure of Abraham and his relationship with YHWH (Gen. 18:16 [22b]-33).[120] However, if the narratives of the ancestors as a whole originated in the postexilic period, then it would appear that the discussion of "election" would have been much clearer in these texts (cf., e.g., Chronicles) and the word בחר (= *bāḥar*) certainly would have been drawn on more frequently to set forth a more exact designation of what was meant.

Thus the narratives of the ancestors, which have no ample parallels in the literatures of the ancient Near East in either form or content,[121] tell the origins of the history of the people of God and speak of the preparatory history which moves with intentionality toward Israel's becoming the people of God (Exodus 1ff.). At the same time, the exodus tradition is older than the tradition of the ancestors within Yahwistic faith. The Joseph Narrative, which in terms of its character and themes is not to be reckoned as belonging to the stories of the ancestors,[122] serves as the bridge between the two traditions. Genesis 50:24, with both its preview of the exodus out of Egypt and the gift of the land and its look back at the oath of God to the ancestors, provides the connection between the books of Genesis and Exodus and therefore between the narratives about the ancestors, Joseph, and Egypt.

The Old Testament wisdom literature, which for the first time in the late postexilic period inserted into its thinking the history of the people of God (Sirach 44ff.; Wisdom 10–12), makes no reference anywhere at all to the ancient ancestors but rather knows as "father" only the beloved father of a group of humans or, better said, of "wise people" or names the teacher "father" while calling his student his "son."[123]

Essential categories of the explication of faith which are expressed in the narratives of the ancestors become integrated into Yahwistic faith, although they originally stood in no direct relationship to it. These hermeneutical categories are preserved there and later acquire significance for the New Testament people of God: the lack of a permanent home, the "dwelling" (John 1:14 original text), the wandering people of God, the presence of God, being under way, and the significance of promises. In order to know God, it is necessary to travel along the path.[124]

Chapter 7. Kingship and Messianic Hope[1]

The institution of kingship[2] was not founded in the beginnings of ancient Israel but rather developed historically there after the conquest and the period of the Judges. Thus the monarchy in Israel was not only a late phenomenon in the context of the ancient Near East, it also was an entity that was not placed at all within the faith of the ancestral groups, the Moses group, and indeed preexilic Israel prior to state formation. However, it is also the case that this later phenomenon of the monarchy was first integrated into the Old Testament as an expression of the faith of election that was itself an integral element of Yahwistic faith, and this integration occurred in a twofold fashion. First, the Old Testament speaks of the first royal figures of Saul and David as individual "chosen ones," what probably was the oldest use of a straightforward, terminologically concise statement of election. Thus Saul is chosen by YHWH (1 Sam. 10:24; cf. Ps. 78:70), then David as well (1 Sam. 16:8ff.; 2 Sam. 6:21), according to certain, ancient witnesses from the the Ark Narrative and the Succession Narrative of David. Kingship was spoken about in such a way (2 Sam. 16:18), and a son of David bore the name Yibhar which was formed from the root בחר = *bāḥar* ("elect").

Later on, the Deuteronomistic History and the texts that were dependent on this corpus took up this theologumenon and used it to refer both to individual kings and to the monarchy as a whole.[3]

In addition to these explicit statements of election, there is a second way that election of the monarchy is expressed. This is in the representations of electing activity and speech acts that describe such a phenomenon without using or even having to use at the same time the word "elect." Here are to be reckoned, for example, the promise of Nathan in 2 Samuel 7, the so-called "Last Words of David" in 2 Sam. 23:1–7, and perhaps Psalm 132 which provides a synopsis of the election of David and Zion and thus combines 2 Samuel 6 with 2 Samuel 7 and finally also 1 Kings 8. E.-J. Waschke has shown that even more ancient traditions are to be sought and discovered behind each of these texts.[4]

7.1 Concerning the Book of Judges

The Book of Judges is placed before the narratives of the origin of the Israelite monarchy and brings together several narrative purposes and a varied content.[5] Judges 17–21, which are clearly addenda to the recognizable concluding chapter, incorporates two narratives that set forth something negative, each in its own particular way, that leads to the monarchy as a necessary consequence of and solution to these problems. "The terrible period in which there was no king over Israel" (Judg. 21:25; cf. also 17:6; 18:1; 19:1) was, on the one hand, characterized by the establishment of questionable sanctuaries which in turn led in a strange fashion to dubious cultic ministers and to acts of the worship of idols that were critically condemned. Among such dubious sanctuaries was that of Dan and its idol (Judges 17–18).[6] On the other hand, this period was a time of evil, cruel deeds that would necessitate at the same time a retributive campaign (Judges 19–21). The "scandal of Gibeah" served as an example of those difficulties which Israel was unable to resolve by peaceful means for all concerned.[7] Since the Book of Judges now exists as part of the Deuteronomistic History, it is already clear through these appendices that the Deuteronomistic movement did not wish to view the institution of the monarchy only in a negative light.[8]

The Book of Judges begins with a retrospective look at the conclusion and result of the conquest (Judg. 1:1–2:5). The uniform guidance of Israel under Moses and Joshua is now a thing of the past (Judg. 2:10), and the Israelites were unable to carry through to completion the total conquest of Canaan. There are spheres of Canaan that remain unconquered (Judg. 1:21, 27ff.), and there continue to be Canaanites in the land who became for Israel a problem viewed in various ways (Judg. 2:21–3:6). At the actual kernel of the Book of Judges stand the so-called narratives of deliverance (Judg. 3:7–16:31) about the charismatic "great judges," as, for example and above all, Ehud, Gideon, Jephthah, and Samson. In addition, in these chapters there are references to the so-called "minor judges" whose function continues to remain unclear.[9] The greater judges (שפט = šōpēṭ), who outwardly "obtained justice" for Israel, led Israel or rather individual tribes or tribal groups into battle and YHWH war (cf. Judg. 4:14–16) against threatening and attacking enemies. The narratives of these deliverers[10] place their thematic emphasis on the securing of possession of the land, on the reports about charismatic individuals, on YHWH's "spirit" working in them[11] (cf. Judg. 3:10; 6:34; 11:29; 13:25; 14:6, 19; 15:14), and on their military accomplishments together with the groups that followed them. An ordered succession of one judge after another is still not provided; however, YHWH raises up the deliverers who become active in saving their nation when threatened by its enemies. These older narratives are now brought into a theological framework of understanding which provides them with a Deuteronomistic introduction (Judg. 2:6–3:6), containing several strata, that describes the period of the Judges as an interplay between human actions and divine reactions. Indeed, Judges 2:11–19 also assumes the form of an "editorial" (J. Wellhausen). According to this, the Canaanites and their religion provide the temptation that leads Israel to its apostasy. The righteous punishment of YHWH follows then this apostasy. When, however, YHWH's people cry out to him, he is prepared to hear them and to raise up a deliverer (מֹושִׁיעַ = *môšîa'*; Judg. 3:9, 15); however, Israel's apostasy does not cease. This narrative structure is often repeated (with modifications), and its contents are often recalled.[12] Furthermore, Gideon is described (in spite of Judg. 8:24–27) as a faithful worshiper of YHWH who destroys foreign cultic symbols (Judg. 6:25–32).

The attempt of Abimelech to set up in Shechem a (Canaanite) city-state (Judges 9) does not endure. YHWH had sent once again his "Spirit," only this time, though, an evil one (Judg. 9:23).[13] The judge Gideon rejects the status of "ruler" that was offered him (Judg. 8:22f.), and the Jotham fable,[14] which is placed in Judg. 9:8–15(a?), also assumes a critical position toward the monarchy (cf. also Judg. 1:4b-7). The monarchy of Saul[15] which then arises (ca. 1012–1004 B.C.E.?) allows one to recognize clearly the problems that would face Israel and its faith with the development of this institution (1 Samuel 8ff.). The ongoing history enables one to see that this problem continues. In spite of all these problems or perhaps even conspicuously justified by them, this institution, along with its experiences, evaluations, and hopes, came to play a large role within the Old Testament. Thus the word "king" (מֶלֶךְ = *melek*), for example, is found in the Old Testament over 2,500 times and ranks as the fourth most frequently encountered term in the Old Testament, even ranking above "Israel" in terms of occurrences.[16]

7.2 The Origin of the Monarchy and Saul

The beginnings of Israel's monarchy did not take place in a mythical or prehistoric time but rather in a historical situation of military exigency resulting from the assault of the Philistines who were beginning to demonstrate their military superiority.[17] The institution of kingship did not "descend from heaven."[18] It was not created then and there at the beginning of the world as a special act of creation by the gods,[19] and it was not given by a god or the gods to the people from the very beginning. In addition, the reign of the first king, Saul, already indicated that the monarchy would become a necessary (Judg. 17:6; 18:1; 19:1; and 21:25)[20] though problematic institution.[21]

Saul's monarchy was one of transition from the still charismatically stamped period of the so-called great judges and deliverers, to a hereditary monarchy, to dynasties that were attempted or established.[22] One can debate whether or not the decisive break first occurred between these judges and Saul or between Saul and David. Saul was still characterized as having charismatic features in what is probably the oldest of the narratives concerning the origin of kingship (1 Sam. 11:1–11, 15; cf. 1 Sam. 10:6). A charismatic dynasty that, for example, could be built upon Saul and then would continue on, is a debated matter in itself. When it is maintained concerning David that the Spirit of Yahweh has been granted to and continues with him because of his anointing(1 Sam. 16:13; cf. 2 Sam. 23:1f.), then this is an intentional theological statement that David has surpassed Saul. This superseding of Saul by David is noted in the separation of Saul's anointing (1 Sam 10:1) from the gift of the Spirit and also by the fact that he did not receive YHWH's Spirit as a continuing gift (1 Sam. 16:14ff.; cf. 18:12).[23]

In addition to 1 Sam. 11:1–11 (15), there are other texts in 1 Samuel that allow Saul's becoming king to be seen in a positive light (1 Samuel 7; 9:1–10:6), and consequently they also mention his anointing (1 Sam. 9:16; 10:1).[24] In contrast to David (2 Sam. 2:4, 7; 3:39; 5:3, 17; cf. 2 Sam. 19:11: Absalom), however, nothing is mentioned about Saul's having been anointed by either the people or their elders. Rather, it is instead only Samuel who anoints him. In contrast to an earlier anointing by the people, the anointing of King David by a prophet at the instruction of YHWH (1 Sam. 16:3) and then finally by YHWH himself is clearly an intentional theological superseding of the earlier tradition in the related prophetic narratives and the corresponding stories of David (1 Sam. 16:13; 2 Sam. 12:7). And it should be stressed that the (Deuteronomistic?) narrator in his editorial work later on intentionally seeks to insert a critical perspective on Saul (1 Sam. 15:1, 17).

In addition to these texts that offer a positive evaluation of kingship, there are other groups of texts that offer a critical view (1 Samuel 8; 10:17–25; 12). Statements about kingship are inserted into a "law of the king" that depict kingship in a strongly negative fashion (1 Sam. 8:11–18). This "law of the king" also designates in an apt fashion certain related social developments that came with the introduction of the monarchy.[25] All of these texts are now component parts of the so-called Deuteronomistic History. They allow one to recognize that this work of history and probably even its subsections as well (cf. 1 Sam. 8:7 with 8:22) do not contain a homogeneous, theological position concerning kingship. The possible strata of the Deuteronomistic History (critical: the Deuteronomistic Priestly stratum?; disapproving: the Deuteronomistic legal stratum?) and the Deuteronomistic History as a whole, even after a lengthy experience with the monarchy, cannot and do not want to bring into uniformity these two conflicting views of this institution.[26] Since human kingship is only rarely mentioned within the Deuteronomistic History as an opposite pole to the kingship of YHWH (1 Sam. 8:7; 12:12),[27] this view of God in the present context is a later development. Even so, this contrast is related to the argumentation in Judg. 8:22f. where Gideon refuses the offer of rulership, even to become the "ruler,"[28] by referring to YHWH's own status as ruler. Often the prophets are the antagonists of the kings.[29] The main tensions, however, appear to have resulted primarily from the conception of YHWH as warrior[30] and the role of the king who logically now, with the origin of the royal institution, should be the military leader (cf. 1 Sam. 11:6ff.; then see 1 Sam. 8:20; 18:17; and 25:28). Thus it could no longer be so clear that, or even how, YHWH alone was to be the liberator from duress (1 Sam. 10:18ff.). Further, while the people had "chosen" the king (1 Sam. 8:18), it was expressly emphasized, nonetheless, that the people are a people of YHWH and continue to be so (1 Sam. 10:1), for they stand under his sovereignty (1 Sam. 8:7; 10:19; cf. Judg. 8:22f.). And in the farewell address of Samuel (1 Samuel 12), this critical position is then stated and reinforced in a more fundamental manner (vv. 1f., 12ff.).

As a result of this, it was actually unavoidable that there would continue to be conflicts of faith about the monarchy. These conflicts were intensified in regard to Saul, because he developed the desire to continue to rule and even to establish a dynasty. Thus Saul's kingship already had officials who served him (1 Sam. 14:50; 17:55ff.; 18:22; and 21:8), the experiment of standing troops with a commander (1 Sam. 14:50, 52), and officers who received ownership of land as payment (1 Sam. 18:5, 13; 22:7). Then Saul sought to bring his sons into play as potential successors (cf. also 2 Sam. 2:8f.). Thereupon, a democratic and charismatic type of kingship that had been established at the beginning was being repressed in favor of a dynastic institution. And when Saul assumed for himself cultic functions and did not carry out the usual measures required by YHWH war (1 Samuel 13 and 15), conflict finally came to the fore. The (Deuteronomistic?) narrator wanted and was able to make clear that Saul was "rejected" by YHWH (1 Sam. 15:23, 26; 16:1, 7).[31] Since Saul prior to this rejection had at least participated in a sacrificial act (1 Sam. 14:33–35), 1 Samuel 13 takes on a decidedly anti-Saul cast, for it originated perhaps within a priestly[32] or more likely a Deuteronomistic circle of storytellers who were, by contrast, inclined to view David in a positive light (1 Sam. 13:14). The later Deuteronomistic references to David attest to this.[33] The Old Testament texts indeed allow one to recognize very clearly that the cultic functions of the king were infrequently performed even later on and that, above all, they were not attested on a regular basis.[34] This was fundamentally different, for example, in ancient Egypt where the pharaoh "up to the period of the Roman caesar (was) regarded as the only person who was qualified and entitled to take part in sacrifice or some other cultic act in the land. Whatever occurred in the temple on behalf of the gods was carried out in the name of the king."[35] In Mesopotamia the king continued to be cultically active during the rituals of the New Year's Festival and the "holy marriage" associated with them.[36] In addition, the Assyrian king was at the same time a priest.[37] The cultic, priestly acts of the king were not completely excluded in the history following Saul that was narrated by the Old Testament witnesses,[38] even though such acts did not belong to the regular activities of the king in Israel and Judah. This was obviously different from pre-Israelite, Jebusite Jerusalem in which the city-state king was at the same time the priest (Gen. 14:18; Ps. 110:4). The late postexilic Books of Chronicles eradicate rather extensively, however, the references to the cultic actions of the kings[39] and allows them to continue to be true only of David and Solomon, thus clearly following the Deuteronomistic evaluations of these kings. Second Chronicles 26:16–21 makes more than clear the criticism of the cultic activity of a king.[40]

Saul's monarchy was a transitional one and thus necessarily possessed features that were rather unclear and unexplained. This is the reason that Saul failed. The problems already emerging with him, however, were in large measure and for all intents and purposes those which were associated later on with the monarchies of Israel and Judah. How can religion and politics, political activity and Yahwistic faith, be reconciled to each other? What may a king do in Israel? What is he not allowed to do (cf. later 1 Kings 21: Naboth's vineyard)? How are the human, that is, royal, subject and the divine ruler related to each other in terms of the necessary military, political, and in many cases also "theological" decisions? Thus the monarchy of Saul already makes it abundantly clear in probably a historical way, and not just in the view of a later narrator, that it was virtually impossible[41] to be a king *over* the people chosen by YHWH and at the same time to be a king *under* YHWH's rule. Already then, on account of this tension which could at times be productive, the monarchy of Israel becomes a topic of Old Testament theology.

One is pressed to ask, last of all, in regard to each king whether and to what extent the ruler stood and ruled in conformity with YHWH, or whether this was not the case. This tension was responsible for leading to the development especially of the view of either the or an ideal king. While this tension was in the position to strengthen the eschatological hope of Yahwistic faith,[42] it was not alone responsible, however, for producing this eschatological hope. This demonstrates, on the one hand, the fact that, in spite of analogous, diverse experiences with the monarchy and the various interpretations of this phenomenon in Israel's cultural environment, its hope in a future ideal king did not develop from the influence of the ancient Near East. On the other hand, this demonstrates that within the Old Testament itself it is not only the monarchy that moved along its own incline toward eschatological expectation but also the tradition of the exodus, the witness of creation, and the tradition of Zion.[43]

7.3   David and Solomon

The way or ways in which David (1004–965 B.C.E.?)[44] became king is told in the narrative of his rise to power (1 Samuel 16–2 Samuel 5).[45] Even as there were differences in the way that Saul became king, so there are variations in the narrative depictions of how David came in contact with Saul and then became his successor. David is described as an experienced player of the lyre (1

Sam. 16:14ff.), as the conqueror of Goliath (1 Samuel 17), and also in a theologically enriched narrative as the elected and anointed of YHWH (1 Sam. 16:3, 8ff., 12f.; 2 Sam. 6:21). However, all of this encompasses a considerable period for both narrative time and narrated time, for the one designated to follow after Saul has and takes on many other things to do. David is shown to be even more qualifed to succeed Saul by the coming together of power, success, and the presence of YHWH (1 Sam. 16:18; 18:12; 2 Sam. 5:10),[46] until he finally then is anointed by the men of Judah (2 Sam. 2:4, 7) to be king over Judah. After Saul's successor, Ishbaal, had been assassinated by his own people, the northern tribes could scarcely do anything other than anoint David later on as king of Israel through their elders. Still, this did require him to have a contract (ברית = *bĕrît*, "covenant") with them (2 Sam. 5:3). The Books of Chronicles begin their new narration of the David stories intentionally at this point (1 Chronicles 11).

That David was anointed both by the people and by Samuel at the command of Yahweh are characteristics of a later theological enhancement of David and a diminishment of Saul.[47] The Deuteronomistic redactors were not only concerned to contrast between the descending Saul and the ascending David but also had a strong and positive theological interest in David which, for example, may be recognized in the references to him in the Books of Kings (cf. below). Brief remarks within the Books of Samuel prepare one to recognize that this perspective is both circumspect and at the same time significant. Thus the Spirit of YHWH indeed left Saul but continued to remain, however, with David (1 Sam. 16:13, 14ff.). Saul as well as David was chosen by YHWH (1 Sam. 10:24; 16:8ff.; 2 Sam. 6:21); however, he rejected only Saul (1 Samuel 15). Saul conducted his wars as wars of the people (1 Sam. 8:20: "our wars"), while David conducted his wars as the wars of YHWH (1 Sam. 18:17; 25:28). After David, this expression is no longer used.

David's significance for the faith of ancient Israel resides first in the fact that the institution of the "monarchy" was firmly established by and under him. Then, David conquered Jerusalem with his soldiers, a Canaanite city that was not taken by the Israelites before him. This city he made into the capital city of his empire. He later took the ark[48] and moved it to Jerusalem in order to increase the value of the city's religious significance and to incorporate it within the faith of Israel (2 Samuel 5–6). By means of these actions, Jerusalem received significance for the faith of Israel and, above all, Judah.[49] Further, David had founded a dynasty that was permitted to rule first over Israel and Judah (only through the reign of his successor Solomon) and then only over Judah for several centuries. The promise of Nathan (2 Samuel 7)[50] pledges to David that his son and then his house will continue and that this dynasty will bear a high degree of theological dignity. Whether older elements have been inserted[51] into this Deuteronomistic text is increasingly debated. However, one cannot any longer attribute to this promise a high degree of power to form and shape traditions, as G. von Rad has done.[52] This is not much different in reviewing the so-called Last Words of David (2 Sam. 23:1–7) and the covenant (ברית = běrît) of David mentioned there. However that may be, the promise of Nathan plays no role at all in the concrete formulation of the succession of David found in 1 Kings 1. And according to 1 Kings 11:13, 32, and 36, the election of David and his house become bound up with the tradition of the elected *city*.[53] Second Samuel 7, nevertheless, gives to the Davidic dynasty a significant promise and also seeks to incorporate this dynasty into the covenant of Sinai. Thus David is intentionally brought into association with Israel in this special pronouncement,[54] leading to the successful combination of kingship, Zion, temple, and Sinaitic covenant. In this way, the final form of the promise of Nathan is unequivocally set forth in the language of Deuteronomistic theology. In addition, it is quite clear from the Succession Narrative of David (2 Samuel 9–20; 1 Kings 1–2)[55] that, even though it speaks critically of the royal family, there was no question that one of the sons of the king would succeed him to the throne even without a special "charisma" and that the monarchy in the meanwhile had come to be regarded as an established institution. The gift of charisma was now lodged more in prophecy.

One probably also encounters a positive evaluation of the Davidic monarchy and empire in the saying about Judah in the Blessing of Jacob (Gen. 49:8–12) and in the Yahwistic oracles of Balaam in Num. 24:5–9, 17 [-19?][56] which both are *vaticinia ex eventu* and describe a "strongly transformed present" (H.-J. Zobel) but not, however, a future. These texts are already rather close to the "contemporary messianism" of the royal psalms.[57] In addition to the incorporation of Jerusalem into the kingdom and into the founding of the Davidic dynasty, David's significance for the later faith of Israel derived, last of all, from the fact that his great empire (2 Samuel 8–10) was remembered as an ideal empire. Thus this faith is often drawn upon in the Old Testament statements of hope.[58]

7.4   The Criticism of Kingship

The critical assessment of the monarchy, which is encountered in the narratives of Saul and somewhat also in the Succession Narrative of David, is found extensively throughout the Old Testament.[59] In addition to sapiential criticism (Prov. 30:27) or the critical evaluation of the royal rule in the Joseph Story (Gen. 37:8), there is the Jotham fable (Judg. 9:8ff.) which is also critical of kingship. In this last example, only the thornbush is prepared to accept rulership after all the other trees had turned down the offer. The fable seeks not to contend with YHWH but rather to "make the monarchy (as such) a joke."[60] To this belongs also Gideon's rejection of the position of "ruler" (משל = mšl) in

Judg. 8:22f.,[61] where then the alternative of human and divine sovereignty is clearly formulated.

To be placed in the list of texts that are critical of kingship are Deut. 33:5 and Num. 23:21 where in both instances YHWH is the king of his people,[62] while the human king is not mentioned. Among the prophets, it is the prophet Hosea who is the first to articulate with great determination a rather open and clearly expressed criticism of kings. When the people "made" for themselves kings, then they did so without YHWH's approval (Hos. 8:4, 10). Eventually, the monarchy shall be removed from Israel (Hos. 3:4; 7:7; and 10:15). A king stands in opposition to YHWH and consequently is unable to offer aid (Hos. 10:3f.). YHWH in his wrath gives Israel a king and takes him back in his anger (Hos. 13:4–11). When the reunification of Israel and Judah is promised, the promise is couched intentionally in language that speaks of this happening under a ראש ($rō'š =$ "chief") and not under a king (Hos. 2:2).

In Isaiah there is a scene of King YHWH in his court (Isa. 6:5) as well as the narration of a critical encounter of the prophet with King Ahaz (Isaiah 7).[63] Jeremiah's oracles concerning the kings in chaps. 22–23 are comparable in many ways to the criticism of rulers in Hosea. However, this criticism is combined with positive statements about them in this collection.[64]

Deuteronomy attempts in its Deuteronomistic, compositional design (Deut. 16:18—18:22)[65] to surround the king with other officeholders and thus to be the first to support the sharing of power. Furthermore, in the so-called law of the king (Deut. 17:14–20), which has no parallel in the other legal collections of the Old Testament, this king is pointedly described as a "brother" in the community of the people.[66] While the only positive action required of the king is that he continue to read this torah, he is made into a "model Israelite" (N. Lohfink). The law is precise in its statement that the nation may not "elect" (בחר $= bāḥar$), for this is something that YHWH does. The sole activity of the people in this regard is that they "set over" (שים $= śîm$) themselves a king, yet only after YHWH has chosen him (v. 15). However, the (Deuteronomistic) promise of Nathan, the favorable assessments of the monarchy in the Deuteronomistic texts of 1 Samuel 7–15, the references to the promise of Nathan and to David,[67] and the positive and hopeful conclusion of the Deuteronomistic History in 2 Kings 25:27–30 (the pardon of Jehoiachin)[68] make it very clear the Deuteronomistic movement still continued to place its hopes in the monarchy even though it was seen in a different way and was given only a rather limited place. The Deuteronomistic movement, however, was obviously neither prepared nor in the position to strike the monarchy fully from its design of the new Israel.

This Deuteronomistic movement's assessment of the monarchy shows accordingly a complex and tension-filled picture that probably is not limited only to different literary strata and redactions. In 1 Sam. 8:7 and 12:12 ff., Samuel is made to speak very critical, fundamental things about human kingship in opposition to the royal nature of YHWH and to question the obedience of kings to YHWH (cf. 1 Kings 2:4; 3:6; 6:12; 8:25; etc.; cf. 1 Sam. 12:14f., 24f.). One then sees in the "sins of Jeroboam,"[69] that is, in his establishment of royal sanctuaries in Dan and Bethel necessary for his new state and in his setting up of the golden calves for the worship of YHWH (1 Kings 12:25ff.), one of the decisive reasons (1 Sam. 8:11–18) for the apostasy of the people from YHWH and consequently the punishment of the exile that had become necessary. However, it is also the case that in the Deuteronomistic History, David can repeatedly be viewed in a positive light,[70] while Solomon is seen as an exemplary worshiper in his prayer for the dedication of the temple (1 Kings 8:22f.). Thus, for some time the hope for the delay or even the turning away of judgment for some Deuteronomists was expressed in terms of "for the sake of my servant David." And this expression was retained as a theological agency of hope even when this hope had turned out to be illusory. David had received a special promise and bequest (1 Kings 2:4, 24; 3:6f.; 6:12; 9:5; etc.). He could also be enlisted as a model of obedience (1 Kings 3:6; 8:17; 9:4; 11:4, 6, 33, 38; 15:11; 2 Kings 14:3; 16:2; 18:3; 22:2; etc.), including even in the new incorporation of the promise of Nathan into the prophecy to Jeroboam (1 Kings 11:36). In this connection, the promise of the continuation of the dynasty and obedience could also be linked (1 Kings 2:4; 8:25; and 9:4f.).[71] Many times, however, David becomes in different ways a positive point of reference, for "YHWH did not wish to destroy Judah for the sake of David his servant, corresponding then to his promise to him that he would make him a *light* before his sons for all time" (2 Kings 8:19; cf. 1 Kings 11:36; 15:4; also 2 Sam. 21:17; Ps. 132:17).[72]

As a whole, the Deuteronomistic History could not, however, see the monarchy in only a positive way (cf., e.g., 2 Kings 21:11–15 in regard to Manasseh; then 22:16f.; 23:2f.: Dtr²?). Nevertheless, in spite of the exile, King Jehoiachin, still alive, is not passed by, but rather his pardon is seen as a sign of a possibly positive future (2 Kings 25:27–30). The declaration about the Davidic covenant that is probably intentionally preserved in the Deuteronomistic History (2 Sam. 23:5; in Ps. 89:4 coupled with the theme of election) underlines once more the theological significance of David and his dynasty.

Even the announcement of the coming savior king in Micah 5:1ff. contains an element of criticism of kingship insofar as the text is emphatically silent in speaking about Jerusalem as the only, real royal residence, but stresses instead Bethlehem. The Book of Ezekiel also contains statements that are critical of the monarchy (Ezek. 12:10–15; 17:1–21; and 21:30–32), and in his program for the future, Ezekiel gives only a very subordinate role to the coming savior king. This book suppresses thoroughly the title of king (cf. 17:19–24), apart from 37:22, 24, and uses instead that of "prince" (נשיא = *nāśî'*; Ezek. 44:3; 45:7f.; etc.).[73] In addition, what is said for all intents and purposes about the shepherds in Ezekiel 34 (esp. vv. 23f.) and about the royal house in the lament of Ezekiel 19 hardly counterbalances the promise of Ezek. 37:15f. What was valid for this ideal David or Davidic descendant was then granted to the high priest in the postexilic period (Zech. 3:7). According to the witness of the postexilic Chronicler's history whose strong duty-bound thinking was indebted to the dogma of the relationship between deed and consequence,[74] each king who sins receives immediately his punishment from YHWH (2 Chron. 12:1; 16:7ff.; 20:35ff.; 21:4ff.; and 26:16ff.). Since the especially sinful King Manasseh was blessed with a long period of rule, the Chronicler had to devise a conversion in the midst of Manasseh's reign (2 Chron. 33:11ff.).

In spite of all the criticism of the monarchy in Israel, a Davidic covenant was placed alongside the covenant of Sinai, even though the former did not stand in clear theological competition with the latter.[75] That the monarchy was viewed critically as an institution still did not prohibit the continuation of a vital promise to David. This points to a way of thinking that expresses belief in the continuation of YHWH's manner of revelation to his people, in his abiding activity and in his persisting journey.[76]

7.5 "Royal Ideology" in the Old Testament

The kingship of David replaced the city monarchy that was present in Jerusalem.[77] Does this mean that Jerusalem would become the gate of entrance for ancient Near Eastern conceptions of the king? Since scholars have often spoken of an ancient Near Eastern *royal ideology* and still continue to speak at times in this way,[78] they have generally assumed that this ideology influenced ancient Israel's image of its king as well as the corresponding texts of the Old Testament. This matter will now be briefly discussed.

The ideas of the so-called Uppsala School,[79] given a predominantly Scandinavian character, and of the mainly English myth and ritual school (S. H. Hooke) provided the foundation and many details for the thesis of a so-called ancient Near Eastern royal ideology. These ideas (in connection with V. Grönbech) propagated primarily a certain understanding of the cult, namely, the cult as ritual drama and, above all, as an activity of the community that led to its strengthening and less so of the individual. Related to this were folklore studies (J. G. Frazer) and the conception of a "soul of the people," which were influential in this regard (J. Pedersen; also S. Mowinckel).

There issued from all of this the all-purpose idea of a "cultic pattern," that is, a ritual schema typical for the ancient Near East in which the divine king may have been the central figure in the important festivals. On the one hand, he was here the representative of the deity in the cult, his "son," and, according to the schools just mentioned, a dying and rising god.[80] On the other hand, he was also at the same time the cultic representative of the people to the deity, thus serving as a legitimate "intercessor." The text of the respective cultic rituals was a dramatized, mythic presentation of the renewal of life, and the most significant festival was consequently that of the New Year's,[81] which included the king, who as the central actor of the ritual drama played the role of or incorporated in himself the dying and rising God, the battle with chaos, the journey to Hades, the "resurrection," the crowning again of the king, the sacred marriage as a dispensing of life, the procession, and much more. The mission of the king is the well-being of the land, and he procures, for example, the fertility of the land as the mediator of blessing.

More recent scholarly investigation of the legitimacy and limits of this ancient Near Eastern royal ideology has primarily concluded that there can be no discussion of a homogeneous royal tradition in the ancient Near East. The theological appraisal of kingship (also as the "son of god") in Egypt, among the Hittites, among the various Mesopotamian peoples, and in Ugarit was not uniform and continued to change during the course of the lengthy history of the institution.[82] The institution of divine kingship (Egypt, though of varying expression), the cultic deification of the king and a priestly kingship (Sumer), the self-deification of the ruler (Akkad), the king as the chosen servant of the deity (Babylonia), and the deification of the king after his death (Hittites) allow one to recognize major differences. Whether in the final analysis the king also functioned in the temple as the only legitimate priest or as the patron of the temple sets forth a further difference.

How does the Israelite monarchy stand in comparison to these? It had no divine and also no mythic origins, and the king of Israel and Judah had no regular cultic functions.[83] In Israel there was no cultic worship of either the living or the dead king, and there the king did not play the role of cultic mediator between God and the people. In addition, there were differences in the assessment and theological view of kingship in the Northern Kingdom of Israel as compared to the monarchy in the Southern Kingdom of Judah. Further, how does a fundamental criticism of kings come to appear within a possible royal ideology that for the Old Testament concerns the typical and significant and not only the individual. Can an Israelite king in some fashion embody YHWH in a cultic ritual drama? The thesis of a dying and rising deity in Israel's surrounding cultures has been disputed (especially for Babylonia and its Akitu festival), and the Old Testament makes no mention of this notion in regard to YHWH.[84] Was there in Israel in fact a similar cult with elements of a ritual drama in which humans performed?[85]

Even though this royal ideology is not attested in a uniform fashion, one cannot dispute the fact that many of the characteristics of ancient Near Eastern ideology presented above in rough outline are also found in Old Testament texts. In the Old Testament, the king is also the son of God (Pss. 2:7; 89:27f.; and 2 Sam. 7:14). During his coronation, he receives a so-called royal protocol (Ps.

2:7; 2 Kings 11:17) and the power of good fortune (2 Sam. 21:10ff.), since his commission includes responsibility for fertility (Ps. 72:16f.). With the introduction and establishment of the monarchy, Israel borrowed and indeed must appropriate elements of royal ideology from its ancient Near Eastern environment. The "courtly style"[86] in the royal psalms, especially Psalms 2; 72; and 110, shows this rather clearly. Genesis 1:27 and Ps. 8:5ff. use democratized royal predicates in their statements about humans as the "image of God."[87] Possibly the only text in the Old Testament in which the Israelite king was actually named "god," Ps. 45:7, is found in a marriage song in praise of a king. However, perhaps one ought to read in this verse an original YHWH in place of the name אלהים (*'ĕlōhîm* = "god"), due possibly to the redaction of the so-called Elohistic Psalter (Psalms 42–83). The Books of Chronicles hope for a king in the late postexilic period who will sit on the throne of YHWH (1 Chron. 28:5; 29:23; etc.). However, this monarch's cultic activity and even priestly representation is expressly excluded (2 Chron. 26:16ff.). Foremost among his functions as the city king of Jerusalem was a cultic, even priestly function carried out by the king of Judah (Psalm 110). Even so, the question arises as to what extent these statements later on have been or are to be taken literally.

The effort has been undertaken often in the past and sometimes in the present to make the Ugaritic texts the connecting link between ancient Near Eastern thought and its gateway into Israelite thinking, that is, the city of Jerusalem.[88] Thus, for example, one has sought to interpret Ugaritic epics or myths as cultic, dramatic texts. However, at present, studies that point to discoveries such as these have grown rather quiet,[89] so that, for example, Isaiah 6, the Servant Songs, Ezek. 37:1–14, and the vision of the Son of Man in Daniel 7 are no longer understood as cultic, dramatic texts, while the expression לדוד (*lĕdāwid* = "for David") in many superscriptions of the psalms no longer is taken to refer to the king as the customary and exemplary worshiper in the Psalter. Consequently, there are only individual elements of ancient Near Eastern royal conceptions that made their way into Israelite thought. Even as there was no uniform royal ideology in the ancient Near East, so it was with Israel. Furthermore, in Israel kingship was not a fixed, static institution.[90] The king of Judah as well as of Israel was not the subject of royal historical writing which centered around his military feats. The Old Testament does not contain any self-report of a king, no apotheosis of the ruler, and no self-justification before the deity. Sacral kingship may not have existed in Israel.

7.6 The Positive Evaluation of Kingship and the Royal Psalms

In addition to a strong criticism of kingship,[91] the Old Testament quite naturally also contains a positive assessment of the monarchy. This positive

evaluation is found in the oracle concerning Judah in the Blessing of Jacob
(Gen. 49:8–12), the Yahwistic oracles of Balaam in Num. 24:5–9, 17 [–19?],
in the promise to David in 2 Samuel 7, and in the promonarchial texts within
1 Samuel 7–15 (1 Samuel 7; 9:1–10:16; and 1 Samuel 11).[92] Furthermore, the
Deuteronomistic History could evaluate in a positive manner kings such as
Hezekiah (2 Kings 18) and especially Josiah (2 Kings 22–23) who largely
reigned in conformity to the will of YHWH and even introduced reforms in order to purify the Yahwistic cult.[93]

Psalm 21:8 and especially Ps. 89:4, 25, 29[94] likewise point in a positive way
to the continuing existence of hope based on the acts of God on behalf of
David, that is, to a promise that refers to the Davidic covenant (2 Sam. 23:5).
This is also the case in 2 Chron. 7:18; 13:5; 21:7; Ps. 132:12; and Jer. 33:21.[95]
The exilic text, Isa. 55:3, by contrast, transfers the "grantings of grace to
David" (חסדי דוד = *hasdēy dāwid*) to the nation (cf. 2 Chron. 6:42), while in
Isaiah 40–55 the title of king is used only for YHWH as the king of Israel
(52:7).[96]

Regulations governing the behavior of the king of Israel/Judah can be derived from Psalm 101 which presents a mirror of the monarch. Moreover, one
may extract from the Old Testament's proverbial wisdom what appear to be
some rules for the behavior and reign of the king (Prov. 16:10, 12ff.; 20:8, 26,
28; 21:1; 25:2ff.; 29:4, 14; and 31:1–9) as well as guidelines for the relationship of human beings, that is, in this context, the "wise," to the king. The wise
were members of an exalted social position and had access to the king (Prov.
14:35; and 16:14f.; cf. 11:14). In addition, one finds in the proverbial wisdom
of the Old Testament sayings that are critical of kings, although the criticisms
argue more from common experiences than from theology (Prov. 30:21f., 27f.;
31:3ff.). The king's caring for the widows, the orphans, and the poor (Prov.
31:8f.) is a prevalent ancient Near Eastern topos. In Israel, this topos was "democratized" through the corresponding commandments of YHWH. The God
that obligated his people to follow these commandments addressed them to
each Israelite (Exod. 22:21; Deut. 10:18; 14:29; 16:11, 14; 24:17, 19, 20f.;
26:12f.; and 27:19; cf. Isa. 1:17, 23; Mal. 3:5; Prov. 23:10f.; etc.).[97]

Similar to the way the Zion hymns speak about Jerusalem,[98] the royal
psalms (Psalms 2; 45; and 110)[99] talk about kingship in ways that transcend
and surpass the reigning human ruler.[100] Thus the king is begotten "this day"
by God, that is, the ruler is the one who at the beginning of his reign is legiti-
mated by the royal protocol (Ps. 2:7)[101] and adopted for sonship. This relationship to God should not be understood in a literal, physical way. Consequently, the king rules in YHWH's place (Ps. 2:7f.). Sometimes the effort is
made at least to derive rituals of coronation from Psalms 2 and 110 (cf. also 1
Kings 1:33f. and 2 Kings 11). One may say with a substantial degree of certainty that this royal ritual may well have contained a promise to the king (cf.

Pss. 2:7 and 110:1), even if, for redactional reasons, one may no longer clearly enlist for this the present Deuteronomistic, final form of 2 Samuel 7.[102] The king was free to offer a petition to YHWH (1 Kings 3:5ff.; Pss. 2:8; 20:5; 21:3, 5). He is, then, the anointed of YHWH (Pss. 2:2, 7; 18:51; 20:7; 28:8; 84:10; 89:27ff.; 132:10, 17; and Lam. 4:20; cf. 1 Sam. 16:13; 24:7; 26:9; 2 Sam. 12:7; etc.),[103] the chosen one and the "shield" (Pss. 78:70; 89:4, 19f.), and the authorized agent of YHWH himself.[104] YHWH is the father, fortress, and shield of the king (Pss. 2:7; 18:3; 28:1; and 89:27; cf. 2 Sam. 7:14a[105]), while the king is also YHWH's servant (Ps. 18:1; cf. 89:51), the light of Israel (2 Sam. 21:17; 2 Kings 8:19), and the savior (Psalm 72). The king's well-being is also the well-being of the nation (Psalms 28; 63:12; 101; cf. 1 Kings 8:30, 59), even as, by contrast, his sins are their sins (cf. 2 Samuel 24; 1 Kings 9:1–9; etc.; see the Deuteronomistic History's description of the "sins of Jeroboam"[106]). The kings of the earth align themselves against the little ruler of Jerusalem when he ascends his throne, while the nations rage and seek to revolt (Psalm 2). Whether or not this reflects a change of the ruler, perhaps in the New Assyrian empire, the psalm still opens up the prospects of a possible casting off of a vassal's status. Moreover, the king is to smash the nations like clay pots with his iron scepter (Ps. 2:9), something that is reflected in similar Egyptian customs mentioned in the so-called execration texts.[107] And if this little king is to rule "from sea to sea," meaning from the Persian Gulf unto the Mediterranean Sea and from the Euphrates unto the ends of the earth (Ps. 72:8), then his kingdom would extend even beyond that of the empire of David (cf. Ps. 18:44–48). This topos, taken from ancient Near Eastern courtly language, makes clear the type of language used when speaking of a king.[108] Royal hymns, which were present in rich abundance in the religious environment of the ancient Near East,[109] allow one to recognize both similarities to and differences from the same type of hymns in ancient Israel. The Old Testament contains not only statements about the office of kingship[110] and others about the perfection and ideal of the monarchy but also expressions of the consequences of YHWH's adoption and legitimation of the Israelite king.[111] These statements carry within themselves the objective of hoping and wishing ever again or even once for all for an ideal king. G. von Rad has used for this the delightful image of an enormous purple coat that was much too large.[112] One must in fact ask each king whether he is finally *the* king or only *a* king.

Thus it is especially the royal psalms with their "present messianism" (G. W. Ahlström) and their inherent tension between the already now and the not yet (S. Wagner) that have pointed to and established the way for the messianic hope. This allows one to stress that the language of the court of the previously mentioned courtly style of the royal psalms also has exerted an influence on the so-called messianic texts[113] (cf., e.g., Isa. 9:1ff. and 11:1ff.),[114] especially since the royal psalms later on (like many messianic texts) were interpreted collectively.[115] The ideal image of the king in these psalms is filled with the content of hope in God, for the Davidic monarchy also represented the earthly sovereignty of the world ruler YHWH (cf. the composition of Psalm 89; then Chronicles).[116] Psalm 21 makes clear that the king owes everything to YHWH and also points out what is mediated by the king to others (vv. 4 + 7).

Moreover, if rulers such as Hezekiah and especially Josiah were described in the Deuteronomistic History to a certain degree as ideal kings (2 Kings 18; 22 + 23), then this prepared the way for the royal portrait in the Books of Chronicles. According to the latter, the Jewish king (there is no mention of the kings of the Northern Kingdom), as the one who assumed the place of God in this world, sat on the throne of YHWH (1 Chron. 17:14; 28:5; 29:23; 2 Chron. 9:8; 13:8; also 6:40–42). However, this was more a strong investment of YHWH in the monarchy than its revaluation.[117] Even the Priestly document cannot completely pass by the subject of the monarchy, for it arranges the promised descendants of Abraham in such a way that kings should come forth from his loins (Gen. 17:6, 16; 35:11: P). Even the writings that are strongly priestly and cultic in character, such as the Priestly document and the Books of Chronicles, held firmly to the messianic hope in spite of the fact they were not knowledgeable of a monarchy in their own time. Thus the promise of Nathan has even a greater significance for the Chronicler than for the Books of Kings, for this promise "describes the actual, divine principle at work throughout the entire history of David" [118] (cf. 1 Chron. 17:11–14; 28:2–7; 2 Chron. 1:8f.; 6:10, 16, 42; 7:17f.; 13:4–12; and 21:7).[119]

While the prophets and the Deuteronomistic History in no case speak of a final rejection of the house of David, Psalm 89 wrestles with this problem. And when these texts speak of the king as the bearer of the Spirit of YHWH[120] (1 Sam. 16:13 and 2 Sam. 23:2; cf. Isa. 11:2), then they contain a specifically Israelite formulation among the positive statements about the king.

7.7   The Messianic Hope

The tensions between the ideal and the real within the monarchy on the one hand and between its presentation and evaluation on the other, the particular features of royal ideology that led to the creation of a present messianism, even more the courtly style that enriched this ideology, possibly even the increasing influence of the promise of Nathan that developed, and the retrospectives on the great period of David are, taken together in their complex and multilayered form, the factors that led to the development of a *messianic hope*[121] in ancient Israel. To point to only one of these factors is insufficient and reductionistic. In addition, the notion of external influences from the ancient Near East to explain the development of messianism in ancient Israel is not necessarily acceptable, even with the revival of the theses of H. Gunkel and H. Gressmann that argue for this view.[122]

The development of the messianic hope and expectation, furthermore, is not the root of Old Testament eschatology[123] but rather one of its component parts. Eschatology has found no parallel in the cultures surrounding ancient Israel. Jewish eschatology has to do with the expectation of a new, last, conclusive, final, and ideal Davidic descendant as the one who brings about the sovereignty of YHWH in its full realization.

On the journey toward this hope one finds a kind of actualized eschatology in the appropriation of the royal psalms (Psalms 2; 72; and 110) with their transcendent courtly style that stood beside exalted statements about the monarchy of David (Gen. 49:8-12; Num. 24:5–9, 17 [-19]).[124] In addition, one should also include in this journey Psalms 89 and 132 with their expectations concerning the Davidic king. Still, the journey moved from experience to hope (S. Mowinckel). The discussion about the ideal king continued to turn more and more toward future expectation. This probably developed in view of many negative experiences with the monarchy and many tensions between the form of kingship that was encountered in actual life and the continually rearticulated, necessary reform of royal sovereignty. This future expectation also developed on the basis of the close connection of YHWH with the king that continued to come to expression. If one experienced kings in a negative fashion or had to describe them in a negative way, then there stood alongside this experience or depiction a contrasting, ideal portrait by which to measure and bring them into line.[125] Texts that speak of a continuing relationship of YHWH with the Davidic dynasty (2 Samuel 7; 23:2–5; Psalms 89; 132) could be added that freely opened up expectations.

When it is said that divine judgment may have been averted on account of David,[126] then this king possesses already the function of a mediator of salvation. When statements are made about the little king of the tiny state of Israel or especially Judah in the royal psalms, which go far beyond the experience of reality,[127] then these statements have to do, consequently, not with the concrete, presently existing king but rather with his ideal portrait, his desired primeval depiction. The Books of Chronicles move with their perspective along a similar course in their identifying the throne of the king with the throne of YHWH.[128]

If, in these ways, these hopes slowly developed within the historical faith of the Old Testament until they focused on the final, eschatological, savior king, they still remained for a long time focused on this world and were connected to a quite concrete situation that would be brought to a final conclusion by this savior king.[129] Thus it is no wonder that most texts that are attributed to the so-called messianic prophecies contain a criticism of the current ruling king or royal house or existing monarchy that stands beside or mostly before the actual statement of messianic hope. Consequently, these so-called messianic texts deal not only with the promise of salvation but with the realization that this salvation must and can take place only through judgment.[130]

Since the Davidic dynasty is a tree that has been cut down, then the new savior king must sprout from its stump (Isa. 11:1ff.). Even as Isaiah has reached back to the ancestor David, so Micah 5:1ff. reaches back to David's city of birth, Bethlehem, and proceeds to criticize Jerusalem as the present residence of the king. In Jer. 23:5f. the promise of the branch receives a royal name. His name, "YHWH is *our* righteousness (our salvation)," is obviously at the same time an implicit, critical, renunciation of Zedekiah (YHWH is *my* righteousness).[131] In addition, there is always a rather strong distinction made between the power of God that is appearing and coming into effect and the personal action of the one bringing salvation. This savior is and continues to be the instrument of YHWH. It is the "zeal of YHWH Sebaoth" who is at work here (Isa. 9:6),[132] and it is YHWH who is acting here (Jer. 23:5f.). Thus, in the Old Testament, this "messiah" is neither a superficial nor even a competitive double of YHWH, even as the Davidic covenant does not stand in tension with the covenant of Sinai.

In regard to the texts that fit now the purpose of this topic, two preliminary remarks must be made. First, the authenticity of these texts, for one thing, is strongly disputed. In this connection, however, some scholars on occasion have lapsed into hypercriticism. For example, that the hope for "the future Davidic ruler" could not have developed until after the Davidic dynasty had come to an end with the Babylonian exile is an often repeated but unproven postulate. Certainly, additions and amplifications expanded these texts of messianic hope. Thus, Amos 9:13–15 was attached to Amos 9:11f., while Isa. 11:6–8, 9, 10–16 was added to Isa. 11:1–5. Micah 5:1–4a is also multilayered. In examining these and other passages, one must argue more carefully in searching for each one's fundamental core than has often been the case. Second, it is undisputed that the assessment of these texts should quite naturally take into consideration the common, current depiction of Old Testament prophecy. The recognition that there obviously are not the same kinds of additions to each prophetic book may also speak for the "authenticity" of many of these texts. Furthermore, it is always to be asked how the texts that speak of messianic hope relate to the common message of each respective prophet. Finally, some of the texts that have been debated were connected to an aspect of their original setting, perhaps, for example, an enthronement ceremony (Isa. 9:1–6), before they were understood to have an orientation toward the future.

Being a Judean, Amos consequently knew something of the Davidic dynasty. One could say that this dynasty may be a "falling booth"[133] as early as the division of the Davidic-Solomonic empire (Amos 9:11f.). There is indeed in Isa. 7:10ff. an announcement of a new king that offers a criticism of the present ruler, although this text lacks the messianic coloring[134] that is present in courtly style in Isa. 9:1–6 and 11:1–5.[135] Isaiah 9:1–6, with the mentioning of the five throne names in Isa. 9:5f.,[136] is at least preexilic[137] and could fit well the situation of 733 B.C.E., while Isa. 11:1–5 does not badly conform to Isaiah's usual proclamation.[138] Micah 5:1–4a takes an implicitly critical stance toward Jerusalem, a position that fits well the other preaching of the prophet.[139] Verses 1, 3a, 4a, and 5b are an ancient kernel, and they promise a decisive new beginning likened to the earlier one. Additions are found also in Hos. 3:5 and Jer. 30:9; 33:14–16a. By contrast,[140] Jer. 23:5f. should not be denied to Jeremiah, even as Ezek. 17:22–24; 34:23f.; 37:24f. (cf. also 21:30–32) should not be disallowed for Ezekiel.[141]

Deutero-Isaiah transfers now the "lasting gifts of grace to David"[142] to the nation (Isa. 55:3; cf. 2 Sam. 7:23f.) and even assigned the title of messiah to the Persian king Cyrus (Isa. 45:1). Cyrus is viewed by the prophet as the instrument of YHWH for the long-awaited period of salvation that is breaking into history. However, the so-called Servant Songs in Deutero-Isaiah[143] are not messianic, for the songs possess their own content and literary form that do not conform to messianic texts.

In their eschatology coming into realization,[144] Haggai and Zechariah (as does Deutero-Isaiah) see Zerubbabel as this "messiah" (Hag. 2:21–23; in Zech. 4:1ff. there are two anointed ones: a priest and a descendant of David).[145] Also, Zech. 6:9–13 originally pertained to Zerubbabel, not to the high priest Joshua.

The way in which the portrait of the messiah changes may be seen in the light of Zech. 9:9f. It is not an accident that these verses, in following Zech. 9:1–8 which probably reflects the victorious march of Alexander the Great, wish to set forth an intentional contrast.[146] The reference to "your king" is connected expressly to well-known expectations.

The character of the Chronicler's discussion of Davidic sovereignty[147] can probably be viewed as a veiled messianic witness. In Daniel 7, however, the "Son of Man" is scarcely a messianic figure. Rather, the chapter sets forth the greatest possible contrast between the Son of Man from on high and the four animals from below who ascended from the sea. They represent respectively the embodiment of Israel and its coming kingdom of God in contrast to the ("animal-like") four world kingdoms which shall pass away.[148]

In the texts mentioned above, the word "messiah" (with the exception of Isa. 45:1 for Cyrus and the metaphorical use in Zech. 4:11ff.) does not occur. Rather, the term refers elsewhere either to the earthly king (1 Sam. 24:7; Ps. 20:7; Lam. 4:20; etc.) or, in the postexilic period, to the high priest (Lev. 4:3, 5; 16:32) and the priests in general (Exod. 28:41) where anointing is viewed as a legal act that transmits power and might.[149] In the places where this anointing is carried out by a prophet and not by the people (1 Samuel 9f.; 2 Kings 9), the prophet demands that the anointed "is to accept the duty of kingship and to acknowledge YHWH's power and sovereignty."[150] The language of these texts is consciously veiled[151] and mysterious. Subsequently, in investigating linguistic use, one should not too quickly postulate the inauthenticity of these texts. Moreover, the expectation of this bringer of salvation went through a lengthy development[152] that has created many recastings and different accents. The messiah was not always expected to be a powerful ruler (cf. Ezekiel 34; Zech. 9:9f.). Consequently, one cannot speak of either a distinct or a uniform portrayal of the messiah in the Old Testament, even if there are continuing, structural lines (K.-D. Schunck), as, for instance, the nearness of the ruling figure to YHWH and his sovereignty and the bringing of peace, justice, and righteousness. Further, the picture of the messiah always sets forth an ideal Davidic descendant, who is especially commissioned and endowed by YHWH either to be a shepherd or to possess unusual wisdom.

Thus, because of multiple tensions in the existing monarchy that nevertheless held promise for the future, the Old Testament inquired after *the* king who, as a human being, is also entirely an instrument of God to bring divine salvation and is and ever continues to be in concord with God. In the postexilic period, it is perhaps the case that many of the messianic texts, resuming in Isa. 55:1–3, are explained by referring them to the nation and pointing out its messianic role.[153] This can be shown, for instance, by a comparison of Jer. 33:15f. with Jer. 23:5f. or by the multiple additions present in Micah 5:1–5. A wider expansion of the Jewish expectation and portrait of the messiah then occurs in the so-called "period between the Testaments." Psalms of Solomon 17 is an especially typical testimony to this (cf. also *1 Enoch* 48:10; 52:4; 4 Ezra 7:28f.).

Christian theologians and readers of the Old Testament on occasion inquire after the "Old Testament witness to Christ." Here it must be pointed out that this Old Testament testimony does not primarily consist of the witness of the messianic texts which Jesus did not fully "fulfill" and which do not possess within the Old Testament the great significance later attributed to them. Rather, here one should inquire after the fundamental structures of these Old Testament witnesses of faith that were later taken up in the New Testament witness to Christ. These structures include, for example, election as a historical act, history as word and promise, the relationship of word and history, and so on.[154]

Chapter 8. The Temple and the City of God
(the So-called Zion Tradition)[1]

Jerusalem was first conquered by David on behalf of Israel. Afterward, he transported the ark there and made the city into the capital of his empire which united the northern territory of Israel with the southern territory of Judah into a personal union (2 Samuel 5–6). The Jerusalem temple was first built by Solomon (1 Kings 6–8). In spite of their later appearance in Israelite history, city and temple took on rather important significance for the faith of ancient Israel. This significance was given even though people knew that what Ezekiel would express about Jerusalem was true: "Your lineage and your birth were in the land of the Canaanites; your father was an Amorite, and your mother a Hittite" (Ezek. 16:3). The non-Israelite prehistory of what became in the time of David the Jerusalem of Israel and Judah therefore was well known. The question then arises as to how the significance of this city was expressed in Israelite faith and then how this expression was related to the overall Israelite faith in YHWH and the God of Israel.

Psalm 68:16f. speaks about this faith[2] in stating that YHWH intentionally took up his residence in Jerusalem (cf. Ps. 74:2), thus making an actual choice in selecting Mt. Zion from among the mountains to be the mountain of God. Here Israel's God dwells in his sanctuary (Ps. 68:36), and the temple mountain is YHWH's נחלה = naḥălâ ("inheritance, possession") (Exod. 15:17). When one seeks to determine how this divine activity was conceptualized, one may point to Deuteronomy, which has spoken of the place that YHWH has chosen (Deut. 12:5f; etc.). Deuteronomistic literature and the later texts that are dependent upon it refer to this specific activity of God in connection with the historical acts of divine election.[3] In this way it becomes clear that election signifies not simply a once for all act of Israel's primeval choosing but also an ever recurring phenomenon. This indicates that election is a fundamental structure for interpreting Old Testament faith. Unlike a mythical event in which, for example, Babylon was created in the pattern of a heavenly archetype,[4] the election of Jerusalem has to do with a historical action.

8.1 Jerusalem—Zion—the City of God

Jerusalem is mentioned 660 times in the Old Testament, including occurrences with descriptive titles or other appellations. Jerusalem is called the "city

of God," the "city of YHWH," the "city of our God,"[5] and the "holy city."[6]
YHWH speaks of Jerusalem as "my city" (Isa. 45:13), but Israel never calls
Jerusalem "our city." Jerusalem as "my city" is expressed by a human being
only in the prayer in Lam. 3:51. Jerusalem is also, quite naturally, the "city of
David,"[7] and it is also called Salem (Gen. 14:18; and Ps. 76:3). In addition, the
city was called "Ariel" (Isa. 29:1f., 7; and 33:7), a term that probably means
an "altar hearth" (Ezek. 43:15f.). Jerusalem is the "throne of YHWH" (Jer.
3:17; 14:21; and 17:12), while in later texts and often in combination with the
temple Jerusalem is the "holy mountain"[8] or "YHWH's mountain" and "his
holy place" (Ps. 24:3). In these latter expressions, Jerusalem is seen as the place
of God's holy presence (Isa. 65:18f.; 66:10, 13, 20).

Jerusalem is called Zion (צִיּוֹן = ṣiyyôn) 152 times even though the name
does not occur from Genesis to 1 Samuel. Zion predominantly occurs in the
sphere of cultic-religious language, and both names are often found in paral-
lelism (Isa. 2:3; 4:3; 30:19; Pss. 102:22; 135:21; etc.). The personal name
Zion, appearing always without a definite article, originally referred only to
the southeast hill of the city, the Ophel. YHWH is closely bound with
Jerusalem, as its designations (city of God, city of YHWH, etc.) show. It is
true, then, that "those who trust in the Lord are like Mount Zion, which does
not move, but rather abides forever. As Jerusalem is surrounded by mountains, so YHWH surrounds his people from this time on and forevermore" (Ps.
125:1f.). Thus the Zion psalms, with expressions that have many parallels in
the surrounding cultures of ancient Israel,[9] can praise the sovereignty of
YHWH's protective presence and succor in this city and utter their confidence
in him (Psalms 46; 48; 76; cf. Joel 2; Zech. 8:22; 12 and 14).[10] One can only
passionately weep in response to the destruction of Zion (Psalm 74; Lamentations). Zion is the city against which the assaults of the raging elements (Ps.
46:3f.), the nations, and their kings shall fail or at least should fail (Pss.
47:7–10; 48:5f.; 68:13ff.; 76:2–7; 99:1; and 110:1ff.).[11] By contrast, it is also
the destination of the pilgrimage of the nations (Isa. 2:2–4; Micah 4:1–3; Isaiah 60; cf. Hag. 2:6–9; Pss. 68:29f.; 72:10f.; Jer. 3:17). Accordingly, the city
of God had significance, then, not only for Israel but also for serving as the
means of the revelation of God to the world, for out of Zion/Jerusalem the תּוֹרָה
(tôrâ = Torah) and the דְּבַר יהוה (dĕbar yahweh = "word of the Lord") go forth
(Isa. 2:3; Micah 4:2).[12]

8.2   Jerusalem in the History
of Old Testament Faith

With the exception of Gen. 14:8ff. (see below), Jerusalem is never mentioned in the Pentateuch. Before David, this city was neither the main city nor
even one of the main cities of Canaan. Rather, it was history, and surely not

its less than advantageous geographical position, that constituted the city's recurring and theological importance. There is no narrative that speaks of the Jerusalem temple's building by a divine action in the primeval period. Rather, the temple's origins were occasioned by David and Solomon in history, not by a divine decision in a prehistorical, mythical time. In addition, the temple was not built by gods, as was narrated, for example, about the Esagila temple in Babylon.[13] David was the one who acquired the building site for the future temple (2 Samuel 24),[14] while the presence of the "Angel of Yahweh"[15] designated this location as the one that had been "chosen" by YHWH. Before this, David had taken the previously unconquered (Judg. 1:21)[16] Canaanite city-state (Josh. 10:1) with his soldiers by means of a politically and religiously clever chess move (2 Sam. 5:6ff.; Isa. 29:1) and then made the city into the capital city of his kingdom. The city was ideally located between the two sections of his kingdom, that is, between Israel and Judah. He then transferred to this originally Jebusite city (Josh. 18:28; 15:63) the ark and YHWH Sebaoth, who sat on the cherubim throne and thus was closely connected with this religious object (2 Samuel 6),[17] thereby bringing into play a new religious focus. Since Jerusalem was connected to neither of these two sections of the kingdom, David sought in this way to avoid tensions that were called forth by the union of two regions. The ark and YHWH Sebaoth who sat upon the cherubim throne were now bound to Jerusalem and to the royal house that ruled there. Jerusalem possibly was and continued to be the "city of David," meaning that the city was not a part of the tribal territories, even though it resided within the sphere of Benjamin's interests (M. Noth; see Josh. 15:8; 18:16). Rather, it lay between Israel and Judah and in the midst of these regions was an independent entity. When Jerusalem and Judah are mentioned next to each other, this separation is probably reflected (Isa. 1:1; 2:1; 3:1, 8; 5:3; Jer. 4:5; etc.).

While in David's time the ark of YHWH was located only under a tent (2 Sam. 6:17), there was a uniform need for the capital city to have a temple for this deity. However, the protest of Nathan against David's intention to build the temple (2 Sam. 7:5–7)[18] shows that the views of faith associated with YHWH, which had developed from a more nomadic background (2 Sam. 7:6ff.), continued to exert their force for quite some time.[19] YHWH did not find it as necessary to obtain for himself a temple as, by contrast, did Baal whose temple was important for his kingship.[20] The fact that David never built the temple presented theological difficulties to the writers of the Books of Chronicles. Subsequently, they wrote that this king, who was so essential in their mind for Israel's cult and worship, at least had prepared the details of the temple and then transmitted to his successor, Solomon, the model of the future sanctuary (1 Chron. 28:11ff.) and the arrangements for organizing its cultus (1 Chron. 18:1–13; 21–26; 28:11f.; and 29). Archaeological excavations, as, for example, in Arad, indicate that there were in Israel and Judah other YHWH sanctuaries both before and during the time of the Solomonic temple.[21]

Old Testament texts corroborate the obvious assumption that the pre-Davidic, Canaanite (Jebusite)[22] city-state of Jerusalem had a cultic and therefore theological tradition during its pre-Israelite existence.[23] The name אל עליון (*'ēl 'elyôn* = God Most High) was mentioned in Gen. 14:18ff. (cf. Ps. 110:4) in connection with Melchizedek, the priest-king of Salem (=Jerusalem; Ps. 76:3).[24] This is the deity whose blessing was placed upon Abraham and to whom Abraham gave his tithe.[25] Here the traditions of the ancient ancestors and Jerusalem were bound together.[26] On the basis of Ps. 85:11 (cf. Isa. 60:17; and Ps. 72:3), one can conclude that the deities Salem and Sedeq were worshiped in Jerusalem. The city name "Jerusalem" is possibly translated "Foundation of (the god) Salem." Further, this divine name is certainly intentionally contained in the name of David's son Solomon who previously was actually named Jedidiah (2 Sam. 12:25). The deity Sedeq[27] is also to be found in the names of the pre-Israelite kings (Gen. 14:18ff.; Ps. 110:4; and Josh. 10:1, 3), and the name of this deity, along with its original function, continues to shine through many Old Testament texts.[28] Moreover, in Jerusalem David took a priest into his service whose name not accidentally was Zadoq (2 Sam. 8:17; 20:25; 1 Kings 1:34; etc.). אל עליון (*'ēl 'elyôn* = God Most High) is called the creator of heaven and earth in Gen. 14:19, thus suggesting that the Old Testament view of the deity as the creator of the cosmos is also influenced by this Jerusalem tradition (cf. Ps. 89:8ff. as a parallel).[29] Jerusalem is the mountain of God that touches heaven and earth, a mountain that also lies to the north of Ugarit and is mentioned repeatedly in Ugaritic texts. This mountain of God is equated with Mt. Zaphon which is closely connected to the god Baal (Ps. 48:3; cf. Isa. 14:13).[30] Streams of water flow out of the temple and the city of God (Ps. 46:5; Ezek. 47:1–12; Joel 4:18; and Zech. 14:8), a depiction that does not strictly conform to the empirical character of Jerusalem's geography. However, this portrayal is similar to the statements found in the texts of Canaan and Syria, as well as elsewhere in the ancient Near East, that speak of the city of god, the garden of god, and the temple.[31] The powers of chaos and the nations that surge against and assault this mountain of God and the city of the great king YHWH[32] (Ps. 48:3) both come to ruin (Pss. 46:6f.; 48:5–8; and 76:5–7; cf. the military element in Gen. 14:20).[33] When Israel speaks then of YHWH, the king of the world, there is here a trace of the influence of the kingship of El[34] (cf. Psalms 47; 93; and 97) whose royal sovereignty indeed extended over the gods of his pantheon. This parallels the way that Psalm 82 now speaks of YHWH.

The temple of Jerusalem was built under Solomon (1 Kings 6–8).[35] A capital city needs its own temple, and the king in his capacity as the city king of Jerusalem can perhaps ignore Israelite misgivings. Although the temple primarily may have been more the royal chapel closely associated with the palace than an actual temple of the kingdom, it still came to have an ever greater significance for the people of Israel and/or Judah and their faith. The description of the appearance of this temple and its construction is reported in 1 Kings 6:1–38 and 7:13–51 (cf. also Ezekiel 41). Built with the help of Phoenician artisans (1 Kings 5:15ff.),[36] the design follows the typical temple pattern of Syria and Canaan, formed with a porch, nave, and inner chamber (1 Kings 6–7).[37] The ancient temple dedication saying in 1 Kings 8:12f. indicates that the temple was at first more a residence (cf. 1 Kings 6:11–13; Isa. 8:18; Pss. 43:3; 74:2; 76:2; Joel 4:21) for the deity than a place for an occasional theophany. This latter understanding is recognized in 1 Kings 8:30f. which clearly seeks to correct the earlier understanding of divine dwelling.[38] The temple became therefore the "house of YHWH," not because he dwelt there, but rather because he may be encountered there.[39]

The "holy of holies" (thus in 1 Kings 7:50; 8:6; and 2 Chron. 4:22), also called the דביר (*dĕbîr*) (thus in 1 Kings 6:22f.; both combined in 1 Kings 8:6; 2 Chron. 5:7), is an inner room in the temple that contains the ark and the cherubim who serve as witnesses to and symbols of the presence of YHWH Sebaoth who is enthroned over them (1 Kings 6:23).[40] This room remains dark, however, and does not have an image of God, even though one came to the temple in order to "look upon"[41] (Pss. 11:7; 42:3; and 84:8) YHWH's "countenance." It was here that one stood before YHWH. The temple was also a sign of election.[42] The temple mountain contains characteristics of Sinai (Ps. 68:18f.). For example, a theophany occurs when the ark is brought into the temple, thus reflecting the theophanies at Sinai (1 Kings 8:10; cf. Exod. 40:34f.). In addition, YHWH's guidance of Israel from his dwelling in Sinai to his sanctuary in Zion is stressed in Exod. 15:1–18. At the same time, this journey is one that led from divine battle to the royal sovereignty of YHWH.[43]

The architectural symbolism of the temple includes decorative elements and pieces of equipment that stem from and are inspired by the surrounding cultures of Israel.[44] These include the bronze sea (1 Kings 7:23–26) and the altar of burnt offerings in the shape of a small ziggurat (thus Ezek. 43:13–17) that took on cosmic characteristics. Accordingly, the temple "possessed cosmic dimensions and was the location in empirical reality where the primeval stabilization of the world was seen to be a phenomenon of present experience."[45] Inscriptions were found on the columns that stood before the temple entrance (1 Kings 7:15–22). They possibly consisted of intercessory words of blessing for the Davidic dynasty[46] and thus underlined the relationship between the temple and the royal dynasty. The God who was worshiped here was the God of Jerusalem as well as the God of Israel, Judah, and the cosmos. This God was the lord of the world, the king of his people, and the deity of the dynasty of David. The Jebusite views of the deity's city and the mountain of god merged with the Israelite conceptions of faith concerning temple theology, the ark, and the cherubim (1 Kings 6:23–28; 8:6–8)[47] in forming what is customarily named the "Zion tradition" in the Old Testament.[48] Thus it was on the basis of these coalescences of theological tradition, which are here clearly seen, that this temple continued to play an important role in the national consciousness.

Through the transfer of the ark to Jerusalem (2 Samuel 6) and its introduction in the temple (1 Kings 8:1–11), the temple and the Davidic dynasty came to be closely bound together, although 2 Sam. 7:5–7 perhaps still sought to negate critically this connection. Moreover, the election of David and of Zion can be mentioned in common (Psalm 132; cf. Psalm 78; 1 Kings 8:16 LXX; 11:13, 32; and 2 Chron. 6:6).[49] The ark, however, continued to surrender its significance[50] to the temple. It was hardly ever mentioned, and not at all when the temple was destroyed in 587 B.C.E. (2 Kings 25:8ff.). Furthermore, its loss was not mourned later on (e.g., in Lamentations).

However, Jerusalem and its temple continued to be important (1 Kings 11:29ff.; later also Jer. 41:5), even after the breakup of the Davidic monarchy's rule over both Israel and Judah in 926 B.C.E. Subsequently, following the division of the empire (1 Kings 12:1–32), Jeroboam I had to set up rival sanctuaries in Bethel and Dan (1 Kings 12:27ff.). There must have been important reasons that Jerusalem remained Judah's capital city in spite of its close proximity to the nation's northern boundary. The effort was made, not to relocate the capital to Hebron, but rather to move Judah's border farther to the north.

Prophetic texts also point to the developing Zion theology, for some of the prophets take up this theology in a positive manner, while others argue polemically against it (Amos 1:2; Micah 3:11f.; Isaiah 6; 8:18; 28:16; 31:9; Jer. 31:6; etc.).

The year 701 B.C.E. became especially important for the further increase in the significance of Jerusalem and the temple, since at that time the Assyrian king Sennacherib laid siege to the city, but for uncertain reasons could not conquer it (2 Kings 18:13ff.; 19 par.).[51] If Isaiah did speak words during this period that touched on this event, something that is more than likely,[52] then it would have been an important new impulse for the developing Zion theology to include the belief that the nations that attacked Jerusalem failed and were shattered, because Yahweh stood by his Zion. Furthermore, although Isaiah also uttered critical remarks against Zion theology when it led to negligence or engendered arrogance, he still presupposed such a "theology" (cf. Isa. 1:4–9; 3:16f.; 8:5–8, 11–15; 10:27b–32; and 29:1–4). Even so, the "authenticity" of additional Zion texts in First Isaiah may be creditably disputed,[53] while others most probably must be denied him.[54] These texts, moreover, are not typical for Isaiah, for they predominantly or exclusively deal with the preservation of Jerusalem against the assault of the nations and reflect new, postexilic hopes that are created out of other sources of Zion theology. Jeremiah must have entered into a dispute with this Zion theology that became an expression of folk piety (Jer. 26:1–6; cf. 7:1–15 in Deuteronomistic editing).[55] Micah's especially critical assault against Zion and its theology (Micah 3:11f.) must have still been known during the time of Jeremiah and could thus be cited to exonerate him during his trial (Jer. 26:18).

Deuteronomy's and the Deuteronomistic History's theology of the name was also significant for Jerusalem. YHWH would elect only *one* place to cause his "name" to dwell (לשכן = *lĕšakkēn*) or to place (לשום = *lāśûm*) his name.[56] In this regard, YHWH's presence in the temple was not at all debated; however, this theology of the name did offer a correction to the theology of presence connected with the ark and the cherubim. This correction had its basis in the historical situation that the exile occasioned and also helped prepare for the Deuteronomistic separation of the dwelling of the name in the temple from the dwelling of YHWH in heaven.[57] While Deuteronomy could not speak directly about Jerusalem, more because it was formulated as speeches of Moses and less because it originated in the Northern Kingdom, its demand for cultic purity by means of cultic unity was still directed first to this city. Also here, then, the discussion speaks of the "election" of this cultic place,[58] not of YHWH's having "created" this location (for instance, even in a more primeval time). Deuteronomistic ideas set forth then other emphases, as, for example, the prayer of the dedication of the temple (1 Kings 8:22–26) shows. According to this prayer, while YHWH's name is present in the temple, he is transcendent and thus is himself not actually present in the temple (1 Kings 8:30ff.).[59] Rather, YHWH dwells in heaven. In this way, YHWH is near to the community that dwells in exile far from Jerusalem and without a temple. Consequently, 1 Kings 8:52f., 59f., for example, states clearly and with a consoling purpose that people may pray to YHWH in heaven (cf. Jer. 29:7, 12–14). Texts dependent upon Deuteronomic and Deuteronomistic thinking likewise take up this kind of evaluation and view of the temple.[60]

The ways in which the cultic reforms of Hezekiah in the eighth century (2 Kings 18:1–7) and then especially of Josiah in the year 621 B.C.E. (2 Kings 22–23) were evoked by the teachings and instructions that led to Deuteronomy or that were connected to what may be seen as proto-Deuteronomy are debated and will not be discussed here.[61] Regardless of how these reforms were carried out, even if they were more politically based and did not essentially take place in the way that 2 Kings described them, they still increased even more the significance of Jerusalem and its temple.

While Jerusalem and the temple are without attestable theological significance in Old Testament wisdom literature,[62] in the Psalms[63] of Zion they are the locations of the presence of YHWH where worshipers encounter the Holy. Here is the place of the *deus praesens* (H. Spieckermann), of yearning, of joy, and of consolation. And here the individual worshiper as well as the community stands before YHWH (2 Kings 19:14) who was and is connected with the ark (Psalm 132). It is the temple where one experiences YHWH's earthly as well as heavenly entrance and ascent (Pss. 24:7–10 and 47:6ff.)[64] and the homage that accompanies them (Isa. 6:3 and Psalm 29). And the temple is where one experiences community with YHWH, for the king and divine warrior "dwells" now on Zion (Isa. 8:18; Joel 4:17–21) and appears here in order to speak (Ps. 50:1–6). From here one awaits and experiences help, life, salvation, and blessing (Ps. 9:15; 14:7; 20:3; 22:3, 20, 23; 36:10; 42:9; 53:7; 128:5; 133:3; and 134:3). Here protection (Psalms 46; 48) and security are maintained (Ps. 23:6). Here one sees, praises, and thanks YHWH (Pss. 30:2–4, 12f.; 65:2; 84:8; 97:8; and 147:12) who is enthroned here (Pss. 9:12; 104:1f.) and is praised as the king of the gods and of the cosmos (Psalms 47; 93; 96; 97; Ezek. 43:7; and Exod. 15:17f.). It is from here that he forms and maintains his world as the creator and world king (Psalms 93; 95; 96; 104; and 148),[65] although it is less a matter of *prima creatio* than *creatio continua* that is in view.[66] Ancient Jebusite-Canaanite traditions are at work in these statements and are articulated in a form and content that have been transformed.[67] Furthermore, it is YHWH's glory (כבוד = *kābôd*)[68] that takes on his presence in the temple (Isaiah 6; cf. Psalms 24; 29; and 102:17). Later on, Ezekiel and the Priestly document sought to speak of the glory of YHWH in spite of the destruction of the temple and the exilic separation from Jerusalem.[69]

According to the message of the preexilic and early-exilic prophets, YHWH's judgment also fell even upon Jerusalem.[70] Lamentations (chaps. 1–5); Psalm 74 (v. 1: "rejected"?); and Psalm 79 lamented, questioned, and reflected on the reality of the experience of this judgment. YHWH himself has "profaned" (Ezek. 24:21) his sanctuary; he became like an enemy to it (Lam. 2:5).[71]

Even after the destruction of the temple, Jerusalem still continued to be an important cultic site (Jer. 41:5). According to Ezekiel (11:16), YHWH became for Israel in exile "a sanctuary for a little while."[72] However, because of the destruction of the actual temple and the reorientation and new orientation that resulted, this prophet is silent about the divine name YHWH Sebaoth and speaks instead of YHWH's glory (כבוד = *kābôd*). Now separated from the temple and able to move about, this "glory" is encountered in the exile far from Jerusalem (Ezekiel 1–3). The prophet promises that the divine glory that has left the temple of Jerusalem (Ezek. 11:22f.) will enter once more into the new temple he envisions (Ezek. 43:1–9) so that YHWH will dwell forever in the midst of his house in Israel.[73] Similarly, the Priestly document makes YHWH's glory mobile and thus can speak of his presence in the "wilderness" where he can accompany, draw near to, and encounter even a murmuring people.[74] This divine glory in P is associated with a portable sanctuary[75] and also is encountered in the key passages of this literary source (Exod. 24:16; 25:8; 29:45f.; and 40:35). The new temple envisioned by Ezekiel is described in the basic stratum of Ezekiel 40–48 as being developed by YHWH himself, although it is never realized in this form.[76]

For Deutero-Isaiah it was more important that YHWH lead his people out of exile and back to Zion, described as the garden of God (Isa. 51:3), and that Jerusalem and its temple be rebuilt (Isa. 44:28; 49:16f.; cf. Zech. 1:16) than it was to speak of the return to the land, a theme that strikes a chord with the theological value placed on the land elsewhere in the Old Testament[77] (Isa. 40:9; 41:27; 46:13; 49:13ff.; 51:3, 11, 16; and 52:7f.).[78]

During the postexilic period, the temple of Jerusalem increased in significance. This may be determined from the call for the reconstruction of what became the new second temple in Haggai and Zechariah (Hag. 1:2ff.; 2:1ff., 15ff.; Zech. 2:14ff.; 6:15; and 8:1ff.), a call made urgent by their promises for the future (cf. Hag. 2:6–9, 18f.; Zech. 1:16; and Pss. 51:20; 102:14, 17, 22; 126:1), and from the temple dedication that occurred in 515 B.C.E. (Ezra 6:6ff.). The temple's increased importance was also due to the Jewish community's assuming a less political and a more cultic form of existence under foreign rule[79] and to its occupying a relatively small territorial sphere.[80] The participation of the Samaritans in the rebuilding of the temple was rejected (Hag. 2:10–14),[81] allowing Zion theology to continue to expand. Zion is the crown of beauty (Ps. 50:2) and is associated with the expectation concerning the messiah (Zech. 9:9f.), while Jerusalem is the object of the pilgrimage of the nations (Isa. 2:2–4; Micah 4:1–3; cf. Hag. 2:6–9; Isa. 60:1ff.; also in combination with the statement about the crushing of the nations in Zechariah 12 and 14) and maintains accordingly its revelatory significance for the world.[82] In the postexilic period, there were some pilgrimage psalms (Psalms 120–134) that sang of the desire for Jerusalem and the journey there, its temple that stands once again, and the blessing that was to be experienced there.[83]

In the Books of Chronicles, the temple and worship become the major goals of the history of Israel, and it is here that the location of Moriah in Gen. 22:1ff. is identified with Jerusalem (2 Chron. 3:1). Further, Israel is organized entirely by reference to the temple as the center of Jewish life, according to the postexilic additions to the texts of the Priestly document and 1 Chronicles 1–9.[84] Deutero-Isaiah's promises become actualized anew (Isa. 60:1ff.), while Zion theology becomes even more significant with the addition of texts to Deutero-Isaiah and Trito-Isaiah and with the redaction of the final form of the Book of Isaiah as a whole.[85] The practice of praying in the direction of Jerusalem is also adopted, possibly as early as the exile (Dan. 6:11). The Book of Daniel and the Books of Maccabees show how great a role Jerusalem played in the controversies of the second century B.C.E.[86] Herod the Great (died 4 B.C.E.) massively expanded the temple which was later destroyed in the fateful year 70 C.E. The Romans made Caesarea the provincial capital in place of Jerusalem, and after the failure of the Jewish rebellion during the reign of Hadrian, Jerusalem became "Aelia Capitolina." Jews were forbidden entrance to this city. The history of Jerusalem and its serving as the location for the temple have not come to an end even unto the present time. In looking at the Old Testament, one can nonetheless say that both Jerusalem and the temple have had a greater influence on the piety of ancient Israel than did the monarchy.

8.3   The "Zion Tradition"

Thus Jerusalem incorporated within itself various functions during the course of its Old Testament history. For a long period, it was a royal residence, the capital of a mostly rather small kingdom, a cultic site, and a city with an increasingly dominating temple. It was then a city of a cultic community that was formed and organized in a strongly theocratic manner. Finally, it was seen to be the new Jerusalem, a city of the expected time of salvation.[87] And with all of these, Jerusalem was the "daughter of Zion," the symbol of both the nation and the community.

Very complex and substantial traditions of faith were developed in this city and connected with it. Associated with the idea of the ark as a portable sanctuary was the conception that God accompanied his people, guided them, fought on their behalf, was with them (Ps. 46:4, 8, 12), and became present in their midst. Since the time of David and Solomon, this understanding of the ark, and this by means of the cherubim,[88] came to be associated with the state sanctuary in Jerusalem that came into being. This state sanctuary was located in what was previously a Canaanite city, took over much from the city's Canaanite traditions of faith, and inserted these elements into the Yahwistic faith, thereby expanding and enriching its content.[89] Texts from the ancient Near East make analogous statements about the temple and city of a deity, although they speak in more detail about both than do, for example, the Zion psalms.[90] This means that the faith in the wilderness God YHWH who has no temple still continues to exert a mild influence. Moreover, Israel and the monarchy were bound to one another for several centuries by means of Jerusalem, thus providing the opportunity to establish a connection between the David tradition and the Zion tradition (Psalms 2; 20:3; 72; 110; and 132). This combination of traditions continued to exert its influence even after the cessation of the monarchy (Zech. 9:9f.; cf. 12:7f.). Now YHWH took up residence in the land and assumed the position of the monarchy. Thus Israelite ideas of faith were permeated by Canaanite ones, as, for instance, YHWH war and the city of God (Psalm 46), Israelite ethics concerning the neighbor and Jerusalem cult theology (Psalms 15 and 24),[91] and statements about YHWH as king of his people along with those about creation and the cosmic rule of God (Psalm 24; YHWH enthronement hymns[92]). The complexes of ideas about the mountain of God and the city of God (Psalms 46; 48; and 76), which transcend in a cultic-mythical fashion the present, earthly Jerusalem and thus participate in helping to place Jerusalem within a developing eschatology, also draw on Israelite statements that had belonged to understandings about Sinai. Thus, as Israel finally is drawn from Sinai to Zion (Exod. 15:13, 17f.), so now Zion is drawn back to Sinai since the Torah goes forth from Zion (Isa. 2:2–4; Micah 4:1-3; cf. Psalm 50). From the city of God go forth many things throughout the world that are necessary for its continuation, including water (Ps. 46:5; Isa. 12:3; Ezek. 28:11–19; 47:1–12; and Zech. 14:8),[93] world order (Pss. 96:13f.; 98; and 99:4), and, above all, peace and salvation (cf. Jer. 14:13; Ezek. 13:10, 16; 34:25; 37:26; Hag. 2:9; Zech. 7:7; 8:10ff.; 9:10; Pss. 29:11; and 122:7f.).[94] However, the deities Salem and Sedeq with their own characteristics and peculiar features continue to exert their influence in these statements. Thus Zion can be addressed as the center of the earth (Ps. 48:3). When the ark and the cherubim eventually are not concealed within the interior of the second temple and when the holy of holies is completely empty, the ancient expressions of faith do not fade.

Whether this complex Zion tradition was kept alive by a festival is no longer so certain as was thought only a short time ago.[95] The regular celebration of a "royal Zion's festival" is not clearly attested either from 2 Samuel 6–7 or from other texts.[96] Moreover, there were "Songs of Zion," at the same time known to the Israelites as "Songs of YHWH" (Ps. 137:3f.),[97] which they could not and would not sing simply at the demand of foreign captors in a strange land.

8.4 Jerusalem in Old Testament Future Expectation

Jerusalem also obtained its place in the Old Testament expectation concerning the future, something that is now to be addressed separately. Thus Isaiah had already expressed his hope for the preservation of Zion.[98] Similar again to the royal psalms, the Songs of Zion in the final analysis always express an element of hope with their words that go beyond the present time. So Zion received in Isaiah 40–55 prominent significance,[99] for YHWH would lead the exilic community back there in a new exodus. The theme of Zion and the hope for both this place and its community, which permeate the whole of the Book of Isaiah, join and hold it together. In the Book of Ezekiel (Ezekiel 40–48), the new temple was precisely designed, and then was built under Haggai's pressing admonition based on promise (Hag. 1:2ff.; and 2:1ff.). Zechariah appropriated Haggai's admonition and promise in a slightly modified form and asked when salvation for Jerusalem would break into history (Zech. 1:12f.; 2:16; 3:2; 8:2; and 12:8, 10). Thus, new promises for Jerusalem were ventured in the exile (Isa. 44:28; and 52:1f.) and postexile (Isa. 4:5; 25:10; 35:10; 54:11–17; 59:20; 60:1ff.; 62; 65:17ff.; 66:5–24; and Zech. 14:9, 14bff.). YHWH would

elect Jerusalem "again" (עוֹד = 'ôd) (Zech. 1:17; 2:16; and 3:2; cf. Isa. 14:1).[100]
The desired eschatological kingdom of YHWH (Isa. 24:23; 33:22; 52:7; Jer.
8:19; Obadiah 21; Micah 4:7; Zeph. 3:15; Zech. 14:9; Pss. 146:10; and 149:2;
cf. Ps. 48:3) was clearly connected to the mountain of God in terms of significance for the world and the nations (Pss. 96:8; and 97:8; cf. Ps. 47:9; 93:3; and
99:2). At Zion one learned that God is "YHWH, our God, forever and ever"
(Ps. 48:15) and that he would ever again deliver Zion, since, as Psalms 46; 48;
and 76 proclaim, the nations that approach Jerusalem are always defeated (cf.
Isa. 30:18–22; 33; Micah 4:11–13; Joel 4:9ff.; Zech. 12:1–8; and 14:12ff.).[101]
In addition to these writings, a few other texts speak of a pilgrimage of the nations to Jerusalem (Isa. 2:2–4; Micah 4:1–4; Isa. 60:1–7) where they receive
instruction from YHWH or bring there their wealth (cf. Hag. 2:6–9).[102] These
texts dealing with the nations point to the final, contrasting position of the Old
Testament on the question as to whether the nations shall be able to take part
in the salvation of Israel brought by its God.[103]

As the monarchy so also Jerusalem with its temple grew together with the
people of Israel and their faith in YHWH. The monarchy and the Zion tradition both enriched this faith and yet endangered it in many spheres, as may be
seen in the prophets' criticism directed toward the kings, the cult, and the temple.[104] On the whole, the combining of elements of Canaanite belief with Yahwistic faith, which is manifested in the Zion tradition, was seen to have positive significance for the religion of Israel. These elements were seen, above all,
in the statements about the "kingship of YHWH" and about creation and the
providential guidance of the world. This coalescence may also be seen in the
hope for shalom that is associated with Jerusalem, a hope that involves more
than simply the cessation of war (Pss. 29:11; 72:3ff.; 85:9ff.; Isa. 9:5f.; 52:7;
and 54:10ff.).[105]

Ancient Israel stood before its God in Jerusalem. In this very same place,
YHWH acted on behalf of his people and his community. It was here that one
experienced YHWH's salvific presence. It was here also that the "problems of
the nearness of God and the distance of God, judgment and salvation, promise
and fulfillment, and covenant and faithfulness to the covenant became pressing issues."[106] The city, "in its observable architectural construction and strong
fortifications, is the emblematic manifestation of the protective power of Yahweh both for it and its inhabitants . . . (and) accordingly assumes for itself a
quality of God."[107] The use of the expression "Daughter of Zion/Jerusalem"
for the city as well as for the nation and the community points in an especially
clear way to the relationship of God, community, city, and temple.[108] These
designations should not be seen only as picturesque and metaphorical descriptions but also as characterizations that were to treat Jerusalem/Zion as "the subject of a gift," a "character," and even a woman who was the object of YHWH's
bequest[109] and who received from him her dignity (Isa. 50:1; 54:6; 2 Kings

19:21; and Lam. 2:13; cf. Ezek. 16:37; and Lam. 1:8). "In spite of all the power of acculturation, what would have happened to the wilderness deity, YHWH, together with the traditions of salvation history associated with him, had he not taken up residence in the Canaanite temples of the land of Canaan, and above all in the temple of Jerusalem?"[110] The so-called Zion tradition demonstrates rather clearly that this discovery of a home involves not only the act of receiving but also the acts of giving and taking. Indeed, the Zion tradition shows that YHWH faith was ever open to a new act of divine "electing."

Chapter 9. Priests and Levites[1]

9.1 Priests and Levites as "Chosen"

The initial survey of Old Testament statements involving election has already indicated that priests and levites were designated as chosen by YHWH.[2] In this survey the reference to the house of Eli (1 Sam. 2:28) was classified as the most ancient text, the statements about the levites in Deuteronomy (Deut. 18:5; and 21:5) were categorized as later, and then the rest of the references to the priests (Num. 16:5ff.; and 17:20), levites (1 Chron. 15:2; and 2 Chron. 29:11), and Aaron (Ps. 105:26) were grouped together as postexilic. Furthermore, the analogous statements about a "covenant" of YHWH with the Aaronide priesthood (Num. 25:10ff.) and the levites (Jer. 33:21; Neh. 13:29; and Mal. 2:4f., 8) are no earlier than the postexilic period. In spite of this, one may determine on the basis of these passages not only that the priests and the levites were the objects of the actions of YHWH's election but also that they were, in addition, the instruments of God on behalf of his chosen nation. He had ordained these priests and levites to their position and orders (Exodus 28f.; 39f.; Leviticus 8; Numbers 3; and 8). For these reasons, it is important to deal with them in more detail.

9.2 Concerning the History and Functions of the Old Testament Priesthood

It is extremely difficult to develop a history of the Old Testament priesthood from the existing sources. Still, one may recognize certain fixed points that provide at the same time some understanding about priestly activities and their various changes.

The Old Testament is familiar only with male priests.[3] This may not have been so, simply by chance. Rather, this restriction may say something about the milieu and the type of religion of the participating groups in ancient Israel. In the narratives about the ancient ancestors, no priest is mentioned.[4] Rather, the "fathers" themselves offered their sacrifices and built the altars for them (Gen. 12:7f.; 13:4, 18; 15:9f.; 21:33; 22:9f., 13; 28:16ff.; 31:54; and 46:1; cf.

also Judg. 6:17ff., 25ff.; 13:16ff.; 1 Sam. 1:3f., 21; and 1 Kings 18:23ff.). The unique scene found in Gen. 14:18ff. (cf. Ps. 110:4) emphasizes that the priest-king of Jerusalem, Melchizedek, comes from the Jebusite-Canaanite region (Salem = Jerusalem according to Ps. 76:3).[5] The mentionings of the priests and levites in Exodus 25ff.; Leviticus 8–9; and Numbers 1–10 go back, not to the Mosaic period, but rather to the exilic Priestly document and to postexilic expansions that are inserted. It cannot be decided whether these texts have taken up older traditions.

First Samuel 2:27–36 may be traced to the premonarchial period.[6] Eli and his sons (cf. 1 Samuel 21: the priests of Nob), who obviously held a hereditary priestly office, were priests in Shiloh who functioned as keepers of the ark[7] and probably as keepers (for Hebrew שמר = *šāmar* in these contexts, cf. also Num. 1:53; 3:28, 32) of the entire sphere of the holy. Judges 17–18 speaks similarly of the levite Micah who is the keeper of the idol and is called "father" (Judg. 17:10). In addition, if the ephod (אפוד בד = *'ēpôd bad*)[8] is mentioned as belonging to the priest and his activity (1 Sam. 2:18, 28; 14:3; 22:18; David wears the ephod in 2 Sam. 6:14 and 1 Chron. 15:27, 29), then the ephod in this context is probably a piece of clothing with a pocket for the oracle. One approached the priest in order to inquire about a divine decision (שאל = *šā'al* = "ask"; Num. 27:21; Judg. 18:5; 1 Sam. 22:15; 23:2; 30:7f.; and Hos. 3:4; cf. 1 Sam. 14:18f., 36f.).[9] Later the ephod, obviously artistically fashioned, became a part of the high priest's vestments (see the description in Exod. 28:6ff. and 39:2ff.). Furthermore, Judg. 17:5, 12 uses the idiom "to fill the hand" (cf. Exod. 32:29; etc.), an idiom also known elsewhere in the ancient Near East,[10] to speak of the act of installing a priest.[11] The idiom may also have referred to the allocation of a portion of the gifts that were the sanctuary's due (cf. 1 Sam. 2:16f.). General presuppositions for priestly service (although probably from a later time) are mentioned in Lev. 21:5ff. (no cutting of bald spots on the head; no trimming of the beard; stipulations concerning marriage; no bodily defects), while specific ones are found in Exod. 30:17–21; Lev. 21:1–5; and Ezek. 44:21 (washings; no contact with corpses; and no consumption of wine when serving in the inner court).[12]

In addition to protecting and caring for the ark, the image of God, and the temple, and administering the oracle lots when inquiries of God are made, early priestly activity also included instruction in YHWH's law, that is, in the knowledge and transmission of his will (Hos. 4:4ff.; Micah 3:11; Zeph. 3:4; Jer. 2:8; and Mal. 2:7; cf. Deut. 31:9; and 33:10). However, the priests early on were not so much involved in offering sacrifices, since the laity themselves largely took responsibility for this cultic activity. The offering of sacrifices as a priestly activity began to gain in significance with the monarchy and reached its height in the postexilic period (Leviticus 1–5; 6–7; cf. Numbers 28–29; and 1 and 2 Chronicles). At least until the time of Saul, cultic activities were not always limited to the priests and levites. That priests had to deliver a war sermon is an idea that belongs more to Deuteronomic and Deuteronomistic ideology (Deut. 20:2–4) than to reality. Nevertheless, the Books of Chronicles, with their militaristic and utopian spirit,[13] picked up this notion of priestly involvement in war and made it even more prominent. Here, it takes only the priests' blowing of the trumpets to cause the enemy to fall dead by the thousands (2 Chron. 13:14ff.).

Presented in the form of a programmatic proclamation of judgment, 1 Sam. 2:27–36,[14] in addition, speaks of the removal of the house of Eli as priests by the Zadokites of Jerusalem. Zadok did not come from the house of Eli;[15] rather, he was a priest of pre-Israelite, Jebusite Jerusalem when the city was taken by David. Zadok's non-Israelite origins were later suppressed, and his legitimacy as a priest had to be established in spite of this background. Thus, according to 1 Kings 2:26–35, it was Solomon who removed the house of Eli as priests and replaced them with the Zadokites.

The formation of the monarchy consequently became significant for the history of the priesthood. Eventually a uniform and structured priesthood was shaped. There was a high priest (2 Kings 25:18; Jer. 52:24; later 2 Chron. 19:11; 26:20; and 31:10) beside whom a "second priest" stood (2 Kings 25:18; and Jer. 52:24). Priestly lineage (e.g., "Zadokites") and geneaology became important.

The Aaronides were active in Bethel (Josh. 24:33; Judg. 20:27f.). Aaron, one of the most controversial figures in the Pentateuch,[16] is mentioned over three hundred times in the Old Testament but outside the Pentateuch only thirteen times. His name, like that of Moses, gives evidence of either Egyptian origins or influence (this was also true of Hophni and Phinehas, the sons of Eli: 1 Sam. 1:3; 2:34; 4:4, 11, and 17). According to Exod. 4:14[17] and 6:20 (P), Aaron was supposed to have been a levite as well as the brother of Moses. However, both of these representations do not inspire much confidence. That Moses and Aaron actually were brothers (Exod. 4:14–16) is improbable in view of Exod. 2:1–10 where Miriam, not Aaron, is mentioned and of 15:20 where the emphasis is placed on Miriam, not Aaron. It is likewise improbable that he was a levite in view of the opposition of the levites against him in Exod. 32:25–29. Aaron does not appear at all in Exodus 13–15 and is mentioned in Deuteronomy only in 10:6 which refers to his death and in 9:20 which obviously draws on an ancient source in Exodus 32. In Exod. 17:8ff. he participates (in a secular or cultic way?) in the battle with the Amalekites. H. Valentin[18] regards this latter text as the oldest source for the presentation of the person of Aaron and sees in Exod. 17:10, 12 (= 15:20; also 18:12?) ancient materials in which he does not function as a priest at all. However, a look at Exod. 17:8ff. makes this dating and interpretation improbable.[19]

The appearance of Aaron with the elders on the mountain of God (Exod. 18:12; 24:1–2, 9–11) is mostly seen as a later insertion. With the exception of the sections that belong to the Priestly document, the references to Aaron within Exodus 5–12 are later additions. P is also the only source that mentions the sons of Aaron (Exod. 6:23).

Aaron later stands in opposition to Moses and to the levites (Exod. 24:14?; 32;[20] Numbers 12) and, according to Deut. 33:8, belongs perhaps to the priesthood of Kadesh (together with his sister Miriam?). Like Moses, Aaron may not enter the land of promise but rather dies on M. Hor (Num. 20:22ff.; 33:38; Deut. 32:50; a different location is given in Deut. 10:6). His death prior to the entrance into the land of Canaan was due to his (unknown, continuing) sin against YHWH, something that was the case with Moses as well (Num. 20:12). There is not a uniform grave tradition for Aaron in the Old Testament, since two contradictory texts deal with his death and burial (Deut. 10:6; Num. 33:38; however, compare Josephus, *Ant.* 4.83).

One is hard-pressed to find reliable, older texts that describe the person and function of Aaron. He has no significance in Deuteronomy 12–26. Consequently, the early history of the Aaronides is rather unclear, and its interpretation is very hypothetical. There is much more discussion of Aaron and the Aaronides in later texts, that is, especially the Priestly document and its expansions. This source is interested in his origins (Exod. 6:14–27 P). Aaron is presented as a fellow actor with Moses in the contest with the Egyptian magicians[21] and as his spokesman (Exod. 7:1ff.; 9:8; and 12:1: P). Aaron was also associated with Moses during the wilderness wandering (Exod. 16:2, 6, 9; Num. 1:3, 17; 2:1; etc.).

It cannot be determined from the texts themselves that all priests in the pre-exilic period were or even had to be Aaronides. However, one may recognize that the Aaronide priests were active in Bethel and dwelt in the region of Judah and Benjamin (Joshua 21; Judg. 20:28). These brief references do not offer anything further about this priesthood's broader history. Did the Aaronides remain in Bethel during the exile? Did they exert influence on Jerusalem, or did Jerusalem influence them? Or did an Aaronide movement develop during the exile for reasons that are unknown to us, a movement that comes to have increasing influence? How did their connection with the Zadokites take place, and how is this relationship to be explained?[22]

It is recognizable that from the period of the Israelite-Jewish monarchy the king himself, in contrast to the cultures surrounding ancient Israel, did not have any regular cultic or priestly functions. Second Chronicles 26:18 says this explicitly in the postexilic period. Only seldom does the Old Testament report that the king offered sacrifice, and then only in rather special circumstances.[23] These narratives at the same time allow one to recognize that there was not a single priesthood with proper jurisdictional authority at the time.[24] However, the text of 1 Samuel 13, the age of which is debated, seeks to report the tensions between Saul and Samuel that provoked a cultic act of the king.[25] In the dedication of the temple (1 Kings 8), Solomon is something approaching the "patron" of the temple that primarily was to have been his royal chapel,[26] and thus he may sacrifice and above all pray there. Also, the reforms of kings Hezekiah (2 Kings 18) and especially Josiah (2 Kings 22–23) were not exclusively cultic actions but also had a political undergirding, if not also a political basis in the dissolution of Assyrian hegemony because of the retrenchment of Assyrian power. Certainly, there is nothing intentionally stated in 2 Kings 23 about Josiah's direct involvement in cultic activity. It is true that he "commanded" the nation to observe the Passover (2 Kings 23:21), and in the resumption of this text in 2 Chronicles 35 it is expressly mentioned that the priests and levites were installed to cultic service by the king. While he gave orders to prepare animals for sacrifice, he himself, however, offered no sacrifice (vv. 6–9; 11–16). In granting the king priestly dignity, Ps. 110:4 on the one hand points back to Gen. 14:18ff. and on the other hand probably refers to his office as the city king of Jerusalem which perhaps allowed later on more latitude for these kinds of cultic activities than had the earlier position of a king of Israel and/or Judah.[27] Progressively, the priests become the only ones who may "draw near" to God at the altar and serve him (Lev. 21:17; Num. 18:7; etc.).[28]

At the head of the kingdom's sanctuary stands "the priest" (1 Sam. 22:11; 2 Kings 12:8; 23:4; Jer. 29:25f.; and Amos 7:10ff.). The cultic reform of Josiah, both in its original form and in its Deuteronomic/Deuteronomistic reformulation,[29] aimed at and occasioned the centralization of cultic places and priesthoods in Jerusalem. Was this also the reason that necessarily brought together Aaronides, Zadokites, and Levites and arranged their various understandings into a systematic arrangement? According to Deut. 18:1–8, which sets forth the programmatic reference to the "levitical priests," all levites should be or continue to be priests. That is, the levites of the land, whose livelihood was now in danger, should find their new support in priestly service in Jerusalem. This claim, however, could not be carried out.[30]

After the exile, and that means especially after Ezra, all priests are Aaronides (Numbers 17). Beginning with Haggai the expression of the activity of the "high priest" appears (Hag. 1:1, 12, 14; 2:2, 4; Zech. 3:1, 8; 6:11; Neh. 3:1, 20; and 13:28).[31] He was also called a "prince" (נגיד = nāgîd; 1 Chron. 9:11; 2 Chron. 31:13; Neh. 11:11; Dan. 9:25; and 11:22) and functioned as the necessary mediator between God and the people, for he entered the holy of holies on the Day of Atonement and carried out his cultic rites dealing with sin (Leviticus 16). The high priest was also anointed for entrance into his office (Exod. 29:4–7; and Lev. 8:6–12).[32] Special regulations for his purity and his marriage (Lev. 21:10ff.) were established for him. His death resulted in the pardon of those who had fled to cities of refuge because they had slain other human beings (Num. 35:25ff.).[33] Wherever the high priest already is encountered in texts belonging to the preexilic or the early periods of Israel, this is due to later redactional insertions (Num. 35:25, 28, 32; 2 Kings 12:11; 22:4, 8; and 23:4).

The tasks of the priests, who according to late priestly texts likewise were all anointed (Exod. 28:41; 30:30; 40:12–15, etc.),[34] include giving instruction about clean and unclean, making decisions in these cases (Lev. 10:10f.),[35] and above all, offering sacrifices accompanied by the small and great blood ritual (Lev. 4:1–35) for the atonement of the people granted by YHWH.[36]

Later on, the Zadokites once again stood alongside the Aaronides at the head of the priesthood.[37] During the struggles for the office of the high priest in the period of the Hasmoneans,[38] the Zadokites were ousted. However, the Priestly document in its arrangement of the cultus at Sinai did not allocate to the Zadokites a legitimate place, although it did seek to associate them in most of the postexilic additions with the Aaronides (see below).

In any case, only an Aaronide is allowed to be a priest in the postexilic period (Exodus 28–29; Leviticus 8–10; and Numbers 16–18).[39] Aaron became the brother of Moses, and both were levites. The Zadokites consequently become connected with the Aaronides as descendants of Eleazar (Exod. 6:23 P; cf. Num. 20:25f.) and Phinehas (Num. 25:11), respectively the son and grandson of Aaron (Ezra 8:2; 1 Chron. 5:30–34; and 6:35–38). Did a compromise in the period of the exile take place between the Zadokites and the successors of David's priest, Abiathar (2 Sam. 15:24; 1 Kings 1:7; etc.), under the general heading "Aaronides"?[40] Ezekiel 44 does not, however, trace the Zadokites back to Aaron. All of these efforts at combining priestly groups, in which often a "levitical" descent plays a role,[41] reflect problems, conflicts, and attempts at solution. However, modern efforts to unravel the actual background and development of priestly groups cannot be successfully carried out. Aaron became the first "high priest" (Ezra 7:1–5) with royal rank and vestments (Exodus 28–29). He became the "prophet" (נביא = *nābî'*) (Exod. 7:1f. P) and "mouth" (Exod. 4:14–17)[42] of Moses who transmits Moses' words to the pharaoh and performs the decisive miracle in Egypt. He performs this miraculous deed with the magical staff that Moses possessed (Exod. 7:9ff., 19ff.; 8:1ff., 12ff.: P). Aaron also became the intercessor (Exod. 8:4) and the organizer of the army (Num. 1:3; 2:1). According to the Books of Chronicles, the Samaritan cult is illegitimate, because no Aaronide priest presides there (2 Chron. 13:9ff.; cf. 11:13ff.).

Thus, one meets in Aaron a late and, especially in the postexilic period, an increasingly more expanded figure (cf. the "house of Aaron" in Ps. 115:10, 12; 118:3; also Luke 1:5). It is possible, even probable, that he was a historical figure, but it is not possible to set forth precisely his location and function, for he hardly would have been capable of making his own way into the different spheres with which he later became important. It has been assumed[43] on occasion that Aaron may have been a representative of a faith that, originally distinct from that of the Moses group, may have taken no initiative toward making an idol and that perhaps may have been a part of the so-called group participating in the wilderness festival (Exod. 3:18; 5:1), a group that joined the Moses group later on. When there were problems, these could have been concealed in the events of Exodus 32.[44] Or perhaps the Aaronides were priests against whom there was preexilic opposition (Exodus 32; 1 Kings 12:25–32). Did these priests suddenly come to stand in the forefront in the postexilic period, since the suspicion arose once again that the Zadokites originated within a Jebusite realm? Were Aaronide priests of Bethel compelled during the exile to go to Jerusalem? However, that the priesthood of the Aaronides did not avoid debate is shown by the polemical texts in Numbers 12 (Aaron's and Miriam's strife with Moses) and Numbers 16 (the rebellion of the "gang of Korah" with that of Dathan and Abiram).[45] In the midst of these contexts, the guarantee of a "covenant of salt" (Num. 18:19)[46] issued to the Aaronides as well as a covenant of priesthood that has as its content the eternal priesthood of the successors of the grandson of Aaron, Phinehas (Num. 25:10ff.), should well support the claims of particular priestly groups. On the whole, only a few of the fundamental features of the history of the Old Testament priesthood may be ascertained. It receives its prominent significance for the first time in the postexilic period and in connection with the expansion of the cult that occurred during this time.[47]

9.3   Concerning the History
and Functions of the Levites

One must also speak of the levites in dealing with the history, function, and theological significance of the priesthood. They were already necessarily and repeatedly mentioned in the preceding discussion, and in several texts they were designated as priests "elected" by YHWH (Deut. 18:5; 21:5; 1 Chron. 15:2; and 2 Chron. 29:11). Unfortunately, what was true of Aaron and the Aaronides[48] was also valid for the levites, namely, that one can say very little with certainty about their origin and early history. Rather, one mainly can only mention hypotheses about these. Just a glance at the levitical genealogies (Exod. 6:16–25; Num. 26:57ff.; 1 Chron. 5:27ff.; and 6:1–32), together with their tensions and diversity, shows even a casual reader the problematic nature of the levites and the research about them.

The name or the appellation לוי (*lēvî*) is probably[49] to be derived from a verbal stem of the same phoneme which can have the meaning "to be/become obligated." Thus the noun can mean "consecrated for" and "adherent, client, and worshiper of." These suggest, further, that the expression לוי אל (*lēvî-'ēl*) means "adherent of God X." In addition, the term could point to a legal and social status as well as a religious specialization[50] that could explain both the loosening of normal familial bonds (Exod. 32:29) and the fact that a levite could not own land (Deut. 10:8f.; and Josh. 13:33). Thus the levites may not have comprised their own tribe either in Israel or before its existence; rather, they may have been a professional association or guild.[51] Additional, important statements are made in Deut. 10:8f. and 33:8–11 (cf. 18:1) about the status and activity of the levites. Levites offer cultic service in the presence of YHWH, utter blessings before the people, instruct the nation in the law, and preside over the casting of lots. Likewise, Exod. 32:25–29 shows the levites to be loyal to YHWH.[52]

That some of the Old Testament enumerations of the tribes of the people of Israel contain the tribe of Levi (Gen. 29:34; 35:23; 46:11; 49:5ff.; Exod. 1:2; Deut. 27:12f.; 33:8ff.; Ezek. 48:31; and 1 Chron. 2:1f.) while some do not (Num. 1:5ff.; 7:12ff.; 26:5ff.; Joshua 13–19; and Judg. 5:14ff.) must not entice one into searching for what was originally a secular tribe of Levi who then perhaps may have perished (thus the so-called "theory of extinction") or may have been transformed into a priestly tribe. This is especially the case, since the texts that have been set forth will not sustain this argument. Thus, Gen. 49:5–7 could not be combined with Genesis 34 to support the theory of extinction,[53] while the existence of a secular tribe of Levi is as hard to prove as the idea that two different groups originally had the same name. Rather, the group of levites was a community of those who were adherents of YHWH (cf. once again Exod. 32:25–29), connected with Kadesh-Barnea, and once upon a time perhaps had attempted to settle in Palestine (Genesis 34; Exod. 17:7; Num. 13:26; 27:14; 32:8; and Judg. 11:16).[54] That there was the ability and desire to name the levites with the name of the individual ancestor "Levi" would speak for the so-called "eponymous theory" where the levites are compressed within the person of the patriarch (Mal. 2:4). In addition to the covenant of Sinai, the Davidic covenant, and the covenant of Noah,[55] there must have been in the view of certain Old Testament texts and the groups that stood behind them a special covenant with the priests.[56] There was neither the ability nor the desire to dispense with this status in the postexilic period even in levitical circles. The entire late text of Mal. 2:4–9 (4 + 8),[57] along with Jer. 33:19–22 and Neh. 13:29, thus speak of a special "levitical covenant," the content of which concentrates on חיים (*ḥayyîm* = "life") and שלום (*šālôm* = "peace/well-being"). In these passages, the levitical covenant is associated with the Davidic covenant or with the priestly covenant. Older texts, such as Deut. 33:9 or especially Num. 25:10–13 (covenant with the levitical successors [!] of Phinehas, the grandson of Aaron), could have been the foundations for these later developments.[58]

One may mention Judges 17–18 as the first, essentially historical, fixed point which undergirds much of what has already been said. It is clear in Judg. 17:17 that the "levite comes from the tribe of Judah" and therefore does not belong to the tribe of Levi. Rather, the levite is a Judean who assumes the function of a levite. Of what this function consists is precisely described in Judges 17. The levite is not immediately a priest, but he does bring along the presuppositions of priesthood and cares for both the idol and its house.

With the beginning of the monarchy, levites were scarcely mentioned for a long time. It is likely that they were suppressed by other (priestly) groups (Zadokites or Aaronides?). The levites were mentioned in a rather detailed fashion once again in Deuteronomy. Thus Deuteronomy was familiar with the "levite(s) in your gates,"[59] that is, the so-called country levites who also probably performed priestly service in the various locations where they were active. According to Deut. 33:8–11, they at least administered the lots for divine oracles, gave instruction in the law of YHWH, and offered sacrifice. The chapters of Deuteronomy that provided the narrative frame for the book and that were often even further shaped by Deuteronomistic features expanded this activity of the levites by making them into those who carried the "ark of the covenant,"[60] stood and served before YHWH, and blessed the people (Deut. 10:8f.; and 27:12, 14), but did not have any portion in the land since YHWH is their נחלה (naḥălâ = "inheritance").[61] The country levites, according to Deuteronomy, were now to continue to be correctly known as "levitical priests,"[62] that is, the country levites, who had lost their means of employment at the local sanctuaries but could now be priests at the central temple as a result of the centralization of the cult (Deuteronomy 12). In addition, in this book all priests were probably also to be levites (Deut. 18:1). Thus, even Moses, Aaron, and Zadok later on were made levites (Exod. 2:1; 4:14; and Ezek. 40:46).[63] This was perhaps more easily carried out, because to be a "levite" originally had nothing to do with membership in a tribe but rather with the status and function of one who was especially loyal to YHWH.

The Deuteronomic entitlement of the levites to share in the priestly service at the central sanctuary (Deut. 18:6–8) could not be carried out.[64] Thus the country levite is one social category of those to whom charity should be given and who should not be abandoned. Consequently, he is often mentioned in connection with other *personae miserae* (Deut. 14:27; 16:11, 14; 26:12f.; etc.). That these levites may have been the bearers of the Deuteronomic and Deuteronomistic traditions overall,[65] or even in a wider role a larger reform and restoration movement,[66] cannot be demonstrated. In Gen. 49:5–7 their status is described from the perspective of their opponents, while in Deut. 33:8–11 there is found, by contrast, their own positive evaluation,[67] although one may still see in v. 11 the opposition against Levi and his claim.

During the exile or shortly thereafter, the Book of Ezekiel assigned the levites in Ezek. 44:6–14 a minor type of cultic service, while the Zadokites reappeared then as levitical priests (Ezek. 44:15). This demotion of the levites was seen here as the punishment for having supported Israel in its idol worship (Ezek. 44:10–12; and 48:11). The assignment of only lower cultic service continues to appear in other postexilic texts (Num. 1:47ff.; 3; 4; 8:24ff.; 18:2ff.; and 35:2ff.; cf. also Ezek. 45:5). This minor role of the levites was also presupposed by the Books of Chronicles which, in addition, certainly endeavored to create a further reevaluation of the levites (see below). According to the prophetic vision of Ezek. 45:5 and 48:13f., there is imparted to the levites a portion in this programmatic, new distribution of the land.

On the basis of the demotion that took place, it is no wonder that the narratives indicate that the levites were not thrilled with the idea of returning to the land when the opportunity presented itself (Ezra 2:40; 8:15–20; Neh. 7:43ff.). The priests were, by contrast, more numerous among those who returned home (Ezra 2:36–39; and Neh. 7:63ff.). After the return, disputes occurred with the members of the priestly class (Ezra 8:15; polemic against Aaron in Numbers 12), leading to the demand for a "common priesthood" for all Israelites (Num. 16:2–7a) and confrontations of the Korahites with the Aaronides (Num. 16:7b-11).[68]

For the postexilic texts, only the Aaronides are priests, while the levites are minor cultic servants[69] who, as such, were "given" to the Aaronides (Num. 3:9; and 8:19; cf. 1 Chron. 6:33). Even so, the theological status of the levites continued to be upheld (Num. 1:47ff.; and 8:5ff.). Indeed, their status was theologically enriched,[70] something that nurtures the suspicion that this could scarcely have been the case in practice. The levites may have been separated from Israel to become the special possession of YHWH and his gift (Num. 8:14, 16; 18:6). They were the ones who stood in place of the firstborn of Israel who actually had belonged to YHWH (Num. 3:11–13, 40–43; 8:16–18).[71] "The example of the enrollment of the firstborn allows one to recognize the little value placed on minor clerics."[72] The rather theoretical, utopian text of Joshua 21 probably also belongs in this connection. This passage about the levitical cities (cf. Num. 35:2ff.)[73] can be placed alongside Neh. 13:10 which mentions levites taking possession of land (Ezek. 45:5; and Lev. 25:32–34).

The Books of Chronicles[74] seek to present then an additional, even practical evaluation of the levitical class. Here the levites, under the continuation of the demands and theses of Deuteronomy (Deut. 10:8f.; and 31:25),[75] become the "servants before the ark" (1 Chron. 16:4; 2 Chron. 35:3).[76] They also are named here the carriers of the ark in places in Chronicles, something that reads differently from its precursor in Kings (2 Chron. 5:4; cf. 1 Chron. 15:2 as a programmatic statement). However, the Chronicler separates the ark from the tent, the "dwelling of YHWH,"[77] and left the tent in Gibeon (1 Chron. 21:29).[78] While the levites were "teachers" (2 Chron. 17:8f.; and 35:3; cf. Neh. 8:7ff.), they were also, during and since the time of David, singers in the temple worship, something they no longer were according to the testimony of the books of Ezra and Nehemiah.[79] They give thanks to and praise the Lord (1 Chron. 16:4; and 23:5), and their singing even helps to win a war (2 Chron. 20:19, 21).

They are both temple singers and doorkeepers who possess prophetic authority (2 Chron. 20:14–17; cf. 29:30; 35:15; and 1 Chron. 25:1–31)[80] and are
"chosen" by YHWH. They receive in the Books of Chronicles the same predicate as the temple city of Jerusalem (1 Chron. 15:2; 2 Chron. 29:11). According to 1 Chron. 23:4f., where their activity is described in summary fashion as serving the house of the lord, as doorkeepers, singers, and musicians,
their number has reached about 38,000. First Chronicles 9:26 mentions, moreover, their oversight over the chambers and treasures of the temple, including
oversight over the cultic utensils (1 Chron. 9:28), a role that they may always
have had. According to 1 Chron. 23:29, the levites must give attention to
weights and measures, a responsibility that was not insignificant in the cultic
sphere. They were also responsible for the temple taxes and their collection
(2 Chron. 24:5f.; and Neh. 10:39f.). The Books of Chronicles brought the
levites more strongly within the sphere of cultic worship than the Priestly document, for instance, wanted to do. Their auxiliary services approached those
of priestly activity (2 Chron. 29:34; 30:16) but did not lead into that activity.
Parallel to the desired reevaluation of the roles of priests and levites is their
strict separation into two groups. For example, only the priests may purify the
inner court of the temple (2 Chron. 29:16),[81] and they are the ones who may
carry the ark into the holy of holies (2 Chron. 5:7). The levites, moreover, as
temple singers obtained a special part in the worship which is understood in
the Books of Chronicles primarily as the praise of YHWH.[82] In addition, they
were given an increasing role in the cultic reforms (2 Chron. 24:6, 11; 29:5,
11, 12–15, 25f.; and 35:3). The levites had classifications and separate
"guilds" (1 Chron. 6:16ff.). Since the Chronicler, moreover, wishes to have
the levites unconditionally in the temple, he alters even ancient reports in their
favor[83] and places within their genealogies wherever possible many famous
men of an earlier time, including, for example, Aaron and even Samuel (1
Chron. 5:27ff.; 6:33ff.; 6:12f., 18). Finally, the levites even became charis-
matics (2 Chron. 20:14–17), for it is only here that the priesthood and the
levitical class are connected with the spirit of YHWH.[84] There are different
indications as to the age of service until retirement. The ages range from
twenty, twenty-five, thirty, to fifty years of age (Num. 4:3ff.; 8:23ff.; Ezra 3:8;
1 Chron. 23:3, 24, 27; and 2 Chron. 31:17).[85]

9.4   Literary Forms from the Sphere
of Priestly Ceremony

In order to grasp the theological nature of the significance and function of
priestly service in a more precise manner, a look at the spoken rituals expressed
to the laity and at the textual forms from the priestly sphere of activity should
prove helpful.[86]

According to Jer. 18:18, the תּוֹרָה (*tôrâ*),[87] that is, the giving of "instruction," is the distinguishing feature and the property of the priesthood. This fact is clearly confirmed by other passages (Deut. 31:9, 26; 33:10; Ezek. 7:26; 44:23; Hos. 4:6; Micah 3:11; and Mal. 2:7). A worshiper approached the priest in order to "inquire" (שָׁאַל = *šā'al*) about the divine will (Deut. 18:11; Judg. 18:5; 1 Sam. 10:22; 23:4; and 2 Sam. 16:23).[88] An example of a priestly torah is found in Hag. 2:10–13[89] (cf. also Micah 6:6–8 which emulates this literary form). Thus, priestly instruction seeks to "instruct" (ירה = *yārâ*) people in the differences between the holy and the profane, clean and unclean (thus in Hag. 2:10ff.), and so forth.[90] It provides, in addition, instruction about what is in accord or not in accord with YHWH's will. This included a determination as to what may be an offense against a particular taboo or what corresponds to the holiness and sovereignty of YHWH.[91] Such a torah the priesthood may not falsify (Jer. 2:8; Hos. 4:6; and Zeph. 3:4; cf. Isa. 33:14–16).[92] This torah is issued in the form of a judgment or an imperative, and what the priest imparts at the sanctuary as torah is the torah of YHWH (Isa. 2:3; and Micah 4:2). The prophetic polemic against the cult is often issued quite intentionally in the style of such a priestly, cultic decision (cf., e.g., Isa. 1:10ff.).[93]

The priests also probably issued a salvation oracle in which a divine promise was given to the worshiper or the worshiping community in the form of a declaration of a divine answer. One may compare this to the well-known about-face from the lament to the certainty of thanksgiving that is found in many psalms (Pss. 6:8ff.; 12:5ff.; 91:14ff.; etc.). Then there are the clear mentionings of promise in Pss. 3:5; 35:3; and 60:8–10 as well as the statement, "You have answered" in Ps. 22:22. In addition, the oracles of salvation in Deutero-Isaiah (e.g., Isa. 43:1–7; and 49:14f.) point in this direction, and it is probable that the exhortation, "Do not fear," introduces a proclamation of salvation much like the one that may be recognized in Lam. 3:57. What followed the exhortation was either an address to the worshiper or a divine testimony that was given in the form of an address. The skepticism often expressed in scholarly literature about this type of ritual speech is unfounded.[94]

The priests used so-called declaratory formulae[95] which stated that a cultic ritual was correctly executed and therefore was valid. For example, these formulae included: "This is a . . . sacrifice" (Lev. 1:9, 13, 17; 2:6, 15; 4:21, 24; 5:9, 19; Exod. 29:14, 18; etc.),[96] "He/she/it is clean (or unclean)" (Lev. 11:4, 35, 37; 13:11, 13, 15; etc.), "This is holy to YHWH" (Lev. 6:18, 22; 7:1), "He is righteous" (Ezek. 18:9), and "This is an abomination to YHWH" (Lev. 11:13, 41). For example, a sacrifice would then be "reckoned" (חשׁב niphal = *ḥāšab*) to the one who offered it (Lev. 7:18; 17:4; and Num. 18:27, 30) by means of the accompanying oral decision. One has often assumed that the "reckoning" of Abraham's faith in Gen. 15:6, although the term is used in a decidedly noncultic way, may belong to this category.[97] However, in this latter context, חשׁב (= ḥāšab) is in the qal, not the niphal, form, and it is not at all clear as to who the subject of the verb is (who reckons what to whom?).[98] Further, priestly judgments are also given about leprosy in its various forms (Leviticus 13–15). The New Testament's "Show yourself to your priests" (Mark 1:44 par.) makes the same connections. By using these declaratory formulae, the priest spoke in a "preformative" manner to the one who *was* pure and/or righteous.

In the cultus, so-called entrance liturgies were also probably used,[99] which, in addition, are called "liturgies at the gate" (in terms of their possible life situation; cf. Ps. 118:19f.[100]) or torah liturgies (because of torah-like stipulations that are set forth). This could pertain to Psalms 15 and 24 (cf. also Isa. 33:14–16). On the one hand, the righteousness of the temple pilgrim is examined (at the temple gate?), and, on the other hand, it is also exhorted. The conditions for entrance to the temple are partially shaped in sentences formed like those of the Decalogue. The basic contours of the correct ethical condition of the would-be worshiper in the temple, that is, a life lived according to the will of YHWH, were especially measured in terms of an ethic of neighborly solidarity.[101] For example, this included the prohibition of the wrongful pursuit of profit. Consequently, both the priests and the cult inquired concerning YHWH's ethical will and attempted to bring about its realization. Whether then (in extreme cases?) the failure to carry out YHWH's will led to the suspension of the cult is not known, but this could be indirectly inferred from Old Testament texts of curses, as, for example, Lev. 26:14ff. and Deut. 28:15ff. Since the prophets also issued their polemics against cultic practices primarily in terms of ethical arguments directed against the worshipers singled out for attack,[102] it can be concluded that the prophetic examination of these cultic participants, reflecting the entrance liturgies, indicated that their ethical behavior was not sufficiently in line with the will of YHWH. It ought not to be overlooked, however, that both Psalm 15 and Psalm 24 connect the participation in the festival event, "not with cultic purity, but rather with the quality of everyday behavior."[103] And these two psalms integrate into the ethos of this event a theological system that brings together Zion theology, the kingdom of YHWH, and creation theology.[104] In addition, Psalm 15[105] perhaps has undergone a secondary influence by wisdom. It probably must remain open as to whether one may actually recognize in Psalms 15 and 24 a cultic "procession" or whether these psalms have a more general orientation in which humans "inquire" of or "seek" YHWH (Ps. 24:6) and wish to encounter him in the cultic activity of the sanctuary, or whether, to ask the question differently, these psalms have to do with an actual "liturgy" at all.[106]

According to Deut. 20:2–4, the war sermon belonged also to the tasks of the priesthood, and in the Books of Chronicles the priests (and levites) are connected with military actions (cf., e.g., 2 Chron. 20:19 in its context). In Chronicles the priests were to blow the trumpets, not only during events of worship, but in other contexts as well,[107] so that this activity could be designed to have very different effects. More important, however, were the efficacious words of the blessing of YHWH (Deut. 10:8; 18:5; and the wording of Num. 6:24–26),[108] which, as Num. 6:27 (even though it is a late text) shows,[109] probably was given under the pronouncement of the name of YHWH. While Deut. 17:8–13 (cf. 1 Kings 8:31ff.) deals with sacral jurisprudence, a cultic judgment of God is from time to time assumed to be the life setting of quite a few psalms (e.g., Psalms 17; 23; and 63).[110] The carrying out of a divine judgment (ordeal) is described in Num. 5:12ff., while Ezra 6:10; 9:5–15; and Ps. 99:6–8 perhaps mention intercession as a priestly activity.

As is the case, for example, in the Ugaritic texts,[111] rituals are collected together in Leviticus 1–5[112] that seek to instruct the laity in the proper performance of sacrificial ritual, while the texts formulated to respond to questions pertaining to these rituals are presented in Leviticus 6–7 as priestly "knowledge" (דעת = *da'at*).[113] To this priestly knowledge belong then also the laws about clean and unclean in Leviticus 11–15. The laity slaughtered the animal for sacrifice, while the priests (Deut. 33:10b), however, reserved for themselves the performance of the significant blood ritual[114] that served primarily to bring about expiation.[115]

The priestly oracle, which was administered from the ephod (Exod. 28:15ff.: a pocket for the oracle?; cf. 1 Sam. 23:9ff.)[116] and was known as the "Urim and Thummim," is attested many times in the Old Testament (Exod. 28:30; Lev. 8:8; and Deut. 33:8; only Urim: Num. 27:21; 1 Sam. 28:6; cf. also 1 Sam. 14:36ff.). However, the details of the administration of this oracle are not provided in exact terms (cf. Prov. 16:33).[117] Were the Urim and Thummim two disks, two dice, two sticks, or even a manipulated arrow? According to Ezra 2:63 and Neh. 7:65, the Urim and Thummim ceased to be used in the post-exilic period, something that may be explained because of the growing significance of the priesthood in this period. "The priest represented God before humans by the oracle and instruction, while he represented humans before God by means of sacrifice and intercession."[118]

9.5 Concerning the Theological Significance of Priestly Ritual

The actions of priests have the objective of bringing about the sanctification of the people of God,[119] to the end that this people would be and continue to be formed anew in the image of YHWH. Priestly thinking and believing has to do with the continuation of an existing order. The maintenance of this order is pointed out in good fashion by such things as the Sabbath which marks the division of time (Gen. 2:1–3), the rainbow as the the sign of the covenant with the entire world of God (Gen. 9:13ff.), and circumcision as the sign of the eternal covenant with Israel (Gen. 17:7ff.).[120] Priestly faith believes more in an empirical verification of the sovereignty of God and in its theocratic actualization,[121] particularly since the reign of God over nation and world has already been celebrated in the cult in its perfect culmination.[122] According to the Books of Chronicles, the past as well as the future new reign of David is very much cultically shaped.

Priests were often opponents of the prophets of doom (Amos 7:10–17; Isa. 28:7ff.; Jer. 26:7ff.; etc.) and became the defenders of tradition, while the prophets newly announced the will of YHWH and his coming. Since there were cult prophets who served in offices and, at least in the beginning, the priestly office was not without charismatic features, one ought not simply to oppose priest and prophet in terms of office and charisma.

The fact that the priesthood did not stand at the center of the Old Testament, indeed was not in the forefront at least until the exile, contrasts with the religious world of the other cultures of the ancient Near East. Omenology, magical actions,[123] rituals of exorcism, and caring for idols[124] were not and did not become constitutive for the Israelite priesthood. Rather, the Israelite priesthood in its various tasks was determined more and more in terms of what was considered to be appropriate to YHWH. The priesthood received special significance for the first time after the fall of the state and the monarchy. Jerusalem became the major city again in the postexilic period. After the exile, the temple was rebuilt in Jerusalem and the high priest lived there. As his clothing and anointing demonstrate, he continued a part of the royal tradition.

Thus the priests had "to apply Yahweh's work of revelation to everyday life and to guide the people spiritually in this manner."[125] "In their performing of the sacramental actions the priests were the guarantee of communion with God. The great danger, actually inherent in the priesthood, was that it made the institutional element of religion into something immutable, something permanent."[126] Living religion does not deplete itself in the preservation of what is transmitted or in the upholding of given orders. Rather, preservation and movement, priest and prophet, institution and event, and static and dynamic belong together in a vital religion. Indeed, what is extraordinary about the Old Testament can best be expressed in terms of its being dynamic and charismatic. In the tension between the priests and the prophets, there is ultimately a tension between the God who has come and the God who is to come.[127]

Chapter 10. The Prophets[1]

10.1 The Election of Israel
and the Message of the Prophets

There is a dearth of statements about election in the Old Testament prophets.[2] In the places where the preexilic prophets come to speak about statements of election or, better yet, traditions about election, they tend to place them critically in question. The preexilic prophets clearly presuppose the existence and importance of these statements and traditions about election. However, they refer to election only in a critical way, and especially when they were constrained to set forth for their audience a contrasting opposition between divine choosing and Israel's current existence. This is clear, for instance, in Amos (Amos 3:2; 9:7; and probably also 5:14) where YHWH's acknowledged election of his people, deliverance from Egypt, and presence with the nation could be taken up only in a critical fashion.[3] In the same way, Hosea described his audience as appropriate successors of Jacob, for Jacob was only a deceiver in the view of this prophet (Hos. 12:1ff.).[4] Jeremiah (Jer. 9:3) argued similarly about Jacob and his descendants, while it is impossible for Ezekiel to make a single positive reference to the traditions of faith (Ezek. 20:5–8; and 33:24ff.). The prophets came to recognize that Israel developed a faith in election that emphasized the status of being the elect and yet that also placed obligation on the chosen (cf. Hos. 1:6, 9; Amos 5:21; Micah 2:6ff.; 3:11; Isa. 28:14ff.; Jer. 4:30; 7; 26; 28; 37f.; etc.). This faith thought it was possible to recall the earlier history with and under YHWH and yet to evade his new demands on the present.

When these prophets confronted Israel anew and firmly with the ethical will of its God, they placed once more the combination of election and obligation[5] in the forefront. The life of the elect, along with their social, cultic, and political behavior, does not correspond any more to the claim of God who had disclosed himself to the community that had made itself responsible to him.

With this, YHWH's relationship becomes important for the ones to whom he has come anew, not just to those who have existed in community with him in the past. According to prophetic conviction, YHWH is the God who has not only presented himself to and claimed his people in the past but also continues to do so in the present by means of his new actions in history. For example, he acts anew in the coming of the Assyrians and the Babylonians which leads to the judgment and punishment of his people (Amos 4:12; Isa. 10:5ff.; and Jeremiah). In connection with this, the prophets find it necessary to treat and to cope with newly emerging theological questions. How does one look at YHWH and the foreign nations as well as YHWH and their deities? Is YHWH actively at work in the Assyrians and the Babylonians, in the "enemy from the north" (Jeremiah), and in the Persians (Deutero-Isaiah)? Is election still valid in terms of the new, judging, punishing coming of YHWH to his people, or must one think about their rejection not only as a possibility but, as is the case with the Book of Jeremiah,[6] also as a reality? How may one describe the character of this new coming of YHWH to his people? Is the punishing activity of YHWH a purging or a destroying activity that brings about a complete "end" (Amos 8:2)?

In their message, the prophets differentiate among those whom they address. The nation and the community, those accepting and rejecting the prophetic message, are now differentiated. The nation is addressed, but at the same time the individual is called to make a faithful decision. In this way, there is a fundamental distinction between the so-called "writing prophets" and, prior to Amos, their predecessors—for instance, Elijah and especially Elisha. In the latter, there is more of a confronting of individuals, chiefly the king, by the prophets. In the writing prophets, it is the nation of YHWH that is threatened with YHWH's punishment and overthrow, because it has opposed and continues to oppose the will of its God. Their message presents a radical threat to Israel, and in the nation's encounter with this message it becomes, in the final analysis, "individualized." It is indeed the nation, as well as each hearer of the prophetic word, who stands both anew and individually before God.

According to their message, these prophets know that they are empowered, commissioned, enlightened, and sent by YHWH himself. They also often say something about their "calling" in order to clarify their legitimation (Amos 7:10ff.; Isaiah 6; Jeremiah 1; Ezekiel 1–3; etc.). However, only a few speak about "election," and this first occurs in later texts (Jer. 1:5; and Isa. 42:1; cf. 49:1). Further, the noun נָבִיא (*nābî'*) probably means "one called," rather than "speaker" or "one who calls out,"[7] and the translation of the term with "prophet" is simply an expediency.[8] The verb that is derived from this noun, occurring in the niphal and hithpael, characterizes the activity of a נָבִיא (*nābî'*), without making more precise differentiations.[9] They are the ones who now interpret the history that happens to Israel and to themselves as the acts of their God, speak of a new unity of history and word,[10] and now "see words" (Amos 1:1; and Isa. 2:1), for they see a new event, more from the perspective of an overarching vista than from the position of foresight, as an address of their God. A new divine history now stands before Israel, new also in the sense that it is a history of judgment and punishment, since Israel is ripe for judgment and deserving of punishment. What the prophets must speak and what they must proclaim is the new dialogical encounter of the God of Israel with his people, a dialogue that is opened by the prophetic word.[11] If one sees in this dialogue only a call to repentance,[12] this would be just as narrow a view as if one seeks the point of departure for prophetic proclamation only in the certainty about the future[13] or only in its critical view and analysis of the present in which, for example, the prophets chide the cult or the society.[14] And if one argues that the prophets do not announce a new coming of YHWH to effectuate judgment but rather only produce the evidence of what YHWH always has done,[15] then the prophetic message, including its background as well as its purpose, may not be fully and completely captured.

How did these prophets come to their message? Who were the prophets and what did they announce as the "word of YHWH"?

10.2 "Prophecy" in Israel's Religious Environment

If one attempts to become more familiar with the phenomenon of "prophecy in the Old Testament" by means of an etymological analysis of the terms that are used for it, then one is often disappointed. Neither the Greek word προφήτης[16] (= *prophētēs;* "one who speaks forth or declares openly"?), nor the Hebrew נביא[17] (*nābî'; "*one who speaks, one who calls forth, or one who is called"?), provides much additional help in seeking to ascertain the nature of Old Testament prophecy. In briefly looking at the Old Testament, one often distinguishes between a more ecstatic type of prophecy that is probably Canaanite in origin and a type of seer prophecy that is more Israelite in character. Ecstatic prophecy is encountered in prophetic groups (1 Sam. 19:20ff.; and 10:5, 9ff. "with music"; cf. 2 Kings 3:15 Elisha and 1 Kings 18:26–29) and has religiohistorical parallels, for example, with the Egyptian Story of the Journey of Wen-Amon (eleventh century B.C.E.),[18] which tells of ecstatic "prophets" who appear in the Syrian port city of Byblos. Most Old Testament (classical) prophecy is a phenomenon that is distinguished from ecstatic prophecy.[19] However, in more recent times, it has been determined that Old Testament prophecy is not without parallels in the ancient Near East. Not only were there Akkadian "prophets,"[20] but, in addition, certain prophetic phenomena were described in reports found especially in letters deriving from the city of Mari and its environs (end of the eighteenth century B.C.E.).[21] Even the so-called messenger formula ("Thus says . . . ") along with the messenger saying[22] is well known at Mari. In addition, the Mari literature describes the appearance and the commission of the prophetic person, may mention a written order, tells of visions and dreams, and speaks of the reception of divine address, but only when the prophet is awake. The prophetic message, often critical in content, is delivered whether requested or not, and goes back to ecstatic as well as to nonecstatic experiences. There is no question that there are structural parallels between this "prophecy" in Mari and prophecy in the Old Testament. However, in Mari there are mostly individual incidents which are interpreted in a "prophetic" manner, but not great, overarching, historical connections. One no longer is able to say that the phenomenon of prophecy existed only in Israel and that it was especially typical for Israel's faith alone. The king, Zakir of Hamath[23] (ca. 800 B.C.E.), received an answer from his god, Baal, through "seers" and those who knew the future (or "messengers"). Similar texts from Egypt are clearly *vaticinia ex eventu,* although they do provide evidence of "prophetic" speaking and activity.[24] Even the Old Testament itself was aware of the existence of prophets outside Israel (Numbers 22–24; 1 Sam. 6:2; 1 Kings 18:18ff.; Jer. 27:9; and Daniel 1ff.). However, we now must ask more precisely about the form and especially the content of prophetic speech.

The Deuteronomistic redaction of Deuteronomy saw in prophecy Israel's particular means of divine revelation in contrast to the practices of the other religions of the ancient Near East. Moreover, this redaction connected this prophecy closely with Moses and wished to see the prophet only as an interpreter, "like Moses," of the Torah (Deut. 18:9–22). This portrait of the prophet, however, is not congruent with the features of classical prophecy.

In any case, it is already clear from these opening remarks that Old Testament prophecy has followed a history that possibly reaches back even to the time before the Old Testament and reaches out to include the surrounding cultures of ancient Israel. It is also clear that even within Israel prophecy was not a uniform phenomenon. Furthermore, the interlacing of the prophets within the history of ancient Israelite faith, a subject still to be discussed, allows one to recognize that they in no way were the great solitary figures they had earlier been depicted to be.[25] They occupy indeed a great portion of the textual strands of the Old Testament, although there are also Old Testament writings and groups of writings in which they are not met and which are totally silent about prophecy. For this, one may point to Job, Proverbs, and Qoheleth as well as Leviticus, Joshua, Song of Songs, Ruth, and Esther. Even in the Psalter, a prophet is mentioned only once, when the exilic psalm, Psalm 74, laments that there is no longer a prophet (v. 9).

10.3   Old Testament Prophecy before Amos

The famous remark in 1 Sam. 9:9[26] (cf. 2 Sam. 24:11 and Amos 7:12 with 7:14) combines the (earlier) seers with the (contemporary) prophet. Consequently, one has often concluded that Old Testament prophecy ultimately may have two roots: the more Canaanite type of prophecy that has prophetic groups

(1 Sam. 10:3ff.; 19:18ff.; and 1 Kings 18:20ff.), ecstasy and group ecstasy,[27] music, cultic dancing (1 Sam. 10:5; 2 Sam. 6:5; and 2 Kings 3:15), and a special garb (2 Kings 1:8),[28] and the more Israelite type of seer prophecy. A glance at prophets, men of God (1 Kings 13:1, 11, 18; 17:18, 24; 2 Kings 1:9ff.; etc.), and seers mentioned in the Old Testament who functioned chronologically before the beginning of so-called writing prophecy, and that means before Amos and before 750 B.C.E., indicates that they indeed clearly belong to the history of prophecy. However, it is difficult to recognize in the Old Testament prophetic classes and continuing streams that clearly contrast with each other. Thus, an example of prophetic groups is found in the circle of Elijah, thus indicating these groups belong to "authentic" Yahwistic faith (1 Kings 19:14). Still the question arises as to whether this mention of these murdered prophets is historically accurate or whether it is a Deuteronomistic topos.[29]

That already Abraham was called a "prophet" (Gen. 20:7 = E?) and is said to have received a prophetic word (Gen. 15:1) are remarks that probably are to be attributed to the narrator who is active here.[30] Moses also received the title of "prophet," not only in a Deuteronomistic context (Deut. 18:9–22) in which the prophet in good Deuteronomistic fashion is the interpreter of the Torah (cf. Deut. 34:10; Mal. 3:22), but also in Hos. 12:14. According to Num. 12:6–8a (which is quite different from Num. 11:10ff.), he is superior to the prophets. By contrast, according to Exod. 7:1 (P) Aaron was the נָבִיא (*nābî'* = "prophet") of Moses. Balaam was a foreign seer (Numbers 22–24),[31] while the Israelite woman Deborah was a prophet, according to Judg. 4:4. Other women prophets included Miriam, according to Exod. 15:20; Huldah, according to 2 Kings 22:14ff.; possibly the wife of Isaiah according to Isa. 8:3;[32] and a certain Noadiah, in Neh. 6:14. Among the four titles given to Samuel in order to be able to lay claim to this key figure for the beginning of Israel's statehood and for the transition so important for the faith from the period of the judges to the period of the monarchy was the title "prophet" (1 Sam. 3:20; and 9:9).

We know relatively little about Gad, the "prophet, the seer of David" (2 Sam. 24:11); he is supposed to have said things that were both supportive and critical of David (1 Sam. 22:5; 2 Sam. 24:11ff.). The prophet Nathan is more clearly presented in his connection with David. Nathan is a prophet of promise as well as a prophet who threatens the punishment of YHWH (2 Samuel 7 + 12).[33] He is then implicated in various intrigues involving the succession to David (1 Kings 1:8ff.). Thus he is shown already to be a prophet who in no way has to do only with questions of faith.

The prophet Ahijah of Shiloh played a specific role in both the division of the kingdom following the death of Solomon and the designation of his Northern Israelite successor, Jeroboam I (1 Kings 11:29ff.). Even so, Ahijah later on issued a judgment oracle against this same king (1 Kings 14:2, 6–18). In 1 Kings 13 there is a narrative about a conflict between two unnamed prophets.[34] Other prophets, moreover, are only briefly mentioned (1 Kings 12:22; 16:7, 12; 2 Kings 17:13, 23; etc.), while the Jonah in 2 Kings 14:25, probably because he was represented as a prophet of salvation, had his name incorrectly given to the character who is the hero in the small Book of Jonah. The prophet Micaiah ben Imlah, as a prophet of disaster, is an individual "charismatic" prophet who is opposed to a group of prophets of salvation who are attached to the kingship (1 Kings 22).[35] There emerges in this narrative the problem of true and false prophecy.[36] The Books of Chronicles are also aware of other prophets. Here they are representatives of God in history, preachers of repentance, and employers of the dogma of retribution so important for the Books of Chronicles.[37]

Of great significance, however, was Elijah[38] (ca. 860–850 B.C.E.; 1 Kings 17–19; 21; and 2 Kings 1–2), whose name is a confession, "YHWH is (my) God," that would conform well to the contest between Yahwistic faith and the worship of Baal. The narrative of 1 Kings 17–18, shaped by the overarching topic of the "appearance and end of a drought," sets forth the victory of YHWH over Baal. YHWH uses Baal's own weapons, rain and lightning from heaven, and defeats him in his very own sphere of divination. In their present state, the texts[39] are styled in an ideal, typical form, shaped in an exemplary fashion, given a Deuteronomistic stamp,[40] and comprised of several strata. Yet they still allow the character Elijah to be clearly recognized. The continuation of the narrative in the story of Naboth's vineyard (1 Kings 21)[41] may have been secondarily inserted into a critical scene between Elijah and Ahab (vv. 17ff.), although this continuation also deals with an important, fundamental problem in a relevant and appropriate manner. In all his activities, Elijah proved the buoyancy of Yahwistic faith in the region of Canaan and in the confrontation with Baal (cf. 2 Kings 1:2–17) and gave his support to the worship of YHWH alone. The title "man of God," worn by both Elijah and Elisha,[42] reflects probably an older narrative stratum in which, for example, the miraculous character of the legitimation of these men of God was narrated.

The miracle was more frequently associated with Elisha (2 Kings 2; 4; 6; and 8), who, while supposed to have been the successor of Elijah (1 Kings 19:15–21 and 2 Kings 2), contrasted rather significantly with him. Miracles were probably more typical for Elisha,[43] who also was more involved in politics (2 Kings 9f.: revolution of Jehu) and in military events, particularly in the conflict with the Arameans (2 Kings 3; 6:8ff.; 6:24–7:20). The latter was likely responsible for his having received the title of honor: "the chariots of Israel and its horsemen."[44] Among the texts associated with Elisha is the narrative of the healing of Naaman (2 Kings 5) which is especially beautiful and is theologically engaging. Here, God is discovered in the standard fashion, while the connection between YHWH and the land is underlined (v. 17).[45] And with Elisha's expression of good wishes as Naaman is departing (v. 19), one finds something of a presentiment of the justification of the sinner that comes only through grace.

The prophetic groups, already found in association with Saul (1 Samuel 10 + 19), are encountered once again in the Elijah and Elisha narratives (2 Kings 2; 4:1, 38ff.; 6:1ff.; and 9:1ff.).[46] Further, Elijah is supposed to have dealt with a great host of Baal prophets, according to 1 Kings 18:4, 19, 22, and 40.

Without preclassical prophecy serving as its precursor, classical prophecy would be unthinkable. Preclassical prophecy incorporates to a large extent a more popular, basic stream of the prophetic tradition. That preclassical prophecy was often the carrier of nomadic tradition (Nathan's protest against the building of the temple? Elijah's protests against the replacement of YHWH by Baal and against the transformation of YHWH into Baal?) and even the vehicle by which charismatic leadership continued to endure[47] cannot be demonstrated with certainty. It can be inferred from many oracles of the later writing prophets that they were familiar with their predecessors and even saw themselves as belonging to the prior history of this prophecy, although distanced from it (Amos 7:14; Hos. 6:5; 12:11; Jer. 2:26, 30; 4:9; 5:13; etc. Amos 2:11 = Deuteronomistic redaction). The approximation of prophetic call narratives to the "calls of the deliverer," which one can find in Exodus 3; Judges 6; and 1 Sam. 9:1–10:16 and perhaps can be related to Jeremiah 1,[48] points more to a typical literary pattern of such narratives than to a close similarity of the prophets to these deliverer figures, including the latter's behavior as well as their commission, for example, that was given in the context of YHWH war.

10.4 The "Word of YHWH" in the Prophets

It is true that the writing prophets since Amos, who are known by means of the sayings, collections of oracles, and "books" that exist in written form,[49] wished to prove from whom they received both their commission and the content of their message.[50] Even so, the preexilic prophets say nothing about the "Spirit of YHWH" having seized or endowed them.[51] Rather, they say (some 123 times) they are given *the* (not *a*)[52] "*word of YHWH*" (דבר יהוה = *děbar yahweh*)[53] (cf. Jer. 1:9; Ezek. 3:10f.) that now may issue forth through them. According to Jer. 18:18, the "word of YHWH" is especially typical for the prophets. Of the 241 times that the combination "word of YHWH" occurs, some 225 occurrences are a *terminus technicus* for this prophetic revelation of the word. Ecstatic phenomena in relationship to the event of revelation in the writing prophets[54] cannot be recognized. Of significance is the fact for many prophets that, although they speak about the "word," seeing and "visions" are the key experiences. A word of YHWH goes forth apparently not by means of hearing (so in Isa. 5:9; 22:14; 40:3–8; 50:4; and Job 4:12–17) but rather by seeing. This is true already for Amos (Amos 7–9; cf. also 1 Kings 22:19ff.), then also for Isaiah (Isaiah 6), Jeremiah (Jeremiah 1), Ezekiel (Ezekiel 1–3), and Zechariah (1:7–6:8). In the time before Samuel, the word of YHWH was seldom received and there was no vision (חָזוֹן = ḥāzôn; 1 Sam. 3:1). The vision and call reports[55] are mostly stylized as first person accounts in order to emphasize that these are not reports by strangers about the prophets but rather are reports presented in the form of self-reflection in which the prophets set forth their experiences in ways that avoid ecstasy. Even the visions themselves give the impression that a very real, perceivable action of YHWH is clearly believed to have happened. The prophets stand in such visions at a point of personal decision and enter into dialogue with YHWH (Amos 7:2, 5; Isa. 6:5ff.; and Jer. 1:6, 11ff.). If one wishes here to speak of ecstasy, then what one has is concentration ecstasy (see J. Lindblom)[56] rather than absorption ecstasy which does not correspond well with the image of God in the Old Testament. The freedom of the prophet continues in spite of what is experienced, so that a prophet can object to what is revealed (Jer. 1:6). Likewise, the private character of each individual prophet continues to exist. The "I" of the prophet is not extinguished; rather, it is taken into service. And if it can be said that these prophets may have "seen the words" of YHWH (Amos 1:1; Isa. 2:1; cf. Micah 3:6f.), this means that to them an event has become a word, that is, an action or occurrence becoming an address that must be weighed. The ancient Israelite, therefore, called both a "word" and an "event" a דבר (dābār).

Thus YHWH has spoken to the prophets through what happened to them, what they experienced and had to experience, and from this address, this situation of disclosure, their own conscience has been overcome and they are empowered and compelled to transmit this "word event." God is linked with reality and address, and with history and language, and the transcendent God becomes immanent through the prophet. The event becomes a symbol.[57] Having to do with a "state of affairs," the event "becomes the essence of YHWH's reality," so that one can correctly translate the so-called formula of the "word event": "the word of YHWH happened to."[58] The messenger formula ("thus says the word of YHWH"[59]) and the messenger oracle make it even clearer that the prophets were understood more as the intermediary of the word[60] than as the speaker encountered by YHWH (cf. Hab. 2:1–3; also Job 4:12–17), for they found themselves both wanting and having to bring to new expression YHWH and his coming. This is and continues to be a completely conscious process. A prophet receives, understands, and believes an insight from divine inspiration without the possibility of the occurrence of a kind of mystical union between God and the prophet. Experiences have transpired, and the hearer should be capable of being directed to have similar experiences. This hearer likewise was to hear what YHWH presently says and has to say. An event becomes an address, a deed becomes a word, because it was YHWH who, residing behind this event of encounter, was newly experienced and believed.[61] While Amos sees earthly, everyday things, as, for example, locusts or a basket with ripe fruit (Amos 7:1–3; 8:1–3), he also sees in them at the same time something more. Because of YHWH and through the prophet's faith in the God who acts to enlighten him,[62] Amos comes to believe and understand these visions to be the transparency that discloses divine revelation. Even as the fruit is "ripe" to eat, so then Israel is "ripe" for judgment, while the "harvest" causes the listener to think of the "end" (Heb. קָיִץ = *qayiṣ;* קֵץ = *qēṣ*). It is not only the Assyrians who are coming as the hostile enemy of Israel but also YHWH who comes to judge and punish his people (cf. Isa. 5:26ff.; 10:5ff.). Later it is not only the Babylonians who come in order to bring about the end of Judah; it is also YHWH who acts to punish his wayward people through Nebuchadrezzar so that this foreign ruler can even be designated the "servant of YHWH" (Jer. 25:9; 27:6). This compares later to the Persian ruler Cyrus who was called the "messiah," meaning that he served as the instrument of YHWH's salvation (Isa. 45:1).

All of this means, then, that this word of YHWH, this word event which was an active power as well as the means of conveying the divine message, was not only a "word" that imparted to the prophet what he or she was to say but also a power that he or she was to experience (1 Kings 17:1; Amos 1:2; 3:8; 7:10; Isa. 9:7; Jer. 5:14; 20:9; 23:29; Isa. 40:8; 55:10f.; and Ezek. 11:13). The word of YHWH also contrasts in a critical fashion with the experience of dreams (Jer. 23:28f.). It is the pathos of YHWH (A. Heschel) that seizes the prophets. YHWH deigns to enter entirely into these prophets, while allowing them to retain their own individual psychological, stylistic, and even theological distinctiveness. When the knowledge of God has permeated thoroughly what the prophets are shown, this then becomes the means of and the basis for the formulation of their message. In this way, the development of a prophetic oracle can be positively compared with the coming into being of a modern sermon.[63] A situation and a "text," that is, a word that occurs within the situation, form the point of departure.[64] This was then placed in relationship to what the prophet himself as well as his listeners normally knew and believed about YHWH. There then followed, in a manner of speaking, a conversation with the traditions of faith in which both the speaker and the listeners live. These traditions are then appropriated or critically addressed anew with a view either to setting forth their meaning for the present or possibly to bringing into question their significance for the completely different situation of those who are now addressed. Then there follows the insertion of the prophetic word into certain established speech forms and genres of texts that conform to what is to be achieved in the concrete situation of communication. All of this involves very conscious acts that do not eliminate the prophet's intelligence but rather engage and then bring into service this intelligence. The fundamental basis for making all of this possible lies in the interaction of word and history that normally is seen to be determinative for the Old Testament's view of God, in the critical interaction of faith and contemporary existence, and less so in the certainty of the prophets' view of the future than in their certainty about a God who is not tied to the moorings of the present.[65] Those who are encountered in this fashion by God then must know and reflect on their own lives. This process leads them to see that their nation is unfaithful to God and to pronounce judgment with a clear conscience. These prophets can only say that YHWH himself comes anew to judge and to punish his people within the course of historical catastrophes.[66] "Prepare, O Israel, to meet your God!" (Amos 4:12).[67] With that, however, the truth or, even better, the legitimacy of this interpretation as well as prophetic competency overall continued to be a point of contention and subject to debate. The presence of the so-called "false prophets" points to and underlines this controversy surrounding the prophets.[68] The "word of God" as such cannot be proven or demonstrated to be true. Rather, the one who hears this word encounters its demand.

A somewhat differently nuanced understanding of the word of God from the mouth of the prophet and a related, likewise differently oriented portrait of the prophet that still is strongly determined by the usual one are encountered in the Deuteronomistic view of prophecy. These prophets are, first of all, the interpreter of the Torah even as Moses was, and they stand within the succession of his office (Deut. 18:15, 18). Then there is the general discourse about "my/his servants, the prophets" within the Deuteronomistic redaction of the Books of Kings, and this discourse is spoken both by YHWH and by the particular narrator.[69] Consequently, the prophets were primarily understood as "foretellers"[70] who proclaim with warnings and threats the coming judgment of YHWH against his unfaithful people and who call them to repentance (2 Kings 17:13). However, in spite of their preaching, they have detected the absence of faith in the nation (1 Kings 14:18; 16:12; 2 Kings 14:25; 17:23; 21:10; etc.). Judges 6:7–10 describes a kind of Deuteronomistic, prophetic, model sermon that here is placed on the lips of a nameless prophet. The prophets have always again "established" YHWH's word (1 Kings 2:4; 6:12; 8:20; 12:15; etc.), and this word hits home, that is, it comes to fulfillment and does not fail. Therein, its truthful character is recognizable (Deut. 18:22; Josh. 21:45; 23:14f.; 1 Kings 2:27; 8:15, 24, 56; and 2 Kings 10:10). It is also quite obviously the exilic reality with which this portrait of the prophet conforms. It was in the exile that the prophets' threat of judgment had come to pass, and yet it was also the time in which they issued the call to repentance.

10.5   The Different Kinds of Texts
in Prophetic Preaching

In their proclamation, the prophets wished to confront those who heard the prophetic word in their customary world and environment and with their ordinary manner of thinking. Thus it is not surprising to discover in prophetic literature texts deriving from a variety of *settings* and situations for communication that are not typically prophetic in and of themselves. Rather, these oral and literary forms were appropriated from other spheres familiar to the prophetic audience.[71]

Thus a priestly torah[72] is imitated (Amos 4:4f.; 5:4f., 21–24; and Isa. 1:10–17), or a funeral lament (Amos 5:2; and Ezek. 19:1–14) or a cry of woe connected to a situation of mourning (Amos 5:18ff.; and Isa. 5:8ff.),[73] or, by contrast, a love song (Isa. 5:1–7). The cry to flee and the call to battle perhaps derive from YHWH war (Jer. 46:3–6; and 48:6–8).[74] Doxological (Amos 4:13; 5:8f.; and 9:5f.) and hymnic elements are also present in prophetic literature (Isa. 42:10–13; 44:23; 45:8; 49:13; etc.). A numerical saying from the sphere of wisdom is heard in the folk sayings of Amos (Amos 1:3ff.), while the sorites in Amos 3:3 — 6:8 also stems from the world of the sages. The lawsuit is mentioned, for example, in Hos. 4:1 and Isa. 1:18, while courtroom scenes are preferred by Deutero-Isaiah (Isa. 43:8–13; 41:21–29; etc.). According to Jeremiah 29, a letter was sent to the exiles in Babylonia, while Isaiah 47 is patterned after a taunt song.

However, the authentic and specific situations for prophetic texts are the prophetic word of judgment, the prophetic word of admonition, and the prophetic word of salvation, all with their own specific features. The so-called messenger formula (כה אמר יהוה = *kōh 'āmar yahweh;* "thus says YHWH")[75] can be inserted in different places into each of these forms of prophetic speech. The prophets are thus seen as messengers who are taken into service by YHWH.[76] They speak, therefore, in the first person form of the one who sends them and with his full authority.[77] Moreover, the fact that one is a messenger does not exclude one's own shaping of the discourse, as, for example, the unfolding of the message in 2 Kings 18:19–35 and the expression in one's own words in Exod. 5:6–13 show. By contrast, the so-called formula of the oracle of the seer (נאם יהוה = *nĕ'um yahweh;* "whisper [?] of YHWH"), belonging to the speech of the seer (cf. Num. 24:3f., 15f.), occurs only in the middle or at the end of the oracle.[78] Often a "call for attention" ("Hear the word of YHWH") is placed at the beginning of or inserted within prophetic oracles. Moreover, it is worth nothing at this point that this "call for attention" appears to stem less from oral speech than from the written redaction of prophetic books.[79]

A prophetic "word of judgment"[80] can be issued against individuals—for example, against the priest Amaziah in Amos 7:16f. Often, however, the word of judgment is directed against the king as the representative of the nation (e.g., 2 Kings 1:3f.; Jer. 22:1–5). Above all, however, the prophetic word of judgment affects the entire nation[81] (Hos. 2:6f.; Isa. 3:1–9, 16–24; 8:5–8; Amos 4:1–3; etc.) or also foreign nations (Amos 1:3ff.; Isaiah 13ff.; etc.).[82] Such a word consists of the actual announcement of disaster (K. Koch: pronounce-ment) and its basis (K. Koch: indication of the situation).[83] In earlier scholar-ship, this combination was often called the threat and the invective.[84] On oc-casion there followed a concluding characterization, either of the nation or of the announced disaster, that sought once more to stress very clearly that the coming punishment of the nation was inevitable (Ezek. 14:23). The function of this type of prophecy, together with its particular theological setting, is dis-puted. Is the intention of this type of prophecy to point out the inevitability of the coming disaster and to make known its requisite nature, or is the purpose to set forth even in this announcement of judgment a last admonition, an im-plicit, final cry to repent or, better yet, to act justly, as may be assumed espe-cially from the argumentation of the proclamation of judgment?[85] Does this type of prophecy not have to do with "the dialogical encounter of the God of Israel with his people that is inaugurated by the prophetic word"?[86]

This question turns on the classification of the actual prophetic *word of ex-hortation*.[87] This type of speech can be issued either with a negative an-nouncement, that is, with a justification for disaster (Isa. 1:10–17; Amos 5:6; etc.), or with a positive proclamation, that is, with the setting forth of reasons for salvation ("Seek me, so that you may live": Amos 5:4f., 14f.; Hos. 10:12; Zech. 1:3; etc.). According to one opinion, these words of exhortation did not represent authentic exhortations any longer but rather intended to make clear how futile the possibility was for repentance and therefore served as evidence of guilt.[88] Thus one can point to Amos 4:6–12 which repeats the clause, "yet you did not return to me." However, is this type of prophetic word also not in-tended to be an authentic exhortation[89] that aims to say that "this word at the least is taking place even now"? "To seek" YHWH (Amos 5:4) happened also through both the consulting of a prophet (1 Kings 14:1ff.; 2 Kings 1:2ff.; and 8:8ff.) and the hearing of his word. This word, in spite of everything else, speaks of "living."

The prophetic *word of salvation* can be subdivided[90] into oracles of salva-tion, promises of salvation, and depictions of salvation. The content of depic-tions of salvation—for example, those which portray the peaceable kingdom of wild animals or the universal peace with the nations—occurs, for instance, in Isa. 2:1–4 and Isa. 11:6–9, and often already contains eschatological fea-tures.[91] A promise of salvation speaks of approaching salvation, and this chiefly for the nation (e.g., Isa. 41:17–20; and Jer. 34:4f.). Sometimes there stands at the end of this promise of salvation a so-called concluding character-ization of God, for such a promise can be grounded only in YHWH alone. At other times, the prophetic oracle of salvation or the promise of salvation (e.g., Isa. 43:1–4, 5–7) resembles a priestly oracle of salvation[92] and pledges salva-tion in the present. In the course of this address, the admonition "Do not fear" is often attached. With regard to all of these oracles of salvation, the rather significant question arises as to whether they originate for the first time in later redactions or whether they can actually be traced back to individual prophets themselves. This question is especially valid for the texts that belong to the corpora of writings of the preexilic prophets.

In addition to the distinctions already mentioned, C. Westermann has distinguished between words of salvation within a narrative report that are thus related to a concrete situation (e.g., Isa. 7:1–17) and words that are present in collections of prophetic oracles and appear to be either later additions to words of judgment (e.g., Micah 2:12f.) or independent oracles of salvation (Isa. 9:1–6; and 35:1–10). In addition, he separates the words of salvation according to their predominant themes, as, for example, the themes of salvific words of liberation, gathering up and bringing back, the return once again of God, restoration, and blessing. All of these differentiations can help one grasp the particular coloring of each oracle. In addition, one should remember that prophetic words directed against the foreign nations often can indirectly be words of salvation for Israel.[93]

Typical genres of texts[94] for prophecy that are found in the prophetic books include *call narratives*.[95] These are misunderstood if one assumes they possess a biographical interest. The event of the call itself takes place *before* the formation of such a text, and nothing historical may be inferred from it. They are, rather, theologically shaped writings of legitimation that often are dependent on what for them is a typical pattern: namely, a divine encounter with an introductory word occurs first in the narrative, is followed then by the prophetic commission, an objection or a reply, the surety of divine presence, and the promise or gift of a sign. A vision, a theophany of YHWH (Isaiah 6; and Ezekiel 1–3; cf. 1 Kings 22:19–23), or a transporting to the divine sphere can be constitutive for the call. Either the sending forth of the prophet or his address by a divine "word" takes place in one of these settings (Jeremiah 1; cf. also Exodus 3 for the call of Moses and Judg. 6:11–24 for that of Gideon). Both types (the sending forth and the divine address) are already interwoven in Deutero-Isaiah (Isa. 40:1–8; 42:1–4).

Then there are *vision reports* (cf. Amos 7:1–9; 8:1–3; 9:1–4; Jer. 1:11–19; Ezekiel 1–3; Zechariah 1–6; etc.). Here one must distinguish[96] between visions of divine presence (e.g., Isaiah 6), visions of symbolic words (Jer. 1:13f.), visions of assonance (Jer. 1:11f.: שָׁקֵד = *šqd;* Amos 8:1–3: קַיִץ = *qyṣ*), and visions of events or occurrences. From the vision reports in Amos to those in Daniel (Daniel 2; 7; 8; and 10–12), one may trace a clear development that can be recognized not only in the increasing number and size of these texts but also in their literary formation and reflective character.[97] Already in Ezekiel there are repeated cases of descriptions of visions that are formed out of verbal images, thus indicating that the vision has now become a means of literary expression (cf. Ezek. 37:11 as the basic root of 37:1–14; Jer. 15:16 as the basis for Ezekiel 1–3; and Isa. 7:20 as the foundation for Ezek. 5:1ff.). Consequently, with this the journey begins that leads to apocalyptic, and the so-called night visions of Zechariah (Zech. 1:7—6:8) already present "fabricated vision reports."[98] Also to be mentioned are prophetic symbolic actions (cf., e.g., Ezek. 24:15–24; 37:15–28) which also reveal a particular literary structure.[99]

In all of these textual genres, the word of God is encountered in the form of human words, even in texts that come from students and redactors. It is hardly possible to separate out the *ipsissima verba* of the prophets from these texts and then, as, for example, G. Fohrer wishes to do,[100] to understand only these actual words of the prophets as the word of God. Indeed, the attempts to isolate these authentic prophetic words are mostly burdened with judgments based on personal taste.[101] Rather, it is important to recognize that even these "authentic" prophetic words would have been filtered through the medium of human thought and speech. A word of God that comes before or after human reflection and formation cannot be separated out from the text. Rather, it has obviously fallen to God to make himself known through humans and their speech, that is, through the construction of a word event. God is revealed through humans who are encountered and affected by him, and through the witnesses of their speech new encounters are created and made possible.[102]

The prophetic word is therefore not only communication or proclamation but also the putting into operation of what is announced. This word is the driving force of history that is not only a word about judgment and salvation but also a power that initiates and brings them both into reality. In the prophetic word, history already appears as the future.[103] It is in the field of history, where YHWH is active, that he makes himself known through human beings. Thus the revelation of God occurs in the entwinement of word and history, of speech and event, and of faith and action, and this word can point ever anew to the course of history: "So that you may know that I am YHWH!" Through the word history receives its unity, its finality, and its character as a conversation between YHWH and his people.[104] Through the word history becomes an address. History is not equated by the word with YHWH, although it is true that YHWH is made concrete through history. As for these prophets, their criticism of the present and their conviction about the future ought not therefore to be played out against each other in a fundamental manner. Through the prophetic word, history is explained, announced, promised, and fulfilled. Subsequently, prophetic preaching already of its own accord points toward eschatology.[105]

The so-called political preaching of the prophets[106] is supported precisely by this very conviction which knew that YHWH and history were bound together. Furthermore, behind this conviction stands the Old Testament's approximation of nation and community, together with the propinquity of religion and politics in many areas, for which the political words of the prophets are precisely a good illustration. And the symbolic actions of the prophets, which extend from the mantle of Ahijah of Shiloh (1 Kings 11:29ff.) to the crown for Zerubbabel in Zechariah (Zech. 6:9–14)[107] and which find their largest number of examples in Jeremiah and Ezekiel, are not just illustrations, representations, or confirmations of prophetic preaching. Furthermore, these symbolic actions are not simply stylistic expressions or literary accoutrements for prophetic words. Rather, these consciously, purposely, and intentionally executed actions authenticate the coming event which already is breaking into history both in them and in the prophetic word. They are an anticipatory proclamation of an action,[108] an active word event. They are an event as word, that is, a word event in the fullest sense of an authentic דבר (*dābār* = "word").[109] Even the prophets themselves could become a symbolic action, that is, an action word, as was the case with Hosea's actions in regard to his wife and marriage (Hosea 1–3), Jeremiah's being denied the right to marry (Jeremiah 16), and Ezekiel's not only being forbidden to weep over the death of his wife but also being instructed to lie on his right and left sides so that he should bear the guilt of Israel and Judah (Ezek. 4:4ff.; and 24:15ff.).

10.6 Judgment and Salvation

The main content of prophetic speech is the announcement of the coming acts of judgment and punishment of YHWH.[110] The need for this approaching, punishing disaster is based on the social, cultic, and political condition of evil that characterizes the nation as well as on the holiness of YHWH, its God. YHWH can and will no longer show mercy (Amos 8:1–3). The prophets' criticism of the present and their consciousness of God blend together at this point.

The approaching judgment could be misunderstood, however, if it should be regarded as an inevitable fact. This is probably not true even of Amos. In addition to his statement, "The end has come for my people, Israel" (Amos 8:2),[111] the prophet ventures, in casting his eyes toward God, a hesitant, reserved "perhaps" (Amos 5:15; cf. Zeph. 2:3 and Joel 2:14) for a merciful action of YHWH for a remnant of Joseph. Since there was no passing allusion to a promise of salvation during the time of judgment but rather only after it was completely finished, and since such a promise was not based upon the nation in any of the prophets, then it is a question as to whether or not everything there may have been completely corrupted and thus ripe for judgment. It is always much more YHWH himself who is able to build the bridges between judgment and salvation in his own way and through his own loyalty (cf. only Hos. 11:8f. or Jer. 31:20). Judgment is not the final purpose, not at all the ultimate goal of YHWH's way with his people. Even if there is no further possibility for the people, one should not assume that the end of YHWH and of his reality has come to pass. Thus one can speak of the coming judgment not only in terms of annihilation but also as purification (e.g., Isa. 1:24ff.) Conditional judgment and unconditional salvation together are aspects of the same message of the approaching God. Both can even stand beside each other, as, for example, in Jeremiah 24 (good and rotten figs). Consequently, one can argue about and answer in two different ways even the most serious and weighty problem, that is, whether YHWH shall or even already has repudiated and rejected his people.[112] And one can beseech YHWH not to do something (Deut. 9:25f.; 1 Kings 8:57; both Deuteronomistic texts; and Lam. 5:22).

Consequently, if one dares at all to speak of salvation, then these words of salvation always have YHWH himself as the intrinsic ground of actualization (cf., e.g., Amos 5:15b; Isa. 9:6c; and Micah 2:12). He shall create salvation and bring his reign to perfection.[113] With this appear all the elements of salvation once again, the very things to which Israel has been directed, only now these things are presented in their complete perfection[114] (a new exodus, a gathering up, a new Jerusalem, a new David or Davidic descendant, a new covenant, peace, and other things). There will be compassion (Zech. 1:16) and liberation (Isa. 40:2), redemption and forgiveness (Isa. 44:22; and Jer. 31:34), restoration and a gathering up, and an increase and renewal of the people (Micah 2:12f.; 4:6–8; Hos. 11:11; Ezek. 36:26ff.; and Jer. 31:31–34). The knowledge of God and the community of God will be fully realized (Hos. 2:16–25; and Ezek. 36:26f.). There will no longer be the worship of false gods (Ezek. 37:23; 43:7–9; and Zech. 13:2), and all war will come to an end (Isa. 9:4; Zech. 9:10; and Micah 4:3f.). Then YHWH will rule from Zion (Zech. 2:14) over a fruitful land (Isa. 4:2–6; and Amos 9:13–15), and, according to the testimony of one text, he will bring about this salvation through a savior king.[115] YHWH will "choose" anew (Zech. 1:17; 2:16; and Isa. 14:1).

10.7 "True" and "False" Prophets

Many of the writing prophets engaged in controversy with their prophetic opponents over the question of salvation and/or disaster. In regard to this question, one often speaks of the "false prophets."[116] It must be made clear at the outset that false prophets do not appear in the Old Testament in the guise of "swindlers" who only pretended to be prophets.

In addition to the more charismatic individuals who meet us, for instance, in the form of Amos, Hosea, Isaiah, or Micah, and who, as is clearly evidenced with Amos (Amos 7:10ff.), had another profession, there are "official," mainly professionally employed state and cult prophets who were temple functionaries with cultic-prophetic duties. However, while such prophets are clearly evidenced in Israel's ancient Near Eastern environment,[117] they are not directly attested in the Old Testament. Rather, they may be inferred to have existed. Thus, there often are reports of individual prophets as well as prophetic associations that are attached to a sanctuary (1 Kings 11:29: Shiloh; 13:11ff.: Bethel; and 2 Kings 2:1f. and 4:38: Gilgal; cf. also 1 Sam. 19:18ff.: Ramah; and 2 Kings 2:5: Jericho), while other prophetic groups were active within the retinue of kings in military expeditions (1 Kings 22:6ff.). In looking at the writing prophets, one should certainly guard oneself against premature combinations and forced theses according to which, for instance, an Amos, a Jeremiah, or an Ezekiel originally may have been the same kind of cult prophet.[118] Amos 7:14 is an often mishandled biblical passage in this regard. Today the books of Nahum, Habakkuk, and Joel are occasionally attributed to the circles of the prophets of salvation, and, in this connection, the present forms of these books (see esp. Nahum and Habakkuk) allow one to recognize later redactions.[119]

The previously mentioned prophetic groups and schools are clearly attested in the Old Testament. Nathan and Gad could have belonged to the court prophets under David. Micah (Micah 3:5–8) and especially Jeremiah (Jer. 23:9ff.; and 27–29) entered into controversy with the prophets of salvation, and this kind of conflict is also found in Ezekiel (Ezekiel 13–14). The following features are characteristic of these cult, salvation, and state prophets: their appearance often in larger groups, a close connection to the monarchy and to sanctuaries, and the preaching of salvation, that is, the total lack of oracles of judgment against the nation. By contrast, it is sometimes asked whether or not the utterance of prophetic words against the foreign nations was once the task of the cultic prophets, but there is no clear answer. In any case, one does not encounter in the persons and the message of these prophets of salvation what is, on the whole, typical for Old Testament prophecy. Here the "office" stood in opposition to the "call."[120]

Numbers 11:16ff. (another's sharing in the spirit of Moses) and Num. 12:6–8 (Moses stands over the prophets) have to do with problems of the proper ordering of prophetic phenomena. In 1 Kings 13, one prophet opposes another, with a deadly result for one.[121] According to 1 Kings 22,[122] the individual prophet Micaiah ben Imlah as the only "true" prophet stands over against a group of some four hundred "false" prophets under their leader Zedekiah. According to 1 Kings 22:21–23, moreover, YHWH himself can be the one who effectuates this false message![123] For that reason, the problem of false prophecy cannot be easily solved. This problem is completely missing in Hosea, while it is suggested in Amos only in 7:14 and in Isaiah only in 3:2 and 28:7–13.

The first explicit mention of prophetic opponents occurs in Micah (3:5–8) where they are unfit on account of their venality. In addition, they are happy to say what the people want to hear (Micah 2:6f., 11). According to Zeph. 3:4, Jerusalem's prophets are careless and full of deceit. Deuteronomy 13:2–6 seeks to identify prophets who summon the people to abandon YHWH. They should be put to death (v. 6). Deuteronomy 18:14–22 mentions, on the one hand, prophecy as Israel's own special possession in contrast to the interpreters of signs in the surrounding cultures and, on the other hand, traces at the same time this prophecy (in good Deuteronomistic theology) back to Moses, thus making the prophets into interpreters of the Torah (cf. Mal. 3:22). In addition, true prophecy is demonstrated by the fulfillment of its proclamations (Deut. 18:21f.). Also for Deuteronomistic theology, prophets are predominantly foretellers.[124] Moreover, the formulation of Deut. 18:21 allows one to recognize rather clearly that the problem of the identification of false prophecy was an existential one.

It is especially, then, Jeremiah and Ezekiel who are concerned with the problems of true and false prophecy, seeing that they lived during the period shortly before and at the beginning of the exile, a time of great struggle with the questions of judgment and salvation. One may recognize in the texts in Jeremiah[125] different forms of argumentation regarding true and false prophecy,[126] although they explore the question of the relationship of historical event and later interpretation in a manner that is scarcely like any other having this theme. That at the time of Jeremiah and subsequent to him the problem of the demonstration of the truth of the "word of YHWH" possessed a particular urgency is shown by the fact that in no other prophetic book does one encounter or find consciously inserted by the redactors with such frequency the messenger formula as well as the formula of the occurrence of the word with their function of seeking to authenticate the prophecy. The Book of Ezekiel presents in chap. 13 (and 14:1–11) a kind of basic reflection on this theme, mentions false women prophets (Ezek. 13:17ff.), and promises in 12:21–25 that no "vain vision" will again be given in the house of Israel.[127] Prophetic opponents do not appear in the text of the prophet of salvation, Deutero-Isaiah. This is even more clearly the case in Haggai. According to Neh. 6:1–14, Nehemiah saw through the scheme of a false prophet, while Zech. 13:2–6 promises either the complete end of prophecy, including false prophecy, or the complete end of false prophecy alone.

It cannot be demonstrated that the false prophets[128] are always prophets of Baal. It is also inaccurate to say that false prophets may have used glossolalia, that is, prophesied in an unknown or unclear language. Hananiah not only speaks in an understandable manner but even says in addition, "Thus says YHWH" (Jer. 28:2, 11). Certainly there were among the "true" prophets ethical differences or even deficiencies. Conversely, dependency upon the king or upon popular opinion or the wish for success must not automatically make a prophet a false prophet. The true prophets have an advantage, insofar as the later reader of the Old Testament is concerned, since they were quite simply remembered for their message of judgment that came to pass through the advent of the exile. In addition, the accounts of the clash between true and false prophets were preserved from the point of view of the "true" prophets, since the Old Testament does not contain a single, transmitted writing that clearly might belong to the circles of the "false" prophets. It is questionable whether the "true" prophet was an independent charismatic and the "false" prophet was an official attached to an institution. Rather, the "false" prophets were the representatives of a national faith in salvation, which was an erroneous view especially in the historic hour allotted to them shortly before the exile. For us to wish to determine from the outside, as it were, the nature of false prophecy is fraught with many perils, and these increase in number when one seeks to place oneself in the role of those who were directly addressed at the time and who, having heard the message, must decide, at the very least soon thereafter, whether they were indeed encountered by the true word of YHWH. "The inner prophetic conflict (prophet against prophet) is the Achilles heel of prophecy."[129]

One (Deuteronomistic) text in Deuteronomy thinks that it has clear categories for dealing with this problem (Deut. 13:2–4). However, which of the prophets that we meet in the Old Testament may have done such things? According to Deut. 18:20 (cf. Jer. 23:32; 28:8f.), a person is a true prophet whose announcement is fulfilled. However, how does a present hearer of a prophetic message determine whether and when it may have been fulfilled? As we have already mentioned several times, one encounters here the Deuteronomistic prophetic portrait of a foreteller which belongs more to the history writing of the Deuteronomistic school than to the differentiation between prophetic spirits. And if one applies the category of fulfillment to the writing prophets, then Deutero-Isaiah would especially be identified as a false prophet because his announcement of the new, great exodus was not fulfilled in the way that he had stated.[130] The ethical dubiousness of the false prophets, which Micah addresses (Micah 3:5–8), could also apply to a Jeremiah who, according to Jer. 38:24ff., lied. Furthermore, is one's personal and moral character any kind of demonstration of or criterion for the truth of what he or she says? Also, one recognizes a true prophet or a false prophet by his or her "fruits" (Matt. 7:16), but unfortunately this takes place considerably later when these fruits have ripened. Moreover, that prophets debated the authenticity of each other's commission by YHWH also does not help the actual listener. And if the prophecy of salvation was or is principally false, then Deutero-Isaiah was for this reason also a false prophet. How can a helpful answer to these questions be found in the Old Testament which filters these clashes to us through a later point of view and through the lense of the "true" (writing) prophets? Is this quest possible at all, or, as G. Quell thinks,[131] could the label of "false prophet" be assigned only by a true prophet and by no one else? More recent scholarship has given up on this question and therefore has often resigned itself entirely to an all-inclusive categorization of false prophecy.[132]

With the exception of Micah 3:5ff. and Deut. 18:22, the content of the message of the so-called false prophets was limited to salvation of an insular kind. This was a salvation without any conditions or demands and without any connection to a preceding judgment. Accordingly, these prophets could be rebuked for having given rest to the wicked (Jer. 23:14, 17; cf. 15:19f.; and Ezek. 13:22). Therefore they preached probably only *on behalf of* humans, not, however, *against* them, or, to use later theological categories, they proclaimed a gospel without law, or cheap grace. This preaching, however, was exactly wrong for the situation that had been presented to them, a situation that, in addition, they consequently evaluated incorrectly. Their preaching was wrong, for it did not correspond to the will of YHWH. YHWH had primarily determined, now and beyond, to bring his presently so disposed nation to judgment, and not, however, only or immediately to save them. He is not only the deity who is near at hand and always helpful and ready to help but also the distant God (Jer. 23:23f.).[133] This points once again to the connection of word and history and of message and situation to the end that the only possible criterion of distinction between true prophecy and false prophecy is, namely, the theological criterion corresponding to the phenomenon of prophecy.[134] Salvation was (and is?) here not to be promised without repentance, while there could (and can?) be no talk of forgiveness unless it is requested. The demonstration of guilt[135] always belongs to the experience of the encounter with God, if one seeks to judge human reality from a perspective that corresponds to God's. Therefore it can be said: "Your prophets have seen for you what is false and deceptive; they have not revealed your guilt in order to restore your fortune" (Lam. 2:14; cf. 4:13). Consequently, during the situation of the punishment of the exile when "false" prophecy had failed, the lament was heard that there may be no more prophets, no more word of YHWH, and no more help (Ps. 74:9; Lam. 2:9).

It was only by looking back at the past that it became obvious who had been a "true" and who had been a "false" prophet. This had to do not only with the fulfillment of pronouncements but also with the correct assessment of the activity of YHWH in a particular situation. All of the Old Testament texts that deal with the problem of true prophecy and false prophecy are now shaped by this retrospective view and operate within the framework of understanding set forth by the canon. The prophets received their place in the canon primarily through the Deuteronomistic portrait of the prophets. This means that the prophets were primarily interpreters of the Torah (Deut. 18:15, 18)[136] whose own literature was placed between the Torah and the "writings" (cf. Mal. 3:22 at the end of the "prophets" in the canon). Subsequently, the question about false prophets was seen especially within this context (Deut. 18:21f.). That the problem for earlier hearers was set forth quite differently was wrenched from view with the formation of the canon.

10.8   Concerning the Message
of the Individual Writing Prophets

Within the contents of their critical message, the individual prophets have made their own particular contribution, and this may be seen in the way their message is grounded, thematized, and shaped, as well as in how and why they refer the previously given traditions of Israelite faith to their own faith and especially to that of their audience.[137]

From the first group of writing prophets, namely, the prophets of the eighth century B.C.E.,[138] the first to mention is Amos.[139] From the traditions of faith, there appear in Amos critical references to the exodus from Egypt in Amos 9:7 and the "being known" by YHWH, that is, election, in Amos 3:2. However, in both instances Amos was constrained obviously by his opposition to these references, and in both instances a positive reference was denied to his listeners. More than likely, this audience had referred to these traditions of election faith, as is reflected elsewhere (Amos 6:1–6, 13). Already here it is rather clearly shown that the prophetic interpretation of these respective traditions of Israelite faith is more important than the fact that these traditions are at all mentioned. It is only in a spontaneous way, so to speak, that Amos mentions the conquest of Canaan by YHWH (Amos 2:9),[140] while perhaps the reference to divine presence (Amos 5:14) is to be understood as having been taken up in an equally critical manner ("just as you have said"). However, Amos is still the prophet who speaks most clearly of the consequences of the coming judgment, indeed of the "end" (Amos 8:2).[141] The "how" of this judgment could still be made distinctively concrete in relationship to the clear "that" (Amos 2:13; 4:3; 5:27; 6:7, 9f.; 7:1, 4, 11, and 17). His visions (Amos 7:1–9; 8:1–3; 9:1–4) led him to his recognition of impending judgment and then moved him to the point of his first skillful intercession. When he provides the reasons for the necessity of judgment, he mentions social injustice, that is, the segregating of the people of God ("my people" = Amos 7:8, 15; 8:2) into the oppressor and the exploited,[142] and into persons of property and those who are destitute. In addition, he mentions the misuse of worship for personal security and as an alibi for antisocial behavior.[143] One recognizes neither a clear reference to the requirements of the divine law nor a clear reference to wisdom in this regard, and it is not necessary to attribute any of this to the "ethic of solidarity"[144] that is associated with the ideas about the people of God. Even foreign nations become subjected to Yahweh's sovereignty over history (Amos 9:7) as well as to his decree and judgment (Amos 1:3–2:3). In his social criticism, Amos does not develop a social program for improvements; however, it is the case for him as well as for other prophets who speak about social matters that this social criticism provides one of the reasons for divine judgment against those who are addressed.[145] The reference point of this criticism is the thinking about the people of God and their social order, which should not allow for the development of opposing social classes. This social criticism as the rationale for judgment is enfolded within the message of the coming of YHWH. This is analogous to the prophetic criticism of the cult.[146] Thus, the Day of YHWH, which appears as a familiar notion to the nation,[147] is not light, as the people hope and say, but rather darkness for Israel (Amos 5:18–20). Further, this is underlined by the cry of woe, a literary form that represents those addressed as already over-taken by death (cf. Amos 5:2).[148] If, in the coming judgment in which YHWH is active (Amos 3:15; 5:17, 27; 7:9; 9:8), there should be a remnant, which is itself improbable (Amos 3:12), then this would take place through the "grace" (חנן = *ḥnn*) of YHWH. Even this grace would be constituted on the basis of only a "perhaps" (Amos 5:15). The term חסד (*ḥesed;* "steadfast love, loyalty"), in contrast to Hosea, does not occur at all in Amos. Indeed, the discussion else-where (Amos 5:3, 16; 6:10, 14; and 8:3) does deal with surviving the judg-ment.[149] Within the concluding verses of the Book of Amos, which seeks also here to transmit a salvific outlook, Amos 9:11–12 is, at the most, to be regarded as deriving from Amos himself,[150] while Amos 9:13–15 is clearly an amplify-ing addition. After the exile, one could not and did not wish to allow Amos to conclude any longer with harsh words of judgment.

Hosea,[151] who likewise belonged to the earliest group of the writing prophets dating to the eighth century B.C.E., is different from Amos in many respects. When he grounds in rich images (cf. Hos. 5:12, 14; 13:7, 8; 14:6, 9; etc.) YHWH's activity of judgment said to be coming, Hosea speaks less about antisocial conditions in Israel (Hos. 7:1; 10:4; and 12:8f.) and more about the nation's cultic apostasy in following the Baals and the "calf" of Samaria.[152] In addition to this, there is the criticism directed against the priests (Hosea 4) and the monarchy.[153] YHWH reacts against all of these negative things with his personal "I" (Hos. 5:14!; cf. 5:2, 12; 7:12; etc.). His people shall be called "not my people" as well as "not pitied" (Hos. 1:6, 9), names given by Hosea to his own children, for YHWH will become the one who is "no longer your God" (Hos. 1:9). If there is mention of Israel's sins, then this is often made specific in terms of forgetting, forsaking, and disregarding the salvific acts of "YHWH from Egypt" (Hos. 12:10; 13:4), for Hosea often alludes to the former history of Israel with its God.[154] In this regard, mention is made even of the patriarch Jacob, but here he can only be regarded as a deceiver who therefore is the le-gitimate ancestor of the contemporaries of the prophet who behave in the same way (Hosea 12).[155] Israel has received its land from YHWH, and this same God, who has led them here, is also the giver of the fertility of this land (Hos. 2:10, 11, 16f.). YHWH, however, struggles with himself over whether or not he can and must only punish Israel (Hos. 11:1–9). Thus, there is found in Hosea not only pronouncements of judgment (as, e.g., in 1:9; 8:13; 9:3; 10:6; and 11:5) but also mentionings of and reflections on the "covenant" (Hos. 2:20;

6:7; and 8:1)[156] that indicate that a new journey back into the wilderness may be followed by a new migration into "YHWH's Land" (Hos. 9:3; cf. 2:16ff.; 8:13; 9:3, 6; and 11:11). The extent to which Hosea's own marriage with his harlot wife (Hosea 1; cf. 3:1–4?) was of significance to him as a kind of key experience for his interpretation of the relationship between YHWH and Israel as his "wife" (Hos. 2:4ff.) is debated, even as the question of the relationship of chap. 1 in Hosea to chap. 3 is disputed. In any event, Israel's sin is often characterized by Hosea with the concrete image of Israel "playing the whore" or exhibiting the "spirit of whoredom" in abandoning YHWH.[157] However, when Hosea, also differently from Amos in this regard, speaks of the possibility of a new acceptance of Israel (Hos. 2:16ff.),[158] the only basis for this (as with Amos) lies in YHWH himself (Hos. 11:1–11).

In his own reasons for judgment, Isaiah[159] is especially akin to Amos. Isaiah is also concerned with the absence of righteousness[160] and with false worship (e.g., Isa. 1:4ff., 10ff., 21ff., 24ff.; 3:1–7; and 5:1–7, 8–24). The Day of YHWH is for Isaiah as it was for Amos a day of destruction that will come upon Israel (Isa. 2:6ff.). However, Isaiah then[161] readily mentions the disbelief of Israel/Judah as a noteworthy sin (Isa. 1:4; 5:19, 24; 10:20; 37:23; etc.).[162] Isaiah is (as a citizen of Jerusalem) closely associated with Zion. In the temple, he received his call (Isaiah 6),[163] while the term "Jerusalem" also occurs frequently in his statements about judgment and words of trust (Isa. 1:27; 3:26; 28:16; 29:1–7[8]; 30:19; and 31:9), for it is YHWH himself who dwells upon Zion (Isa. 8:18). There also are cries of woe in Isaiah (Isa. 5:8–24; 10:1–4a), for, according to his message, it is Assyria who fights against Judah (Isa. 5:26ff.; 10:27ff.). Afterward, however, Assyria itself shall fall victim to the judgment of YHWH on account of its arrogance (Isa. 10:5–19). Occasionally, it appears that Isaiah has seen the coming judgment, not as annihilation, but rather as purification (Isa. 1:24ff.). To be sure, when a "remnant" often is discussed in Isaiah 1–39, this is always due to exilic and postexilic additions that originated from the self-understanding of the community that addresses this topic (Isa. 4:3; 6:13; 10:20–22; 11:11, 16; and 28:5).[164] The name of Isaiah's son, which has offered the connecting point for the later remnant theology, is, in all probability, not to be translated "Only a remnant shall return," that is, it is not to be interpreted as a promise (Isa. 7:3). Among the texts that speak then about the history of a "plan" or "work" of YHWH, at least the passage of Isa. 5:11–17, 18f. belongs to the preaching of Isaiah.[165] Whether or not one can attribute to this preaching Isa. 9:1–6 and above all 11:1–5, at least the latter text should be weighed seriously.[166] Also so for Isaiah, "the true continuity between disaster and salvation . . . ultimately exists in God himself,"[167] and this God does not only "thresh" (Isa. 28:23–29) when he performs his "work" (Isa. 28:21).

Typical for Micah[168] as well, whose authentic preaching should be found especially in chaps. 1–3, the pronouncement of judgment is once again based on the antisocial conditions that exist among the people of God (Micah 2:1ff.; 3:1–4) and on the corruption within its leading circles (Micah 3:9–12). It is in this regard that Micah is seen in clear opposition to the prophets of salvation (Micah 3:5–8). His threat, "Because of you Zion shall be plowed as a field" (Micah 3:12), was still familiar at the time of Jeremiah and could even be quoted (Jer. 26:18). Micah 1:1, 6, 9, 19, and 12ff. says that it is not only Jerusalem that shall encounter disaster but also Samaria and the cities of Judah. Micah disputes the belief that Yahweh may surely be in the midst of Israel, an affirmation that derived from Israel's/Judah's own self-confidence. In Micah 6:8 there is the appeal to what has been "told," that is, to the law of YHWH known by the nation, "justice in the gate," and "justice and righteousness" (cf. Amos 5:14f., 24). The same kind of unmistakable references to the justice and law of YHWH[169] is seldom found in the preexilic prophets,[170] although such references may often be discovered, by contrast, in exilic (Ezek. 18:5–9; 20:13ff.; and 22:6ff.) and postexilic texts (Zech. 1:6; 7:12; and Mal. 3:22) as well as in the Deuteronomistic editions of the prophetic books (Amos 2:4f.; and Jer. 16:10f.; cf. 9:12; 32:33; and 44:10, 23; see also the addition of Isa. 8:20).

A second group of prophets, from the seventh and the beginning of the sixth centuries, is comprised of Nahum, Habakkuk, Zephaniah, Jeremiah, and Obadiah. Considerably different in orientation from the prophecy of a Micah is that of Nahum[171] who was active between the conquest of Thebes by the Assyrians in 663 B.C.E. and the fall of Nineveh in 612 B.C.E. and who especially proclaimed to the empire of Assyria its speedy dissolution. This prophetic book was also redacted; for example, the psalm embedded in Nahum 1:2–8 is a later addition.

The prophet Habakkuk[172] likewise appears to have had the fall of Assyria in mind when he announced judgment against a foreign nation by another (the Babylonians?). A large portion of his words are placed in the style of laments of the prophet and answers of YHWH to these laments (Hab. 1:2–2:4). In addition, the cries of woe in Hab. 2:6–19 are directed against a foreign power, although, like Hab. 1:2–4, 12a, 13f. earlier on, these in fact are redacted and enriched by references to Israel/Judah. On the other hand, however, an ongoing redaction history has been assumed[173] in which internal Jewish grievances have been modified into words directed against Assyria and about Babylon. From the Book of Habakkuk the question, "How long?" which refers to the problem of the delay of divine intervention into a negative present (Hab. 1:2; and 2:3), as well as the mention of the faith of the righteous (Hab. 2:4), because it is later referenced by Paul (Rom. 1:17; and Gal. 3:11), came to have a continuing, influential significance. In Hab. 2:1–3 (cf. Isa. 21:8), an experience of revelation (in the temple?) is perhaps described. Accordingly, Habakkuk could have been a cult prophet.

In more recent study, only fifteen oracles of the three chapters of the Book of Zephaniah are considered to be original.[174] The words against foreign nations (Zeph. 2:4–15) and the words of salvation at the end of the book (Zeph. 3:11–20) certainly were already spoken earlier, mostly by prophets active in the time of Josiah (639–609 B.C.E.). Besides the words of judgment against Judah and Jerusalem, due for example, to their practical "atheism" (Zeph. 1:12), the passage concerning the great Day of YHWH, especially the underlying words *dies irae, dies illa,* continues to be influential (Zeph. 1:7–2:3; see 1:14f.). From the secondary verses in 3:9–13, the characterization of the poor, patient remnant also became significant. This prophetic book has also undergone a redaction that, while especially recognizable in Zeph. 1:1, 4–6, is seen throughout the entire book.[175]

In the proclamation belonging to the early period of his activity (Jeremiah 2–6), the prophet Jeremiah[176] is close to the preaching of Hosea.[177] This proximity is shown by the image of the marriage between YHWH and his people, the wilderness period as the time of first love (Jer. 2:1–3), the mention of the exodus and the gift of the land (Jer. 2:4ff.), the sin of Israel/Judah seen chiefly in terms of the cultic apostasy from YHWH ("to play the harlot," Jer. 3:1–3, 6f., 9, etc.), YHWH's love for his people, and the criticism of kings (Jer. 21:11 – 23:8). There is also a similarity between Jeremiah's embodiment of his message and Hosea's acting out his preaching through his marriage. Jeremiah can only characterize the nation's apostasy from YHWH as inconceivable (Jer. 2:10f., 22). YHWH even forbids the prophet to make intercession on behalf of the nation (Jer. 7:16; 11:14; 14:11; and 15:1ff.), and thus he suffers both with God because of the sin of the people (Jer. 4:19–22) and with the nation standing under the acts of divine judgment. The "enemy from the north" (Jer. 1:13f.; 4:5ff., 19ff.; 6:3ff.; etc.) will bring devastation, the sword, and deportation (Jer. 4:7, 26f., 31; 6:1, 15; 13:19; and 22:22). In his laments (e.g., Jeremiah 8 + 9; 14:17f.), Jeremiah brings the distress of his people, occasioned by the threatening and impending judgment of God, before YHWH. According to the Book of Jeremiah, YHWH is a God who himself weeps over his people and land (Jer. 12:7–12). Jeremiah expresses the distress of his prophetic office and personal existence before God in the so-called confessions.[178] These confessions, both individual and collective in form, weave together the sufferings of the righteous, the sufferings in the prophetic office, and the sufferings of the community. While they provide evidence of redaction and further rethinking, they do not reflect exclusively a later handling of these problems. It becomes rather clear that in his clash with other prophets (Jer. 23:9ff.; 27–28),[179] Jeremiah expects YHWH's punishing activity will lead to the subjugation of the nation. Subsequently, the Babylonian king Nebuchadrezzar can be called not incorrectly the "servant of YHWH" in certain passages of the Book of Jeremiah (Jer. 25:9; 27:6). In respect to YHWH's acts of judgment, Jeremiah can still look forward to his acts of salvation after having lived through divine judgment. This expectation is indicated in the symbolic act in Jeremiah 24 where the good and the bad figs standing next to each other represent salvation and disaster,[180] in the narrative placed into the form of a vision report in Jeremiah 32 (vv. 1–15; the purchase of the field) that recalls the visions of Amos,[181] and in the letter to the exiles (Jeremiah 29; esp. vv. 5–7; cf. vv. 10–14: secondary?).[182] In addition, other words of salvation must also go back to Jeremiah (Jer. 3:12, 21–25; 4:3). Furthermore, the famous word of promise in the new covenant passage (Jer. 31:31–34; cf. 32:37–41) now exists in at least a Deuteronomistic edition. To be ascribed to this Deuteronomistic edition of the Book of Jeremiah,[183] among other things, are the frequent mentionings of repentance in the framework of a so-called "alternative sermon" (e.g., Jer. 11:1–14; 17:19–27; and 18:1–12) as well as the struggling with the question of whether, in respect to the experience of election, one is now to reckon with God's rejection of his people (Jer. 33:24, 26; cf. Lev. 26:44; Lam. 5:22; and Ps. 89:39).[184] In this connection, an "authentic" word of Jeremiah is often attached (Jer. 6:30; 7:29; 14:19, 21; and 31:37). There are texts in the Book of Jeremiah that, while post-Jeremianic, are not, however, Deuteronomistic (e.g., Jer. 10:19f.; and 30:5–7, 10f.). Nevertheless, they often take up and transmit materials containing the thoughts of the prophet.[185] Jeremiah is not only to "tear down" but also to "build up" (Jer. 1:10; 24:6; 31:28; 42:10; and 45:4).[186]

In a mocking word of judgment, Obadiah,[187] the "smallest" and last of the preexilic prophets in the Old Testament, prepares the nations for military action against Edom (vv. 1–14, 15b) and threatens this nation that had assaulted Judah (probably during the collapse of 587/586 B.C.E.) with the Day of YHWH as its punishment (vv. 15a, 16–21). The purpose of this punishment, however, is to effectuate salvation for Israel (vv. 17f.) and to establish Yahweh's sovereignty (v. 21c). At the least, vv. 19–21 may be a later addition.

Ezekiel[188] is the first among the third group of prophets who belong to the period of the exile. He was among those deported to Babylonia following the first Babylonian conquest of Jerusalem in 597 B.C.E. It was in Babylonia that he received his call. It was the case that YHWH's "glory"[189] had left the temple and moved toward the east (Ezek. 11:22ff.), but it was now present among the exiles in Babylonia where Ezekiel was allowed to see it in a vision (Ezekiel 1–3).[190] The prophet's first concern exists in the fact that he is to make clear to his fellow exiles as well as to those who remained at home (Ezek. 11:15) that the judgment recently experienced was just and that still other punishments may be at hand (Ezekiel 4–5; 7; and 15). He presented concretely Israel's sin as the abandonment of YHWH and the worship of other gods who make them impure (Ezek. 5:11; 6; 8:7ff.; and 14:3ff.). Israel, the vine that is fetched from Egypt by YHWH, is nothing other than an unusable piece of wood (Ezekiel 15). In the historical reviews (Ezekiel 16; 20; and 23),[191] Ezekiel points out that the entirety of Israel's previous history, which he also portrays as a "marriage" between the nation and YHWH (Ezekiel 16; 23; cf. Hosea and Jeremiah) and which began in the exodus from Egypt, has been a history of sin. Israel was always, as Ezekiel was wont to say, a "rebellious house" (Ezek. 2:5f.; 3:9, 26f.; 12:2f., 9, 25, etc.),[192] and as the "watchman of Israel" (Ezek. 3:16ff.; 33:1–9) he labored on behalf of the exiles for new righteousness and new life (Ezek. 18; 22:6ff.; and 33:11). When the messenger came to the exiles with the report of the second conquest of Jerusalem by the Babylonians (Ezek. 32:21f.), Ezekiel's proclamation, according to the present form of the redaction of the book, turns about, and he promises that, after the judgment, there would be new salvation, new human beings, a new David (or Davidic successor) (Ezek. 34:23f.; 37:15ff.; cf. 17:22ff.; 21:32), and the restoration of the nation (Ezekiel 36–37). True, he was able earlier to speak of a new exodus, but not apart from the element of a purifying judgment (Ezek. 20:32ff.). The "Day of YHWH" as the day of judgment now lies behind those addressed (Ezek. 7:1ff.; 13:5; and 34:12), and YHWH desires not the end of his people but rather the doing of justice and repentance. He desires "life" for each individual, not death (Ezekiel 18). Also, the kernel of the description of the new temple along with the partitioning of the land in Ezekiel 40–48 could still go back to Ezekiel himself. The bridge between judgment and salvation is, for Ezekiel, only YHWH himself (cf. Ezekiel 34 as a "Good Shepherd"), for his statement, "You shall know that I am YHWH,"[193] is true not only for judgment but also for the salvation that has been announced. YHWH wills to act on behalf of himself (Ezek. 36:22; cf. Isa. 43:25; and 48:11) and is moved to pity for the sake of his name. While Israel had desecrated his name, he will "sanctify" it (Ezek. 36:21–23).

As is true of Jeremiah, symbolic actions are typical also for Ezekiel (Ezek. 3–5; 12; 21; and 37:15ff.). When his wife dies, he is not to mourn (Ezek. 24:15ff.), for he himself, in like manner to Hosea, Jeremiah and the servant of God in Deutero-Isaiah, was a "sign" (Ezek. 12:6, 11; and 24:24; cf. 21:11). Like Jeremiah, Ezekiel must confront the problem of false prophecy (Ezekiel 13–14). On the whole, Ezekiel, "through his unrelenting pronouncement of judgment and the promise of coming salvation, was without doubt substantially concerned, both before and after the brink of disaster in 587 B.C.E., that Israel survive this catastrophe and receive an additional future."[194] Through his overviews of history, the special form of his vision descriptions (with the intimating "something like," or the accompanying and explicative "man" in Ezekiel 40ff.), and the form and content of chaps. 38–39 (Gog and Magog), Ezekiel, like Deutero-Isaiah, has been important for the shaping of many elements of later Old Testament apocalyptic.[195]

Isaiah 40–55 is usually attributed to the prophet Deutero-Isaiah,[196] who, following Ezekiel, was active during the Babylonian exile after the deportees were brought there. This prophet spoke no longer of judgment, for Israel had already experienced its punishment and received its forgiveness (Isa. 40:2). Thus, this prophet proclaimed in an often strongly hymnically shaped speech an imminent salvation that was even now breaking into history. He announced that a new exodus was to take place, only this time the departure would not be in haste (Isa. 52:12; cf. Exod. 12:11; and Deut. 16:3). This new exodus would be from Babylonia under the leadership and guidance of YHWH and would be bound up with the transformation of creation (understandable only as an eschatological event) (Isa. 40:3f.; 41:17–20; 43:16–21; 48:20f.; 49:10f.; 51:9f.; and 52:7–10, 11f.), even as creation, history, election, and salvation are bound together in Deutero-Isaiah overall (cf., e.g., Isa. 43:1, 7, 15; 44:1f., 21, 24; and 54:5).[197] The "new" is approaching and goes far beyond the "former" (Isa. 41:22; 42:9; 43:9, 18f.; 52:12; etc.). In the disputations between YHWH and his people (e.g., Isa. 40:12–31; 42:18–25; and 44:24–28) as well as in the judgment scenes between YHWH who is the sovereign over history and the foreign gods who are proven to be powerless and speechless (e.g., Isa. 41:21–29; and 43:8–13), the prophet with his message of salvation tries to set aside the disbelief of the hearer and speaks of future salvation as though it were already realized at the same time that he promises it (e.g., Isa. 40:1–8; 41:17–20; 43:1–7; and 44:1–5). This salvation, that is, YHWH's "righteousness" as his saving act,[198] will be so overpowering that even foreign nations will come forward and be included in the salvific event (e.g., Isa. 41:17–20; 45:1–7, 14–17, 22–24; and 49:7, 14–21, 22f.).[199] The Persian king Cyrus, who appears as the liberator of the exiles, can be designated as the "messiah" (Isa. 45:1),[200] while the promises about the Davidic dynasty are now related to the people (Isa. 55:3; cf. 2 Chron. 6:42).[201] YHWH, who alone is truly God (Isa. 44:6, 8, etc.) and sovereign over history (Isa. 41:2, 4, 22f.; 43:9, 22–28; etc.), shall as the king of Israel lead back his people to his Zion (Isa. 40:9–11; 49:14–17; 51:3, 11; 52:1, 2, 7–10; etc.). His powerfully active word continues to prevail (Isa. 40:8; 55:10f.).

These were great words by which this prophet felt empowered. That the fulfillment of his promises fell far short of what was assured was a substantial reason for many problems of faith that appeared in the postexilic period that followed, as especially Trito-Isaiah, Haggai, and Zechariah 1–8 show. With this, the way leads to the fourth group of prophets, namely, to those of the postexilic period.

After the start of the return from exile, the prophet Haggai[202] had to exhort the people to start rebuilding the temple by promising (Hag. 1:2–11; and 2:15–19) the arrival of the riches of the nations (Hag. 2:1–9). The Judeans were hesitating because of their unsatisfactory economic situation. For Haggai, the time of salvation would soon break into history, an inbreaking that Haggai thought was so near that he provided Zerubbabel with messianic qualities (Hag. 2:20–23). It is debated as to whether Haggai, in his priest-like torah in

Hag. 2:10–14 that speaks of infectious impurity, meant that his own people or a foreign, mixed population (cf. Ezra 4:1–5; and 5:1–5) could not participate in the rebuilding of the temple.[203] The Book of Haggai also shows traces of later redaction.

The prophet Zechariah (= Zechariah 1–8),[204] who was perhaps active at the same time as Haggai and who is mentioned with him in Ezra 5:1 and 6:14, promises more forcefully than he admonishes, or, better, he bases his admonitions on his promises (Zech. 1:3). He can say in his (presently eight, originally only) seven night visions (Zech. 1:7–6:8) that lead to the symbolic act of the coronation of the high priest Joshua (Zech. 6:9–15, originally probably Zerubbabel) that salvation and new community with YHWH are already prepared or, better, have already received their design, even if there is no trace of them on earth. In view of the salvation that has drawn nigh, the former fast days that were observed should now be abolished (Zech. 7:1–6; 8:19). According to the night visions, the judgment against the nations, the glorious expansion and securing of Jerusalem, and the purification of the land and community shall shortly be fulfilled. The original fourth night vision is shaped by this expectation of the nearness of salvation (Zech. 4:1–5, 10b–14), for, with the lampstand and two olive trees, it characterizes as two "messiahs" (Zech. 4:14) Joshua the high priest (cf. to him also the addition in Zech. 3:1–7) and Zerubbabel the political ruler. With many elements of his proclamation, including, for example, the angel who provides interpretations, the symbolic language, and the cycle of visions as a sequence, Zechariah is already on the path to apocalyptic.

The texts assembled in Isaiah 56–66 (Trito-Isaiah)[205] do not derive from one writer. They preserve glimpses into the questions of faith (Isa. 59:1, 9), the problems, the shaping of groups, the hopes, and the disappointments of the postexilic community (Isa. 56:9ff.; 57:1ff.; 59:1ff.; and 60:1ff.). More frequently, earlier texts (especially from Deutero-Isaiah) are interpreted anew and repeatedly stressed in order to search out the blame for the failure of the final salvation promised for the nation and its sin. Many texts in this section of Isaiah have received their place in the structure of the redactional history of the entire book and its Zion theology.[206] Isaiah 60–62 is often viewed as the kernel of the collection of texts in Trito-Isaiah and as the work of a writer who is close to Deutero-Isaiah. However, this writer saw his purpose to be the resumption of Second Isaiah's message of salvation in a loyal and powerful manner (Isa. 61:1).

The minor prophet Malachi[207] (more likely an anonym), however, is a prophet who no longer appears before his audience with a "Thus says the Lord" but rather takes up in six words of discussion[208] their doubting questions, discusses with them the pros and cons of each, and seeks to supply a solution. Even the Day of YHWH is viewed here as the answer to pressing questions (Mal. 3:16–21). The book in addition is not a collection of originally oral words; rather, it is an authentic piece of prophetic writing.[209] There are additions at the end of the book that, on the one hand, relate the prophets to the law of Moses and, on the other hand, seek to make concrete the eschatological expectation (Mal. 3:22–24). These additions place the text within the common redaction of the prophetic books in the postexilic community.[210]

The Book of Jonah[211] is not a collection of prophetic oracles; rather, it contains a prophetic narrative in which only Jonah 3:4a is a prophetic saying ("In four days, Nineveh will be destroyed"). This narrative presents the experiences of a prophet (taken from 2 Kings 14:25?) and his word. Jonah, who according to the command of YHWH is to announce judgment against the pagan city of Nineveh, seeks to avoid this commission by fleeing. However, he is not able to escape from YHWH who makes use of pagan mariners and a great fish[212] to turn Jonah around and to bring him to Nineveh. There Jonah, against his own expectation and theological preference, must learn that this heathen city, together with its king and its animals, is to be spared. This city is spared when it does penance because of the sermon on repentance by the prophet and because YHWH himself repents of the disaster he had announced. Thus YHWH is also "merciful" and "compassionate" toward the heathen (Jonah 4:2; cf. Exod. 34:6).[213] Jonah pouts at God and becomes increasingly weary of life. The open and remaining question to Jonah as well as to the reader of this little book ends the narrative (Jonah 4:11): May God not also show mercy to so many pagans? All of this probably indicates that the Book of Jonah is either a small, narrative, didactic sermon or a kind of midrash about the repentance and salvation of the heathen and the merciful love of YHWH that is not limited to Jewish orthodoxy. This book, taking up many earlier Old Testament texts and motifs and placing them within a new interpretive framework, is addressed to a postexilic Israel that restricted YHWH's compassion too narrowly to itself. Israel also has a mission to the nations, because YHWH wills to effectuate salvation for them as well.[214]

While Ps. 74:9 laments the fact that there may no longer be any prophets, Zech. 13:2–6 speaks of the coming end of prophecy.[215] It is unclear what the precise background and the concrete meaning of this latter text may be. It perhaps offers an intentional contrast to Joel 3:1f.[216]

The remaining texts of postexilic prophecy, such as Zechariah 9–11; 12–14; Joel; and Isaiah 24–27, already lead to emerging apocalyptic, a topic that will be addressed elsewhere.[217]

PART FOUR. THE RESULTS AND CONSEQUENCES OF ELECTION EXPERIENCED IN HISTORY

What YHWH had done for his people according to the witness of the Old Testament must and should have consequences. Election is not only an outward action but also an internal event. The gift of election in history was bound up with the duty of responsibility. Israel was to recognize this duty, to take it on, and to live it out concretely in life. YHWH opened himself to community with his people and in so doing placed upon them responsibility. Israel's ethos was consequently determined by election and responsibility (chapter 12), along with its hope (chapter 14) and its view of other nations (chapter 15). Its cult was shaped by election and obligation (chapter 13) as well as by its view of human beings (chapter 11). The experience of the activity of God sets into motion thinking about faith, something that already became evident in Israel's view of history and of creation.[1] It is now time to investigate Old Testament thinking about the areas mentioned above.

Chapter 11. The Israelite and His Relationship to God (Anthropology)

11.1 Human Being as Creature (Biological and Biographical)

The Old Testament allows one to recognize a great deal about how individual persons as well as the social groups that surrounded them were viewed at the time. One should expect that there were a variety of views and assessments of anthropology present in the many strata of the Old Testament and in the diverse social expressions existing at the time. We shall first give attention to what the Old Testament thought in general about this subject.[2]

a. From Birth to the Family

According to a not unimportant theological bon mot, a human being must first be born before he or she is able to be born again; he or she must first exist, before he or she can be theologically characterized. This truism may be introduced by first looking at the "biological" life of the Old Testament human being and then followed by the questions of theological anthropology. In doing so, one should note that much that interests us in the area of cultural history may be mentioned here only in passing and cannot be described in detail. In addition, Old Testament Israel was also woven into the fabric of its cultural environment. With these preliminary remarks in mind, what can be reconstructed in essence about the external appearance of the Israelite male and female from the Old Testament?[3]

They belonged to the genus of people known as Mediterranean, had primarily black or dark-brown hair, and were, as skeletal finds indicate, 1.65 m. to 1.70 m. (male) and 1.60 m. (female) in height. The Israelites were often viewed as smaller than other peoples (Num. 13:32f.; Deut. 1:28; and Amos 2:9), and when they were compared with the complexion of the Edomites, who were ruddy (Gen. 25:30), they must have classified themselves as somewhat lighter. According to the ideal for what was beautiful in 1 Sam. 16:12,[4] David, however, was "ruddy, had beautiful eyes, and was beautiful in complexion" (cf. Cant. 1:5f. for the complexion of the woman as well as Gen. 6:2; 12:11;

and 24:16 for her beauty in general). And the comparison of the goat's black hair to that of the woman was considered to be a compliment (Cant. 4:1; and 6:5). The ideal of female beauty (as also for the male: Cant. 5:9–16) was expressed in images and metaphors to which we are often unaccustomed: the eyes are grapes, the teeth are like sheep, the neck is like the tower of David, the nose is like the tower of Lebanon which looks out toward Damascus, the breasts are like towers (Cant. 8:10) or twin gazelles, while the male has legs like marble columns (Cant. 5:15). The womanly figure consists of round hips and a wide lap (Cant. 7:1f.) and is compared as a whole to a palm tree (Cant. 4:1–7; 6:4–7; and 7:2–6, 8). The upshot of this reads: "You are altogether beautiful, my lover, and nothing spoils your appearance" (Cant. 4:7),[5] although this beloved one is also compared to a mare (Cant. 1:9). Even so, a woman, however beautiful, is like a golden ring in a sow's snout, if she is shameless (Prov. 11:22). People mostly wore their hair long, while men sported beards, which, if disfigured, could be the basis for war (2 Sam. 10:4). When the ideal male is imagined, then once more it is David who is the example, for he is skilled as the player of a stringed instrument, did not come from an entirely poor family, knew how to fight and to speak, was beautiful in form, and YHWH was with him. Also, he was successful by virtue of divine presence (1 Sam. 16:18; cf. Gen. 39:3, 5).

In regard to external characteristics, however, one cannot and ought not to speak of a "Semitic race," since, first of all, "Semitic" (since A. L. von Schlözer, 1781) is a linguistic term, and second, the Israelite people consisted and continued to consist of mixed races. The tribal mothers of the sons of Jacob were Aramaeans (Gen. 28:5; and 29:23, 28). Ephraim and Manasseh were the offspring of an Egyptian mother (Gen. 41:50ff.; cf. 48:5), while Moses himself married a foreigner (Exod. 2:21f.; and Num. 12:1). Ezekiel knew of the originally non-Israelite origins of Jerusalem and its inhabitants (Ezek. 16:3). The existence of "mixed marriages," which there consequently were, became a significant problem for the first time in the postexilic period (Ezra 9:1 – 10:44; and Nehemiah 13).

The average life expectancy of the Israelite of those times, who probably was more passionate than many people today (cf. Jonah),[6] was fifty to sixty years.[7] When one lived longer than that or when one approached the age of eighty, this exceptional feat was considered worthy of mention (Ps. 90:10). The enormous life span mentioned in Genesis 5, which is dependent on the Babylonian list of "primeval kings,"[8] and the unusual longevity attributed to the ancestors Moses, Aaron, and Joshua were to prove that in those times the power of life was greater when community with God was closer. Then humanity's longevity began to decrease, as the declining numbers in Genesis 5 were supposed to prove.[9] Later on, the discussion is entirely of a more normal life span,[10] and a levite could retire when he reached the age of fifty (Num. 8:25). Due to the fact that Num. 14:29 and 32:11 presuppose that a twenty-year-old man already had sons, the custom was to marry at a younger age than today. This could result in the fact that one indeed could live with an extended family "unto the third and fourth generation." This means that it was not seldom that great-grandparents shared life with their great-grandchildren.

Psalm 139:13, 15 and Job 10:8–12 depict how a child is formed within a mother's womb (cf. Isa. 44:2; Jer. 1:5; etc.).[11] What occurred after a normally painful (Gen. 3:16) birth (Gen. 35:16f.; Ps. 22:10f.; Job 1:21; and Qoh. 5:14) can be extracted from Ezek. 16:4. After the birth, there followed the giving of the name which, according to the Old Testament, was more frequently done by the father than the mother.[12] And every name expressing a wish, offering thanksgiving, or providing protection contained normally a so-called theophoric element mostly comprised of יהו (*yāhû*), יה (*yâ*), or אל (*'ēl*).[13] The baby was raised under the care of the mother and was nursed considerably longer than is customary today (1 Sam. 1:22–24). The Old Testament does not indicate that childhood was a wonderful time when the children were treated in an especially genial fashion and particularly valued (true even for Ps. 8:3). The play of children is mentioned only in the promise concerning future salvation (Zech. 8:5). However, that children of the time also could be impertinent is evidenced by 2 Kings 2:23ff. Here, for example, children disrespectfully call the "man of God" a baldhead, seeing that he could not catch them. Earlier on, children were already put to work in their families and their mostly small farmer existence (1 Sam. 16:11; 17:17ff.; 2 Kings 4:18; Jer. 7:18; cf. even Judg. 8:20). The boy increasingly came under the charge and guidance of his father, while the girl remained more with the mother and was involved in her activities. In this manner, children were introduced to the world and to the problems of adults. The mortality of children was high, so that it was something noteworthy if the father not only produced children but also reared them (Isa. 1:2). Whether there was already a more formal education in a school is uncertain. Rather, it is more likely that the father as well as the entire family contributed to the necessary practical and theoretical knowledge of children. For sons of scribes and "officials," who at the same time were their potential successors, this is probably the case, although there is no textual support for this conclusion. Some excavated texts have been classified as writing exercises.[14] Although the Canaanite-Hebrew alphabetic script was considerably easier to learn than, by contrast, the Egyptian or Mesopotamian writing system, the mention of the literate boy in Judg. 8:14 is probably an indication of an exception to the general rule that "I cannot read" (Isa. 29:12). It is probable, at least in the family circle, that more was narrated and orally transmitted than was written down (cf. Ps. 78:3–7). If the Deuteronomic/Deuteronomistic movement especially placed on the shoulders of the father the task of transmitting religious tradition (Deut. 6:20–24; cf. Exod. 12:26f.; 13:14; Deut. 4:9f.; 11:19; and Josh. 4:6f.),[15] this had to do also with the situation of the exile, with its lack of an official cult, and with the collapse of larger, social groups. The father, who is now facing these conditions, seeks to inquire of the tradition of faith (Deut. 32:7), and the responsibility of the teacher is impressed upon him (Deut. 11:18f.). The Book of Proverbs allows one to recognize that the pedagogy of that time included firm discipline (Prov. 13:24; 19:18; 23:13f.; 29:15, 17), something that by analogy was supposed of God (Prov. 3:12; 2 Sam. 7:14; and Deut. 8:5). That such a father was no tyrant is made clear in not a few places that speak of paternal love (Gen. 37:3f., 34f.; 2 Samuel 13; etc.), and YHWH also loves his people as he would a son (Hos. 11:1). He has compassion for his people, even like a father who has compassion for his children (Ps. 103:13; cf. Prov. 3:12). And he is called father who, at the same time, is the redeemer (Isa. 63:16).

The human beings of ancient Israel suffered greatly and often from illnesses,[16] such as those which were especially caused by the climate (rheumatism) and the environment (diseases of the eyes). Broken bones quickly made people cripples (2 Sam. 4:4), while blindness and illnesses of the skin ("leprosy"; Leviticus 13–14; and Deut. 24:8f.)[17] were more frequent than they are today. Childhood illnesses often led to death (2 Sam. 12:15; 1 Kings 14:1ff.; 17:17; and 2 Kings 4:18ff.). Doctors, who were obviously present in Egypt (Gen. 50:2), were hardly known among the Israelites (Jer. 8:22) and, in addition, were not very popular (Job 13:4). Thus, for a long period of time, the sick and injured sent rather for the "man of God" (1 Kings 14; 2 Kings 4:18ff.; 8:7–9; and Isaiah 38), or they were brought to him (2 Kings 5), and even as late as 2 Chron. 16:12 the visit of doctors was still very harshly judged. Sirach 38 is the first text to sing the praises of the physician.[18] The (Deuteronomistic) self-declaration of YHWH: "I am YHWH, your physician,"[19] however, causes one to recognize that one could think of and wish for good doctors. At the same time, however, it is also clear that one regarded illness as the punishment of God and as the consequence of sin (Exod. 9:14f.; Num. 12:9ff.; Ps. 38:2–9; etc.) and disobedience.[20] This was also customary in Israel's cultural environment at the time.[21] The performance of many astonishing physical feats by Hebrew men is narrated,[22] while Hebrew women are said to give birth to their children easily, quickly, and before the arrival of the midwife, much to the distress of the pharaoh who had commanded the murder of all male nurselings (Exod. 1:15–22). Moreover, a woman who did not give birth to children and, above all, did not bear sons (Ps. 127:3) met with less favor, as one can see in the cases of Sarah, Rachel, and Hannah (Gen. 11:30; 30:1; and 1 Samuel 1). Indeed, she even regarded this as the punishment of God (Gen. 20:17f.; 2 Sam. 6:23).

Circumcision was likely at first a puberty ritual that was carried out with a stone knife (Exod. 4:25; and Josh. 5:2).[23] The word חתן = ḥātan ("bridegroom") is derived from חתן (ḥātan), which probably once carried the meaning "to circumcise."[24] According to Gen. 17:25, Ishmael was thirteen years old when he was circumcised, that is, at the time of puberty. It was in the exilic and postexilic periods, when texts in Jeremiah, Ezekiel, and the Deuteronomistic edition of Deuteronomy called for a circumcision of the heart which would bring into conformity an external ritual with the inner will of human beings (Deut. 10:16; 30:6; Jer. 4:4; 9:25; and Ezek. 44:7, 9). Circumcision, according to the witness of the Priestly document, became a ritual for children that was interpreted as a "sign" (אוֹת = 'ôt) of one's belonging to the covenant (Gen. 17:1–4 P).

From the "child" (יֶלֶד = yeled) came the "youth" (נַעַר = na'ar or בָחוּר = bāḥûr)[25] and then the "man" (אִישׁ = 'îs)[26] who was then able to participate in the cult, to marry, to be held legally accountable, and to bear arms. He set up a family and entered into the circle (סוֹד = sôd) of legally responsible men. As was usual in those days, the nature and character of his family was endogamous, patrilineal (as the genealogies show), patriarchal, patrilocal, and polygamous.[27] Consequently, the man preferred to marry wives who came from his relatives (cf. Gen. 11:27, 29; 22:23; 24:47; 28:1f., 9; 36:3; etc.), something that also probably had to do with the preservation of property and equality of status. Marriages to unrelated women led to unhappy experiences (Gen. 26:34f.). The genealogy was calculated through the father's line. The father was the lord and master of his family. The man took his wife to his own house (Deut. 20:7) and did not enter hers,[28] and he was allowed to have several wives. The extended family was called the "house of the father" (בֵית-אָב = bêt-'āb),[29] an expression that did not exclude the high value placed on the wife and mother. Those who belong to a "house of the father" may be recognized in Gen. 7:7 and 45:10 (cf. the figures in Gen. 46:26). Whoever had to leave the family, as, for example, Abraham (Gen. 12:1), had considerably less chance of survival. In the religious sphere, as, for example, during the Passover (Exod. 12:3f., 46) or during a pilgrimage festival (1 Sam. 1:3f.), the extended family sustained its members. And within it, the גֹּאֵל (gō'ēl = "redeemer") acted, if the occasion arose, to redeem and protect other family members (Ruth 2:20; 3f.; Lev. 25:49; and Jer. 32:7). The high value placed on the family is reflected also in the fact that Israel in the Old Testament not only regards Jacob as its ancestral father and sees itself as the descendants of the sons of Jacob but also envisions the nations together as one great family (Gen. 9:18f.; 10).

b. Marriage

While the Old Testament has no word for "marriage"[30] (the same is true for "history" and "freedom"), the practice was nonetheless self-evident. And it was the male or his family who took the initiative. The male "took" a wife (Gen. 4:19; 11:29) and "ruled" over her (Gen. 3:16). It was rare for one not to marry, as was the case with Jeremiah whose decision to remain single was due to YHWH's will (Jer. 16:2). Whoever finds a wife has found something good (Prov. 18:22), and YHWH himself was the one who brought the woman to the man (Gen. 2:21–24). The man and the woman were both created in God's image and blessed by him (Gen. 1:27f.). "To become fruitful" stands under divine judgment as "very good" (Gen. 1:28, 31), and to become "one flesh" (Gen. 2:24) accords with the divine will.[31] Normally, a man looked for a suitable wife among his relatives (cf. Num. 36:10f.), since one was at least somewhat known in this circle and these kinship connections promised a good marriage (cf. Gen. 20:12; 24; 28:9; 29:16ff.; and 36:3). If the choice of the marriage partner was determined and regulated more by custom and family (Gen. 21:21; Judg. 14:3; and 1 Sam. 18:17), there still could be indications of personal love and affection (cf. also Cant. 8:6f.). Thus Jacob loved Rachel, but not Leah (Gen. 29:20), and Paltiel, who, when his wife was taken away, ran after her weeping (2 Sam. 3:15f.; cf. in addition Judg. 14:1–3).

A marriage was considered to be concluded with the act of betrothal (cf. Hos. 2:21—אָרַשׂ = *'rś*), even if not yet consummated. There was no religious rite that was performed with the concluding of the marriage, although there was probably a feast (Gen. 29:27; Judg. 14:10; etc.). A betrothed maiden was considered legally to be a married woman (Deut. 22:23ff.).[32] Compensation was paid to the father of the maiden for his loss of her labor ("dowry": מֹהַר = *mōhar*; Gen. 34:12; Exod. 22:16; and 1 Sam. 18:25; cf. Deut. 22:28f.), which should not be confused with the wedding gifts (Gen. 24:53; and 34:12). A portion of the dowry was for the benefit of the wife in case her husband divorced her. The dowry could also be replaced by the performance of labor (Gen. 29:15ff.), which could be accepted on occasion in strange forms (1 Sam. 18:25: one hundred Philistine foreskins). Polygamy was allowed because numerous progeny were sought in order to increase the family's labor force and because this provided a support system for as many women as possible as well as for aged parents later on. That things did not always proceed in a friendly way between the (seldom more than two)[33] wives is demonstrated by Rachel and Leah as well as by Hannah and Peninnah (Genesis 29–31; and 1 Samuel 1). Monogamy was the normal practice, particularly since not every man could or wished to support several wives. That this type of monogamous marriage prevailed in later times is shown in the portrait of marriage in Hosea and Jeremiah as well as in Mal. 2:15. Jacob's marriage to two sisters (Leah and Rachel) represented a union that was forbidden by later law (Lev. 18:18). The taking of concubines, mostly slaves in this status, was allowed (cf. Genesis 16: Hagar; or Gen. 35:25f.: Bilhah and Zilpah). Written marriage contracts are not found in the Old Testament, although they are evidenced elsewhere in mostly later contexts (e.g., Tob. 7:13). Coming to maturity more quickly "moves . . . the generations closer together; indeed, it pushes them past one another and makes the commandment concerning marriage concrete and necessary in a way that hardly comes within our purview (Leviticus 18)."[34] For example, a father, advanced in age, nevertheless had still married a young wife. After his death, his son from an earlier wife is already over thirty years of age. He now must consider whether or not he should marry his father's young widow who pleases him. Divorce was possible, and indeed was rather easy. However, in normal circumstances, the divorce proceedings could be initiated only by the husband who would speak the divorce formula (Hos. 2:4a) or later on would have to give a letter of divorce in order to settle many legal problems (Isa. 50:1; Jer. 3:8; and Deut. 24:1–4). It was customary to provide certain financial support of the divorced woman.[35] The so-called levirate marriage (marriage to a brother-in-law; Deut. 25:5–10)[36] at first sought to make certain that a deceased husband would still be able to have future offspring and then later to provide support for the widow.

c. Work

Human labor,[37] according to the Old Testament, took place for the well-being of humanity, not for that of the gods,[38] and it is the destiny of humans to work from the very beginning (Gen. 1:26, 28f.; 2:5, 18). That this labor is often vain and arduous (Qoh. 3:9f.; and Ps. 127:1) is (according to the witness of the Yahwist) the result of divine curse which afflicted humanity because of human transgression of the divine commandment (Gen. 3:17f.). Thus labor is nowhere especially valued in a positive way; rather, it is something that man and woman have to do (Ps. 104:23; and Prov. 31:15, 18) in order to meet the requirements of life's necessities (Gen. 1:29; 2:15; Ps. 128:2; Prov. 14:23; and 16:26). And standing alongside labor is the gift (Gen. 2:1–3) and commandment (Exod. 20:8–11; etc.) of the Sabbath,[39] which, with its emphasis on rest (even for slaves),[40] creates an important counterbalance to the usual evaluation of labor.

d. Aging and Dying

To die young was seen as a punishment of curse (Ps. 109:8, 13; cf. Isa. 38:10ff.), so that the Books of Chronicles,[41] which are grounded in an ideology of exact retribution, must find additional reasons why good King Josiah died young while evil King Manasseh could reign for a long time (2 Chron. 35:22; and 33:12–20). However, if one does become old,[42] infirmity sets in, a condition about which Qoheleth is not the only one to speak in an impressive manner (Qoh. 12:1–7; cf. further Ps. 71:9, 18; and Job 30:1).[43] At that time, one would rather become old than be old. Women become incapable of bearing children anymore (Gen. 18:3), while the hair of men becomes gray (Isa. 46:4), their vision decreases (Gen. 27:1; and 48:10), and they see their powers decline (Hos. 7:9). The one who reaches the age of eighty is incapable of correctly distinguishing things from each other and is unable to enjoy life (2 Sam. 19:36–38). An old man cannot warm himself in bed, so that, even if he is a king, an attendant must care for him (1 Kings 1:1–4). The fact that Moses' old age was different from this deserves mention in Deut. 34:7; by contrast, the Book of Job denies there is anything positive about becoming old (Job 12:12; and 32:7–9). The son is commanded by God to take care of and to attend to his aged parents himself when they have become weak (Exod. 20:12; Deut. 5:16; and Prov. 23:22). When one must go the way of all the world (Josh. 23:14; and 1 Kings 2:2)[44] and die, perhaps even "old and full of days" (Gen. 25:7f.; 35:29; and Job 42:17), it is hoped that one has placed one's house in order beforehand (2 Sam. 17:23; and 2 Kings 20:1) and has made provisions for one's assets (Deut. 21:16). Nowhere does the Old Testament report about the assistance provided for the dying by those who remain behind. However, it is probable in this regard that the one who is dying consoles those who remain behind and utters on their behalf words of blessing (Gen. 48:1ff.; 50:18ff.; and Deuteronomy 33).[45] Nevertheless, one understandably is aware of the anxiety over death (Psalm 88), so that prophetic promises, which made old age a relative matter or even portrayed it in a beautfiul way, certainly found their audience (Isa. 65:20; and Zech. 8:4–6).[46]

The dead likely were buried on the day of their death by their relatives (Amos 6:10) and, if possible, were placed in the family grave (Gen. 23; 49:29ff.; 50:7ff.; 2 Sam. 19:38; etc.). One performed the death rites[47] and laments (2 Sam. 1:1lff., 19ff.; 3:31f.; Jer. 16:5ff.; 48:36ff.; and Amos 5:16) for the dead over a seven-day period (Gen. 50:10; cf. Job 2:13; for Moses and Aaron, however, thirty days: Deut. 34:8; and Num. 20:29). To this belonged the customs of the tearing of the clothing and fasts (Gen. 37:34; Lev. 10:6; Judg. 11:35; 2 Sam. 1:2, 11; 1 Kings 21:27; etc.), as well as the shaving of the hair to make a (bald) head and the beard (Lev. 21:5; Deut. 14:1; 21:12; Isa. 3:24; 15:2; Jer. 16:6; 41:5; etc.). One also strew dust upon the head (1 Sam. 4:12; and 2 Sam. 1:2), dressed in "sackcloth" (2 Sam. 3:31; Isa. 22:12; Jer. 4:8; and 6:26), sat down in the ashes, and cut gashes into the flesh (Lev. 19:28; 21:5; Jer. 41:5; and 47:5). These ritual acts were significantly present in and connected to the religious world of Israel's environment, although in Israel they were often criticized and even forbidden. These acts were originally intended to make those who remained behind unrecognizable to the dreaded spirits of the dead. Mourning and mourning rituals were more strongly oriented to their objective performance, although subjective feelings quite naturally were not excluded. A priest was allowed to participate in these mourning rites only if the deceased was a very close relative (Lev. 21:1–4). The high priest, however, could not at all participate personally in these rites (Lev. 21:11), since anything dead is "impure" and thus taboo.[48] The presentation of mourning bread and cup of consolation (Jer. 16:7 conjectural; and Ezek. 24:17, 22) probably did not belong to these "rites of self-deprecation" but rather were a component part of protecting from attacks by the dead (spirits) those who remained behind, served the purpose of making the living unrecognizable, helped them to avoid the food from the house of the dead, and accordingly originated still in animistic thinking. The Ugaritic texts provide evidence of the popularity of these rites in Israel's environment (cf. Jonah 3:5–10).[49] Consequently, they must have fallen victim to Israel's complete break with Canaanite culture, certainly in the later texts and legal collections, and were forbidden and declared unclean. Contact with the unclean dead and their sphere was subsequently excluded from the cult.[50]

One prefers to be buried with the ancestors, with whom the dead are "gathered" or "laid down," or to whom they "went."[51] Cremation was done only in special cases (1 Sam. 31:12f.; deleted in 1 Chron. 10:12) and was customary when criminals were executed (Josh. 7:25; Lev. 20:14; and 21:9). A good burial was desired and was regarded as a reward for a good life (1 Kings 14:13; and 2 Kings 22:20). To remain unburied was considered to be a terrible fate.[52] The dead person is therefore (Job 14:10) in his or her grave as well as in the kingdom of the dead, that is, in Sheol (שאל = *šĕ'ōl*), from which there is no return. How the kingdom of the dead was seen and how the grave and this world of the dead were related to each other have already been discussed.[53] Offerings to the dead appear to be mentioned only in an indirect way in Deut. 26:14 (cf. Ps. 106:28). This is to be distinguished from grave offerings, which were common, were not so sharply criticized, and were not prohibited.

e. Woman

What was the "place of the woman"[54] in the ancient Israelite family and society? "Throughout her entire life the Hebrew woman was placed under the care of a male guardian, first the father and then the husband." When she became a widow, she was placed under the care of a male relative. In spite of this, the Old Testament speaks of independently acting, significant women, such as Miriam (Exod. 15:20f.; etc.), Deborah (Judges 4f.), Ruth, Esther, Athaliah (2 Kings 11), Huldah (2 Kings 22), and Judith, as well as of the often important role of the queen mother (גבירה = *gĕbîrâ*).[55] "Wise" women are also especially mentioned (2 Sam. 14:2; 20:16). "Whatever is legally required can still provide the bounds for free movement in everyday life; and we see the Hebrew woman in this free movement everywhere. However, there are still two worlds: that of the man and that of the woman."[56] Custom, law, and (the official) cult[57] attribute to the woman a place of subjection to the man and point to her dependency upon him, something that was true for all ancient society at that time, for it possessed a patriarchal character.[58] The wife belonged to the property of

the husband; he was her "lord" (בעל = ba'al; or ארון = 'ādôn; Gen. 18:12; and
20:3), was to "rule" over her (משל = māšal; Gen. 3:16),[59] and, according to
Lev. 27:1–7, was worth twice as much as the wife.

Somewhat differently nuanced statements do not fundamentally alter this
picture. The woman provided for the husband appropriate, partnerlike support
that also included help with labor (Gen. 2:18). She was also created from a part
of the man (Gen. 2:21) and was "(finally) bone of my bone and flesh of my
flesh," as the man joyfully determined (Gen. 2:23; cf. Gen. 29:14). Thus, both
were then "one flesh" (Gen. 2:24) in the act of sex and in the bearing of children, and in their fellowship overall each finds happiness in the other (Deut.
24:5). The most important task of the wife was the bearing of children (Gen.
24:60). Should she remain infertile, then the husband could take to himself a
concubine.[60] Genesis 2:23 wishes to stress with its folk etymology the close
connection of the man and the woman, even though איש and אשה ('îš and 'iššâ
= "man" and "woman") do not derive from the same root. According to Gen.
1:26f., the man and the woman are both created in the image of God (see below), something that, nevertheless, does not keep the Priestly theology from
barring women from cultic activities. Menstrual blood was not interpreted to
be a potent power but rather an impurity (Lev. 15:19–33; cf. Gen. 31:35; 1
Sam. 21:5; and Isa. 64:5). In addition, originally only men came to the festivals (Exod. 23:17; 34:23; and Deut. 16:16; the married woman is also absent
in Deut. 16:11). A vow made by a wife must be honored by her husband (Num.
30:4–16). Is it an accident, an intention, or an unalterable necessity that the
married woman is not mentioned in the commandment concerning the Sabbath
(Exod. 20:10; and Deut. 5:14; in contrast to Deut. 29:10f. regarding the
"covenant") that releases people from working on this day?[61] When a woman
in response to the question of her husband as to why she wishes to ride away
simply answers with a "שלום" (šālôm = "good-bye"; 2 Kings 4:23), then this
is surely something noteworthy. How far the legal power of disposition belonging to the husband or the head of the family extended over the woman, son,
and daughter is made shockingly clear in several texts (Gen. 19:8; 22; Exod.
21:7; Judg. 11:29ff.; and 19). In addition, adultery is assessed differently in regard to the wife than to the husband (Gen. 38:24): in every case, the husband
commits adultery only with the wife of another man, and this is forbidden him.
However, he does not commit adultery if he has an extramarital affair. This is
not true, however, in terms of the wife. Divorce is initiated by the husband
(Deut. 24:1; Isa. 50:1; and Jer. 3:8; cf. Hos. 2:4 as a possible divorce formula)
but not by the wife (Judg. 19:2–10).[62] The removal of the wife from being the
special possession of the husband, which is carried out by the Deutero-
nomic/Deuteronomistic interpretation of the Decalogue (Deut. 5:21), was rescinded by the later Priestly understanding of the Decalogue (Exod. 20:17b), a
view that was close to the general (de)valuation of the woman in the postexilic

period. There is no indication within the entire Old Testament of any developing improvement of the position of women. Following the birth of a girl, the mother was unclean for a longer period than when delivering a boy, and her purification sacrifice for giving birth to either can be offered for her only by the priest, not by herself (Leviticus 12). By contrast, according to the rituals described in Leviticus 1ff., the husband himself is able to offer sacrifice or at least can be active in its performance. Thus, nowhere in the Old Testament are sacrifices mentioned in which women act independently in making the offerings (cf. 1 Samuel 3–5). In the court for the women in the second temple and then especially the Herodian temple, women are separated from the holy.[63] When independent activities of the woman are described in Prov. 31:10–31,[64] this is the exception, not the rule, in the Old Testament. Perhaps these activities of the woman in Proverbs 31 represent those women who belonged to the rich upper class, or perhaps we have here the ideal woman described from the viewpoint of the husband who wanted as much as possible to delegate to her much of his work. Similarly not mentioned elsewhere is the erotically active role of the maiden or the woman that is present in Canticles. Is it the man who wished her to be so? In any case, Canticles allows one to recognize clearly that prudery was not normal or even expected. Certainly it was expected (according to a male double standard?; cf. Exod. 22:15f.) that the maiden was to be a virgin when she married (Deut. 22:13ff.).[65] That a man leaves his father and mother in order to be with his wife (Gen. 2:24) scarcely refers to the man's taking up residence in the house of his wife's family; rather, it refers to setting up a common household.[66] Late texts (Numbers 27 and 36) are the first to ensure that women will have a limited right to inherit property. The Old Testament is not very helpful to the modern, legitimate efforts for women's emancipation, and the history of the Old Testament and that of early Judaism both point more to a growing curtailment of women's rights than to their liberation.[67]

11.2 Anthropological Terms

How does the Old Testament person speak about himself or herself? Which ideas are used in order to describe human existence, life, behavior, and experiences?[68]

In the Yahwist's narrative of creation and disobedience (Gen. 2:4b-3:24), יצר אלהים יחוה = *yahweh 'ĕlōhîm yāṣar* ("YHWH Elohim forms") humanity, that is, the man (אדם = *'ādām*), like a potter from the אדמה = *'ădāmâ* ("land"; Gen. 2:7).[69] With this image, the connection between humans and the soil is stressed, while, at the same time, the important significance of the inhabited land for the Yahwist is emphasized. This latter emphasis, assuming the form of the so-called אדמה (*'ădāmâ* = "soil, arable land") motif,[70] runs through the entire primeval history (Gen. 2:19; 3:19; 4:2f., 10f., 14; 6:1, 7; 8:8; and 9:20) and enters into and combines with the ancestral narratives, beginning with the important text in Gen. 12:3. The interpretive addition, "dust" (עפר = *'āpār*; Gen. 2:7), which likely stems from Gen. 3:19, emphasizes that humans are frail, for they are "dust and to dust they shall return," as it is written in Gen. 3:19 (cf. Qoh. 12:7), where "dust" (עפר = *'āpār*) also appears together with אדמה (*'ǎdāmâ* = "soil, arable land"). Similar conceptions of the creation of humanity by one or more deities from clay or earth are known in Israel's cultural environment.[71]

When the frailty, powerlessness, and weakness of humanity are addressed or are to be addressed, the term בשׂר = *bāśār* ("flesh") is used, a term that consequently does not appear once in the statements about God.[72] Moreover, "flesh" in the Old Testament is not at all used in the sense of the Pauline σάρξ = *sarx* ("flesh"; cf., e.g., Gal. 5:16f.), that is, it yet does not characterize "flesh" as the special location of sin.[73] This also is not even implicit when the sexual organs of both male and female are included under the term "flesh" (Lev. 15:2f., 7, 19; Ezek. 16:26; and 23:20). The male member describes a power and potency that one uses in making an oath by placing the hand under the thigh and on the loins (ירך = *yārēk*; Gen. 24:2–4, 9; and 47:29).

יהוה אלהים = *yahweh 'ělōhîm* ("YHWH Elohim") breathes into the nose of the human being fashioned out of the earth the "breath of life" (נשׁמת חיים = *nišmat ḥayyîm*) and in this way the person became a living being (לנפשׁ חייה = *lěnepeš ḥayyâ*; Gen. 2:7).[74] Whoever translates the statement as "The man became a living soul" completely misunderstands what is meant, for Old Testament anthropology is familiar neither with the dichotomy of body and soul nor a trichotomy of body, soul, and spirit.[75] What is designated the "breath of life" in Gen. 2:7 is breath (1 Kings 17:17; Isa. 2:22; Prov. 20:27; and Dan. 10:17), something that, according to Gen. 7:22, the animals also possess. God is the one who gives this breath of life, meaning that life is dependent upon him and his gift (cf. Isa. 42:5). In the Old Testament, this breath of life is more often called רוח = *rûaḥ* ("wind, spirit"), and both expressions occur beside each other in Isa. 42:5; 57:16; Job 27:3; 32:8; 33:4; and 34:14. When someone ceases breathing, then both נשׁמה = *něšāmâ* ("breath") and רוח = *rûaḥ* ("wind, spirit") are used for this expression (Dan. 10:17; and 1 Kings 10:5 = 2 Chron. 9:4). When God withdraws this breath of life from a person, then he or she dies (1 Kings 17:17ff.; Job 27:3; and 34:14f.). And when no נשׁמה = *něšāmâ* ("breath") remains, then life no longer exists (Josh. 11:11; cf. 10:40; 11:14; and Deut. 20:16). The Old Testament is not familiar with any part of the human person that continues beyond death.[76] All that has or still has breath praises YHWH (Ps. 150:6).

The word רוח = *rûaḥ* ("wind, spirit"), previously mentioned, consequently can have a breadth of meaning (as does the corresponding Greek equivalent πνεῦμα = *pneuma*), ranging from wind (Exod. 10:13, 19; 14:21; and Isa. 7:2),

to breeze (Gen. 3:8), to breath, to spirit (Isa. 19:3; and 29:24), and to the phenomenon itself as well as to the power that causes it to move.[77] Accordingly,
רוח = *rûaḥ* stands for both the vitality of the human person (cf. Gen. 45:27;
Judg. 15:19; and 1 Sam. 30:12) and simply his or her breath (Isa. 42:5; 57:16;
and Zech. 12:1), something that is designated as the "breath of life" in Gen. 2:7
that God breathes into the man. In Ezek. 37:1–14, where most of the wide range
of meanings belonging to רוח = *rûaḥ* is displayed, the term refers to the action
of the רוח = *rûaḥ* (Ezek. 37:6, 9f., and 14) that then issues forth through the
word of the prophet. Further, the רוח = *rûaḥ* as breath cannot be limited only
to humans. The animals also share it (Gen. 6:17; 7:15: P), for "all flesh" contains it (Num. 16:22; and 27:16; cf. Job 10:12; 34:14; Qoh. 3:19, 21; 12:7; Pss.
104:29f. and 146:4). When God withdraws and takes back to himself the רוח
= *rûaḥ* or נשמה = *nĕšāmâ*, humans as well as animals die (Pss. 104:29f.; 146:4;
and Job 34:14f.). Humans and all creatures continue to be dependent on God.
Consequently, dead idols do not contain breath in themselves (Hab. 2:19). רוח
= *rûaḥ* designates further the human will ("spirit"). Ezekiel 11:19 and 36:26
(here together with לב = *lēb* ["heart"], as in Exod. 35:21; Deut. 2:30; Ps. 51:12,
14; etc.) are typical examples. Further, one may point to, for example, Gen.
41:8; Isa. 26:9; Jer. 51:11; Ezek. 11:5; and 20:32 where the term refers simply
(as does נפש = *nepeš*; see below) to humanity. It can also be used to mean "I"
(Pss. 31:6; 77:4, 7; and 143:7).

נפש = *nepeš*, a common Semitic word that frequently is found in Israel's
Near Eastern environment, is not what one understands by the word "soul"[78]
in Greek, Hellenistic, and perhaps even modern thought. Nor does the term נפש
= *nepeš* approach the meaning of its predominant translation in the LXX,
ψυχή = *psyche*, that is, something that probably is immortal as over against
something corporal, and is more precious than the body. Such an understanding, found in the LXX, is first present in the early Jewish text, the Wisdom of
Solomon (Wisd.), which seeks to combine Hellenistic ways of thinking with
Old Testment wisdom (Wisd. 2:22f.; 3:13; 4:10–5:23; 8:19f.; and 9:15). Moreover, that נפש = *nepeš* has nothing to do either with "soul" or with "immortality" is demonstrated by the Old Testament expression נפש מת = *nepeš mēt*
("dead *nepeš*") which simply designates the entire human person as a corpse
with its dreadful power (Lev. 19:28; 21:11; Num. 5:2; 6:6; etc.). נפש = *nepeš*,
which also can simply mean a "person,"[79] stands concretely for "throat" (as
does its Ugaritic equivalent; cf. Isa. 5:14; 29:8; Jonah 2:6; Ps. 23:3; Prov. 10:3;
13:25; 16:24; 25:25; 28:25; and Qoh. 6:7), as well as for the breath that passes
through it (cf. נשמה = *nĕšāmâ* or רוח = *rûaḥ*; Gen. 35:18; 1 Kings 17:21f.; Jer.
2:24; and 15:9). The verb נפש = *npš* (niphal) means "to draw a deep breath,"[80]
and אף = *'ap* ("nose") as the human instrument for breathing and blowing (Isa.
2:22; and Job 4:9) not accidentally means "nose" as well as "anger" (Prov.
30:33; Deut. 9:19; etc.). All living creatures have this breath, not just humans

(Gen. 1:20, 30). In Gen. 2:7 the breathing into the man results in his becoming a נפש חיה = *nepeš ḥayyâ* ("living being"). However, this expression is found frequently within priestly thought also in regard to the animal world (Gen. 1:20; 9:10, 12, 15, 16; Lev. 11:10, 46; and Ezek. 47:9). One understands "soul" to mean the interiority of humans, their feelings, aspirations, and their life force, but it is not a component of human nature that is separate from the human person. It is the case then that one can render נפש = *nepeš* with the word "soul" in some places in the Old Testament[81] (cf., e.g., 1 Sam. 1:15; Ps. 42:5; and Job 30:16). Above all, however, נפש = *npš* occurs in those places which have to do with human longing (Deut. 23:25; Prov. 16:26; 23:2; Micah 7:1; etc.)[82] and with the human being's vital self (H. Seebass); (Gen. 12:13; 19:19f.; Prov. 8:35f.; and Job 19:2). "My soul" (נפשי = *napšî*) stands for "my life" or for "I" (1 Kings 20:32; Pss. 103:1f.; 104:1; etc.; cf. Pss. 6:4; 42:6f.; 43:5; Jer. 4:31; etc.).[83] One is to love YHWH with one's entire "I" (נפש = *npš*; Deut. 4:29; 6:5; 10:12; etc.; used of YHWH in Jer. 32:41!). For all intents and purposes, "life" is meant when נפש = *npš* is spoken about.[84] In a less colorful way, נפש = *npš* stands frequently (both for male and female) for "someone."[85] The Old Testament mentions a נפש = *npš* of YHWH only in Jer. 32:41 and 1 Sam. 2:35, while נפש = *npš* in Isa. 1:14 probably refers only to his "I."

Important still is the combination of נפש = *npš* and דם = *dām* ("blood"; Gen. 37:21ff.; Lev. 17:11; Deut. 12:23). When the breath departs, life ends. When the blood flows, life flows with it. Life, however, belongs only to YHWH. Consequently, humans do not have the power of disposal over blood, even when they are allowed to consume animals following the flood (Gen. 9:4f. P; cf. Lev. 3:17; 7:26f.; 17:10, 12, 14; etc.). For the purposes of atonement, accorded by YHWH and not produced by humans, blood may be used in the so-called blood ritual (Lev. 4:5–34; 16:14–19; and 17:11).[86]

The heart (לבב/לב = *lēb/lēbāb*; a common Semitic term), according to the people's understanding in the Old Testament (however, e.g., also to that of the ancient Egyptians),[87] was the seat not only of the emotions and feelings[88] but also of the will, of thought (Judg. 16:17f.), and of the understanding (Deut. 29:3: understanding heart).[89] Solomon prays for a "hearing heart" (1 Kings 3:9), that is, for a will that is willing to be obedient. "Without heart" signifies not "heartless" in our sense but rather "without insight" (Hos. 7:11). And even when the beloved is told by his lover that she has stolen his heart, he understands as an Old Testament human being that she has destroyed his wits. Thoughts of the heart can also be evil (Gen. 6:5; and 8:21), so that the will in addition to the intellect is involved. The phenomenon of blood circulation was probably not completely unknown. Moreover, heartbeats are mentioned in Ps. 38:11. In the first two chapters of Genesis, rich in anthropological statements, לב = *lēb* ("heart") is not mentioned. However, the fact that לב = *lēb* ("heart") stands not only for the interiority and spiritual nature of humans is shown by the statement that eating and drinking make the heart strong (Gen. 18:5; Pss. 22:27; and 104:15). "Heart and kidneys" as a word pair designate the thought and feelings of humans as a whole (Jer. 11:20; 17:10; 20:12; Pss. 7:10; and 26:2). Thus, as only YHWH really knows the heart and kidneys of humans, so his activity and knowledge have a special affinity with the לֵב = *lēb* ("heart") of human beings.[90] The human person sees what is before his or her eyes; however, YHWH looks into the heart (1 Sam. 16:7). YHWH is also the one who places a thought into the human heart (Ezra 7:27; Neh. 2:12; 7:5; and Qoh. 3:11: late texts). Therefore, in Hebrew thought "heart" and "speech" are closely connected.[91] However, the human לֵב = *lēb* ("heart") is also obstinate or can become obstinate.[92] A pure, different, and new heart is nothing but thinking that includes a correct decision of the will and right action (Ezek. 11:19f.; 36:26; Pss. 51:12; 73:13; Prov. 20:9; and 22:11; cf. Matt. 5:8). To say that one's heart is not present means that he or she is not honest (Prov. 23:7). However, when people do something with their "entire heart," then this takes place with their entire will and all of their feelings (Deut. 6:5; 10:12; etc.). Thus YHWH inscribes the Torah on the human heart, that is, places it into the will that is the center of human emotions. In so doing, the Torah is fulfilled (Jer. 17:1; and 31:33; cf. 1 Kings 8:58). And even YHWH himself has a heart, that is, feelings, will, and desire (Gen. 6:6; 1 Sam. 2:35; 13:14; 1 Kings 9:3; 2 Kings 10:30; Jer. 3:15; 7:31; 32:41; Ps. 33:11; etc.), and this has positive significance for humans (Hos. 11:8f.).

רוּחַ = *rûaḥ* ("spirit, wind"), נפשׁ = *nepeš* ("soul, mind," etc.), and לב = *lēb* ("heart") can all be used to refer to the emotions, including, for example, anger, vengeance, vexation, and fury (Exod. 15:9; Deut. 19:6; Judg. 8:3; Isa. 25:4; Ezek. 16:27; Ps. 27:12; etc.), mourning or pain (Isa. 57:15; 65:14; etc.), love (Gen. 34:3, 8; 1 Sam. 18:1; 20:17; and Cant. 1:7; 3:1–4), joy (Prov. 2:10; and Isa. 55:2), courage (Num. 14:24; Josh. 2:11; etc.), pride as well as humility (Lev. 26:41; Isa. 57:15; 61:1; 66:2; Ps. 131:1; Prov. 16:19; 18:12; 29:23; etc.), patience (Qoh. 7:8) or impatience (Exod. 6:9; and Job 21:4), passion (Deut. 24:15; Jer. 22:27; and Ps. 84:3), desire (Deut. 12:15, 20; 1 Sam. 2:16; and Micah 7:1), and jealousy (Num. 5:14, 30).

The Old Testament is not aware of a particular word for conscience. Probably, however, the phenomenon of a bad and thus restless conscience is impressively described in Psalm 32. On occasion, לב = *lēb* ("heart") is used in these connections (1 Sam. 24:6; 25:31; 2 Sam. 24:10; 1 Kings 8:38; and Job 27:6), and sometimes also the kidneys (Ps. 16:7).

Liver (כבד = *kābēd*; only in Lam. 2:11) and kidneys (כליות = *kĕlāyôt)* stand for organs to which the feelings were attributed. The kidneys are so important that they are especially mentioned as being created by YHWH (Ps. 139:13). They are the object of punishments (Job 16:13; and Lam. 3:13) and the seat of feelings (Jer. 12:2; Prov. 23:16; Job 19:27; and Ps. 16:7; together with the heart: Jer. 11:20; 17:10; and Pss. 7:10; 73:21).

The frequently found proximity of these just mentioned terms[93] as well as their intersecting meanings makes it clear that the Old Testament has a rather holistic view of humanity. The individual terms are related to each other (as, e.g., the "United States": Robinson), for in referring to each respective organ the Old Testament is not attempting to describe only one particular part of the human person. Rather, in the reference to an individual organ the Old Testament seeks to set forth the particular "feature under which the human person at that specific moment appears." Further, "the nature of the human person comes to light in his 'behavior'; what the human person is is 'expressed' in what he does."[94]

11.3   Genesis 1:26ff.:
Humanity as the Partner of God

Several Old Testament texts contain theological statements about humanity that are set forth in a conceptually expanded form. To these belong, first of all, Gen. 1:26ff. where God creates humanity according to his own image.[95]

In a speech that, with its "let us," is directed to his court[96] as well as to himself (cf. Gen. 3:22; 11:7: J) but does not point to or even suggest the notion of the Trinity, God commands the creation of humanity (אדם = 'ādām) בצלמנו כדמותנו = bĕṣalmēnû kidmûtēnû ("as our image, according to our likeness"). The LXX translates צלם (= ṣelem; "image") here with εἰκών = eikōn ("icon, image"; Vulgate: imago; "image"), while it translates דמות (= dĕmût; "likeness") with ὁμοίωσις = homoiōsis ("likeness"; Vulgate: similitudo; "likeness"). The occurrence of these terms in the LXX already points toward the importance which they came to have in the New Testament (2 Cor. 4:4; and Col. 1:15) and in the Christian history of dogma and dogmatics. However, what do these terms mean in the context of Genesis 1?

First of all, one should point out that these terms also occur in additional places in the Old Testament, namely, in Gen. 5:1, 3 and 9:6, that is, two Priestly texts that occur respectively after the fall and the flood. Since the Bible does not treat the subject of what humans have lost (entirely or only partially) because of the fall, there is no indication of how humans after the flood, including the ancient as well as contemporary readers of the Old Testament, are to relate these statements to themselves. Furthermore, these predications are mutually true of both male and female (Gen. 1:27). In this regard, however, the Priestly theologians themselves did not persist in carrying out a program of equality for male and female. This fact is indicated by the cultic legislation. צלם (= ṣelem; "image"), preceded by a b (beth essentiae = "as our image"), means more an external representation, for example, a statue (2 Kings 11:18) or a figure. However, it is understandable that, for a theologian like P (or better Pᵍ), this term may no longer have to do only with the external form of appearance. In addition, this notion of external appearance does not fit the Priestly statement in Gen. 9:6. The abstract term דמות (= *dĕmût*; "likeness"), which is added here and coupled with an attenuating כ (*k;* "according to"), further reduces the impression that the idea first or primarily involves external appearance (cf. Gen. 5:1, 3 which has ב = *b* instead of כ = *k*)[97] and keeps one from reaching an understanding that is oriented only to the external.[98] Thus the translation of כדמותנו = *kidmûtēnû* would be "something that is similar to us."[99] Further, both terms occur together and are to be interpreted in relationship to each other. The human person is the "image and likeness," that is, the image of the divine primeval archetype[100] in a way that is analogous to the relationship between the tabernacle and the heavenly temple (cf. Exod. 25:9, 40; תבנית = *tabnît*, "pattern").

Since these terms alone do not explain what being in the divine image more precisely implies, it is time now to look at the context. According to the context, the human being is the recipient of the blessing of God, is to multiply, fill the earth and take possession (כבש = *kābaš*) of it, and is to look after the animal world (רדה = *rādâ*; cf. Ezek. 34:4; Ps. 49:15).[101] P several times makes reference to the commission to multiply, an activity that enjoys divine blessing, in the promises of increase in the history of the ancestors (Gen. 17:2, 20f.; 28:3f.; 35:11; 47:27; and 48:3f.), and this history finds its (primary?) purpose in promising that Israel will become a great nation (Exod. 1:7 P; cf. Gen. 47:27; and Lev. 26:9). Also the commission to take possession of the earth is related to Israel and its land (in Num. 32:22, 29; and Josh. 18:1; cf. also 1 Chron. 22:18f.). This has to do neither with a general commission to have dominion nor with a license to exploit the earth.[102] "Dominion," if one wishes to use this term, can never refer to absolute dominion, according to Old Testament understanding. These commissionings are connected with the blessing of God and, more than that, to the God who issues them. Responsibility is to be lived out, and it is in this way that the image-like quality and the likeness of humans to God are expressed. Humans were taken into service as the "partner" of God, a word that probably best and most comprehensively translates the meaning of "image" and "likeness." These terms make no statements about the nature of human beings but rather intend to describe humanity's function as willed by God. Humans represent God in a prescribed realm and receive for this purpose certain qualities, which do not make them godlike (the כ = *k* elucidates this) but rather elevates them to be the partners of God. Humans are to be the feudal partner of God in his formation and administration of the creation. While they are the partner of God in a legitimate way, they are not regarded as the "crown of creation." Indeed, God's work for seven days does not culminate with humanity; rather, rest is the final act of God that brings to conclusion his activity of creation. Thus, it is the Sabbath that is the crowning climax of the whole of creation (Gen. 2:1–3),[103] and it is the ordinance of the Sabbath that is founded in creation and blessed and made holy by God.[104] This was and became the day for Israel's communion with God, since it is on this day that both YHWH's glory took up residence in their midst and his call was issued (Exod. 24:15b–18a P; cf. also Exod. 39:32, 43). Consequently, humanity is, according to Gen. 1:26–2:3, not only the partner sharing in the sovereignty of God but also his conversation partner who, hearing YHWH's call and acknowledging his sovereignty, was to live responsibly before him. YHWH and Israel both depended on and gave meaning to the other. The one may not and could not exist without the other, and the one could not be properly fashioned without the other. The *dominium terrae* is no carte blanche for the exploitation of the world. If one has (unfortunately) (mis)understood this in this way, this is not intended in the text itself. Rather, what is intended is the commissioning of humans to participate in divine sovereignty over the earth.[105] One may see rather clearly in all of this the formative power of Yahwistic faith at work in the portrait of humanity (cf. later to J, etc.). The creation is to be secured and to be set in order, and humanity has to live in dialogue with God. As his partner, humanity has to bring God into the conversation in this world.

Thus, according to the witness of the Old Testament, something was promised to all humans in general that, elsewhere in the ancient Near East, was appropriate only for kings. It has been correctly noted that P is also here dependent on previous tradition. For example, *ṣalmu* was a royal predication in Akkadian. This term does not mean the appearance; rather, it designates the position and office of the king. The king was the representative of the deity, and this was as true of Akkad as it was of Assur and of Egypt.[106]

What mostly in Israel's cultural environment was stated especially about the king (although not exclusively, as, e.g., Egyptian texts show),[107] the Old Testament for all intents and purposes attributed to humanity. Further, Gen. 1:26ff. stands in obvious proximity to Psalm 8, although this psalm shows no evidence of dependence on Genesis 1. Rather, both texts go back to an older tradition that was prior to each of them.[108] In addition, what is said in Gen. 1:28 states in an obviously intentional, more extenuated fashion what was expressed about the sovereignty of the "royal" human in Ps. 8:7. Therefore, not only is God imagined in anthropomorphic terms,[109] humans also are believed to be theomorphic. In humanity, God is to continue to effectuate acts of creation, and Gen. 1:28 is God's "preliminary design" (N. Lohfink)[110] for what is to come, that is, for what P narrates later on. This preliminary design for what is to come is already said by God to be "very good" (Gen. 1:31). In this divine assessment of "very good," the sexuality of humanity is also included. The image and partnership mark the dignity and at the same time the dependency of humanity as well as its divine commission and responsibility before God. What are present here are statements of relationship between God and humanity, not expressions about something that exists within human beings. Whoever chooses to speak of God must therefore speak at the same time of humanity, and whoever wishes to speak correctly about humanity must also speak about God. All of this is true for both male and female, according to Gen. 1:27. Both genders are to be partners of God in the ordering of the world. There is in addition to this, at least implicitly, the addressing of the work of humanity, something that is more directly spoken about in Gen. 2:5 and 3:19. Humanity's work in the producing of culture and civilization forms a partnership with God's activity in the ordering of his world.

11.4 Humanity according to the Witness of Different Groups of Texts

One cannot fully interpret the statements about humanity in Gen. 1:26ff. without looking at all of the theological positions and statements of the basic Priestly text. This inquiry must now be intensified and expanded by examining other corpora of texts in the Old Testament.

a. Priestly (Basic) Source

We continue now with the image of humanity in the Priestly source.[111] That this document desired initially to see humanity in a positive light already becomes clear both in the statements about blessing and rank in Gen. 1:26ff., which indicate that humanity's place is the "incarnation of the ordering power" in the world,[112] and in the predicate "very good" which also includes humanity (Gen. 1:31). This positive view is underlined by Gen. 9:1–17 where God establishes a universal בְּרִית = *bĕrît* ("covenant") with humanity in general as the descendants of Noah (together with the animal world: vv. 10, 12, and 15f.). This covenant has a rainbow as its sign. This bow is to remind God (!) of his eternal covenant with all flesh (vv. 15–17), and the covenant contains the promise that henceforth no other primeval flood is to come. Further, the spillage of human blood is placed under the punishment of death (Gen. 9:6). Animal flesh may be eaten in the future; however, the blood is removed from the authority of human disposition (Gen. 9:4).[113] Moreover, the act of violence, which, according to P, brought about the primeval flood (Gen. 6:12f.), is abolished. Violence is not to be and indeed cannot be expressed. Also for P, humanity no longer continues to be "very good." God gives even to wicked human beings the means to sustain themselves in his various cosmic orders, as, for example, the rhythm of time (the Sabbath), the separation of chaos from the cosmos, and the course of the stars which serve only to provide directions (cf. Gen. 1:14ff.). Chaos in the future shall not endanger or even lay siege to the cosmos. God has given life, and he wills also to support it (Gen. 9:1–17). This is especially true of the humans who are "righteous and pious" like Noah and who "walk with God" (Gen. 6:9). "Only the Noachic human being shall survive beyond the exile,"[114] says the basic Priestly document to its contemporaries, and it admonishes them by noting that God has already provided his means of support and given his promises to make this possible.

For Abraham and his descendants, being pious remains important, even if they are no longer "with God," as were Enoch and Noah (Gen. 5:24; and 6:9 P), but rather only walk "before" him (Gen. 17:1). However, in the positive and expansive promises of the important speeches of God, the significance of the eternal covenant of Abraham is brought out, as in the promise of the land, not only for Abraham himself but also for his progeny (Gen. 17:7–10). In particular the assurance of multiplying is issued (v. 6), which takes up anew and with the promises of kings (Gen. 17:16; and 35:11) even surpasses Gen. 1:28.[115]

Through circumcision (Gen. 17:10f.),[116] which is explained as the sign of the Abrahamic covenant, attention is drawn to the preparatory cultic event that, like the Sabbath in Gen. 2:1–3, is so important for P and its view of humanity. The covenant of Abraham extends through Isaac and Jacob to the people of Israel, to the descendants of Jacob who is blessed (Gen. 35:11f.; 48:3; Exod. 1:7: P),[117] and not through Ishmael who is placed outside it (Gen. 17:20f.). The positive gifts that God had earmarked for humanity to flourish are meant to be especially reserved for Israel and this people who stand within the Abrahamic covenant.[118] This is underscored by the Priestly narratives about the exodus and Sinai. In the miraculous salvation at the sea, YHWH seeks to exalt himself in the eyes of the Egyptians so that they are to know that he is YHWH (Exod. 14:4, 17f.). Decisive for P, however, is God's action on behalf of his people. God heard the cry of his oppressed people, remembered his covenant with Abraham (Exod. 2:23–25), brought them forth in order to give them the land (Exod. 6:6–8), made possible the Passover as a cultic remembrance, festival, and eternal order (Exod. 12:14), and imparted to Israel the glorious revelation of deliverance (Exod. 14:22f., 26, 27). P speaks of the glory of YHWH once again in Exod. 16:10 and above all in Exod. 24:15–18. It is this glory which, through YHWH's appearance on the seventh day, culminates in making possible the atoning cult of Israel. It is here that the call of YHWH goes forth: YHWH dwells in the midst of his people as a cultic community and is their God (Exod. 29:42ff.; cf. 6:7). Exodus 40:34 combines then the "glory of YHWH" with the priestly "tent of meeting,"[119] so that YHWH's appearance is made possible through this preparation (Lev. 9:4). Here everything reaches its culmination in an anthropological way when the people, seeing YHWH's presence, rejoice and offer worship (Lev. 9:24). "The Priestly source says that it is humanity, defiled yet called, who comes to the place of atonement where God himself wills to be present in the midst of history."[120] "The fundamental endowment of humanity in creation, that is, its identity as the 'image of God,' comes to programmatic fulfillment now in the idea of priestly humanity in the 'people of God': the priestly cultic community is *the* guarantee for continuation in the order of creation far removed from the threat of chaos, because YHWH himself has taken up residence in their midst."[121] In the Priestly understanding, as also in 1 Chronicles 1–9, Israel becomes the means for sustaining the human race. "Because the creator God, as a good king ruling over his earth, will not allow himself to abandon this world and leave it to its destruction, Israel can rest secure upon the promise given to Abraham and actualized at Sinai."[122] The God of Israel is also the creator of the world, the covenant of Noah supports the covenant of Abraham, and the divine blessing is no longer connected to Israel (as was the case in J; see below) but rather is "anchored in creation as the function of the powerful activity of God."[123] And God "does not forgo any act of salvation for creation."[124] God's bow in the clouds is to make this known to all humanity (Gen. 9:12ff.).

b. The Yahwist

The Priestly document displayed an image of humanity that to a large extent indicated a positive orientation. This document sought to console and comfort the exilic community, secure its stability, and direct it toward a new future. The older Yahwist source,[125] by contrast, could not and would not speak in such a predominantly positive way about humanity to people of his day. While he indeed held in high regard his own period, that is, the time of the (Davidic -) Solomonic empire,[126] a perspective reflected, for example, in Gen. 12:1–3; 25:23; 28:14; and Num. 24:5–9, 15–19, this was less true of his contemporaries who perhaps suffered the tyranny resulting from the rise of the empire. "Not human accomplishments, but rather the action of Yahweh, including his promise, have led to the establishment of the empire. The Yahwist holds nothing back from his critical portrayal of humanity set forth in his primeval history."[127]

According to the Yahwist, YHWH has well equipped the man (Gen. 2:7), has given him a task (Gen. 2:15), and has provided him with a helper that corresponds to himself (Gen. 2:18f.).[128] God also wishes here to take the man as his partner and allows him to participate in his creative activity (Gen. 2:19f.). However, this first pair overstepped the bounds of YHWH's first commandment (Gen. 2:16f.), wishing that they could "be like God" (Gen. 3:5) and not creatures standing under God and responsible to YHWH who had formed their lives. For the Yahwist, it was only due to the grace of YHWH that they were not punished immediately with the death that had been threatened (Gen. 2:17).[129] However, they experienced life-diminishing cursings (Gen. 3:15ff.) and were expelled from the garden of God, thereby forfeiting eternal existence (Gen. 3:22ff.).[130] However, even here YHWH proves to be a caring God in that he makes them garments from skins and clothes them (Gen. 3:21). Thus the Yahwist can and will not only speak of humanity as the creature of God (Genesis 2), but he also must speak of human disobedience (Genesis 3). Analogously, Gen. 11:1–9 stands after Genesis 10, each with its differently accented verdict about the world of the nations. Already among the sons of the first human pair and thus the first brothers there was dissension and murder (Genesis 4), while the descendant of Cain, who bore the name of Lamech, sings a boasting song by which he glorified his greatness (Gen. 4:23ff.). By constrast, YHWH himself supports even Cain, the fratricidal murderer, by placing upon him a mark (Gen. 4:15), even though he would obtain no portion in the land (Gen. 4:12, 16). Then comes the primeval flood, because YHWH was grieved, having been forced to recognize regretfully about his human creation that: "The evil was great upon the earth, for the thoughts and efforts of humans are evil from their youth" (Gen. 6:5).[131] While the primeval flood concludes with the repeating of this reason (Gen. 8:21), YHWH promises that such an event is never to happen again. Rather, he will maintain the continuation of the world (Gen. 8:21b, 22). This means that he has not altered human nature. Rather, YHWH again shows unfathomable mercy to human beings (cf. Gen. 6:8; 19:19), who, even after the flood, continue to be evil. Reckoned among them are the Yahwist's contemporaries and indeed all readers of the Old Testament. That humans do not understand each other anymore is a further penalty of YHWH assessed to them because of their arrogance in stepping over the boundaries that God had established. This is how the Yahwist probably would have understood the narrative of the Tower of Babel (Gen. 11:1–9) that appropriates the multifaceted, prevalent topoi of building inscriptions.[132]

As is the case with P, the Yahwistic primeval history seeks to describe a fundamental story that not only narrates the past but also continues to have an effect. Thus the Yahwist continues to play back the fundamental event of the primeval history for a present humanity. In Gen. 12:1–4a and beyond, including the election of Abram which is described, the theme of "blessing" comes once more to expression and is taken up several additional times (Gen. 24:35, 60 [J?]; 26:24; 27:29; 32:27, 30; and Num. 24:9f.). YHWH sets forth for humanity the new possibility of blessed existence, and the narrative stresses at the same time that every positive attainment of humans in his own period results from the gift of YHWH's blessing, not from their own personal accomplishment. "This is the human person: one who is richly endowed because of God's compassion, a fallen creature under profound curse because of alienation from God, and yet one who has begun with God a new, mysterious history through which is to stream forth a new blessing for all generations of the earth."[133] Indeed, even the ancestors cannot be described only in a positive fashion. This is as true for Abram (Gen. 12:10–20; 16*[134]) as it is for Jacob (Genesis 27; 30). However, even for a Jacob who does not speak straightforwardly and appropriately about God (Gen. 27:20), the promise of divine presence and guidance (Gen. 28:13–15; cf. 30:27, 30) is valid, for, in spite of everything, YHWH brings to fulfillment all of his promises (Gen. 21:1a; and 25:21).

If now the Yahwist and Priestly sources, with their so differently accentuated depictions of human nature, are woven together in the Old Testament, something that is not only true for the primeval history,[135] and if both clearly combine this primeval history with additional narratives that follow, then one may ascertain, first of all, that both see humanity as the creature of God and place upon this creature the burden of responsibility before the creator. Second, both sources stress that an individual human being who has no partner is no human being at all. Then, however, the split right down the middle occurs in the perspective about humanity (the more positively evaluated creature, the more negatively seen "sinner"), a dichotomy that all later readers of the Old Testament encounter: creature, but also sinner, blessed but also under curse, obligated to the orders of God, yet sustained by YHWH's grace. The human being can only be the "image" of God because God made him accordingly. The human being, however, is also a sinner, because he (she) himself (herself) wills to be. To be allowed to be the partner of God excludes, not includes, equality with God. If the Priestly source, however, tells of YHWH's atoning cult as the goal of his journey with Israel and the Yahwist speaks of YHWH's blessing as the ultimate, divine purpose, then both sources are not at odds, moreover, in their view of the objective toward which the action of YHWH, the God of Israel, strives: YHWH wills a positive future for his own. According to the Yahwist (Gen. 8:21f.) as well as the Priestly source (Gen. 9:1–17), the preservation of our present world as well as its human creatures is due to God's promise that he would continue to sustain it. The human being is, as God's creature, always dependent upon God. Through his activity on behalf of Israel, YHWH has (according to both J and P: Exodus 13–14) demonstrated that he is able to save and liberate his own, can chose them to enter into community with him, and can preserve them as a faithful and gracious God even when the people abandon him or, murmuring and disbelieving, they turn against him. In similar fashion, the Deuteronomistic History likewise not only narrates a history of human sin but also opens up a new confidence in a new future through YHWH's promises, his continuing guidance, and his call for repentance and new obedience.[136]

c. The Law and the Prophets

In Old Testament law, as in the Covenant Code (Exod. 20:22–23:19), in the so-called Law of YHWH's Privilege (Exod. 34:10–27), in Deuteronomy, in the Decalogues (Exod. 20:1–17; Deut. 5:6–21), and in the Holiness Code (Leviticus 17–26), the divine "I" or an authorized human speaker addresses Israelite humans about their responsible conduct of life and their ethical duties.[137] According to the Covenant Code, for example, each person is responsible for his own action. He is not able to transfer his guilt to anyone else. The theological location of this requirement is especially made clear by the anchoring of all these texts in the context of the event at Sinai and associating them with Moses. The one who lays claim to humans is the God of the saving exodus, the God of the guidance through the wilderness, and the God of the community founded by him. History and law are linked together, meaning that responsibility can be lived out only in a this-worldly fashion, since ancient Israel did not know of any retribution in a future existence. When the prophets[138] speak of humanity, they do not always have in mind Israelites, as the so-called oracles against the nations demonstrate.[139] They especially speak about humanity when they indict humans and point to their guilt, indicating that humans have not maintained their ethical, interpersonal responsibility to each other, that the chosen people do not live in community and carry out the obligations that accompany their election, and that persons in the eyes of God are and have become guilty of being oppressors and exploiters of their fellow human beings (Amos 3:9–11; 5:7, 10–12; 6:12; 8:4–6; Micah 2:1–5, 6–11; and Isa. 5:8–10). Those in positions of leadership no longer give consideration to justice, are open to bribery, and pull the wool over the eyes of the poor (Micah 3:1–4, 9–12; 6:9–16; Isa. 1:23; and 3:12, 13–15). The one who otherwise is considered to be strong as a human being shall be able to do nothing before the God who comes to judge his people (Amos 2:13ff.; Isa. 1:31; 2:12, 17; and 3:25). Even the ideal of feminine beauty does not escape prophetic criticism and indictment. Beautiful women are called cows of Bashan. They imbibe and harass their husbands, so that no good fortune is promised them (Amos 4:1–3; cf. 8:13). The beautiful daughters of Zion shall lose their jewelry with which they adorn themselves, and they must go forth tied in rope, bald, and dressed in sackcloth (Isa. 3:16–24). Seven women shall fight for one man (Isa. 4:1). Israel is a virgin, however, she is already consecrated for death (Amos 5:2). Those who are at ease, the privileged, and those who live in luxury must go into exile (Amos 6:1–7; 7:17; and Micah 1:16). The previous order of the human community shall be inverted (Isa. 3:1–7). Whoever takes pride in his or her own power shall faint with exhaustion (Amos 6:13f.). Moreover, it is true that: "He has told you, O human being, what is good and what YHWH requires of you: nothing other than to practice justice, love kindness, and to walk humbly with your God," as a later prophetic interpretation of a related word states it (Micah 6:8). Thus people are called to the practice of justice and to the learning of what is good (Isa. 1:16f.). However, whoever thinks that a human person could hide from YHWH or could escape him shall experience the very opposite (Amos 9:1–4; cf. Psalm 139). The prophetic "woe" oracle, stemming from the death lament, resounds over those who are wise in their own eyes (Isa.

5:21). When, however, Isaiah gives voice even to a love song and sings the intimate words from love lyrics about a beloved one and his vineyard, then one thinks finally one is able to hear something human and beautiful from the mouth of the prophet. Still, all of this results in an indictment (Isa. 5:1–7). When, however, the prophet of the exile, Deutero-Isaiah, said that "all flesh" is grass, then this provides only the somber background from which springs forth the contrasting and comforting promise that "the word of our God" shall be successful in shaping the continuation of life (Isa. 40:1f., 6–8). Moreover, humanity is primarily critically seen and negatively evaluated by the prophets as a consequence of the message of judgment that is paramount in their writings. Only YHWH himself is able to alter humanity by the efficacy of his spirit (Ezek. 36:26ff.; and Jer. 31:33f.).[140]

d. The Book of Psalms

In the psalms and prayers,[141] humanity can be spoken about in different ways depending on the genre as well as the occasion and purpose of the text. Moreover, since it is here that Old Testament persons themselves bring to expression their own understanding of humanity in an especially impressive way and do so within the context of their place before God, a look at these texts will be helpful.

It is in Israel's psalms and prayers that humanity is praised as a royal creature who stands under the special blessing of God. In addition to the individual psalmist, the congregation also announces in words its confirmation and praise in both an elementary and definitive manner (Psalm 8).[142] This human being, who is the object of YHWH's special attention (Ps. 8:5; cf. 144:3f.), can be placed within the order of creation and not simply praised as the one who stands over against creation and rules over it (Psalm 104). This is especially so, since there are sinners in God's beautiful and ordered creation, a point noted in a later (certainly remarkable) addition (Ps. 104:35). In Israel one cannot speak of humanity as creature together with his sinfulness and leave out of consideration the question of salvation. YHWH looks upon all inhabitants of the earth and directs their thoughts, an affirmation that is evaluated positively (Ps. 33:13ff.). The human being, who has experienced YHWH's affection and support, gives him thanks for things that are both spiritual and physical, seeks to help others to have the same experience (Psalms 9; 34; 65; 92; 107; and 138), and prays anew for his blessing (Psalms 67; 85). Then the psalmist's trust is called forth in order to awaken it anew and to strengthen it (Psalms 16; 23; 27; 56; and 91). The psalmist in this connection speaks openly before a purported community of God; he does not pray inwardly while lacking confidence, nor does he break forth in public prayer while filled with uncertainty: "With you is the source of life" (Ps. 36:10).

Above all, however, the psalms in their most frequently represented genre, the individual lament, acknowledge the dependence of all humanity upon God. It is not only one aspect of human persons that suffers but indeed their entire being (Psalms 6; 22; and 31; cf. 63:7; 84:3; etc.). Also, every dimension of the human person praises YHWH (Pss. 35:28; 51:10; and 71:23f.). Even the eyes can stand for the human being as a whole (Ps. 13:4; cf. 17:8). The mouth as well as the lips praise YHWH (Pss. 8:3; 34:2; 49:4; 51:17; 71:8, 15; 81:11; 89:2; 109:30; 119:108; etc.), and yet they, along with especially the tongue (Pss. 52:4; 57:5; 64:4; 140:4), also disseminate disaster and deceit (Pss. 22:8, 14; 35:21; 59:8; and 107:42). Here the needs of the human being come to expression and are brought before YHWH, including illness, tribulation occasioned by the experience of anguish and distance from God, and distress caused by the hostility of other people.[143] Yet there is also the certainty of divine comfort[144] and presence.[145] The psalmists turn anew to YHWH, thinking he has forgotten or abandoned them, and prays for the intervention of divine deliverance and salvation (Psalms 13; 22; 31; 54; 57; 59; 69; and 77). In order to move YHWH to such interventions and to underscore the psalmists' need for help, they often speak of themselves as a "poor person" (עני = 'ănî; ענו = 'ānāw; דל = dal),[146] for one knows that YHWH raises and lifts up even the poor and lowly (Pss. 34:7; and 113:7; cf. Isa. 14:32). Similarly, the psalmists frequently call themselves the עבד = 'ebed ("servant") and intend thereby to characterize themselves as persons dependent on YHWH's kindness and generosity. Thus, especially in the laments of the individual, the psalmists strive to obtain YHWH's help[147] (cf. Ps. 31:17: "Let your face shine upon your servant"). They believe that YHWH desires the salvation of his servant (Ps. 35:27). With this, the psalmists reach back readily for support to the previous experiences with YHWH, which both they and the ancestors have had (Pss. 22:4–6; 44:2; and 77; cf. 71:19f.). The individual person stands before YHWH as a worshiper who belongs to Israel, the people of God, a point that is often affirmed within the prayers and is underscored through additions that expand the individual features into collective ones (Pss. 3:9; 9:15; 25:22; 28:8f.; 29:11; 31:24f.; 34; 39:13; 40:4; 44:2; 59:6; 66; 69:31ff.; 75:10; 111; and 130). The individual "I" thus turns into a collective "We" or "Us" (Psalms 103; 121 [v. 4]; 123; 130 [vv. 7f.]; and 131), if not also the congregation as well, while the reverse also happens (Psalm 137: from "We" to "I"). The people lament and give thanks (Psalms 33; 44; 68; 74; 79; 80; 85; 89; 107; 115; 124; 126; 135; 149; and 150) or are brought into dialogue with YHWH (Psalms 8; 81; and 118). One thirsts after God and thinks always of him (Psalm 63), prays for his help against hostility and accusations (Psalms 59; 64; 70; 109; 120; and 140), and calls upon oneself נפשי = napšî ("myself") to give praise to YHWH (Pss. 42:6, 12; 43:5; 103:1; and 104:1). נפש = nepeš also stands for the whole of the human self, the "I," in the Psalter. In other words, the term means purely and simply "life" (Pss. 6:5; 7:2ff.; 22:21; 26:9; 42:3; 55:18; 57:2; etc.). When one calls on YHWH, offering a lament while in need, one also requests at the same time a further instruction for the future journey (Psalms 27; 86; and 143). One knows and characterizes the "heart," which YHWH alone knows, examines, and has formed (Pss. 7:10; 17:3; 26:2; 33:15; etc.) as the central location of feelings, thoughts, and the will (Pss. 4:5, 8; 10:6; 13:6; 15:2; 19:9; 20:5; 22:15, 27; 25:17; 28:7; 34:19; 38:9, 11; 51:19; 55:5; etc.). While רוח = *rûaḥ* ("spirit, breath") stands normally for the breath of life when these texts deal with human nature (Pss. 104:29; and 146:4), it can come very close to approximating the "heart" (לב = *lēb*) (Pss. 32:2; and 77:7; cf. 51:12). It becomes especially clear in these psalms, as, for example, in Psalms 16 and 30, how one has seen and evaluated life, sickness (Psalms 38; 41; and 88), old age (Psalm 71), and death (Psalms 39; and 88).[148] Also there especially are psalms that permit one to have a look at what the Old Testament worshiper expected of his God.[149] One prays for guidance and direction and knows quite well his own weaknesses (Psalm 25) and limitations (Psalms 31; 39; 90; and 103:15). The psalmist also prays for his or her own sins, for the succor of forgiveness that is requested or experienced (Psalms 6; 25; 32; 51; 103; and 130), and for the strength derived from divine blessing (Psalms 127; and 128). Thus the worshiper purely and simply prays for life (Ps. 143:11), and the psalms allow one to recognize quite well that what is meant is a vigorous and full life (Pss. 33:19; 34:13; 41:3; 61:7; 66:9; 91:16; 115:15; 118:17; and 133:3). Such a life exists, however, only in community with YHWH in this present world, for the dead do not praise YHWH (Pss. 6:6; 30:10; 88:11; 115:17f.; and Isa. 38:18). Because of one's tribulation and negative experiences that are expressed to God in prayer, "humans," by contrast, can be designated collectively as liars (Ps. 116:11) on whom one cannot depend, as evil (Pss. 119:134; and 140:2, 12), and as those who can endanger the worshiper (Pss. 56:2; and 124:2). However, he or she is certain that, with divine help, this will not happen (Pss. 56:12; 118:6). The psalmist seeks through prayer to overcome the distress occasioned by the good fortune of the evildoers (Psalms 37; 49; and 73).

Thus Old Testament human beings are revealed in their prayers as those who throw themselves on the mercy of God, are dependent upon him, live with him in dialogue, and are supported by him (Psalm 34). When one considers in the Psalter the motif of the hearing of prayer,[150] which is the object of human desire and striving, much of the incorporation of the individual worshiper into the congregation and into the history of the people of God becomes yet clearer. Here, the psalmists recount earlier experiences of deliverance and express their conviction of being heard and receiving help. This conviction is based on existing in community with God, the sustaining experience of the worship of God,[151] and the knowledge of YHWH's "righteousness,"[152] that is, his works of salvation. YHWH also has taken the worshiper from his or her mother's womb (Ps. 22:10f.). The psalmist and the people say "my God" and "my king" (Ps. 74:12; cf. 145:1) or the combination "my king and my God" (Pss. 5:3; 44:5; 68:25; and 84:4),[153] whether they are expressing confidence, making confession, offering a lament, or engaging in praise. In the psalms, feelings of alienation as well as closeness are joined together. The psalmist and the congregation also address God as "my refuge" (Pss. 31:5; and 142:6) and "my light and my salvation" (Ps. 27:1). The worshipers are aware of the demands that YHWH makes of them (Pss. 24:3ff.; 27:11; 41:2; 109:4f.; 119:115; and 143:10), and they acknowledge their fear of God (see below). They acknowledge their sins, together with their power and consequences,[154] pray for forgiveness even for their unknown sins (Ps. 19:13), and learn now and again that YHWH must truly create them anew (Ps. 51:12ff.). Since many of the psalms are actual prayers or can be used as such, the human person is discussed primarily in the psalms in terms of his or her relationship to God. Since the one who prays the psalms is a member of the nation and the congregation of Israel, however and wherever this worship takes place or the prayer is spoken, these relationships of the worshiper or of the worshipers to the people of God and to the congregation are time and again brought to view or at least reside in the background.

e. The Book of Proverbs

The sages by contrast speak more about humanity in general[155] than they do about human beings as Israelites who are members of the people of God and also of the cultic community.[156] However, since many statements are made about "humanity" in the Old Testament wisdom literature, its views of human nature should be explored here. The social community in which the sages are to be viewed (Prov. 5:14; and 26:26) and to which their words are directed is hardly precisely named. One can only deduce from the sayings themselves that the social groups included the family, the tribe, the settled community, and members of the same status or even the same class. The identification of the "neighbor" remains very general.[157] The individual person with his or her everyday problems is brought more prominently into view. Therefore the understanding that the human person is a sinner is seldom discussed in a significant way.[158] Consequently, the notion that individuals are in need of a new creation is something of which the sage is not absolutely convinced (in spite of Prov. 20:9, which appears to revolve around self-purification or a good conscience;[159] cf. Prov. 16:2). The sage indeed knows of his or her responsibility to YHWH (Prov. 14:2, 21, 31; 17:5); however, that this is not the sage's primary theme may be determined on the bases of the themes as well as the distinctive character of the kinds of texts present in Proverbs. The sage sees himself or herself not as a clearly autonomous person but rather as the one who has been endowed by YHWH, is responsible for the order which serves to sustain the world, and is integrated into this order.[160] Also, the sage knows there is much that has been concealed from him or her in this world, because it is YHWH in the final analysis who leads and directs everything. Thus, success is not always guaranteed (Prov. 16:1, 9, 33; 19:14, 21; 20:24; and 21:1f., 30f.). The sages are aware of their limits, and this is why they are wise (Prov. 21:30; 26:12; and 28:26). However, as a whole, they still trust to some extent their own wisdom, knowledge, and education (Prov. 1:1–6; 3:13ff.; 13:14; and 19:20). In later wisdom (Proverbs 1–9), insight, prudence, and knowledge are seen as the gift of YHWH more clearly than in Proverbs 10–31 (Prov. 1:7; 2:5; 3:5; etc.).[161]

Thus one is confident that the counsel of the sage and the invitation and admonition of wisdom will be efficacious (Prov. 1:10, 20–23; 4:1–9, 10ff.; 5:12ff.; 6:20ff.; 7:1–5, 24–27; 8:1–11, 12–21, 32–36; 13:14; and 22:17–21), while one also knows from experience that the invitation of Woman Folly or of the seductress leads to failure (Prov. 5:1–23; 6:24ff.; 7:5, 6ff.; and 9:13ff.). The warning about transgressors is a prevalent topos (Prov. 1:10–19; 2:12ff.; 4:14ff.; etc.), although it is often not clear what the nature of the transgression is (Prov. 12:5; 13:5; and 15:8f.: the sacrifice of the transgressor is an abomination to YHWH).[162] Transgressors threaten other humans (Prov. 12:6; and 24:15), but they shall be punished by the very same misfortunes caused by their sin (Prov. 10:6, 11; 11:5; 13:6; 21:7; 24:16, 19f.). According to Prov. 10:27, the transgressor does not possess the fear of God. Within the sapiential admonitions and sentences that readily set forth comparisons (for pedagogical reasons?), the reducing of humans to categories or types quite naturally demonstrates an inclination toward a black-and-white portrayal (wise–fool;[163] righteous–transgressor;[164] diligent–indolent: Prov. 10:4f.; 12:24; 13:4; and 15:19; and poor and rich: Prov. 10:15; 14:20; and 18:23). Similarly, the righteous person can be contrasted to the fool (Prov. 10:21), and the righteous person is naturally also the sage (Prov. 23:24). Probably serving as a deterrent, a rather strongly negative portrait is drawn of the fool, the transgressor, and the indolent which contrasts with the positive depiction of the sage, the just, and the industrious. Many generally valid statements in wisdom literature resonate with the same kind of typology that is used to express the sages' views of humanity and the world. These statements point to a widely held conviction that there is a clear and unequivocal relationship between deed and consequence,[165] especially since YHWH is seen to be involved. However, it is clear to the sages that there is a "degree of incalculableness" in this relationship, even when YHWH is mentioned. A righteous sage is patient and does not wear his or her wisdom as a sign for display.[166] However, the Old Testament sage could hardly accept totally the idea that "the human being is reminded of his limits, . . . his autonomy is given up."[167] As a thesis, this statement places too much of a burden on all of the wisdom texts. While it hardly corresponds to the common depiction of humanity within this Old Testament corpus, it may reflect the views of God and of humans expressed by the friends of Job (in Job 3–27), views that represent very much a closed, hardly an open, system. It is not the case that in wisdom literature "orders are formulated under the aspect of provisionality" which as "the wisdom of the next step . . . continues to be bound to time and moment."[168] Rather, these orders are issued as very general rules for human behavior.

The contrastive typologies have their place above all in chaps. 10–15 of the Book of Proverbs where antithetical *parallelismus membrorum* is especially frequent. In the strongly general and, from chap. 16 on (especially to chap. 21), wider-reaching ethical instructions of wisdom literature,[169] there is more about the arrangement of complex, individual and communal, everyday life. However, the woman occurs only as an object, not as a subject, of sapiential statements. She speaks only in the role of the seductress (Prov. 7:14ff.). She is seen only from a male perspective, including even Prov. 31:10ff. Consequently, no sapiential counsels or admonitions are imparted to the woman regarding her association with the male.

It is on the basis of the general rules for life and behavior that the extensive spheres of human life and everyday existence are explored and properly shaped. These rules are important for the sphere of anthropology, showing, for example, that a rather emotional person is viewed in a critical way (Prov. 14:17; 14:29; 15:18; 19:18; 20:3; 22:24; 25:28; 26:17, 21; 27:4; and 29:11, 20, 22). Legitimate wisdom, by contrast, can lengthen life and protect one against a premature or sudden death.[170] The young and the old are placed opposite each other, evaluated comparatively, and related to one another (Prov. 20:29; cf. Ps. 37:25; Prov. 16:31; 17:6; 22:6; 23:22; as well as Qoh. 11:9–12:7 for old age). Correct speech and proper silence are often the objects of deliberation and the subjects of exhortation. Indeed, wisdom literature frequently reflects on the power and form of language; and consequently self-control, the lips, the mouth, and the tongue are often mentioned.[171] This has its basis, not only in an originally illiterate culture, but also within the sphere of sapiential reflection. Further, the sages often come to speak in this connection of the "heart" of human beings,[172] attributing to this organ both thinking and speaking (Prov. 15:7, 14, 28; and 16:1), while a "pure" heart is associated with the gracefulness of the lips (Prov. 22:11). In the literature of Proverbs and in Qoheleth,[173] the "heart" stands namely for the center of the will, for thinking and especially planning, for wishes and their limits, and indeed for whatever very much occupies the minds of the sages.[174] YHWH can direct where he will even the heart of the king, which to humans is inscrutable (Prov. 21:1; 25:3). However, the "heart" also stands for the location of the emotions, as, for example, joy (Prov. 14:13, 30; 15:13, 15, 30; and 17:22), anger (Prov. 19:3), and uncontrollability (Prov. 21:4). And YHWH is the one who examines the heart (Prov. 17:3; 21:2; and 24:12; cf. 15:11; and 16:2). This later idiom perhaps goes back to the Egyptian conception of the judgment of the dead where the human heart is examined on the scales and weighed against Ma'at.[175] Then too the sages are intimately familiar with the language of the eyes, and they know that one can recognize in a glance the nature or intentions of a person.[176] If even YHWH has eyes (Prov. 24:18) that carefully keep watch over knowledge (Prov. 22:12), he is also the one who has created the organs of the eyes as well as the ears which, for the sages, are decisive for their ability to know (Prov. 20:12; and 28:9). Heart and eyes (Prov. 23:26, 33), the heart as the seat of thoughts that are spoken and the ear for hearing, also stand side by side (Prov. 22:12; cf. the "hearing heart" that Solomon requested for himself: 1 Kings 3:9),[177] as do the heart, lips, and kidneys, together with thinking, speaking, and feeling (Prov. 23:15f.). Also in this literature, נֶפֶשׁ = *nepeš* ("breath, self, being") stands for "throat" or "palate" (Prov. 16:24) as well as for human striving and desire (Prov. 21:10).[178] It is frequently the case that wisdom generalizes and simply speaks about "humanity" on the whole. Thus certain things are said to be typical of human beings ("How can the human being understand his or her way?" Prov. 20:24), who commonly do something or cause something to occur,[179] in spite of the fact that the sages recognize that humans are different (Prov. 27:19).

f. The Book of Job

In its critical disputation with the thinking and the tradition of wisdom, the Book of Job[180] is no longer able to see in a positive way the human person and his or her life, fortune, thinking, planning, and place before God. In contrast to the pious and patient Job of the narrative frame (cf. Job 1:21; and 2:10), the Job of the dialogues (Job 3–27) rebels against God. He curses the day of his birth (Job 3:1–10; cf. Jer. 20:14–18) and wishes several times that he had been stillborn (Job 3:11ff.; and 10:18–22), for in death there is rest, peace, and equality (Job 3:17ff.). Consequently, several times Job yearns for death, something that for him is even an expression of hope (Job 6:8f.; 7:6; cf. 3:21f.; 10:21f.; 14:19f.; 17:1, 13–16; 19:10; and 30:20, 26).[181] Further, the exalted statement about humanity in Ps. 8:5 has the opposite meaning in the mouth of Job. That God attends to humans is no longer an expression of good fortune and thus the basis for praise and thanks; rather, now it is an indication of oppression and thus the occasion for lament and accusation (Job 7:11), because Job sees himself placed under a standard of judgment by which he cannot be found to be righteous and which, in any case, will not be fairly applied to him. In fact, Job thought that God actually did not even have need of him (Job 7:20f.). Consequently, Job can only speak in a largely negative way about humanity (Job 7; 14). Whoever must go to where the dead are never comes back (Job 7:7–10), and for Job it is true of human life in general when he says: "Leave me alone, for my days are only a breath" (Job 7:16). Humanity cannot be righteous in the eyes of God, indeed cannot answer him once in a thousand times (Job 9:2f.). The distance between the impotent creature and the mighty and powerful creator, a point that the friends can emphasize in their opposition to Job (Job 11:7–12), is for Job himself also oppressive (Job 9:4ff.; 12:7ff., and 16ff.). "Your hands have formed and prepared me; therefore will you turn about and seek to destroy me" (Job 10:8)? The creating of humans from clay and their return to the dust in Gen. 2:7 and 3:19 is reflected in Job 10:9, followed then by a look at the engendering and development of an embryo (Job 10:10f.). In his argumentations against the friends as well as against God, Job knows that he, both as a human and as a sage, is not entirely dumb and without understanding (Job 12:2; 13:1f.). He also knows that one can deceive other humans, but not God (Job 13:9). Confident of this, he nonetheless challenges God to a legal disputation (Job 13:18ff.; and 23:1ff.) and reflects again on the transitoriness of human life and the irreversible wasting away of death (Job 21:23–26). Consequently, humans are subject to God always and in everything (Job 14:1ff.). Job's human flesh (בשׂר = *bāśār*) feels pain (Job 14:22; and 21:6), and his "soul" (נפשׁ = *nepeš*) mourns (Job 14:22; cf. 12:10; 13:14; and 19:1; נפשׁי = *napšî* also simply can mean "me"), while God runs like a warrior against him (Job 16:9ff.). Here one even now sees the bodily appearance of Job (Job 16:15–17). Thus Job describes himself with all the negative features of human existence he can name (Job 19:9ff.), for he can only hope that God in the last minute shall become cognizant of his creature's mortal existence and still be his גאל = *gō'ēl* ("redeemer"; Job 19:25f.). Job continues to hope in God, in spite of God (Job 23:1–17; and 30:20ff.), because humans, especially, those who are young, now laugh about him and mock him (Job 30:1, 9f.). He has always fulfilled the ethical duties and customs of a righteous and pious sage which he lists in Job 29 and 31. When Job comes to speak about his human nature in his laments and accusations against his friends and against God, he does this in a manner that underlines his frailty and his distance from the creator. He does this in order to move this God to turn about and to acknowledge his divine superiority, which must be newly, although not unconditionally, demonstrated in the fortune of an individual, weak, and, in Job's opinion, guiltless human being.

The friends by contrast argue that Job has to be an unrighteous person, otherwise God would not allow him to suffer. Thus, "how can a person be righteous before God or a human person be pure before the one who has made him?" (Job 4:17). The human person creates his or her own disastrous fortune (Job 5:7), while the person whom God chastens is blessed, for he both saves (Job 5:17ff.) and gives long life and descendants (Job 5:25ff.). God is not unjust and shall hold upright once more the person who turns to him. One knows this from tradition (Job 8) as well as from the wise, the gray-haired, and the aged (Job 15:10) who give advice accordingly (Job 11:13ff.). Eliphaz also reaches back to Psalm 8, although he turns it against Job: "What is a mortal that he can be clean, or how can one born of a woman be righteous?" (Job 15:14). Job is warned of the characteristics of the wicked and the fate that results from their behavior (Job 15:25ff.; 18:5ff.), and it is pointed out to him that, since humanity was created, never has a transgressor lived long and well (Job 20:4ff.; cf. 27:7ff.). Even the ideas of the friends that operate within the framework of anthropological ideology serve consequently only to support their explanatory scheme that places the suffering of Job within a rigid system of retribution. In Job 25:1–6 (cf. already 11:7–12), there is in addition the indication of the distance between the creator and the creature, where the human being is designated as a maggot and a worm. When YHWH turns to Job and answers with words in the God speeches (Job 38:1–42:6), he indeed speaks comprehensively of his might and power as the creator.[182] However, in these speeches he does not answer with a word about humanity, much less a word about Job; rather, he lapses into the style of a divine hymn of self-praise.[183] Job's friends as well as Job himself are not vindicated by the majestic God. Not everything, which God has created and supports, revolves only around humanity. And the human question of meaning is not the only question that demands unconditionally an answer.[184] Job accepts this, even though his own questions were not directly answered (Job 42:1–6). When YHWH then restores Job and gives him new children[185] and new wealth, greater than before (Job 42:10ff.), it is not for the reason that the pious Job must receive now his just reward,[186] since YHWH's approval of Job precedes his restoration (Job 42:7). Job has spoken directly to God, not just about him, something that, at the same time, distinguishes him from the friends and their arguments.

g. Qoheleth[187]

It is striking that, proportionately speaking, the Book of Qoheleth takes up the general topic of "human beings" within its twelve chapters more often than the thirty-one chapters of the Book of Proverbs do. In the critical disputation that Qoheleth pursues with the wisdom tradition, sapiential thinking, and the ideal of life, he asks what profit there may be to human beings in the final analysis from all their effort (Qoh. 1:3; 3:10f.) and the striving of their thoughts (Qoh. 2:22). Qoheleth wished to drink wine, while still retaining his understanding (לב = *lēb*;[188] 2:1, 10), which he himself highly valued (Qoh. 1:16; and 9:1), until he might see what was good for the children of humanity to do during the appointed period of their lives (Qoh. 2:3). Qoheleth often says to himself something "in his heart," that is, his capacity to think and reason.[189] This idiom means that he considers, reflects on, and thinks about both life and the world (Qoh. 1:16; 2:15; and 3:17f.) and in doing so, often finds for himself no rest at night (Qoh. 2:23). While he despairs in his thoughts and "in his heart" (Qoh. 2:20), his heart also remains open to the feeling of joy (Qoh. 5:19). He reaches the conclusion: "All is absurd and a chasing after wind. There is no gain under the sun" (Qoh. 2:11).[190] Also the sapiential knowledge of God has its limits (Qoh. 8:16f.). Following the parody of the king in Qoh. 1:2–2:4, the sage speaks once again[191] and concludes that the one who comes after the king can only do what already and always has been done (Qoh. 2:12). One must leave behind to someone else the things over which one has labored during one's life (Qoh. 2:18–21; cf. 2:26). If the heir can be a wise person as well as a fool, while the testator is a person who toils and then must leave everything to another who has not labored at all for what is left, what therefore is the purpose of it all? The power of human disposition is limited (Qoh. 2:24; and 3:13), for it is God who gives to a person who pleases him wisdom, knowledge, and joy (Qoh. 2:26). Furthermore, for Qoheleth the correct time is not known to humans. This means, especially, that they neither know the time of birth and the time of death, nor do they have any control over them (Qoh. 3:2). Additional matters of human life and behavior are assessed under the same categories and lead to similar conclusions (Qoh. 3:1–9; cf. 8:6–9; and 9:12). However, the human being is so constructed that he or she is not simply resigned to whatever happens but rather must and wants to inquire concerning the future. Even so, this desire to know the future does not make accessible to humans any meaning in life (Qoh. 3:10f.; cf. 11:1–8). Rather, people are to enjoy life to the extent that they can, which means enjoying eating, drinking, and other material things, and also to take pleasure in one's wife whom one loves.[192] The extent to which humans experience joy from what they create (Qoh. 3:22) is what remains to them. What they are to enjoy to the full (Qoh. 3:13; 5:17–19; 7:14; 8:15; 9:7–9; and 11:9f.)[193] is that which is their only earthly, limited "portion" (חלק = ḥēleq; Qoh. 2:10; 3:22; 5:17f.; and 9:9).[194] The disillusioning recognition about humans declares that they have no special place, but rather are like cattle (Qoh. 3:18f.), and this means that they are both mortal even though they each are given the same רוח = rûaḥ ("spirit") (Qoh. 3:19; cf. 12:7 as an addition; then Gen. 6:17 P; and Ps. 104:29). That this spirit (רוח = rûaḥ) of humans at their death "ascends upward" is not at all certain (Qoh. 3:21), even though one could express this because of the hellenistically influenced way of thinking at the time.[195] With respect to human mechanisms of oppression, the dead, or, even more fortunate, the ones who are not yet born, are better off than the living (Qoh. 4:1–3). Indeed, Qoheleth knows also that it is not good for a person to be alone (cf. Gen. 2:18), for two are better than one so that one may help the other when he or she falls. Or they can warm and support each other (Qoh. 4:9–12). However, this partner can at the same time become his or her opponent. And all who live in a great crowd become a mass of people easily influenced, whose public opinion, what is more, is not resolute (Qoh. 4:13–16). Religious practice is also among the areas that Qoheleth mentions, and in his critical opinion, it is typically a sphere of activity for fools (Qoh. 4:17–5:6). Riches have no great worth, since a person comes into the world naked and departs the world naked (Qoh. 5:10–19; esp. vv. 14f.). If a person always yearns for more and more, this becomes a great burden weighing upon him or her (Qoh. 6:1ff.). Qoheleth, as did Job, also considers it better to have been an aborted birth than to have (even a long) life with numerous descendants. Longevity and many descendants was one of the ideals of life in the Old Testament (Qoh. 6:3f.). It has certainly been determined what humanity is, namely, mortal, so that humans cannot argue with death which is stronger than they are (Qoh. 6:10).[196] Many words do not bring any advantage to humans; no one knows what ultimately is good for him or her; no one can say to a person what shall be after him or her (cf. Qoh. 7:14). What value does all wise counsel have (Qoh. 6:11f.; cf. 7:23f.; and 10:1, 14), especially when a sage, faced with the oppression from one who unfortunately has the power over him or her to do evil (Qoh. 8:9), cannot make a clear judgment (Qoh. 7:7), and when the counsel of a poor sage is despised (Qoh. 9:13–16)? Since there is neither a clear connection between deed and result (Qoh. 8:10–14) nor an equalization or retribution in the future life (Qoh. 9:1–10), it is correct to maintain a position of moderation between the righteous and the wicked (Qoh. 7:15–18).[197] We have already noted that Qoheleth expressed very negative views about old age (Qoh. 11:9–12:7) in rather impressive literary images. As also noted previously, it is probably no accident that these views occur at the end of the book to form the conclusion.[198] Although "the human person is on the way to his or her eternal home" (Qoh. 12:5), life is still worth living "before the silver cord is torn, the golden bowl is shattered, the pitcher at the well is smashed, and the wheel is broken in the well" (Qoh. 12:6).[199] The verse (v. 7) that comes close to defining death in anthropological terms ("the dust returns to earth, the spirit returns to God") is probably an addition, even though the characterization is correct according to the Old Testament. Qoheleth was in fact a sage, as the epilogue records, and he wrote correctly well-formulated words (Qoh. 12:10). He demonstrated to human beings their limits ("God is in heaven and you are on the earth," Qoh. 5:1) as well as those of his own self-realization and quest to come to a comprehensive understanding of the world. Qoheleth makes clear that the human person is not allowed to secure his or her existence, while the shock of finitude is consciously provoked even as the limits of the human ability to do and to plan are also effectively recalled. The voice of Qoheleth concerning the view of humanity has an important part in the choir of Old Testament witnesses,[200] even though it is not altogether typical for the Old Testament sentiment of life.

h. Basic Structures Held in Common

Leaving aside the question of any dependence on the portrait of humanity in the ancient Near East, what do the Old Testament witnesses with their differently nuanced images of humanity hold in common and what can count as the fundamental structures[201] of the Old Testament witness about human nature?[202] Overall, the Old Testament answer is the basic dependence (עבד = *'ebed;* "slave or servant") of the human creature upon his or her divine creator, a view that includes human ephemerality. "The texts transmitted in the Old Testament desire to know humans overall as nothing other than standing before the 'face' of their God."[203] Then one should mention the dialogical responsibility before God, that is, human obligation (for Qoheleth this is hardly a theme). God's claim (cf. the law that has only *one* God as the basic authority behind it and not also a king) and approval[204] ("a human being does not live by bread alone, but rather by all that proceeds out of the mouth of God," Deut. 8:3)[205] are of fundamental significance for humanity. Where these have disappeared (Job; Qoheleth), humanity enters into a crisis of existence that becomes a crisis of faith. "Hearing" (Deut. 6:4) what is said by God (Micah. 6:8) is, for the Old Testament person, an important manner of behaving that corresponds appropriately to his or her humanity.[206] That the king has a higher human quality than the normal person is a concept not found in the Old Testament (Pss. 89:48f.; and 144:4). Consequently the Old Testament does not tell of a special, even primeval act of divine creation of the king.[207] Human beings have God as their antithesis,[208] are tied into their contemporary generation, and are not individuals in and for themselves but rather are formed for community, being destined to exist with others as they are with God.[209] More clearly than may be discovered in the ancient Near Eastern environment of Israel, the Old Testament person was tied into the community of his or her family, tribe, and nation. The greater significance of history for Old Testament faith entered into this as well.

Birth as the gift of life, and death as a boundary set forth by God, both serve as indications of divine sovereignty, for they each come from the hand of God. Therefore life is ethically as well as temporally removed from human control. Even Job and Qoheleth will not entertain the possibility of suicide. According to the witness of the narrative literature of the Old Testament as well as the works of the prophets and many of the psalms, humans are taken by their God into a history which transmits to them a stability, an orientation, and a future direction, a history in which they are to find success. Life is predominantly seen not as a stringing together of more or less meaningful or meaningless accidents but rather as divine guidance and providence which, while not demonstrable, nevertheless, is believed. Thus the whole of the Old Testament is to be seen in this way, especially if one places greater emphasis on the narratives, the Book of Proverbs, the Song of Songs, and many psalms, and not chiefly on the books of Job and Qoheleth. There is a predominantly life-affirming attitude toward existence that is endemic to the Old Testament human being.[210] The personal names as well as names of thanks and confession make this rather clear.[211] In the obligation demanded of the Old Testament person who belonged to the chosen people, it was clear that he or she was still a guilty person,[212] a third characteristic that may be determined in addition to dependence and responsibility. In spite of this guiltiness ("before you no one living is righteous": Ps. 143:2), which especially the prophets stress (however, see, e.g., also the words of curse in Deuteronomy 27f.), there is still security for this dependent and guilty person, as the psalms, for example, make clear in an exemplary fashion. There is also hope,[213] indeed hope in and through God upon whom one is dependent, before whom one is and becomes guilty (J; Deuteronomistic History), and who one perhaps at one time did not understand (Job; Psalm 73).[214] The God of Israel desires to enter into community with humans. For that end he has chosen his people. What he does for Israel stands as an example of his will and way with humanity in general.

11.5 The Language of Humans

The frequent sapiential observations regarding the theme of language, and the Old Testament assessment of understanding, speaking, and hearing as a whole,[215] lead to the question concerning the view and value of human speech as one of the fundamental features of human nature. In regard to the Old Testament, this subject may be discussed to a large extent only in connection with many problems as well as characteristic features of Hebrew.[216] In addition, one must be mindful that we have before us only a relatively small slice of language that is stamped especially with the peculiar nature of religious discourse, and even this occurs only in written form. Moreover, from the evidence of other Northwest Semitic languages, extrabiblical occurrences of Hebrew, and the Qumran texts, it is now perfectly clear that "biblical" Hebrew is not simply a later work of art; it is quite comparable to the spoken language of the pre-Christian era and, above all, incorporates within itself its own linguistic world.[217]

How highly Old Testament Israel thought of language and of the human capacity for speech is shown already in Gen. 2:19f. (J) where the human person is distinguished from the rest of creation through the ability to speak and where the naming of the animals by the human creature completes the creation of the animal world. At the same time, naming is a sovereign act that points to the human being as the lord of the animal world. Whoever gives a name or was in a position to alter it was the superior who exercised sovereignty. The renaming of Jewish kings by foreign rulers makes this very clear (2 Kings 23:34; 24:17).

The manner in which language could work in a negative way is shown in Genesis 3. The "calling" of God, including his acts of naming in creation (Gen. 1:5, 8, 10), makes it clear that names were not "sound and smoke, the befogging glow of the heavens," but rather that the *nomen est omen*.[218] Further, the numerous Old Testament folk etymologies, which are attempted in the explanations of biblical place-names and especially personal names, do not allow either the modern reader or even theologians to put together a similar etymological theology. Whoever wished to become something at the royal court must be eloquent (1 Sam. 16:18). Then there is the tragic fact that humans and nations could not live in concert with each other, since they speak different languages, a reality that is understandable only in turns of the punishment of YHWH (Gen. 11:7, 9).[219] One perceives already in ancient Israel something of the view that language also sets forth a paradigm for understanding the world. We say today that language, as a virtual *langue* with its available code, influences both the view of social reality, thinking and speaking and the faith of the person who manipulates these areas in concrete linguistic usage as *parole*.

The Hebrew that comprises by far the greatest part of the Old Testament[220] is the so-called biblical Hebrew or, to avoid more precise differentiations, so-called old Hebrew. This Hebrew is different from the middle Hebrew of rabbinic writings and the new or modern Hebrew *Ivrit*. However, even old Hebrew still embraces a duration of a good eight hundred to a thousand years, from the Hebrew of the Song of Deborah (Judges 5) to that of Qoheleth and the Book of Daniel. In other words, old Hebrew includes the periods ranging from the social features of early Israel before state formation to the hellenistically influenced, cultured class of Jews in the third and second centuries before the common era, all having their respective situations of communication. Since this development and history[221] of the Hebrew language is concealed, even if not fully, by the common written language of the Old Testament, we can only slightly comprehend all of this.[222] However, it is not purely accidental when, for example, YHWH's act of liberation in the exodus is variously described as his military action, or as his leading out of or bringing up from Egypt, or as his redeeming and setting free from Egypt. And it is not simply a chance matter when this act is hymnically confessed and actualized in narrative by a Judean or by a Northern Israelite, or when certain terms are used, such as the word ברית = *běrît* ("covenant"), and provided particular emphases.[223]

The designation "Hebrew" does not occur in the Old Testament; rather, it appears for the first time in the Prologue of Sirach and then later in rabbinic usage. When the Old Testament speaks of the "language of Canaan" (Isa. 19:18) or of יהודית = *yěhûdît* (Judahite) (2 Kings 18:26), it appropriately designates with this expression the language of Israel/Judah as a Northwest Semitic dialect that stands close to other languages of the neighbors of Old Testament Israel, for example, the Moabite and Ugaritic languages. This is the language that is first spoken by Israel probably after its settlement in Canaan and its contact with the earlier Canaanite population.[224] Consequently, Hebrew was not a special "holy" language of the people of YHWH honored by the revelation of the one true God.[225] As a linguistic system with its "common structure of elements of expression and conception,"[226] this Hebrew naturally has its own particular characteristics. However, these are not determined in such a way that Hebrew was especially or perhaps even exclusively in a position to bear witness to God's revelation to and in Israel.[227] Hebrew shares many of its characteristics with other Semitic languages (and a good deal also with Egyptian), so that our modern language of faith must not necessarily be Hebraized in order to express correctly in language what is meant in the Bible. Here it is much better, even necessary, to set forth an interpreting translation too in our contemporary languages. Language is not linguistically practical enough to grasp reality itself; rather, it conveys its portrayal of reality as the comprehension, classification, and formation of the world of experience. Language does not have a direct relationship to this reality; rather, it expresses the system of meaning and activity of the society to which it is bound. In addition, this means for the Old Testament that one is to search after the special character of religious language.[228]

It is unclear which language or which dialect the Israelites (in their different groups) spoke prior to their immigration to Canaan. It may have been an old Aramaic dialect (Deut. 26:5), especially since many synonymns are found in Hebrew that appear to have belonged to two originally different dialects (cf., e.g., דבר = *dābār* and מלה = *millâ* for "word"; and ארח = *'ōraḥ* and דרך = *derek* for "way").[229] Because of the spread of so-called royal Aramaic as the common language for everyday speech, it became necessary for the postexilic community to utilize interpreters or Aramaic translations (Targumim) when Hebrew was used, for instance, in the readings during worship.[230] In 2 Kings 18:26 there is evidence that Aramaic is already known as early as 700 B.C.E. During the period of the persecution under Antiochus IV Epiphanes (175–164 B.C.E.), when the final form and many parts of the Book of Daniel originated, the use of Hebrew, moreover, signified a *status confessionis,* an act of loyalty to holy tradition. This means that chaps. 1 and 8–12 of the Book of Daniel, which frame now the older portion of the Book of Daniel (chaps. 2–7) composed in Aramaic, are consciously written once again in Hebrew, being displayed here in a sense as a "holy" language. Second Kings 18:26, 28 (par.) among others, with its references to יהודית = *yěhûdît* (i.e., the language of Judah), and the variants of pronunciation, סבלת/שבלת = *sibbōlet/šibbōlet* (Judg. 12:6), allow one to recognize that there were still local dialects within Old Testament Hebrew. The finds at Qumran (second century B.C.E. to first century B.C.E.) have shown that Hebrew at the time was pronounced differently in many regions, being far more varied than the considerably later Masoretic pointing system now makes evident to us. For the even earlier time, for instance, of an Isaiah, there was probably also a similar variety of pronunciations, and this would have been true even for the pronunciation of individual consonants, not just for the words with a possible shifting of accents.

Hebrew[231] has only two genders (masculine and feminine), and, in addition, it has singular, plural, and dual numbers. Especially significant is a three-radical root that constructs, with prefixes, infixes, and suffixes or preformatives and afformatives, individual parts of speech and grammatical forms that extend the root's meaning into different areas. Naturally, Hebrew also has primitive nouns, as, for example, אַב = *'āb* ("father"). Case endings no longer exist, and a genitive relationship is expressed by the position of words (*casus constructus*). Further, Hebrew has only a few abstract nouns, and these are found more frequently in later and poetic texts than in prose ones. Where they appear, they are often connected with an active verb: "Loss will come over him" (Prov. 28:22); "Sorrow and sighing shall flee away" (Isa. 35:10); "who drinks unrighteousness like water" (Job 15:16); and "Righteousness dwells in it [= the city of Jerusalem]" (Isa. 1:21). Thus abstractions are brought to life.[232] By contrast, some subjective terms also are objectified. מוּסָר = *mûsār* means both "chastisement" and the activity of "discipline" and may even stand for insight or wisdom.[233] "Joy" can designate the sensation as well as the subject of joy (Isa. 60:15); פַּחַד = *paḥad* is fear as well as what one fears (Ps. 31:12; and Prov. 1:26f.). The Old Testament person has no particular word for "thinking." Instead, he or she spoke of "speaking in the heart" (= in the mind)[234] or "being bent on something" (חָשַׁב = *ḥāšab*). Hebrew, which was lacking in descriptive words, did not have many adjectives. Thus it is always pointed out that the rather picturesque Psalm 23 does not contain a single adjective in its Hebrew text, while the German (and English) translation usually endeavors to have perhaps as many as five adjectives (green, fresh, right, dark, full). Conjunctions likewise are not very frequent in Hebrew, and the ones that occur must be employed to cover a broad range of meanings (cf. כִּי = *kî*, "because, if, when"; or אֲשֶׁר = *'ăšer*, "who, which, what"). For that reason, parataxis outweighed hypotaxis. The most frequently found part of speech in the Old Testament is the verb, while in modern German and English the noun is. The verb in the Old Testament therefore has been designated as the "prince of the clause" (K. H. Miskotte), and one has spoken of the "triumph of the verbal clause,"[235] that is, the main clause. It is in a conspicuous place at the beginning of the clause that the verb by rule regularly stands. If the subject stands at the beginning in a so-called inversion, then it is especially emphasized. The predicate and the fulfillment of the action coincide (יהוה מָלָךְ = *yahweh mālak;* "YHWH has become king").[236] In this connection, a sentence can consist of only a single Hebrew verbal form. In the series of the imperfect consecutives present in the framework of Old Testament narratives, the impetus is shown to be on movement, on the narrative as action, and not on the requiescence of reflection, of pauses, or of description that requires instead the formation of nominal sentences. Hebrew "tenses," of which there are perhaps only two, or more precisely at least four,[237] show in the roles of emphasis or of aspects that are connected with their use another relationship to time than we perhaps have,[238] and the variable counteraction of the conjugations underlines this further. These roles of emphasis and of aspects include the use of "before" and "after" and of "past" and "future" that differ from our own use. For the description of a condition, one selected either the nominal sentence or the participial form of the verb. Within narratives, these do not continue the action; rather, they expound, modify, or develop. The so-called imperfect (prefix conjugation) expresses a movement or designates both an action that is in progress or a condition that is complete. However, the imperfect can do all of this in the past, present, or future according to the slant of the text, its structure, and its temporal sequence. In addition, the imperfect stands in relationship to the other actions or circumstances that are expressed or imagined. Without ו $= w$ in its simple, isolated form, the imperfect can be translated as present, as future, and as a wish.[239] The so-called perfect (suffix conjugation) is best translated by a present or a perfect in German and English when it stands in narrative sentences without a ו $= w$ and refers to a completed action or a continuing condition. The temporal sphere of the verb is determined more precisely by its context. The perfect stands there unrelated, establishing, and independent. In speeches with ו $= w$, it designates the future, consequences, or a demand, or else a continuing, repeated event in the past.[240] In addition to every kind of conjugation, the place of the verb (first position or not) is of significance for the verb's function in the sentence.[241] Also significant are syndesis and asyndesis, recognizable by the presence of a ו $= w$ in its various functions before a verb.[242] The verb in its conjugations in Hebrew is used consequently rather differently from its use in German or English.

In regard to nouns, it is important that the grammatical genders (masculine and feminine) not only have to do with male and female, that is, sexual distinctions, but also, for example, with the collective (masculine: "song" in general) and the singular (feminine: "a [certain] song") noun. The plural noun finds use also as a so-called abstract plural (e.g., זקנים $= z\check{e}qun\hat{i}m$; "old age") or as a so-called plural of amplification in order to express the intensification of the meaning of a word (e.g., מסתרים $= mist\bar{a}r\hat{i}m$, "thorough hiding place"; so also אלהים $= $ '$\check{e}l\bar{o}h\hat{i}m$, "God"?).[243]

The (still not yet sufficiently researched) semantics of Hebrew[244] are not identical with those of German or other Western languages. However, they are made more and more accessible especially by the works in *THAT* and *ThWAT*. One asks no longer about individual words but rather about word fields, the semantic reference system of the word in question, its functions in texts, and what the word brings to the text and how it is used there. For the Hebrews, plants were probably not animated, while stars and other things, by contrast, were (Pss. 114:3–6; 148).[245] If we translate the Hebrew עלמה = 'almâ as "virgin" (perhaps on account of the taking up of Isa. 7:14 by Matt. 1:23) and think of this as a chaste virgin, then we would have to overlook the fact that Hebrew has a word for virgin, בתולה = bĕtûlâ.[246] In addition, in the linguistic usage of the day "virgin" was a title of dignity that one assigned, for example, to a goddess such as the Ugaritic Anat, although there was no possible doubt about the sexual behavior of this mother of several children.[247] The word "son" was used (as, e.g., Gen. 4:17, 25f.; Exod. 1:16; etc.) to designate not only one's physical male offspring[248] but also the grandson (Gen. 31:28; etc.), the relationship of the teacher to the pupil (Isa. 19:11; 1 Sam. 3:6; Prov. 1:8, 10; 2:1; 19:27; etc.), another close affiliation and intimate relationship (Ezra 4:1; 6:20; Qoh. 10:17; Ezek. 40:46; etc.), and a title of dignity (1 Kings 22:26; Micah 1:16; Ps. 2:7; Exod. 4:23; Hos. 11:1; etc.).[249] If we always translate צדק/צדקה = ṣdq/ṣdqh with the word "righteousness" and think of it as having to do with punishment or retributive justice, then much of what comes from the Old Testament (and New Testament) witness will not be understood.[250] The verb שפט = špṭ conducts itself in the same way, for it means not only "to be right" but also "to set right, to help someone get his or her due." The verb היה = hāyyâ means "to be" as well as "to become, to happen."[251] Does it make any difference whether רשע = rēša' is rendered "godless," "transgressor," "sinner," or "rightly condemned," or whether all of these are connected? עון = 'āwôn comprises both guilt and punishment, while צדקה = ṣedāqâ means loyalty to the community in terms of behavior as well as its result. What does it mean for the interpretation of biblical texts that the Israelite of that time had no terms for historical truth and intellectual error or doubt?[252]

Some of "Hebrew thinking," especially about anthropology, is disclosed when one gives attention to the characteristics of the Hebrew language. If the theologian consequently has to be an interpreter, an intepreter primarily of biblical texts and the biblical message, it is necessary for him or her to be familiar with certain features of the Hebrew language and also of Hebrew thought in order to be able to translate appropriately the meaning of biblical texts, not just to recite or to repeat them.[253] One's own linguistic world is naturally a different one from that of the Old Testament, a fact that is to be considered and overcome and not covered up and denied.

The "word" is therefore very highly valued in the Old Testament.[254] For example, Genesis 1 makes clear that it is an active word, a language event that is an action. When the New Testament says in John 1:14 that the Word became flesh, then this is understandable from its Old Testament background.[255] The New Testament has actually been able to express its message largely in the language of the Old Testament, as, for example, the words righteousness of God, faith, sin, forgiveness, grace, and others, and their usage within the biblical texts point out.

11.6 Pain and Fortune

Encountering pain was and is a part of human existence. How did Old Testament human beings experience pain and fortune? How have they seen themselves in regard to sorrow?[256]

Here there is less to do with the general, creaturely pain that, for example, shepherds experience in the heat of the day or in the cold of the night (Gen. 31:40)[257] or that human beings experience from the failure of a rich harvest (Joel 1:17; Jeremiah 14; etc.). Different even is the pain of the parents over the death of their children (Gen. 37:35; 2 Sam. 19:1; 21:10; and 2 Kings 4:27) or of women over their lack of children (1 Samuel 1; Sarah, Rebecca, and Rachel), or over the death of beloved humans overall (2 Samuel 1; and 2 Kings 4:27), or concerning one's own impending death (Psalms 39; 88; Job 14; Qoh. 3:19ff.; 9:12; 11:8; and 12:7). Naturally, one suffers frequently from illnesses (Lev. 26:16; 2 Sam. 4:4; 24:15; 1 Kings 8:37; Psalms 38; 41; 88; 91:3, 6; etc.; cf. Job 2:4f.)[258] that afflict both body and soul in like manner (Prov. 18:14), and "the social situation of the sick was deplorable in the Old Testament period."[259] It is, however, YHWH who here strikes and tears; yet he also is the one who heals and binds up (Job 5:18; cf. Hos. 6:1f.; and Deut. 32:39). The Old Testament speaks less about natural human suffering than of the pain that humans receive from other humans. One suffers under tyrannical kings (Jeremiah 22 and Ezekiel 34). Enemies and war bring about pain (Josh. 6:21; Judg. 1:7; 1 Sam. 11:2; 2 Sam. 24:13ff.; 2 Kings 6:28ff.; 8:12; 25:7; Amos 1:3–2:3; Ps. 137:9; etc.).[260] Slavery is a painful fate (Joseph; Jer. 48:7; Joel 4:6; and Amos 1:6), as is corvée labor in servitude (Exod. 1:13f.). When the Old Testament wisdom literature (Proverbs), the presentation of the social law, and prophetic social criticism speak up for the poor, then one is already familiar with the pain associated with certain societal structures prior to having been called to act in ways that will fundamentally alter these structures. The loss of property brought pain (Amos 2:6; Micah 2:2; Isa. 5:8; Job 1:13–20; and Neh. 5:1–5). The psalms reveal the pain of the innocent offering a lament (Psalms 7 and 35) who suffer because of their enemies,[261] whoever they were or however they may have been understood.

One also was familiar with the pain of self-blame (Psalm 32; David) and spoke of "coming to nothing," "going astray," and setbacks,[262] that is, of failures and the resulting disappointments and suffering. The prophets seek to elucidate in a limited way to the nation their painful existence through their own suffering (Isa. 1:5f.; 9:12; Jer. 4:18; 7:13; etc.).[263] Pain consequently was primarily expressed in the Old Testament as pain that resulted from someone or from something (Judg. 16:21; 2 Sam. 3:16 as concrete examples; Amos 2:6; and 5:7, 12 in prophetic criticism). It is not explained as resulting from the natural world, from human imperfection, or as a form of human existence in general. There is less about *the* pain of human beings than about the fact that *they* suffer. Israel suffers in living, not as a condition of being alive.[264] It suffers within concrete occurrences, both physically and psychologically. Since the Old Testament does not know other gods for Israel besides YHWH and especially does not want to know them, it also relatively seldom speaks of demons.[265] Thus, evil powers or particular gods only very rarely are mentioned as the ones who cause pain, that is, especially illnesses, in contrast, for example, to the Mesopotamian religions[266] or to Egypt[267] (Pss. 59:7, 15; 91:5f.; Job 18:11–15; and 33:19ff.). These powers, who stand under YHWH (Ps. 78:49), include the "destroyer" (Exod. 12:23; cf. 2 Sam. 24:16), the evil spirit (1 Sam. 16:14ff.: music works against it in a healing way, 1 Kings 22:21), and the Satan (Job 1).

Thus the Old Testament by reason of its monotheism necessarily comes to the declaration[268] that distress comes from YHWH,[269] that he also brings about evil (1 Sam. 2:6f.; 16:13f.; 2 Kings 6:33; Isa. 45:7; Amos 3:6; Job 1:21b; 2:10; Qoh. 7:13f.; and 2 Chron. 25:8), that pain has something to do with him, and that it in some way represents him. This conviction of faith extends through narrative literature, prophecy, the psalms (cf. only Psalms 22; 44; 74; and 89), the confessions of Jeremiah that are very similar to them, and the wisdom literature. Most declarations of confession that occur here are not efforts to express a general explanation of the world and interpretation. It cannot be maintained on the basis of the textual evidence[270] that in distress it is only the absence of the so-called "personal God" that is experienced.[271] YHWH, of course, is God (Isa. 45:3ff. in the context of Isa. 45:7), and no one can ask him what he is doing or why he does something (2 Sam. 16:10; Job 9:12). Through this firm association of distress and God and of the beautiful and the fearful, both of which issue forth from the hand of God,[272] the Old Testament protects its faith from dichotomizing its image of God and from the collapse of piety and trust, belief and experience, and God and reality.

This does not exclude but rather includes the fact that one ever again seeks to explain pain as coming from God. This leads one to ask then what God wishes to say about suffering and what he wants to bring about. The most frequently given answer (from Gen. 3:16ff. through the prophets to 2 Chron. 26:19 as well as in the connection between deed and result[273] which is an especially typical form) is expressed in an unequivocal as well as troubling form: pain is the punishment of God (cf., e.g., Jer. 32:19; Job 34:11; Ps. 68:12; and many additional psalms), and this is true for the individual as well as for the people (cf. Deuteronomy 28). This explanation should and would probably lead also to confession and repentance, and it also is connected with the Old Testament conception of wholeness according to which evil creates a sphere that strikes back at the perpetrator of evil. While the explanation that pain was to serve the process of purification is seldom mentioned, it is found (besides in the Joseph Story and in Isa. 1:25 and Jer. 6:29) especially in texts of the exilic and postexilic periods that look (back) at the pain that afflicts or afflicted the nation in and during the exile (Isa. 48:10; Jer. 31:15; Micah 4:10; Ps. 66:10–12; and Lamentations). Deuteronomistic texts mention pain as a testing of the people (Deut. 8:2; and Judg. 3:4), while other texts speak of pain as a testing of the individual (Genesis 22; and Job 1–2). The Old Testament often speaks of pain as an educational activity of YHWH (cf. Isa. 43:24) in function and in effect, while the question concerning the "Why?" of suffering is stronger than the "What for?"[274]

Deuteronomistic texts speak of the vicarious suffering of an individual on behalf of or in solidarity with others by referring to Moses (Exod. 32:32; 34:9; Deut. 3:24f.; and 9:25–29). Here belongs also the suffering of Jeremiah that is expressed not only in his confessions[275] but also in both his destiny in general (cf. Jeremiah 16) and in the laments that otherwise come from his mouth.[276] Further, one should point to Ezekiel (Ezekiel 12; 24) as well as to the suffering of the Servant of God (Isa. 50:4–9; 52:13–53:12).[277] For two reasons the last-mentioned text assumes a special position within the Old Testament witness to pain. On the one hand, this text stresses that in pain there is the nearness of God, not his remoteness. On the other hand, suffering is explained as a guilt offering for the many (Isa. 53:10; אשם = *'āšām*).

From all of this it follows that the devout persons of the Old Testament suffer and can suffer because of God himself. This is true of Samuel (1 Samuel 8) as well as of Job, Moses (Exod. 14:11–15; 15:24ff.; 16:2ff.; 17:2f.; Num. 11:11ff.; 12; 14; and Deuteronomy 9), Hosea (Hos. 9:7–9), and Jeremiah. A communal lament cries out: "It is because of you that we are being killed" (Ps. 44:18–23). Not everything can be explained in this way even as God himself is not understandable in every way (Jer. 31:29; Ezek. 18:2; Lamentations; Job; Psalm 73; Isaiah 53; and 55:6ff.). Pain also continues to be mysterious, for it has to do with God, who himself continues to be mysterious.

Thus, numerous individuals experienced pain, as narrative texts of the Old Testament from every period demonstrate. Each person would experience his or her pain, and no other person would stand in that person's place (Prov. 14:10). Laments are so constructed[278] that individual worshipers or even the people as a lamenting community could be found time after time in these texts. In order to call forth more strongly for YHWH's helping intervention and to depict oneself even more clearly as the one who expects divine help in and from pain, the worshiper described himself or herself as the suffering *righteous person* (so especially in Psalms 7; 18; 35; 38; and 69).[279] Then there is the pain of the individuals that results from YHWH's setting them apart and commissioning for divine service,[280] including Moses (e.g., Exod. 32:30–33), Elijah (1 Kings 19), Micaiah ben Imlah (1 Kings 22), Amos (Amos 7:10ff.), Isaiah (Isa. 28:10, 13), Jeremiah (e.g., Jeremiah 20; 37–39; and 43; then in his confessions), and the Servant of God in Deutero-Isaiah. Here the pain of the messenger of God symbolizes the resistance of the hearers to the message. Pain during eschatological persecution is known in the apocalyptic texts (Isa. 26:7–19; Daniel 1; 3; 6; and 11:33f.). The people experience pain in Egypt (Exodus 1; 3:7; and 6:5f.), and in another form also during their wandering through the wilderness (Exodus 15ff.). Above all, however, it is proclaimed to the people (from Amos to Ezekiel) that they suffer on account of their sins and guilt and will suffer even more. The Deuteronomistic History also writes the history of Israel from this point of view.[281] "The failure of the people of God is a theme of the Old Testament to the same extent that their election is."[282] Here belong also the Deuteronomistic evaluations of illness (Deut. 28:21–35, 58–61) as well as the (Deuteronomistic) statement about YHWH as the physician of his people (Exod. 15:26).[283] Consequently, it is no wonder that the events around 587/586 B.C.E. and then the reality and experience of the exile provoke reflection over suffering (Isa. 40:2; Lamentations; Ezekiel 16; 18; and 23; the *people* as the Servant of God in Deutero-Isaiah), and cause people to question the relationship between former guilt and present pain (Jer. 31:29; Ezek. 18:2; then Ezra 9:14f.; Neh. 1:6f.; 9; Lam. 5:7; later: Daniel 9 and Psalm 106). That one did not simply accept the fact that the innocent must also suffer along with the guilty is shown in 2 Sam. 24:17 and the later text of Gen. 18:22ff.

Finally, the Old Testament also knows something of the suffering of God,[284] from his suffering among the people as well as his commiseration with them. This begins in the testimony of Hosea (Hos. 2:25; 4:6; 5:15; 6:4; and 11:8) and continues through Jeremiah[285] (Jer. 4:19–22; 8:18–23; 10:19–22; 13:17; 14:17f.; 23:9ff.; and 31:20; cf. Micah 6:3), 1 Sam. 8:7 (Deuteronomy), Isa. 63:10, to Jonah 4:11.

The Old Testament worshiper found comfort[286] in pain through the priestly promise of salvation in the cultus[287] ("You have answered me": Ps. 22:22; cf. Ps. 3:5; 1 Sam. 1:17; Lam. 3:57; Isa. 43:1; and other passages in Deutero-Isaiah). Then there is the looking and waiting for the future fate of the transgressor as well as for the time when one hopes for both an answer and help (Psalm 73; Job 20:15ff.; also Ps. 62:4). One takes comfort in the fact that it will not be better for others (Ezek. 16:54; 31:16; and 32:31), and one hopes also for a turn of events that God will bring about (Isa. 25:8). One seldom finds in the Old Testament the belief that community with God and the nearness of God occurred in the experience of pain until it was turned aside (Ps. 73:23: "Nevertheless, I am continuing with you"; cf. Job 1–2; 42:7ff.). And God's presence and activity in the fortune of the suffering, unsightly servant of God (Isa. 53:1ff.) was neither recognized nor assumed but rather must be first revealed by God himself (Isa. 52:13ff.; and 53:10bff.). These statements about the abiding community of God were prepared or accompanied perhaps through assurances as "Your grace is better than life" (Ps. 63:4) or "YHWH is my portion" (Ps. 16:5). The hope for "translation" (לקח = *lāqaḥ*) is affirmed neither in Ps. 49:16 nor in Ps. 73:24; rather, both cases have to do with an earthly deliverance from the sphere of death, that is, a preservation from dying.[288] The comforting prospect of a possible future life continued for a long time to be precluded from the view of the Old Testament. Job and Qoheleth both knew nothing about this, and Qoheleth even expressly disputed it (Qoh. 3:21).[289] Elsewhere, however, a clearly developing, eschatological hope[290] endeavors in the postexilic period to solve earthly problems, to answer the question of theodicy, and also to provide comfort in earthly pain (Isaiah 35; 61:1ff.; and Mal. 3:16ff.).

Prayer[291] had an important function in seeking to bring about the cessation of pain and to provide comfort. Among the prayers it is naturally the lament (cf. Ps. 102:1) that presents us with the most commonly occurring genre in the Psalter that addresses this concern, although it does not always indicate that it has found an answer. Exodus 3:7; 6:5f.; and Deut. 26:7 mention paradigmatically this cry of lament to YHWH, a cry that here is bound up with the situation, so important to the faith, of the people in Egypt and their subsequent rescue. Spoken by either an individual or the community, the lament is addressed to God from whom earlier salvation has been received and from whom calamity is presently experienced. And the psalmist is not inhibited in using language that challenges God (Ps. 22:2; and 63:19bff.). Here the questions concerning "why"[292] or "for what purpose" as well as "how long" have their place.[293] Not being able to answer these questions, the psalmist directs them to God, although in these prayers and therefore in the personal discourse of the worshiper with God the efforts to explain pain were continually undertaken.[294] One regards oneself as a sufferer positioned before God himself, a sufferer who is attacked by him and yet still trusts him at the same time so that expressions of trust are blended into the laments, and trust is reinvigorated by the desired review of earlier activity of divine salvation. Consequently, it is prayer where reflection about pain appears rather frequently. In this regard, then, the praying, lamenting language inquires of the divine, personal You. Faith expressed in prayer is not reflection from a distance that extrinsically asks for the explanation of a matter in which there is no personal involvement. The lament is already itself an act of new trust and of new hope.

There were then in Israel two crucial periods that especially required reflection over pain. There was, first, the crisis of the threatened exile (Jeremiah) that was breaking into history (Jeremiah; Ezekiel) or had already come to pass (Ezekiel; Deutero-Isaiah; and Lamentations). This crisis required Israel to move from the position of accusing God to the recognition and acknowledgment of its own guilt that would lead to divine acquittal.[295] Moreover, the individual worshiper, who saw himself or herself as a "suffering righteous person" (Lamentations 3), as well as the people as a whole (Lamentations 1–2; 4–5), lamented and yet also sought to explain and then to accept the history that was experienced.[296]

The postexile, which posed for Israel the second critical period mentioned above, witnessed the so-called crisis of wisdom that was reflected in Qoheleth and the Book of Job. Qoheleth placed fundamentally in question the connection between pain and guilt (Qoh. 4:1; 7:15; 8:14; 9:2, 11; and 10:5–7). He speaks of chance (מִקְרֶה = *miqreh:* Qoh. 2:14f.; 3:19; and 9:2f.; in the rest of the Old Testament only in 1 Sam. 6:9; and Ruth 2:3),[297] and reflects on enigmatic fate (Qoh. 6:10; 8:6–8; and 9:2f., 12) and time that is not at one's disposal (Qoh. 3:1–8).

In the (multilayered) prose narrative frame of the Book of Job,[298] Job experiences and undergoes many difficult types of suffering, although he continues to hold fast to YHWH and demonstrates therein the unselfishness of his piety. In this manner, he probably is supposed to stand here as an example. In the dialogue portion of the book (Job 3–27), Job and his friends both hold fast to the view that suffering is due to divine punishment.[299] Moreover, Job concludes from this that he appears to suffer as a clearly righteous man under an unjust God, who seems to destroy the pious as well as the transgressor (Job 9:15–23; 16:12–17; 19:6; 23:15f.; etc.). The friends argue, in the meantime, that Job could be a sinner and indeed would have to be a sinner for suffering so, and they demand that he finally confess his sinful condition (also before God) (Job 4:7; 5:6; 8:5ff.; 11:15; 18; 20; etc.; cf. Ps. 41:7f.). From time to time Job expresses aloud his doubts about the theory of divine punishment (Job 9:22; 19:6; and 21:7–15). The speeches of God[300] do not offer a direct answer to the questions about the meaning of pain, indeed pointedly do not desire to do so. These divine addresses to Job signal, moreover, that this question of meaning cannot and could not be answered comprehensively and in general. YHWH is also a hidden God[301] and the lord of the world, not the guarantor of its harmony, while human beings should not and cannot understand everything (cf. Isa. 55:8f.). The solution to the question consists in freeing oneself from the posing of the question,[302] that is, in liberating faith as trust from its tendency toward constructing a worldview. These speeches are primarily not to give instruction about a correct comprehension of suffering or of God but rather to teach about life in pain that is lived under God. For this, Job is even a kind of representative of the problem. However, as is the case in the Old Testament and in the New Testament as a whole, pain is not separated from God. The God of personal destiny is not differentiated from the God of history and the God of the journey with his people. The mystery of pain as well as of the God of Israel is left intact. That the battle against pain, which humans blame on others, does not receive short shrift is reflected especially in the voice of the Old Testament prophets.

11.7   Life, Death, Resurrection

In connection with the Old Testament witnesses to existence, the way of life among humans, and illness,[303] dying and death must also now be mentioned. YHWH is, to be sure, the one who brings death and makes alive (Deut. 32:39; and 1 Sam. 2:6; cf. Isa. 45:7).

a. The Value of Life

Since all life[304] is dependent upon YHWH, comes from him, and stands under his direction, true life is possible only in community with him. This community is seen only in terms of an existence that is this-worldly and earthly. The Old Testament word for "life" (חיים = *ḥayyîm*), as an intensive plural, already indicates that the earthly life was seen as an important, indeed as the most important, good. In addition, חיים = *ḥayyîm* ("life") can also stand for "fortune" (Prov. 3:17f.), and it is then in fact synonymous with שלום = *šālôm* ("peace, well-being"; Mal. 2:5). Actual "life" for Old Testament human beings is healthy, long (Ps. 21:5), full, and whole[305] (cf. Isa. 38:9–20), and חיה = *ḥayâ* ("to live") is tantamount to meaning "to become healthy, to become powerful again."[306] According to Deut. 30:15–20[307] (cf. Lev. 18:5), life is closely connected, on the one hand, with the word of YHWH (Deut. 8:3; and 32:47) and the doing of his commandments, and, on the other hand, with blessing. In the context of Lev. 18:5 (and probably also Deut. 30:15, 19), life is connected also with the cult that transmits it to the community.[308] Wisdom itself and the results of its counsel transmit life to the individual.[309] "The teaching of the wise is a fountain of life to avoid the snares of death" (Prov. 13:14). When Ezekiel (in chap. 18 and 33:10–20) associates the possibility of "life" with the word of approval, "he is righteous," for the one who repents (Ezek. 18:32), he is probably making connection with the cultic, priestly, and legal consecration of life (cf. Ps. 36:10: "With you is the source of life, and by your light we see the light"[310]). However, in the situation of the exile, this necessarily now occurs far from the cult and temple.[311] The imitation of a cultic exhortation to life, which separates the seeking of YHWH even from the visiting of the sanctuaries, is found in Amos 5:4–6. According to Amos 5:14, "life" is made full with YHWH's presence and his mercy. In Ezekiel, as elsewhere then, the greatest opponent of life is death which often stands in opposition to it.[312] All that a person has, he or she will give for his or her life (Job 2:4).

b. Death

When Old Testament persons fall ill, this signifies to them that they already are actually within the sphere of death, for death[313] is, according to the witness of the Old Testament, not only the temporal point of departure but also a sphere and a power that also extend into life. שְׁאוֹל = šĕ'ôl (Sheol),[314] which with reason is paralleled to death (Isa. 28:15, 18),[315] likewise is not only a place but also a power, and threatens to devour humans (Isa. 5:14) and reaches with its "hand" (Pss. 49:16; and 89:49) into human life. If people are weak or ill, they are already in the power of Sheol, standing, so to speak, with one foot in the grave (Pss. 31:13; 88). If they become healthy again, then they are "alive" once more.[316] Thus they can say that YHWH has rescued them from the sphere of death, that is, from שְׁאוֹל = šĕ'ôl (Sheol), and has brought them forth from the pit (Pss. 30:4; 71:20; and 116:8). Thereupon they look upon YHWH in the land of the living (Pss. 27:13; 116:9; 142:6; and Isa. 38:11, 16). These texts do not deal with resurrection from the dead but rather with protection from the finality of death, "with redemption from an existence that is threatened by a calamitous death."[317] Old Testament persons do not confront death for the first time when their lives reach their biological end. "To be drawn out of the depths" (Ps. 30:2)[318] is identical with the expression "to make well" (Ps. 30:3). As is the case in Israel's cultural environment, for example, in Mesopotamia, divine healing of the sick can be described as a "giving life to the dead."[319] This expression, along with another one, "to be taken from the dead," does not mean resurrection but rather indicates "to be supported in life" and to receive healing. The meaning is identical with the reviving of life (Ps. 30:4; cf. 9:14; 68:21; and Job 33:28) and with deliverance from the sphere of death. Both of these idioms are the cause of rejoicing (Pss. 16:9; and 30:12), particularly when God restores to life several times (Job 33:29f.). The diminishment of life that befalls worshipers, a lessening which they experience as estrangement from God and which has transported them into the sphere of the dead, has been repealed. The healthy worshipers, who no longer are driven into the pit, give thanks for healing and deliverance and can praise YHWH as a living person. The dead do not praise YHWH, for they are separated from his sphere of interests. They do not have, nor are they able to have, community with YHWH (Pss. 6:6; 30:10; 88:11–13; 115:17f.; and Isa. 38:18).[320] YHWH is a God of the living, however, not of the dead (Mark 12:26f.). Psalm 88 makes completely clear how one saw and experienced the wasting away of sick persons as the encroachment of death that was threatening them, a death that already had those ill in its power.[321] Since illness often results in exclusion from worship, the separation of sick persons from YHWH was for this reason also underscored. In the cult, YHWH hands out life, indeed his life (Pss. 36:10; and 84:11).

When YHWH, who holds in his hand the lifetime of a person (Pss. 31:16; 139:16; and Qoh. 3:2), takes back the spirit of life, that is, breath from a person (Ps. 104:29; and Job 34:14f.) and causes the individual to die so that he or she returns once again to dust (Gen. 3:19; Pss. 90:3;[322] 146:4; and Qoh. 12:7), and when the giver of life takes it back again,[323] then a human being is shown to be like water that is poured out upon the earth so no one can gather it up again (2 Sam. 14:14).

That death is the recompense for sin or that human mortality is the punishment of God is not a conviction of Old Testament faith,[324] for according to the present text of Gen. 2:4b—3:24 as a whole the humans in paradise were already mortal (Gen. 3:22).[325] What was later made known to them was the fact that they *must* die, not just that they *shall* or *might* die, meaning then that their mortality is also a necessity. Even with this view, it is striking that the fact of death and of having to die was not necessarily seen in the Old Testament as a great problem or a tremendous cause of anxiety. This attitude was manifest even though there was a great mortality rate among those in their younger years. Death was considered to be a negative only when one died suddenly or especially when one died a premature death (Isa. 38:10; Ps. 102:25). One attempted to avoid these types of death as well as dying in a foreign country and thus in an unclean land.[326] Especially the "sage" issued many admonitions about this subject (Prov. 13:14; and 14:27),[327] and wisdom and a communal lament flow together in Psalm 90 which concerns the acknowledgment of the finality of life (Ps. 90:12) but not deliverance from death. Sapiential counsel concerning death Qoheleth did not consider to be helpful. Death is, according to him, the great equalizer, the incalculable opponent of humanity (Qoh. 3:19ff.; 5:13ff.; 6:2f.; 8:8, 10; and 9:3ff., 10). People continue to live then through their descendants (Ruth 4:10; and Isa. 53:10b; cf. 2 Sam. 14:7; and Job 18:17–19), whom they blessed as they were dying (Gen. 48:16, 21), or through human memory (Prov. 10:7; and Ps. 112:6). The critical Qoheleth, however, contests even the positive affirmation (Qoh. 2:16ff., 21; and 8:10).

That the sphere of death was stripped of any sacred character[328] and remained for a long time a theological vacuum[329] from the perspective of Yahwistic faith is astonishing in view of the character of YHWH and the Old Testament image of God. It is obvious that this sphere, which was heavily interspersed with conceptions that played a role in Canaanite religion, was held separate for a long time from the presence and activity of YHWH. That everything associated with the dead and death was in addition viewed as "unclean" also belongs to these connections.[330] Here belong also the expressed prohibitions against a cult of the dead and, in addition, the frequent criticism of the customs of this cult which also existed and presumably were practiced at the same time in folk religion.

In Deut. 26:14 the Israelites, in the setting aside of their tithe, must make their confession that they have not offered any of it to the dead. What is probably meant here is a sacrifice to the dead (cf. Ps. 106:28). To be distinguished from this are the grave offerings which were customary but were not so sharply criticized and prohibited. However, the conjuration of a dead spirit (אוֹב = '*ôb*) stands under a taboo (1 Samuel 28; cf. Lev. 19:31; Deut. 18:9–13; Isa. 8:19f.;

and perhaps Exod. 22:17).[331] The mourning customs connected with laments over the dead,[332] including self-inflicted lacerations, shaving (part of) the head, putting on "sackcloth," the tearing of garments, the sprinkling of dust on the head, and the offering of the bread of mourning and the cup of consolation (Jer. 16:7 conjectural; Ezek. 24:17, 22), are, first of all, rites that are practiced in other cultures. Second, their original meaning certainly did not point only to mourning or to the performance of "rites of self-diminishment" but also to their role as constituent elements of the securing of oneself against the attacks of (the spirits of) the dead.[333] These rites served to make the mourners unrecognizable, to enable one to avoid food from the house of the dead, and perhaps also to make an offering of the hair. In addition, these rites stemmed from animistic thinking.[334] Moreover, these rites were practiced in Israel's ancient Near Eastern environment (cf. Jonah 3:5–10), a fact to which the Ugaritic literature gives testimony,[335] so that they must have fallen victim to Israel's eventual resistance to its religious environment. This is clearly evidenced for the first time in later Old Testament texts and its law codes where such rites were prohibited and explained as unclean. Contact with the unclean dead and their sphere was consequently excluded from the cult.[336]

Therefore, when a human being has departed this life (Job 14:10) and no longer exists (Pss. 39:14; and 103:16), then that person is in the land of the dead from which there is no return (Job 7:9f.; 10:21; and 14:14; cf. Ps. 89:48f.). The Mesopotamian[337] could also speak of the kingdom of the dead and of eternal life which is inaccessible to human beings,[338] while the ancient Egyptian, whose sun-god also visited by night the world of the dead,[339] viewed the future life and therefore death in a positive way.[340] In Egypt a differently accented faith in the gods, a divergent assessment of the monarchy, a contrasting anthropology, and a unique understanding of the cult with its cult of the dead formed the basis on which a positive view of the afterlife was made possible.

c. Translation

The final, not just temporary, translation[341] of a living person before death to the divine, future world or to God, as in the case with pious people such as Enoch (Gen. 5:24) and Elijah (2 Kings 2) who were set apart, was a conspicuous and distinguishing exception. The exilic Priestly document perhaps wishes in a conscious way to use Gen. 5:24 as a positive signal to indicate that for the pious there is always hope, while the notice about Elijah belongs to the anti-Baal tendencies of the Elijah narratives: not Baal but rather YHWH has control over life and death.[342] Psalms 16:10; 49:16; and 73:24 talk not about translation but about being delivered and protected from death so that the worshiper will not have to see (yet) the "pit" (Ps. 16:10). The redemption of God consists in being taken (לקח = *lāqaḥ*) out of the power of שאול (= *šĕ'ôl*; Ps. 49:16),[343] and God's removal (לקח = *lāqaḥ*) of the worshiper is also viewed as an honor for him (Ps. 73:24; cf. Job 19:25).[344] One sees the references to translation in Israel's contemporary world,[345] in Mesopotamia, not in Egypt, that is, in a culture where (analogous to Israel, but contrasting with Egypt) one viewed the future life and the fortune after death in negative terms. Translation to the divine world was, then, actually a reward for the one who took part in this action, although this translation may also be only temporary.

d. Resurrection

What has been said above about the long, continuing separation of the sphere of death from Yahwistic faith is valid also for the hope in "resurrection."[346] This is different from Elijah's and Elisha's awakening of people from the dead that served to legitimate that these were men of God (1 Kings 17:17–24; 2 Kings 4:31–37; cf. 13:21), for resurrection is not followed by a new death. Israel had first dared to speak of resurrection in a still very hesitating manner when there was no longer present a natural misunderstanding deriving from Canaanite religion. By contrast, Israel also gave historical expression to this declaration of faith by closely and exclusively associating it with YHWH. Resurrection was understood not as the dying and coming back to life of the dead in the world[347] but rather as a solution to the problem of theodicy and as the participation of humanity in the salvation of the coming kingdom of God. Among other things, "resurrection" also presupposes that the question concerning the fortune even of the individual had become important. Additionally, resurrection must actually be understood as a new creation and as the resurrection of the entire human being (already Ezek. 37:1–14), since Old Testament anthropology knew nothing of anything that was immortal about or within human beings. Hence, this view of human nature did not associate immortality with the revival of a human being.[348]

There are Old Testament texts that allow one to recognize how Israel was led to its hope in resurrection. While beginning to develop only in an embryonic fashion in the Old Testament, resurrection hope first clearly unfolded in early Judaism. That the kingdom of the dead itself stood under the power of YHWH was stated from time to time (Amos 9:2; Job 26:6; and Ps. 139:8). One only knew that YHWH had not willed to exercise this power, since he had no interest in the dead. Thus, in Israel one was not supposed to speak as the Canaanites did about "resurrection," above all in regard to Baal.[349] In YHWH's case, it is not true that the "sun following the rain" was automatic (Hos. 6:1–3). Ezekiel 37:1–14 points to the power of YHWH and his reviving spirit over a people, who exist like a field of bones of the dead and have no hope (v. 11). When YHWH asks the prophet whether these bones, which describe the people of the exile, can "live" again, Ezekiel can only return this question to YHWH. While

humans could still not believe such a thing, YHWH, however, is able to re-
suscitate those who are desperate. Thus, Ezekiel 37 may have pointed in the
direction of resurrection hope and also may have prepared to a degree the pathway by which this hope would later achieve its final destination. Ezekiel 37 itself, however, may have in mind only the revival of the nation, through the
spirit of YHWH,[350] from the death and burial of the exile.[351] This same spirit
was active in the preaching of the prophet. According to Isa. 53:8–10, YHWH
will yet restore the servant of God after his death, although it must be and continue to remain unclear how one is to conceive of and hope for this (Isa.
53:10ff.). Job did not hope for his own resurrection (cf. Job 7:9f., 21; 10:21f.;
14:10, 12, 14; and 16:22); rather, he hoped that he would see that God would
prove to be his counselor and redeemer (גאל = gō'ēl) and would restore him
(Job 19:25–27; cf. 16:19–21).[352]

   There are questions of theodicy, problems concerning the justice of God in
regard to injustice and pain in the world, which seek to be heard in these texts
ushering in the hope in resurrection. However, it is exactly these very same
problems that have led finally to the actual hope in resurrection itself. These
problems are addressed in two late-postexilic, apocalyptic texts of the Old Testament that are shaped by the expectation of the end, the situation of persecution, and martyrdom.[353] "Israel did not naturally come to its faith in resurrection; rather, it has struggled hard with it."[354] In regard to what is apparently the
persecution under Artaxerxes III between 350 and 348 B.C.E. that led to the
martyrdom of the pious,[355] who might be excluded from the immanent coming kingdom of God that was expected, YHWH promises in a lament: "Your
dead shall live again, my corpses shall be resurrected."[356] And it is also the case
that these people who have been resurrected will take part again in the praise
of YHWH (Isa. 26:19), for indeed the dead shall not sound forth in praise.[357]
However, when the eschatological evil had become so very strong during the
period of persecution under Antiochus IV (i.e., 166–165 B.C.E.), then one is no
longer able to grant to those who produced this evil simply an escape into
death. There is a resurrection of the "many" (cf. Isa. 53:11) who include the pious who have died as well as the martyrs who have been killed. These shall be
resurrected to eternal life, while the wicked, by contrast, shall be resurrected
to eternal dishonor and shame (Dan. 12:2). Also, resurrection solves what has
here become a two-sided problematic of theodicy. The hope in a resurrection
of *all* the dead developed during the period between the Testaments. That
YHWH would destroy death forever, according to Isa. 25:8, was an expression, in the apocalyptic realm, of the hope of the expectation of the great meal
of the nations to be celebrated on Mt. Zion (Isa. 25:5–8). This is a view that
did not think in terms of resurrection but in terms of the idea that the power of
YHWH shall no longer have any boundaries.[358] If one may emend the obviously corrupted text in Ps. 22:30, changing דשני (*dišnēy*) to ישני (*yĕšēnēy*), as

often has been suggested, then one would find also here a hope in resurrection embedded within the apocalyptic addition to Psalm 22, in vv. 28–32.[359] Second Maccabees 6:30 and 2 Maccabees 7 later speak of a hope in resurrection "in heaven."[360]

Subsequently, "resurrection" is a daring hope within the eschatological-apocalyptic horizon of understanding that is based on YHWH as the God who has his way and who does not abandon his own. This hope is the consequence of Yahwistic faith and the risk of faith in the God who still comes unto his own on the other side of death and helps his worshipers to receive (physically) their justice. In addition, resurrection serves the eschatological restoration of the covenant people and is the consequence of election faith as faith in the God of Israel who also establishes his lordship against the appearance of death. The supposition of an influence from Israel's ancient Near Eastern environment is not demonstrable for the more limited sphere of the Old Testament; it is also unnecessary. It may not be disputed that in early Judaism[361] Persian and Hellenistic influences have made themselves equally felt. In regard to Hellenistic influence, for instance, the Wisdom of Solomon expresses the hope for a future life for the immortal soul which awaits a future compensation, since the earthly system of retribution was not empirically functioning in a proper way.[362] However, Hellenistic influence did not prove to be any more decisive in settling this issue.[363]

11.8 Humanity before God

How did the Old Testament human beings see and describe their place before or under God? What did they say when they spoke of the proper behavior toward the God of Israel that YHWH desired of them? Obligation belonged to election (cf. Vol. I, chap. 3.5), while the community bestowed by God on his people required a life appropriate to that community. J. Hempel spoke about the association between feelings of alienation and feelings of solidarity when he wished to characterize the contrast between God and humanity in the Old Testament.[364] This indeed is not an unfounded explanation, although these expressions are not Old Testament words. M. Luther came much closer to Old Testament linguistic usage with his "fear and love" added to the commandments each time as an introductory explanation, something that has already been pointed out. G. Fohrer[365] spoke about the sovereignty of God and the community of God as well as of the connection between fear and trust.

a. Hearing—Serving—Loving—Following

The Priestly document can (in Gen. 6:9 and 17:1) simply say that a man like Noah and a righteous Israelite like Abraham should be or was "perfect" or "whole." Others translate the word occurring here (cf. also Deut. 18:13; and Josh. 24:14), תמים = tāmîm, as "pious," something the term, provided no further explanation here or elsewhere, may imply.[366] Actually, the root תמם = tmm designates something that is "in order"; however, when and how is a person "in order" before YHWH? It is only asserted and stated about Noah that he found favor before YHWH (Gen. 6:8 J), without any reason being given as to why. It was required of Abraham to be תמים = tāmîm. In both places it was obviously clear what the meaning was, only it is not clear to the modern reader. Does the term mean complete devotion or unconditional obedience, or does it mean both of these? In Deut. 18:13 the required תמים = tāmîm includes turning away from the "abominations" of the nations (Deut. 18:9–13), while in Josh. 24:14 the term involves the rejection of strange gods and total service to YHWH. Consequently, תמים = tāmîm is made concrete in Deuteronomic and Deuteronomistic passages by other statements belonging to Deuteronomistic theology,[367] something that the Priestly document unfortunately does not do.

The Deuteronomic/Deuteronomistic movement emphasizes, on the other hand, more the idea of hearing[368] (cf. Deut. 6:4; "Hear, O Israel!") and makes this concrete (in the form of a cultic exhortation?) as "hear and fear," "hear and do," and "listen to YHWH's voice" (Josh. 24:15) which expresses his commandments, namely, the Decalogue and Deuteronomy as its interpretation.[369] In this regard, "hearing" is important also in the context of Exod. 24:1–11,[370] where the assertion of hearing is made in v. 3 and the doing follows in v. 7. A psalmist can affirm solemnly that God does not desire sacrifice, for he has "opened my ears" (Ps. 40:7; cf. 1 Sam. 15:22). Receptive obedience that leads to action is to be (at least according to the Deuteronomic/Deuteronomistic movement) a basic attitude of the Old Testament person before YHWH.[371] The Priestly document also sets forth hearing as an essential element of correct piety (Num. 9:8; and Deut. 34:9), while it characterizes not hearing as misguided conduct (cf., e.g., Exod. 6:9, 12, 30; 7:13, 22; and 16:20).

Likewise, one finds especially in Deuteronomic/Deuteronomistic contexts discourse that one should "serve" (עבד = 'ābad) YHWH"[372] (e.g., Deut. 6:13f.; 10:12, 20; 11:13; 13:5; 19:9; 30:17; and 31:20). This stands in relationship to the prohibition against serving other gods and also against praying to them[373] instead of fearing YHWH.[374] The contexts and combinations of verbs make it clear that this service not only involves cultic worship but also means a way of living in which there is an obedient relationship to YHWH and his will. Consequently, not much more can be said about service than what was also fully required by תמים = tāmîm or by hearing.

Often אהב = 'āhab ("love") stands in close connection with עבד = 'ābad ("serve").[375] Service should include love that draws on love for YHWH.[376] "Love" is encountered as a description of the (correct) relationship to God[377] already in the conclusion (debated in terms of literary criticism) of the Song of

Deborah (Judg. 5:31), so that one should not think too narrowly or too quickly of the image of marriage as the background or even origin of "love." This is true, especially since Hosea is indeed the first to shape the image of marriage between YHWH and his people and speaks only of the love of YHWH for this people (Hos. 3:1; 9:15; 11:1, 4; and 14:5; cf. Jer. 2:2; 31:3; Mal. 1:2; and 2:11). Deuteronomy requires that the people[378] also love YHWH.[379] However, within Deuteronomic/Deuteronomistic theology, "love" is only another term for obedience toward YHWH in the sphere of the relationship with God. To be commanded to love stands therefore in connection with "to fear" God (see below), "to serve him," and "to walk in all his ways" (thus Deut. 10:12).[380] With this obedience, the love of this people is concretely expressed as a requited love for its God. Certainly, this love seeks to motivate obedience on an emotional level. Psalm 119, which often speaks of the love of the worshiper for YHWH's commandments and for his Torah, is, as is Neh. 1:5, in this way a true student of the Deuteronomists.[381] The only other texts that speak of a love for YHWH (in part textually uncertain) are the passages of Pss. 31:24; 116:1; and 18:2 (here רחם = *rāḥam;* "to have compassion/feelings") and, following Hosea, the Book of Jeremiah. Jeremiah's description of the early period of Israel points to Israel's love for YHWH, a love freely given that was not demanded of the nation (Jer. 2:2). His description of the present, in this regard, contrasts strongly with the early period, since Israel now loves strange gods and the stars (Jer. 2:25; and 8:2). According to Jer. 31:3f., however, YHWH shall answer with love.[382]

Often "following after" is mentioned as a characteristic of the correct worship and obedience to YHWH who has elected his people and has led them out of Egypt.[383] Yet, to "follow after" is given concrete form almost exclusively as a sin and as a warning not to "follow after" other gods.[384] This expression is employed with the "forgetting of YHWH"[385] or the "abandoning" of him (e.g., Deut. 29:24; 31:16; Isa. 1:4; Jer. 22:9; and Hos. 4:10).[386] These expressions make clear through negative connotations the contrast between the behavior that actually is expected and what is required.

b. Fear of YHWH/Fear of God

The previously discussed expressions, which are attributed mostly to particular groups of texts or writings, of the correct attitude of worshipers before their God already point time and again to contacts and common features with the *fear* of YHWH or with corresponding verbal formulations.[387] The "fear of God (YHWH)/to fear God (YHWH)" is also an idiom that extends to and has found use in many areas[388] of the Old Testament for the delineation of the human attitude toward God. However, what is the content of its meaning and what is circumscribed by this expression?[389]

A statistical overview[390] points to three main centers of gravity for the discourse about the fear of YHWH, namely, the Book of Deuteronomy, the Psalter, and the Book of Proverbs. The discourse involving the statement that one ought to fear YHWH is once more found primarily (more than thirty passages)[391] within the Deuteronomic/Deuteronomistic literature of the Old Testament. In terms of content, the fear of YHWH is comprised of and defined as the worship of YHWH, serving him, not other gods, with not only a cultic but also an obedient life, hearing his voice, and being obedient to his voice.[392] The fear of YHWH is fully integrated into Deuteronomic/Deuteronomistic theology. This fear concerns loyalty to the God who elected Israel, walking on his pathways, keeping his commandments, and loving him.[393] Not to fear God is sin (Deut. 25:18); to fear YHWH is connected to the obedience set forth in Deuteronomy (Deut. 28:58; and 31:12f.). The fear of YHWH is additionally connected with the experience of the historical acts of YHWH's grace for his people Israel (cf. also Exod. 14:31)[394] and with the response of this people to those acts.[395]

Finally, the fear of YHWH is teachable and learnable.[396] The fear of YHWH is related to the people, for it is associated with his commandments, with Deuteronomy as the proclamation of his will, and with Israel's history. On the whole, the fear of YHWH brings to realization the primary Deuteronomic/Deuteronomistic commandment. In the emphasis on what can be taught and learned and in the motivating promise of a long life here certainly related to life in the land of promise, the sapiential influence on Deuteronomy may be detected, an influence, moreover, that is spread out and integrated into the book.

A second important collection of texts that often discusses the "fear of YHWH" (noun)[397] and "to fear YHWH" (verb) is the psalms.[398] In the wake of Deuteronomic/Deuteronomistic literature, those who fear YHWH once more are primarily those who are faithful to the law.[399] Whoever fears YHWH takes delight in his commandments (Ps. 112:1) and travels on his paths (Ps. 128:1) which he shows to the God-fearers (Ps. 25:12). Then YHWH merits fear from humans, because he is majestic as the creator and as the mighty ruler of the world.[400] All the world fears YHWH, that is, acknowledges him (Pss. 33:8; and 67:8). All humanity shall recognize what YHWH has done and become afraid (Ps. 64:10). Jerusalem shall be rebuilt again in order that the nations shall fear the name of YHWH (Ps. 102:16). The fear of YHWH is also here the activity of divine help and an act of grace.[401]

With YHWH there is forgiveness so that "one may fear him (you)" (Ps. 130:4). The righteous shall see the destruction of the oppressor, become afraid, but then laugh at him (Ps. 52:8; cf. 40:4). The fearers of YHWH are also then a group of persons, although they are hardly proselytes.[402] Rather, they are the pious (cultic) community.[403] They wait on YHWH who takes pleasure in them

(Ps. 147:11). They do not rely on their own power; rather, they seek YHWH, see the pious one and rejoice (Ps. 119:74), trust in YHWH's name, and call on him. His covenant is with them (Pss. 25:14; and 111:5), they praise him (Ps. 135:20), and they fulfill their vows (Ps. 22:24, 26). YHWH helps them (Pss. 34:8; 85:10; 111:5; and 145:19), and his grace and his compassion are with them (Psalm 103). They love YHWH (Ps. 145:20), and the worshiper may continue in their midst (Pss. 61:6; and 86:11). The fear of YHWH is here simply a designation for piety, a word that certainly is more precise in terms of its content even though it also has different emphases. Further, the fear of YHWH is associated with an emphasis on the community, on worship, and on the *tremendum* deriving from the encounter with the holy.

In the sayings of Proverbs,[404] the fear of YHWH[405] is expressed mostly in the form of a substantive. This is almost always the case when used in the ethical sphere. In addition, this expression is not normally used to describe the character or behavior of people in the plural,[406] as is the case in the Psalter, since wisdom literature has to do with individuals, not with the community (as is the case with the Psalter) and the people of God (as is true in the Deuteronomic/Deuteronomistic literature). Proverbs 1:7, as the first saying after the introduction, immediately emphasizes that the fear of YHWH is the beginning, foundation, and presupposition of wisdom and knowledge, while wisdom is the consequence of the fear of YHWH (Prov. 1:29; and 2:1–5). The first collection (Proverbs 1–9) is framed at its conclusion (Prov. 9:10) by a similar statement, while Prov. 31:30 (cf. Ps. 128:3f.), the next to the last verse of the book, takes up once more the same theme and, with this inclusio, confers on the entire book the fear of YHWH as the emphasis that is determinative for the final redaction. What does the fear of YHWH mean in this context? The fear of YHWH is the means to obtain wisdom even as humility is the means to acquire honor (Prov. 15:33; cf. 22:4). The fear of YHWH serves as the source of life (as does wisdom: Prov. 13:14)[407] in order to avoid the snares of an untimely death. The reward of humility and of the fear of YHWH is riches, honor, and life (Prov. 22:4; cf. Ps. 34:12f. in a wisdom psalm[408]). To those who aspire to the fear of YHWH, their hope does not come to naught (Prov. 23:17f.). The fear of YHWH secures fortune in life (Prov. 14:26), provides protection (Prov. 15:16),[409] increases the length of life (Prov. 10:27), and provides healing for the flesh (Prov. 3:7f.). One becomes satisfied, can sleep safely, and is not afflicted by evil (Prov. 19:23). People are to fear YHWH and the king in order that they not be inflicted with danger by either one (Prov. 24:21). The fear of YHWH becomes the subject of reflection (Prov. 10:27; 14:27; and 19:23; cf. 8:13) under these points of view. Finally, the fear of YHWH stands in general for ethical change.[410] Accordingly, the fear of YHWH is a designation for piety in general, without presenting, however, in a clear or even in a thematic form, its content and its relationship to the cultus, the law and commandments of

YHWH, and the nation and community. This fear of YHWH is integrated further into the sapiential relationship between deed and consequence[411] and wisdom's view of life. The fear of YHWH here has nothing in and of itself to do with contact with the numinous. It is the property of a rational, natural, and religious life, but it is also especially piety as a means to an end. Last of all, it serves especially the wise and helps them to achieve many positive things for which they strive. The "fear of God" is also a frequently used expression in extra-Israelite wisdom literature.[412] Although the "the fear of God" becomes the "fear of YHWH" in the Book of Proverbs, this divine name still yields no Israelite or Yahwistic content in this literature.[413] Rather, the consequences of the fear of YHWH after which one strives are detailed as its content.

The Book of Qoheleth,[414] which avoids the name YHWH and speaks only of "(the) God" (often with the article), consequently offers no passage that deals with the fear of YHWH, although there are several texts that take up the fear of God (verb, not substantive).[415] In Qoh. 7:18b[416] and 12:13,[417] it is clear that one has additions of orthodox redactors whose presence may also be determined elsewhere. In Qoh. 8:12b[418] + 13, traditional school wisdom is cited according to which it will go well with those who fear God. By contrast, those who do not practice the fear of God will not live long. In Qoh. 8:10, 11, and 12a, Qoheleth himself reported his observation and then drew his own conclusion. The concluding sentence of Qoh. 5:6 ("rather fear God") looks very much like an addition at the end of 4:17–5:6 which could stem from the spirit of Qoh. 12:13 in the attempt to cast a final anchor of deliverance. Accordingly, there remains in the book actually only Qoh. 3:14 as an authentic Qoheleth passage for the fear of God. Thus God does everything in order that one should fear him. Such a statement conforms well to Qoheleth's normal portrait of the deity in which the feeling of distance regarding "the God" outweighs the unconditional subjection before him (cf. also Qoh. 8:12f.). Qoheleth expects nothing from fearing God in the way that Proverbs does, and he exudes a sapiential, critical attitude also in this selection of passages. The additions attempted through the fear of God to restrain this thinker who was, for many, too critical, and they derived the full content of the fear of God from other spheres (Qoh. 12:13) or even from the sapiential school tradition which Qoheleth directly criticized (Qoh. 7:18).

The passages for the fear of God in the Book of Job[419] add nothing more to the previously reconstructed picture of the sapiential witness to this topic. These texts characterize, on the one hand, Job in his piety and moral behavior (Job 1:1, 8f.; 2:3; and 6:14; cf. 9:35), yet bring to expression, on the other hand, good, sapiential, traditional school theology when presented as coming forth from the mouth of the friend Eliphaz (Job 4:6; 15:4; and 22:4[420]). Accordingly, this sapiential thinking retained its character wherever it spoke of the fear of YHWH or the fear of God.

That the Elohist also designates the fear of God as an important predicate of a person who is right before the Almighty[421] hardly associates this document with wisdom, since in the Elohistic texts the fear of God is replete with different meanings in the various contexts of the same source. In this source, nothing is gained through the fear of God as was true in the sayings of Proverbs. Rather, the fear of God (Gen. 20:11) expresses "reverence and regard of the most elementary moral norms, whose severe guardian was everywhere considered to be the divinity."[422]

If "the ones who fear God" in Exod. 18:21 had been shaped by wisdom, then Deuteronomy, connected with sapiential thinking, would not have replaced this expression in Deuteronomy 1:15 with "the wise." According to Gen. 22:12, the fear of God is obedience even toward the obscure, terrible commandment of the God of Abraham, and for Joseph (Gen. 42:18) it is a "guarantee of a reliable word existing among humans."[423] And when the Hebrew midwives were referred to as God-fearers (Exod. 1:17, 21), then it was because they were not prepared to follow the Egyptian king's order to kill the male infants immediately after their birth. "The fear of God stood at the cradle of the Israelite nation,"[424] while Moses was afraid to look at God (Exod. 3:6b). The element of the numinous was preserved in the fear of God, and the people's fear of God is to be expected from the divine-human encounter that tests them (Exod. 20:20). "On the basis of the traditions of salvation history, the Elohist wants to lead Israel to new obedience and to new disobedience during the tribulations of his time,"[425] a period that can be understood in terms of the cultic, political, and social trials[426] occurring during the time of Elijah (cf. 1 Kings 18:3, 12; and 2 Kings 4:1).[427]

If, then, the "fear of YHWH/fear of God" in the Old Testament is the most frequently named designation of the right relationship of the individual as well as of the community and the nation with YHWH, then the expression does not mean "terror before God" which leads one to flee from God, even though the consciousness of the numinous or of a *tremendum* still often resonates in the term, and the feeling of distance from the deity continues to compel obedience (disregarding the texts in the Book of Proverbs). YHWH, however, is not only the one who excites fear (cf., e.g., Gen. 28:17), but he is also marvelous[428] and as such even merciful (Dan. 9:4; Neh. 1:5; 4:8; and 9:32). The fear of YHWH stands also for religion, and quite simply for piety. The fear of YHWH is reverence, in which one submits to him. It is not only an attitude of the heart but also an external deed. A godless person who does not fear YHWH has reason to fear (Job 15:20). Whoever fears YHWH need have no anxiety, however (Prov. 14:26). The fear of YHWH, therefore, already has something of the trust in God, so that to fear YHWH can be associated not only with "to walk in his ways" but also with "to love him" (Deut. 10:12) and "to believe" him (Exod. 14:31).

c. Faith

The discourse in the Old Testament about faith in YHWH as an attitude of a person toward and before God occurs more seldomly than might be expected by a reader of the Old Testament who is conditioned by the New Testament's and perhaps also Paul's understanding of faith.[429] Wherever this does occur, however, there are important statements that already show that the verb אמן = 'mn hiphil ("to believe"), which is formed[430] and appropriated from the root אמן = 'mn ("to be firm, certain, and trustworthy"; in contrast to בטח = bṭḥ ["to trust"], see below), is used only in regard to the God of Israel and not other gods. In addition, this fact indicates that in the Old Testament, "faith" is expressed only in a verbal form,[431] and "to believe" is seen as a process and deed."[432] In addition, in the religious sphere of usage, the word is related only to persons or their words (most with ב = b or with ל = l).[433] How does Hebrew, that is, "the actual soil from which sprang the idea of faith"[434] for both the New Testament and Christianity, speak of faith?

It is often the case that in the Old Testament a topic is narrated without already having been conceptually defined. This is true, for example, even in the sphere of "election."[435] Thus there are also Old Testament texts that tell about and describe faith without using or having to use the word itself.[436] This is analogous also to trusting in YHWH, which Psalm 23, for example, knows how to describe in such a beautiful way without the verb "to trust" even making an appearance. In effect, Noah builds his ark (especially according to the testimony of the Yahwist) "in faith," that is, in trusting obedience (Gen. 6:8),[437] since he does not know why and for what reason. When Abram, on the basis of the command and the promises of YHWH, abandons his homeland and relatives and therefore the social securities that were decisive for that time in order to set out for a land unknown to him (Gen. 12:1–4a J), then this is an act of obedient faith, that is, of believing trust in the guidance of this God and in the fulfillment of his promises. Consequently, this is a faith that is grounded in the word of promised action. These narratives were also transmitted in order to provide examples of faith and to beckon and to encourage similar kinds of trusting obedience. In addition, this scene in Gen. 12:1–4a introduces a history of YHWH that provides a new beginning after the primeval history concludes in such a negative way (Gen. 11:1–9). This history has as its object YHWH's people Israel and through them the other nations (Gen. 12:3) and thus works to bring to conclusion an old history and to open up a new one.

If we take seriously the wider context of the Abram stories, then this faith of Abraham, which is mentioned once more as an example in Heb. 11:8ff., is at the least not a constant one. Rather, this "father of the faith" had a much more erratic faith, as the contiguous narratives graphically describe.[438] The obedient, faithful Abram soon becomes anxious about his life and lies in order to secure his existence (Gen. 12:10ff.), and later he cannot get along in an equitable way with Lot (Gen. 13:5f.). In addition, these events still do not fulfill any promise but rather only relate their renewal (Gen. 13:14–18).[439]

What was only implicitly described in Gen. 12:1–4a[440] was theologically more greatly enriched and then brought to expression in the much later chap. 15[441] which already provides a summary for the Abraham traditions. The first scene (Gen. 15:1–6) describes a revelation to Abram with a new pledge and a new promise that was pronounced on the basis of a doubting, question pointing to the nonfulfillment of the past promise (vv. 2–3). This promise was to receive support by the response in v. 5, but finally demanded of Abram an even greater faith. While the reference to progeny, like the number of the stars in heaven for a childless man who has in the meantime become old, not only and primarily is certainly to make faith stronger, it also can actually awaken even a greater doubt. There is presupposed here a situation of need and of justified doubt in YHWH's promise, a tension between the world of experience and "righteousness" as salvation.[442] Verse 6 places next to the statement that Abram "believed" the comment that "he reckoned it to him [in content as well as in logical sequence] as righteousness." This righteousness is correct behavior involving the proper relationship[443] between the community, God, and humanity, and perhaps even is an act of salvation (Gen. 15:6). The New Testament returns three times (Rom. 4:3–5; Gal. 3:6; and James 2:23) to this faith of Abram where it is clearly presupposed that YHWH is the one who reckons to Abram his faith as righteousness. And in the New Testament, it is Abram whose faith is regarded as an appropriate reaction within the divine-human relationship (cf. Deut. 6:25; and 24:13). Consequently, the[444] question may provoke astonishment as to whether one actually is to view this Old Testament text in such a way, for a change in subject is not intimated in v. 6. Therefore, according to the judgment of the (Deuteronomistic?) narrative, is it YHWH who reckons to Abram something or is it Abram who plainly regards what YHWH has promised as righteousness, something that is equivalent to a salvific act of YHWH?

The customary understanding of Gen. 15:6 is forged by the New Testament references. However, seeing that the "and" at the beginning of v. 6a is a connective, not a contrastive conjunction, one would have to translate it as "however." Further, the section of the verse (part b) that moves on with the narrative obviously relates back to part a of v. 6 without a change in subject being indicated ("for he believed it was a salvific act for himself"). The "it" does not refer to the faith of Abram; rather, it refers back to what was said in a positive way about YHWH in the preceding scene (vv. 1–5).[445] In addition, "to believe" in Gen. 15:6 is expressed by a perfect verb with a ו (*waw*) *copulativum* (והאמִן = *wĕhe'ĕmîn*), hardly a (*waw*) *consecutivum,* and not by a simple imperfect *consecutivum* that continues the narrative (as, e.g., in Exod. 14:31; and 1 Sam.

27:12). "A sequential narrative perfect designates a condition from which and on which the event recounted in the narrative takes place."[446] Hence, the event somehow ensues from what has preceded and is contrasted somewhat with the things that have been related in the narrative. Thus one could translate v. 6: "And then (thus) Abram depended on YHWH and assessed the promise previously given by YHWH (לֹ = lô) to be for him (i. e., Abram) a salvific act." This shows that Abram's fundamental attitude, which appeared earlier, is now renewed.[447] In addition, v. 7 directly continues with YHWH as the subject.

That one might reckon something to YHWH *as* something is certainly an infrequent linguistic usage (Mal. 3:16); however, it is not impossible.[448] Only it could be asked what is meant by "to reckon" (חשׁב = ḥāšab). It must not be a cultic, priestly linguistic usage for a reckoning by YHWH[449] that was fully loosened from its cultic background, as G. von Rad has assumed.[450] This cannot be the case, since the verb in cultic texts is used in the niphal (Lev. 7:18; 17:4; and Num. 18:27), while it occurs in the qal in Gen. 15:6, a fact that von Rad did not consider. Also to take into consideration are the instances of the verb ḥāšab in Num. 18:30 and Ps. 106:31, as well as its colloquial occurrence in 2 Sam. 19:20 (cf. Prov. 27:14). The term is provided theological content in Ps. 106:31 in a rather analogous way to Gen. 15:6.

As is true in Isa. 7:9 and 28:16 the hiphil of אמן = 'mn is used in Gen. 15:6 as an intransitive (or inner-transitive) absolute without an object.[451] The context, which may not be overlooked in the use of the verb that is without an object, makes clear, on the one hand, that what is meant is considering the contents of the promise to be true,[452] while, on the other hand and at the same time, also meant is a trusting acceptance of the promise that is actualized in the performance of life. Overall, these two aspects of faith are very closely related. "Faith in the Old Testament sense does not mean: to think something about God, but rather it means: to expect something from God."[453] Consequently, one shall once again see, in looking at the Old Testament statements about hope,[454] the Old Testament witness to faith. This witness is illustrated in Gen. 15:6 by Abram and his believing, trusting, hopeful reference to the promised act of YHWH's salvation.

In the scene in Gen. 15:7–21, which originally was once independent from Gen. 15:6, "the sentence of faith receives an additional narrative interpretation," for "the *believing* Abraham now receives a sign of the highest significance."[455] However, after these high points of faith, Abram (in Genesis 16) falls back once more to an alternative solution in addressing the question raised about the promise of descendants, thus demonstrating a behavior that is not very strong in the faith. However, he is encountered once more in Genesis 22 as the obedient, God-fearing, trusting father toward a God who one thought could or must be depicted as issuing a divine commandment that placed a human being under the sacrificial knife. However, within the stories of Abraham introducing the narratives of the ancestors, Gen. 15:6 has maintained a significant place insofar as he already openly represents as the first ancestral father of Israel an exemplary believer (cf. Neh. 9:8 and 1 Macc. 2:52 as references).

Faith (here together with "to fear YHWH"), understood as the consequence of the experience of an act of salvation, is the contribution that the summarizing, concluding notice of the narrative of the deliverance at and in the sea makes to the theme: "So YHWH delivered Israel that day from the power of the Egyptians . . . , and Israel saw the mighty work which YHWH did against the Egyptians; and the people feared YHWH and believed in both YHWH and in his servant Moses" (Exod. 14:30f.). In v. 30 (+ 31a?), the so-called Yahwist[456] speaks. Does he also speak in v. 31(b)? The discussion about faith had already taken place in Exod. 4:31 where the nation "believed" on the basis of what Moses (and Aaron[457]) narrated, and they prayed to the God who had done and directed everything. Exodus 4:31 has a concluding, framing notice that functions like Exod. 14:31, especially since in Exod. 4:1 Moses asks in a doubting fashion as to whether the people would then believe him (cf. vv. 5, 8, 9[458]). After he has been able to perform authenticating signs, then they do believe him. This faith in Moses, which in Exod. 14:31 is so remarkably related to the faith in YHWH (Ps. 106:12 erases this relationship) and which exalts Moses as no other person, is a faith[459] that is both accepting of and trusting in the power and word of the spokesperson called by YHWH (cf. Exod. 19:9) who is his instrument in the coming, promised liberation of the people from their slavery,[460] something that is completely fulfilled in Exod. 14:31. The faith of the people is the result occasioned by the event.[461] They are prepared to trust in the God who reveals himself as YHWH. Thus, he has fought on behalf of his own (Exod. 14:13f.) and for no reason (Exod. 14:13) other than that they should fear him.[462]

That this was no foregone conclusion[463] can be recognized from Num. 14:11 where YHWH is allowed to say that "this people" spurned him and, in spite of all kinds of miracles that he performed in their midst, did not believe in him (cf. Pss. 78:11, 22, and 32). That Israel or even Moses and Aaron (Num. 20:12 P) during the wilderness wandering "did not believe" is frequently mentioned in Deuteronomistic texts (Deut. 1:32; 9:23; and 2 Kings 17:14), in texts dependent upon them (Pss. 78:22, 32; and 106:24), and in texts that belong to the "murmuring" tradition of the sinful and thankless people.[464]

If one attempts an initial evaluation, the result is that none of the previously considered passages is to be clearly seen as an earlier, older text. Numbers 14:11 (in Num. 14:11ff.) is regarded mostly as a later, inserted piece,[465] as is Exod. 19:9.[466] Numbers 20:12 belongs to the Priestly source. That the people did *not* believe YHWH is also a Deuteronomic/Deuteronomistic accent in the use of the word "to believe" (Deut. 1:32; 9:23; 2 Kings 17:14; etc.). Genesis 15:6 is a later text. Exodus 14:31 repeats much of the content of v. 30. Moses as the "servant of YHWH," and the "seeing" and the "doing" of the divine hand, are evidenced in Deuteronomic/Deuteronomistic texts (Deut. 3:24; 11:2; and 34:12). Exodus 4:5, 8f. and 19:9 go with Exod. 14:31, while Exod. 4:1 could perhaps be the older point of departure for the mentioning of faith in the contexts concerning Moses and the exodus. Consequently, it may be difficult to find pre-Isaianic passages for the religious idea of faith in the Old Testament.[467] There are in the Old Testament, much more, the presence of textual notices that make theological judgments that approximate Deuteronomic/ Deuteronomistic thinking and that also have learned a great deal about faith from Isaiah.[468]

That "faith" in the Old Testament is a rather infrequent word is shown in the fact that, within the prophets, it appears only in First and Second Isaiah. Moreover, faith has a more significant richness in First Isaiah. This sparsity of references to faith in the prophetic literature is probably due to the prophets' regarding a believing trust as very suspect in their time, a faith that did not seem to them to be possible in view of the coming judgment of God. Often the scene involving the encounter between Ahaz and Isaiah in Isaiah 7 is seen as the hour of the birth of faith (B. Duhm). Here the prophet declares that the attack of kings Pekah and Rezin on Jerusalem and against King Ahaz will not succeed. However, this text, in the form of a word of judgment against the two foreign kings, does not concern an unconditional promise of salvation for Judah that is then made conditional by an admonition with a wordplay involving the root אמן = '*mn* ("If you do not believe, then you will not remain": Isa. 7:9). Rather hortatory tones (v. 4) to the vacillating followers of Isaiah are already heard in Isa. 7:4ff., so that v. 9b can appropriately follow and does not have to be understood only as a word to the later reader of the "memoir" (Isa. 6:1–9:6 or 8:23).[469] In addition, the context with its own particular situation is important for the interpretation of what "faith"[470] in an absolute sense means, both here and in Isa. 28:16. Faith involves, on the one hand, a self-abandonment to the announced action of YHWH (v. 7) and, on the other, the trusting acceptance of the prophetic word. These two dimensions are related to each other, while the anxiety mentioned in v. 2 and the subsequent seeking of help from the Assyrians, mentioned in 2 Kings 16:7 and here only presupposed, are excluded.[471] The analogous saying in Isa. 28:16 from the later period of Isaiah's activity has a similar background and takes a corresponding position, since it rejects participation in the emerging uprisings against Assyria (cf. Isa. 30:15). A reference to the promise of Nathan (cf. Isa 7:2a: "house of David" and 2 Sam. 7:16a[472]) must not be assumed in this connection. Any such reference also would only reinforce, not alter, what had been said before. It is equally true that a relationship of the "faith" to YHWH war and an oracle that comes from this context cannot be demonstrated.[473] אמן = '*mn* ("faith") hiphil does not occur in these settings. If the prophet Isaiah, who possibly stood close to the wisdom

circles, was the one who actually had made "faith" into a theologically important key word, then one could also point to different sapiential texts (Prov.
14:15; and 26:25) that speak of faith between persons and perhaps provide another origin for this concept. However, it may be difficult to discover an original situation in life for הַאֲמִין = *h'myn* ("to believe"). The oracle of salvation[474]
that H. Wildberger endeavored to use as the life setting offers, as he himself
sees, very little evidence for this and provides no direct support for the idea
(Pss. 27:13f.; 31:24f.; and 116:10; also Isa. 7:9).

As for Deutero-Isaiah, faith is, in Isa. 43:10, the objective of the disputation
between YHWH and the nations. Here a blind and deaf nation, who is the servant of YHWH, appears as a witness. However, at the same time, the nation itself is to be led to believe and acknowledge the singular nature of the divine
being of YHWH who had no origins and who does not perish (Isa. 43:8–13).
Belief is here already imbued with a much more robust content. According to
Isa. 53:1, no one has believed the message,[475] which, no doubt, was connected
with the nature and activity of the servant of God and then was raised through
the interpretive word of God in the structure of Isa. 52:13—53:12 to another
level.[476]

Faith as trust comes to expression in passages of the psalms (Pss. 27:13; and
116:10; cf. Dan. 6:24). Its content is more like trusting obedience in the psalm
on the law (Ps. 119:66). In Jonah 3:5 the faith of the people of Nineveh is fear
at the preaching of Jonah and a sign of their repentance that is then concretely
carried out (v. 9).[477]

Thus an activity of YHWH in word and/or deed precedes human faith. In
faith a person should and can "rest secure," considering what is believed to be
reliable. God's existence is not a question for Old Testament faith, and to believe in him consists primarily of expecting something from him and not thinking something about him. YHWH himself is the truthful God, the God of the
"amen" (Isa. 65:16), and the God of loyalty (Pss. 30:10; 57:11; Hos. 2:22; and
Deut. 32:4).

d. Trust

A look at the use of בָּטַח = *bṭḥ* ("trust") may provide yet a supplement to
what has been said.[478] The verb can describe the act of trust as well as trust itself, and it can describe certainty as both an inner and an outer condition. In
this connection, it is especially striking that the lack or failure of בטח = *bṭḥ*
("trust") frequently stands for futile, disappointed trust in the sphere of human
interaction.[479] In addition, one should not trust in strange gods, in false gods
and their images (Isa. 42:17; Hab. 2:18; Pss. 115:8; and 135:18), even if Assyrian negotiators demand it (Isa. 36:4, 7; cf. 37:10). "Another, even clearer
linguistic usage stands over against this plain literary usage: in YHWH his

community can know for certain that it can rely upon him."[480] "Whenever a human being is disappointed by other people, he or she may certainly be aware of the care of God."[481] Therefore one says that the ancestors trusted in God (Ps. 22:5f.), laments over the failure to trust (Zeph. 3:2; and Ps. 78:22), affirms that the king trusts in YHWH (Ps. 21:8), and also states that "blessed is the person who trusts in YHWH" (Jer. 17:7; cf. the contrast in v. 5; cf. Pss. 40:5 and 84:13). There is the discussion of the lack of trust in the prophetic laments (Jer. 13:25; 28:15f.; Ezek. 16:15; and Hos. 10:13).[482] Sapiential texts emphasize the significance of this trust (Prov. 3:5; 14:16; 16:20; 22:19; 28:25; and 29:5 cf. Pss. 32:10; 37:3, 5; and 112:7). The cultic community is called on to exude a trusting self-abandonment (Pss. 4:6; 9:11; 40:4; 62:9; and 115:9–11; cf. Isa. 26:4; 50:10; and Jer. 49:11). The admonition to trust found in Isa. 30:15 runs parallel to much of what is said about faith in Isa. 7:9. The discourse about trust in YHWH is especially common in prayers. Thus, confessing, lamenting worshipers praying the psalms wish to leave, are able to leave, must leave, or even have left their situation of need with YHWH.[483] Finally, "dwell securely" (שכב לבטח = *škb lbṭḥ* or ישׁב = *yšb* or similar) is a readily expressed and fitting promise especially in the period when the exile was threatened, just beginning, or had already commenced.[484] The psalmist acknowledges in thanksgiving that YHWH allows or may allow him to dwell in safety (Pss. 4:9; and 16:9; and Isa. 12:2), while wisdom promises this to the one who listens to its teachings (Prov. 1:33; 3:23; 10:9; and Job 11:18). Trust in YHWH, however, is readily associated with the connection between deed and consequence in sapiential texts,[485] according to which such trust is disbursed in life (Prov. 16:20; 22:19; 28:25; and 29:25; cf. 16:3; 18:10; 20:22; and 30:5). "[Therefore], there is always a relationship in view to which trust directs itself; *bṭḥ* means almost without exception a process that constitutes existence."[486] That there was, however, also a false trust in YHWH and his protective presence in the temple is made clear by the Deuteronomistic temple speech in Jer. 7:3–15 (vv. 4 + 14) that inquires after obedience and an ethically correct behavior.

Old Testament Hebrew also uses for "trust" the verb חסה = *ḥsh*, from which is derived the noun מחסה = *maḥăseh*.[487] This verb and the noun also have their place especially in prayers,[488] for example, in order to bring into the laments the motif of trust in the utterance of prayer.[489] In addition, they appear in the hymnic and thanksgiving components of the songs of lament[490] as well as in actual hymns and thanksgiving psalms themselves (Pss. 18:3, 31; and 118:8f.), in general songs of trust (Pss. 11:1; 16:1; 62:8f.; and 91:2), in a song of trust about Zion (Ps. 46:2; cf. Isa. 14:32), and finally in statements of hope.[491] Trust in YHWH includes renunciation of self-reliance (Psalm 11) and is an attitude that determines the whole of one's existence (Psalm 31). It also has to do here with hope in YHWH's deliverance. In Psalm 25, בטח = *bṭḥ* and חסה = *ḥsh* stand alongside each other (Ps. 25:2, 20), while trust is aligned with joy and singing (Ps. 64:11). Who trusts in YHWH finds refuge under the shadow of his wings, that is, security (Ps. 57:2). Here a reference to the sanctuary and its function in providing asylum is possible (cf. Pss. 36:8; 61:5; and 91:4; cf. Ruth 2:12), especially when the fundamental import of חסה = *ḥsh* is assumed to mean "to take shelter." Also חסה = *ḥsh* can be used in reference to other gods (Deut. 32:37), and in Ps. 34:8–11 a righteous worshiper is described who fears YHWH, trusts in him, and experiences the fruits of this attitude of faith (cf. Ps. 5:12f.). A trusting worshiper experiences protection, consolation, and redemption. The prophet polemicizes against false and illegitimate trust in political powers and his or her own power as well as against a trust in YHWH that is groundless (Isa. 28:15; and 30:1–3). Moreover, the positive expressions of trust belong overwhelmingly in the language of prayer, so that first person speech stands in the foreground as lament, petition (Pss. 17:7; and 31:20), thanksgiving, and confession ("I trust in you, shelter me with you").[492] Wherever the plural is used, the community is in view.[493] The macarism (Pss. 2:12; and 34:9, 23) stands close to this language of prayer.

e. Righteousness

In Gen. 15:6 (and Hab. 2:4?), faith and "righteousness"[494] are related to each other. How does righteousness look to YHWH who himself is declared to be *righteous*,[495] and when is a person righteous before him?[496]

Does the discourse about צדק = *ṣedeq* point to a condition and quality and צדקה = *ṣĕdāqâ* to one's concrete action, while צדיק = *ṣaddîq* is an adjective that is used of an individual person? If so, then, analogous to the "righteousness of YHWH," righteousness means less a general, normative behavior that, for instance, is oriented to the divine commandments and more a behavior that is especially related to the community (e.g., "to be found innocent of the accusations of others"; Deut. 25:1ff.). Thus, as is predominantly the case with divine righteousness which often is closely connected with that of the human being (cf. Psalms 111 + 112), righteousness means beneficial behavior (Gen. 20:4f.; 1 Sam. 24:17f.; and 26:23). Within the election and obligation of the God of Israel, the righteous person lives in a right and proper relationship with God that is like the corresponding relationship to his or her human community.

Consequently, such righteousness is expected of and practiced by the king who is responsible for the nation (2 Sam. 8:15; 15:4; 1 Kings 10:9; Pss. 45:5, 8; 72:1–3, 7; Prov. 16:12f.; 25:5; 31:9; Isa. 32:1; and Jer. 22:13, 15).[497] One expects righteousness from the coming king of salvation (Isa. 9:6; 11:4; and Jer. 23:5f.). This topic is further addressed in legal texts where the innocent have to be and have to continue to be "righteous" in a just pronouncement of judgment and the guilty are to be declared guilty (Exod. 23:1–3, 6–8; Lev. 19:15; and Deut. 1:16; 25:1; cf. 16:18–20; 1 Kings 8:32; Pss. 58:2f.; and 82:3).

That this is no longer the case is denounced by the prophets (Isa. 1:21, 24; 5:7, 23; 29:21; Amos 2:6; 5:7, 24; and 6:12). Whoever performs the command-ments of YHWH (Deut. 6:25; cf. 4:8; Pss. 19:10; and 119[498]) returns to a debtor his or her surety, is "righteous," and behaves righteously in terms of the con-ditions of the community that require such activity to be currently in force. Within these communal conditions, scales, weights, and measures are to be ac-curate, that is, "in order, righteous" (Lev. 19:36; Deut. 25:15; Ezek. 45:10; and Job 31:6). That this linguistic usage does not always correspond to our con-ception of righteousness is shown by the action in Genesis 38 according to which Tamar was righteous, but Judah was not (Gen. 38:26), for Tamar en-gaged in "conjugal relations . . . in order that the name of her husband might survive."[499]

The Old Testament has readily said that one may have practiced, ought to practice, or may not have practiced justice (משפט = mišpāṭ) and righteousness (Gen. 18:19; 2 Sam. 8:15; 1 Kings 3:6; 10:9; Jer. 22:3, 15; etc.). This language especially has its place in the speech of the prophets,[500] in Hos. 2:21 in the framework of a promise of divine action, and in Job (34:5) in the form of re-buke and indictment. Justice is that which suits and befits an indiviudal when righteousness commonly presides in and is practiced by him or her. Thus, in the Priestly source "righteous" and "pious, whole, complete" are used to-gether (Gen. 6:9: Noah; cf. Deut. 32:4 for YHWH), characteristics that are present already in the word "righteous" when used as a predicate of a human being (cf. Hos. 14:10). The term "righteous," in addition, is encountered also in the Psalter (Pss. 1:5f.; 32:11; 33:1; etc.), for righteousness is mediated also through the cult in which YHWH works to create salvation (Psalm 33; cf. Pss. 32:11; 118:15; and 142:8). Further, righteousness and loyalty (אמונה/אמת = 'emet/'emunâ) or righteousness and goodness/kindness/mercy (חסד = ḥesed) can be appropriately bound together because of the content of righteousness in the Old Testament.[501] "Righteousness" is not only just a deed, it is at the same time the consequence that results from its activation (Pss. 58:12; 112:3f.; etc.).[502]

Righteousness as a beneficial deed and result is, in addition, the content of Old Testament hope (Isa. 1:26f.; 9:6; 11:4–9; Jer. 23:5f.; 31:23; 51:10; and Hos. 2:20ff.). Since the salvation promised by Deutero-Isaiah (also called "righteousness": Isa. 46:13; and 51:5) brings about forgiveness, one seeks the reasons that necessitate for this forgiveness and discovers them in the absence of human righteousness. Human righteousness, for which one contines to hope and await, is now newly demanded (Isa. 56:1;[503] and 58:2; cf. 58:8; 59:14; 60:17; and 61:10f.). And when godly people, who have pointed out to others the pathway of righteousness, die (Dan. 12:1–3), then one hopes within the framework of apocalyptic expectations concerning the end that they will be resurrected.

The placing together of examples in Pss. 15:2–5; 24:3–5;[504] Job 31; and, above all, Ezek. 18:5–9 demonstrates that the practice of justice and righteousness has to do not only with individual deeds but also with a general behavior expressed in many kinds of actions. In the last-mentioned example (Ezek. 18:5–9), the thematic framework (in vv. 5 and 9) formulates in detail the judgment that is appropriate for and that issues from behavior of various kinds. Here, behavior toward God and behavior toward one's fellow human being are placed side by side,[505] and the verdict of "צַדִּיק הוּא" (= *ṣaddîq hû'*) (Ezek. 18:9) is the upshot of the interrogation.

The late Deuteronomistic passage of Deut. 9:4–9[506] assumes a special place in the testimony about human righteousness, according to which Israel is not to attribute to its own righteousness the (new) gift of the land. When YHWH still gives the land to a stiff-necked people, then it is only due to his, that is, "YHWH's[507] faithfulness to the promise he had sworn to the ancestors." Psalm 143:2 also stresses that no living person may be righteous before God (cf. Isa. 43:9, 26; and 45:25), and in its laments and accusations the Book of Job asks in similar fashion whether one could be righteous before the deity (Job 4:17; 15:14). Thus one comes to recognize that it is actually only YHWH who can bestow (Isa. 61:11; and Ps. 99:4) or impute righteousness (Ps. 106:31). It has often been maintained that there was a close relationship between "righteousness" and "covenant."[508] However, there is no Old Testament passage in which both terms appear together. Actually, it is only in Ps. 111:3, 5, and 9 that one can endeavor to discover a relationship between the two terms insofar as they relate to YHWH. Here, his "covenant" and his "righteousness" are both described as enduring forever.

In the wisdom literature and in the comparison of typical human beings as well as situations popular there, the "righteous" person stands over against the "wicked" person (רָשָׁע = *rāšā'*),[509] as does the wise person and the fool. The wise and the righteous are those (Prov. 9:9; 11:30; and 23:24) who practice justice and righteousness (Prov. 1:3; 2:9; 8:20; and 21:3; cf. 16:8). Wisdom provides to the sages what the cult also conveys. While the sages are less interested in cultic phenomena, they are especially interested in a fortunate life that results from everyday decisions. Good fortune comes to them and their righteousness rewards them, since the relationship between deed and event[510] is at work according to the understanding of the wise (Prov. 10:3, 25, 30; 11:4, 5f., 18f., 28, 30; 12:28; 13:6; 14:34; 21:21; 28:1; 29:6; etc.) and to the friends of Job (Job 8:6; 17:9; 22:2f., 19; 27:17; and 36:7). While Job describes his own righteousness (Job 29 [v. 14]; cf. 27:5f.; and 31), he was to determine nonetheless that God is not righteous toward him and consequently allows him to suffer as an innocent man. The other revelation, that no human is righteous before God (Job 9:2; and 40:8), is integrated with this thinking, since God would not otherwise bring punishment (Job 9:1 — 10:22). Qoheleth fundamentally contests the view that the righteous may have a better fate than the wicked (Qoh. 3:16f.; 5:7; 7:15; 8:14; and 9:2). Thus, for him it is better neither to be too righteous and wise nor too wicked and foolish (Qoh. 1:16f.).

f. Knowledge of God

Finally, mention should be made of the "knowledge of YHWH" within the Old Testament discussion of the human relationship to God.[511] While "knowledge" can stand here for piety, it is already thoroughly clear that this kind of knowledge does not have to do with an intellectual, cognitive process but rather with a process of life, that is, with an awareness that derives from the experience of living. This is recognizable in not a few passages through other, concrete expressions that are related to ידע (*yāda'* = "to know") (1 Kings 8:43; Isa. 11:2; Pss. 36:11; 91:14; Prov. 1:7; 2:5; 1 Chron. 28:9; etc.). "Not to know" YHWH is also a designation for sin (1 Sam. 2:12f.; Isa. 1:2f.; [6:9!]; Jer. 9:5; Hos. 4:10; and Job 18:21). Initially, Hosea and Jeremiah[512] were especially those who spoke accusingly of the absence of the knowledge of God or who, in a positive fashion, admonished or even promised the actualization of such knowledge.[513] The Deuteronomic/Deuteronomistic literature then follows with a warning to those whom it addresses.[514] According to Hos. 4:1–6, the priests were especially the ones who had the responsibility to transmit the knowledge of God and were to teach the correct behavior toward YHWH based on this knowledge (cf. Jer. 2:8; and Mal. 2:7). Other gods, by contrast, Israel did not know, nor was it supposed to know (Deut. 11:28; 13:3, 7, 14; 28:64; 29:25; 32:17; cf. also Jer. 7:9; 19:4; 44:3; and Dan. 11:38).[515]

11.9 Sin and Guilt

The psalms lament over the presence of hostility and attacks from "enemies" and "evildoers." In the wisdom literature, the wicked stand in contrast to the righteous (cf. also 1 Kings 8:31f.: Deuteronomistic). It goes well with the one who does not commit sin, as with the case of Job (Job 1:1). However, at the same time, when illness and suffering afflict Job, he must lament over the fact that God seeks to discover in him sin and guilt, having surely known that Job is innocent (Job 10:6f.). Prophets rebuke Jacob for his transgressions and Israel for his sins (Micah 3:8).[516] They accuse the nation as well as individuals of not acting in conformity with either YHWH or the community. The narrative literature sets forth examples of actions that were evil in YHWH's eyes and that were not pleasing to him, that were harmful to their fellow human beings and therefore were unjust before YHWH. Subsequently, the Old Testament sees human beings, like the whole of the nation of Israel, not only as creatures and mortals before God but also as sinners. Israel is seen not only in terms of election resulting from YHWH's action but also as a people and as individuals who refuse to live responsibly before this God. How does the Old Testament speak about the sin and the guilt of humans?[517]

a. Narrative Texts

The Yahwist saw it necessary at the beginning of his work not only to tell the story of the creation of humanity and the surrounding world but also to combine this scene immediately with another one in which the first humans received the initial commandment of YHWH while they were still in the garden of God in Eden (Gen. 2:4b–3:24).[518] This commandment was to make clear that humans are not "like God" but rather stand under God, that is, are responsible to him and are to acknowledge him as lord. And the adherence to this one commandment forbade the consuming of the fruit of the tree of knowledge, which the Yahwist interpreted as the tree of life (Gen. 2:16f.). The Yahwist immediately placed the transgression of this imposed commandment, which actually was not necessarily oppressive and difficult, into the context of his first large narrative unit on "creation and fall" and interpreted it accordingly as the human primeval event. And in the redaction of the Pentateuch as well as in the entire Old Testament, this narrative retained its place. This narrative not only tells how the first transgression of a divine commandment took place but also how it continues to occur. There were and there are no other humans than those who are described here.[519] Yet the expression "sin" occurs nowhere in this narrative. Its content is not defined but rather narrated. "Sin" in Genesis 2–3 consists of the desire of humans to be autonomous, to use their God-granted freedom to make the decision (Isa. 1:18–20) to decide against God. Sin is also understood as the failure to recognize the authority of God and as preferring to discuss the divine word rather than to observe it (Gen. 3:1–3). People vitiate even the divine commandment so long as or because they think it does not affect them, or they question whether it may be an intrinsically good commandment (Gen. 3:4f.), or they hope they may themselves become like god (cf. Isa. 14:14; and Ezek. 28:2), that is, their own lord who is not responsible to God. When the final decision regarding the tree and its fruit occurs, the serpent is silent, leaving the human[520] alone to make his decision, and the transgression of the commandment is almost obvious, almost self-evident. This transgression expands (Gen. 3:6b), for sin follows sin, from one sinner to another. As in the rest of the Old Testament,[521] there is here nothing of an "original sin" in the sense that sin or being a sinner is inherited,[522] perhaps not even by means of the sexual act.[523] The Old Testament also nowhere appeals to Genesis 3 in order to explain or to elucidate sin in some way. Probably, however, the Old Testament is aware of what R. Rothe[524] named the kingdom of sin where sin continued to be active and infectious. Indeed, the Old Testament knows of a solidarity existing between sin and guilt, because the descendants as well as their primeval ancestor, the sons as well as the fathers, have all sinned.[525] The Old Testament knows that all humans are sinners (Gen. 6:5; 8:21; Isa. 6:5; Pss. 51:7; 143:2; etc.; see below). The transgression of the divine commandment leads then not to the promised positive results but to disillusionment (Gen. 3:7), to the futile effort to flee from God (Gen. 3:8), and to an encounter with him. In this encounter, after the attempt to shift the blame for the guilt for the transgression, the guilt before God comes forth with all its worldly, interpersonal, and negative results (3:14ff.). The reach for autonomy led to the diminishment, not to the mastering, of life. It is masterfully told how sin comes into the world through human beings,[526] how sin takes place, and how sin leads to certain consequences. These things happen even though a term for sin has not yet appeared. Narrative theology occurs here that offers psychologically splendid, theological interests and statements in the form of story and discloses for its own present both etiological explanations as well as exemplary, typical, fundamental structures of human existence.

In the narrative about Cain and Abel (Gen. 4:1–16), which follows Genesis 3, the story tells about the first murder that, for God sake, also occurred as an act of fratricide. Here there comes forth from the mouth of YHWH (in v. 7) for the first time a reference to a dangerous sin (חטאת = ḥaṭṭā't) which lies in wait for human beings. This is the sin that once again addresses human responsibility (cf. Genesis 3),[527] but it is also a sin that the human being should master. However, the fact that humans are not able to rule over sin makes clear its power and the desire to sin as well as the weakness and the evil nature of humanity. Then, as the upshot of the narrative from the mouth of the evildoer Cain, there follows for the first time a confession of sin, where, moreover, a significant change in the meaning of the term occurs: "My guilt (עוני = 'ăwônî) is greater than I am able to bear (נשא = nś')" (Gen. 4:13). Thus, the narrator has the evildoer himself offer up a confession before and to YHWH. Sin, guilt, and punishment are seen here as one. The Old Testament thinking about unity as well as the connection between deed and result becomes clear. YHWH had the ability to remove the guilt; however, he did not do so. Rather, he places it fully upon the shoulders of the evildoer, who must bear responsibility for it in spite of the fact that he thinks he is not able to bear it. The consequences also here are narrated (Gen. 4:15f.). However, here as well (cf. Gen. 3:21) the narrative does not dwell only upon punishment; rather, it points to divine grace, for YHWH preserves even this "sinner" and protects him "only by reason of grace" (Gen. 4:15b). Thus, Genesis 4 is not only the first narrative about sin and guilt that compresses the action into particular terms, it is also at the same time a narrative of forgiveness that unfolds at least in rudimentary ways. This means, then, that in a similar way the discourse about forgiveness certainly is not yet conceptually compacted into particular terms. The remarkable new entrance of YHWH in his issuance of the general promise in Gen. 8:22 and then especially in his interaction with Abraham, including in particular the divine promises given him (Gen. 12:1–3), brings about the decisive change, contrasting with the divine judgments rendered to humans both before and immediately after the primeval flood in Gen. 6:5 and 8:21 (J).[528] Human sin, guilt, and hopelessness do not have the last word.[529]

The Priestly source was not familiar with a "fall due to sin," and probably in a conscious way did not narrate such a story because of its emphasis placed on a positively shaped view of human nature.[530] Rather, this document signals a steady movement of humans into a form of existence that is no longer fully related to God. This change in human existence is indicated by means of the decreasing length of life of the early human beings (Genesis 5) and then certainly by the surprising mention of the acts of violence (חמס = *ḥāmās*) and injustice that humans commit against each other and that subsequently trigger the primeval flood. With the judgment from the mouth of God (Gen. 6:13) that "the end of all flesh has come before me," P even takes up a word of Amos (Amos 8:2; cf. Ezek. 7:2),[531] although it shifts, moreover, this "end" to a distant past and in particular to the primeval flood. Moreover, in its final assessment of humanity, preparations for which were made by the negatively accentuated story of reconnaissance (Num. 13:32; and 14:36) and by the narrative about the disbelief even of Moses and Aaron (Num. 20:12), the Priestly document is not different from the Yahwist source, since for P the sacrificial cult and atonement are necessary for the human beings that it addresses and describes.

An additional narrative description of sin is 2 Samuel 11 which describes David's adultery and his crime against Uriah whom he dispatched in an evil manner. These actions were "evil in the eyes of YHWH" (2 Sam. 11:27b). David is confronted by the prophet Nathan, who implicates him by telling a paradigmatic story[532] at the conclusion of which the king himself renders judgment: "As YHWH lives, the one who has done this is a child of death" (2 Sam. 12:5). The famous "You are the man!" and the following announcement of punishment (2 Sam. 12:7–12) bring David to make the confession: "I have sinned against YHWH" (חטאתי ליהוה = *ḥāṭā'tî lĕyahweh*).[533] Thereupon, the prophet utters a word of forgiveness for David, while also announcing that the death of the child that has thus been conceived will take place. Here the deed of David not only is described as an evil action involving human beings but also at the same time is declared to be a sin against YHWH. And this is compressed into an Old Testament term for "sin" and "to sin," as was the case in Genesis 4.

The narrated sin of the people is then encountered in the so-called murmuring tradition present in the accounts of the wilderness wandering,[534] as well as in the Deuteronomistic descriptions of the history of Israel. These Deuteronomistic accounts begin in Deut. 1:24f. with the narrative about the faithlessness of the people regarding the (new) gift of the land and then are found especially in 1 and 2 Kings which tell of the apostasy of the kings and in general of the nation from YHWH. An especially important example of this occurs in 1 Kings 21 (Naboth and Ahab). In addition to these examples of Deuteronomistic narratives, other cases are present in Ezekiel 16; 20; and 23 as well as in the psalms that trace the history of Israel (Psalms 78 and 106). Israel obviously saw it necessary to describe and then to acknowledge its rebellion against and apostasy from YHWH. This probably goes back to the judgment of the preexilic prophets (Amos 4:6–12; Hos. 2:4ff.; Jer. 2:4–13; and 3:21–4:2) who, in their accusations, not only could and wished to see the present as sinful but also considered the past as exemplary for their contemporary situation. "The prophets have made sin into a theme of history."[535]

b. Terms

The Old Testament possesses many words to designate "sin." On the one hand, these are found mostly in contexts that have a profane sense, while, on the other hand, in defining what sin is, they provide it with their own particular accent. Among the (perhaps 25![536]) terms[537] that are present in the Old Testament semantic field for sin, that is, terms that express a deed or an attitude that YHWH condemns, the verbal and nominal words formed from the root חטא = ht' are the most frequent (verb חטא = ht'; substantive חטא = $h\bar{e}t'$; חטאה = $het'\hat{a}$; חטאה = $h\breve{a}t\bar{a}'\hat{a}$; חטאה = $hatt\bar{a}'\hat{a}$; and חטאת = $hatt\bar{a}'t$), after the more general term רעה = $r\bar{a}'\hat{a}$ (see below). This former term (ht'), which occurs also in colloquial speech for "mistake or failure" as in the failure to hit the mark or to reach an objective (Judg. 20:16; and Prov. 19:2) or as the transgression of a norm (1 Sam. 14:33ff.), means in the religious sphere chiefly an act, a transgression that harms a communal relaltionship either with a human being or with YHWH (Exod. 10:17; 1 Sam. 2:17, 25; 15:24; 1 Kings 8:46; and Jer. 16:10–12). This term can also signify transgressions of norms and concrete commandments, as, for example, David's transgression of the prohibition against adultery (cf. also Lev. 20:20; 1 Sam. 14:33ff.; 24:12; and Hos. 4:1, 6–8 as a concrete example of another kind).[538] David's confession, "I have sinned" (2 Sam. 12:13), was probably the usual form of such an admission, since this formula occurs frequently in the Old Testament.[539] The people spoke in a similar way when uttering their penitent confession, "We have sinned." "This forms the presupposition for the turning point in a situation of need and stands in close connection with the putting aside of strange gods and with the communal lament."[540] As a direct address in the second person singular or plural or in the third person in the form of an accusation or conviction, the formula establishes the basis for judgment.[541] Who sins must bear the consequences.

Sin reverberates back against the sinner, because YHWH wills and ordains it to be so.[542] However, according to several important witnesses, it should not, at the same time, affect the innocent (Gen. 18:17ff.; Num. 16:22; and Jer. 31:29). The call to repentance of sin is also important (Ezek. 3:20; 18:21, 24; 33:10, 14). The questions concerning the relationship of individual guilt to the corporate whole (Gen. 18:23ff.;[543] and Num. 16:22), questions that are associated with the Old Testament's thinking about wholeness in general (cf. Gen. 6:13; 9:22; 13:13; 20:9; Judges 19f.; and 2 Sam. 24:16), and the experience of present punishment for past guilt come to be viewed as difficult ones and are eventually answered in the negative, something that is clearly quite new (Deut. 24:16; Ezek. 18:2, 22f.; according to Jer. 31:29f., however, this has to do with the future).[544] Grace prevails with YHWH (Exod. 20:5f.; 34:6f.; and Jer. 32:18). He can cover over, wipe clean, bear away, and think no more on sin, and many other things[545] that the worshiper asks of him. When it is indeed said that one may have "sinned against you (YHWH) alone" (Ps. 51:6f.), and when sin and forgiveness stand more in the forefront than illness and healing (Psalms 51 and 130; cf. also Psalm 32), then sin is more deeply reflected upon here than elsewhere. The uncovering of sin and the accusations that are issued on the basis of sin stand in the foreground in the prophetic preaching,[546] although the concrete contents of sin receive different emphases in each individual prophet.

"The most important expression within this linguistic family is *ḥeṭ'* which indeed occurs only thirty-three times. However, especially in the Deuteronomistic and Priestly spheres (some eight times), the word designates an unforgivable burden of sin that reaches beyond individual acts. This burden of sin leads inevitably to death because of the principle of the relationship between the deed and its consequence."[547] חטאת = *ḥaṭṭā't* can designate, in addition to "sin," a sacrifice that is mostly translated as a "sin offering."[548] The passages for this term are found mainly in texts belonging to the Priestly document and to Ezekiel. "Through his instructions issued at Sinai, YHWH has in wise foresight provided for human sinfulness by allowing an Israelite sinner henceforth to be able to dispose of his sphere of sin at the sanctuary" (cf. Lev. 5:7). "There the animal in a literal sense becomes the sin through the offering in the actual presence of YHWH, meaning that the *ḥaṭṭā't* sphere is concentrated upon the animal and becomes, as it were, the flesh of an animal"[549] (cf. Lev. 4:3, 28). Atonement results, and, after the sacrifice, the forgiveness of the sinner who brought the offering is mentioned.[550] "Pervaded by the conviction that humans always will be entrapped by sin and, at the same time, driven by the concern that the future Israel united with its God around the tabernacle (Exod. 29:43–45) could again lapse into a history of degeneration as had once been experienced by the preexilic people, the warding off of sin becomes a decisive element of each great cultic act in the Priestly statutes."[551]

The term עָוֹן = 'āwôn ("offense, guilt"),[552] occurring also in the profane sphere, on the one hand, is used more in particular (early as well as late) literary contexts for the willful, intentional offense[553] against the law,[554] while, on the other hand, within the Old Testament thinking about wholeness that is dynamically shaped and that corresponds to the connection of deed and consequence, the word designates sin as a deed, as imputed guilt,[555] and especially as the punishment that results and consequently encompasses the entirety of the event.[556] So it is that through deed and guilt the individual and the community as well as the ancestors and their descendants are bound together,[557] for sin has consequences not only for the evildoers themselves but also for others.[558] In prophetic proclamations of judgment and the bases for judgment עָוֹן = 'āwôn is also obviously mentioned.[559] YHWH says that he may have become tired of and wearied by the guilt of Israel (Isa. 24). On the other hand, the mention of עָוֹן = 'āwôn has a privileged place in the statements of confession (e.g., Ps. 51:6f. or Ps. 90:7f.; cf. Gen. 4:13; 44:16; 1 Sam. 25:24; and 2 Sam. 14:9), in laments and thanksgivings,[560] and in cultic language and rituals in which something like this was addressed.[561]

The Hebrew term פֶּשַׁע = peša' designates primarily the legal concept of "crime"[562] and originated in judicial contexts. That the relationship of the community is wounded by an intentional and willful misdeed corresponds to Old Testament thought. In prophetic preaching (cf. already above, Amos), פֶּשַׁע = peša' is used in pronouncements of judgment and accusations.[563] It was often regarded as the most important, most severe, Old Testament word for sin. It is true, however, that this term "perhaps in Amos . . . (became) therefore the most severe Old Testament word for sin, because Israel's relationship to Yahweh was shaped in a most clearly defined way in the legal sphere."[564] Thus פֶּשַׁע = peša' has to do with a (criminal) break with YHWH who punishes the evildoer for his or her sin. Here one may point to a development from פֶּשַׁע = peša' as a single deed to that which is comprehensive. The latter is often expressed by the plural[565] or in combination with כֹּל = kōl ("all") or רֹב = rōb ("many").[566]

Rather frequently, however, sin is also very generally designated by "to be evil" or "to do evil."[567] To be "bad" and "evil" are also considered in Hebrew and in the thinking about the whole to be misfortune and wickedness.[568] If one does "evil in the eyes of YHWH,"[569] as especially the Deuteronomic/Deuteronomistic movement and texts dependent upon it often say, then this means that one has abandoned YHWH for Baal or other foreign gods or has constructed maṣṣēbôt and 'ašērôt or other "images" (Deut. 4:25; cf. 9:18). This is shown especially by the frequency of these passages in the Deuteronomistic condemnations of kings in the Books of Kings. According to a formula assigned to Deuteronomic legal texts,[570] Israel also was to "eradicate the evil from its midst, or from Israel." Behind this stands the Deuteronomic/Deuteronomistic conception of the pure, holy, people of God, for here the one who should be exterminated by the death penalty[571] is each time an apostate, one who entices others to abandon YHWH, a false witness (Deut. 19:19), an incorrigible son (Deut. 21:21), a dishonorable maiden (Deut. 22:21), and a kidnapper (Deut. 24:7). Cult and ethics are also both taken into consideration here. The apparent use of the expression "evil" before Yahweh, in a more general way in Gen. 38:7; Isa. 65:12; 66:4 and Ps. 51:6, shows that the more Deuteronomistic meaning of "evil" before YHWH as cultic apostasy may not be commonly put forward. This is also true, for example, for Gen. 6:5; 8:21; Isa. 56:2; Mal. 2:17; Ps. 34:17; etc., where none of the contexts even once provides an indication of what the evil consists of. Apart from Deuteronomic/Deuteronomistic linguistic usage, sin consequently may consistently be characterized most generally as an act of evil. Expressions such as "We were not willing to listen" and "We were not willing to travel the right path" (Jer. 6:16f.), as well as the specification of sin as apostasy (Isa. 1:4; and Jer. 2:5), rebellion (Num. 14:9; Isa. 30:9; and Ezek. 2:3), and a breaking of the covenant or the dissolution of the marriage between God and the people (Isa. 24:5; Jer. 3:8; 11:10; Ezek. 16:23) seek to make sin concrete. If an inquiry is made (and this occurs relatively rarely) to discover the basis for human sinfulness, then one may point to the weakness of human nature (Job 4:20; 25:6; Pss. 78:38f.; and 103:13f.).

Striking about the Old Testament discussions of sin on the whole are the facts that the distinguishing features of "sin" (as, e.g., also with "revelation")[572] do not need a special, religious language and that both cultic and ethical offenses are of equal rank in being marked and referred to as sin. YHWH's will is undivided, and there is *one* divine will that is active in all spheres. Sin was also no moral deficit or moral defect; rather, it has to do with doing something that displeases YHWH and that does not correspond to his will.[573] The consequences of sin relate not only to the sphere of human relationships (cf. only Genesis 4) and the earthly fortune of the evildoer, including, for instance, pain as punishment or illness,[574] but also to the reaction of YHWH within history. Both coincide in the principle of the relationship between deed and result,[575] for the thinking concerning the context of the sphere of action and the thinking about YHWH as judge[576] are seen as intertwined.

11.10 Atonement and Guilt

Every Hebrew term for "sin" that has been mentioned also occurs in the context of the rejection of forgiveness or the petition not to forgive.[577] The unforgivable nature of sin, therefore, is (disregarding חטא = *ḥēṭ';* see above) not emphasized through a particular, preferred term reserved only for this concept. Above all, however, the understanding of forgiveness is encountered rather in the petition for absolution or more usually, for instance, in speech that grants or promises forgiveness. This is true for the derivations of words from the roots of אטח = *ḥṭ'* ("sin"),[578] עו = *'āwôn* ("offense, guilt"),[579] and פשע = *peša'* ("crime"),[580] roots that also often occur in connection with each other. More-over, the verbs used for "forgiveness" are, above all, נשא = *nś'* ("to take away"), סלח = *slḥ* ("to forgive, pardon"), and כפר = *kpr* ("to cover, atone"). Thus the Old Testament not only is familiar with sin and guilt but also can tell about repentance,[581] forgiveness and atonement,[582] and even forgiveness with-out the appearance of a corresponding terminology.

a. נשא = *nāśā'*

We have already discussed in other contexts the fact that YHWH's grace exceeds his will to punish (Exod. 20:5f. par.) and that he "is compassionate and gracious, patient, and abounding in goodness and faithfulness" (Exod. 34: 6f.).[583] One encounters the verb נשא = *nāśā'* ("to bear, take away") together with several words for "sin," namely, עו = *'āwôn* ("offense, guilt") and de-rivatives from the root אטח = *ḥṭ'* ("sin"). This verb had the meaning "to bear" in various kinds of textual locations. However,in clearly recognizable, origi-nally cultic-declaratory speech,[584] the term is used of someone's[585] having to bear or being unable to bear the sin, the guilt, and subsequently the conse-quences that one's act had placed on him or her.[586] In this connection, substi-tution is possible according to some texts:[587] the priests in Exod. 28:38 (cf. Lev. 10:17?), the sons of the guilty in Num. 14:33, the prophets in Ezek. 4:4–6, and the servant of God in Isa. 53:12. The removal of sin through the sacrifice of an animal (Lev. 10:17 [?] and Lev. 16:21f.) probably has nothing to do with substitution but rather with elimination.[588] The verb נשא = *nś'* ("bear, take away") came to be used in the petition for forgiveness (cf. Gen. 50:17; Exod. 10:17; Num. 14:18f.; and 1 Sam. 15:25),[589] in (mostly later) doxologies,[590] in paraenesis (Exod. 23:21; and Josh. 24:19), and in prophetic proclamations of salvation as well as disaster (Isa. 2:9; 33:24; and Hos. 1:6). And the verb can stand isolated (elliptic) without an object (e.g., Gen. 18:24, 26; Isa. 2:9; Hos. 1:6; and Ps. 99:8). The remark that "our God" is praised as a forgiving God in Ps. 99:8 and, above all, the doxological-rhetorical question of the redeemed, postexilic "remnant"[591] in Micah 7:18f., "Who is a God like you who for-gives/takes away עו = *'āwôn* ('transgression, guilt')?" demonstrate that in these contexts one must have known and then stated that such forgiveness from a deity was nothing normal (cf. Ps. 130:4, "With you there is forgiveness, so that you may be feared"). That the relationship between guilt and punishment would come to break through the principle of the connection between deed and result was not at all an obvious development. That YHWH as the Lord of this principle of the connection between deed and result could break through it and did break through it by means of forgiveness, that is, by "bearing away" guilt and not "leaving one to die" (Pss. 16:10; and 141:8; cf. Pss. 86:13; and 118:17f.), was worthy of thanksgiving and praise. Thus it is no accident that the discourse of forgiveness[592] has its place especially in the petition,[593] in the thanksgiving, and in the doxology, and this is true not only for the use of the verb נשׂא = *nś'* ("to carry, take away").

b. סלח = *sālaḥ;* כפר = *kāpar;* פדה = *pādâ;* גאל = *gā'al*

In a more narrow sense, "forgive/forgiveness" of sins and guilt by YHWH is expressed some forty-six times in the Old Testament by the word סלח = *sālaḥ* and its derivatives (three times). This term occurs neither in secular usage nor in expressing forgiveness between human beings. Except for 2 Kings 5:18 (?) and Amos 7:2, all of these passages belong to the exilic and postexilic periods. A very small selection of texts that look back on certain particular offenses and are to be dated to the (early-) exilic period says that YHWH does not (Jer. 5:7; and Lam. 3:42), did not, and will not forgive (2 Kings 24:4; and Deut. 29:19).

The promise of forgiveness primarily has its place in prophetic (conditional as well as unconditional) promises of salvation to Israel/Judah/Jerusalem (Jer. 5:1; 31:34; 33:8; 36:3; and 50:20). With the exception of Jer. 5:1, all of these passages belong to the Deuteronomistic redaction of the Book of Jeremiah (Jer. 33:8) and still later literary strata. Forgiveness is the presupposition as well as the content of salvation. In Isa. 55:7 and 2 Chron. 7:14 (without parallel in 1 Kings 9), repentance and forgiveness likewise are coupled.

The first of the prayer texts to mention is Neh. 9:17 where, on the one hand, God's nature is trustingly set forth as that of a (and even always: Ps. 86:5[594]) forgiving God. On the other hand, his historical actions for his people are mentioned as a concrete expression of his acts of forgiveness (substantive plural). Daniel 9 (vv. 9 = 19) is a prayer text that is closely related to the text in Nehemiah 9. Forgiveness introduces salvation (Ps. 103:3) as becomes clear in the context of the request for forgiveness in Ps. 25:11 that is central to the entire thrust of the psalm (cf. vv. 17–20).

In prayers of intercession,[595] Moses asks for divine forgiveness for the people's culpable deeds as well as for their lack of trust (Exod. 34:9; and Num. 14:19: Deuteronomistic interpolation?), and he points to earlier instances of forgiveness of "this people" as the motive for hearing the prayer (Num. 14:19b with נשׂא = *nś';* "to carry, take away"). It is no wonder that Solomon's prayer for the dedication of the temple, as a kind of Deuteronomistic programmatic text from the late-exilic period, often asks for the forgiveness that is so central to the entire text. This request is frequently made in order to abrogate punishment and to help to open up a new future (v. 30!) for the nation that has become guilty (1 Kings 8:30, 34, 36, 39, and 50 = 2 Chron. 6:21, 25, 27, 30, and

39). The community between YHWH and his people should continue to be preserved or restored. Amos was successful in the uttering of his initial visions, for YHWH did grant a reprieve from punishment (Amos 7:2). However, the prophet ceased his intercession later on in the sequence of the visions.

Finally, according to 2 Kings 5:18, even the Syrian military commander Naaman, as a non-Israelite, offered his prayer, and at the forefront of his petition was forgiveness. He asked for forgiveness, because he knew that when he returned to his homeland it would be necessary for him then to worship his own native gods in addition to YHWH, whom he knew as the only true God.[596] "The fulfillment of this petition indeed is not stated *expressis verbis*. Still, one may derive indirectly from the answer of Elisha a guarded promise so that not only is the petition a singular one within the Old Testament but so is the answer that is associated with the worship of strange deities."[597]

The frequent combination of סלח = *slḥ* ("to forgive") and כפר = *kippēr* ("to atone") allows one to recognize that forgiveness was also something that one through the cult strove to obtain and experience,[598] chiefly with the חטאת = *ḥaṭṭā't* ("sin") sacrifice and the אשם = *'āšām* sacrifice.[599] Leviticus 4:20 relates the event as well as the statement of forgiveness to the entire community, even though it is only the person who is offering the sacrifice (in Lev. 4:22 the נשיא = *nāśî'* ["prince"]) who is at issue. Up to Lev. 5:26 (cf. the larger context of Lev. 5:21–26), sins are propitiated and forgiven that are committed without willful intent (Lev. 4:2, 22, 27; cf. 4:13).[600] Forgiveness in association with a ritual of atonement is next mentioned in Lev. 19:20–22 and Num. 15:22ff. The verb סלח = *slḥ* ("to forgive") occurs here in the niphal in a formula that completes the execution of the ritual, something that may be especially well recognized in Lev. 4:31.[601] Here it must be YHWH who is considered to be the subject, and it was probably the priest who pronounced forgiveness. Forgiveness without a rite of atonement occurs according to Num. 30:6, 9, and 13 within the sacral-legal findings pertaining to the nonfulfillment of a vow by a woman when the reason resides not with the woman herself but with the annulment of the vow by the father or her husband.

The association of atonement and forgiveness with the activities of sacrifice that are a consequence of human sin is not to be understood either in terms of atonement creating the presupposition for the forgiveness of human guilt or in terms of humans first doing something to which God responds and reacts. Rather, atonement and forgiveness are gifts and actions of God that proceed from him and benefit human beings.[602] Atonement and forgiveness comprise the purpose that is realized in the act of atonement. YHWH effectuates atonement that mediates forgiveness, while the priest (only) carries out the atoning act.[603]

God's action of forgiveness is conveyed not only by נשא = *nś'* ("lift up, bear") and סלח = *slḥ* ("forgive") but also by numerous other expressions.[604]

YHWH is petitioned to "allow to pass" the sin (2 Sam. 24:10 = 1 Chron. 21:8—העביר עון = *h'byr 'wn;* cf. Micah 7:18 עבר = *'br* qal), and both the promise of forgiveness (2 Sam. 12:13; cf. Zech. 3:4) and the request for it (Job 7:21) can thus follow as a consequence. Guilt is covered over (כסה = *kissâ;* Pss. 32:1; and 85:3), and sin is wiped clean or washed away (מחה = *mhh;* Isa. 43:25; 44:21f.; Jer. 18:23; Neh. 3:37; Pss. 51:3f., 9, 11; and 109:14). That these expressions complement, interpret, and perhaps even attract one another is shown by their association in Psalms 25 and 51. Psalm 103:12; Isa. 38:17; and Micah 7:19 offer other, rather especially impressive images (to allow sin to be as distant as the sunrise is from the sunset, Ps. 103:12; to cast sin behind the back, Isa. 38:17; and to cast sin into the sea, Micah 7:19). Then YHWH "remembers" the sin no more (זכר = *zkr;* Isa. 43:25; 64:8f.; Jer. 31:34; and Ps. 25:7), or "he does not take it into account" (חשב = *hšb;* Ps. 32:2). "To heal" (רפא = *rp'*) can finally be the sign of forgiveness as well as the act of forgiveness itself (Pss. 41:5; 103:3; 107:17, 20; Hos. 6:11 + 7:1; 14:3f.; Jer. 3:22; Isa. 6:10; 53:5; etc.).[605]

Since YHWH is "merciful" (Exod. 34:6 par.), "to be merciful" (or "to grant mercy") is expressed as an action by him.[606] In the context of Exodus 32–34, the granting of the mercy of divine accompaniment from Exod. 33:12ff. is a sign of forgiveness following the apostasy of the people. "Be merciful to me" is a frequent petition in the psalms,[607] shows a close proximity to the petition for forgiveness (cf. only Pss. 41:5; and 51:3f.; also 25:16), and makes it once again clear that this request for forgiveness is a favorite place in which the Old Testament worshiper speaks of forgiveness by YHWH. The expression of the possibility of hope in 2 Sam. 12:22 (מי יודע = *mî yōdēa'* ["who knows?"]) speaks of the chance of God's "being merciful" in the context of sin and forgiveness. Amos 5:14 has a more timid request of YHWH: "Perhaps, YHWH, God Sebaoth, shall be merciful to the remnant of Joseph" (cf. Ezra 9:8).

In Ps. 26:11, the verb פדה = *pdh* ("to redeem")[608] stands beside חנן = *hnn* ("to show mercy, grace"). That פדה = *pdh* ("to redeem") originally in its profane use contains within itself something of a legal action (e.g., ransom with the provision of an equivalent value) becomes less important in its religious use when YHWH is the subject of "redemption." This term, which in and since Deuteronomy[609] is used to interpret the liberation of Israel from Egypt as an act of justice that sets free (cf. esp. Deut. 24:18), is not so much a military event[610] as it is a divine action of forgiveness of the nation (Hos. 7:13) as well as of the individual (Job 33:27f.). That פדה = *pdh* ("to redeem") also is found in expressions of hope is indicated by Jer. 31:11; Isa. 51:11; and the text that is dependent upon these passages, Isa. 35:10 (cf. also Isa. 1:27; and Zech. 10:8). That such a hope in the exilic period was not self-evident is demonstrated by the question of YHWH in Isa. 50:2. As seen in Ps. 130:8, the hope in a final redemption finds expression also in prayer. Moreover, the present conclusions of two psalms point to redemption. These conclusions, more than likely added by a later hand, in one instance pray for the redemption of Israel (Ps. 25:22), while in another serve to confirm the certainty of this hope in salvation (Ps. 34:23). That פדה = *pdh* ("to redeem") consequently can be used to refer to the past liberation of the nation from Egypt, the deliverance of the individual (cf. also 2 Sam. 4:9; 1 Kings 1:29; Pss. 26:11; 31:6; 71:23; etc.), the promised salvation of the prophet (Jer. 15:21), and the anticipated setting free of Israel in the future[611] is not unimportant evidence when one inquires about theological correlations. The individual Israelite is embedded within the history of his people and drawn into the hope that is borne by the God who works in it. Psalm 49:8f. knows that a person cannot "redeem" either another individual or even himself. However, this psalm also knows that God[612] is able to do this (v. 16).

The verb גאל = *g'l* ("to redeem")[613] is often placed together with פדה = *pdh* ("to redeem"). In distinction to פדה = *pdh* ("to redeem"), the activity that גאל = *g'l* ("to redeem") denotes is a personal, even familiar (Lev. 25:48f.) bond between the parties involved.[614] The Book of Ruth (Ruth 2:20; 3:12; and chap. 4), Jer. 32:6ff., and the legal stipulations in Lev. 25:25ff., 47ff. enable one to recognize this quite well. Like פדה = *pdh* ("to redeem"), גאל = *g'l* ("to redeem") is also used for both the redemption of the individual in the past as well as in the present and the deliverance of the nation in the past, present, and future.[615] Then גאל = *g'l* ("to redeem") was used, probably since the exile, for the interpretation of the liberation from Egypt (Exod. 6:6; 15:13; Pss. 74:2; 77:16; 78:35; and 106:10). Hope for other, analogous acts of redemption is then founded upon this primal act of liberation (Isa. 63:9). The first exodus from Egypt forms the basis for hope in a new exodus from Babylon (Isa. 51:10f.; cf. 48:20; and Micah 4:10), as indeed Deutero-Isaiah readily uses the verb גאל = *g'l* ("to redeem") for the description of the delivering act of YHWH.[616] In assurances of salvation and promises, whether as YHWH speeches containing hymnic self-predications and as prophetic oracles or adjoining confessions uttered by the people ("our savior": Isa. 47:4), YHWH, for the first time in the Old Testament, is designated as the גאל = *gō'ēl* ("redeemer") of Israel in order to establish the basis of the prophet's message of consolation and to make it concrete. In addition, "he anchors the end of Israel's history in its beginning."[617] Salvation and the forgiveness of sin are promised together (Isa. 44:22f.). Trito-Isaiah is also a collection of writings that seek in regard to this very point to hold fast to what Deutero-Isaiah has asserted as well as to think about it once more in a new situation (Isa. 59:20; 60:16). In Isa. 63:9 past, present, and future are considered together under the same, major, theological theme of liberation from Egypt (cf. Ps. 106:10). YHWH's salvation is expressed in thankful praise (Lam. 3:58) or becomes the desired object of a petitioner's prayer (Ps. 119:154). Job confesses YHWH as his גאל = *gō'ēl* ("redeemer") who becomes the basis of his hope for the authentication of his integrity in his last hour (Job 19:25), while the psalmist in Ps. 19:15 expresses trust in YHWH as "my savior."

On the whole, "forgiveness" is not an exclusively exilic and postexilic theme in its various forms of expression, but it is witnessed in these periods in a considerably frequent number of occurrences, and it receives then an obviously more substantial interest than in the preexilic period.[618] The postexilic period is the exclusive location for the expression "sin." On the one hand, this is connected with the experience and the interpretation of the exile as the punishment of YHWH as well as the new beginning that is the object of hope and gift. On the other hand, this is associated with a strengthened awareness of sin and feeling of human alienation from YHWH.[619] Several observations support this impression. One is the fact that it was considered necessary even in these times to say that YHWH's Spirit was needed to transform rather fundamentally both humanity and nation.[620] Another is the combining together of both the forgiveness of sin and the gift of the Spirit for the purpose of transformation in Psalm 51, as well as forgiveness and new obedience in Jer. 31:31–34 and Ezek. 36:26f. The experience of forgiveness in the Old Testament on the whole is bound up with the positive transformation of the outer circumstances of life, above all a change that leads to the ending of the experience of punishment. This often signifies the transformation of need into support, of illness into healing, and of slavery and hostility into liberation and restitution. YHWH was indeed also the God who plainly had saved and released from bondage the lord who had bound himself to his own and the savior of the living who had yoked himself to mortal beings. This worldliness of the Old Testament (W. Zimmerli) is one of the many positive features of this book. Liberation and freedom cannot only be inner and spiritual qualities.

Thus the Old Testament describes and even requires the human being to be a worshiper who fears God. The meaning of this fear of God includes a variety of nuances. For example, the Old Testament describes the fear of God in the sense of faith that is portrayed as active involvement, while it is also expressed as accepting trust. The person who lives among the chosen people of God is to live in harmony with this community, that is, is to behave in a "righteous" way, since his or her God is also a righteous being whose works of righteousness bring about salvation. This has to do, not with absolute norms, but with life that is lived in a personal relationship with God who has made himself accessible to the community. The fear of God has to do with mutual loyalty between the people of Israel as well as with well-being that is reciprocally demonstrated. If God elects a people and makes accessible to humans community with himself, then there also occurs in the Old Testament the acceptance of the sinner and of sinners, even if, as is often true, this is narrated more than it is conceptually expressed. The action of God precedes that of humans, even as election goes before obligation and as divine turning toward humanity is prior to the response of obedience (cf. Exod. 19:3–8). It is not the following of the commandments and the obedient life in the covenant that first makes the Israelites members of the people of God. However, it is probably the case that they can be removed from this community. Primarily, however, Old Testament piety is responsive in nature, but it does not seek to attain something. What God does to Israel (cf. Deut. 7:6–11), and what results consequently for the humans who belong to the Old Testament people of God, is the model for what God desires purely and simply for all human beings. For example, what happened to Jacob as an assumed deceiver (Genesis 27ff.; and Hosea 12) was something that was analogous to what Israel experienced under the God of Jacob (Isa. 41:8, 14; 42:24; 43:1, 22; and 44:21–23), and the God of Israel/Jacob is then the God also of the nations (Isa. 44:1–5; 45:1–7; and 49:5f.). These are norms that God has established to order the behavior of human beings in the Old Testament and to impart to them both stability and orientation. Acceptance by God involves the experience of both forgiveness and life, something that chiefly occurs in the cult and as the consoling word. And all this occurs for the guilty in spite of their guilt. There is the experience of the new turning of God toward humans in spite of their own mortal failure in responding to his demanding will. And there is the guidance toward salvation that passes by way of apostasy and judgment and comes to realization through the new work of YHWH's creation and the doing of his justice (cf. once more the psalms in general; then see Exodus 33f.; Psalms 51; 130; Ezekiel 18; 36:22ff.; 37:1–14; Jer. 31:31–34; and Deutero-Isaiah). YHWH forgives on account of the honor of his name and because of his nature as God (Ps. 79:9f.; cf. Pss. 74:18; and 115:1f.). His turning toward humanity is grounded in himself alone. Thus the individual worshiper, who is the first to confess that there is no living person who is righteous before YHWH, offers the petition: "Do not enter into judgment with your servant" (Ps. 143:2). Consequently, already in the Old Testament it is clear that within the particular, fundamental structures of Old Testament piety[621] there already exists what Paul calls the justification of the sinner.[622]

Chapter 12. The Life of the Elect
(Foundational Questions for Ethics and Ethos)[1]

It is also the case that in regard to the question of ethics one expects or hopes to find a great deal of instruction from the message of the Old Testament. However, it must be remembered that the ethical instructions within the Old Testament originated in a period of time that is a great distance from us and in a form of a society that often is very alien to us. These instructions are directed to members of a nation at that time and to a community that is always identical with that nation. Whether these teachings can be transferred as generally valid concepts to the sphere of universal human life is a question that now is to be concretely asked but not presupposed. For example, Old Testament laws about war, commandments concerning the ban, and regulations regarding purity (Deut. 7:1ff.; 20; and Leviticus 11ff.) bring out this difficulty rather clearly. Even so, the Decalogue, which is always and again valued as so central to the Old Testament, found a new and continuing interpretation in the Sermon on the Mount and later on, for example, in Luther's catechisms. Thus, as one considers the matters now to be discussed, it is the case that the present project is intentionally and primarily descriptive in nature and thus will largely exclude contemporary evaluations.[2] Nevertheless, one may suggest that in the area of ethical instructions the "interplay between Yahwistic faith and society"[3] especially can be of general interest for ethical questions in the modern period. Thus, fundamental questions and some substantial problems of Old Testament ethics will be treated here. However, one cannot avoid the fact that this endeavor will represent more of a systematic overview than the subtleties of historical analysis.[4] The latter would be scarcely possible, in any case, because of the nature of the sources.

12.1 Election and Obligation

The election and obligation of the people of God by their God YHWH belong together, as much as the exodus and the covenant, the covenant and the law, faith and action, and historical action and the law that is based upon and appeals to it. "The law of the Old Testament that is consequently understood as given by God has its foundation in the relationship of God to Israel that is constituted through divine election."[5] The preambles of the Decalogue in Exodus 20 and Deuteronomy 5 make this entirely clear, and the statement, "All that YHWH has said we will hear and do" (Exod. 24:7), with its characteristic sequence of verbs that is peculiar to the Old Testament, underscores the importance of doing. The relationship between YHWH and his people is also supposed to be an ethical one. The chosen nation is "made holy," for YHWH has separated this people out (Deut. 7:6), and they are to live and even now live as a holy nation (Lev. 20:7; and Deut. 14:21). "Be holy, for I am holy" it reads (Lev. 11:44f.; 19:2; and 20:26), and the statements "I am holy" and "I am YHWH" appear more often as a pronounced final clause in ethical instructions (Lev. 18:5, 30; 19:4, 10, 12, 14, 16, 18; etc.). Israel also was to "walk with YHWH" in an ethical way (Micah 6:8). YHWH's love for his people occasions love in response (Deut. 7:8; 10:12; etc.). All of this means, not only that ethical diversity in the Old Testament is related to a particular point and then organized by it, but also that, in the Old Testament, there is no fully autonomous ethic, and this is true even for wisdom literature.[6] Rather, what is central to ethics in the Old Testament is the emphasis placed on service to God. Israel's election to service is the "waking call . . . to service in the kingdom of God."[7] A God who has revealed himself in history cannot be indifferent toward ethics. "Now such a God overcomes the anonymity of uncertain obligations."[8] This is indicated by the primeval history (Gen. 4:9) as well as by the narratives of the ancestors, the Decalogues as well as the early historical writing, and prophecy (Amos 3:2) as well as cultic texts (Psalms 15 and 24). Thus all "laws" are also known at Sinai and attributed to Moses.[9] In this way, all the laws are related to election and obligation, even when the molding of individual ones by YHWH is still decidedly different, something that a comparison, for instance, between the Covenant Code (Exod. 20:22—23:19) and the Book of Deuteronomy indicates. "The law grows, so to speak, within the context of faith."[10]

Thus, even YHWH can become the *object* of choosing, while the people and even the individual (Ps. 25:12) appear now as the subject (Deut. 26:17–19; and Josh. 24:15, 22; cf. Judg. 5:8; and 10:14 for the choosing of strange gods). This involves the nation's and/or the individual's willing acceptance of divine election, the election of life through YHWH's law (Deut. 30:19), the doing of his will (Josh. 24:14), the traveling along the path where YHWH leads and also wishes to provide moral guidance (Ps. 119:30, 173, etc.; Zech. 1:3), and ethical community with this God. The ethos is such that the people of God can even expand what had been the limits of their former boundaries (Isa. 56:4: e.g., castrated men who, however, observe the Sabbath). Thus, even in the area of ethics the free gift of the chosen community is openly acknowledged and lived, and the ethics of Israel increasingly become the ethics of response (J. L'Hour),[11] a life lived in freedom, righteousness, and communal loyalty both required and given by YHWH, and a choosing of the right way that is in accordance with the divine will.

If now, however, life is supposed to stand in service to the God who elects, then this God clearly points the ones inquiring after the ethical dimensions of the divine will once more to history, to their fellow human beings, and to their responsibility for their world and their creation. According to the Old Testament, this knowledge is the strongest impulse for moral action: it is YHWH who is the one who addresses ethically both us and me.[12] The motivations in the Old Testament legal collections[13] allow one to recognize this ever more clearly in their historical development. The joy in the law (Psalms 1; 19B; and 119) calls one to responsibility before the God who elects, whose gift consists of the announcements of his will. Where YHWH rules, humans stand within his community that requires obligation. Thus the rest of God as gift and the social responsibility of Israel as duty stand beside each other and comprise the different rationales for the commandment of the Sabbath (Exod. 20:8–11; and Deut. 5:12–15). Since YHWH himself is righteous, and that means he behaves faithfully toward his community (Deut. 32:4; Pss. 11:7; 25:8; 116:5; etc.),[14] he desires to see such righteousness actualized among those who are his own (Isa. 1:17; 5:7, 18ff.; 28:17; Jer. 21:11f.; Micah 3:9–12; Pss. 18:21ff.; 103:6ff.; etc.). Beyond this, Deut. 9:4–6 found itself compelled to deliberate on the fact that Israel could certainly never successfully obtain this level of righteousness.[15] The commandments, which concern the behavior of humans toward God, are, in terms of value and substance, not to be separated from those which concern fellow humans, something that the Decalogues likewise show. "You shall not hate, but rather you shall love — for I am YHWH" (cf. Lev. 19:15–18). "You shall rise before those with gray hair — for I am YHWH" (Lev. 19:32). These theological statements concerning the identity and authority of YHWH can become the central argument for Old Testament ethics. The other type of statement forming the rationale for Old Testament ethics is an anthropological and communal one: "as you" (Deut. 5:14; and Lev. 19:18). One is also able to see how important this ethical sphere was and is for Yahwistic faith and therefore for Old Testament piety, for there is always the appeal to an action that is appropriate for YHWH and for the people of God. This ethical sphere continues to say, "You shall do or not do this!" but never once does it demand, "You shall believe or not believe this!" Israel is elected by YHWH and daily is "to choose" anew YHWH as its own God. It is to declare itself a follower of YHWH through its activity on YHWH's behalf and to confess his divine activity that takes precedence over human action both in substance and in time. It is then in the Book of Deuteronomy, and above all its frames that are Deuteronomistically formed, that these associations are above all clearly articulated (cf., e.g., Deut. 6:10–25; 8:1–6, 7–20; and 11:1–32), while the Holiness Code follows it in this regard (Leviticus 17–26). One can clearly recognize the influence of the prophets' ethical requirements on this development of the Old Testament's ethical instructions and their developing argumentations that continue to gain in importance during the exilic and postexilic periods. It was and is YHWH who demands the good that "is stated" to Israel (Micah 6:8), and the right conduct toward YHWH belongs to the ethos of Old Testament human beings, a conduct that can be characterized in a variety of different ways.[16] However, this conduct continues to be the basis for all that follows and all that was closely connected with it (Job 1:1). This is seen, for example, in the initial commandments of the Decalogue as well as in the ritual commandments and prohibitions.

12.2   Ethos and Morality

The Old Testament wisdom corpus and especially the Book of Proverbs, closely related in its ethical instructions to similar literature in ancient Israel's cultural environment, allow one to recognize that the Israelite ethos was partially shaped by the "sages," who stand behind this sayings wisdom, were educated, and also were socially better situated. This ethos involved a behavior that at the time was generally one for which a person strove.[17] This, however, applies to other spheres of Old Testament literature that point to recurring, ethical ways of behaving, that is, to what might best be called *customs*.[18] Thus Abraham treated Abimelech in a manner that "a person should not do" (Gen. 20:9), when he passed off his wife Sarah as his sister. The narrator probably in a conscious way allows this judgment to be made by a non-Israelite. In the rationale provided for the announcement of disaster against the foreign nations, among others the prophecies against the nations by Amos (Amos 1:3–2:16) also appear capable of reaching back to a very basic awareness of right and wrong.[19] Thus, as pertains to ethical conduct in ancient Israel, there was much that was regulated and determined by custom and habit. In respect to the national consciousness, certainly this was also true: "In the whole of ethical ideas, religion and morals have merged."[20] This means they permeate each other. The law of hospitality, for instance[21] (Gen. 18:3ff.; 19:1, 6ff.; 24:14; Judg. 19:3ff.; 1 Kings 17:12; 2 Kings 4:8ff.; and Job 31:32; as a contrast: Judg. 5:24ff.), something that is never expressly mentioned in any of the Old Testament legal collections, belongs to these cases involving custom, as does the law of blood vengeance[22] (Num. 35:19; and Deut. 19:12). While the latter continued to be practiced for a long time when there was a murder or an act of manslaughter, the law was first circumscribed in Deut. 24:16.[23] Its frequent mention in legal texts as well as in narrative literature shows, however, that this practice was not exceptional.[24]

12.3   An Ethos Shaped by YHWH

Above all, Israel's ethos was to be shaped by Yahwistic faith and determined by the character of its God. YHWH's authority that obligates his followers stands behind the Decalogue and the law. Whoever YHWH seeks must also seek the good (Amos. 5:4f., 14f.). Even agriculture is determined in its course by YHWH's character (Isa. 28:26–29). Further, the narrator has the king's daughter say to her half-brother who is sexually abusing her, "One does not do this in Israel!" (2 Sam. 13:12f.), although marriage between the two would have been normal in Egypt. One says that this may be "a scandal (נבלה = *nĕbālâ*) in/to Israel" (Gen. 34:7; Deut. 22:21; Josh. 7:15; Judg. 20:6, 10; and Jer. 29:23; cf. Judg. 19:23f.; 20:3; and Exod. 22:2). It is necessary to eradicate the evil "out of Israel," "out of your midst."[25] This often has to do with sexual offenses, a sphere in which Israel probably consciously and often wanted to be set apart from its cultural environment. Israel ought not and desired not to live as the Canaanites did in this area of life (Lev. 18:3; Exod. 23:34; and Jer. 10:1f.; cf. Lev. 18:22ff.; and 20:13–33). The so-called Law of YHWH's Privilege (Exod. 34:10–27)[26] also shows how Israel's faith and its order of society regulated by him stands in opposition to the Canaanite order of city-states. In addition, decisions and setting boundaries are essential marks of the Israelite ethos.[27] The religious-ethical term "(an) abomination (for) (תוֹעבה = *tô'ēbâ*)" (or plural, and in the Old Testament the term occurs both with and without "to YHWH"), attested also in Israel's cultural environment, courses its way throughout the wisdom literature[28] and is intensified in Deuteronomic and Deuteronomistic thought and related literature.[29] However, the term is not found at all in the Covenant Code. Nevertheless, "abomination" designates both cultic taboos and ethically negative practices and makes the explicitly ethical consequences of YHWH faith recognizable and obligatory. YHWH's character and actions are to determine Israel's own conduct (Exod. 20:11; Deut. 5:15).

One who is a debtor, whose pledge has been withheld, may call upon YHWH, who then will hear him (Exod. 22:25f.). Likewise the poor person may cry out to YHWH, if and when a loan is refused him (Deut. 15:9). The oppressed may and ought to turn to YHWH in any event, for to him the ethical action of his people is not a matter of indifference. Therefore the correlation between the human and the ethical is not insignificant (Exod. 22:20–22; and Deut. 24:14f.). A creditor, by contrast, who returns to the debtor his or her pledge acquires through this means righteousness from YHWH (Deut. 24: 10–13).

Israel should be formed and sustained as the people of God by the ethical regulations of the Old Testament's collections of laws, and thus it ought not to conduct itself in the manner of the pagan nations (Lev. 20:24b; Deut. 12:29ff.; 1 Kings 14:22–24; 2 Kings 16:3; 17:7ff.; Ps. 106:35; etc.). An individual sinner contaminates the entire nation (Joshua 7; 1 Samuel 14; and Judges 19–20). Thus the "you" of the legal collections addresses the individual Israelite as well as the nation, something that Deuteronomy can underscore in its present form, for singular and plural forms of address stand beside each other in this book. In their actions, the Israelites are also concerned about the deeds of their ancestors, and they are united with them through the specific "today" of the divine address and claim (Deuteronomy). The Old Testament is also familiar with both the love of God (Deut. 6:5) and the love of neighbor (Lev. 19:18),[30] and the summation of the two in the twofold commandment of love is clearly anchored in the Old Testament. The prophets use this as the basis for their indictment when and if evil is done to the neighbor (Isa. 3:5; Jer. 5:8; 9:7; 22:13; and Ezek. 22:12).

In the Old Testament legal collections, it is probable that at first only the things that were disputed in their solutions and consequences were codified. What remained, the so-called "gaps in the law," were regulated by custom for a time, until a legal decision that clarified a dispute had to be added. Research has indicated that it is indeed probably the case that the Israelite (as well as the ancient Near Eastern) legal collections contain decrees or even protocols of judgment about once debated legal cases.[31] The Old Testament's locating all of these legal collections at Sinai, including the Decalogue, the Covenant Code, and the Holiness Code, and its understanding of them as an interpretation of the Decalogue (Deuteronomy) make them into regulations of divine law, since YHWH is also the defender of justice and morality. There is no distinction at all between morality, law, and religion. Since the exile, a great deal of tradition, including, for example, the Sabbath and circumcision,[32] had to be more clearly connected with the character and will of YHWH on account of election and its preservation as a teaching (cf. Gen. 2:1–4a; 17: P). One asked more and more whether and how he or she could be obedient to YHWH in such areas as the law of hospitality, the law of the family, or even general morality. The earlier multiple expressions of morality, which in part were due to the different groups and strata of population that were bound together in Israel, became uniformly shaped. Certainly it must be recognized that we know scarcely anything about this presumed multiplicity. Was there, for example, a popular folk morality that stood beside a system of conduct that was more strongly shaped by Yahwistic religion? Did Israel have only *one* kind of ethic? Were not also rather significant differentiations made in the area of ethics as were, for example, in the public as well as in diverse forms of "believing in YHWH"?[33] We know far too little about the sociology and developing social history of Israel to be able to say anything more precise about the area of its possible or actual ethics. What exists for us now in the form of the texts of the Old Testament has in all probability undergone an ethical standardization, so that, for example, especially the Deuteronomistic view of law and obedience appears to be determinative.

Moreover, some basic principles may be recognized that evidently were determined by the character of Yahwistic faith and the concomitant conception of Israel as the people of God who are elected and obligated by YHWH. Thus, economic differences within the people of God that especially developed since the establishment of the monarchy were not to lead to social divisions or to the contrast between exploiters and the oppressed. This problem is recognizable already in the Covenant Code (Exod. 21:4–11, 16, 18-32; 22:20–26; and 23:1–9). Then it was especially the social criticism of the prophets[34] that spoke to this issue and saw in the antisocial behavior of those addressed by it an essential basis for YHWH's punishing intervention. Social manifestos and programs were not a part of this social criticism; rather, it had to do with opposing the division of the people of God into the oppressed[35] and those who rule and into the exploited and the exploiters. The beginning of the royal period and especially the time of relative quiet and economic prosperity under Jeroboam II had evoked the experiences of a particular kind of primitive capitalism and luxury (Amos 3:12, 15; 4:1; 5:11; 6:4; and Isa. 3:16–24). At the same time, there arose the transformation of YHWH into Baal so that, in addition to Amos,[36] also Hosea appeared and had to speak. If there was perhaps an orientation to earlier ideas of a segmentary, or a stronger egalitarian society[37] and also the rejection of many Canaanite,[38] Assyrian, Babylonian, and Hellenistic foreign influences in the course of Israelite history, there was also the example of the Rechabites with their pure morality that was oriented entirely to the "earlier," nomadic way of life (Jeremiah 35). This type of existence rejected the drinking of wine, viticulture, dwelling in houses, and so forth. Even so, for Israel and in Israel, this type of existence was not the normal experience that was desired by God. Even the Nazirite, who was "consecrated to God," who rejected the drinking of wine, who refused to cut his hair, and who practiced other injunctions, was a unique type of person in Israel.[39] One also wished to continue on one's ethical journey with YHWH (Deut. 5:33; 10:12f.; Jer. 5:4;[40] Micah 6:8; etc.).[41] If one traveled along YHWH's pathways and sought as well as was obligated to "follow after" him instead of after strange gods,[42] then this journey was one that also encountered new, ethical challenges that were to be decided according to YHWH's will. Israel's changing and developing law concerning the land offered, for instance, a typical example.[43] Thus Israel's ethos was also historically shaped, and responsibility before God primarily was to be lived out ethically by relating Old Testament religion to this world.

In the Old Testament legal corpora as well as in the ethical demands of the prophets,[44] no argument is made anywhere that clearly points to some form of thought concerning natural law.[45] Also, the Old Testament is not familiar with the concept of doing good for the sake of the good; rather, it is YHWH's will that lays claim to human lives. Fixed orders are established by God, including the sphere of justice (צדקה = *ṣĕdāqâ*), faithfulness to community (חסד = *ḥesed*), and the connection between deed and result.[46] However, disregarding the last area mentioned, these orders, which, for example, also extend over the entire creation and incorporate both animals and plants (Psalm 104), are not the subject of direct theological reflection. Further, it is the Old Testament portrait of humanity that also contributes to its ethics, for apart from Gen. 9:6 there is in no legal clause a direct reference to humanity's being made in the image of God (Gen. 1:26ff.).[47]

However, YHWH was and is the one who, for example, freed his people from slave labor in Egypt (Exod. 1:14; 2:11; 3:9; 5:7–9, 10–18; and 6:5f.). Therefore from now on this nation should also live as a liberated people and, in addition, as a people freed from slavery. Consequently, this people revolted against slave labor and the introduction of taskmasters (Deut. 5:15; 1 Sam. 8:11–18; 1 Kings 4:6; 5:27f.; 9:15ff.; and 11:28). It was not by chance that this very same theme led to the partitioning of the empire into the kingdoms of Israel and Judah after the death of Solomon (1 Kings 12:4ff.), and one has King Jeroboam I, certainly not accidentally in this connection, point to the God of the exodus (1 Kings 12:28). For the Book of Deuteronomy and the Holiness Code which is dependent upon it (however, this is not so for the Covenant Code), all members of the people of Israel are "brothers,"[48] including the prophet as well as the king (Deut. 17:15, 20; and 18:20). Further, orphans, widows, foreigners, and the levites[49] as social classes are expressly commanded to be the recipients of public assistance from everyone, not only from the king, who in Israel's cultural environment was responsible for this[50] (Deut. 14:28f.; 24:17, 19–21; 26:12f.; and 27:19; cf. 16:11, 14; and Exod. 22:21). YHWH is the defender and father of widows and orphans (Ps. 68:6), and their protector who requires their preservation (Deut. 10:17f.; cf. Pss. 10:14ff.; 82:3; 146:9; and Hos. 14:4). This is why the position of a slave, which continues in and of itself, can nevertheless then be improved in certain situations in contrast with Israel's ancient Near Eastern environment (Exod. 21:26f.), while the Book of Deuteronomy, in clear opposition to the ancient Near Eastern laws concerning slaves, demands that one may not have to hand over a slave who has fled to his former master (Deut. 23:16f.). Providing for a poor person is a social objective.[51] In addition, it is striking that, again in contrast to the cultural environment in which (high!) interest was customary,[52] the Old Testament sees only in a negative way the charging of interest. Charging interest of members of the people of God was forbidden,[53] even if the actual practice was to have looked different. A stand was taken against the falsification of weights and measures, against the enslavement of small farmers, and against debt slavery and bribery. However, it is remarkable in this connection that the argumentation is more theological than charitable or even economical in nature.[54] "The brotherly ethic is a consequence of being liberated to brotherhood."[55]

Manslaughter committed against slaves is to be punished (Exod. 21:20). Kidnapping is forbidden (Exod. 21:16; probably also Exod. 20:15 par). The relationship between humans and their fellow humans is shaped by the relationship with God and receives therefore a deepened seriousness,[56] since more is involved, then, than mere social approval or disapproval. Thus election and history are fundamental principles of Old Testament ethics where one walks the pathway of YHWH, travels with one's God, and lives before him. The ethos is, therefore, also popular and practical, and not timeless and theoretical.[57] Even political decisions are religiously determined (Isaiah 7). And since God, who has acted in history to elect Israel, is also believed to be the creator of the world,[58] ethics can be argued theologically on the basis of creation, although considerably less so than is the case with salvation history (cf. Gen. 9:6; and wisdom literature).

12.4   An Ethos Related to Community

The relationship of the Israelite ethos to YHWH is at the same time the relationship to the community. This has already become clear in much of what was previously brought out and is conditioned by the fact that YHWH elected a people to enter into community with him whose life now is to be formed under his lordship. The Old Testament legal collections as well as the proclamation of the prophets[59] allow one to recognize so well that here the ethos occurs within the form of solidarity[60] and that the purpose of ethical action is less the good fortune of the individual[61] than the welfare of the community. In such good things as salvation, peace, the enrichment of children, and the like, community with God is known and the blessing of YHWH is experienced. It follows, then, that divine blessing must also be accountable for the reception of these good things. Accordingly, for example, "salvation" (שלום = šālôm) encompasses good things that are religious, historical, and natural.[62]

The stipulations for life within the extended family and clan were regulated and defended by apodictically formulated legal principles (Exod. 20:14; and 21:12, 15, 16f.). The law of the levirate and solutions of problems such as blood vengeance[63] worked in the direction of maintaining solidarity and faithfulness to the community,[64] and casuistic legal stipulations were added as developments and applications of fundamental regulations. When the state "came to overlay the primary communities,"[65] social differentiations and conflicts developed, leading to the need for inquiring more often and more generally about the law and its now also stronger theological basis.

In these connections, then, righteousness (צדקה = ṣĕdāqâ) and justice (משפט = mišpāṭ)[66] are readily used terms and become important ideas that often appear in a reciprocal relationship. These terms occur especially in the message of the prophets (Isa. 1:21, 26f.; 5:7; Jer. 5:1; 9:23; 22:3; Hos. 4:1f.; 6:6; Amos 5:7, 15, 24; Micah 6:8; Zeph. 2:3;[67] etc.). The fact that this message has to do with life that is related to community and with justice that the individual has within the community demanded that this communal basis of existence is not to be contested (Isa. 3:14f.; 5:18; 10:1; Jer. 6:13; etc.). Rather, once again this community has to do with YHWH (Pss. 17:2; 37:6; 111:7; Isa. 49:4; etc.), and it is in this community that things happen in the "right" way. Also חסד = ḥesed ("loyalty, steadfast love")[68] is used for this behavior that is related to and in conformity with the community, behavior, however, that in turn is also determined by YHWH's own חסד = ḥesed ("loyalty, steadfast love"; Exod. 15:13; 34:6; Jer. 31:2f.; Psalm 136; etc.). Israel became and was certainly a community of faith, and not only a people,[69] and this occurred through the religious experience of the community associated with the exodus and then through the nation's ongoing history under and with its God. It was from this experience that communal life became a matter of faith and along with that of religious ethics. Freedom could not primarily then be the freedom of the individual to make personal choices between different possibilities; rather, it was tied up with social responsibilities and remained in the visible world with which ethical conduct was associated. And since behavior had to do with ethical confirmation and formation in the context of history, a general concept of morality and ethos was also foreign to the Israelite. In spite of the principal requirements of the Decalogue, which were not already uniform and furthermore which aimed at and pressed their way toward interpretation and concretization,[70] the will of God was no absolute and objective norm. Rather, the divine will had to do every time with the practice of justice and being just in contrast to being a concrete demand placed in a concrete situation or a concrete demand among one or more other possible demands. Genesis 38 and the description of the conduct of Tamar, characterized in v. 26 as "righteous," demonstrate well that this woman, although she had even made herself into a "prostitute," still acted appropriately according to the concrete requirement of the community.[71] Old Testament ethics, therefore, cannot be only a moral system of thinking. Rather, the evildoer (רשע = rāšā') is one whose conduct is contrary to the community, who in a particular case is unjust or behaves wrongly. The commandment to love the neighbor (Lev. 19:18)[72] involved first a kind of solidarity of the people.[73] In addition, with the exception of much in the wisdom literature,[74] there is no ethos of personality with its own moral development; rather, Old Testament ethics have to do with the community historically determined and established by God. The so-called human rights of "freedom, equality, and brotherhood"[75] as well as the fundamental values of freedom, righteousness, and solidarity are good Old Testament rights and values. In comparison with fundamental constants that extend into the anthropological sphere, ethos and law are variable in particular areas of the Old Testament, as the different legal collections of the Old Testament demonstrate. The Old Testament *never has to do with an absolute, established law with which one must comply.* Yet one must be concerned with the private rights of the *individual.*"[76]

Since the Old Testament legal community wants to and should be preserved, its commandments are thus mostly shaped in the form of prohibitions. "You are not to do injustice in rendering a legal judgment. You are not to show partiality to a poor person" (Lev. 19:15). Disturbances are to be kept far from the community, or they are to be removed from it ("You are to remove the evil from Israel/out of your midst," Deut. 13:6; etc.). First in Deuteronomy and then in later texts there is in the legal sentences an instruction that provides a more paraenetic thrust and makes a strong theological argument concerning just actions that is readily attached then to the rationales.[77]

A good example for the relationship of the Old Testament ethos to the community is the Old Testament evaluation of lying. M. A. Klopfenstein[78] has pointed out that in Old Testament literature all the terms used for "lying" are oriented to presuppositions and norms of the life of the community: שקר = *šqr* in regard to contract law, כחש = *khš* for sacral and profane law, כזב = *kzb*, רמה = *rmh* for the sphere of everyday activity and behavior, and also שוא = *šw'* for the realm of magic.[79] This explains why, then, in the Old Testament there is no general prohibition against lying and why there does not occur in the Old Testament a general demand in principle for truthfulness in our sense of the term. There lying is not so much condemned in terms of itself but rather is condemned on account of the adverse consequences for another person with whom one stands in community. Bearing "false witness," of which the ninth commandment in the Decalogue speaks, means false testimony in the legal proceedings of the law court and is therefore damaging to the community, and this is the decisive element for understanding the meaning of this law. The condemnation of lying "has to do primarily with destroying the community between God and his people, between God and human beings, between members of the nation, and between human beings. *Lying is contrary to community.*"[80] Thus, even Jeremiah could lie (Jer. 38:24ff.), because he actually harmed no one with his false statement (cf. Exod. 1:19). Even in certain cases of stealing in foreign communities, this appears to have been similarly the case (Exod. 3:22; 11:2; and 12:35f.?).

This reference of moral action to a larger entity, either the "people" or the "community," in which the individual finds himself or herself and which provides him or her a religious structure, is scarcely found elsewhere in the laws of the ancient Near East. Consequently, it was in this sphere that Israel found itself once again shaped by Yahwistic faith, be it in the election of a people by this God, in regard to his divine personality, or in the direction of the community ethically ordered by him.

The consciousness of individual responsibility was also embedded within this communal sense, for there was solidarity between the individual worshipers or members of the group and of the community itself,[81] and the prophetic message summoned the people as well as the individual to this responsibility. In addition, one can ask about the mind, that is, about the "heart"

(Isa. 29:13f.; Ezek. 36:26; and Lev. 19:17; cf. Pss. 73:1; 139:4, 23f.; Zech. 7:10; 8:17; and 1 Sam. 16:7).[82] Ethics involving action also have in view the mind (Pss. 15:2; and 24:4), and the last prohibition of the Decalogue, "Do not covet," especially in its Deuteronomic formulation, probably goes beyond "to strive after something through concrete actions" (Exod. 20:17f.; and Deut. 5:21).[83] The Covenant Code already is responsible for addressing individuals on the basis and grounds of this solidarity. Talion[84] (Exod. 21:24f. par.) is limited to the individual and circumscribes blood vengeance (Deut. 19:11–13; 24:16). In the Covenant Code, which demonstrates in its present, Deuteronomistically redacted form that it combines cultic with moral commandments and incorporates within itself both moral and cultic dimensions (cf., e.g., Exod. 22:17–19), the language that comes forth from the mouth of YHWH who establishes justice is of "my people," of his liberating action (Exod. 22:20; and 23:9),[85] of the "poor who are beside or with you" (Exod. 22:24; cf. 23:6), and of the mantle of the fellow citizen (Exod. 22:25). Lord and slave stand, last of all, in the same place before YHWH (Exod. 21:2, 6), and the rights of the slaves were expanded (Exodus 1–11). YHWH, who is compassionate (Exod. 22:26c), will listen to the cries of the oppressed (Exod. 22:26), and since Israel also was an oppressed sojourner in Egypt, the poor, the sojourners, widows, and orphans were not to be oppressed (Exod. 20:22ff.).[86] Ethical demands can be required even of the enemy (Exod. 23:4f.). Here law becomes ethics.[87] E. Otto[88] has shown how on the whole the "subjection of the norms of everyday life under the will of God" was secured by redactional and traditiohistorical means especially in the Covenant Code. YHWH is, as a deity who establishes justice, also the defender of justice (Exod. 22:22, 26; also cf., e.g., Isa. 56:1f.). In an increasingly socially fractured society, this "theologizing of the law keeps the law, which is intended to be an instrument for all, from becoming an instrument for the few. In addition, this theological reflection, which viewed the law as the means to protect the socially weak, identified it with the will of God in that YHWH was introduced as the subject who is to carry out this law."[89] This is, for example, also made clear by the scene that is added to the one about Naboth's vineyard in 1 Kings 21:1–16. This scene classified the previously narrated action as unjust before YHWH (v. 25), so that Ahab must now hear the divine-prophetic announcement of punishment (vv. 21f.). "One should write the history of Israelite justice as the history of the integration of justice into the will of God."[90] The continuing history of Israelite justice, extending from the Covenant Code, through Deuteronomy, to the Holiness Code (Leviticus 19–26), clearly justifies this view, particularly in the theological and paraenetic groundings of legal sentences in these law codes.[91] Just actions stand under the blessing of YHWH but unrighteous ones under his curse (Leviticus 26; Deuteronomy 27–30). The individual experiences this, and the nation must experience this in its history. A direct request for a reward for a morally good deed, however, is seldom found in the Old Testament. Job does seek to set forth his earlier good conduct toward God (Job 29; cf. also Job 31). Otherwise, however, moral action is simply borne of the conviction that YHWH, the trustworthy deity, has commanded this action, and he has promised his blessing upon the one who acts according to his will.

12.5 Strength for Moral Activity

Only hesitantly and seldomly does the Old Testament provide information for the question as to where the worshiper or the community derived the power for moral action. The paraeneses and legal grounds point, first of all, to the acts of YHWH for his people that take precedence temporally and essentially over human action. These acts of YHWH include the liberation of the community of sojourners from Egypt, the gift of the land, and so on.[92] The freedom bestowed by YHWH is to be preserved; one is to live in and out of it. Then one should point to the cultus,[93] where the community of God, strengthened and experienced, received its blessing (cf., e.g., Psalms 97; 99; 132; 134; etc.) and where divine faithfulness to the community that brought about salvation was encountered.[94] It was the festival community during the sacrificial feast that obtained "righteousness" (Deut. 33:19; Pss. 4:5f.; 22:26f.; and 51:18, 21), since YHWH is also the one "who makes you holy" (Lev. 21:8).

Thus, moral questions and commandments are tied into cultic formulae (Psalms 15 and 24; Micah 6:6–8; Isa. 33:14–16; and cf. Deut. 26:13ff.; and Ezek. 18:5ff.). However, ethics do not establish the relationship with God; rather, this relationship derives from the divine gift of community which God has established and maintained. It is this freely given community that was the presupposition for and continuation within the covenant and communion with God. Also, it was in the field of ethics that the Israelites were aware that they were dependent on YHWH's continuing, new acts of grace, even as these occurred in paradigmatic fashion in the cult. If YHWH were to abandon his people, then the doing of justice and morality (Deut. 28:20ff.; and Lamentations 5) would be abolished. The worshiping event has a decisive function for the proximity of YHWH to his people. The exile and the reality of its punishment were due to the prior weakness of the people in their faithfulness and obedience to YHWH. Thus the people certainly came to know more about the impotence of the human will ("heart") and of their sinfulness. Since that time, the Old Testament thus said more about the idea of YHWH having to give of his Spirit[95] in order to strengthen the moral fabric of the individual as well as of the community. What appears as a requirement in Ezek. 11:19 becomes with intrinsic necessity in Ezek. 36:26ff. a divine promise (cf. Jer. 24:7; 31:31ff.; and Psalm 51). One had only to experience clearly the deficiency of one's own righteousness (Deut. 9:4–6).

In looking at the individual, Israel also continued to be level-headed concerning the person's level of moral performance. Israel told not only of saints but also of sinners, as, for example, Jacob and David, and the material transmitted in individual legends often presented its moral judgment through the changing context, something to which the Jacob stories are able to attest. Not only the Deuteronomistic History but also the "murmuring traditions,"[96] attached directly to the exodus and the Sinai covenant, point out that God at best works with what may be seen as broken instruments (Gen. 32:10f.), while Israel saw itself as an altogether unthankful and sinful people. When Israel tells the story of its ancestors or its earlier history, it seldom has to do with ethical models. Rather, there are more divine examples, indications of God's disposition as well as of his school to which he takes individuals (from "Jacob" to "Israel"), when they were exhorted to analogous action (Hosea 12). It was the community of solidarity under YHWH that issued requirements to, strengthened, and shaped the individual.

12.6   Some of the Contents of the Ethos

When examining some of the contents and materials of the requirements of Old Testament ethics,[97] one should point out first of all that conduct toward YHWH belongs here, for one is to love (Deut. 6:5), know (Hos. 4:1), and fear him (Job 1:1).[98]

For the ethics between human beings, the Decalogue with its fundamental requirements is essential, as is the social-critical message of the prophets[99] (Exod. 20:2–17; and Deut. 5:6–21; cf. also the pre-Deuteronomic, so-called Law of YHWH's Privilege, Exod. 34:10–26).[100] Here the freedom given by YHWH is to be preserved (Deuteronomic) or grasped and then proven in new obedience (Deuteronomistic).[101] Alongside and following the commandments and prohibitions mentioned in the Decalogue that determine conduct toward YHWH is the grown son's responsibility for elderly parents from whom he receives life (Exod. 20:12; and Deut. 5:16). Murder, and thus killing that was illegal and was under the purview of the community, is forbidden (Exod. 20:13; and Deut. 5:17; cf. Exod. 21:12; and Gen. 9:6). Adultery is no purely private matter but rather disturbs the community (Exod. 20:14; and Deut. 5:18) and is a sin against YHWH (2 Sam. 12:13).[102] Private property is presupposed[103] and protected (Exod. 20:15, 17; and Deut. 5:19, 21; cf. Lev. 19:11; Jer. 7:9; and Prov. 30:9).[104] The prophets reflect then on the just use of this property and speak of its limits. For instance, a prophet such as Amos argues that these limits reside at the place where evil and destructive social differences enter into the people of God.[105] Texts leading to the Decalogue are present in Hos. 4:2 and Jer. 7:9 (cf. Psalms 15 and 24) and point out that earlier than the time of the Deuteronomic/Deuteronomistic School or of P the same type of moral series has been attempted for the regulation of human interaction. Similar texts, furthermore, are Lev. 19:13–18 and Deut. 27:15–26,[106] while Decalogue-like texts are contained in Leviticus 18 that seek to prohibit disturbances in the extended family through evil sexual relationships.[107] E. Otto has described how bodily wounds (Exod. 21:18–32) in Old Testament law were evaluated differently and also independently (e.g., regarding the protection of the slave) in cuneiform laws.[108] In Exod. 23:1ff. there appears to be something like a judge's code, and the incorruptability of those who have to render judgments continues to be inculcated (Isa. 1:23; 5:23; Micah 3:9ff.; etc.). In the countries of Israel's social environment the already mentioned[109] care for widows, orphans, and the poor (cf. Exod. 22:21–23; Deut. 10:18; 14:29; 16:11, 14; 24:17ff.; etc.) was a special task of the ruler, as is shown particularly well in the Prologue and the Epilogue of the Codex of Hammurabi.[110] However, this task becomes "democratized" in Israel and placed on the heart of each member of the nation, for it is now King YHWH who rules protectively over these persons. In order to make a conscious demarcation from the manner of life and faith of the Canaanites as well as to secure their own Israelite identity,[111] the sharpening and practicing of certain kinds of sexual behaviors continued to be addressed time and again (e.g., Gen. 9:22f.; Hos. 4:13f.; Jer. 2:20ff.; and Leviticus 18).

Human labor[112] is something that is taken for granted in the Old Testament; therefore it is nowhere expressly and completely made into a theme.[113] Man and woman have to work (Ps. 104:23; and Prov. 31:15, 18), and their work serves the purpose of acquiring the necessities of life (Gen. 1:28f.; 2:15; 9:2f.; Ps. 128:2; Prov. 14:23; and 16:26; cf. Sir. 17:1ff.). Forced labor, moreover, was viewed with a critical eye, for YHWH has freed his people from such conditions (Exod. 3:9; and 6:6; cf. 1 Kings 11:10f.).[114] However, the changing social situation in the government and country under the kingship brought with it the danger of exploitation and oppression of the workers by the monarchy, as the prophetic social criticism demonstrates.[115] Nevertheless, humanity, and this means not only the slave, still was to labor according to the will of God (Exod. 16:26; 20:9; Deut. 5:13; and Qoh. 3:9f.), mostly from morning until evening (Pss. 104:23; 128:2; and Prov. 31:10ff.). This was already the case in the Garden of Eden where the humans had to cultivate and maintain this garden (Gen. 2:15 J; cf. Gen. 1:26, 28f.; 2:5, 23; and 9:2f.). When the humans were driven from this garden, there were consequences for them, although not for YHWH. This did not have to do with placing their forthcoming labor under a curse; rather, this impending labor (Ps. 127:1f.; Qoh. 3:9f.; and Sir. 7:16) was to be futile and tiresome (Gen. 3:17–19, 23). Human labor was not considered to be a burden relieved by the gods, either in the garden or afterward, as it could be narrated and believed to be in Israel's Near Eastern environment.[116] Rather, humans worked for themselves and for the acquisition of what both they and the communities where they lived required in order to live. A direct relationship between the "labor" and the "work" of YHWH[117] and the labor and the work of human beings is nowhere set forth in the Old Testament,[118] even if the agricultural labor of humans in Isa. 28:23–29 is described by a comparative reference to the activity of YHWH. The sayings literature of wisdom is convinced that human industry produces positive fruits, although divine blessing is needed (Ps. 127:1f.; Prov. 10:22; Qoh. 3:9–15; etc.), while, by contrast, laziness results in harm.[119] Even in the promised time of salvation labor will not cease. One shall once again plow and reap (Amos 9:11ff.), reforge weapons (Isa. 2:4; Micah 4:4), and bring in the harvest (Isa. 9:2). Moreover, this future time always evaluates labor in a positive way and presents it as successful. In the Old Testament apocalyptic texts, human labor naturally no longer approaches a theme.[120] That labor comes closer to being a theme in the primeval history and the wisdom literature than in other writings of the Old Testament connects these two textual traditions in a way that provides another example of correspondence with Israel's Near Eastern cultures, for in these cultures one can also determine an analogous relationship.[121] Numbers 21:17f. and Isa. 16:10 mention songs of labor. An important corrective to labor and its Old Testament value is the Sabbath as both gift (Gen. 2:1–3) and commandment (Exod. 20:8–11; etc.),[122] since it makes rest possible even for slaves.[123] A devaluation of bodily labor in favor of spiritual activity is found for the first time in Sir. 38:25ff. Thus, human life exists according to the will and character of YHWH (Gen. 2:1–3), and not only from work. Rather, rest is the gift of God to his human creatures and to his world. Rest is not just a privilege reserved for the deity.

12.7 The Place for Animals

According to the Priestly source, humans were permitted to eat only plants for nourishment in the original scheme of things (Gen. 1:29f.). This certainly does not provide the theological basis for vegetarianism, since in Hebrew thought plants were probably considered to be inanimate.[124] According to the Hebrew perspective, the animal,[125] however, has a נֶפֶשׁ = nepeš ("soul, being, life force"),[126] which was probably associated with the blood, for it was here that the נֶפֶשׁ = nepeš took up residence (Lev. 17:11, 14; Deut. 12:23). God indeed spoke in Genesis 1 about the animals, although he spoke about humans in a directly personal discourse (Gen. 1:26–29). The human being was to rule over the animals (Gen. 1:26; cf. Ps. 8:7–9). What this lordship entails is not at all very clear according to Genesis 1, since animals are not yet permitted to be eaten. Perhaps what stands in the background here is the ancient Near Eastern concept of an original peaceable kingdom at creation.[127] In any case, animals are placed under humans, although the lordship according to Old Testament thought could not be a despotic-tyrannical subjugation. The verbs used in Gen. 1:26, רדה = *rdh* ("have dominion") and כבשׁ *kbš* ("subdue"), are not, then, to be translated with "trample" and "tread underfoot."[128] These terms mean, rather, the taking possession of something, that is, "to place one's foot on something" (cf. Josh. 18:1) and "to put to pasture and to lead about,"[129] so that the human being therefore is viewed as a shepherd (cf. similar images in Psalms 23; 78:20ff.; and Ezekiel 34). There is no discussion of the exploitation of the contemporary world by humans, even though this verse has been misunderstood in this way for a long time. One also finds, according to Gen. 1:20ff., that much from the animal world stands under the blessing of God. And while in Gen. 1:26ff. the enjoyment of flesh was still withheld from humans, there is permission given for animal nourishment for the period after the primeval flood (Gen. 9:3). However, blood was withheld once again from human consumption and reserved for God (Gen. 9:4f.). With this it becomes clear that the animal world is still not left fully to human discretion. God's covenant is valid also for animals (Gen. 9:9f.).

According to Jonah 3:7f., the animals, together with the human beings, did penance in Nineveh, and a "great fish" functions as the instrument of YHWH for this prophet (Jonah 2:1). Human being and animal live together in a community of good fortune, even as the narrative of the primeval flood shows in an exemplary fashion, that is, in community both in judgment and in deliverance and new beginning. As a consequence, even the animals may and should rest on the Sabbath (Exod. 20:10; 23:12; and Deut. 5:14), while conversely an obstinate ox may be condemned to death (Exod. 21:28ff.). Many stipulations of Old Testament law concerning animals emit a certain "humanizing tendency" (Exod. 22:29; and Deut. 22:6f.; not to separate immediately a young calf from its mother; to allow the mother of young birds to live), even though the second example may be accompanied by a pragmatic interest. The actual point and the religiohistorical background of the prohibition against cooking a kid in its mother's milk are debated (humanitarian? polemic against the cult? a taboo prescription that excludes something that could offend the gods?).[130] When the land bears fruit during the Sabbath year, fruit that humans are not allowed to harvest,[131] animals, in addition to the poor, are to make use of it (Exod. 23:10f.; and Lev. 25:7). The ox and the ass, which have strayed, are to be returned to the owner, even if he is the enemy of the finder (Exod. 23:4f.). One is not to muzzle an ox while treading the grain (Deut. 25:4), something that Paul relates in a thoughtful way to the apostle and his livelihood (1 Cor. 9:9; cf. 1 Tim. 5:18). "The animal therefore stands under the protection of the law, as does the person who is legally weak,"[132] and Gen. 1:20ff. consequently positions, not without consideration, the creation of animals close to that of humans. Although certainly after the Old Testament's issuance of the law of the cult[133] not a few animals were continually sacrificed while others were supposed to have been exterminated at the court of Solomon in "legendary" numbers (1 Kings 5:3). Still the Old Tesament person nowhere reflects over the fate of the animal world that surrounds him or her. There is no indication of his or her compassion, something that stands in contrast to YHWH (cf. Jonah 4:11 which ends with a concluding, open question to the reader). An animal must die in order that the human firstborn may be "ransomed" and live (Exod. 13:13, 15; 34:19f.). Genesis 22:13 was later on viewed as the basis for this practice.

According to Gen. 2:4bff., the animals were also viewed as helpers for human beings, and they practiced a kind of lordship over the animals through giving them names.[134] Humans also experience animals, moreover, as a power that threatens them. In this regard, one shall have to think less on the serpent in Genesis 3 than on the chaos monster which bears various designations in the Old Testament.[135] A human could become "animal-like" (Dan. 4:12ff.), and many different animals could be dangerous. Genesis 9:2, with the animal world's "dread and fear" of humans, probably serves as an intended contrast. Animals appear in Old Testament proclamations of judgment (Amos 3:8, 12; Hos. 5:14;[136] 13:7f.; Joel 1:4ff.; and Lev. 26:22). Animals stood as symbolic figures for the animal-like, hostile world kingdoms (Daniel 7–8), and only YHWH can play with Leviathan (Ps. 104:26; cf. Job 40:29).[137] One knows that God also cares for the animals (Pss. 36:7; 104:14, 21, 27f.; 136:25; and 147:9), and the righteous person acts in a similar manner (Prov. 12:10). On the whole, however, the relationship of the Old Testament worshiper remains "objective and cool" toward the animal world that surrounds him or her,[138] even though the discussion within the Old Testament is not only about humanity's lordship over the animal world and presents more positive and theologically intrinsic views about the reality animals share with humans.[139]

Ravens provide for Elijah (1 Kings 17:4, 6). Balaam's ass sees more of God's intervention than does its master (Num. 22:23), and for this reason the ass complains bitterly when Balaam strikes it (Num. 22:28ff.; cf. 1 Sam. 6:7–12). A single lamb was mentioned in the sermon of repentance directed toward David (2 Sam. 12:1–10), and it is stressed there that its master held the lamb like a daughter (2 Sam. 12:3). Tobias was accompanied not only by an angel but also by his dog (Tob. 5:6, 16ff.; 6:1; and 11:9) who functioned then as a messenger. God even uses animals, which he indeed knows (Ps. 50:10), as his instruments on behalf of and against human beings. He is also the one who takes away their lives (Ps. 104:29f.; Job 34:14f.; and Qoh. 3:19) and causes them to experience his judgment (primeval flood; Joel 1:20; and 2:22). The animals also praise YHWH (Ps. 148:7, 10). Their division into "clean" (i.e., those which may be sacrificed and eaten[140]) and "unclean" animals (Leviticus 11; and Deut. 14:3–20) is not provided a more precise rationale elsewhere. But this division even then more than likely was no longer obvious, and for us today it may not be sufficiently inferred. It was simply YHWH's commandment. The situation of salvation at the end of time will bring complete peace between human beings and animals as well as within the animal world (Lev. 26:6; Isa. 11:6f.; 35:9; Ezek. 34:25; and Hos. 2:20).[141] In Israel, however, there was a time already present when the ox and the ass indeed knew their lord and his crib, but Israel itself ("my people") did not (Isa. 1:2; cf. Jer. 8:7). One can learn from the animals (Job 12:7, 10; and 39:1), even from the small animals (Prov. 6:6), although it may only be that humans as well as animals are mortal (Qoh. 3:19ff.; and Ps. 49:13, 21). The animal world, finally, makes clear that the human person is not the only creature of God. An indication of this is found in the divine speeches in the Book of Job that place in question all thoughts of humans as the center of creation (Job 38:39ff.; 39; and 40:15ff.),[142] and, according to Qoh. 9:4, a living dog is better than a dead lion, a point Qoheleth makes in regard to his sapiential evaluation of death. According to the Old Testament witness, the world of animals consequently is closely bound with human beings as well as with YHWH, its creator and sustainer, something then that also has its ethical consequences.

12.8   The Ethics of Wisdom Literature

The ethical admonitions, sayings, and instructions of the wisdom literature are not to be seen as belonging to the covenant of Sinai, as part of the obligation of the people of God chosen through YHWH's historical action, or as a teaching understood as the commandment of YHWH or as deriving from it.[143] Rather, wisdom literature more decidedly presents the individual in his or her everyday problems, and not the people of God in its fundamental obligation to the covenant. From time to time, this individual naturally appears as an Israelite, although not in a decisive way. Naturally, these ethical teachings are directed to a conduct that takes place within a community (cf. Prov. 5:14; 11:10; and 26:26), and often the "neighbor" is in view, although not, however, the stranger or the foreigner[144] (Prov. 6:1, 3; 11:9; 17:18; 18:17; 24:28; 25:8f., 18; and 29:5; in 3:29 and 25:17 it is the neighbor). There are, however, also texts that enable one to discern a reference to the development of individual personality.

Sapiential ethics are primarily the professional ethics of a circle of "sages" who are more well-to-do and belong chiefly to the propertied class, often that of court officials. There are in Israel very different social groupings that exist side by side and not in any chronological sequence. Israel also was not ethically homogeneous.[145] Even though the sapiential teachings demonstrate a closeness to the legal texts, the sages have apparently attempted to live out their own form of Yahwistic faith. The often asserted propinquity of apodictic legal sentences to the so-called tribal wisdom overlooks many differences between these textual forms,[146] even if the "elders" perhaps represented a bridge between the "sages" and the other Israelites and between sapiential rules of life and the Old Testament will of God, and even if the elders were connected with both of these polarities, thus causing sapiential ethics and the law to be mutually influenced by the other through means of "justice at the gate." It is certainly no accident that there was a frequent discussion in Proverbs of the correct handling of judgments, witnesses, and corruptibility,[147] matters that were certainly also topics in the wisdom literature of the ancient Near East. The wisdom texts allow one to recognize that there were "sapiential" rules of life proceeding from the mouth of the *pater familias* as "clan wisdom" for the common life within the extended family or clan that was different from the wisdom that was directed more toward professional education.

However, Deuteronomy represents the first programmatic attempt to bring into close relationship the law of YHWH and wisdom, an effort carried out by the circle standing behind the book.[148] In spite of the close similarity of sapiential teachings to the exhortation used elsewhere and to stipulations of the law, the sentence wisdom of the older sapiential texts, and that means especially in Proverbs 10–30 (31), is not understood as the word of YHWH. Rather, these older wisdom sayings are viewed as the advice of the sage that will help others to discover sapiential insight and to learn how to conduct life wisely. Moreover, one cannot speak of a fully autonomous ethos even when wisdom has more to do with the development of a personality that conforms to world order or the order of existence in a good and life-promoting fashion.[149] Seeing the world as a cosmic and ethical order was specifically purported to be the foundation and purpose of wisdom. This order was established and maintained by YHWH. While the wisdom texts are not silent about YHWH, he is brought into play in a way different than is the case in Old Testament legal texts that seek to give a rationale for their demands.[150] Old Testament sayings literature has to to more with everyday matters and ways of behaving that often require no legal stipulation. What does this sapiential view and conduct of life look like that may be deduced from the statements, judgments, and admonitions of the proverbial literature?[151]

The counsel of the sages (Jer. 18:18) and the teaching of the elders (Prov. 6:20) or of the wise (Prov. 13:14; 28:4, 7, 9; and 31:26) point to insight for living and to the formation of a balanced, good, and consequently successful life within the then recognized orders of the world that were to be actualized anew. Thus, the sage is a person who has self-control (Prov. 5:23; 14:17f., 29f.; 15:18; 17:27; 25:28; and 29:11),[152] who knew the right time to speak or to be silent at the right time, who valued the good word, and who thereby revealed as well as put to use his insight for living.[153] Among the characteristics of the sage, one finds, for example, the previously mentioned interest in the education of his or her own character.[154] Proverbs 16 and following, which in contrast to Proverbs 10–15 are less characterized by an antithetical style, especially have to do with the formation of the complex, everyday existence of human beings and their social interactions. The sages recommended the enjoyment of life (Prov. 27:9; and 31:6f.), although they advised at the same time moderation (Prov. 20:1; and 23:20f.). They recommended married love (Prov. 5:15; and 18:22; cf. even Qoh. 9:9) but warned against marrying too early (Prov. 24:27); they exhorted their students to choose the right spouse (Prov. 12:4; 19:14; 30:23; and 31:10ff.), because spouses were not viewed only in a positive light (Prov. 11:16; 19:13f.; 21:9, 19; 25:24; 27:15; and 31:3). Further, the sages frequently warned against the strange woman, who was probably a foreign woman rather (?) than the wife of another man and who represented a danger that was not forcefully and consciously enough exposed.[155] The principles of life practiced by the sages have much in them that are patriarchal (Prov. 13:24; 22:15; 23:13f.; and 29:15, 17), although this is certainly not customary only among circles of the sages. The sages quite naturally and intentionally dealt with poverty and wealth (Prov. 10:2, 16; 13:22; and 20:21), and they sought to find for the wealthy an appropriate way (Prov. 5:9f.; 11:24; 14:20; and 29:3) to assist the poor.[156] The wealthy's acts of goodness and charity in turn led to their own well-being.[157] In lending to the poor, one ultimately lends to YHWH (Prov. 19:17), something that really means that this act of charity is repaid in a positive manner. It is striking that the sojourner, who elsewhere is mostly mentioned along with the widow and the orphan, does not appear in Old Testament wisdom literature. One is exhorted to work hard and is warned about laziness because of its possibly terrible consequences.[158] Extravagance brings about disaster (Prov. 21:17; and 23:20f.), and there is only a warning issued about pledges (Prov. 6:1–5; 11:15; 17:18; 22:26f.; and 27:13), something that causes one to envision once again affluent sages. In business one is to be honest and without deceit (Prov. 11:1; 16:11; and 20:10). Correct conduct toward the king, to whom the sage consequently had access, or toward other superiors, is urged (Prov. 11:14; 14:35; 16:14f.; 22:29; 23:1; and 24:21f.), and a friend is to be chosen with careful deliberation (Prov. 17:9, 17; 18:24; 19:4, 6f.; 20:6; and 27:6, 9f.).

"Beside the counsel, 'Be wise!' the sages place the admonition, 'Be good,' or better—'... Avoid evil in order that you may continue to be preserved from misfortune and ruin.'"[159] Subsequently, not only is there the striving for an ethical conduct that is oriented toward the successful life but also a moral behavior that incorporates certain norms for ethical decisions and activities. There are, then, connections between wisdom and morality, between what a wise person does and what was socially customary, between wisdom and the law of YHWH, and naturally also between Old Testament wisdom and the wisdom in Israel's ancient Near Eastern environment. Subsequently, the connection of wisdom to the law of YHWH or to YHWH as the creator should not be too one-sidedly set forth as the foundation of this ethos.

In the final analysis, all ethical behavior was borne by the conviction that there is a connection between deed and consequence that was established and preserved by YHWH (Prov. 24:12; and 25:21f.).[160] That this was valid "occasionally" or "from time to time" is not said. Apart from that, the discussion is of YHWH,[161] for example, of him as the creator (Prov. 14:31; 16:4; 17:5; 19:17; and 22:2). However, these texts are silent about YHWH's actions in history and about his action on behalf of his people. YHWH functions more as the originator of an order that brings reward (Prov. 12:2; 16:3; and 22:4), and the ethics of the sages continue within and argue from within that order. Both the righteous and the godless are "requited" on the earth by YHWH (Prov. 11:31). No harm affects the righteous, although the wicked are filled with misfortune (Prov. 12:21).

When the discussion pertains to a person's not increasing his or her substance through unjust profits[162] and not being enticed to remove the boundaries of his or her property (Prov. 22:28; and 23:10f.), the perspective is linked to similar prohibitions or accusations in legal and prophetic texts of the Old Testament (Deut. 19:14; 27:17; Isa. 5:8; Hos. 5:10; and Micah 2:2). However, such admonitions belong to the common material of Old Testament wisdom literature and legal collections, as is also the case in the rejection of false weights and measures.[163] And the legal clauses[164] want certainly to secure what is traditional and not to set forth something that primarily is new.

One finds rich evidence that Old Testament wisdom's discourse corresponds to that of ancient Near Eastern wisdom literature, even when the sages make a more strongly theological argument. This is true, for instance, when taking into consideration the fear of God that then becomes in Old Testament wisdom literature the fear of YHWH.[165] This similarity is also true in respect to other ways of arguing. Thus an ethical, however, not cultic,[166] activity is "a delight" to YHWH, while an unethical one is an "abomination" to him.[167] In addition, this has to do, not with what is "a delight" to YHWH as such, but rather with the well-being of the one who has acted.[168] "An abomination or loathing" is also found in ancient Egyptian wisdom texts,[169] while the use of this expression in Deuteronomy[170] introduces other, especially cultic and sexual spheres of taboo. Wisdom also exhibits here an ethos that, in terms of its particular interests, does not conform fully to the rest of the Old Testament. Therefore one can hardly say in such an emphatic and one-sided way that the grounds for the sapiential admonitions and warnings point to and enter into the sphere of the revelation of the God of creation.[171]

It is, then, not without significance for this sapiential view of YHWH, the world, and piety of the sage that Qoheleth[172] later on subjected wisdom's entire worldview and practice for life to a radical critique, concluding that they produce no actual profit (Qoh. 1:3; 2:11; 3:9; etc.).[173] Hard work and riches bring about nothing,[174] and life with a wife is not as wonderful as one might think (Qoh. 7:25–28).[175] The ability to know the correct time and thus to act accordingly in the right way is denied to human beings (Qoh. 3:1ff.). The relationship between righteous action and a good result, a teaching presupposed and readily affirmed in wisdom thinking, is likewise unfounded.[176] Even the pleasure and joy of life, the only positive element of life that continues, according to Qoheleth,[177] is in the final analysis also "vain" (Qoh. 2:1).

The Book of Job,[178] in the framing chapters (1f.; 42:7ff.) and especially in the critical dialogues of Job with his friends who are so completely chained to their sapiential worldview (Job 3–27), takes part in this critical perspective on wisdom's view of life. In the context of this book, there are two chapters that are significant for Old Testament ethics. When Job describes his earlier fortune in chap. 29, he mentions also the wealth he once had, but adds at the same time that he had used these resources especially for the welfare of the poor. In addition, one may elicit from this text a great deal about the life style of a rich and pious sage. And when Job sets forth his so-called oath of innocence before God (Job 31),[179] one is able to recognize in this "human introspective examination of conscience prior to confession," as the chapter has also been named, much of what at that time was customary. One also learns that Job, as a good and righteous sage, in no way thought only of himself but rather felt connected with and obligated to the community.

Consequently, there is in the ethos of wisdom more about the individual and its everyday problems, meaning then that one may see overall that the place of the sage was indeed among the community, but not the community as the nation or congregation of God. Wisdom has to do, not with the obligation of the chosen in the sphere of the law of God, but rather with conduct for everyday life, and this also strongly within the structure of professonal ethics that approximate the ethics of the sages in Israel's contemporary ancient Near Eastern world. While this ethos does not reject a relationship to the will of YHWH, this appears to be, however, looser and this means there is not an expressly stated referral to the commandments of YHWH. Rather, wisdom sees ethical conduct more particularly through the principle of the relationship between deed and result.[180] The limitations of such a practice of life and faith occasionally emerge already in the Book of Proverbs where it can be noted that the the connection between deed and result is not always readily apparent to a person.[181] Qoheleth and Job then make these limits completely clear, and the further development of Israelite wisdom literature (Sirach and the Wisdom of Solomon)[182] shows that this wisdom necessarily underwent many alterations and enhancements for its preservation and continued corroboration.

12.9 The Limits of Old Testament Ethics

Moreover, there are clearly still other limitations of Old Testament ethics that may be noted.[183] Slavery[184] was, as was also the case in the New Testament, not completely overcome (Jer. 34:8ff.). Although no male or female Israelite was to be a lifetime slave[185] to another Israelite (Exod. 21:2;[186] cf. Deut. 15:13f.), this is something that both Leviticus 25 (setting free after forty-nine years) and Amos 2:6 and 8:6 confute.[187] Many "slaves" are also a blessing (Gen. 24:35). Nehemiah sought to abolish debt slavery (Nehemiah 5).[188] However, it is Job who still had to determine that the slave is free for the first time in the kingdom of the dead (Job 3:19). The Old Testament ethos is, and this is true according to the Old Testament wisdom literature, primarily the ethos of the male, that is, of the free male.

Consequently, the cultic (cf. only Leviticus 12), legal, and social place of the woman[189] remains more narrowly restricted than that of the male[190] and so on. Thus, as with the slave, scarcely any other thing except work can be expected of her (Lev. 19: 20–22; Job 31:10; and Neh. 5:5). She belonged to the property of the man (Exod. 20:17f.), and the effort in the Deuteronomic/ Deuteronomistic interpretation of the Decalogue (Deut. 5:21a) to extract her from these possessions was rescinded in the later, postexilic interpretation of the Decalogue in Exod. 20:17.[191] Polygamy is nowhere fundamentally debated or overcome (Deut. 21:15ff.), and the sexual morality of the man is contrasted with what is required of the woman. The male even "rules over" the woman (Gen. 3:16).

Furthermore, the Old Testament ethic remains a rather nationalistic ethic (cf., e.g., Deut. 14:21; and 23:20f.), even though the Old Testament does not contain a commandment that requires the defense of this national honor.[192] Blood vengeance[193] is not fully overcome (cf. still 1 Macc. 9:38–42).

Even ancient Israel had already recognized that much was certainly conditioned by time, was variable, and would be eventually surpassed. This is true especially in the practice of the ban,[194] even if the Book of Esther (Esth. 9:15f.), at least in a literary way, falls back on this ideology and the Books of Chronicles breath a rather militaristic spirit. It must not be forgotten that it was a people with its own political and sociological structures and problems that YHWH himself had elected to be his community.

Thus, the ethical instructions of the Old Testament are model examples of the effort at that time to make concrete and to practice faith in YHWH as a living faith, even though these examples are shaped by a historically, socially, and politically different environment and by convictions of faith held in those times. It may not, however, be unimportant that Jesus could answer the question about the chief commandment (Mark 12:28–34) with two commandments from the Old Testament (Deut. 6:5; and Lev. 19:18).[195]

Chapter 13. The Worship of Israel (Cult)[1]

13.1 Concerning the Evaluation of the Old Testament Cult

"Happy is the one whom you elect and allow to live in your courts. We shall be satisfied with the good things of your house; 'holy' is your temple" (Ps. 65:5).

According to the Old Testament's own understanding,[2] the event of worship is a new experience of historical election and the concomitant establishment of the community of God. In the cultus, election was newly awarded and lived, and it was in the cult that election was also answered and invigorated as faith.[3] This is demonstrated by Israel's festivals, prayers, the Sabbath, and sacrifices. Israel's worship of God also continued to live as a result of the historical election of the nation and its sanctuary by YHWH.[4] The historical acts of YHWH's election are the intrinsic basis of the Old Testament cultus and its contents, something that is made especially clear in Israel's festivals.[5] At the same time, the historical election demanded the negation of foreign cults and cultic practices and included in essence their rejection. Magic and divination were forbidden in Israel, as were the worship of ancestors and cultic prostitution. Things that are foreign to Yahwistic faith and that endanger it are eliminated as "unclean" or as "an abomination to YHWH."[6] These prohibitions can be justified directly with the indication of Israel's election as the people of YHWH or with the holiness of the people created by that election and transmitted to them by their God (Exod. 22:17; and Deut. 14:1f.; cf. 14:2–21 [v. 21!]; 23:18f.; and Leviticus 11; 19:26–29). One is to adhere to a commandment, for it is YHWH's commandment, since the reasons for these exclusions and boundaries as well as for the "impurity" of certain kinds of animals are not named and are only to be deduced with difficulty.[7]

The congregation gathered for worship can be designated as the "elected" of YHWH (Pss. 65:5; 105:6, 43; 106:5; 1 Chron. 16:13; and Isa. 65:9 [cf. vv. 15 + 23]), even as the priests and levites working in the cult are chosen for this service by YHWH.[8] Even the city of God with its temple is characterized as historically elected.[9]

In order to found a cultic site, YHWH must appear first. A person then builds an altar (Gen. 12:7; 28:10ff.; Judg. 6:11ff.; 2 Sam. 24:16ff.; etc.). Furthermore, it is YHWH himself who establishes cultic places with the commemoration of his name in order that he may come to human beings and bless them.

According to the Old Testament conception, the cultus consequently is founded and ordered by YHWH. The regulations concerning the "tabernacle,"[10] the legislation for sacrifice, and other things in the large section of Exodus 25 through Numbers 10 show this very clearly. It is YHWH who seeks and then makes possible this divine service. According to the testimony of the Priestly narrative, the cultus of Israel grew out of the history of God with his people and is anchored there. Indeed, the cultus is even the goal of the entire work of divine creation.[11] "From you comes everything, and what we receive from your own hand we give back," 1 Chron. 29:14 is able to say. YHWH is the one who confers upon the cult and its sacrifices their meaning. "The life of the flesh is in the blood, and I myself have given it upon the altar in order to make atonement for you" (Lev. 17:11). Thus, even this brief look at the passages and spoken rites[12] that were used in the cultus has already allowed us to recognize the sacramental form of the Old Testament cult that was determined by the actions of YHWH. Likewise, this early look has also allowed us to see that cultic acts do not work *ex opere operato,* while questions concerning the condition and life of the cultic participant are not left unasked (Psalms 15 + 24).[13] Cultic and ethical commandments and prohibitions stand next to each other with equal status and value (cf. Exod. 23:1–19; or Lev. 19:26ff.). In addition, YHWH also reacts as a punishing God against violations of ritual commandments, as, for instance, Lev. 7:22ff.; 17:8f., 14; etc. demonstrate.

Thus one shall not be able to say with L. Köhler[14] that the Old Testament cultus may be placed under the superscription "The Self-Redemption of Humanity." Furthermore, the view of J. Wellhausen, according to whom the Old Testament cultus may be in truth the ethnic element in Israelite religion,[15] shall have to undergo corrections. That dangers existed in these directions is not to be denied. The polemical words of the Old Testament prophets issued against the cult allow one to recognize rather clearly that its operation was misunderstood, that people thought they could use it for their own security, that YHWH's grace was believed to be accessible there, that ethics and cultic performance were separated, and that people thought they could continue to contaminate the cultus of YHWH with foreign elements.[16] This polemic, in addition, often makes use of intentional, cultic terminology and is issued in the form of a perverted, cultic decision.[17] However, this has nothing to do with the rejection of the cultus in principle ("since Amos and Wellhausen") but rather with a concrete criticism of a false cultus against which the prophets spoke and which they opposed because of its especially wrongly formed attitude toward its operations. Furthermore, one shall have to distinguish between the "state cult" and the "family cult," that is, between cultic rituals of diverse groups operating with different motives, even though one expression did not exclude the other. The Old Testament, both as a whole and in its present redactional form, moreover, wished to move progressively toward the imageless cult of the only God YHWH,[18] the God who had revealed himself to his people by means of his acts of election in history.

In the cult, Israel encountered the free gift of YHWH's grace and its dispensation.[19] YHWH had founded this cult, given it to his people, and ordered it as the means of their sanctification. According to the testimony of the Old Testament, the cultus did not establish Israel's relationship to YHWH; rather, Israel is made vital, actualized, and strengthened by the cultus. This means that the cult is primarily therefore a sacramental event, not, however, first and foremost a sacrificial act. The cultus, according to the Old Testament, is first of all beneficial, and not primarily sacrificial, for it occurs "for and before YHWH" and brings Israel into the memory and commemoration of God.[20] The expressions "for YHWH" and "to serve him"[21] do not mean only or even primarily service on behalf of YHWH in the form of exerting influence upon him or placating him; rather, they mean service in his honor.[22]

In the face of multiple cultic actions, Old Testament Israel still did not find a comprehensive expression that would cover all activities of worship. There is often the discussion of עבדה (*'ăbōdâ;* "service, work"),[23] which comes close to a comprehensive term. Yet one should note that this term never once is used as a designation for the worship of strange gods but stands rather in general for "labor."[24]

13.2 Cult—History—Revelation

Today it is no longer debated that cultic ritual and event are indispensable for a religious community as well as for the life of faith of the individual.[25] Cultus and group, worship and congregation belong together. It is no longer hostility toward the cult that is regarded as the mark of all legitimate religion, and no one speaks anymore of a cult-free primeval origin of religion. Rather, one now seeks to determine more precisely how cultic ritual and action theologically were construed in the Old Testament. Does the cult provide a conduit for blessing to enter into the common soul of the nation or of the cultic community?[26] Was the cult a creative drama that renewed reality?[27] How did myth and cult interact with each other, or, said in a more Old Testament kind of way, how did history interact with the cultus? Was myth reconstituted in the cult or was it something that was newly actualized? Was the Old Testament cultus, above all, the actualization of the revelation of Sinai[28] or the miracle at the Reed Sea?[29] Was there in ancient Israel something like a cultic theophany of YHWH,[30] perhaps even a cultic-ritual drama in which the ark eventually came to play a role (Pss. 24:7–10; 47; and 132)?[31] What occurred in the cultic celebration of the kingship of YHWH? How did his "ascension to the throne" take place?

That we know unfortunately far too little about all of this becomes depressingly clear when these questions are formulated differently, for instance as follows: How does the cultus interact with revelation? Does the *deus absconditus* become in the cultus the *deus revelatus?* Is the cultus indeed[32] the only legitimate location of divine revelation, and not the conscience, nature, and history? May the above perhaps be correct in regard to the conscience but not, in the Old Testament's view, history as well as nature and its orders?[33] Is there not testimony in the Old Testament cultus to the further actuality of the historical acts of YHWH's election, even though this activity or even event is not reenacted (dramatically in the cult)?[34] Was the theophany ritually reconstituted again in the Old Testament cultus, was it "performed," so to say, or was it "only" present each time as a word event? "Our God comes and is not silent" (Ps. 50:3). "I desire to hear what YHWH will say" (Ps. 85:9). Does such a reductionism to the Word alone perhaps derive too strongly from modern Protestant premises, or, on the contrary, was the Word for the Old Testament worshiper more than it mostly is for us today?[35] One requested such a coming of God (Ps. 50:3a: בוֹא = *bô'; cf.* Ps. 144:5ff.), knew of YHWH's coming to or descending upon (יׇרׇד = *yrd*) Sinai/Horeb/Mountain of God (Exodus 19 = J, E, and D; 24:15ff. = P),[36] had experienced YHWH's coming from the south (Judg. 5:4f.; Deut. 33:2f.; and Ps. 68:9), and spoke about such in other, analogous ways.[37] However, it still cannot be overlooked that the Old Testament texts make no clear or indeed frequent statements about a regular, cultic appearance of YHWH but rather continue especially to mention a coming of YHWH (1 Kings 8:10). Or is the theophany in the cult presupposed as obvious and well known?

As one looks at the Old Testament, the first thing to be said is that the participants in the cult have been decisively shaped by the defining activity of YHWH in their and their ancestors' previous history, and not, however, primarily or indeed only by its cultic actualization and representation. The theological statements about Israel's festivals[38] and their content and the narrative literature of the Old Testament make this entirely clear. The cultus accordingly is an opportunity, made possible through the work of YHWH for the new actualization of divine action. And the cultus, according to the Old Testament, offers the opportunity of a new encounter with God, the experience of a new, even hymnically realized presence of YHWH made possible by historical activity and the accompanying revelation that occurs. The cultus, however, is not exclusively or even primarily the possibility that makes revelation conceivable. However, it is probable that there were developments that took place even in the assessment and experience of the Old Testament cult and that YHWH's (or perhaps beforehand El's) "present salvation" was experienced and interpreted differently. Nevertheless, typically and to a large extent, this is traced out only by conjecturing omissions in Old Testament texts.[39]

The historical traditions of Israel, such as the exodus from Egypt, the wandering in the wilderness, the election of Zion and the temple, and later the Sinai event, receive, as it will be shown, their setting within the cultus of Israel. This is not true of universal myths that were isolated and did not achieve integration into Israelite faith. A battle with chaos, for example, is neither reenacted nor actualized in a cultic drama. Rather, YHWH's acts of history can be described with mythic images (Isa. 51:9f.; Ps. 74:13ff.; and 77:15ff.).[40] "There was no room for the development of a cult regulated by myth,"[41] and YHWH's royal dominion was declared and celebrated in other ways than was the case, for example, with Baal.[42] The historical acts of YHWH's salvation for his people also were not (cyclically) repeatable.[43] One can only hope for an analogous event, for example, for a new exodus; however, this hope was not exclusively or primarily determined by the cult, for it was heard even in the period of the exile when the temple was far away. What is more, this fundamental activity of YHWH was most likely actualized in the cult in such a way that one spoke of divine action in new language, that is, in the language of promise and command, as occurs, for example, in the Book of Deuteronomy, even if this text may not be attributed directly to the cultus. Deuteronomy 31:10–13 presents a programmatic text for the regulation of the reading of the Book of Deuteronomy and does not represent an actual event. There were, however, evidently a narrative re-presentation of the past,[44] a sermon-like realization and remembrance of the salvific acts of YHWH, and, along with these, a new and further testimony to the continuing actuality of what was thus narrated and delivered. During the exile, when the previous and customary cultus was no longer possible, these narrative re-presentations evidently moved from the cult into the family as the bearer of tradition. The "father" must now narrate, "when his son asks him," what YHWH had done on behalf of his people. In addition, it was the "today" of Deuteronomy and its textual components as "sermons" that came to assume the contemporary functions of re-presentation.[45] It was certainly no accident that in all of the so-called "catechetical texts" of the Old Testament that may be mentioned[46] the exodus from Egypt was regarded as the fundamental act of YHWH's salvation.[47] Nevertheless, in and according to the Old Testament, the cultus is not limited to being only the "answer" of Israel or only the worship of YHWH that includes thanksgiving offered him. Rather, the cultus is also, and this chiefly, the new consignment of salvation and, with this, both election and obligation.

Consequently, with all the rootage of the Israelite cultus in the thinking and action of its ancient Near Eastern environment, a topic we shall pursue in more detail momentarily, one shall have to ask what was specifically Israelite in all of this. The cults in the neighboring kingdoms were organized differently. This has already been seen in the cultic role of the king[48] as well as in the significance that the divine images and their caretaking had in these locales.

Furthermore, each portrayal of the divine pantheon was shaped either by the marriage of the gods or by the descent of individual deities into the kingdom of the dead. All of this could play no role in Israel. In looking in another direction, however, one must keep from trying to illuminate too much the cultus of ancient Israel by reference to primitive, for example, animistic cults. Worship in Israel was no natural, magical renewal of life. The תרועה (tĕrû'â; "shout, cry") was no orgiastic ecstasy, neither was there cultic inebriation. Rather, the cult was a place of the clear encounter of YHWH with his people.[49] Since this God, moreover, is not an unknown deity but rather is one who is intimately known from history, one does not first have to make preparations for the encounter with YHWH. Nor does one have to introduce a prayer to him[50] with long lead-ins. The "Be joyful before YHWH" and the concomitant socially responsible action of the participant in the cult are not accidentally mentioned beside each other (Deut. 16:11f., 14; etc.), for YHWH is known not only as the God who elects but also as the one who imposes obligations. If "I am YHWH, the one who sanctifies you" is true of the cultus as well as of the ethical requirements of YHWH,[51] then one cannot say that the Old Testament cultus represented works, but not grace, or was an act of self-help but not a component of God's salvation.[52]

13.3   Concerning the History of Old Testament Worship

Even a glance at the statements of the Old Testament that point to the *historical development of the Israelite cultus*[53] can clarify something of what is involved in comprehending the major problems of ancient Israelite worship.[54]

While only the Sabbath is specifically named as the gift of God to the world in the primeval history of the Priestly document (Gen. 2:1–3),[55] it does include a cultic law in the so-called Noachic commandments (Gen. 9:3–6), although it does not designate it expressly as such (v. 3). However, the Yahwist already mentions sacrificial rituals in his version of the primeval history. In Gen. 4:3 (J), certainly no cultic interests appear in the foreground, even if the relationship between cultus and culture shines through when each of the brothers offers a gift from his sphere of labor. Moreover, when Genesis 4 tells now of the offering of a sacrifice, this signals at the same time that the direct intercourse of humans with God, at least as it is described in Genesis 2–3, is at an end. YHWH has also now become a distant God. The type of sacrifice called here the מנחה (minḥâ; "cereal offering? gift offering?")[56] is just as little the object of reflection as is the type of sacrifice of Noah (Gen. 8:20ff. J) whose offerings are called the עלת ('ōlōt; "sacrifices, burnt offerings"). The sacrifice of the primeval flood hero following his deliverance, moreover, was a topos in the tradition of the primeval flood narratives of the ancient Near East that preceded the Yahwist.[57] The Priestly document neither could nor would narrate anything about this, since for P the distinction between clean and unclean animals was not yet possible at that time (Gen. 7:2ff.). P held that the legitimate Yahwistic cult was first founded at Sinai.[58]

The stories of the ancestors[59] mention unabashedly different cultic places[60] which the ancestors either founded or frequented: Shechem (Gen. 12:6f. J; 33:18ff. E), Mamre (Gen. 13:18; cf. 23:17–19; 25:9; 49:30; and 50:13),[61] Beer-lahai-roi (Gen. 16:4), Beersheba (Gen. 21:22ff., 33; 26:23ff.; and 46:1–4), and Bethel (Gen. 12:8 J; 28:10–22 JE; 35:1–9, 14f. E?). The mention of Jerusalem is limited.[62] It is striking that a priest is not referred to once in these stories of the foundings of cults and offerings by the ancestors. Indeed, the Priestly document does not even mention these ancestral cultic activities. Elsewhere, the "ancestors" perform cultic activities themselves. It is probable that among the mentioned sanctuaries there are fewer that are newly founded by the ancestors than there are that are already occupied cultic sites that are taken over by new tribes and groups. This is indicated by the names and designations of deities that are connected with these sites.[63] The burnt offering (עוֹלה = ʿôlâ) plays no role here. This type of sacrifice is mentioned as required by God only in Gen. 22:2f. (cf. Noah's sacrifice in Gen. 8:20). That Abraham can offer a ram in place of his son (Gen. 22:13) in the present context no longer has to do with replacing the sacrifice of a child with the offering of an animal. Genesis 31:54 mentions a meal offering (זבח = zebaḥ) at the end of a sacrificial meal associated with the concluding of a contract between Laban and Jacob.[64] And Gen. 31:19, 30ff. mentions the household gods (תרפים = tĕrāpîm)[65] as something that is self-evident, although at the same time not without disparaging considerably their suspect treatment.[66] In addition, stones and trees were mentioned in connection with the cultic sites and rituals (Gen. 12:6; 13:18; 18:1; 21:33; 28:10ff.; 31:45ff.; and 35:4). Whether the narrative of the concluding of a covenant along with its associated ritual in Gen. 25:7ff. preserves an old tradition is debated.[67] Moreover, Genesis 17 and the mention of the covenant with Abraham, along with circumcision (including the children: v. 12) as its sign, are to be attributed initially to the basic Priestly document of the exilic period.[68]

It is also not possible to say anything more precisely than this about the cult of the Moses group and the Mosaic period.[69] In connection with the effort to obtain the release of the enslaved Israelites in Egypt, several times mention is made of their desire to celebrate a sacificial festival for their God YHWH and therefore the request for their (temporary?) release (Exod. 3:18; 5:1–8, 17; 8:4, 21ff.: always with זבח = zbḥ; "sacrifice"). Although the Passover is the subject of discussion in Exod. 12:1–13:16, most of what comprises this section derives from later hands (Deuteronomic and Priestly). Thus these texts permit one to recognize the later transformation of what was originally a ritual of a New Year's Festival into the remembrance of the exodus. The thesis of L. Rost,[70] that the Passover[71] originally was a ritual concerning the departure of nomads of small herds to summer pasture places in inhabited country, possesses a great deal of probability.[72] According to Rost, the Passover ritual originally served to protect the herds and their owners and thus possessed an apotropaic character (cf. 12:23?).

If the so-called Kenite hypothesis[73] should likewise be given some degree of probability, a hypothesis that many support, then the notice of the sacrifice of Jethro to the God of Israel (Exod. 18:12) could possibly have some actual validity.

That a cultic event was at the same time connected with the Sinai covenant[74] is not suggested by the ancient text of Exod. 34:10 (J). Exodus 24:9–11 by contrast speaks possibly of a "covenant meal before YHWH" (not "with" him; cf. Exod. 18:12). That this should be a repeated occasion, however, is not said. In any case, the verses in Exod. 24:3–8 describe an event that occurs once; the ritual portrayed here also has no parallels in the rest of the Old Testament. The blood ritual (vv. 6 + 8), with the "blood of the ברית = běrît" (cf. Zech. 9:11)[75] and the word of explanation, joins together the partners (God and people) into a close and continuing community of mutual responsibility,[76] although there is no discussion about any atoning significance given to this ritual.[77] One may not overlook the fact that sacrifice, blood ritual, and covenant theology are placed together only here.[78] Moreover, with the references to the people, the Covenant Code, the twelve stones that correspond to the twelve tribes of Israel (v. 4), and the (in. v. 5) concentration of sacrificial terminology, the text points clearly to later additions if not also to a later origin. The older texts of the Sinai pericope still do not contain an elaborated covenant theology.[79]

Exodus 32 is less shaped by its basic source (vv. 1–6, 15a, 19f., 30–34?) than it is by its continuing redactions that reflect the event mentioned in 1 Kings 12:25ff. that takes place under Jeroboam I. Therefore, Exodus 32 provides only limited consideration for the cultic questions of the time of Moses.[80] Every now and then the thesis is presented[81] that, concealed behind this narrative, there is a conflict between the Moses group and an Aaron group over the problem of the imageless worship of YHWH. It is, however, very questionable whether this text returns so far back to the past that it presents accurate, historical information.

By contrast, the sayings of the ark (Num. 10:35ff.) are capable of indicating that a portable, accompanying symbol of the presence of YHWH belonged to the Moses group or to another group of the wilderness period that later went up to Israel.[82] Even the older texts, which were written prior to the Priestly document and which speak of a tent for the encounter with YHWH (Exod. 33:7–11; Num. 11:16f., 24–30; and 12:4f., 10),[83] can point to another sanctuary that reaches back into the wilderness time and perhaps belonged to another group that was later incorporated into Israel.[84]

That the bronze serpent[85] mentioned in Num. 21:4–9 was supposed to have stemmed from the time of Moses is improbable, since it scarcely then would have been removed by Hezekiah from the temple in Jerusalem (2 Kings 18:4). The serpent would have been, rather, a Jerusalem cultic symbol (symbol of healing?) of Canaanite mediation with possibly an Egyptian origin and background.[86]

Especially debated is the question whether the imageless worship of YHWH along with the expression "no other gods besides him" belonged to the religion of the time of Moses or to the Moses group. Was YHWH at this time already a "jealous God" (Exod. 20:5; 34:14; and Deut. 5:9)? It is true that today the worship of YHWH alone and the imageless nature of this faith are ever more frequently given a late origin. However, these views are open to criticism by the fact that one cannot explain many things in the development of Israelite faith without a certain and already early impulse of a Yahwistic faith shaped in these ways. Nothing is to be said for obvious reasons about the date of the formulations of the first and second commandments as they presently exist.[87]

In the texts that seek to report about the period between the conquest and state formation, several sanctuaries are mentioned together. Shechem was of special significance (Josh. 8:30f.; 20:7; 24; and Judg. 9:4, 37), and close to it Shiloh (Josh. 18:1; Judg. 18:31; 21:19ff.; and 1 Samuel 1–3; 4:3f.), where the ark[88] was to have stood and where a "festival" was celebrated (Judg. 21:19–21). First Samuel 1:3ff. allows one to assume that there was the custom of a pilgrimage there. Also mentioned, then, are Gilgal (Joshua 3 + 4; 9:6; Judg. 3:19; 1 Sam. 7:16; 11:14f.; 13:7ff.; and 15:12ff.), Bethel (Judg. 20:18ff.; and 21:2ff.; 1 Sam. 7:16; and 10:3), Mizpah, Gibeon, Ophrah, and Dan.[89] In addition, Mt. Tabor was probably a location for a sanctuary for some Northern tribes, namely, Zebulun, Naphtali, and Issachar (Josh. 19:22, 34; Deut. 33:19; and cf. Judg. 4:6, 12).

Consequently, there were a large number of sanctuaries in this period, some of which were more significant than others.[90] However, there was no central sanctuary with a cult carried out in common by "Israel." This is indicated also by the sacrificial activities of Samuel in different sanctuaries (1 Sam. 7:9f.; 10:8; 11:15; 13:12; and 16:2, 5). It is completely plausible that it was already Yahwistic faith that bound the tribes together. However, this had still not led to a central sanctuary, and the previous, well-represented thesis of an "amphictyony" of this earlier Israel, that is, of a sacral tribal league with a central sanctuary and cultus serving as the unifying bond, must submit to some attenuations and modifications.[91] One shall have to consider, in addition to this, the so-called militaristic Yahwism, that is, the wars conducted under YHWH by tribes and tribal groups, as a unifying bond for these groups.

Consequently, sacrifices are mentioned time and again, although in different cultic places,[92] and so are, in addition, constructed altars (Josh. 8:30f.; 22:10ff.; Judg. 6:24; and 1 Sam. 7:17), sacred trees, and cultic objects (Judg.

6:11; 8:27; 9:6; 13:19; and 15:19). Priests are at times mentioned in connection with the sacrifices and the altars (Judges 17/18; and 1 Samuel 1–2; 4), although at other times not (Judg. 6:25ff.; 13:15ff.; and 1 Sam. 16:5). First Samuel 1–2 permits one to look at the customs of pilgrimage and sacrifice, and in this connection the Elides are mentioned as priests in Shiloh.[93] From the sphere of (Canaanite?) agriculture, agrarian festivals were taken over during the pre-state period and progressively integrated into Yahwistic faith.[94] Also, particular kinds of sacrifices, especially the burnt offering, not familiar to either the tribal groups immigrating into the land or to those tribal groups which developed in the land prior to the formation of Israel, were first thoroughly known in the land of Canaan and that means also by other population groups. The terms for sacrifice in Ugaritic[95] suggest a great similarity between the cultus practiced there and the Old Testament's cultic practices, even though these terms communicate nothing about a specific understanding of sacrifice.[96] First Samuel 9:12 and 20:6 allow one to recognize, by contrast, the meaning of זבח = zebaḥ ("sacrifice") for these groups. 'Ašērâ and maṣṣēbâ (wooden pillar and stone monument respectively),[97] as components of cultic places (במה = bāmâ), likewise probably go back to Canaanite influence.

The kingship of Saul was of no particular significance for the history of Israelite worship. If the controversies between Samuel and Saul narrated in 1 Sam. 13:7b-15 and 1 Sam. 15:1–25 are limited to cultic matters, then these two texts, which clearly are later, offer no irreproachably reliable material for the period of Saul. Rather, these points provide data only for the later (Deuteronomistic) view of certain constellations of problems that concern the kingship of Saul and the cultic activity conceded to be exceptional for kings as a whole.[98] According to 1 Samuel 4–6, the ark[99] that was brought from Shiloh as a sign of the presence of YHWH among his fighting people was a war palladium that accompanied Israel in its battle against the Philistines.

Among the first significant actions of David was the transfer of the ark to Jerusalem after he had conquered the city (2 Samuel 5–6), for this introduced or more closely bound this city and the Davidic dynasty that was now reigning there to Yahwistic faith. Pre-Israelite Jerusalem cult traditions found entrance into Yahwistic faith, even if modified in many ways. The development of the so-called Zion tradition[100] and particular aspects in the assessment of the (Davidic) dynasty[101] were set in motion. These elements strongly shaped theologically the worship of Israel, as shown by the (even if also later) Zion hymns,[102] the royal psalms,[103] and the YHWH enthronement hymns.[104] The extent to which the ideas of YHWH (Sebaoth) as king (via the ark or cherubim?) were brought together already as early as Shiloh[105] is a question that to this point has not been clearly answered.

When David introduced his reign in Jerusalem and also added at the same time Canaanite regions to enlarge his sphere of rule (Judg. 1:27–35; and 1 Sam.

24:5–7; cf. Solomon according to 1 Kings 4:17–19), these acts certainly necessarily led to the reciprocal permeation of "Israel's" faith with that of the
"Canaanites."[106] Later prophets such as Elijah, Hosea, and the early Jeremiah
continued to form a front against these developments.[107] Deuteronomistic
thinking saw in this one of the main sins of Israel and gave an extremely positive assessment to the cultic reforms (1 Kings 15:12f.: Asa; 2 Kings 18:4:
Hezekiah; and 2 Kings 22–23: Josiah) that sought to eliminate some of these
Canaanite influences and to correct various matters.[108] In these controversies,
it was the Rechabites (Jeremiah 35) who maintained a religion that was
strongly loyal to YHWH and practiced an associated ethos that was strongly
hostile to the society and culture of the settled villages and cities. Their "zeal
for YHWH" rejected the ownership of farms and vineyards as well as the cul-
tivation of land and the enjoyment of wine, and they lived in tents instead of
houses. It is worthy to note, however, that this rigorism was not the normal pattern of life and was not interspersed among the common practices of faithfulness to YHWH.[109] First Samuel 21–22 mentions in reference to the priesthood
of Nob some of the cultic customs practiced there, including the shewbread (1
Sam. 21:4ff.), the ephod (v. 10),[110] and the inquiry of the priest or, rather, of
God (22:15).

After David already had procured the plot of land, designated as chosen by
YHWH through the appearance of the "Angel of YHWH"[111] for the temple
building that had been planned but not executed (2 Samuel 24), Solomon was
the one who built and outfitted it (1 Kings 6–7).[112] That, therefore, in the new
capital city and in the seat of the king a cultic place was created that became
significant for the entire worship of Israel/Judah, even if this temple was not
exactly a kind of main or even central sanctuary, needs only to be mentioned.

For the view of the royal period that is present in the Deuteronomistically
redacted Books of Kings, the first thing to mention is the assessment of the
"sins of Jeroboam."[113] Jeroboam I caused images of calves to be erected in the
sanctuaries of Bethel and Dan to serve as counterweights to the sanctuary in
Jerusalem (1 Kings 12:25ff.). The calf images were to serve for the worship of
the deity of the exodus, thus for the worship of YHWH (1 Kings 12:28c). They
were certainly not meant to be pictorial representations of this God, who instead was to stand or sit enthroned over or upon them. This "sin," however,
was put forward as the main reason that the Northern Israelite part of the state
must face collapse. The kings who succeeded Jeroboam were judged according to whether they had walked in these "sins of Jeroboam" and whether they
had abolished the "high places" or tolerated them.[114] Further, these high places
(במה = *bāmâ*),[115] which consisted especially of an altar that often stood on a
raised platform, a stone monument (מצבה = *maṣṣēbâ*)[116] that probably was the
symbol of a male deity, a wooden post (אשרה = *'ăšērâ*)[117] standing for a female deity, and one or more trees, fell under the criticism of the Deuterono-

mistic editors for being cults that were syncretistic in their eyes.[118] That this was not always seen in this way is demonstrated by the unproblematic mentionings of these cultic places (1 Sam. 9:13ff.; 10:5) and cultic objects (Gen. 28:18, 22; 31:13; 35:14, 20; Exod. 24:4; etc.) in other areas of the Old Testament. In addition, these calves as well as amulets, figures of idols, and so forth frequently have been discovered in Israel, something that one might believe was otherwise the case on the basis of the first and second commandments. However, these archaeological discoveries continue to point to this idolatry in an increasingly frequent way.[119] The destruction of the *maṣṣebôt* is commanded already in the older texts (Exod. 23:24; and 34:13), and not for the first time in the later texts (Deut. 7:5; 12:3; 16:22; and Lev. 26:1).

Likewise, more recent discoveries indicate that it is not clear-cut that only YHWH himself was worshiped or that he was worshiped everywhere in the same way. These discoveries, which presumably date from the eighth century B.C.E., appear to classify him ("poly-yahwistically"), on the one hand, with designations of geographical locations ("YHWH of Teman," "YHWH of Samaria"), something, however, that, is not so entirely new if one recollects the "YHWH from Hebron" in 2 Sam. 15:7 or "your gods [plural!] who have brought you out of Egypt" (1 Kings 12:28b). However, the Deuteronomic/Deuteronomistic movement with its "YHWH is one" (Deut. 6:4) and its demand for only one legitimate cultic site for YHWH (Deuteronomy 12) objected strongly to this. On the other hand, the new texts from Khirbet el-Qom and Kuntillet 'Ajrud mentioned alongside YHWH "his" Asherah,[120] although this scarcely means that Asherah is the wife of YHWH, since personal names with suffixes are unusual. Rather, these texts simply placed YHWH together with an Asherah who was a cultic pole and was of a "comparable height standing by his side."[121] In texts of the fifth century B.C.E., from the Jewish colony on the Nile island of Elephantine in Aswan, we encounter later the deity Asim-Bethel, the goddess Anat-Bethel, and the "Queen of Heaven" in addition to YHWH[122] as the deities worshiped by the Jewish colonists, certainly far from Palestine and Jerusalem.[123]

The sympathies of the Deuteronomists were clearly on the side of the kings who had been active in reformations of the cult and, at the same time, removed the "high places" (2 Kings 18:4, 22; 23:8, 13, 15, and 19). This is only briefly reported of the Jewish king Asa in 1 Kings 15:9–15 (cf. 2 Chronicles 14) and likewise of Joash in 2 Kings 11:13ff. (cf. 2 Chronicles 24). More fully narrated is the cultic reform of Hezekiah (2 Kings 18:3f.), a text that is even more generously elaborated by the Chronicler (2 Chronicles 29–31). Hezekiah presumably sought to rescind what his father, Ahaz, had introduced because of Assyrian cultic influence (2 Kings 16:10–18). This was more easily possible because of the difficulties surrounding the throne after the death of the Assyrian king Sennacherib (681 B.C.E.). That this cultic reform had, therefore, its center of gravity in the attempted political and therefore also religious dissolution of Assyria[124] is more than probable.

The cultic reform of Josiah in the year 621 B.C.E. (2 Kings 22:3–23:25)[125] is narrated with a heightening of the theological dimension present in Deuteronomistically redacted texts[126] that are strongly interested in reforms and reporting about them. If "this book of the law" (2 Kings 22:8) was actually found in connection with the political as well as the religious attempts of Josiah at secession and reform, then it could have been only a precursor of the present version of Deuteronomy, although in a Deuteronomistically redacted and shaped form.[127] According to 2 Kings 23:4ff., Josiah was to have carried through comprehensive standards of cultic reform, including among them the abolishment of Canaanite and Assyrian religious and cultic influences[128] and especially the centralization of the legitimate YHWH cult in Jerusalem (2 Kings 23:8f.). It is logical that in this connection the "high places" as well as the altar (erected by Jeroboam I) in Bethel were also destroyed (2 Kings 23:13–15). That the reform was not so fully carried out or was not so comprehensive as the Deuteronomistic scribes conclusively portray it to us is shown, for example, by the references to the "Queen of Heaven" in the Book of Jeremiah (Jer. 7:18; and 44:15–27).

Since the time of Hezekiah (725–697 B.C.E.) and Josiah (639–609 B.C.E.), the Deuteronomic and later the Deuteronomistic movement[129] was at work both literarily and theologically. Their goal was a cultic one, namely, to attribute to one God (YHWH) only one legitimate cultic place among his people, in order to create cultic purity (Deut. 6:4ff.; 12) by way of the unity of worship and thus to reduce the number of gods (Jer. 2:28) as well as altars (Hos. 10:1). The Covenant Code had not arranged matters in such a way but rather had seen the possibility of several cultic sites for YHWH (Exod. 20:24ff.). Deuteronomy programmatically required that all festivals, including especially the Passover[130] formerly practiced by families, be carried out at the central sanctuary (Deuteronomy 16). The reason that this cultic site in Deuteronomy is still not called "Jerusalem" but rather always is referred to as the "place which YHWH has chosen in order to cause his name to dwell/to place his name there,"[131] is to be sought more in the Deuteronomistic conception of Deuteronomy as the speeches of Moses and less in the (also debated) possibility that components of Deuteronomy can be traced back to the traditions of the Northern Kingdom or that another cultic location was previously in view. Also the section about Josiah's concluding the covenant (2 Kings 23:1–3) offers an idealized scene for the heightening and legitimizing of the authority of Deuteronomy and can be considered only in a very limited manner as a witness to a covenant renewal festival customarily, even regularly practiced during the preexilic period.

Probably under Assyrian or Babylonian pressure and influence, a change in calendars was undertaken (in the eighth or seventh century B.C.E.). The new year now began, no longer in autumn, but rather with the beginning of our own New Year, so that Israel's autumn festival now fell in the seventh month of the year.[132]

What the conquest of Jerusalem by the Babylonians, the destruction of the temple, and with this the end of the existing cult in 587/586 B.C.E. meant for Israel's and Judah's faith can be extracted from Lamentations (Lamentations 1–5). In the exile, one was in an unclean land (Amos 7:17) and could sing there only in a movingly mournful way a Song of Zion (Psalm 137), since one was not prepared to honor any request by the captors to sing such a song (Ps. 137:3). For the ones who had remained back in the land it was, as before, both possible and worthwhile to make a pilgrimage to Jerusalem (Jer. 41:4f.). Was there on the ruins of the temple a certain cultic enterprise (cf. also Lam. 1:4) put into operation or maintained? Ceremonies of lament took place both in the homeland and among the exiles (1 Kings 8:33; Zech. 7:1ff.; 8:18f.; and Lamentations). The laments that were loudly sung in these cultic settings were answered by Deutero-Isaiah, possibly toward the end of the Babylonian exile, with his announcements and promises of salvation. Collective songs of lament, such as Psalms 44; 74; 79; and 89, could be sung only in this setting. One prayed in the direction of Jerusalem (1 Kings 8:48; and Dan. 6:11), for prayer also was pointed out to be a possibility for turning toward YHWH even in a foreign land (Jeremiah 29).[133]

All time was YHWH's time, even if it was the exilic period in Babylon. Every place was YHWH's place, even if it was Babylon. Deutero-Isaiah[134] likewise made it clear that the Babylonian gods were not to be the victors over YHWH and therefore also were not to pose any challenge or danger for the exiles. And Ezekiel, who had to see the "glory of YHWH"[135] abandon the Jerusalem temple (Ezek. 11:22f.), encountered this glory and therefore the presence of YHWH among those who had been led away, a group to which he himself belonged (Ezekiel 1–3). The observance of the Sabbath (Gen. 2:1–3; cf. Exod. 24:16 P) and circumcision (Genesis 17 P) were made newly important by Priestly theologians during the exile as signs of the devotion and attachment to YHWH. And one met here and there in small groups in order to listen to the word of YHWH (Ezek. 33:30–33), so that many scholars see in this the beginning of the later worship of the synagogue that is oriented to the word. Some appear to have regarded Josiah's reform as a mistake (Jer. 44:17). Others outlined models for the new temple and the new worship, as one hoped they would be in the period following the return home (Ezekiel 40–48; Exodus 25–31 par.[136]), when the exiles might be brought back to Zion under YHWH's guidance even as Deutero-Isaiah promised. In addition to the prophets of the exile, the Priestly theologians also had for their exilic community sustaining instructions and saw this world as created by the God of Israel, not, for instance, by the Babylonian god Marduk, and as permeated by the sus-

taining orders of the God of Israel. To this belonged the chronological struc-
turing of the course of this world (Gen. 1:1–2:4a) and the covenantal sign of
the rainbow (Genesis 9).[137] Theologians of the Deuteronomistic School looked
now beyond YHWH's necessary judgment of his people and outlined a new
constitution for the people of God (Deut. 16:18–18:22) and correct orders for
worship (Deuteronomy 12 + 16). They spoke of new obedience that could
make possible a new conquest, particularly since YHWH would remain loyal
to his oath to the ancestors[138] and to his promise, his covenant, and his grace.
The Holiness Code belonged also to these plans and outlines for a new, cultic
order (Leviticus 17–26)[139] and desired, for example, to regulate the possibility
of the profane slaughter of animals (Lev. 17:13ff.), but in a different way than
took place in Deut. 12:20ff.

During and after the slow return from exile that occurred in individual
waves and according to the warnings and promises of the prophets Haggai and
Zechariah (Zechariah 1–8), the returnees gave their attention first to the erect-
ing of an altar (Ezra 3:2–6) and then, with the permission of the Persian king
(Ezra 5:6–6:12), to the rebuilding of the temple (Exodus 25–32). This second
temple, which Ezekiel (in Ezek. 40:1–44:9) had outlined in a vision, did not
appear to have been realized in the way he had seen it. Yet it was still dedicated in 515 B.C.E. (Ezra 6:15–18), after which a Passover festival was celebrated (Ezra 6:19–22). The outfitting of this temple is not fully congruent with
its Solomonic precursor. This is especially noted in the fact that the holy of
holies was not the location for the ark but rather was empty. Exodus 25–31 and
Exodus 35–40 say a great deal about the furnishing of the temple. Moreover,
more programmatic expressions are treated in these corpora of texts that could
not fully be put into practice.[140]

The autumn festival was divided into three festivals in the postexilic period.[141] As for the Priestly theologians after the exile, which had been experienced as punishment and had rather strongly awakened the consciousness of
guilt, their thinking about atonement became especially important and formative for the ensuing postexilic (sacrificial) cult.[142] In addition, the cultus increasingly became the business of the priests. The systematization of the cult
now being introduced and the theological reshaping of the different sacrifices
were connected with these and other reasons.[143] In their present form, the rituals of sacrifice in Leviticus 1–5 + 6–7 clearly originate in the postexilic period. The Chronicler's historical work, by contrast, wishes to see that the worship of its late postexilic community under the musical leadership of the levites
as singers[144] is understood more as the praise of YHWH. Moreover, we
scarcely know the exact nature of the particulars of the performance of the
postexilic, cultic activities. Rather, we are able to access these only in part.
Thus it is certain that an expansion of the temple music took place, something
for which the Books of Chronicles are a witness.[145] David as the great singer

of psalms is also the intiator of the worship, according to the Chronicler. However, the Book of Malachi, for example, allows one to recognize that cultic activity in the postexilic period was not always Yahwistic (Mal. 1:6ff.; 2:1ff.).

When the withdrawal of the Samaritans from the Jerusalem cult begins, presumably under Alexander the Great,[146] although it will not reach its full conclusion until later, the Chronicler does not yet write off those who are cultically separated.[147] Rather, the Chronicler anticipates they will come back again to Judah. Thus this "remnant" would make fully complete once again the people of God.[148] And when especially Jerusalem and, above all, its temple suffered a terrible misfortune in the religious persecution under Antiochus IV in 169 B.C.E. and the years following (Dan. 11:31ff.; 1 Macc. 1:17ff.), the thinking and action of those who rose up against this oppression chiefly revolved around these two locations and their cultic renewal. The festival of Hanukkah keeps alive even unto today the memory of the new dedication of the temple on the 25th of Kislev (= 12, 14) of the year 164 B.C.E. (1 Macc. 4:36ff.; and 2 Macc. 10:1–8). Finally, the Festival of Purim is to keep alive the memory of the event described in the Book of Esther, and this is even the stated purpose of the book (Esther 9:17ff.). This festival is also mentioned in 2 Macc. 15:37 and later in Josephus (Ant. 11.6, 284ff.).

13.4   The Festival Calendar and the Festivals

Festivals (חַג = *ḥag,* or מוֹעֵד = *mô'ēd*) are constitutive for a cultus.[149] In Israel there were not a few of these. There festivals of victory and communal laments are mentioned (1 Sam. 15:12; Joel 2:12; Zech. 7:5; 8:19; etc.) as well as familial festivals such as the shearing of sheep (Gen. 31:19; 1 Sam. 25:2ff.; and 2 Sam. 13:23ff.), weaning a child (Gen. 21:8), marriage (Gen. 29:22ff.; and Judg. 14:10ff.), and later probably also circumcision (Genesis 17). The day of the New Moon and fast days were mentioned.[150] In the postexilic period came the Festival of Purim (Esther 9:17ff.), the festival of the rededication of the temple (Hanukkah),[151] and the day of Nicanor (1 Macc. 4:59; and 7:48f.). The prophets also mention festivals.[152] The "(sacrificial) festival for YHWH in the wilderness," which is programmatically mentioned in Exod. 5:1–8; 7:16, 26; and 8:4, 22ff. by those held prisoner by pharaoh, can be only a festival of shepherds and not an agrarian festival, if it was intended to be real.[153] In addition, YHWH is in this way clearly designated as a deity of the wilderness.

The most important festivals of Israel from the Old Testament period, however, which are clearly comprehensible in their theological significance and development, are named in the Old Testament's calendars of festivals. These festival calendars are found in the Covenant Code (Exod. 23:14–17), in the so-called Law of YHWH's Privilege (Exod. 34:18–24 J and JE), in Deuteronomy (Deut. 16:1–17), in the Holiness Code (Lev. 23:4–44), and in the postexilic reformulations of the Priestly document (Numbers 28–29). The sequence of the festival calendars and their historical succession of origin are described as follows.

The oldest and also rather brief text in the Covenant Code (Exod. 23:14–17) mentions three agrarian pilgrimage festivals (חג = ḥag) during the year which males are to celebrate in honor of YHWH ("me"; cf. Lev. 23:6, 28, 34, 40). The Mazzoth festival (מצות = maṣṣôt) is the first. Occurring in the month of Abib, this festival is celebrated by the eating of unleavened bread ("mazzah"). This festival is already associated with the exodus from Egypt in this first calendar.[154] By contrast, the Passover, certainly no agricultural festival, is not yet mentioned. However, it is possible that v. 18 and v. 19b are connected to this festival. The second festival mentioned is the "harvest festival" (חג הקציר = ḥag haqqāṣîr) which concerns the firstfruits of the harvest (cf. Num. 28:26) and thus probably points to the beginning of the wheat harvest, while mazzoth occurs at the beginning of the harvest of barley. The third festival occurs in autumn at the end of all of the harvests, including also of oil and wine. This is the "festival of ingathering" (חג האסף = ḥag hā'āsip), and it occurs at the brink of the beginning of the new year that "goes forth" (v. 16). In the Covenant Code, there are mentioned in addition to these three agrarian festivals of pilgrimage, which are not given a sanctuary for their destination, the Sabbath, the sacral fallow land for the well-being of the needy (שמט = šmṭ as a verb, "lie fallow"),[155] and other cultic commandments and prohibitions (Exod. 20:22f., 24–26; 22:19, 30; and 23:10ff.).

The second festival calendar (Exod. 34:18–24; more exact: vv. 18, 22f.) within the framework of the so-called Law of YHWH's Privilege[156] also speaks of three agrarian festivals of pilgrimage for men, as does the calendar embedded in the Covenant Code, and orders matters for Mazzoth in a similar fashion to Exod. 23:15. In Exod. 34:25, however, the Passover is mentioned (פסח = pesaḥ), although this festival is still not fully connected to Mazzoth. However, this association is suggested here.[157] The exodus out of Egypt is once again mentioned in association with the Mazzoth festival (Exod. 34:18), and here as well as previously in Exod. 23:15 Mazzoth is the first festival to which is assigned a historical act of YHWH. It may be no accident at all that reference is made here for the first time to the "primeval election of Israel,"[158] namely, to the exodus event. The "Festival of Weeks" (חג שבעת = ḥag šābū'ōt) is now clearly determined as the beginning of the wheat harvest, while the regulations given concerning the harvest of ingathering (Exod. 34:22) are once more similar to those in Exod. 23:16.

In the third festival calendar (Deut. 16:1–17),[159] it is primarily no longer Mazzoth but rather Passover that is emphasized in detail and treated at the beginning. As had been the case with Mazzoth, Passover is now associated with the exodus from Egypt and is explicitly transferred from houses to the sanctuary (vv. 5 + 7). This sanctuary is to be used not for every possible festival but only for those which have been chosen by YHWH. In v. 8, Mazzoth is mentioned in a way that is suggestive of what previously had been stated, and Passover and Mazzoth are now closely interwoven. The notice concerning the date does not yet mention a specific day. The month that is mentioned, Abib, includes the period from the latter part of March to the middle of April and later is given the Babylonian name Nisan. More precise explanations and indications are given for the mazzah bread and for the slaughter of the Passover lamb. The Festival of Weeks is once more a harvest festival. Moreover, it was now (v. 12) to serve as the time in which Israel was to remember its slavery in Egypt and, in so doing, became now the second festival taken from the exclusively agricultural sphere into which a historical act was inserted. The date for this festival is mentioned in terms of occurring seven weeks after the barley festival. The third festival receives here only the name "Tabernacles" (סֻכּוֹת = *sūkkôt*), for which no reason is provided. This festival occurs again at the end of the entire harvest. However, the circle of participants is emphasized and programmatically expanded in all the festivals. In addition to the earlier, customary, full citizens are the son, the daughter, and even the servant, the handmaiden, the levite, the sojourner, the orphan and the widow. And the statement "Be joyful before YHWH" is underlined in the festivals of Weeks and Tabernacles (vv. 11 + 14).[160] In addition to the expansion of the circle of participants, the requirement of centralization, and the emphasis on the Passover, this statement is also an important peculiarity of the Deuteronomic/Deuteronomistic festival calendar and its understanding of the cult.

The festival calendar of the Holiness Code (Leviticus 17–26) is found in Lev. 23:4–44, a text that has several strata.[161] According to this text, all three festivals last a week (in Deuteronomy 16 only Passover/Mazzoth and Tabernacles). Also, the Holiness Code contains an interweaving of calendar and ritual because the offering of sacrifices is also introduced. Precise dates are established, what is to happen and when "in the sanctuary." Passover/Mazzoth are now clearly a combined twofold festival, a rationale for which is no longer necessary. This twofold festival begins on the fourteenth and fifteenth of the first month. Accordingly, the beginning of the year is moved to the New Year, something that probably occurred under Assyrian influence.[162] The Festival of Weeks is expanded into a harvest festival with the offering of the first sheaf, along with burnt, cereal, and drink offerings. And no bread made out of new wheat is to be eaten up to the beginning of this festival (vv. 9–14: a later expansion?). Verses 15–22 determine more precisely the date when the first sheaf is to be offered: some seven weeks after the offering of the sheaf (probably the barley sheaf). Thus it would appear that this festival also may have undergone some kind of transformed character in the same way that the Festival of Tabernacles was regulated. The autumn festival was divided into three festivals beginning with Leviticus 23. On the seventh day of the first month (thus also here according to the new calendar), the New Year's Festival (designated by the term שַׁבָּתוֹן = *šabbātôn*) is to be celebrated (cf. Num. 29:1ff.; and Neh. 8:2),[163] while on the tenth day of the seventh month the Day of Atonement (יוֹם הַכִּפֻּרִים = *yôm hakkippūrîm;* Leviticus 16) is observed for which rest and fasting are enjoined (vv. 26–32) and which serves the purpose of the expiation of sins (v. 28; לְכַפֵּר עֲלֵיכֶם = *lĕkappēr 'ălêykem*). On the fifteenth day of the seventh month, the festival week for Tabernacles begins which now is connected likewise with the history of Israel. The festival is supposed to serve to bring to mind the wilderness period during which one was to have dwelt in tabernacles (vv. 39–42). Nothing in the Old Testament's understanding inquires about the historical possibility or even probability of tabernacles in the wilderness for even a small group of participants (Exod. 12:37; 38:26; etc.).[164]

The festival calendar in Numbers 28–29 is found in the context of post-exilic additions to and continuations of the Priestly document (Num. 28:16–29:39). Here there is an exact calendar that also prescribes a relatively detailed ritual for sacrifice, so that this late and most comprehensive festival calendar of the Old Testament has more the character of sacrificial regulations than festival ones. Passover and Mazzoth are once again combined; however, they are not dated. New Year's on the seventh day of the first month (29:1ff.), the Day of Atonement on the seventh day of the tenth month (29:7ff.), and Tabernacles beginning with the fifteenth day of the seventh month (29:12ff.) likewise receive precise regulations for sacrifices. And these are especially detailed and comprehensive for the festival week of Tabernacles. Rest from labor is enjoined for the festivals, and each is described as a "sacred convocation" (מִקְרָא-קֹדֶשׁ = *miqrā'-qōdeš*).

Another text that concerns the festivals of Israel is found in Ezek. 45:21–25. It is chronologically to be placed probably after Numbers 28–29 and contains as a special feature sacrificial stipulations for the (also mentioned in Ezekiel 40–48) "prince" (נָשִׂיא = *nāśî'*) in regard to the "sin offering" (חַטָּאת = *ḥaṭṭā't*).[165]

If one looks over the festival calendars in relationship to each other and in sequence, then the following is worthy of note: the stipulations become increasingly comprehensive, since they wish always to become more precise and more detailed in regard to dating as well as sacrifices. The festivals are gradually brought within the dimension of "salvation history" out of the agricultural sphere and therefore, insofar as this goes, are made progressively Yahwistic.[166] Festivals are combined (Passover/Mazzoth), although later are also split apart (autumn festival). They become centralized in a sanctuary, due to Deuteronomy as well as a result of Deuteronomy, and they become lengthened in their duration. It is not clear whether the expansion of the circle of participants that Deuteronomy sought to achieve was successful. In addition, the sacrificial regulations gain increasingly in significance as well as in size. During the course of the history of Israel's cultus, a change in the calendar eventually had to have taken place.

If one looks at the diachronic sequence of the festival calendars in terms of the individual festivals and their development, then one is able to understand in an approximate way the following.

Mazzoth[167] (מצּוֹת = *maṣṣôt;* Exod. 23:15; 34:18; 12:15ff. P; and 13:3ff. Deuteronomistic; then connected with Passover) was originally a festival independent of Passover and had probably to do with the beginning of the barley harvest. In this festival, one ate the first "unleavened" bread, that is, the first bread from the new harvest of barley.[168] Initially this festival was not given a precise date but rather could be arranged according to the circumstances at the time. However, was this festival originally an agrarian one that Israel had then been able to appropriate once in the land of Canaan? Placed at the beginning of the different festivals, it was probably the first to be connected with an event of Israel's history, namely, the exodus from Egypt. If the corresponding text in Exod. 23:15 was an addition, then this association would have been carried out for the first time in Exod. 34:18. This association further exists in Exodus 12 (according to v. 15 it is Mazzoth); however, in terms of literary and redactional analysis, one finds here an association that is later. Then Deuteronomy and later the Priestly document came to associate Mazzoth and Passover, and this combination "may go back to the approximate, temporal coincidence of the practice of offering the Passover sacrifice and the celebration of the Mazzah festival. Perhaps this combination may have been especially suggested by the fact that in the Passover meal it was customary to eat 'unleavened bread with bitter herbs' (12:8)."[169] The combination was certainly also assisted by the fact that Mazzoth and Passover later became two chronologically closely adjacent (pilgrimage) festivals.

Scholarship has produced no precise results about the early history of Passover[170] (Heb. פסח = *pesaḥ;* Aram. פסחא = *pashā'*). In its origins, this festival did not have to do with the sacrifice of the firstborn or the firstborn's substitution in the form of an animal sacrifice; rather, it had to do with the custom of taking up residence ("house," not "tent," is mentioned) when an apotropaic blood ritual was conducted to drive away an angel of plague ("Destroyer," Exod. 12:23)[171] who, seeing the blood, would mercifully "leap over" (פסח = *pesaḥ*) the threshold of the house that had thus been protected. The oldest text[172] on the topic does not permit one to recognize the often earlier assumed situation of a biannual change of pasture (transhumance) connected with the ritual of Azazel.[173] However, there likely is the endangerment of the house and its inhabitants by a demon (Exod. 12:21–27; vv. 21–22a, 23b = J? JE?).[174] The ritual was by nature not originally connected to a sanctuary, not to mention a single and central one, but rather the practice was oriented to a family, tribe, and group (cf. Exod. 12:2ff. P). According to the later (Deuteronomistic and Priestly) texts, nothing of the slaughtered animal was burned. Rather, it was eaten in its entirety, and its blood was used for apotropaic purposes. Perhaps this ritual was even the oldest form of Israelite sacrifice before Israel's contact with Canaan (cf. Exod. 12:27: זבח פסח = *zebaḥ pesaḥ*).[175] It was Deuteronomy (Deut. 16:1ff.; cf. Ezek. 45:21ff.) that wanted to see a sacrifice within the Passover festival, that tied closely together Passover and Mazzoth, that moved the festival to the central sanctuary, and that set it on its course to develop into the main festival of the postexilic community. According to Josh. 5:10–12 (Deuteronomistic), Israel celebrated a Passover after the crossing of the Jordan and the entrance into the land of promise. The regulations concerning Passover in Exod. 12:1–20, 40–51 (P) represent several strata that are connected to different concerns, interpretations, and periods.[176] These texts, such as Exod. 13:1–16 which either leads to or stems from Deuteronomic/Deuteronomistic thinking, clearly have in view a recurring festival of remembrance (Exod. 12:14a; 13:3) that is a "Passover for YHWH" (Exod. 12:11, 14, and 27). However, it is also true that an older ritual text (in Exod. 12:3b, 6b*, 7a, 8a, and 11bβ) shines through here, and Exod. 12:1–14, 28 is probably the oldest section within the composition attributed to P. At this point, the Priestly document had to be disloyal to even its own theological conception that the legitimate cultus began at Sinai, although, in contrast to Deuteronomy, P presented the family as the *Sitz im Leben* of this festival (Exod. 12:3f.) and saw in the Passover not an act of sacrifice but rather the beginning and the actualization of YHWH's fundamental act of liberation.[177] The reasons already mentioned above in regard to Mazzoth[178] facilitated its combination with Passover. The most significant factor was the common reference to the exodus from Egypt.[179] For P, the blood of the Passover lamb no longer possessed any apotropaic significance but rather is a "sign" (אות = *'ôt;* Exod. 12:13), and P connects by this means Exodus 12 to the covenant of Abraham and its sign of circumcision (Gen. 17:11; cf. also Gen. 9:12f. P: the rainbow as the sign of the covenant of Noah). According to 2 Chronicles 30, the Passover of Hezekiah was significant, while according to 2 Kings 23:21ff. and 2 Chronicles 35 it was the Passover of Josiah who was supposed to have done something of a great service in celebrating this festival that was so important to Deuteronomy as well as to the Deuteronomic/Deuteronomistic School. Passover belongs now once again to the temple, even if the festival did not include a sacrifice (in spite of the ritual of blood: 2 Chron. 35:11). That the levites were to be active in the slaughter of the Passover lamb (2 Chron. 30:15–17; etc.) was a view that no longer found acceptance.

The harvest festival (חג הקציר = *ḥag haqqāṣîr;* Exod. 23:16) or the Festival of Weeks (חג שבעות = *ḥag šābū'ôt;* Exod. 34:22; Deut. 16:9f.)[180] occurred seven weeks after Mazzoth and was connected with the beginning of the harvest of wheat. Isaiah 9:2 and Ps. 65:10–14 perhaps referred to this. Deuteronomy 16:9–12 made this festival into a pilgrimage festival to the central sanctuary. Whether the programmatic ritual of the offering of the gifts of firstfruits from Deut. 26:1–11 (in one of its previous forms?) once had its location here or whether this offering in terms of time as well as place was still unrelated is difficult to determine. In early Judaism, the Festival of Weeks became connected with the events at Sinai and therefore also with "salvation history." The dating in Exod. 19:1 was probably of significance in connection with this (cf. also 2 Chron. 15:10).[181]

The Autumn festival, or rather Tabernacles,[182] as a festival of ingathering (חג הָאָסִפ[י]ף = ḥag hā'āsîp/hā'āsip; Exod. 23:16; and 34:22), was originally the festival for the conclusion of the harvest of grapes, figs, and olives (Deut. 16:13) and thus was purely and simply a harvest festival. Its Canaanite origin is shown in Judg. 9:27. Since it often was simply named "the festival,"[183] it was at first the most significant festival in the course of the year, and not (yet) the Passover. The name "Festival of Tabernacles" (סֻכּוֹת = sūkkôt) stemmed first from Deut. 16:13ff. (cf. Zech. 14:16ff.), while in Lev. 23:42f. (cf. Neh. 8:17) one finds for the first time the basis for these tabernacles in the practice of the wilderness period. However, the name "Tabernacles" originated from the custom of constructing huts in the vineyards and gardens during the gathering of grapes and other fruit in order to keep watch and to spend the night. By means of the festival calendar of the Holiness Code (Leviticus 23) and the additions to the Priestly document (Numbers 28–29), this festival was expanded, separated into various parts, provided with a ritual for atonement, and enriched with the adding of salvation history (Leviticus 16; 23:42f.; and Num. 29:12–38). According to Zech. 14:16, the survivors of the nations each year will be drawn to Jerusalem in order to celebrate there the Festival of Tabernacles and to prostrate themselves before King YHWH.

In addition to the Day of Atonement,[184] one of the festivals that was separated from the Autumn festival (later on Festival of Tabernacles) was the New Year's Festival.[185] The festival calendars in Exodus 23; 34; and Deuteronomy 16 still do not mention it. Moreover, Exod. 23:16 enables one to recognize that the autumn festival was celebrated at the "going forth (= at the beginning) of the year." The beginning of the New Year consequently was still connected here with the (Canaanite) agarian festival periods. Under the influence of the introduction of the new (Assyrian or now Babylonian influenced?[186]) calendar, the Israelite New Year fell at the beginning of the seventh month (first of Tishri), and thus was celebrated in the autumn according to the evidence of Lev. 23:24f. and Num. 29:1–6 (cf. Exod. 12:2; and Ezek. 45:18–20 here in both the first and the seventh month). Important cultic activities were carried out on this day according to the accounts of postexilic (!) texts (2 Chron. 5:3: dedication of the temple; Neh. 8:1f.: renewal of the covenant). If one looks more closely, one sees that the *beginning* of the year (Ezek. 40:1) gives evidence to Israel's own New Year's *festival* in Leviticus 23 and Numbers 29 (however, also here without these names). Rest from work, cultic assembly, and sacrifice are decreed for this festival. Thus one has concluded that the Israelite autumn festival may have contained some or even many elements that were constitutive for the important New Year's festival in the ancient Near East, for example, in Ugarit[187] and Mesopotamia.[188] These included the renewal of creation and its maintenance along with the closely connected (new) ascension of YHWH to the throne.[189] Now the Old Testament passages that actually speak of the New Year's festival are quite few.[190] One can assume, moreover, on the basis of the festival's significance in the ancient Near East, that it was celebrated also in Israel/Judah (within the structure of the autumn festival?). The festival first received its real significance, however, within (early) Judaism.

All previously mentioned festivals provide no evidence of a dramatized myth that was the foundation of its rituals. Rather, these festivals are bound up with the course of the agricultural year and continue to be adapted to the history of Israel. Where texts permit a precise look into the execution of the festival, they indicate that the spoken, narrated word that pointed to YHWH's historical acts of redemption was important (Exod. 12:26f.) .

In Joshua 24 (the assembly at Shechem), 2 Kings 23:1–3 (covenant conclusion by Josiah), and perhaps also Nehemiah 8 (reading of the law under Ezra, with the concluding celebration of the Festival of Tabernacles), there is evidence for festivals on the occasion of the *renewal of the covenant.* Yet, only a few times in the history of Israel is this covenant renewal mentioned. This took place each time during both historical and theological junctures and in addition is evidenced only in Deuteronomistic and dependent literature. Deuteronomy 26:16–19 sketches for this covenant renewal a programmatically ideal scene (cf. Deut. 5:2f.; and 27:9). But Deut. 31:10f., according to which Deuteronomy was to be read publicly every seven years, does not offer much in the way of a "festival" to mark the occasion, especially since this custom of public reading is nowhere mentioned as actually being practiced. The efforts made, from time to time, to discover in Psalms 50 and 81 evidence for a covenant renewal festival are overweighted. Thus one is to be wary about the thesis that there may have been a regular covenant renewal festival in Israel,[191] and that this festival may have been connected with or a part of the autumn festival. Therefore, not without reason, the conversations about trying to discover such a covenant renewal festival have become rather quiet within more recent Old Testament scholarly discussion.[192]

The existence of an enthronement festival of YHWH has often been derived from the YHWH enthronement psalms (Psalms 47; 93; 96; 97; [98]; and 99),[193] if not also from other psalms and texts such as Isa. 52:7 in the fashion of S. Mowinckel in previous times.[194] Following other scholars, S. Mowinckel placed the enthronement of YHWH in the New Year's Festival which was it-self a part of the Autumn Festival already in the preexilic period. Mowinckel saw this enthronement of YHWH occurring during the Autumn Festival as a cultic drama. The kingship of YHWH in addition was seen by him to have close parallels to similar ideas in Israel's ancient Near Eastern environment along with the myths and viewpoints that were associated with this subject (creation of the world, the battle with chaos, and the removal of a crisis).

Now YHWH's kingship, especially in its full expression of his being king of the entire creation, of the nations, and also of the gods, was certainly cele-brated cultically. This kingship was experienced in the temple cult, made pre-sent, and hymnically praised, something about which Psalm 47 speaks. YHWH's kingship has to do with the preservation and maintenance of the world from the threat of chaos (Psalms 93; 95; and 96). Also, one should not be able to see any opposition between YHWH's *becoming* king and *being* king, between being and event, or between the ascent and enthronement of YHWH on his throne on Zion and on his throne in heaven. Moreover, one cannot de-rive from the Old Testament passages that tell of the sovereignty of YHWH evidence for an enthronement festival of YHWH. An enthronement festival could have been only an aspect of the Autumn Festival or the New Year's Fes-tival,[195] and this kingship of God was oriented to and therefore in many ways influenced by the continuing reign of the god El but not the victorious reign of the god Baal always newly obtained in battle.[196]

While YHWH's sovereignty always exists and is not mythically founded, at the same time it continues to be newly actualized. This is why several of the YHWH enthronement psalms, such as Psalms 96 and 97, already possess es-chatological coloring. This has to do with how YHWH's sovereignty is active in the past, present, and future. YHWH does not struggle for his kingship; rather, he demonstrates it (cf. Ps. 93:1–4).[197] Also 2 Samuel 6 (the transferring of the ark to Jerusalem by David) as well as 1 Kings 8 (the dedication of the temple by Solomon) cannot be considered as texts that point to an enthrone-ment festival, since both set forth descriptions of particular events that occur once for all, and, in addition, both know nothing at all about any enthronement of YHWH. The frequently maintained parallel between 2 Samuel 6 and Psalm 47 cannot be sustained.[198] One also cannot make 2 Samuel 6 and 7 into the foundation of a "royal Zion festival," for these are two texts that in their nature belong to rather divergent sources and different situations.[199] Further, Psalm 132 is overweighted with such themes. That there possibly occurred in the Jerusalem cultus either an ark procession or an ark entrance (Psalms 24; 47; and 132; perhaps also Psalm 93; cf. Pss. 46:9; 48:13; and 66:5?) is not as cer-tain as has been maintained.[200] And nothing could be said on the whole about a cultus that involved a cultic drama of actualization, for example, the ritual of the repetition of the creation of the world. There is, however, "the presence of

YHWH concealed in the temple that guarantees the salvation of the world and its order."[201] The "presence of the world king," who is enthroned in heaven, is experienced in the temple. The temple is the "cosmic place located in empirical reality . . . where the primeval stabilization of the world is discerned as an event presently experienced."[202] Further, God's presence is actualized in the hymnic praise offered by the cultic congregation.[203] There his "witnesses" (Pss. 93:5; and 95:7)[204] shout, for the enthronement of YHWH "signifies the taking possession of Zion by the royal God."[205] The "enthronement" of YHWH was therefore the celebration of his continuing royal rule that was observed probably in connection with the Autumn Festival and New Year's Festival. Since many of the texts that speak of the "kingship of YHWH" are to be assigned to cultic activity and "since the cultic congregation proclaimed YHWH's becoming king is now occurring or has already occurred (Ps. 47:6, 9), the cult became the place of the inbreaking of the kingdom of God, the place in which the royal rule of YHWH existing 'since now and forever' breaks into . . . the present world reality and becomes certain. 'Cultic actualization' means then: the cult depicts the being of God as becoming, as a present and future event, and makes the celebrating community like the 'shields of the earth' (Ps. 47:10) certain of the presence of the coming divine king."[206] The "cultically present" and the "eschatological" meaning of the YHWH enthronement psalms are then no longer in opposition.

An especially important festival in the postexilic period was separated from the Autumn Festival in the festival calendar of the Holiness Code in Leviticus 23. This festival, the Day of Atonement, occurs not at all in the older festival calendars (יוֹם הכפורים = *yôm hakkippûrîm:* Lev. 23:27–32; 25:9; and Num. 29:7–11; not in Ezek. 45:18ff.). The early text, Leviticus 16, is in itself not uniform.[207] This also had its basis, for here various matters (purification of the sanctuary, purification of the priests, the scapegoat, and Azazel) along with different rituals could be joined together.[208] After an introduction (vv. 1–2a), there are regulations about the Day of Atonement (vv. 2b-28), followed by a paraenetic instruction (vv. 29–34a) and a note about carrying out these matters (v. 34b). The frequency of the verb כפר = *kippēr* (as a so-called resultative Piel with the following, various prepositions: בעד = *b'd,* את = *'t;* and על = *'l*) in the text allows one to recognize the significance that is given here to "atonement."[209] Moved to this festival is the activity in the temple's holy of holies (v. 2) where the high priest (here "Aaron") effectuates atonement first for himself and then for the people. In addition to this, there is a so-called rite of elimination that is evidenced also in Israel's cultural environment[210] with the laying on of both hands (v. 21)[211] and the sending out of the "scapegoat" into the wilderness for (the demon) Azazel (vv. 8–10, 21f.). Everything is actually narrated or decreed twice, since vv. 2b–10 are set forth in a more general way and vv. 11–28 present the specialized instructions. Atonement and purification take

place for both priest and congregation with the carrying out of a blood ritual
(vv. 14–16)[212] on and before the כפרת = *kappōret* ("a cover plate"? or an
"atonement monument"?[213]). The ever new mention of sin offerings, burnt offerings, and atonement makes clear the main features of the text as well as of
the festival. Whether the Azazel rite (vv. 8, 10 and esp. vv. 20b–22; there, however, without the name "Azazel") was original here or was later connected to
the rite of the scapegoat (vv. 8, 10, 21f., and 26?) and had its own prehistory is
difficult to clarify, although the idea of its being original is plausible.[214] The
goat for Azazel,[215] in any case, now has the function of "bearing" guilt (נשא =
nś'; v. 22; cf. also John 1:29), meaning that an older (?) rite of elimination was
incorporated into the event of atonement. The themes of sin and guilt, as well
as of atonement and cultic and ethical purity, are postexilic. This means that
after the experience of the punishment of the exile, the sins and guilt of the exile were especially made known and led to the asking of expiation for the
priests, the nation, and the congregation (v. 30!). Expiation is now, however,
as Leviticus 16 also makes clear, no punishing act of God, nor is it rather a human performance to bring about results. It is, rather, a divine act of salvation,
YHWH's removal of guilt, that makes possible expiation.[216] This institution
and gift of YHWH is to be employed precisely according to order by the high
priest; the intrusion of disorder is banned. Consequently, as is the case with the
Old Testament cultus in general, this rite has nothing to do with human self-
redemption[217] but rather with YHWH's gracious act of salvation for his congregation. Israel was to become assured of reconciliation with its God and of
the resulting, newly established order between God and the congregation of the
nation. There are predominantly postexilic problems and questions that were
to be overcome by means of Leviticus 16 (vv. 29, 31, and 34). One does not
wish to be deprived again of this gift of atoning activity that creates salvation.

The rites of purification to be carried out by the priests have a similar purpose and character, namely, they are founded and regulated by YHWH who
acts through the priests. However, we certainly know very little about these
rites. Numbers 19 describes the production and application of the "water of purification." The sacrifice of an animal, a blood rite, and ablutions were required
in the producing of ashes necessary for the "water of purification." The "hys-
sop ([?] אזוב = *'ēzôb*)"[218] mentioned in Lev. 14:4, 6, 49, 51f.; and Num. 19:6,
18 is also referred to as the brush of purification for sprinkling in Ps. 51:9 (cf.
Exod. 12:22). Isaiah 1:18 likewise mentions ablution (כבס = *kbs*), as did in a
similar way Israel's ancient Near Eastern environment.[219]

What happened to Isaiah probably also belongs to this context. Because of
his "unclean (טמא = *ṭm'*) lips, the prophet could not join in the threefold utterance of "holy" by the seraphim.[220] An act of expiation is performed by one
of these seraphim who touched Isaiah's lips with a glowing coal (cf. the purifying fire in Num. 31:22f.) from the incense altar (?).[221] It is YHWH who in

the temple freely provides through one of the figures in his heavenly realm forgiveness that atones and purifies.[222]

13.5. Sabbath and Circumcision

With the establishment of a regularly recurring day of rest, the Sabbath (שׁבת = *šabbāt*) continued to increase in significance within the Old Testament and even beyond.[223] This day of rest to this point is not evidenced elsewhere in the religious world of Israel's ancient Near Eastern neighbors. References to this day are already present in the oldest legal collections of the Old Testament as a time of rest (שׁבת = *šābbat;* "to cease"[224]), as the interruption of labor for both humans and animals (Exod. 23:12; and 34:21). However, in these collections, there is no specific mention of the name "Sabbath," and no theological basis is provided. In Exod. 23:12 the day of rest is said to have the purpose of providing "respite." In the wisdom literature, the Sabbath finds no mention at all. In each of the two decalogues, the Sabbath commandment or the commandment to rest from labors on the seventh day is issued in apodictic form but receives a different rationale. In what is probably the older[225] Decalogue, the heavily expanded Sabbath commandment stands in the middle point (Deut. 5:12ff.) and offers an interpretation that contrasts with that in Exodus 20. In Deuteronomy 5 the Sabbath receives a rationale and an intention that combine social elements with salvation history. Here the Sabbath rest is even for the slave (cf. already Exod. 23:12), since Israel also was a slave in Egypt. The rest of YHWH[226] on the seventh day (vv. 8–11) in the Decalogue in Exodus 20, by contrast, receives a theological rationale that is theocentric and grounded in creation (cf. Gen. 2:1–3 P). In Genesis 2:1–3 the Sabbath as the gift of God to his newly created world is the goal and the culmination of the divine activity of creation. Here, the temporal order for humanity and the cosmos is structured by YHWH and is accompanied by blessing.[227]

Older references to the Sabbath are found in the preexilic prophets (Amos 8:5; Hos. 2:13; and Isa. 1:13) as well as elsewhere (Exod. 16:29f. J?; 2 Kings 4:23; and 11:5, 7, 9), where it is often mentioned along with the day of the New Moon, although the two are not identical[228] (cf. also Ezek. 45:17). Amos 8:5 allows one to recognize that a particular circle already held a critical view of resting from labor on the Sabbath. Thus the Sabbath certainly had already been known in preexilic Israel, probably in the sense of a day of rest for humans from labor (Exod. 23:12 and 34:21)[229] and less as a holiday in honor of YHWH (so in Hos. 2:13; and Isa. 1:13?).[230] However, 2 Kings 4:23 already mentions that one was in the habit of consulting a man of God on this day, when one wished to do so. The rhythm of seven and the emphasis on this number, which obviously has special significance for the divine and thus for the cultus, is also evidenced elsewhere.[231] A marriage (Gen. 29:27f.) as well as a period of mourning (Job 2:13) lasted seven days. The servant of Elijah went to look for rain seven times (1 Kings 18:43). On the seventh day of marching around Jericho, the seven trumpets were blown (Josh. 6:4ff.). Several cultic actions were carried out seven times (Lev. 4:6, 17; 14:7; etc.). A particular impurity lasted seven days (Lev. 12:2; etc.). A fast could last seven days (1 Sam. 31:13), and a festive meal could continue for seven days (Esther 1:5; etc.).[232] In Ugaritic religion, the number seven also possessed significant prominence.[233] The arrangement of seven stood obviously for a superordinated, larger, yet also distinctly visible period of time that, as a small round number, possessed great importance and was to be noted in the workings of the gods and in the actions of humans oriented to it. Whether the origin of the rhythm of the Sabbath, then, is to be sought in market days (E. Jenni), in travel, or elsewhere is unclear and debated. However, this question is without relevance for the grasping of the theological significance of the Old Testament Sabbath.

In the Old Testament, the Sabbath (independent of the phases of the moon) is a kind of "tithe on time."[234] It occurs "for YHWH" (Exod. 20:10; and Deut. 5:14), and it is the time that both humans and animals devote to him. Since a temple and sacrificial cult was not possible during the exile (especially for those who were a part of the Golah), the significance of the Sabbath was enhanced (cf. besides P also Ezek. 20:12, 20; 44:24; 46:1–4, 12; and Lam. 2:6). Here it became a kind of mark of being set apart, an act of confession, and a sign of the covenant (Exod. 31:13–17 P; cf. Num. 16:31 for the Sabbath as a "commandment").[235] The Sabbath is not only the day that God has blessed and through which he blesses. It is also the day sanctified, that is, set aside, for and by him (Gen. 2:3 P), as well as the day of God's presence with his community (Exod. 24:15b-18a P; cf. 29:45f.; 39:32, 43; 40:17, 33b, 34).[236] The Sabbath is perhaps also in the context of the exile a conscious contrast to the Babylonian *sapattu* day, that is, the day of the full moon which was also a day of bad luck. This was the day on which one avoided work for fear of failure and misfortune.

In the Old Testament Sabbath, creation is already aimed at and directed toward Israel and its time, and the relationship between work and rest was carried out. "Rest" is no longer limited to being the privilege of the gods.[237] God places his rest within creation, giving it to humans, who certainly are his "image" and partners.[238] Divine rest is both gift and example, and this is true even for the male slave and the female slave, the sojourner, and livestock (Exod. 20:10; and Deut. 5:14).[239] That the name "Sabbath" is lacking in Gen. 2:1–3 is due to the "consideration that the Sabbath is valid for Israel but not for humanity,"[240] that is, the Sabbath first achieves in Israel its full efficacy. Here then the creation reaches its purpose in the cult.[241] In addition, this Sabbath was as well the day for humans, who are free to participate in worshipful community with God. Humans are to be the partners of God in having dominion over creation (Gen. 1:27f.) and are to be conversation partners with him as well. In addition to the Priestly sections in Exodus 16[242] (cf. also 35:1–3), according to which God himself is concerned that his people also receive provisions on this day of rest, one should not undervalue the significance of Exod. 24:15b-18a; 31:12–17 (probably an addition to P); and 39:32, 43 (P) for the Priestly appreciation of the Sabbath,[243] since the open-ended conclusion in Gen. 2:3 allows one certainly to inquire as to the purpose of this day's now being "sanctified." Also, to "remember" the Sabbath in Exod. 20:8, in comparison to "keep" the Sabbath in Deut. 5:12, points more to the cultic sphere. The fact that the seventh day has no evening in contrast to the preceding six days is no accident in the Priestly language that is so precise and deliberate. While the various works of creation must be compressed into the first six days, the seventh day was free of any further labor. This means that the significance of what is "created" on this day is clearly underlined. Does one hear a faint hope in the never-ending rest with God as the purpose of creation? It is no wonder, then, that this theologically filled Sabbath, in terms of both Deuteronomy 5 from the Deuteronomistic School and Exodus 20 from Priestly thinking, became important also for the exilic community. God brings to completion through "rest," and his final work of creation is the rest transmitted through Israel's Sabbath as his gift to his world.[244]

Other exilic as well as certain postexilic texts point to the increasing significance and transformation of the Sabbath (Lev. 16:31; 23:3, 32; 26:34f., 43; Isa. 56:2–6; 58:13f.; 66:23; and Jer. 17:21–27), and Nehemiah sought to support its observance (Neh. 10:32, 34; and 13:15–22). The Sabbath appears in the festival calendar (Lev. 23:3), and sacrifice was even introduced for this day (Num. 28:9f.), which later appears then as a natural practice in the Books of Chronicles (1 Chron. 9:32; 23:21; 2 Chron. 2:3; 8:13; and 31:3; cf. Ezek. 45:17; and 46:12). Psalm 92:1 points out that there were Sabbath songs. During the Maccabean wars, it had to be decided, because of tragic experiences, that one indeed must fight and defend oneself on the Sabbath, although one could not pursue the fleeing enemy (1 Macc. 2:32, 37–41; 2 Macc. 8:26ff.; 15:1ff.). However, it appears that this self-defense interpretation of the Sabbath was not often consistently pursued (2 Macc. 6:11).

Circumcision[245] was an early practice of Israel, a fact indirectly documented by the designation of the Philistines as the "uncircumcised" (Judg. 14:3; 15:18; 1 Sam. 14:6; 17:26, 36; etc.; cf. Genesis 34). During the exile, this ritual became, like the Sabbath, an important religious practice. Because of the strong influence of Priestly thought, circumcision became a sign of the covenant (אוֹת בְּרִית = *'ôt běrît;* Gen. 17:11) of Abraham accorded to the people of Israel.[246] Originally a puberty ritual that served as a kind of consecration for marriage, circumcision according to P (Gen. 17:10ff.) had to be performed now on children, and not on men (cf. Gen. 21:4; and Lev. 12:3). These circumcised children were to be enumerated among the "descendants of

Abraham" who stood within the Abrahamic covenant that was so important for the theological thought of P. In addition to the Sabbath, it was circumcision, also performed independently of the temple cult, that increased in significance during the exile.

In other contexts, the expression "to circumcise" (מול/מלל/מולה = *mûlâ/mll/ mûl*) is used also in a metaphorical way to convey the idea that one's heart and ears have been circumcised.[247] Accordingly, "bodily" circumcision is not devalued; rather, it is continued while the image is used to refer to personal purification from sins, devotion, and repentance, characteristics that are appropriate for a community of YHWH.

Besides the Sabbath and circumcision, the distinction between "clean" and "unclean"[248] (cf. already Gen. 7:2f., 8 J?), that is, between what could be sacrificed as well as eaten over against what could not, was also significant for the total life of Israel and not just its cultic existence. It was also the case that these regulations became more important for the postexilic community (Deut. 14:3ff.; and Leviticus 11). It is no longer very clear which animals were "unclean" and why they were considered to be so.[249] YHWH had commanded this dichotomy between clean and unclean, and this by itself was decisive. Leviticus 12–15 also contains additional stipulations concerning purity that pertain to women and childbirth, leprosy, the arena of death, and secular matters.[250]

13.6 Sacrifice

According to Amos 5:25 and Jer. 7:22, the Israelites were supposed to have been unaware of sacrifice in their early period. Now it is true, however, that these statements were clearly formulated in an overstated polemic. Even so, they may have preserved the celebrated, authentic kernel inasmuch as Israel first put into effect an expanded sacrificial system[251] in the land of Canaan. This is confirmed by the fact that many Old Testament terms for sacrifice are also found in Canaanite-Syrian religion which confronts us in the Ugaritic texts.[252]

In the history of religions, one distinguishes between communion sacrifices (with ideas about solidarity), sacrifices that are gifts, and sacrifices for sin.[253] This rather rough categorization also turns out to be valid for the kinds of sacrifice mentioned in the Old Testament and described more precisely in Leviticus 1–7 and Numbers 28–29 (cf. also Exod. 29:10–37).[254] In these texts (as well as Lev. 14:10–32; 17; 22:17–30; and 27), the various types of sacrifices are presented with their rituals.[255] Among these, Leviticus 1 and 3 are especially closely connected. There is no mention of the motivations for each sacrifice, as the Old Testament nowhere offers a rationale for sacrifices or a general theory of sacrifice.[256] One can only infer sometimes the occasions and backgrounds from narratives or now and then from prophetic texts. While a sacrifice originated in some concrete motive, such as thanksgiving,[257] this offering continued to become a regularized ritual.[258] Further, the priest came to replace the laity, and the central cultic site came to take the place of various sanctuaries.

For the Israelites, sacrificial animals were domesticated animals whose sacrifice represented something that actually had to be "given away." These animals included, above all, bulls, rams, lambs, and goats; doves were provided as an offering by those who were poor (Lev. 1:14–17; 5:7–10; 12:8; and 14:21–31). The rituals in Leviticus 1–5 allow one to recognize that the so-called declaratory formula, for instance, "This is a (valid) burnt offering" (Leviticus 1:9), belonged to the performance of the rite of sacrifice[259] so that it could be regarded as "well-pleasing" and "credited" (רצה/רצון = $r\bar{s}h/r\bar{a}\hat{s}\hat{o}n$, חשב = $\dot{h}\check{s}b$, חפץ = $\dot{h}p\dot{s}$).[260] Prior to this, the worthiness of the one desiring to offer the sacrifice was more than likely explored.[261]

The oldest type of sacrifice probably was the communion sacrifice (זבח = $zb\dot{h}$;[262] cf. Exod. 12:3f.; and 1 Samuel 1–2) which is mentioned some 162 times in the Old Testament. Ancient texts,[263] which mention this sacrifice, include Exod. 34:15; 1 Sam. 9:12; 20:6; and probably also Exod. 24:11. Genesis 31:44–54 shows that a communion meal was part of the ceremony involving the establishment of a ברית = $b\check{e}r\hat{i}t$ ("covenant, treaty") between people who perhaps also were called "brothers" (v. 54). The ritual of the זבח = $zb\dot{h}$ ("communion sacrifice") from the later period is described in Leviticus 3 and 7:11–21. The manner in which a זבח = $zb\dot{h}$ ("communion sacrifice") took place in the ancient period can be determined from 1 Samuel 1–2. It was a sacrificial slaughter as well as a communion meal, for only portions of the animal were burned. The fat portions belonged to YHWH (1 Sam. 2:13ff.), while most of the animal was consumed by the participants in the meal and distributed among their community (1 Sam. 1:4, 21). That originally the deity himself was considered to be one of the participants in the meal and that the ones offering the sacrifice sought to have a portion of the life's power of the animal sacrificed for themselves cannot any longer be recognized in the Old Testament texts. In the Old Testament, one eats at the most "before YHWH," however, not *with* him (Exod. 24:9–11). Further, the one offering the sacrifice and YHWH stand beside each other in the ritual of the זבח = $zb\dot{h}$ ("communion sacrifice"), meaning then that no priest is necessary. However, these were also the reasons that this kind of sacrifice, which was especially used during offerings of thanksgiving and the fulfillment of vows, steadily diminished in importance. When the שלמים = $\check{s}\check{e}l\bar{a}m\hat{i}m$ ("peace offering") was added later, the $zb\dot{h}$ ("communion sacrifice") continued to be deprivatized, neutralized, and increasingly supplanted. Furthermore, several quite different texts (such as Leviticus 17; and Ezekiel 40–48) point as well to these supplantings[264] with the additions of the priest, the priestly portion, and the ritual of blood.[265]

The Priestly texts (however, cf. in addition Exod. 24:5) neutralized the word זבח = *zbḥ* by making it simply a generic term for "sacrifice" and by placing it some fifty times in construct with שלמים = *šělāmîm* ("peace offering"?)[266] which served as a specific qualification, that is, "peace" (cf. Leviticus 3 and 7:1ff.; then, e.g., cf. also Lev. 19:5; and 23:19 in the Holiness Code).[267] This was encouraged by the fact that שלמים = *šělāmîm* ("peace offering"?) was only rarely encountered by itself in older texts but appeared more frequently in combination with other terms for sacrifice.[268] Moreover, what שלמים = *šělāmîm* ("peace offering"?) actually meant originally is unclear and debated. One thinks of a sacrifice of closure, a communion sacrifice, and a covenant sacrifice,[269] but whether this offering at times was a separate category of sacrifice is debatable as well.[270] In addition, 1 Sam. 11:15; 1 Kings 8:63f.; 2 Chron. 29:35; Prov. 7:24; and Amos 5:22 (only here in the singular) do not give an explanation, and a look at the *slm(m)* sacrifice evidenced in Ugarit does not provide much help.[271] שלמים = *šělāmîm* ("peace offering"?) also occurs next to עולה = *'ôlâ* ("burnt offering") even in texts outside the Priestly document and the Chronicles (Exod. 20:24; 32:6; etc.), as well as beside other terms for sacrifice (1 Kings 8:64; 2 Kings 16:13; etc.). Thus it can be asked whether it did not always represent a kind of "sacrifice of closure" and moreover was especially connected with the עולה = *'ôlâ* ("burnt offering"). Later on, then, it would have also been joined with זבח = *zbḥ* ("communion sacrifice") (cf. already 1 Sam. 10:8). However this addition of שלמים = *šělāmîm* ("peace offering"?) was accomplished, the זבח = *zbḥ* ("sacrifice") eventually became a priestly sacrifice. According to Leviticus 3 (cf. in addition Num. 6:13–20), זבח-שלמים = *zebaḥ-šělāmîm* ("peace offering"?) was a bloody sacrifice that included the offering, laying on of hands, slaughter, blood rite, and conflagration, thus standing parallel to the עולה = *'ôlâ* ("burnt offering"). The difference was mainly in the fact that in the שלמים = *šělāmîm* ("peace offering"?) only the fat portions were burned. It can no longer be ascertained what the שלמים = *šělāmîm* previously was. Perhaps it was a cultic meal, but who is to say? The sacrificial character of זבח-שלמים = *zebaḥ-šělāmîm* ("peace offering"?) was more strongly stressed and expanded in later texts, as a comparison between the passages in the Chronicler's historical work with those in the Deuteronomistic History makes clear.[272] The character of a communion sacrifice by comparison continued to recede into the background and was robbed of its own weight by its more frequent combination with other kinds of sacrifice (cf. the Books of Chronicles or Numbers 7) and especially by the insertion of the blood rite required by Priestly theology.[273]

In terms of the phenomenology of religion, the gift sacrifice (מנחה = *minḥâ:* Gen. 4:3–5; 1 Sam. 2:17; and 3:14) stands in close proximity to the communion sacrifice. Certain Old Testament texts still suggest that the gift offering to the deity was originally (and thus also in Israel's cultural environment[274]) viewed as the direct feeding of the deity. That YHWH needs feeding had to be rather directly denied (Judg. 13:16; and Ps. 50:12f.; cf. Isa. 44:16ff.). Moreover, the flesh of the sacrifice was still cooked (Judg. 6:19f.; and 1 Sam. 2:13) and salted (Lev. 2:13; and Mark 9:49). Then there are mentionings of "God's food" (Ezek. 44:7; Lev. 21:6, 8, 17; 22:25; and Mal. 1:7; cf. Gen. 18:5ff.), and of bread placed before YHWH's "face,"[275] something that is not entirely satisfactorily translated by "shewbread" (Exod. 25:30; 1 Sam. 21:7; 1 Kings 7:48; etc.). Further, the gift offering was also a gift of sanctification (cf. Deut. 26:1ff.), which could be connected with thanksgiving and praise. It is obvious that this gift by contrast could easily have been (mis)understood to have the sense of *do ut des*. However, there is little about this (mis)understanding that may be traced within the Old Testament. The classification of sacrifices to which the gift sacrifice belonged was also expanded and came to include the sin offering.

Among the gift sacrifices is to be named, first of all, the עוֹלָה = *'ôlâ*,[276] the so-called burnt offering.[277] This main form of the gift sacrifice is mentioned 286 times in the Old Testament and probably was appropriated by Israel from the Canaanites. God simply received the sacrifice which produced also the "smoke of appeasement" (רֵחַ נִיחֹחַ = *rēaḥ nîḥōaḥ*).[278] The priest received only the skin of the sacrificial animal. The sacrifice was burned and ascended to the deity in the smoke (עלה = *'lh* in qal and hiphil). The rite of this type of sacrifice is described in Leviticus 1 and 6:1–6. Older texts mention this type of sacrifice in Gen. 8:20; Exod. 20:24; Judg. 6:26; Isa. 1:11; and Hos. 6:6. According to Leviticus 1 and 6, the priest is always necessary, there must be an altar, and the distance between God and humans is made much clearer by this type of sacrifice. The burnt sacrifice is later offered daily (Numbers 28) in addition to special festival days and occasions. It also becomes a "royal sacrifice" (1 Kings 3:4, 15; 9:25; and 2 Kings 16:15).[279] Since the cultic laws that we currently have primarily come from the postexilic period, it is no wonder that the עוֹלָה = *'ôlâ* was the predominant type of sacrifice and replaced the זבח = *zebaḥ*.

The major components of the עוֹלָה = *'ôlâ* ("burnt offering") are the "bringing near" as a priestly act (קרב = *qrb,* hiphil; in Lev. 1:2, 3a the laity do this), the laying on of hands (סמך = *smk*) as an act that identifies the sacrificial animal with the one offering the sacrifice in order to bring about his or her well-being,[280] the slaughter of the animal (שחט = *šḥṭ*), the blood rite (זרק = *zrq*),[281] and the conflagration (קטר = *qṭr*). Among these various components, the laying on of the hands and the blood rite were probably added from the sin offering. All of this indicates that the individual sacrifices tended to influence each other, that the priestly responsibilities increased, that the blood rite grew in importance, and that the practice of sacrifice was ever more systematized. Finally, Lev. 1:14–17 provides regulations for the so-called bird (עוֹלה = *'ôlâ*).[282]

The oldest expression for a gift sacrifice is probably מנחה = *minḥâ*[283] (cf. Gen. 4:3ff.; 32:14; 1 Sam 2:17; and 3:14), something that also simply means "present" or "gift,"[284] and then later became the designation for "cereal offering." מנחה = *minḥâ* occurs in Leviticus 2 and 6:7–11 to describe a priestly multilayered ritual and is often called an "offering" that is approximate to the קרבן = *korbān*. That the מנחה = *minḥâ* was defined as a vegetable, grain offering consisting especially of wheat flour with oil, or of baked goods made from these ingredients, together with incense[285] is likewise secondary as, for example, Judg. 13:19 and 1 Sam. 2:17 show. Wheat flour, oil, and incense are also the components of the so-called אזכרה = *'azkārâ*, [286] that is, that portion of the מנחה = *minḥâ* ("gift offering") which was burned upon the altar. The מנחה = *minḥâ* ("gift offering") does appear by itself (Lev. 6:12–16; and Num. 5:11–31), but it is found in Priestly texts especially as a sacrifice that accompanies the עולה = *'ôlâ* ("burnt offering"). As is clear in Num. 15:1ff.; 28:12, 31; and 29:6, the מנחה = *minḥâ* ("gift offering") functions in the form of an offering of food and drink that accompanies the עולה = *'ôlâ* ("burnt offering"). Other texts (Leviticus 1 and 3) give evidence of this "attached" character, even if it is also clear that sacrifice does not consist only of animals and blood (cf. also Cain and Abel in their concurrent offerings: Gen. 4:3f.). The sacrifice is prepared, the אזכרה = *'azkārâ* is taken and burned, and the priests then receive the main portion. Last of all, the מנחה = *minḥâ* ("gift offering") is often accompanied by a libation, that is, a drink offering of wine, water, or oil (Heb. נסך = *nesek*;[287] cf. Lev. 23:13; 18:37; etc.). In addition, this kind of sacrifice was once an independent drink offering (Gen. 35:14; Jer. 7:18; and 19:13).

In Lev. 6:15f., the "whole sacrifice" (כליל = *kalîl*) is described that elsewhere is mentioned only in Deut. 33:10. This type of sacrifice seldom occurs next to the עולה = *'ôlâ* ("burnt offering") (1 Sam. 7:9; Ps. 51:21) and was probably absorbed by it.

While not so in the consciousness of those who gave the offerings, the growing significance of the blood ritual within the theory of sacrifice and its practice makes one think that in Priestly theology in the postexilic period sacrifice must have been less understood in terms of thanksgiving, sanctification, veneration, and entreaty. Rather, sacrifices in Priestly understanding must have been viewed more as the means of removing sins and guilt that came more strongly to the fore during this period. Thus sacrifice came to be interpreted as the means for expiation (כפר = *kippēr*). It was probably the fate of the exile that necessitated this perspective and the consciousness of sin that accompanied it. One desired a new subsiding of sin and guilt and with that to avoid the punishment threatening anew. Blood is indeed life,[288] and life belongs to God (Gen. 9:4f., 9; and Lev. 17:11; cf. Lev. 3:17; 7:26f.; Deut. 12:23; etc.). If now blood continues to be used in the sacrificial cult (Exod. 29:20f.; Lev. 4:6; 8:23f.; 14:4, 6f.; etc.), that it "is given for you on the altar" (Lev. 17:11), then this takes place because YHWH has ordained that blood may make atonement possible. YHWH is the one who guarantees atonement for the worshiper by means of his or her offerings of sin and guilt.[289] Moreover, atonement is not an act that placates God but rather expiates the sinner through divine action.

Israel is certainly threatened by YHWH's zeal (Lev. 10:6; Num. 1:53; 17:11; and 18:5) and his "plague" (Exod. 12:13; 30:12; Num. 8:19; 17:11f.; and Josh. 22:17), according to the view of the Priestly document. It is possible that thinking about atonement was already known even in the preexilic period;[290] however, even Deut. 21:8, which is secondary to Deut. 21:7, points to the Deuteronomistic, exilic sphere of theological thinking.

The "sin offering" (חטאת = *haṭṭā't*)[291]and the probably old "guilt offering" (אשם = *'āšām*),[292] which has less significance, are not clearly differentiated from each other in terms of their use as well as meaning. Nevertheless, both have their prominent place in the Priestly theology of sacrifice. Their rituals are described in Leviticus 4 and 5 (cf. Lev. 6:17–22; and 7:1–10), although, especially true of the אשם = *'āšām* ("guilt offering"), they are less clearly organized than the rituals in Leviticus 1 and 3 and certainly are multilayered. Constitutive for the so-called sin offering are the presentation of the animal sacrifice, the laying on of hands (with confession of sins: Lev. 5:5; and Num. 5:6f.), the slaughter and the blood ritual, and then the burning and disposal of what remains. Sin offerings as well as guilt offerings are probably genuinely Israelite in origin and predominate in the postexilic period. The sin offering[293] was used more for sins that were "unintentional" (בשגגה = *bišgāgâ*) (Lev. 4:2, 22, 27).[294] The Old Testament offered no atonement for conscious and grave sins (ביד רמה = *běyad rāmâ;* with a "high hand"; Num. 15:30). The guilt offering (cf. also Isa. 53:10 for this) appears to have been reserved for those occasions when injury was inflicted, thus intensifying the offense, in comparison with situations that involved no injury.[295] In connection with both of these types of presentation of sacrifices, the occurrence of YHWH's forgiveness is spoken about in connection with the act of atonement.[296] The request for forgiveness accompanying these sacrifices reached its climax in the exilic and postexilic periods.

According to 2 Kings 23:10; Jer. 7:31, and 32:35, the sacrifice "for Molech" (למלך = *lěmōlek*) was offered in the Hinnom Valley, a practice that was strongly condemned. למלך = *lmlk* probably designates not only a sacrificial term but also a deity, "Molech" (cf. Lev. 18:21; 20:2–5; 2 Kings 23:10; and Jer. 32:35).[297] In the Old Testament, the sacrifice of children was probably indicated by this term (cf. Lev. 20:5f.; Deut. 18:10; 2 Kings 17:17; and 2 Chron. 33:6), for this sacrificial expression points to this in Israel's cultural environment (Deut. 12:31; 2 Kings 23:10; Jer. 32:35; and Ezek. 16:20f.). In addition, this meaning is evidenced by the required prohibitions (Lev. 18:21; 20:2–5; Deut. 12:31; and 18:10) and clearly by 2 Kings 23:10; Ezek. 20:25f., 31;

23:37ff.; and Isa. 57:5 (also Hos. 13:2?; cf. Jer. 19:5 "for Baal" and 2 Kings 17:31). Micah 6:7 and 2 Kings 3:27 illustrate a ceremony of lament and petition that is extremely intensified by the reference to human sacrifice.[298] However, these texts also, in line with the previously mentioned prohibitions, issue indictments of this practice. In addition to the texts already mentioned, Judg. 8:21; 11:31ff.; 1 Sam. 14:45 [?]; 15:33 [?]; and 1 Kings 16:34 witness to the existence of the sacrifice of children and of human beings (also in Israel's cultural environment: 2 Kings 3:27), mostly on the occasions of extraordinary events.[299] Moreover, nowhere in the Old Testament are there indications that this practice was fundamentally and completely rejected (Exod. 22:28b). It is clear that Gen. 22:1–17 now contains more theological commentary than the providing of a rationale for replacing human sacrifice with the offering of an animal. An older, redacted basic narrative in Genesis 22 may, however, have had this purpose.

Genesis 28:22 and Amos 4:4 speak of the cultic contribution of the tithe[300] of the harvests for the sanctuary in Bethel. Amos 4:4 also speaks of this gift for Gilgal, while Gen. 14:20 does so for Jebusite Jerusalem, although with regard to the latter instance it is probable that Abraham and Jerusalem were already connected together.[301] Deuteronomy 14:22ff. shifted the giving of the title to Jerusalem, where this offering, moreover, may be consumed by the presenters themselves. Every third year they are to distribute it to the socially powerless in their place of residence (cf. Deut. 26:12ff.).[302] According to Num. 18:20ff. (P), the tithe is a contribution to the cultic personnel, here the levites. Later it is expanded to include the tithe of herds and flocks (Lev. 27:32f.; and 2 Chron. 31:4ff.).

The contribution of firstlings, which later came to consist only[303] of firstfruits of the harvest (Exod. 23:19) and the firstborn of the cattle and sheep (Gen. 4:4; and Exod. 34:19), stands often next to the tithe. Deuteronomy 8:8 specifies the most important kinds of fruit in this regard, and Deut. 26:1–11 mentions a prayer[304] that is to be presented when this offering is dedicated. While the offering of firstlings was to emphasize that YHWH is to be worshiped in thanksgiving as the giver of what is good (cf. Prov. 3:9), the tithe was considered more as priestly support or, according to Deuteronomy, as at least temporary social assistance.

That various kinds of sacrifice could be mentioned or even frequently combined is seen, for example, in Lev. 23:37; Num. 29:36–39; and Deut. 12:6. Many sacrifices were, in addition, accompanied with the burning of incense,[305] or a component of their rites was designated as "incense burning." Subsequently, utensils for incense not only were mentioned in the Old Testament (1 Kings 7:50) but also have been brought to light in great numbers by archaeologists.[306]

One can also well name a sacrifice in the Old Testament a "prayer which is acted."[307] תּוֹדָה (*tôdâ*) designates both the thanksgiving offering and the thanksgiving sacrifice (Lev. 7:12; Amos 4:6; Pss. 95:2; 100:4, etc.). What is clear now from the[308] Old Testament's psalms and prayers is that the worshiper, when he or she prays, is already found to be in a decisive relationship with God and the community of God. The worshipers establish this relationship neither with their prayer nor with their sacrifice; rather, they seek to strengthen this relationship and to purify it. The means to accomplish this have been made ready and arranged by YHWH himself in these sacrifices.[309] If one neither distorts nor curtails the significance of a sacrifice in a manner incongruent with the Old Testament, sacrifice, according to the Old Testament, is a feature of the sanctification of the people of God.

13.7 Prayer

Cultic activities include not only sacrifices (Isa. 1:11, 13; and Amos 4:4f.) and songs (Amos 5:23) but also prayer (Isa. 1:15),[310] that is, the "calling on YHWH." Old Testament Israel had different expressions for "prayers" (תפלה = *těpillâ;* תודה = *tôdâ;* and תהלה = *těhillâ*), and the verbs used for "praying" cover a wide range (קרא = *qr';* זעק = *z'q;* צעק = *ṣ'q;* ידה = *ydh;* עתר = *'tr;* פלל = *pll;* etc.).[311] Recent investigations of prayers of lament and petition[312] have shown that one also here can and must differentiate between the official temple or even state cultus of the general community from the "casual small cultus"[313] of the primary social group, especially encountered in the family.[314] Even the prayers of lament and petition used more for private worship, as well as the texts assigned to the great cult, were written by "experts," and both kinds were meant to be used by other individuals as well as by people in the larger community. In regard to this larger community, one should not always think, however, only of the gathering of great cultic assemblies that were determined officially or by the course of the year,[315] particularly since a sick person could not always make his or her way to the great cult and, as an "unclean" person, would scarcely be admitted to its precincts. Rather, one shall have to inquire about the more private prayers in Israel.[316] The private nature of prayer is underscored by the numerous prayers that are disseminated throughout the Old Testament in its narrative and prophetic literature and thus are encountered outside the collections of prayers in the Psalter. Similarly, the prose prayers also carry (in the Deuteronomistic texts?) the Old Testament designation תפלה = *těpillâ* ("prayer"; 2 Sam. 7:27; and 2 Kings 20:5). However, in and of itself, תפלה = *těpillâ* ("prayer") means more the "cultic, formalized prayer coming forth from the celebrating group."[317]

Prose prayers dispersed through other textual contexts are not, for example, always arranged according to the classical formal structure of many psalms, although they do contain several of their major elements (address, lament, and petition). Examples are present in Gen. 32:10–13 (Jacob's prayer before his encounter with Esau)[318] and in Josh. 7:7–9 which contains a brief lament to YHWH. The "crying out" to YHWH by the Israelites in a prayer that contained a confession of sins (Judg. 10:10, 15) is important for the Deuteronomistic theology, for, as Israel's history demonstrates, this petition contains the dimension of hope.[319] 1 Samuel 12:10 (Deuteronomistic) "cites" a petition that is based on hope, as the continuation of the petition demonstrates. David prays and gives thanks (2 Sam. 7:18–29), while Solomon's prayer of dedication of the temple (1 Kings 8:22f.) allows an in-depth look at Deuteronomistic theology and the problem of the exile. Elijah and David can utter a fervent prayer (1 Kings 18:36f.; and 2 Sam. 15:31), and, in addition, similar texts show that these were not unique occurrences in Israel (Num. 12:13; and Judg. 16:28). Brief prayers such as laments of petition are found also in Judg. 13:8 and 15:18. King Hezekiah prayed for deliverance (2 Kings 19:15–19) and health (Isa. 38:1–3). More comprehensive and theologically programmatic prayers are also found in Ezra 9; Nehemiah 9; and Daniel 9.[320] Moses was also presented as a great intercessor.[321] He prays for the nation (Deut. 3:23–25; 9:25–29, Deuteronomistic; then Exod. 5:22f.), even for the pharaoh,[322] and especially for murmuring and apostate Israel during the wilderness wandering.[323] Samuel also "cries out" to the Lord on behalf of Israel (1 Sam. 7:9).[324] Even Amos was active for a time, meaning that while both of his first visions were intercessions (Amos 7:2, 5), he did not venture to offer subsequent ones later on. The so-called confessions of Jeremiah[325] are, in the final analysis, also prayers, which certainly ought not and cannot be associated with autobiographical expressions but rather are texts in which later worshipers want and should continue to find themselves. Intercessory prayers, moreover, were forbidden to Jeremiah (according to Jer. 7:16; 11:14; 14:11; and 15:1). They were, therefore, customary and possible, as other texts demonstrate (e.g., Gen. 18:22ff.; 20:7, 17; Josh. 7:6–9; 1 Sam. 7:8f.; Isa. 53:12; Joel 1:14; Job 1:5; and 42:8). The overall general root used for "to pray" (עתר = '*tr*)[326] probably originally designated intercession and contained something that was rather pressing. Prayers are even inserted into the Books of Chronicles (2 Chron. 14:10; and 20:6–12).[327] Then one finds traditional "psalms" that are reconfigured as prayers and interspersed in narrative texts in Exod. 15:1–18; Deuteronomy 32; 33:2–5, 26–29; 1 Samuel 1–2; 2 Samuel 22 (= Psalm 18); Isaiah 12; Habakkuk 3; Jonah 2; and in the montage of psalms in 1 Chronicles 16.[328] Standing here together and in relationship to each other are cultic as well as noncultic prayers.

When the Old Testament worshipers pray three times a day, according to Ps. 55:18 and Dan. 6:11, they stand, kneel, throw themselves down on the ground, bow, and humble themselves.[329] There is, in the final analysis, no uniform posture when praying. Then people spread out their hands (1 Kings 8:38, 54; and Isa. 1:15) and lift them up (Ps. 141:2). Graphic depictions from the cultural environment of ancient Israel clarify this activity very well.[330] Occasionally such prayers were accompanied by sacrifices (Job 42:8; cf. תּוֹדָה = *tôdâ* as thanksgiving and sacrifice) and by laments and fasts[331] (Ezra 8:21, 23; 10:1; Neh. 1:4; and Dan. 9:3f.: entirely postexilic), since, as was analogous to the ancient Near Eastern environment of Israel,[332] the worshipers considered themselves to be forsaken by God by reason of need, illness, or misfortune. God was experienced as hidden, not responsive, and not helpful (Pss. 22:3; 28:1; 35:22; etc.).

In a brief look at the Psalter,[333] where not accidentally the name YHWH appears most frequently in the Old Testament,[334] one can only deal here with the common basic structures and essential features and characteristics[335] of some of the prayers that are collected there.[336]

The so-called lament of the individual is the type of text most often represented in the Psalter. Typical examples of this *Gattung* are Psalms 6; 13; 14; 22; and 142. What is most striking about these psalms is that the worshipers do not first have to put into the right mood the deity who is addressed by their petition. Rather, the address proceeds rather briefly (Ps. 13:2: "YHWH"; and Ps. 22:2: "My God, my God").[337] Furthermore, magical elements and conjurations are absent. Every Old Testament prayer indeed has in view a God who alone has come to Israel and has revealed himself to this people. So, no prayer is uttered to any kind of intermediary being, intercessor, or something of the like. The worshiper's immediacy to God is here a fact of life. The differences between prayers in the cult of the small social group and those in the temple are not revealed by this dimension. The "personal God" is also the God of the nation and of the congregation.[338] And as the worshipers always turn themselves toward YHWH, so it is that YHWH is the one who is believed to respond to such prayers and allows himself to be moved by them, even if on occasion they must cry out to him for a long time. At times the worshipers must cry, "How long?" since YHWH at times is experienced as a distant God.[339] The people of Israel witness that YHWH will respond since their fundamental experience is the liberation from Egypt where they have seen him act to deliver them by reason of their crying out to him from their situation of distress (Exod. 2:24; 6:5; and Deut. 26:6f.). It is also clear from this that one can and is to call out to God as YHWH, for his name is known and he himself is well known (Exod. 3:15). One does not have to pray to him as "a god or goddess whom I do not know."[340] YHWH helps and is called upon "for his name's sake"[341] and on the basis of his nature, his character which is well known to the worshiper, his compassion, and his loyalty (Ps. 25:6f.). This does not mean that YHWH would be at the worshiper's disposal. The worshiper knew also about the distant as well as the hidden God. The lament can become also an accusation against God (thus already Exod. 5:22f.; then Job).[342] The contrast between the worshiper's feeling of distance from God and the feeling of bondedness with him is a matter of concern in Old Testament prayer. And it is the latter type of prayer, grounded in bondedness, that still allows it, with every feeling of separation, abandonment, and lack of understanding, to find its way to become a prayer of trust. The confession of confidence has therefore its fixed place even in the laments of the individual as well as those of the nation. This confession of confidence occurs also in those texts which reflect the punishment of judgment experienced during the exile (cf. Pss. 13:6a; 22:4, 5–6 10f.; 44:1ff.; 74:12ff.; etc.).[343] In addition, the worshiper's attitude of piety is also decisively expressed. YHWH is the king of Israel and of the world as well as "my king" for the individual worshiper.[344] And YHWH's saving righteousness and his will to save are imparted to both the nation and its individual members.[345] The worshiper is "poor," thus is in need of the help of YHWH who especially attends to the poor.[346] He is like one who is sick unto death and requests from YHWH, who is the God of the living and maintains no relationship with the dead, salvation from illness and from the emaciation of death.[347] And when even YHWH himself laments, then this demonstrates something about the God who suffers with his people (Jer. 2:10–13, 31f.; 3:20; 8:7; 12:7–13; 15:5–9; and 18:13–15a).[348]

The psalms, with their imagistic language which is open to various interpretations and with their many kinds of typical expressions in petitions and laments, seek both to enable and to facilitate the worshipers' efforts to find themselves in these prayers. They are in these ways comparable to our hymnals, even if the formal description of the Psalter as the "hymnal of the postexilic community" compels some skepticism. As rhythmically and probably also metrically formed texts, psalms are a powerful, compelling word and effective speech. And the most frequent *Gattungen* of the psalms, like the lament and the hymn, are not only types of texts but at the same time they are attitudes of piety.

When the worshipers speak of their "enemies" in a way that is often apalling to the modern reader[349] and pray that much evil will befall them, then in this manner this adverse world of the worshipers is summoned forth and its circumstances are described to be as bad as possible in order to move YHWH to take action. People certainly cannot rid themselves of their enemies in Israel through means of magic. Faith is always also a threatened faith, meaning that the glimpses at the enemies accompany the observations about the worshipers themselves and about God. Indeed, these glimpses and observations provide the frames of reference in which human existence is fully examined.

In contrast to the lament, however, YHWH is the one who sits enthroned over Israel's songs of praise (Ps. 22:4) and who is himself praise (Ps. 148:14). He is praised in the hymns in ways that both describe and tell about him (cf., e.g., Psalm 33). This means: "Israel's praise of God is a reflection of divine action, and is not to be interpreted in entirely human terms."[350] This understanding can be traced from Exod. 15:21 to the expanded texts in Psalms 135 and 148. When a hymn, other than, for example, Ps. 89:10–17, is not directed specifically toward YHWH but rather speaks of him in the third person, then it takes aim at the world that is to join in this praise. Also, God is indirectly glorified by the wondrous nature of his creation. Praise induces both joy and a feeling of being safe (Psalm 8), and it mediates and sets forth a certain, positive feeling about the world. And in praise, the perspective of the worshiper moves beyond his or her own interest. Life is the praise of God; the dead praise God not at all (Pss. 6:6; 88:11–13; cf., as a contrast, Isa. 26:19, where the dead will rise and give praise. Such praise is offered in view of divine works in both creation (Psalms 104; 139; and 148) and history (Psalms 135; and 136). Praise also is uttered in view of the royal sovereignty of YHWH that is experienced as well as anticipated (Psalms 47; 93; 96; and 99) and his presence in the temple and the city of God (Psalms 46; 48; 76; 84; and 87). It is to be acknowledged that Israel came to no understanding of prayer that worked automatically. There were laments with petitions that were and were not heard, and the actual elements of the lament's description of need are for the most part considerably briefer than was true, for example, of Mesopotamian prayers.[351] One knows also that one must continue to call upon YHWH frequently and for a long period of time (1 Sam. 7:8; Pss. 55:18; 88:2; 92:3; and Neh. 1:6). Besides the individual worshipers, the nation and the community also utter their laments (cf., e.g., Psalms 44; 60; 79; 83; 85; and 89). It would be rewarding to conduct a precise investigation of the individual and communal laments that would denote the specific motives of trust that actualizes salvation and of the hearing of prayer.[352] These would be the motives mentioned by the worshiper that provide the basis for his or her confidence in YHWH and the reasons he or she expects to receive divine succor. The psalmist/worshiper becomes here a witness to faith, meaning that a "kerygma" is also found, then, in these prayers.[353]

The Songs of Thanksgiving (e.g., Psalms 30; 66:13ff.; 116; and 138), which often were connected to a thanksgiving offering (תּוֹדָה = *tôdâ*), especially show this. They belonged probably to a cultic activity that took place with a circle of participants (family? cultic congregation?) (cf. Pss. 30:5; 32:11; 34:4; and 116:18) and included a sacrifice that was offered as the fulfillment of a vow,[354] because a dire threat was now averted (Pss. 22:26; 56:13; 66:13–15; 116:17f.; and Jonah 2:10).

The worshipers of the psalms also knew consequently something of YHWH's preceding acts of salvation, of his acts of election performed for his people and the congregation in which they now stand and in which they often found themselves strongly embedded. However, mystical prayer that strives to achieve union with the deity was unfamiliar to Old Testament Israel. There were, however, the so-called psalms of salvation history (Psalms 78; 105; 106; cf. also Deuteronomy 32) that either as praise or as a confession of guilt brought to expression in prayer God's history with his people. In the exilic and postexilic psalms, one prayed more expressly than in the older texts for the forgiveness

of sins (Psalms 51; and 130). And Psalm 23 ("The Lord is my shepherd . . . ")
is rather frequently used as a so-called psalm of trust.

Thus, Old Testament prayer is a part of a lived, not simply striven after,
community with God, a community that was graciously given and that even
the worshiper who considered himself or herself abandoned by God (Ps. 22:2)
could still call upon: "Our ancestors hoped in you, and since they hoped, you
delivered them. Unto you they cried and were saved, they hoped on you and
were not put to shame" (Ps. 22:5f.). The history of Israel with its God maintains its paradigmatic character also for the prayer of the individual worshiper.
The God, who has disclosed himself to his own, desires to answer prayer, for
he "allows himself to be moved by entreaties" (Gen. 25:21). The location of
the Psalter within the Old Testament, after the Torah and the Prophets, makes
conspicuous these two canonical perspectives.

13.8   The Cult in the Wisdom Literature

The questions about the cultus do not play a great role in Old Testament
wisdom literature.[355] Since the sages were occupied especially with matters of
everyday ethics and were oriented to the secular community,[356] they did not
take into consideration the cultic congregation. Thus this literature nowhere
mentions, for example, Israel's great festivals or the congregation gathered together in the temple. The temple as the "house of God" is mentioned only in
Qoh. 4:17, and here the listener is more important in Qoheleth's view than sacrifice. A priest appears only in Job 12:19. Naturally, the sage was also a worshiper; however, in the Old Testament wisdom literature, cultic matters were
mentioned more in passing. Perhaps the circle of tradition bearers of wisdom
literature also developed and sought to cultivate a somewhat differently oriented piety. They were obviously not just oriented to the program which, for
instance, the priesthood or the Books of Chronicles had outlined for the postexilic community. Postexilic Judaism was therefore a complex entity.

Qoheleth can mention only fools when he thinks of sacrifice (Qoh. 4:17),
and in speaking of this topic, he concludes that to sacrifice or not to sacrifice
has no influence on the fortune of human beings (Qoh. 9:2). Vows and thanksgiving offerings that accompany them are mentioned by the Strange Woman
when making her invitation (Prov. 7:14), and Qoheleth is again the one who
offers a general warning, this time in regard to making vows (Qoh. 5:3–5). One
may add to this also Prov. 20:25. Proverbs 31:2 speaks about a "son of my
vows." Job several times is admonished by his friends to turn toward God and
to confess the sins he denies he has committed (Job 5:8ff.; 22:21ff.; etc.). In
this connection, the discussion is also about vows (Job 22:27). Proverbs 17:1
mentions in passing that one could have a house full of sacrificial meat; however, a dry morsel in peace may be, nonetheless, preferable to much meat with

strife. And in every case, justice and righteousness are more preferred by YHWH than sacrifice (Prov. 21:3), and the sacrifices of the godless are (probably for YHWH) an abomination (Prov. 21:27). In Prov. 15:8 the contrast to this is the prayer of the righteous that is well-pleasing to YHWH (cf. Prov. 15:29). However, the prayer of anyone who does not listen to sapiential instruction is even an abomination (Prov. 28:9). The firstfruits that one is to offer to honor YHWH are mentioned together with the consequential well-being of the sage (Prov. 3:9). The Book of Job mentions sacrifice in its framing chapters in order to show that this pious, justice-creating, and God-fearing man, Job (Job 1:1), was also a worshiper of God in making these offerings (Job 1:5; 42:8). If there are in wisdom texts discussions about "clean" or "unclean," of atonement, and other similar things, it is doubtful whether the cultic sphere still actually dominates this use of language (Prov. 14:9; 16:6; 30:12; Qoh. 9:2; and Job 1:5). Even the so-called oath of innocence uttered by Job (Job 31) characteristically mentions no cultic obligations. "With this list of texts, it is still to be noted that only a very few of the ones mentioned actually impart cultic counsels, while the remainder either only touch on cultic matters in a cursory manner or even evaluate them in a rather critical way."[357]

In the Book of Jesus ben Sirach, which belongs to early Jewish wisdom literature and has received some theological "infusions" (A. W. Jenks), there is set forth a different, more positive relationship to the temple, the cult, and the priesthood.[358] In view of the crisis that appears in Job and Qoheleth, Ben Sirach's wisdom can be newly and better established. In connection with Ben Sirach belongs probably also Psalm 15 which combines the cultic and the sapiential.[359]

13.9 The Theological Location of the Old Testament Cult

The meaning and the main purpose of the Old Testament cultus are consequently the ongoing, new sanctification of the people of God and their members. The sacramental outweighs the sacrificial, while beneficence outweighs sacrifice.[360] In the cult, light, life, and righteousness are experienced and dedicated. Here also humans experience YHWH's presence along with the new stabilization of their world. Here as well the "I am YHWH, your God" is delivered, blessing is received from YHWH, and hope is newly strengthened. It is here that a person can experience atonement, because YHWH is willing to cause this to happen. And the necessary means for atonement is present to a human in the releasing of the blood that belongs alone to YHWH (Lev. 17:11). This cultus of Israel had absorbed pre-Yahwistic elements (Passover lamb?), integrated Canaanite features (many sacrifices, agrarian festivals, and the presence of YHWH in the temple), and sought to insert also theologumena from the worship of El (often reshaping this; e.g., YHWH as king). The actual

Yahwistic elements were salvation history (the festivals) and the image of God in history (the festivals) and the law (psalms). The pagan substructure of the cultus experienced, therefore, its Israelite reshaping and expansion. In contradistinction to the cults of the surrounding cultures, Israel excluded the sexual-orgiastic element, rejected magic and conjuration, and made clear the influential role of the experience of history and its mediation of the gracious gift of God over against a religion bound more to natural phenomena. Thus the narrative texts of the Old Testament contain few or even no cultic rituals; rather, in the form of narrative and praise they comprise the repository of a historical but not prehistorical-mythical event. Further, cultic activities in Israel were accompanied by the spoken word[361] and were not seen as working *ex opere operato,* even though, as the prophetic polemic against the cult shows,[362] popular piety was readily widespread even in the cult and could and would interpret matters very differently.

Thus the cultus in Israel is connected, not only with the cosmic order and its cultic, ritual expression, but also with historical election and obligation, the freely given community of God, and God's own taking of responsibility for Israel in turn. It was not myth that issued forth in the cultus;[363] rather, the cultus continued to be strongly shaped by historical traditions. This is demonstrated by Israel's festivals, prayers and psalms, the Sabbath, even circumcision, and their respective interpretations. God provides in the cult for his people the possibilities to strengthen, purify, and maintain community with him, in spite of the fact that this community is always one that exists between the holy God and sinful human beings. This YHWH is, however, the "Holy One of Israel" who grants community to his people and accepts them as his partner. The cult bestows "righteousness" and "life" which create salvation,[364] and in the cultus the individual as well as the congregation, so to speak, enters into the sphere of this righteousness.[365] And when Ezekiel in exile, far removed from temple and cultus, was asked about the possibility of righteousness, he mentioned the things that already had been heard in the cult as the demands of YHWH (cf. Ezek. 18:5–7; and Pss. 15:2ff.; 24:4ff.). The cult as the consecration of divine righteousness, which includes YHWH's acts of salvation and his work of redemption, first brings approval and then intends to contribute to the sanctification of life and to enhance existence within this community of God. Cultic action and experience are, for the Old Testament worshiper, the encounter of blessing (Num. 6:24–26; Pss. 24:5; 129:8; and 133:3) and, in addition, the source of power for moral action.[366]

Thus it is also true of the Old Testament cultus what Luther said about Christian worship during the dedication of the castle church at Torgau: "For nothing other happens here but that our dear Lord himself speaks with us through his holy word, and we in turn speak with him through our prayer and praise" (*WA,* 49:588).

Chapter 14.   The Future of the People of God (Expectations concerning the Future, Eschatology, Apocalyptic)

Whoever approaches the questions concerning the "eschatology of the Old Testament"[1] encounters shaky ground and a contested field.[2] How appropriate is this term in describing Old Testament phenomena, and how well does the full complement of the content of eschatology correspond to Old Testament data? What is the relationship of (contested) eschatology to (uncontested) future expectation or to rising above and transcending the present, and what is the relationship between eschatology and apocalyptic? Where does the eventual, fundamental grounding of Old Testament eschatology reside? How does one describe the possible development of eschatology, and how is this development to be evaluated theologically? Is there a flight into the future that has been initiated by deficiencies of or disappointments with the present? Were there religiohistorical influences from the outside? The answers to many of the questions listed here, in addition, are closely connected with the specific view of prophetic proclamation.[3] And since prophecy also involves the association of judgment and salvation, literary-critical and redactional questions come into play.

14.1   Concerning the Conceptions of Future

In looking primarily at the term "eschatology," at least as far as the Old Testament is concerned, one recognizes that a general consensus has developed in scholarship. It is certain that, for Old Testament thinking, this term should not be used in the sense of Christian theology, that is, as a "teaching about last things."[4] On the one hand, Old Testament eschatology does not allow itself to be summarized under a dogma, and, on the other hand, it does not have or at least did not have to do with something like "last things" until the very end of its development when it merged into apocalyptic (see below). Now there actually does exist toward the end of the Old Testament an eschatology that has to do with the end of history and a future age. However, what at one time had previously earned the designation of eschatology in the assessment of earlier scholars is now viewed clearly and in particular as something that is internal to history and this-worldly. In addition, one should certainly ask whether or not

Old Testament apocalyptic with its eschatology that included a future world and dualism had precursors leading to its development. That is, can or even must there not be assumed a development in eschatology?

A second consensus of contemporary scholarship exists in the fact that, in spite of all the problems that the term "eschatology" causes when used to refer to Old Testament phenomena, one indeed cannot simply dispense with the word. Among other things, this has its basis in the fact that much of the content of New Testament and Christian eschatology, as, for instance, the "Day of the Lord," or the "sovereignty of God" as the content of hope, originated in the Old Testament although not only in Old Testament apocalyptic.

As a result, if one steps back and takes a look at undisputed Old Testament apocalyptic which expresses a particular form of eschatology, then one recognizes first that this apocalyptic has developed within and from Old Testament prophecy. Zechariah 9–11 and Zechariah 12–14; Isaiah 24–27; and the Book of Joel point clearly to this transition from prophecy to apocalyptic. Prior to these texts are Haggai, Zechariah 1–8, and Deutero-Isaiah, which have been correctly assessed as possessing an actual or actualizing eschatology,[5] because they testify to an outspoken, imminent expectation in which they mention, for example, a Cyrus or a Zerubbabel as the messiah (Isa. 45:1; Hag. 2:20–23; Zech. 4:1ff.; and 6:9ff.)[6] and an already inbreaking or directly imminent salvation. Consequently they qualify their own contemporary period as an eschatological one. In inquiring even farther behind these texts, one is pushed almost back to the prophetic preaching of judgment and salvation where the legitimate question emerges as to whether and why one might be able to designate even it as "eschatological." Did the prophets think, for example, that the judgment they announced was a final one, and, if so, for whom: for Israel as a people, as a state, or as a community facing the end of its relationship with God; for the addressees; for all the nations; or even for the "world" (however one thinks of it)? Is there a "thereafter" for these prophets, and once again, if so, for whom, how, and why? That there are now some texts in the prophetic books which lie before us that have "eschatological" content is not to be debated (e.g., in Isa. 11:1–16). The only question is whether they had already originated or could have originated with the same prophets in whose collections and books these eschatological materials are found. One can think of Amos 9:(11?) 13–15; Hos. 2:20–24; Isa. 2:1–4 par.; etc., perhaps as well as Isa. 9:1–6; Jer. 31:31–34; and Ezek. 36:22ff. How did the preexilic prophets understand judgment? How do they view the possibility or impossibility of salvation after this judgment? At the least, this twofold aspect of their message, which should not too quickly be made unilateral,[7] shows that it is a possible basis for the development of an eschatological message and expectation.

Then there are other texts that speak in a way that transcends or goes beyond their own present or even events or persons given prominence in the past.

One may be inclined to see these texts as already eschatological or at least as pointing in this direction. Here belong, for instance, the so-called royal psalms (e.g., Psalms 2; 72; and 110) or texts such as Gen. 49:8–12 and Num. 24:5–9, 17–19.[8] The last two texts probably indeed describe the empire of David in enhanced images, while the royal psalms, in their superordinate, "courtly style," move beyond the king who is presently addressed.

As a result, one perhaps cautiously can agree with the view of Th. C. Vriezen,[9] who has attempted to outline the development of Old Testament eschatology over the course of four distinct periods. For the pre-prophetic period with its political and national movement extending beyond the past or present (Genesis 49; Numbers 24), Vriezen speaks of a pre-eschatological time. He then speaks of a proto-eschatological period in reference to the preexilic prophets. If one makes clear that eschatology here has to do with indications of something later on and that the term can actually be used in a very broad sense, then this approximate identification offers some help in the classification of understanding. To the first period belongs then, for example, the expectation of a "Day of YHWH" presupposed by and thus already existing before Amos. This "Day of YHWH" prior to the preexilic prophets had been viewed as the time of YHWH's salvation for Israel (Amos 5:18ff.). The prophetic message of judgment and salvation belonged, then, to the second period.

In comparison to the above, one should best speak of an actual eschatology beginning with the experiences of 597 and 587 B.C.E. and the resulting exiles that are reflected in the writings of Deutero-Isaiah, Haggai, and Zechariah.[10] This means that one should speak of a so-called actualized eschatological hope (Th. C. Vriezen) from this time forward, a hope that then continued to be developed into apocalyptic in the postexilic period and that was connected in part to the earlier efforts proclaimed by these prophets. This development, furthermore, sought to master the problem of the "final theophany yet to appear." "What is new primarily resides in the view that one does not any longer await the future as a possibility within the continuum of history, but rather hopes for YHWH's new intrusion into present history."[11]

For the entire development of eschatology, the fact that Yahwistic faith had always had an expectation concerning the future must not be undervalued. The break between the preexilic and the postexilic periods ought not be seen as too extreme. This connectedness to the future is made clear, for example, in the promises of the land to the ancestors and to the Moses group (Gen. 12:7; 28:13–15; and Exod. 3:7–10) and in the declarations of hope in the psalms and prayers of the Old Testament.[12] Was it not the case that Israel in its journey with YHWH always was in the position of being newly under way and that this was due to the fact that it continued to expect more and greater things from its God?[13] Whether these expectations always possessed an inherent degree of finality, as argued, for example, by H.-P. Müller, must remain open. He has attempted to demonstrate how this degree of finality was related to the spheres of the intrusions of God into history, blessing, and covenant.[14] When problems and doubts arose about these and related matters, their solutions and expectations were pushed into and then anchored in the future. According to Müller, this led eventually to an eschatology that took up and promised to fulfill these expectations shaped by their feature of intrinsic finality. Hope in a "final" salvation, in an act in history that bears the character of finality (G. von Rad), is likely evident for the first time in Deutero-Isaiah. Therefore one can point to elements of faith in the Old Testament that tended toward complete redemption and fulfillment. Here one is to think chiefly of the notion of the sovereignty of YHWH.[15]

Accordingly, the always newly undertaken effort[16] to remove the term "eschatology," insofar as it pertains to the contents of the Old Testament, from the sphere of the theological confusion of tongues (G. Wanke) may still be necessary. It certainly is not at all clear that one should initially lay aside this term and, as Wanke suggests,[17] then insert into the description of texts the most general understanding of "eschatological" that is possible. What would be the criteria for this to happen? Circular reasoning would appear to be unavoidable. Thus a precise differentiation would perhaps be more helpful.

14.2 The Question concerning the Fundamental Root of Old Testament Eschatology

This first orienting look at the development of Old Testament eschatology has already shown that its fundamental root, its origin, and its development must not be traced to foreign, religiohistorical influences. Earlier theses of this kind, for instance by H. Gunkel[18] and H. Gressmann,[19] cannot be substantiated. The pattern of the sequence of disaster and salvation was as infrequent in the ancient Near East as was eschatology. The few texts that, for very clear-cut reasons, had dared to think initially about the possibility of the end of the world during the so-called First Intermediate period in Egypt have continued to remain the notable exceptions.[20] An influence by Persian religion, assumed by A. von Gall,[21] can be indicated for the first time in Old Testament and early Jewish apocalyptic. However, Persian influence is not the deciding factor in solving the problem of the origins of Old Testament and early Jewish apocalyptic but only assists in this effort. The Ugaritic texts do not allow one to recognize anything approaching eschatology, as is true also of the religions of Mesopotamia.

S. Mowinckel has attempted to show that the cult may be the fundamental root of Old Testament eschatology,[22] and he thought of this especially in connection with the enthronement or New Year's festival.[23] He argued that it was in this festival that Israel may have traveled the path from event to hope and may have embarked upon its journey into the future, when and because the discrepancy between cultic experiences and everyday reality became too great. However, was there not also this tension, this disparity in the experience of things as they stood in Israel's ancient Near Eastern environment? Was there not also among the other nations the worshiper who was disappointed because of the everyday reality that turned out so differently from what was expected? Why, then, did eschatology not also develop among these nations? Nevertheless, Mowinckel discovered actual "eschatological" concepts for the first time within exilic and postexilic texts of the Old Testament, while G. Fohrer[24] held that these concepts belonged to the proclamation (of salvation) of a reconstituted cultic prophecy during the postexilic period. For this reason, he also evaluated them as the epigonous degeneration of Old Testament faith.[25] Nevertheless, he sought to discover inner-Israelite roots for Old Testament eschatology in the same way that others before him had attempted to do, although certainly with different evaluations of its worth (E. Sellin;[26] L. Dürr;[27] and O. Procksch[28]). The inquiry after the fundamental root of Old Testament eschatology has often been connected with this problem of evaluation, as is especially clear in the thinking of G. Fohrer. Is it possible to provide additional clarity for addressing these problems?

14.3. Yahwistic Faith and Future Expectation

As already mentioned, O. Procksch had pointed to the character of Old Testament faith in God as the basic foundation that made possible Old Testament eschatology. One can go into this judgment more deeply and make it more precise.[29]

It is already the name YHWH that points to the pervasive presence and the self-evidence of this God in future activity. Exodus 3:14 provides the only explanation in the Old Testament of the name YHWH, "I am who I show myself to be," and sees this as the typical meaning.[30] In addition, the Old Testament witnesses to YHWH as a God who succeeds (largely at first in a military fashion) on behalf of his own people (Exodus 14; 15:21; and Judges 5). He is also the one who acts in history to rescue (Joshua and Judges), who promises and then fulfills (the ancestral narratives; Exodus 3), and who accompanies and leads purposefully (guidance in the wilderness, the murmuring narratives, and the conquest). If history inquires after its future and if the knowledge of YHWH occurs here, then the frequent statement, "You shall know that I am YHWH," is directed toward a future action of YHWH in history and refers Israel to this action.[31] Promised blessing yearns for actualization even as the sovereignty of YHWH longs for total completion. Election seeks the perfection of the community that is founded by divine action in history.[32] One awaits the accomplishment of the reign of this God, his new activity in history, his new proving of himself in judgment and salvation, and the complete communion with him. "Throughout the Old Testament there is a forward look."[33]

To await YHWH, then, is never once an epigonous deterioration of faith that transforms an earlier, better "either-or" of the decision of faith into a "before-after" that is viewed in an even more negative way.[34] Rather, both descriptions of "either-or" and "before-after" belong together. To believe in YHWH always means to expect something of him, to hope in what is expected, and to believe that he will perhaps even entirely and finally prevail. Thus, in this context, expectation is the attitude that best corresponds with and is most original to faith. The future of God is an essential part of the certainty that is given life by his action in both the past and the present.

If one consents to such a description even in an initial way, then the question of the development of Old Testament eschatology is not dependent only upon the "authenticity" of one or more texts of the Old Testament. Rather, this development has to do on the whole with the fundamental structures of the faith in YHWH. V. Maag's thesis[35] of eschatology as a function of the experience of history should be considered and taken up in its entire depth. He argues that the exodus event,[36] for example, was not only the beginning of Israel's relationship with God but also its continuing, intrinsic foundation. Whoever has experienced God in this event was ready and in the position to hope for something new and even grander from him. In the Song of Miriam (Exod. 15:21), hope in this God is expressed in praise, while any reference to either the setting or the concrete naming of the enemy (both for now and in the future) is consciously not mentioned.

Then there are the Priestly generations and the figures of the ancestors who are arranged in a chronological and linear succession. Here the look at the former generations is also linked to the future ones, even as the previous activity of YHWH was also a type for other actions that were to follow.[37] Thus an understanding of history as linear and consequently purposeful is both implied and always newly called forth. One can speak of the "plan of YHWH."[38] The promise of land gives issue to the hope in the (also new) conquest of Canaan, while the experience of the Davidic empire raises the hope for a new Davidic successor or successors. The exodus produces hope for an analogous action in a new exodus, as does the sealing of the covenant for a new covenant. One speaks here of themes of correspondence (G. Fohrer)[39] or of the transposition of themes (H. Gross)[40] or of the eschatologizing of traditions (G. von Rad).[41] Perhaps the statement "in the beginning" (Gen. 1:1) already carries within it a possible "end," is aware of the "end" brought about by God in the primeval flood (Gen. 6:13 P), and perhaps even reaches beyond that "end" to the qualified "end" in Amos 8:2 (cf. Ezek. 7:2). The last-mentioned text consciously assigns this end to the past as a judgment of disaster that God had already rendered.[42] In contrast to the six days preceding it, the Sabbath has no "evening," according to Gen. 2:1–3, thereby providing an element of hope, for it remains open to the rest of God as the purpose of creation.[43] When the hope for a new creation is expressed,[44] this is to bring about not only the renewal of the old creation but also its increasing enhancement. This hope is then combined, for example, with the vision of a new, fully restored Jerusalem/Zion and thus the culmination of Israel's journey. This "golden age" of the peace of creation resides for Israel, not in the past,[45] but in the future.

In the final analysis, one experienced with YHWH not only a deficiency in the fulfillment of his promises and a diminishing of one's own hopes but by contrast a surplus as well, for these promises point beyond themselves to the future, thus indicating the prospects of an even greater destiny.[46] One learned not only that but also how one's own hopes in God himself and his action were surpassed time and again. Hope in God is indeed never free from disappointment, but it is still removed from the dejection that disappointment usually produces. Where one knows of YHWH, there also emerges from the possible disappointment of faith a faith that is new in hopeful anticipation.

In this sense, then, not only is it true that Yahwistic faith always bore within itself a future expectation, but the related thesis is equally true: eschatology is the legitimate development of this future hope, not its deterioration. "Thus the God confessed by Israel is the God who carries things to their completion. This he has done and continues to do within the context of history. Consequently, Old Testament eschatology is the explication of Yahwistic faith in its application to history."[47]

14.4 Statements of Hope

The more general explanation provided above can be enhanced and made more concrete by a look at the statements of hope expressed by Old Testament worshipers as well as the various corpora and writings in the Old Testament. W. Zimmerli has described these statements of hope in a brief study,[48] while C. Westermann has investigated every verb and substantive that expresses hope in the Old Testament.[49] The especially important verbs are קוה = *qiwwâ* ("to wait for"), שבר = *śibbēr* ("to wait, hope"), חכה = *ḥikkâ* ("to wait, await"), יחל = *yḥl* ("to wait for, hope for"), and צפה = *ṣph* ("to keep watch"), while the significant substantives are תקוה = *tiqwâ* ("hope"), אחרית = *'aḥărît* ("end, future"), כסלה = *kislâ* ("confidence")/כסל = *kesel* ("confidence"), and תוחלת = *tôḥelet* ("hope").[50]

What faithful individual Israelites hoped, expected, and wished for themselves in their everyday existence is found in the statements of hope in the Book of Proverbs, statements that no doubt were made by members of a particular social class who took part in a view of life and the world shaped by wisdom.[51] The Book of Proverbs occasionally argues in a very self-evident manner, similar, for example, to Psalm 37, a wisdom psalm, and analogous to the friends of Job (in Job 3–27; and 32–37; see below). In making this argument, the freedom of God is not fully preserved.[52] In this book, hope in YHWH is mentioned only in Prov. 20:22 and then in connection with the principle of deed and consequence expected to be guaranteed by YHWH.[53] Elsewhere the sage hopes for a good future, a beautiful life, and joy (Prov. 10:28; 11:23; 23:17f.; and 24:13f.). In such a sapientially ordered, continuing life, the wise person hopes to avoid a premature death,[54] while only evildoers and fools have no positive future.[55]

These hopes shaped by wisdom also play a role in the Book of Job. Here Job's friends draw these hopes within the substance of their argumentation, while Job, by contrast, negates their validity as he seeks to work out a possible interpretation of his own.[56] The friends offer Job hope, if only he will become and then live a life that is good, wise, and righteous (Job 4:5–9; 5:15f.; 8:11–13; and 11:18, 20). However, Job can and will "hope" now only in his death that will occur because of the unrighteousness of God which, in Job's own thinking, he has experienced (Job 6:8f.; 7:6; and 17:13). For Job, God himself certainly brings to ruin all hope (Job 14:19f.; 19:10; and 30:20, 26). Even a life beyond death is not open to Job; rather, he can only wait expectantly, hoping then in the last moment of his life to still experience an encounter with God. God, in spite of everything, still turns out to be his "redeemer" (גאל = gō'ēl), and the one who maintains his right (Job 19:25f.).

In the midst of his own critical assessment of wisdom, Qoheleth raises his voice quite naturally against the sapiential view of hope.[57] Asking then whether such a hope can actually survive on the basis of the sapiential view of existence and the experience of a successful life, he responds with an inexorable negation. Humans are denied the ability both to influence and to take a calculated look into the future (Qoh. 3:10ff.; and 9:1ff.). Even the sage, like every other person, will and must die and cannot control the time to come.[58] Qoheleth even contests the idea of immortality (of the soul? Qoheleth uses the term רוח = rûaḥ), which is probably being discussed in Hellenistic circles during this period (Qoh. 3:21).[59] The shock of finality is consciously provocative. The dead certainly now have no hope at all (Qoh. 9:4f.; cf. Isa. 38:18). Is it an accident that the various traditions and content of the faith of Israel, which, according to the testimony of other Old Testament texts and writings could mediate hope and disclose the future, do not come to expression and thus carry no weight in the wisdom literature? Moreover, the psalms in the variety of their literary forms allow one to recognize well how much hoping, looking, and waiting for YHWH were components of the Yahwistic faith of both individuals and the nation.[60] In these texts, it is clear how hope and hoping are a "process of existence"[61] insofar as the verbal element in the expressions of hope along with its personal character therefore dominate. The *lex orandi* points also here in a decisive way to the *lex credendi*.

The worshiper awaits YHWH, his action, and his answer, for he is indeed "the hope of Israel."[62] The worshiper awaits YHWH's word (Ps. 119:43, 49; etc.). Hoping and trusting stand in close proximity to each other.[63] For the worshiper, YHWH is the "God of my salvation,"[64] intimately known by reason of his name and his goodness. On account of YHWH's qualities that make hope possible, the worshiper looks to him as the one who will and ought to provide help and as the one who should "remind" himself of his own character, compassion, and loyalty (Ps. 25:6f.). And the worshipers themselves also remind YHWH of his deeds (Ps.74:1f.) in order to pray through to new hope.[65] The act of remembering creates hope. Thus the nation also hopes (Jer. 14:22), and the resorting to earlier acts of YHWH's salvation (e.g., Ps. 22:5), indeed to earlier hopes (Pss. 22:5; 40:2; and then Psalms 44 and 88 in the laments of the nation, as well as Ps. 106:4), awakens new hope and makes it possible. YHWH may yet appear or act as before (Pss. 3:8; 16:1f.; 40:2; etc.). Hoping and waiting stand under a special promise[66] that becomes the basis both for the exhortation to hope and even the worshiper's own appeal.[67] To hope is simply and finally the defining characteristic of the relationship with God. "It is well with everyone who waits on him!" (Isa. 30:18).[68] "May your goodness be upon us, O YHWH, as we hope in you" (Ps. 33:22).

Consequently, hope is encountered in the Psalter, not as a by-product of the relationship with God, but rather as the foundational structure of Yahwistic faith. Psalm 119:49 can express it in this way: "(on which) you have made me hope." One was never at an end as long as YHWH was one's God. The power of hope based on him is shown even in periods of crisis. This is especially true of the Babylonian exile which points in hope to a new future with the expression of its new theological formulations that originated and took root during this critical time.[69] Thus, in this period, one speaks in Deuteronomistic circles of YHWH as the "rock" and the "God of faithfulness" (Deut. 32:4; cf. Ps. 31:6).

The binding of hoping, awaiting, and expecting to faith in God shows, in addition, that hope cannot and may not be seen as something humanly existential where the capacities to transcend and to move beyond one's situation simply are a dimension of human nature. Rather, these capacities are grounded much more in the character and activity of God and are directed toward him. Here human beings not only take upon themselves anew the experiment of hope in the face of their own limitations or show their openness in principle to the future but also express hope both in and from their relationship to God and as members of the people of God. Thus Yahweh sets apart for himself here and there the individual human being as well as the nation of God. Both are present in Psalm 90 and both characteristically and typically are interwoven. This hope also allows God to have his freedom: verbs with the naming of a concrete object of hope, disregarding texts such as Psalm 37 that are influenced by wisdom, seldom occur in the Psalter. Thus hope is in no way a hope for a rapid change. The worshiper cries out for a long period of time and is ever waiting (Ps. 69:4; and 119:84). "Wait upon YHWH" (Ps. 27:14) means to take heart, or it can mean that "Israel hopes in YHWH" (Ps. 130:7). A refrain containing this exhortation occurs throughout Psalms 42 and 43.[70] Thus hoping and hope are not a principle, a condition, or a possession. They are never without disappointment or crisis, so that expressions of hope have then their place chiefly in the lament and in prayer. This means they have their place where faith is actualized, that is, in a speech to God, a speech in and from personal wonderment, and a speech within the I-Thou relationship. "I hope for this, because you are so gracious" (Ps. 13:6). "My God, upon whom I hope" (Ps. 91:2; cf. 25:2, 15).

14.5 Concerning the Development
of Old Testament Expectations of the Future

Within the narrative literature of the Old Testament, the Yahwist[71] attests to a theology of hope by the fact that he permeates the primeval history (Gen. 11:1–9) with life-diminishing curses (Gen. 3:14–19; 4:11f.; and 9:25)[72] that contrast with the promise issued in Gen. 8:21f. However, he then follows this primeval narrative with the story of the ancestors containing promises to them that establish hope in YHWH's word and deed. However, even in the narratives of his primeval history in Genesis 2ff., the Yahwist inserts indications of YHWH's preserving and supporting grace amidst all the punishment (Gen. 3:21; 4:15; and 8:21f.). Indeed, even the threat of death issued in Gen. 2:16f. is not carried out. Even here there is concealed an indication of a God whose grace will continue to show mercy. The barren Sarah can still become a mother (Gen. 18:14), and from the deceiver Jacob there can still become one who contends with God (Genesis 27 and 32). Promises of land (Gen. 12:7; 28:13–15) and promises of blessing (Gen. 12:1–3; and 28:14) point toward the future. YHWH protects and guides the destiny of Joseph, and, hearing the cries of his people, he gives them a future (Exod. 3:7f.). He does not even withdraw his devotion from a mumuring people; rather, he leads them into the land (Exod. 3:8; and 33:12ff.) that he has promised to them. Wanderings and breakings of camp leading to a new destination under the promise and guidance of YHWH are constituent elements of the Yahwistic interpretation of history.

The Priestly narrator,[73] by contrast, seeks to bring about trust that is directed toward the future through his emphasis on the sustaining and orienting order of creation (Gen. 1:1ff.). For him, this order is directed toward the Sabbath that serves as the culmination and goal of creation. The Sabbath in P is understood as the gift of God to his world which, through Israel, obtains its special significance.[74] This emphasis on effectuating a trust directed toward the future is likewise served by P's emphases on the covenants of Noah (Gen. 9:1–17) and Abraham (Genesis 17). Indeed, P presents the latter as an eternal covenant and asserts several times that it is valid for Abraham's descendants.[75] P seeks to transmit to the exilic community new hope in its God through the description of the miracle at the Red Sea as a revelation of mighty YHWH (Exodus 13–14) and through the construction of the tabernacle that YHWH promises will both contain his presence and allow him to dwell among his people (Exod. 29:43ff.). With the tabernacle, YHWH establishes the cultus that will make possible Israel's further community with its God.[76] It has often been thought that P's hopes crystallized into one great hope, that of the return from exile. The cave in which the ancestors are buried is indeed a legally acquired earnest for the eternal possession of the land (Genesis 23) that provides hope for a new distribution in Joshua 13–21 (P).[77] The statement, "You shall know that I am YHWH, the one who has led you out of bondage in Egypt" (Exod. 6:7), becomes the sum and substance of the message of the Priestly source. It is probably not inappropriate to see in the mention of Egypt a transparent reference to "Babylon."

The Deuteronomic and especially the Deuteronomistic movement has spoken about the exodus from Egypt in a similarly transparent manner.[78] YHWH hears the cries of lament coming from his people and can turn toward their need (Deut. 26:5–9), and the Deuteronomistic narratives of the conquest (Deuteronomy 1–3) several times point to the exilic hope of new conquest.[79] According to the description of this multilayered Deuteronomistic History, Israel within its history has burdened itself with grave guilt that had to lead to the punishment of the exile. Since Israel has abandoned the covenant that YHWH had granted and commanded them to keep (Deut. 29:24),[80] he has abandoned his people (Deut. 31:17f.). Israel had to experience YHWH's wrath (Judg. 3:8; and 10:7) but also had to be allowed to see that he had heard the cries of his wayward people,[81] had opened up a new future, and had continued to delay the prophetic judgment proclaimed against his nation (Judg. 6:7–10; etc.) on account of the "sins of Jereboam." YHWH delayed this punishment because he remembered David and the promises made to him. Thus he provided "for the sake of his servant David" a "lamp" that would continue to burn and postponed his punishing action.[82] However, in the meantime, both YHWH's good and his evil words had been fulfilled (Josh. 21:43–45; and 23:14–16), for Israel had done not only what was good "in the eyes of YHWH" but also what was evil (Deut. 31:29; etc.). However, since the Deuteronomistic History now concludes with the mention of the act of mercy extended toward the Jewish king Jehoiachin (2 Kings 25:27–30)[83] that occurred in 562 B.C.E. when he still was a member of the exilic community, then this somewhat reserved narrative technique provides another, although disguised and perhaps even dilatory, indication of hope in a future that remains open (cf. Jer. 29:11).

Other texts and probably also other strata of the Deuteronomistic History speak of the possibility of a "return" that is based on promise (Deut. 4:25–31; 30:1–10; and 1 Kings 8:46–53), or they characterize the previously mentioned "crying out" to YHWH as one way that had already provided access to God in Israel's history and wished to point to this way as a possibility of hope for contemporary Israel. In addition, the discussion can be about the promise that Israel will express a renewed obedience that is given concreteness by compliance with the Deuteronomistic Decalogue and the Book of Deuteronomy that interprets it. This obedience can occasion the dwelling again in the land.[84] This promised, "good" land, sworn by YHWH to the ancestors and their descendants, can be described in effusive terms (Deut. 6:10f.; 7:13; 8:7b-9; and 11:10–12).[85] There Israel shall find the "rest" that it presently does not have.[86] Thus, even during the exile, Israel hoped in its God, YHWH, with whom "perhaps" there was indeed hope (Lam. 3:29; cf. vv. 22f.).

Deuteronomy 32[87] reflects the relationship of history, judgment, and possible salvation and serves as a kind of summary of Deuteronomistic theology which, moreover, appears here in its late-exilic expression that has been influenced by Ezekiel and Deutero-Isaiah. This characteristically occurs under the two-sided viewpoint of the faithfulness of YHWH and the unfaithfulness of the nation. Thus the effort is made to transmit hope even during times of judgment, since YHWH's faithfulness will overcome the faithlessness of the nation. The God of faithfulness (Deut. 32:4; cf. Ps. 31:6) is also here once more the one who opens up this possibility of hope and a positive future. Thus, in and with the Deuteronomistic History, sin is confessed and repentance is carried out. YHWH is conceded the right to administer justice in his acts of judgment, although one hopes at the same time to receive grace from him, because he is known and continues to be known as the God who gives both hope and future and who ultimately will not reject his chosen people.[88]

Exilic songs of communal lament request that YHWH might still "remember" his congregation whose history he has shared (Ps. 74:1f.), and they ask how long the enemy was to ridicule the name of YHWH and his power (Ps. 74:10, 18; cf. 44:10ff.; and 79:4). The history of the nation was regarded as sinful, even though YHWH may always have acted in a salvific manner (Psalm 78;[89] cf. 106). Psalm 77 also belongs to these contexts where the worshiper during his or her time of present need remembers the former period and earlier acts of YHWH in order to garner new confidence. And one may recognize in the postexilic Psalm 126 how resorting to the "turn of fortune" (v. 1) in the exile raises new hope in an analogous act of YHWH.

Further, the awareness that humanity in general and the people of Israel in particular are creatures between judgment and salvation is also encountered in the Old Testament in narrative literature and in the Psalter (cf. yet Psalms 51; and 130). The murmuring narratives (within the large context of Exodus 15 to

Numbers 21),[90] already often mentioned, further make rather clear how unthankful and sinful Israel saw itself to be. In the final analysis, these texts are
also a kind of confession of sin by Israel to its God who guided and sustained
his people, while the nation rebelled against him and his guidance, wished for
a different leadership, and did not trust in him.[91] Therefore the murmuring narratives of Israel operate almost as though they were applications of Genesis to
the nation as a whole. Consequently, Israel saw itself already at the start of its
journey as not being worthy of God's turning toward them to save. It was no
accident, then, that apostasy (Exodus 32) followed soon after the concluding
of the covenant (Exod. 24:1–11). YHWH's answer, however, consisted in the
fact that he "is to remain faithful to his cause and to his promise,"[92] although
he obviously always found his people to be a burden. His intention to eradicate
the people (Exod. 32:10; and Num. 14:12) did not come to pass, and this was
something exemplary in and of itself. Yahweh allowed himself to be persuaded
by the intercession of Moses.[93] Faith in YHWH finds and makes possible hope
in the future.

14.6 Rejection by YHWH?

The election of the nation also signifies its obligation, for it is Israel's election that plainly sets forth and encompasses its responsibility. Israel's liberation by YHWH resulted in being bound to him. YHWH's gifts expected obedience in return, and beside divine blessing stood also the possibility of divine
curse (Leviticus 26; and Deuteronomy 27ff.). However, it was, above all, the
prophets who saw it especially necessary to take up the questions concerning
judgment and salvation.

In their writings as well as in the Deuteronomistic History and the texts that
are dependent on it and mostly stand in close temporal proximity to the exile,
the question is therefore broached as to whether YHWH would and could *reject* the very people whom he had elected. From the distant past[94] the same
question was raised in multiple ways about Saul and his peculiar problems (1
Sam. 15:23; and 16:1),[95] for he was also described as a king who did not master the tensions and problems in his kingship and was found wanting (according to the meaning of the Deuteronomistic movement)[96] in certain areas of his
rule. Also the rejection of the sanctuary at Shiloh by YHWH was to have been
final (Jer. 7:12; 26:6; and Ps. 78:60, 67), but this was something that continued
to be mentioned as an example and a warning.

However, in other places it is said that YHWH may have rejected or wished
to reject his city Jerusalem, the priests, or even his entire nation.[97] That YHWH
could elect as well as reject is also reflected in Deutero-Isaiah (Isa. 41:9). However, Israel struggled with this problem, especially during the exile (Pss. 74:1;
89:39; and Lam. 5:20–22), and it was neither ready nor in a position to allow

the validity of only a negative answer. This is shown by statements that expressly deny the thought of a possible rejection of the nation (Jer. 31:37; 33:19–22; cf. 2 Kings 21:14 with 1 Sam. 12:22). And even where the category of curse must become the leading theme of the exilic explanation of history (Deut. 28:15ff.), other intonations are heard on its periphery, including, for example, those of the possibility of a return (Deut. 30:1ff.; cf. Lam. 5:21) and new obedience. The idea of rejection is not frequently encountered in the Old Testament, and it is even on occasion emphatically denied.[98] However, the idea is still brought into consideration as a possibility. It already appears in Hosea as a threat issued on the basis of an offense (Hos. 4:6; and 9:17).[99] And it is found as a question in Lam. 5:22 (cf. Jer. 14:19), as Lamentations on the whole brings into the expression of prayer the problems of the exile, the guilt of Israel/Judah, the justified punishment of YHWH, but also the hope in a new beginning (cf., e.g., Lam. 2:20ff.; 5:1ff.). In also dealing with this problem, Psalm 60 directs it toward YHWH. Similar are the (Deuteronomistic) prayers in Deut. 9:25ff. and 1 Kings 8:57 that beseech YHWH not to give up his people (cf. also Psalm 44). Psalm 89 speaks of the rejection and repudiation of the Davidic king (vv. 39ff.) and yet continues these thoughts in making a new petition to YHWH (vv. 47ff.). Psalm 74:1f. laments that YHWH may have "rejected forever" his people but prays at the same time that he ought to remember his congregation. Also for Psalm 78 Israel's rejection is not final (in spite of v. 59), as the continuation in vv. 67 through 68ff. shows. If for clearly obvious reasons that are closely related to the time period of the exile already in progress the (Deuteronomistically redacted) Book of Jeremiah and the Deuteronomistic History most plainly struggle with the problem of rejection, then its limits are circumscribed by reference to "this generation" or something similar (Jer. 7:29; cf. 31:35–37) in order to attempt to mitigate the effects of this problem. In addition, it is the Deuteronomistic historical review of the community, which continues to exist in spite of everything, that inserts the category of "rejection" into its explanation of history. This historical review signals at the same time that this concept of rejection is not intended to be the last word in regard to either the community's own existence or the knowledge given it. The Northern Kingdom of Israel was "rejected," and YHWH had threatened the same for Judah (2 Kings 17:18; and 23:27 Deuteronomistic). This also had now taken place. However, the fact that one could reflect theologically and retrospectively on one's own reality (cf. Josh. 23:15) at the same time opened up the possibility of precluding one's own final rejection. On the contrary, the possibility that this rejection by YHWH could occur is expressly contested and vehemently denied in language that, not without reason, is in part formulated as YHWH's own (Lev. 26:11, 44; 1 Sam. 12:22; Isa. 41:9; and Jer. 14:21). All of this indicates that the problem broached was not an easy one to master. This was indeed obviously so in regard to the preexilic prophetic preaching of judgment, the justification and fulfillment of which had now proven itself. YHWH's most original nature, his "I am YHWH," must prevail (Lev. 26:44). YHWH ought not to reject his people for "his/your name's sake" (cf. 1 Sam. 12:22), a reason not rarely brought before him in the form of prayer (Jer. 14:21; cf. Ps. 94:14; and Lam. 5:22). A certificate of divorce does not exist (Isa. 50:1). YHWH seeks rather to have compassion for his people (Jer. 33:23–26). One can appeal to his divine presence when asking why all of this may have happened to "us" (Judg. 6:13ff., Deuteronomistic).

In these connections, the discussion then is often about the *wrath of YHWH* or analogous figures of speech.[100] This expression occurs in the context of narratives (Exod. 32:10) in which the jealousy of YHWH does not fully come to culmination because of intercession (Exod. 32:11f., 14), in the interpretation of history that is examined in retrospect (Ps. 78:58f., 62; Deut. 2:15; 9:19; 29:26f.; Judg. 2:14, 20; 3:8; 10:7;[101] and 2 Kings 17:18), and also in "threats" that are closely associated with the explanation found in Deuteronomistic thinking (Deut. 4:25; 7:4; 11:17; and 1 Kings 8:46). Prophets spoke about this subject in their threats of judgment (Isa. 5:25; 9:11; 10:4; 30:28; Zeph. 1:14ff.; Jer. 4:4, 26; 6:11; 7:20; 21:12; 23:19; 25:37; and Ezek. 21:36), while (predominantly exilic) communal laments pray for the averting of the experience of divine wrath.[102] YHWH may not even conceal his "face"[103] any longer as he had done when angry;[104] rather, he is to turn his face toward his congregation (cf. Isa. 8:17).[105] For Deutero-Isaiah, YHWH's wrath is indeed an active event, although it is now abating and passing away (Isa. 42:25; 47:6; and 54:7f.). YHWH may no longer be then a "hidden God" (Isa. 45:15).[106] The exilic and postexilic passages of Isa. 14:1; Zech. 1:17; and 2:16 speak then of a continuing or rather a new election. One knew from them that YHWH's wrath does not continue to endure (Ps. 30:6; cf. Exod. 34:6f.; Pss. 37:8; 60:3; 85:4, 6; 90:11; and 103:9).[107]

14.7 Judgment

The struggle over election and rejection is only one dimension of what results from the prophetic announcement of judgment and the reality of the experience of the exile. It is the prophetic message of judgment itself[108] that now must be more closely examined. What is the basis of the prophetic announcement of judgment, and how is it to be understood? What is the relationship between judgment and (possible?) salvation? How and on what grounds can the prophets speak about salvation at all?

The first appearance of prophets with a message of judgment that addresses the entire nation of Israel corresponds with the rise of the Assyrians in the middle of the eighth century B.C.E. and their growing ambition for power over Syria and eventually Palestine. Was it this experience of upheaval and threatening danger occasioned by the Assyrians that shaped current experience into the expectation of judgment? What role did these prophets' consciousness of God play in this regard? What role did their possible certainty of the present and new coming of God to his people have to play?

When Amos first speaks of the impending punishment of YHWH and of the judgment of Israel,[109] the "that" of this judging activity of YHWH stands in the foreground. "Be prepared, O Israel, to meet your God" (Amos 4:12; cf. 3:2; and 8:1f.). Rather different statements can be made about the "how": war, deportation, earthquakes, probably also epidemic disease, forces of nature, and so on.[110] It is deliberately stressed that YHWH, on the very "Day of YHWH" (Amos 5:18–20) when the people expect salvation, is the one who is coming in judgment against his people. The "motto" (Amos 1:2) directly at the beginning of the Book of Amos also makes this clear, and the use of the divine "I" as the subject of the threatened actions underscores the point as well (Amos 3:14f.; 4:12; 5:17, 27; 6:8, 14; 7:9; and 8:9).

This is not different in Hosea. Here it is true of YHWH that he is "like a lion to Ephraim" (Hos. 5:14) and like a mother bear (Hos. 13:7f.). Israel is "not my people" (Hos. 1:9) and receives "no pity" (Hos. 1:6), and YHWH is no longer present for the nation (Hos. 1:9).[111] In the land, there is neither faithfulness, nor love, nor the knowledge of God (Hos. 4:1); rather, there is apostasy from YHWH, the whoredom of "prostitutes" who forsake him, and the worship of the calves (Hos. 4:4–19; 8:4–6, 11–13; 10:1–8; 13:1–3; etc.). Thus the days of affliction are come because of Israel's incurrence of great guilt (Hos. 9:7, 9). In different ways Hosea also concretely depicts the punishing activity of God.[112] However, the prophet can also speak of the educational effect of punishment that should lead to repentance (Hos. 2:8f.; and 3:1–5), because YHWH himself is prepared to change, because he is God and not a human being, and because "he is the holy one in your midst" (Hos. 11:8f.).[113] He also creates a new salvation that shall lead a transformed Israel, after a new beginning in the wilderness, back to the land of promise to experience a new betrothal with its God (Hos. 2:16ff.).

For Isaiah it is chiefly the Assyrians who function as YHWH's instrument of judgment (Isa. 5:25ff.; and 10:5ff.). YHWH, the "Holy One of Israel" (Isa. 1:4; etc.[114]), is the one who whistles for the enforcers of judgment to come (Isa. 7:18–20) and to serve as the rod of his wrath (Isa. 10:5; and 30:32; cf. 5:25).[115] Micah says that YHWH devises disaster "against this generation" (Micah 2:3), and announces that Samaria will be destroyed (Micah 1:6). He says that Jerusalem will be a heap of ruins and Zion will become an unplowed field (Micah 3:12), and, since he was a contemporary of Isaiah, Micah also may have viewed the Assyrians as the ones who would carry out this destruction. Jeremiah spoke of the "enemy from the north"[116] who later became concretely identified as the Babylonians (Jer. 4:5–9; 20:4ff.; 25:9; 27; etc.).

The "evil" that displeases YHWH consequently includes both social and cultic misdeeds (Hos. 7:15; Jer. 1:16; 2:13; 5:28; 7:30; 35:15; etc.; also see Zech. 7:10; 8:17; Isa. 56:2; and Neh. 13:17–27). He reacts to this by doing "evil" himself, that is, by bringing disaster as punishment (Josh. 23:15; 24:20; Isa. 31:2; Jer. 1:14; 2:3; 4:6; etc.; and Ezek. 6:10), since there is "no field of human activity and plans that stand outside the judging activity of YHWH. . . . It is probably indeed divine freedom . . . that makes it possible for the prophecy of judgment to challenge the very roots of the salvific activity of YHWH when this leads to the notion of the human possession, control, and determination of the limits of salvation and disaster from the hand of YHWH."[117]

When reasons are attached to prophetic announcements of judgment, something that is usually the case, and have as their purpose the legitimation of the threat against the nation, then what is specifically characteristic of each individual prophet and his message may well be recognized in these reasons, in these "invectives" present with the "threats," and in these "indications of the situation" that accompany the "announcements."[118] Thus the arguments of Amos, Micah, and Isaiah are strongly social-critical in nature (e.g., Amos 2:6ff.; 5:11; 6:1ff.; 8:4–6; Micah 2:1–5; 3:1–4; etc.; Isa. 1:21–23; 5:7, 8ff.; etc.). On the other hand, Hosea speaks more about cultic apostasy (Hos. 2:4, 7; 4:1–3, 11–14; 8:5; etc.), as does Jeremiah later on (Jeremiah 2). Isaiah by contrast speaks about political misdeeds that derive from a lack of trust in YHWH (Isa. 7:9; 28:16; and 30:15). What finally makes judgment necessary is the notably incompatible coexistence of the manifested behavior and character of the sinful people and the nature of its God. As a God who is not indifferent to the condition of the individual members of his community and who asks about "justice and righteousness" among his people (Isa. 1:17, 21; 5:7, 23; Jer. 5:1, 28; 22:15; Amos 5:7, 15, 24; Micah 3:9; etc.), especially since he is a God of justice, YHWH now can only pronounce judgment *against* the nation (Amos 3:2). He now can only conduct a war *against* and no longer *for* Israel and Judah,[119] since his people have continued to commit apostasy and have repeatedly negated their claim to the title of the community of God that he has given them. Indeed, already in their earlier history, the people have shown themselves to be disloyal, as, for instance, is recounted in the "murmuring narratives" or in the (Deuteronomistic) Book of Judges. Thus, for the prophets of the eighth century B.C.E., YHWH comes against his nation to judge and to punish by means of the feared Assyrians who are well known for their military conquest and the practice of deportation. For Jeremiah, this instrument of divine judgment takes the form of the Babylonians. The prophets derive their explanation of history from their consciousness of God. They make use of the meaning of the larger history to interpret the meaning of the history of Israel and Judah.

In this regard, the question now arises as to what function the proclamation of judgment by the preexilic writing prophets serves in their announcement and grounding of YHWH's approaching action of punishment. Does this proclamation of judgment provide evidence for the necessity and unavoidability of judgment, or for insight into its legitimation, or for the acceptance of punishment? Moreover, are there texts that clearly support these understandings of the proclamation of judgment, especially from the prophets of the eighth century B.C.E.?[120] Or does the demanding God place in the announcements of judgment a final invitation to repent or to alter one's misdeeds? Said in another way that sharpens the point: Is the announced judgment an unavoidable fate, or is there also a living God at work in this judgment?[121] Is judgment also perhaps a passageway (certainly a necessary one) that leads eventually to a possible salvation? Or may one or can one ask such questions? In any event, one cannot point to or uncover any passages that suggest that these prophetic words of judgment had their origin as well as their life situation in the cultus. Further, one cannot point to a cultic background to account for or to motivate the change from judgment to salvation.

Prophetic words of judgment contain not only announcements but also, as already mentioned, evidence of guilt, a threat, and an indication of the situation. They involve not only the imminent coming of YHWH to judge and to punish but also the announcement of its necessity. "There is an irrevocable connection between guilt and disaster."[122] A true prophet uncovers both transgression and sin (Micah 3:8), and the discovering of misdeeds and the announcement of disaster are "two sides of the same coin."[123] However, the prophetic words of judgment at the same time contain a call to repentance, a call to practice justice, and a call to abandon both antisocial activity and the making of evil political pacts attacked by the prophets (Hosea; Isaiah; and Jeremiah). Consequently, for these reasons it is clear that the prophetic message does not have to do only with the inevitability of a coming judgment. Accordingly, in spite of judgment, the possibility of salvation at the very least is not fully excluded.

Isaiah 17:12–14; 29:1–8; and Jer. 29:11 speak of judgment as a transition to a time of salvation that will follow. The exile threatened by a number of prophets does not automatically lead to the annihilation of the deportees, although "annihilation" can stand for "exile," since there one is as good as dead.[124] When the message of the second fall of Jerusalem proves true, Ezekiel in exile may have and could have gone from announcing a message of judgment (now especially in Ezekiel 5 and 8–11; yet also transmitted in 22:1–16) to one of salvation (Ezek. 33:21f.; then chaps. 34ff.). Thus this prophet took up (in Ezek. 7:2ff.) the message of the "end" from Amos (Amos 8:2) but went beyond it in order to see in this a conclusive finality.

Consequently, the prophetic books also contain authentic words of admonition, although there are not many of them in this corpus.[125] These admonitions not only seek to explain a wasted opportunity but also actually intend to call people back to YHWH, even at the last minute (Amos 4:6–12).[126] Thus the power and honor of YHWH come to completion in the carrying out of judgment. Yet it also has both its limits and its positive goal. Whether one should subsequently recognize in the prophetic announcement of judgment the "character of finality"[127] appears questionable. However, the postexilic community, by its redaction of the Old Testament as a corpus of writings, presented both judgment and salvation within the prophetic books as a proclaimed possibility. By means of this redaction, this possibility of judgment and salvation was presented not only in a temporal sequence (e.g., in the form of the so-called "three-part eschatological scheme"[128]) but also as existing side by side. This makes it clear that and how both stood before Israel as a further possibility.[129] Moreover, eschatology involves the fortune of individual humans in "only an implicit" manner.[130]

14.8   Remnant

Mainly encountered in the prophetic books, "remnant"[131] refers to those who continue to endure and thus, so to say, to those who build a bridge between judgment and salvation. This notion can be drawn upon in only a very limited way to support the view that the judgment announced by the prophets was a catastrophe that was not always regarded and only seen as annihilation and therefore as a final "end."

Among the preexilic prophets it is (not Amos 3:12 but rather) only in Amos 5:15 that the thought of a remnant is ventured, and then only a remnant that "perhaps" would be rescued by YHWH. Isaiah 1:8, which mentions the surviving Daughter of Zion, is a possible second passage that could have become part of the nucleus of the later, fully developed conception of the remnant. Similar to this is the name of Isaiah's son, Shear-jashub (Isa. 7:3). However, this name later was no longer understood as a threat ("only a remnant shall return"), as it was probably originally meant, but, rather as a promise ("A remnant shall return"). All other texts, for example, Micah 4:7; 5:6f.; Zeph. 2:7, 9; 3:12f.; as well as those in First Isaiah (e.g., Isa. 4:2f.; 6:13c; 10:20–23; 11:10–16; and 28:5f.), prove to be additions upon close examination and, more precisely, exilic and postexilic interpretations. These interpretations qualify with the word "remnant" this exilic and postexilic community as a single community. This community has experienced and then lived through the judgment and now sees in itself the nucleus of the new beginning after the exile. Clearly exilic texts (Isa. 46:3; also Deut. 4:27; and 28:62?) and postexilic texts (Zech. 8:6, 11f.; Ezra 3:8; 6:16; 9:15; etc.) support this view. It can be the Golah that is viewed as this remnant, or it can be also the entire postexilic community, or it can be even (in the Books of Chronicles) the Samaritans as the "successors" of the earlier Northern Kingdom (e.g., 1 Chron. 13:2; and 2

Chron. 34:21) who must join the Southern Kingdom once more in order to have an "entire Israel." However, when such is ascertained, then the following is true: "With the existence of the remnant, in no way is the final state of salvation attained. So long as the nation is designated as a remnant the two entities of judgment and salvation may be newly and presently experienced and professed. . . . History is also seen in addition . . . as an entwinement of judgment and salvation."[132] That a fissure runs through the people of God is brought to expression more frequently and preferably without the use of the word "remnant" (cf. Isa. 65:1–16; and 66:1–4, 5f.).[133]

14.9   The Day of YHWH

It is different with the "Day of YHWH" which likewise is mentioned relatively frequently in prophetic proclamation.[134] A hope for salvation in and for Israel that is connected with this expression becomes clear through the contrast in Amos 5:18–20 where "this day" is mentioned for the first time. However, the understanding given to this day by Amos is just the opposite of the salvation for which the people hoped. Among the other books of the preexilic prophets, this "Day of YHWH" is then mentioned in Isaiah (Isa. 2:12; 13:6, 9; 22:5; and 34:8), Zephaniah (Zeph. 1:7, 8, 14–18; and 2:2f.), Jeremiah but only in 46:10, and Obadiah 15.[135]

In Ezekiel the "Day of YHWH" refers not only to a future day as was true in previously cited texts (Ezek. 7:7, 19; cf. 30:3), but also to the judgment against Jerusalem residing in the past (Ezek. 13:5; and 34:12). The Book of Joel takes up in detail the theme of the Day of YHWH as an event of judgment but once (Joel 1:15; 2:1, 11; 3:4; and 4:14), while in additional postexilic texts this day is mentioned only in Isa. 61:2 (cf. 63:4); Zech. 14:1; and Mal. 3:(2), 19, 23f.

Consequently, one first encounters in the "Day of YHWH" the people's expectation of salvation, a view that is opposed by Amos. This Day will be and will bring darkness for Israel, not light (Amos 5:18–20). Isaiah continues to see the content of the Day of YHWH in terms of an event of judgment, but he expands this to include a cosmic dimension (Isa. 2:12ff.). Zephaniah adds to this understanding by seeing in this Day a day of judgment that affects the entire earth and all the nations. According to the Book of Joel,[136] which is already on the way to apocalyptic, the Day of YHWH now has a sign, namely, a plague of locusts described as a mighty army (Joel 1:15; and 2:1, 11), that affects nature and history, Israel and the nations. However, the Day of YHWH becomes once more a day of salvation for those from Israel who return to YHWH (Joel 2:12f.). For Mal. 3:23 the Day of YHWH offers a solution to the question of theodicy raised by the distress mentioned in the book.

According to numerous passages, the prophets who proclaimed the Day of

YHWH saw it as "near at hand."[137] According to Isaiah 13, this day is directed primarily against the nations, as is the case in the present redactional context of Obadiah 15. However, in Obadiah the occasion was the behavior of the brother nation Edom that had committed an indecent assault against Judah. That the Day of YHWH was a time that had already affected Israel during its past is mentioned not only by the previously noted texts in Ezekiel (Ezek. 13:5; and 34:12) but also in Lam. 1:12; and 2:1, 21f., that is, in texts of the exilic period that look back to the past.

One named such a day the "Day of YHWH" probably because it was or could be entirely determined by and filled with the activity of this God. That one also spoke in a similar manner about other days in terms of the events that occurred during them is demonstrated in such expressions as the "Day of Midian" (Isa. 9:3) and the "Day of Jezreel" (Hos. 2:2) which were days of military actions, and the "Days of the Baals" (Hos. 2:15) which refer to cultic festival days devoted to this deity in his various manifestations. However, as concerns Israel, this day has less to do with the cult and more to do with history. This day is primarily a day of YHWH's action in history, originally for the benefit of his people. According to the view of many prophets of judgment, however, this day is characterized by an event that is directed *against* Israel. It is a day of YHWH's wrath, fire, and fury. Thus the concept of the "Day of YHWH" entered into the prophetic message, where it was reshaped and expanded. Here it receives a proclivity toward eschatology.

In a similar way, the expressions "on that day" (ביום ההוא = *bayyôm hahû'*) and "at the end of the days" (באחרית הימים = *bĕ'aḥărît hayyâmîm*) are also incorporated into the prophetic message and made useful. "On that day" did not primarily always mean the "Day of YHWH" but rather served as a purely temporal formula of linkage or envisioned some period of time (Exod. 32:28; Judg. 3:30; etc.) that was to emerge from the context. Often the formula was also introduced in redactional additions (e.g., Isa. 4:2; 10:20; and 11:10). It is similar to the formulae "in that time," "in those days," and "Behold, the days are coming."[138]

Also, the expression "at the end of the days"[139] primarily designates simply the future, a subsequent time, and the time of descendants (Gen. 49:1; Deut. 4:30; 8:16; Isa. 46:10; Prov. 29:21; etc.). Even the word "end" (קץ = *qēṣ*)[140] primarily stands for a temporal or spatial distance (Job 28:3; and 2 Kings 19:23). In Amos 8:2, the word is used for the threatened "end" of Israel. Ezekiel 7:2–6 takes up this term but does not give it the meaning of an absolute end (cf. Lam. 4:18). Genesis 6:13 (P) shifts this "end" to the distant past, prior to the primeval flood.[141] Habakkuk 2:3 allows one to recognize not only that but also how the phenomenon of the delay of the expected intervention of God, already familiar in the Old Testament prophets as a time of distress, was addressed. The "end of days" is first spoken about in Isa. 2:2–4 (par.) and then in

Ezek. 38:16, especially Dan. 2:28 and 10:14, and perhaps already also in the addition in Hos. 3:5. Consequently, even the word "end" as such now becomes for all intents and purposes in the Book of Daniel the term for the end of the world in view of the inbreaking kingdom of God (Dan. 11:27; and 12:6f., 12f.).

Thus it is good to recognize in all of these phenomena how the contents of the faith of Old Testament Israel integrates into the future expectation of Yahwistic faith and from there is taken into developing eschatology (and apocalyptic).

14.10   The Expectation of Salvation and the Promise of Salvation

Consequently, if there is the possibility of salvation,[142] then the basis for this is found only in YHWH. Amos makes this clear with the unique, hesitative "perhaps" of possible grace that resides only and entirely in YHWH and that could benefit only a remnant (Amos 5:15; cf. Zeph. 2:3; Joel 2:14; and Jonah 3:9). Hosea, on the one hand, has a final judgment in view,[143] but, on the other hand, he speaks of divine pedagogy in this judgment (Hos. 2:4–17; and 5:15) of purification and education,[144] and of repentance (Hos. 2:9, 18; 3:5; and 14:2).[145] As is the case with the Yahwistic testimony to the primeval flood,[146] it is YHWH himself who changes (Hos. 11:8f.) and therefore makes salvation possible. Isaiah also announces the coming judgment (Isa. 5:16f., 25–29; 9:7; 10:3f.; etc.), and recognizes it as a process of purification (Isa. 1:21–26).[147] He struggles with the question of the possibility of judgment and salvation (Isa. 28:23–29), since YHWH's nature is similar to that of a farmer who not only destroys through excessive threshing but also provides nourishment. A deliverance for, as well as to, Zion, where YHWH still dwells (Isa. 8:18), is perhaps in view (Isa. 14:32; 28:16; 29:1–7, 8; and 30:15–17). It is "the zeal of the Lord Sebaoth" who does this (Isa. 9:6; cf. 28:29). In the Book of Micah possible salvation is addressed only in the later additions (as, e.g., Micah 2:12f.).[148] In the Book of Jeremiah, the twofold mission of "plucking up and tearing down" and "building and planting" (Jer. 1:10) can be mentioned in this regard.[149] It is possible that Jer. 3:11–13, 14–17a, 21f.; 4:3f.; 6:27ff.; 23:1–8; 24:1–10; 29; 31:4f., 15–20; and 32 are to be regarded as formulations of an expectation of salvation[150] that does not revoke judgment against Judah but rather confirms how both judgment and salvation are alone grounded in YHWH's works.[151]

Ezekiel says therefore that YHWH will create such salvation not for the sake of Israel but rather for the sake of his own holy name (Ezek. 36:22f.). Also, the nations should not be able to say that YHWH may be powerless and may not be able to change destiny (Deut. 32:26f.), lest they be victorious not only over Israel but also over its God. This has to do with YHWH's honor. Salvation originates also as a wonder of God's new creation (Ezek. 36:26ff.; and 37:1–14; cf. Ps. 51:12ff.) and on the basis of YHWH's faithfulness (Isa. 14:1).

It is the divine "I" that is always the emphasized subject (cf. Jer. 31:31–34). It is YHWH himself who shows compassion to his people in judgment, who suffers under his own punishing action (Hos. 11:8f.; 14:5–8; and Jer. 12:7f.), and who again turns toward his people after the judgment is concluded (Hos. 2:21f.). It is in Amos (Amos 5:15), Isaiah (Isa. 28:16, 24–29), Ezekiel (Ezek. 20:32–44; 33:11; 36:16ff.; and 37:1–14), Hosea, and Jeremiah that the depiction of God opens up the positive perspectives concerning the future. It is Yahwistic faith as future expectation.

Pledges or promises of salvation[152] in the writings of the preexilic prophets are therefore not to be regarded principally as secondary. Nor are they always to be assigned to the postexilic community and its self-understanding or view of history. Moreover, the fact that this salvation must pass through the darkness of judgment and the recognition that there is no simple continuity are, for example, precisely indicated throughout. Many words of salvation not only presuppose aspects of judgment but also are incorporated within them. Thus the word of darkness in Isa. 8:23 stands before the promise of light in Isa. 9:1–6, the word of striking and disfiguring comes before the word of the king of salvation who shall come from Bethlehem (Micah. 5:1ff.), and the declaration of the return of the wife to her first husband in Hos. 2:8f. occurs in the context of the declaration of judgment in Hos. 2:7–15 (cf. the addition of Hos. 3:5 after Hos. 3:4). Subsequently, one ought not to smooth out too quickly the complexity existing within the prophetic proclamation of judgment and salvation.

Only Deutero-Isaiah,[153] as the "evangelist of the Old Testament," is no longer aware of a word of judgment against Israel. According to him, the nation has already suffered its punishment (Isa. 40:2) and has drunk the cup of wrath (Isa. 51:17). YHWH has expunged their sins for his own sake (Isa. 43:22ff.; cf. 48:11). Now it is time to announce comfort and salvation. What YHWH has previously proclaimed has dawned in its fullness (Isa. 42:9; 44:24ff.; 45:18f.; 49:14ff.; etc.), and therein YHWH demonstrates his power over history over against the speechless, powerless gods (Isa. 41:21–29; 43:8–13; and 45:18–25). Rather, the discussion is of YHWH's activity of salvation and of his "righteousness" (Isa. 42:6; 53:11; 41:2; 45:8, 13, 18f. 23,; 46:13; etc.).[154] In a new exodus out of Babylon, which in importance will surpass considerably the earlier exodus out of Egypt, YHWH himself will lead his people back to Zion. In so doing, he will demonstrate his sovereignty once more in Zion.[155] In this way the knowledge of YHWH will come to pass, indeed not only in Israel but also among the nations. They will join Israel on the basis of what has happened there and what they have seen.[156] "Not through a new obedience, not through new cultic ordinances, and not at all through human plans, but rather the future of the new people of God is here consolingly presented only through the promise of the new and now salvific coming of YHWH to his people."[157] The "I" of YHWH and his "I am YHWH" are newly and emphatically underlined (Isa. 41:4; 42:8; 43:11ff.; 44:6; 45:5–7; 48:11; etc.), for only he is able to create such salvation, a salvation that is grounded only in him.[158] Texts in Isaiah 56–66 (esp. Isaiah 56–59 and 65) then show by contrast that later on the question continued to be raised anew concerning the inbreaking of the announced salvation and its failure to appear. This absence of salvation was attributed to human behavior not in accord with the will of YHWH in the postexilic community. By contrast, Zechariah possessed the view on the basis of his night visions that this salvation might already be prepared in heaven (Zech. 1:7–6:8).

If the presently pledged or promised salvation for the future was to be made concrete, then this was possible only by reaching back to a former deed of YHWH. This salvation can only be declared by and through YHWH. It cannot be fulfilled by human wishes. The YHWH who elected David and made promises to him shall send a new Davidic ruler or rulers.[159] A new covenant[160] will surpass the earlier covenant of Sinai (Jer. 31:31–34), a thought that Hosea had already set forth (Hos. 2:20–25) and that Ezekiel and his students had carried forward in their own way (Ezek. 34:25; and 37:26). Also a new exodus will take place, a view that in Ezekiel was connected to a judgment of purification (Ezek. 20:32ff.) but in Deutero-Isaiah, by contrast, was entirely now a salvific gift.[161] Hosea's formulation had already led in this direction (Hos. 2:16ff.;[162] 11:8b-9; 12:10; and 14:2–9). The nation will be made new (Ezek. 36:26ff.;[163] 37:1ff.; Isa. 65:20–25; and 25:8), as will its temple (Ezekiel 40–48). The hope in an entirely new creation[164] is characteristically not withdrawn: in it the new Jerusalem preserves its significance (Isa. 65:17–25; 35:3–10; and 40:1–8, 9f.). YHWH's Spirit[165] will be that which creates this perfected people (Ezek. 11:19f.; 36:26f.; 39:29; Isa. 32:15; 44:3; 59:21; and Joel 3:1ff.). Becoming new is no longer only a demand that is addressed to Israel (Ezek. 18:31; cf., by contrast, Ezek. 36:26f.). Rather, in addition, this expression of YHWH's will encounters both the nation and even the world in a new way.[166] Portraits of peace among the nations (Isa. 2:2–4 par.) and among the beasts (Isa. 11:6–8; Hos. 2:20; etc.) blend together with colors from the representations of paradise. However, when such expressions are made, they open a vista that stretches, not backward to a golden age that has disappeared, but rather forward into the future.[167] The coming salvation is predictable only in exaggerated motifs of equivalence, since it has been located only in the sphere of divine possibilities and can obtain content and form only from God and his constitutions of salvation. Thus this salvation is portrayed either in elevated highlights or by denial that excludes previous negative experiences. Jeremiah 31:31–34 can serve as the model for both.

If prophetic words of salvation receive justifications, then they consequently can point only to YHWH, since all promises have their basis only in him. Also YHWH's forgiveness shall be then completely "eschatological" (Ps.

130:8; Isa. 35:10; 51:11; Jer. 3:22; 31:34; and Ezek. 36:25ff.), for he is the one who brings about the decisive turn of events and the one who "changes destiny." The expression used for this, שׁוּב שְׁבוּת = *šûb šĕbût,* for this reason has YHWH as the subject. The object is always a plural, and the goal that is pronounced is also positive (with the exception of Job 42:10).[168] "Thus one shall be able to judge that the future expectation, in all of its thematic variation, has its basis, center, and finally its purpose in reference to the divine 'I' and its exclusivity."[169] In this connection, it is then no longer really decisive or fundamental for the comprehensive understanding of Old Testament hope whether certain words of salvation are first attributable to a particular stratum (dependent upon Deutero-Isaiah) or to later redactions.[170]

The prophetic message in its developing eschatology comes to stand against ritual and cult as the attempt to secure completely human existence in the same way that prophecy comes to oppose the priesthood in general.[171] The outer and the inner ways of the eschatological message stand over against the inner and the outer ways of ritual,[172] for the eschatological message brings to an end the striving of humans to obtain the security of their own identity.

The prophetic books are redacted to follow the so-called two-part (judgment—salvation) or three-part (judgment against Israel, judgment against the nations, salvation) eschatological, schematic structure, and thus are shaped by this eschatological conviction of faith, here clearly that of the postexilic community.[173] The Book of Isaiah (Isaiah 1–35; chaps. 1–12; 13–23; and 24–35), the Book of Ezekiel (chaps. 1–24; 25–33; and 34–48), the Book of Jeremiah in the LXX version, and the Book of Zephaniah follow this latter structure, although each certainly only in a very rough way.

14.11   The Origins of Old Testament Apocalyptic

The fact that Old Testament apocalyptic developed primarily out of prophecy and not, as G. von Rad thought,[174] from wisdom is already indicated by the recognition that the first "apocalyptic" texts are found as additions to or redactions of prophetic writings and not wisdom literature. Indeed, Old Testament wisdom literature shows no acquaintance whatsoever with "eschatology."[175] In this connection, one thinks first of the description of war in Micah 4:11–13, then the prophecy about Gog and Magog in Ezekiel 38–39,[176] and after that the additions in Trito-Isaiah (Isa. 60:19f.; 65:17–25; and 66:20, 22–24) and some of the psalms (Pss. 22:28–32; and 69:31–37).[177] One cannot draw a sharp line at all between prophecy and apocalyptic, as the texts brought together in the books of Joel and Zechariah (1–8; 9–11; and 12–14) demonstrate, for not only has Zechariah 9–14 been viewed as standing under the influence of emerging apocalyptic but also Zechariah 1–8 has been portrayed as the first apocalypse.[178]

Zechariah 9–11 and 12–14 allow one to recognize clearly the conceptual influence of apocalyptic.[179] Since the nations were very much regarded as a menace to the Jewish community endangered by them, their own annihilation is threatened. The collapse of world power is announced by the use of metaphors (the cedars of Lebanon, and the oaks of Bashan; Zech. 11:1–3). Zechariah 11:4–17, the so-called allegory of the shepherds, is in the final analysis a kind of survey of history with a negative slant, while Zechariah 12–14 looks more into the promised future and the end of history. Again the pagan nations, which threaten Jerusalem,[180] are annihilated, while the land is freed from all impurity. However, the time of the prophets (or only the false ones?) is also now at an end (Zech. 13:3–6). The style of the book is more readily interpretation than prophetic discourse, and accordingly one is also on the way to apocalyptic. The present period is a time under sin. While the world power must be annihilated, Israel, however, must be gathered and liberated. Past prophecies of earlier prophets that had not yet been fulfilled are now brought to pass. A consciously archaic and also veiled linguistic usage was in the offing. Here prophecy has approached the threshold of apocalyptic. One awaits the entirely new, interprets afresh the old on the basis of the new, and sets forth new interpretations that lead into the fourth century B.C.E. However, all of this is done anonymously.

The Book of Joel, which is to be regarded as a unity,[181] likewise exhibits characteristics that clearly point to incipient apocalyptic. Because of the many references to earlier prophetic texts, the prophet, who is not designated as such, proves to be an interpreter who is actualizing these texts anew (e.g., Joel 1:15; 2:11, 13; 4:5; etc.). Furthermore, the book treats contemporary and sequential occurrences of disasters incurred by both nature and the nations and characterized by both cosmic and historical tribulation. The "Day of YHWH"[182] receives a universal character, and the new salvation, for which the prophet hopes, will come from YHWH in the form of his renewing spirit (Joel 3:1ff.) and shall be realized at Zion (chap. 4). In the Valley of Jehoshaphat, "world judgment" is to be carried out, the pagans are to be annihilated, and thereby Israel will learn that YHWH is its God (Joel 4:17). Even Isa. 2:2–4 is obviously corrected in a certain manner. As a whole, the Book of Joel is an entirely literary product where the concrete event (a plague of locusts?) signifies a portent of the end close at hand. In addition, the inbreaking of this end shall then bring the solution to the many questions that presently trouble the emerging apocalyptic seer.

The so-called Apocalypse of Isaiah (Isaiah 24–27)[183] is a textual conglomeration of eschatological announcements (e.g., Isa. 24:1–3, 21–23; and 25:6–8: the banquet of the nations on Zion, 27:1, 12f.), permeated with hymnic-like fragments (e.g., Isa. 25:1–5; 26:1–6; and 27:2–6) which in turn refer to laments, or, said in another way, the prayers of lament and hymns respond in different ways to the prophecies. However, the "situation" is not at all clear, although it involves the hardship that surrounds those who speak out here. The concrete temporal background is probably a persecution of Jews, like the one that occurred under Artaxerxes III (358–338 B.C.E.), and the "city" mentioned frequently in Isaiah 24–27 could be Samaria which was destroyed by Alexander the Great in 331 B.C.E. The fall of this city is considered to be a sign and prefiguration of the end time that is breaking into history, and during the persecution there obviously were martyrs who received the promise of resurrection,[184] a teaching that appears here for the first time in the Old Testament (Isa. 26:19).[185] A weakly emerging eschatological expectation was to become strengthened. Supplements show that new efforts continued to determine the drawing nigh of the eschatological present and to encourage people to see things through to the end in order to provide eschatological consolation during periods of tribulation.

14.12   Old Testament Apocalyptic (the Book of Daniel)

Old Testament apocalyptic[186] began first to take shape in additions and redactions (Trito-Isaiah; Zechariah 9–14) and then in small collections of texts (Isaiah 24–27; Joel) that were on their way to apocalyptic. However, it is not until the Book of Daniel,[187] originating in the second century B.C.E., that one finds the first and only "apocalypse" in the Old Testament.[188]

"*'Apocalypse' is a genre of revelatory literature with a narrative framework, in which a revelation is mediated by an otherworldly being to a human recipient, disclosing a transcendent reality which is both temporal, insofar as it envisages eschatological salvation, and spatial insofar as it involves another, supernatural world.*"[189]

Apocalyptic is therefore both an intellectual movement that was not limited to Palestine, let alone then to Israel, and a group of literary creations, that is, "literature of the end time." In this case, the Book of Daniel incorporates materials and texts from the time of the beginning of the second century B.C.E. to the period of the Maccabean revolt under Antiochus IV. The book achieves its final form sometime between 167 and 164 B.C.E., for it is not aware of the rededication of the temple and the death of Antiochus. While these texts still do not reflect in all of their parts the harsh situation of persecution under Antiochus IV, they do permit one to recognize that and how more isolated cases of trial and persecution first came about.

As an apocalypse, the Book of Daniel is a so-called "macro-*Gattung*" in which are incorporated various subordinate *Gattungen*. To these belong the vision reports,[190] which often are shaped like allegories, are given a very elaborate form, and attempt to comprehend history in a sweeping overview. As the four vision reports especially show (Daniel 7; 8; 9; and 10–12),[191] which here are clearly a stylistic instrument, the Book of Daniel is to be assigned more to the so-called "apocalyptic event" that exists alongside the so-called "apocalyptic report."[192] In the latter, the seer, for example, sets out on a heavenly journey and then describes what he may see in the heavens. Emotional, poetic, and metaphorical language involving symbols and images is preferred, and the influence of the mythological is recognizable. So Isa. 27:1 echoes something of the primeval battle with the dragon, while Daniel 4 (cf. Ezekiel 31) reflects much that has to do with the cosmic tree. In Daniel 7, the four animals from the deep reflect both contemporary and mythological features.

The historical surveys in the form of the future (Daniel 2; 7; 10–11) have their precursors in the summaries of history in Ezekiel (Ezekiel 16; 20; and 23; cf. also Acts 7:2–50). In these, "prophecies after the fact" (*vaticinia ex eventu*) are popular[193] (cf. Dan. 10:1–11:39), where history can be attested as meaningful and directed by God. Standing beside these are didactic narratives with examples for proper faithfulness in periods of affliction (Daniel 1; 3; and 6) and reports of war (cf. also Ezekiel 38f.; Zechariah 14; and Joel 4), which, for example, in Daniel 11 in many cases derive their pictorial material from earlier descriptions of the "Day of YHWH." Within the narratives, one also finds texts that already approach very closely the later martyr legends (Daniel 3 and 6). These texts contain indirectly for the reader(s) ethical admonitions. The present evil is coming to an end and the period of well-being is breaking into history in the form of the kingdom of God (Daniel 2; and 7). It is important to endure and to be faithful until this future arrives. Linear, inner-historical eschatology is here becoming end of time apocalyptic.

The Book of Daniel is the only apocalypse within the Old Testament. This kind of text found its further development, however, in early Judaism. Within this development, Persian influence first makes itself clearly noticeable.[194] Texts from the so-called *Ethiopic Book of Enoch,* such as the so-called Vision of Animals (*Eth. Enoch* 85–90), can in this connection be even older than the texts now incorporated in the Book of Daniel.[195] Between 250 B.C.E. and 150 B.C.E., perhaps as many as fifteen such apocalypses were formed in early Judaism. They were always understood as a "book," that is, as literature, and as a book of mystery that often contained instructions for the initiated scribes (Dan. 12:9ff.) and that wanted to be read and their secrets unlocked. Thus they are no longer oral texts. However, when they are able to be read, when they are "opened," then this is also a sign for the immanent end that is breaking into history (Dan. 12:4, 9). The apocalyptic seers understand themselves as initiated, "wise" interpreters of images, visions, dreams (Daniel 2 + 4), and secret writings on the wall (Daniel 5). Above all, however, they are interpreters of prophecy and can actualize it for their own present (Daniel 9). Thus the seventy years of Jer. 25:11ff. and 29:10 can be related and directed to the seer's own time as well as to that of his readers and followers. While the seer needs for his own understanding an interpreting angel (Dan. 4:10ff.; 7:16; 8:15f.; 9:21ff.; and 10:5ff.), he also stands out from the crowd of other "savants" (Dan. 11:33, 35; and 12:3) because of his knowledge and own individual destiny (Dan. 12:13). The readers also belong to such savants or are at least to be or to become ones. This knowledge is not the understanding that occurs in wisdom literature, meaning then that one does not seek the roots of apocalyptic in this corpus. Rather, apocalyptic has to do with a type of mantic wisdom,[196] a knowledge of the end time, a period in which one now lives. The end time, through interpretation, is and becomes recognizable as such. Investigations of the history of the form of apocalyptic as well as its world of images point rather to prophecy and here especially to Ezekiel and Deutero-Isaiah as the fundamental root of Old Testament apocalyptic.[197]

History is seen as a purposefully directed unity, although with a sequence of negative descents, something indicated by the statue's metals that become increasingly less valuable (Daniel 2).[198] Moreover, this history, which one now experiences as a time of suffering and of evil to which one does not acquiesce, is moving toward its end (Daniel). And the inbreaking kingdom of God stands in complete opposition to the kingdoms of history. The kingdom of God opposes them like a stone that is cast, but not by a human hand, against a multi-layered statue standing on very brittle feet. The statue standing on these feet refers to the present situation of the apocalyptic seer under the Diadochi, and the falling stone that topples the statue points to their collapse and end as a whole. Or the kingdom of God is likened to "a human form from heaven" that stands against "*four* beastlike creatures from below, that is, from the waters of chaos" (Daniel 7). The "Son of Man" from above stands as the greatest possible opposition to the four animals from below. This "Son of Man," according to Dan. 7:27, stands also for the "people of the holy ones of the Most High" who are to obtain a share in this kingdom of God. One places the eschatological counterforce of God against the situation of the experience of oppression with its power. The heavenly archetype, as, for example, the battle of the angels (Dan. 10:13), corresponds to its earthly likeness, and the heavenly event at the same time anticipates the corresponding earthly one, consoling thereby those who understand. During this temporal situation, when the kingdom of God is breaking into history, the initiated are at the same time the very ones threatened and are now called anew to faithfulness and obedience and to become strong in their hope. For this reason, the author preferred to remain anonymous and probably by necessity was required to do so, for he borrowed the name of a great saint from the past. That this was reputed to be "Daniel" is indicated by Ezek. 14:14, 20 (cf. 28:3) and probably also the Dan'el texts from Ugarit.[199] For the Enoch literature, one can point to Gen. 5:21–24.

Along with these polarities of the heavenly and earthly world, and of the kingdom of God and human kings, there is already present in the Book of Daniel a dualistic, otherworldly eschatology that is an important feature of apocalyptic thought. This is so even if the Book of Daniel does not explicitly speak of the contrast between the present (העולם הזה = *hā'ôlām hazzeh*) and the coming aeons (העולם הבא = *hā'ôlām habā'*),[200] but rather, it seems, of the vanquishing both of history and of the opposition of the world kingdoms that are passing away and of the coming kingdom of God. As a consequence, apocalyptic is occupied with the present in the face of a pending future, and this within the horizon of world history and cosmology. Here, personal, political, and cosmological eschatology flow together, for the coming kingdom of God will also bring about the resurrection of the dead (Isa. 26:19; and Dan. 12:1–3), even though Old Testament apocalyptic has not yet conceived of a general resurrection of everyone.[201] The Book of Daniel deals with the reckoning of the "times" (Dan. 7:25; 8:14; 9; 11:11f.; and 12:7)[202] and the "end" (קץ = *qēṣ;* Dan. 8:17, 19; 9:26; 11:27, 35, 40; and 12:4, 9, 13), while Daniel now has to grapple with the problem of the "delay of the parousia" and has to extrapolate the announced date (Dan. 12:7, 11, 12). Moreover, the goal is the eschatological sovereignty of God (Daniel 2; 7; 8:23; and 11:36). This can be called a sovereignty that is decisive not only and indeed primarily for the coming age but for the present one as well (Dan. 3:33; 4:14, 22, 31f.).[203] It is only a matter of a short time before this sovereignty is to be fully realized. Also in this double aspect of the discourse about the sovereignty of God is shown apocalyptic's consoling function. Resignation is resisted, and perseverance admonished. Consequently, apocalyptic does not exclude ethics but rather qualifies them, and the legends and visions that are united in the Book of Daniel are now joined together in such a way that the entire book speaks about trials and loyalty in view of the expectation of the kingdom of God.[204] For this reason, the Book of Daniel readily reverts from the Aramaic language of the older legends in Daniel and the first vision (Daniel 2) that concludes this earlier collection (Daniel 2–6; 7) to the "sacred" Hebrew language in the programmatically added first chapter and the concluding chapters of 8–12.[205]

If the announcement of the sovereignty of God can be placed even in the mouth of heathen rulers who praise the God of Israel as the only true God (Dan. 2:47; 4:31–34; and 6:27f.; cf. 3:29), then not only apocalyptic but indeed the entire Old Testament carries the conviction that he leads his own to salvation and successfully brings about the final establishment of his sovereignty. One places one's hope in YHWH who continues to be the God who in freedom comes to give aid (Dan. 3:17f.), who has the power to save, although he does not have to do so, and who is not to be renounced should he not intervene to provide help. The Old Testament awaits the sovereignty of God, even as Judaism later on awaits it as well. Christianity awaits this sovereignty together with both of these and offers the prayer, "Thy kingdom come." The one who has learned this prayer was aware that through his or her language and actions the kingdom of God was dawning. This tension is to last until YHWH will be entirely accepted as king and will be revealed "on that day" (Isa. 2:17; Zech. 14:9; cf. Obadiah 21).

Chapter 15. The Chosen People of God and the Nations[1]

If it is the case that the Old Testament witness finds its center in the affirmation that YHWH opens himself to community with human beings through the historical election of Israel (cf. Vol. I, pp. 27–39) and that this divine action moves beyond this nation by its serving both an exemplary and intercessory purpose, then he is shown by this election of a people to be a God whose power extends over the world. This means then that election is not only election "from" (Deut. 7:6; 10:14f.; 14:2; cf. Isa. 41:8f. and already Amos 3:2) but also election "to."[2] In other words, Israel's "election is for service."[3]

15.1 A Comprehensive Overview of Election

When YHWH led the people out of Egypt and thereby consummated their primal election,[4] he had proved himself to be Lord over a foreign nation and a hostile land. In the course of negotiations between Moses (together with Aaron) and the Egyptian pharaoh, the question, in the final analysis, already concerns whether YHWH will prevail or whether the Egyptians and their gods will triumph. The Yahwist and the Priestly document take up this question, each in its own way, within the literary contexts of the exodus event. According to Exod. 12:32 (J), Moses and Aaron are to pray for a blessing for pharaoh, while according to Exod. 12:12 (P), YHWH shall execute a judicial punishment against the gods of Egypt.[5] If YHWH then led Israel into a land that was possessed by other peoples, he must show himself to be the Lord also of these nations. The books of Joshua and Judges intentionally narrate the story of this lordship. If Israel was to be constituted and then maintained in this new land, it must live both in opposition to these nations and with them. The prophet Hosea, Deuteronomy, and the texts that reflect[6] the so-called Zion tradition may be mentioned in reference to the problem that has been noted.[7] If one could speak of an assault of the nations against the city of God, or of a gathering of the nations to pay homage there, or of a pilgrimage of the nations to this sacred place,[8] then the relationship of Israel as well as of its God to these peoples came into view. If one sang about or hoped for YHWH's kingship over the world,[9] then this had to do with his sovereignty over the nations. If the prophets could invoke the foreign nations as the instruments of YHWH's judgment against his own people,[10] or could call the Babylonian king Nebuchadrezzar a "servant of YHWH" (Jer. 25:9; 27:6; and 43:10), or could point to the Persian king Cyrus as the messiah who was the instrument of YHWH's salvation, then it becomes clear that the question concerning the nations, including both their salvation and their destruction, is often addressed within the writings of the Old Testament.

The election of Israel neither signaled YHWH's renouncement of the other nations nor involved their rejection in any way, a fact that Deutero-Isaiah later makes clear when he explicitly shapes this affirmation into a leading theme.[11] According to the Table of Nations in Genesis 10, a type of literary document that is without analogy in the ancient Near East, Israel enjoys vis-à-vis the nations no preeminence due to creation, mythology, or prehistory. According to Amos 9:7, Israel in addition was given no historical primacy. Israel stood in the center of the world and "humanity (formed) a concentric circle with the chosen people as the middle point"[12] for the first time in the Chronicler (1 Chron. 1:1–2:2). YHWH's assignment of the nations to other gods or, vice versa, the stars as gods to other nations (Deut. 32:8f. conjectural;[13] 4:19; cf. Psalms 58; 82; 89:7ff.; and Isa. 24:21) represents one of the few systematic attempts to give theological expression to Israel's and YHWH's relationships to the nations and their gods. Even so, according to Amos 9:7, YHWH has set not only Israel but also other nations on a historical journey under divine guidance.

Election faith and thought tend toward a certain universalism. In Deutero-Isaiah yet again, this is especially well recognizable. If the servant of God[14] mentioned in Deutero-Isaiah is also the "light to the pagans" (Isa. 42:9; 49:6) and if various statements about YHWH, Israel, and the nations are especially clustered together in both this text and the texts and writings that are dependent upon it, then it is evident at the same time that there was an ever clearer, developing monotheism. In the search for God, this developing monotheism had and must have had a progressive and illuminating influence on both Israel and the other nations and their gods. However, if it can be assumed that already in its early period Israel had accepted a certain YHWH-only worship,[15] then it is probable that the question concerning the relationship of the foreign nations to the God of Israel quickly emerged. A look at the development of this issue[16] shall corroborate this. Already according to the Yahwist, Israel is a blessing to the nations (Gen. 12:3; etc.; see below), and its election is both a gift and a mission for this people. Election and the kingdom of God belong together, but not election and a restrictive, exclusive well-being.[17]

15.2 A Historical Look at "Israel and the Nations"

Israel saw itself as different from the peoples in its social milieu, as a nation that did not have magicians or soothsayers, and that did not reckon itself among the other nations (Num. 23:9, 23).[18] It spoke differently from the way they spoke about the king,[19] had a significantly different conception of God, increasingly rejected idols, and so forth. However, Israel also had integrated a great number of things from these nations into its faith, although it more or less reshaped what it borrowed. These things included the value it placed on the city of God and the temple, and its view of the cultus, the world, and the realm of the dead. Thus Israel's position toward the nations during the course of its history continued to vary and to change in many ways.[20]

According to the Song of Deborah, one of the oldest texts in the Old Testament, YHWH fought on the side of Israel against the kings of Canaan (Judg. 5:19; cf. 4:12ff.). Israel, even as its God, stood in military opposition to the former inhabitants of the land. Israel's conquest, including the manner in which it occurred and the identity of those who may be numbered among and who belonged to this "Israel," had to be waged against other nations that dwelt in the land before its arrival and then continued to inhabit the land afterward. Joshua 2–11 depicts this conquest as especially a military undertaking, while the following period of the Judges, with the efforts to secure the land, is replete with military conflicts with attacking neighbors. During these conflicts, Israel found itself being pulled ever closer together, something that reached its culmination during the time of Saul and David. These two rulers were also very active in military engagements and had to be.[21]

However, it was probably the Yahwist who was the first to consider the relationship of Israel to the nations. In the words of Noah in Gen. 9:18f., Noah not only named his God in invoking a blessing over Shem (the ancestor within whom Israel was also concealed) but also clearly demarcated him from cursed Canaan. In the Yahwistic portion of the Table of Nations (Genesis 10*), Israel nowhere appears. It is simply not incorporated into the world of the nations but rather stands in opposition to this world so that from Genesis 12 on, the story of Israel and its uniqueness could be told. In this narration, the Yahwist, who belongs to the period of the Davidic-Solomonic empire,[22] sets forth the relationship of Israel to the nations. This relationship is portrayed as one in which Israel serves as the conduit of YHWH's blessing to the nations (Gen. 12:3; 28:14; 26:24b [secondary?]; and 22:18 [secondary]; cf. Isa. 19:24f.; Jer. 4:2), although from time to time this blessing was obtained in a rather negative manner (Gen. 19:30–38).[23] What the Yahwist means here is more a life that blesses than an action (cf. Exod. 9:16), more a continuing effect of the power of blessing imparted to Israel, along with the gifts and the character of God, than an active mediation of blessing in the form of imperative and commission.[24] What YHWH does to and for Israel is the genuinely marvelous deed (Exod. 34:10 J), and thus even the Egyptian king asks Moses and Aaron to procure for him the blessing of the God of Israel (Exod. 12:31f.). According to Exod. 7:17; 8:18; and 9:29 (J), the pharaoh (certainly for him with negative consequences) is also to come to a knowledge of YHWH. YHWH is therefore present even in Egypt, and even this land belongs to his sphere of activity.[25] With the exception of the Book of Job (Job 7:20; 10:14; and 33:27), where certainly Job and his friends are not Israelites, only the Yahwist is familiar with a confession of sins made to YHWH that comes from the mouth of a foreigner (Exod. 9:27; 10:16; and Num. 22:34).[26] However, the fact that at the same time nations are conquered and the persecutors of Jacob are destroyed by YHWH (Num. 24:8, 18f.: J) indicates already that even here no single point of view was expressed about the nations. It was the empire of David, which was expanded by military means, that the Yahwist also is interpreting here. In addition, he has described Israel's fundamental experience of the salvation at the sea (Exodus 14) as an act of YHWH war, with the Egyptians as the victims.[27]

The Elohist is yet again more clearly restrained, since for him the concern for Israel's distinctiveness vis-à-vis its social environment is more important (Num. 23:9, 21–24). The Elohist does not state that Israel performed the role of mediating blessing to the nations. And to be sure, he does not narrate a primeval history, since he wants to establish a far more distinct boundary between the thought and faith of Israel and the thought and faith of its ancient Near Eastern environment. He wishes necessarily to be able to avoid any borrowing of material from this cultural environment, and thus he begins his story with Abraham and what is specifically Israelite.[28]

Texts that are possibly ancient tell of the admission of foreigners to the nation and to the congregation of Israel (Josh. 2:9f.; 9:9f.), making clear that this Israel was not a tightly closed community.[29] Genesis 34:21–23 permitted Canaanites and Israelites to live together, if the former allowed themselves to be circumcised. It is scarcely possible to elucidate the chronological background as well as the intent of this text.[30] Is it the case that the "foreigners" in Shechem were admitted to the congregation of Israel (Joshua 24)?

Amos summoned the nations immediately neighboring Israel to YHWH's judgment (Amos 1:3–2:16),[31] the basis for which is not entirely limited to the crimes they committed against Israel, a point made in Amos 2:1–3. Amos does not reflect upon the reason that these nations stand under the judgment of YHWH, but he obviously presupposes one. However, it is true that what is especially singled out is their brutality in the conduct of war.[32] Does Amos think that YHWH's power in history and his will extend beyond Israel to other nations? Does this text in Amos not have to do with the recognition of a general, obligatory, fundamental ethic for all nations? Or were these (authentic)[33] oracles directed against the nations that once had been a part of the great empire of David and therefore could have known something of YHWH?

For Hosea, the nations did not provide a theme, although he probably wanted to see the religion and ethos of the Canaanites more strongly demarcated from those of Israel (Hos. 2:4ff.; 4:12ff.; 8:1ff.; 10:5ff.; etc.). Micah also was silent when it came to the nations,[34] although, like his contemporary, Isaiah, he did give some thought to the Assyrians, for he speaks about the coming, military event that is directed against Israel, Judah, and Jerusalem (Micah 1:5ff., 10ff.; 3:9ff.). However, it is a later redactor who (according to Micah 1:2) expresses the view that this happens before the eyes and ears of the nations.[35]

Isaiah clearly sees in Assyria the instrument of YHWH's judgment against Israel. However, in view of Assyria's hubris exhibited because of this role, it too will fall under the judgment of YHWH (Isa. 10:5ff.; 14:24–27). Along with this, Isaiah examines the topic of the nations[36] in their relationship to Judah. While the nations are reputed to be Judah's helpers, it should not rely upon them (Isa. 7:1–9; 8:1–4; 28:14–22; etc.). Although the assault of the nations will break forth upon Jerusalem and Zion, YHWH will shatter them, for he dwells there and still lays claim to his city and his temple (Isa. 8:9f., 18; 17:12–14; 28:16). Even here the ideology of YHWH war continues to have its effect. However, the promise that the nations will go in pilgrimage to Zion (Isa. 2:1–4) is secondary and postexilic.[37]

In the Book of Isaiah, one finds for the first time since Amos a collection of sayings dealing with the nations (Isaiah 13–23) that is, however, considerably more detailed than this earlier one. One also can add to this collection the so-called Isaiah apocalypse (Isaiah 24–27).[38] Moreover, this collection of sayings about the nations consists chiefly of secondary material and sets forth rather different evaluations of the foreign nations as a whole and of individual ones. One has ever again introduced into these collections (cf. Jeremiah 46–51; Ezekiel 25–32; 35; and Zeph. 2:4–15) experiences, hopes, and wishes concerning the nations that derive from Israel's continuing history. Since Israel has shaped its history to a large extent by reference to the foreign powers and since most of this history must have been experienced as suffering, what predominate here, therefore, are the words of judgment against the other nations.[39] The contexts in which these oracles concerning the nations originated are often no longer recognizable, since the texts, as, for example, Isaiah 13 + 14,[40] have been largely transformed into what is generally typical. Thus the Babylonians, for example, become purely and simply the symbol of the enemy of God, and thereby the enemy of Israel. In addition, one can find the hope expressed for the conversion of the Egyptians (Isa. 19:18ff.) and an extension of Israel's blessing to Egypt and Assur, which stands at the same time alongside a word of judgment against Egypt (Isa. 19:1ff.). Oracles against the Philistines (Isa. 14:28ff.) and Moab (Isa. 15:1ff.) could have derived from Isaiah himself. However, while Babylonia (Isaiah 13; 14; 21:1–9), Tyre, and Sidon are also mentioned (Isa. 23:1ff.), it is remarkable that no speech is directed against Babylon in the oracles of the exilic Ezekiel.

According to Zephaniah (2:4ff., 8ff., 12, 13ff; and 3:6–8), judgment shall be carried out against the Philistines, the Ammonites, the Ethiopians, and the

Assyrians. This judgment will annihilate these nations, while Israel will be puri-fied. Additions to Zephaniah in 2:11b and 3:9f. speak of salvation for those peo-ples who are restored. For Habakkuk, the "Chaldeans" (= Neo-Babylonians) are YHWH's rod of discipline against Israel (Hab. 1:5ff.), and Nahum turns his words almost entirely against a foreign nation. This judgment against Nineveh, and thus against the Assyrians, will bring salvation to Israel (Nahum 2:4–3:19). Within these oracles concerning the nations in the minor prophets, material is found that either derives from or is given different emphases by a good deal of secondary or redactional editing.[41]

That the nations are able to receive a positive portion in the activity of YHWH is often stated in relationship to the existence of Zion from where this salvation goes forth. At the same time, however, it is this same Zion by which the nations will be broken (cf. Psalms 46; 48; however also 47:10; Isa. 2:2–4; Micah 4:1–4; and Jer. 3:14–18).

The major ideas of Deuteronomy revolve around the actualization of the proper people of God. Here the neighboring nations immediately to the east in the Transjordan, along with their land, are especially not counted any longer in the land promised to Israel (Deut. 2:1–3:11). Furthermore, in this book, the non-Israelite nations and previous inhabitants who have settled in the land ap-pear primarily as a religious threat to Israel (Deut. 6:14; etc.). Consequently, YHWH will and Israel should drive them out (Deut. 4:38; 9:4f.; 11:23; and 18:12 Deuteronomistic; cf. Exod. 23:32f.)[42] or annihilate them through the ban (Deuteronomy 7; etc.). Here one encounters a stratum of the Deuteronomistic School that continues to consider this issue. This stratum concludes that the ban is valid and is something that should be used in order to eliminate the temp-tation to apostasy and thus to escape the resulting punishment of the exile.[43] The separation of Israel from the nations and their customs is required here, and this demand was to be assisted by militant means. Thus Deuteronomy con-tains laws for the conduct of warfare (Deuteronomy 20).

The so-called law of the congregation (Deut. 23:2–9), by contrast, is a post-exilic text, added to (the Deuteronomistic) Deuteronomy, that describes the na-tions on the basis of their genealogy and seeks to determine Israel's self-understanding vis-à-vis foreigners as well as its position toward them. This text, which perhaps has appropriated an older, basic source,[44] does not ask the question of what the "congregation of YHWH" (קהל יהוה = *qhl yhwh*) consists. Rather, it asks who can join this congregation, and how it is to preserve itself as the pure people of God. Here the provisions concerning Moab and Ammon from Deuteronomy 2 are revised. All of this points to a theme that comes close to the problems of mixed marriages (Ezra 9:1–4; 10; and Neh. 13:23ff.).[45] Also later than Deuteronomy proper are the texts of Deut. 32:8f. (conjecture) and Deut. 4:19f., according to which YHWH has assigned the foreign gods to their respective nations, something that then is applied to the cult of the stars.[46]

Also according to the Deuteronomistic History, the nations are especially a threat to the faith of Israel (Judg. 2:3; 2:6–3:6). Here one is compelled to reflect explicitly on why it was that Israel could not drive out or annihilate them and to do so presumably according to the will of YHWH. If Israel becomes "like the nations" (1 Sam. 8:5; Deut. 17:14 Deuteronomistic), then the punishment for this falling away (cf. also Amos 5:26), like sin, shall be a constituent part of the judgment itself. The consequences of this judgment will lead to Israel's and/or Judah's being scattered among the nations, becoming the object of their mockery, and being forced to serve there their false gods (Deut. 4:28; 28:36, 64; and 1 Kings 9:7; cf. also Lev. 26:33; Jer. 9:15; and Neh. 1:8). Thus it is clear that an exilic reality is reflected here.[47] The statement that the nations shall voice their derision in view of the catastrophe overtaking Israel, Judah, and Jerusalem is a frequently found motif in the Deuteronomistic literature. However, these nations will not be allowed to say: "Where now is their God?" Israel and YHWH as well should not become the object of the nations' scorn. Consequently, with the indication of this unseemly situation facing YHWH, the attempt is made to move him to change the fortunes of Israel.[48] In addition to the Deuteronomistic passages, there are likewise primarily exilic texts that argue in this same fashion. Threatened by events that had just transpired in the preexilic period, Judah faced the possibility of becoming the object of the nations' scorn.

Second Kings 5 describes an individual case within the Deuteronomistic History in which a high-placed Syrian official not only receives healing from the Yahwistic prophet Elisha but also through this act comes to believe in his God. However, because this Syrian cannot serve YHWH back in his own homeland, he takes soil with him from Israel.[49] Furthermore, since he cannot escape from his duty to attend temples of his former gods, he is sent away by the prophet in peace that carries with it a pronounced tolerance. The prophet's statement, "Depart in peace" (לך לשלום‎ = lēk lĕšālôm), resists all purism and radicalism. This does not simply free one to decide what is right; rather, it expresses the desire for an obedience based on freedom. This statement already exhibits something of the belief in the "justification of the sinner" by God, and this in regard to a non-Israelite.[50]

Jeremiah proclaims the message of the "enemy from the north" that also and above all points to the Babylonians as the instrument of YHWH's judgment against Judah. Because he speaks of war against Judah (Jer. 4:5–6:30), he receives from all sides increasing opposition from his contemporaries and comes to experience a growing, personal anguish. His message is contested *expressis verbis* by other prophets (Jer. 23:9ff.; 27–28). That Nebuchadrezzar, the Babylonian king, can receive the title "servant of YHWH" (Jer. 25:9; 27:6; and 43:10) is fully in line with Jeremiah's proclamation, even if this designation may belong to secondary texts. That Jeremiah was also to have been a "prophet to the nations" (Jer. 1:5) is not a statement that is to be taken literally in spite of the oracles concerning the nations that are collected in the book (Jeremiah 46–51).[51] In regard to these oracles, those against Babylon (Jer. 50:1–51:58) and Damascus (Jer. 49:23–27) certainly do not belong to the preaching of Jeremiah, while the word against Egypt (Jer. 46:3–12) could indeed have come from him. Moreover, in speaking of the cup of drunkenness and the sword (Jer. 25:15ff.), Jeremiah utters a word of judgment that offers the sure results of what will happen to the nations.

The prophet Obadiah in the year 587 B.C.E. turns against the neighboring nation of Edom which had enriched itself by means of the catastrophe of Judah and had looked down upon its brother nation. Whether these statements reflect reality or contain slander that had by now become a literary topos cannot be resolved here (cf. also Ezek. 25:12f.; 35:1–15; Joel 4:19; and Ps. 137:7).[52]

According to Ezekiel, even the nations are to "know that I am YHWH."[53] Corresponding to this, Ezek. 3:6 indicates that the pagans rather than Israel would hear the message of Ezekiel. YHWH's activity in history shall be the means of this knowledge, and YHWH acts for the sake of his honor as well as his name which he does not desire to see defamed before the nations.[54] Among these nations, a critical stance is taken especially toward Egypt (Ezekiel 29–32), because it had enticed Judah to rebel against Nebuchadrezzar and thus to join it in its downfall. In addition to this, there is an extensive oracle against Tyre (Ezek. 26:1–28:19) which shall fall under judgment because it rejoiced over the fall of Jerusalem. In addition, the oracles of judgment against the neighboring nations of Ammon, Moab, Edom, and the Philistines (Ezekiel 25 and 35) are joined together because of their common stance against Judah during its collapse and destruction. However, Babylon does not receive an oracle of accusation or of judgment, for Israel still had to bow the knee before Babylonian power.

The Priestly source (Exod. 7:5; and 14:4, 18) states that the Egyptians are to know "that I am YHWH."[55] Accordingly, this knowledge most assuredly will not lead to the punishing act of YHWH but, in clear proximity to Deutero-Isaiah, to the mighty deed of YHWH's leading Israel out of "Egypt." Although P is normally "rather strongly linked to Israel,"[56] it also designates the covenant of Noah (Gen. 9:1–17) as one that concerns "all flesh" (Gen. 9:15), while elements of P may also be found in the Table of Nations in Genesis 10.

In Deutero-Isaiah the Persian king Cyrus astonishingly is designated the "messiah" (Isa. 45:1), meaning that he is the (even eschatological?) instrument of YHWH's salvation of his people. Further, the prophet announces that the exiles shall be led home to Zion in a new exodus from Babylon, an act of redemption that the nations themselves shall see. This too shall entice and lead them to the knowledge of YHWH.[57] While Deutero-Isaiah was able to feature the election of Israel by YHWH (Isa. 41:8f.; 43:10; and 44:1f.) as no other prophet did,[58] he also was the one who at the same time expresses a positive view of the nations. Election here is unequivocally both an election "from" and an election "to." Since the nations were included within the activity of YHWH's salvation, Israel becomes YHWH's witness to them (Isa. 43:10; 44:8; and 55:4). Israel and the chosen servant of God are the "light to the nations" (Isa. 42:6; 49:5f.; cf. 51:4). However, this is not (yet) to be understood as an active call to mission.[59] Rather, YHWH's activity on behalf of his people shall possess the power of attraction (cf. Isa. 60:1–3) that works outwardly in an enticing fashion (Isa. 55:4f.) to demonstrate the truth of YHWH before the rest of the world. And the prophet risks promising and declaring all of this during the situation of the Babylonian exile when Israel has hit rock bottom! Courtroom scenes between YHWH and the nations or their gods make precisely clear YHWH's uniqueness and powerfulness over history. One is to recognize that these foreign gods do not possess these divine features but rather are thoroughly impotent (Isa. 41:21–29; 43:8–13; 44:6–8; and 45:18–25). It is both striking and significant that in Israel's conflict with the nations their gods, not only here in Deutero-Isaiah but also elsewhere, either play a subordinated role or are just simply passed by (compare to this only the sayings of Amos against the nations).[60]

According to Haggai, it is only the wealth of the nations that will be brought to Jerusalem in order to accelerate the rebuilding of the temple (Hag. 2:6–9), while according to Zechariah, YHWH will liberate from the power of the nations those exiles who have not yet returned home (Zech. 2:10–13). However, close to this word of liberating judgment stands another in which other nations "on that day" also will attach themselves to YHWH. Even so, there will be no opposition to Judah and Jerusalem continuing to retain their special place (Zech. 2:15f.). Zechariah 8:23 testifies to this in a similar way, while in 8:13 it can be said that Judah will very well be a blessing to the one who utters its name and no longer a curse. Genesis 12:3 appears to be taken up here.

A similar reference to Gen. 12:3 is possibly present also in Ps. 47:10 where the princes of the nations are assembled as the people of the God of Abraham. The chronological context of Psalm 47, and the questions of its uniformity and lastly its precise interpretation, are contested issues.[61] In any case, the positive reference to the nations is connected with the kingship of YHWH over all the earth, a kingship that came to be in primeval times and now is cultically actualized anew (Deut. 33:5).[62] However, in addition to this, this psalm prefers to think more of an attachment of these (princes of the) nations to the God of Abraham and their recognition of him (cf. Josh. 24:2ff.) than of Israel's serving as the conduit of blessing to the nations in the sense of Gen. 12:3.[63]

How complex the Old Testament position toward the nations is and continues to be can be demonstrated in an exemplary fashion by reference, on the one hand, to Isaiah 56–66[64] (cf., e.g., Isa. 56:3ff.; 59:18–21; 60:3, 8ff.; 63:1–6; and

66:15–23) and Zech. 12:1–13:6, and, on the other hand, to Zech. 14:1–21. According to the last-mentioned text from the Book of Zechariah, the nations shall be smashed to pieces at Jerusalem. However, they shall first conquer Jerusalem and only afterward will they be annihilated. In spite of this, the text can still speak of those from the nations who have survived and who then make an annual pilgrimage to Jerusalem (Zech. 14:16f.). While they are not named, those who do not participate in this pilgrimage will consequently experience punishment (Zech. 14:17–19).

In the Book of Malachi, it is surprising to find in Mal. 1:11 the statement that YHWH's name is great everywhere among the pagans (Ezek. 36:23; and Ps. 113:3f.) and that in various and sundry places sacrifice actually is offered in his name (cf. Isa. 19:19). Even if it is not easy to determine either the period in which (consciously placed after Mal. 1:10) this addition (Mal. 1:11–14)[65] was made or how it is to be concretely fulfilled,[66] this statement still remains an isolated, climactic thesis within the Old Testament. Micah 4:5 (as also a postexilic text) determines by contrast that each nation walks in the name of its God. Over against this, Israel ("we") walks forever and ever in the name of YHWH.

According to Joel 3:1, an outpouring of the Spirit of YHWH comes "over all flesh" in connection with the eschatological turn of events that is promised here. In contrast to this, the Chronicler's History and the books of Ezra and Nehemiah are not especially interested theologically in the nations. Rather, these writings strive primarily to achieve the consolidation and circumscription (cf. בדל = *bdl* in Ezra 6:21; 9:1; 10:11; Neh. 9:2; and 10:29) of the postexilic congregation as the "true Israel."[67] 1 Chronicles 16:8, 20, and 28 are verses appropriated from the psalms that have been inserted into this context; 2 Chron. 6:32f. follows almost entirely 1 Kings 8:41–43, although 1 Kings 8:42a is omitted. According to Ezra 6:12, Darius threatens each nation with death that hinders the building of the temple (cf. Esth. 8:11). Nehemiah 9:22 reaches back to Numbers 21, while Neh. 9:24, 30, and 32 looks at Israel's historical experiences with the nations. On the basis of Ezra 9:1–4, mixed marriages with foreign women were forbidden in Ezra 10:1ff. and Neh. 13:23ff. The separation from foreigners is explained as a principle in Neh. 9:2 and 13:30. Later in the *Book of Jubilees,* this program of separation is expanded.[68]

The books of Ruth and Jonah oppose the narrowness of the postexilic community. On the one hand, even an ancestress of David is derived from Moab (Ruth 4:17) and also is spoken about in a positive way. On the other hand, heathen sailors offer better prayers than does the Israelite prophet, while the evil city of Nineveh responds openly to his preaching. In Nineveh the heathen human beings and even their animals do penance because of the preaching of Jonah (Jonah 3:5ff.), while YHWH "repents" over the evil he had resolved to carry out against them.[69] Moreover, there is the contrast between Jonah who is angry over things of no consequence and the God whose mercy extends to the pagans (Jonah 4:1f.).[70] With the question about the justification of this divine compassion toward such a large number of ignorant heathen still open for the reader to ponder (Jonah 4:11), the Book of Jonah brings its narrative to a conclusion in a manner that is both significant and skillful.

According to the Book of Daniel, the world kingdoms that are viewed in this changing situation stand in absolute opposition to the sovereignty of God (Daniel 2 and 7) and are annihilated when he comes (cf. Dan. 11:40ff.). Moreover, the Babylonian king is able to come to the knowledge that the God of Daniel and his companions, therefore the God of the faithful in Israel, is the God over all other gods and the king over all other kings (Dan. 2:47; cf. 4:34). This God alone is able to deliver (Dan. 3:29), and his sovereignty exists now and forever (Dan. 3:32f.; 4:31f.; and 6:27f.). The heathen king looks, in the final analysis, through to the true situation and describes the outcome of every event. While Israel suffers under this foreign power, the indication of the true state of affairs comes forth from the mouth of its ruler, pointing to the turn of events that is to be introduced and made possible by YHWH. The God of Israel continues still to work, and even now in the time of eschatological tribulation, he is directing history once again through foreign rulers and nations.

The Old Testament wisdom literature has not taken up the position of Israel or of Israelites toward the nations as one of its themes. This literature was itself "international" in character and possessed a general, human orientation to life. Wisdom had as the center of its interest the individual person in his or her everyday existence. However, missing is any theme involving individual Israelites approaching their problems of faith and life on the basis of their special identity as Israelites,[71] at least not until later in the books of Jesus ben Sira and the Wisdom of Solomon. Job and his friends were purposefully left or identified as non-Israelites (Job 1:1; 2:11), and in their dialogues (Job 3–27) they speak neither about nor to YHWH[72] but rather use more general designations such as אל = 'ēl, אלוה = 'ĕlôah, אלהים = 'ĕlōhîm, and שׁדי = šadday.[73]

Finally, the Book of Esther sees in the opposing power of the Persians the great threat against Israel. The plan to murder the Jews was prevented, and the countermeasure of their actually murdering their own enemies was permitted (Esth. 9:15), something that was carried out in a frightful manner (Esth. 9:16).

Old Testament Israel has endured its history much more than it has shaped it. It had experienced oppressive foreign domination, and it had to try to resist more powerful opponents. It was led by its God to a land that was settled by other nations, had to conquer this land (in any case according to the description in Joshua 2–11) by military action, and had to defend itself against hostile neighbors, according to the testimony of the Book of Judges and of 1 Samuel. Accordingly, if the "military camp" was experienced "as the cradle of the nation,"[74] where the Man of War Yahweh (Exod. 15:3) was present and active, then as a result the nations were experienced mostly as opponents and as a danger and threat to Israel. These experiences and Israel's continuing problem of securing its own identity make a lasting impact on the disjunctive position of the Old Testament toward the nations. However, it is all the more astonishing[75] when other voices are registered within the Old Testament that consider the possibility of salvation both for the nations and especially for "strangers," although less astonishing when these voices do not say only negative things about "foreigners."

15.3 The Foreigner and the Stranger

It is a rare occurrence in the Old Testament writings when something positive is said about the "foreigner" (נכרי = *nŏkrî;* also זר = *zēr*).[76] The foreigner does not come from the people of Israel but rather is often either a nonresident merchant who is of some means (Neh. 13:16) or a soldier (thus mostly identified as a זר = *zēr;* cf. Isa. 1:7; 29:5) from a distant land who hardly desires to become a resident. The foreigner is not a brother to the Israelites (Deut. 17:15; cf. 15:3) and indeed worships "foreign" gods (Deut. 31:16; 32:12; Mal. 2:11; etc.). Foreign women represent a danger to Israel's loyalty to YHWH, something that can be seen in the case of Solomon (1 Kings 11:1; cf. Neh. 13:26).

Whether the "strange woman" often warned about in the Book of Proverbs is a foreigner or simply the wife of another Israelite cannot always be clearly decided (Prov. 2:16; 5:20; 6:24; and 7:5). Or should one take this warning to be "consciously ambiguous"?[77] Moreover, it is conspicuous that she is designated as a נכריה = *nokriyyâ* ("foreign woman"), a term that does not lend itself well to viewing her as a "wife of another (Israelite)." However, the question arises as to whether the (certainly in Proverbs 1–9, later, post-exilic) wisdom that is presented here is consciously Israelite or whether it resonates with what is a more universal aversion to strangers.

According to Deut. 15:3 and 23:21, one may exact a loan from a foreigner even in the Sabbath year and receive interest. Loans and the charging of interest to foreigners, especially those who were merchants, were thoroughly familiar practices. These practices involve foreigners and thus require special handling by and within Israel, since they do not affect "the solidarity within the clan and the tribe."[78] One may even sell to the foreigner (and to the stranger) an animal that has not been ritually slaughtered or even one that was dead (Deut. 14:21; differently in Lev. 17:10–16). In the postexilic period, Israelite men were prohibited from marrying foreign women (Ezra 10:2ff.; Neh. 13:26f.; cf. Mal. 2:11), although the Book of Ruth shows that sanction was not followed everywhere (Ruth 2:10!). "Of all the people with whom the Jew has social contact he treats the *nŏkrî* the worst."[79] Also here the Book of Ruth draws a clear contrast, for the Israelite Boaz behaves in a friendly, chivalrous, and gracious manner toward the foreign woman Ruth who is connected sympathetically to the Israelite faith (Ruth 1:16) so that the two for good reasons eventually discover each other.

According to Exod. 12:43 (P), foreigners could not participate in the Passover, for they are uncircumcised non-Jews, and according to Ezek. 44:7, 9 they quite naturally cannot become priests. Also, foreign slaves who stand in the service of Israelites must be circumcised (Gen. 17:12, 27: P). Further, Israelites are to guard themselves from acquiring sacrificial animals that had been sold by foreigners (Lev. 22:25).

Set against these largely negative and ostracizing expressions, alongside of which may be placed in addition Isa. 60:10 (foreigners must build the walls of Zion) and Isa. 61:5 (foreigners must perform the heavy manual labor, while the Israelites shall be "priests"), Isa. 56:6f. is conspicuously positive. According to this passage, the foreigner who embraces YHWH may come to the temple which is the "house of prayer for all nations" and join the temple congregation. First Kings 8:41–43 also refers to this situation. Here the foreigner comes to the temple "for your name's sake" in order to pray, because he had heard of YHWH's great name and his mighty hand. YHWH may then hear this prayer and do all that he is asked to do in order that all nations may come to know his name and fear him. The (Deuteronomistic) prayer of the dedication of the temple in 1 Kings 8:23–61 has Solomon utter the prayer that is shaped in part by Deutero-Isaiah and therefore is significantly far-reaching in its character. Solomon says that "all nations on the earth know that YHWH is God and no other." In these texts of the late-exilic or early-postexilic periods, the Old Testament, probably because of new questions of openness, exclusivity, and encounters with people who wanted to "join" the congregation, looks in a positive manner beyond the boundaries of its people Israel, even if this thinking did not influence much of the Deuteronomistic History, to which the important text of 1 Kings 8 belongs.

The "stranger" (גֵר = gēr)[80] likewise was the foreign immigrant who was not related to the Israelites by blood. However, the gēr referred not only to one who wished to enjoy the law of temporary hospitality but also to one who sought continuing protection and wished to become a resident alien (cf. Judg. 17:9–11) for different reasons (war or famine in his or her own land, the threat of debt slavery, etc.). The gēr can easily be admitted to the Yahwistic faith and congregation (Deut. 29:10; 31:12). He experiences the help of God and human beings (Deut. 10:18; 14:29), and, along with the poor, the widows, and the orphans, the gērîm ("strangers") are entrusted to the community for support.[81] Already the Book of the Covenant contains a (now expanded; see below) regulation for protecting the strangers (Exod. 22:20–23) that assumes the style of a speech by YHWH and takes on the manner of his argument. In its paraenetically enriched legal texts, Deuteronomy speaks often of "your stranger" (Deut.

24:14; 29:10; and 31:12; cf. 5:14 and Exod. 20:10), a topic that perhaps is motivated by a severe refugee movement during the times in which Deuteronomy originated. According to Deut. 10:18f., YHWH has loved even the stranger, so that Israel also ought to love him or her (according to Lev. 19:34, "as yourself"). Thus the stranger ("who is in your doors") may take part in the Sabbath rest (Deut. 5:13f.; Exod. 20:10) as well as in the joy of worship (Deut. 16:11, 14; 26:11; differently Lev. 23:42) and also may be present at the reading of the law (Deut. 31:12). Even so, the stranger does not receive his own land to possess and consequently continues not to have legal status. However, together with the widows and the orphans, the stranger receives the tithe every three years (Deut. 14:28f.) and shares the right to gleanings (Deut. 24:19–21; Lev. 19:10; and 23:22). While Israelites were forbidden to do so, the strangers (and the foreigners; see above) were allowed to eat a slaughtered animal that was not ritually flawless (Deut. 14:21). That the strangers, however, had to follow certain commandments of YHWH is indicated, for example, in Lev. 17:8f., 10, 12, 13, 15; 18:26; and Ezek. 14:7. They could also participate in the sacrificial cult, according to Lev. 22:18 and Num. 15:14ff. If the stranger was circumcised and in this way actually became a member of the people of the covenant by means of the covenant of Abraham (Genesis 17 P), he may then take part in the Passover (according to the Priestly document's stipulation in Exod. 12:48). It is striking that the positive argumentations and regulations concerning the stranger become more frequent in the exilic and postexilic texts. Is this connected with the fact that Israel in the exile had experienced once again the same type of existence as strangers and was forced to have contact with them?

Within the Old Testament commandments and regulations that deal with the stranger stands the motivating reference that Israel itself was once a "stranger" in Egypt.[82] This reference is found already in the theologically expanded (Deuteronomistic?) arguments of the Covenant Code that address Israel with the plural "you" (Exod. 22:20; cf. 23:9) and then more frequently in later literary contexts. Moreover, the discussion has to do with "being a slave in the land of Egypt."[83] This manner of argumentation is seldom found in the history of religions and is relatively atypical for a nation's perception of its own history, if not actually unique. A nation does not normally describe its early history in negative terms. Therefore this contrast is a rather decisive one. For Israel, YHWH has delivered his people, or rather those groups who were sojourning in Egypt at the time, from their original status of slavery and social subordination (Habiru/'apiru?), freed them, elected them to be his people, and placed them under obligation. Israel confessed in the final analysis that it possessed no intrinsic worth that would have provided the basis for this initiative of YHWH's redemption and election. Rather, this initiative lay within this God himself, that is, within his nature and within the structure of his own capacity to decide.[84] The reference back to this characteristic of early Israelite, fundamental history, that is, Israel's early existence as "strangers" in Egypt, is to serve both as a reminder that leads to thanksgiving and as a motivating instruction from which a corresponding ethical practice is to grow. That this resorting to Israel's existence as גרים = gērîm ("strangers") intends to evoke the memory of more "social unrest or conflict" is improbable.[85] Moreover, the fact that these arguments are frequent in the Deuteronomic/Deuteronomistic literature may result, not only from a period of increasing numbers of refugees toward the end of the monarchial periods of Israel and Judah,[86] but also from the experiences of the exile and the return home, anticipated as well as undergone, to a land that is now settled by others.

Upon the basis of these connotations, then, the statement that a human being is simply a stranger and a sojourner on the earth like all of his or her ancestors (Ps. 39:13; cf. 119:19; and 1 Chron. 29:15) is not a surprising one. Therefore the image of being a stranger is carried over from the spheres of the land and the law to describe the common, mortal existence of human beings. That this can happen shows that the "stranger" was not viewed in a completely negative way, although he or she was not a legitimate, full citizen of Israel. This person needed assistance and protection in his or her life, and God "like a patron"[87] grants him or her support.

The "sojourner" (תושב = tôšab) is often mentioned next to the "stranger" (גר = gēr),[88] and is especially frequent in the Priestly source and the texts dependent on it.[89] Elsewhere "sojourner" occurs in Ps. 39:13 and 1 Chron. 29:15. The attribution of both terms does not allow one really to recognize a clear distinction between them. While Exod. 12:45 must have in mind a foreigner who is excluded from the Passover festival, תושב = tôšab ("sojourner") elsewhere designates "probably from an economic perspective the same person who is also referred to as a גר (gēr) in denoting legal status. The soujourner, having no land of his or her own, therefore is one who is taken in by an Israelite who enjoys full citizenship."[90]

15.4   The Destruction of the Nations (Judgment)

Old Testament Israel experienced the nations sociologically, politically, militarily, and religiously as a threat to its existence and its manner of life. Nations such as the Philistines and the Assyrians were purely and simply a danger to Israel's existence, and yet there were nations that were also a danger to its way of life, to its living out its faith in YHWH (Canaanites: cf. Gen. 9:25f.; Assyria). A considerably greater power often confronted a small group. For this reason, it is not surprising if a universalism had to recede into the background while the tendency toward a nationalistic religion, by contrast, often continued to break through once again.

Whether an actual occurrence or a later programmatic, revisionist history, the annihilation of the nations in the land of promise was required or "carried out" (Deuteronomy 7 par.), an activity on which the ancient war oracle of YHWH quite possibly would have continued to make an impact.[91] Further, these nations metaphorically were powers of chaos threatening Israel, its king, and Jerusalem (Psalms 2; 46; 48; 68; 76; 84; and 93:3f.; cf. Joel 4; Zechariah 12 + 14; and Ezekiel 38f.). Prophetic threats of judgment against the nations are at first often connected with Israel (cf., e.g., Deut. 25:17–19; Isa. 7:4ff.; Jer. 49:1ff.; and Ps. 137:7–9),[92] or a prophetic judgment against Edom (Obadiah; Isaiah 34) or Babylon (Isaiah 13) is later expanded to a cosmic judgment. Often it is Israel itself which will carry out this judgment against the nations, although in view of the actual power relationships, these declarations may have more the character of wishes and hopes (e.g., Isa. 41:14–16; Micah 4:13; 5:7f.; Lam. 3:64–66; and Ps. 149:6–9; later 1QM; 1 Cor. 6:3; and Rev. 2:26f.).

In connection with statements about Zion as the city of God and the mountain of God[93] and the testimonies that are dependent upon them, the discourse is of YHWH as the lord of the world and as the world king.[94] Accordingly, he is the one who sustains Zion, thereby demonstrating and actualizing his lordship and power over the nations, for he enters into judgment against them (Isa. 24:21ff.; 33; Joel 4:9–17; Zechariah 12 + 14; Psalms 46; 47:4, 9f.; 96:13; 97:6f.; and 98:9). The same type of announcement of judgment, grounded in universal claims, is found, for example, also in Isa. 10:5ff.; 14; 34; 66:15–17; and Jer. 46:7ff.

If the nations therefore are summoned and placed under the judgment of YHWH,[95] then often either their concrete or general guilt is mentioned (Jeremiah 48; Ezekiel 28; 29:3; 31:10; 32:2; and Zech. 9:3), whereby frequently their hubris and their spiteful glee about Israel (Micah 7:8; Isa. 14:29) are set forth as the basis for judgment (cf. also Isa. 10:13f.; 19:11f; 47:7, 10; Ezek. 29:3; and Zeph. 2:8, 10). If one can also speak of the final annihilation of the nations, then this is to occur less on the basis of thoughts of revenge or hopes for retribution and more on the basis of the affirmation that the wicked in the end are not to be victorious. This affirmation has to do with the hope in the realization of the sovereignty of God (Daniel), while after the exile this wickedness, which in the final analysis becomes intrinsic to a developing, dualistic worldview, is located more outside of than within Israel. In addition, the nations increasingly become a theme viewed through a critical lens, because even postexilic Israel/Judah was seen by them merely as an object of their rule and as a people under the foreign dominion of great powers (the Persians, Greeks, Diadochi, and Romans) that continued to be perpetuated.

Naturally then, the salvation promised to Israel can be actualized only when its achievement is coupled with the annihilation of its opponents (cf. Zeph. 3:19f.; Jer. 46:25f.; Isa. 63:19–64:3; and Isaiah 34–35[96]). This has a certain analogy to the deliverance of the individual worshiper from his or her often-mentioned "enemies" in the prayers of the psalms. Consequently, there are prophetic oracles of salvation that carry out this coupling almost by necessity.[97] Also, textual additions are made that carry this sense (Isa. 10:12; 60:12). If YHWH "creates justice" for his people, then this can also mean that he is holding judgment (Ezek. 39:21; Pss. 9:17; and 119:84), and if he helps Israel, this help can also consist of his crushing the nations (Isa. 59:15b–21; 63:1–6). The function of these promises is to provide consolation for a distressed Israel so that such forceful words, for this reason, are understandable (Isa. 34:2, 6f.; Zech. 9:15; and once more Isa. 63:1–6). YHWH says: "Whoever touches you, touches the apple of my eye" (Zech. 2:12). YHWH has himself chosen a people and is, above all, the God of this nation and intervenes on its behalf.

The inbreaking of the kingdom of God is at the same time the necessary end of the kingdoms of the world, for they shall then be annihilated (Daniel 2; 7). Consequently, it is perhaps not too surprising that the term (!) שָׁלוֹם = šālôm ("peace") has no theologically decisive significance for the relationship of Israel to the nations.[98] This notwithstanding, the return home of the (postexilic) Israelite diaspora often is brought into association with not only the destruction but also the salvation of the nations from where the liberated captives will or are to start out (Isa. 11:11–16; 27:13; 60:4; and 62:10–12). The problem of the experience of salvation by the nations, most of whom were in conflict with Israel, was a problem for its faith, proving thus often to be a troublesome matter that found no clear-cut solution in the Old Testament.

15.5   The Nations as the Spectators of YHWH's Salvific Activity

Some texts indicate that YHWH's action on behalf of Israel may be paradigmatic so that what happens to it takes place before the world and for its sake (cf., e.g., Deut. 2:25; Josh. 2:9ff.; and Mal. 3:12). This means that the nations will not be annihilated but rather are and continue to be spectators of the divine action. According to the Book of Ezekiel, even the nations are to "know that I am YHWH," something that indeed does not have any concretely mentioned consequences that extend beyond this knowledge itself.[99] However, this does make clear that YHWH's activity on Israel's behalf in the final analysis also has the purpose of other nations coming to know and acknowledge him as God. Thus YHWH's activity on his people's behalf is exemplary of his intention for his world. In this matter, Israel is the messenger of YHWH and his witness to the world (Isa. 42:19; and 49:12, 26), and the salvation that happens to Israel is a "sign" for the nations (Isa. 62:10–12). The nations, moreover, cannot and are not to continue to be spectators only of the judgment against Israel (Ezek. 25:3ff.), and when YHWH turns the fortunes of Israel, it will be said among the nations that "he has done great things for them" (Ps. 126:1f.). However, YHWH's activity of judgment against Israel also occurs according to the testimony of not a few texts as an example to the nations, so that in this way Israel shall indeed become a reproach among them[100] as well as a witness to the seriousness of YHWH's judgment and his holy will (Deut. 28:46; 29: 23–27; 1 Kings 9:7ff.; Pss. 44:14f.; 79:4, 10; Joel 2:17; and Lam. 2:15ff.). Every once in a while it also happens that, under the impress of what has taken place, the nations themselves (then, however, mostly as those who had been judged) "convert" to YHWH, that is, are allowed to join his people, so that Israel in the final analysis works in turn, if also indirectly, as a witness in a "missionary" fashion (cf. Isa. 45:3ff., 14–17; and Jer. 18:7f.). However, according to Isa. 45:14, this acknowledgment is also to take place "in chains." The different positions taken on the destruction or salvation of the nations or at least on many of them are in part occasioned or harmonized by speaking (as, e.g., in Isaiah 65 and 66) of a distinction that is made within the world of the nations.

15.6 Salvation Also for the Nations—"Mission"?

On the basis of these early efforts and their differentiating as well as differing views of the world of the nations, some of the Old Testament periods and writings are not far from affirming that also the nations could join in the salvation of YHWH. However, these are mostly statements about the promised and expected state of fulfillment, therefore a part of eschatology, and it continues to be the case that Israel is the real recipient of salvation, while the nations may form a secondary circle, so to speak, around Israel and its Zion. There is no salvation for the nations that passes Israel by or that occurs without Israel, and this salvation for the nations does not come to fruition either as a clear, conclusive testimony in the Old Testament or as its definitive climax. The Old Testament continues to be of two minds in its expressions, hopes, and expectations when it comes to the salvation of the nations and the destiny of the world of the nations.

It is first Zion that plays an essential role in most of the postexilic texts that deal with the salvation of the nations.[101] Thus the nations come in pilgrimage to Zion in order to obtain there the instruction and the word of YHWH and then to walk in his ways.[102] Not only will the nations bring their treasures (Hag. 2:6–9; cf. Isa. 18:7) or their wealth to Zion together with the Jewish Diaspora (Isa. 60:1ff.;[103] Jer. 3:17; Zeph. 3:9f.; and Zech. 2:15) but also peace will course its way from there into the entire world.[104] YHWH's royal lordship goes forth from Zion over all the earth (Psalms 47; 96; and 97).[105] The temple will become a house of prayer for all nations,[106] while according to Zeph. 2:11 (cf. 3:9f. and Isa. 19:23–25) each nation, by contrast, will worship YHWH in its own place (cf. Mal. 1:11; Isa. 19:21). "Egypt" will become the people of YHWH and "Assyria" the work of his hands. Israel will be the third partner in this covenant to serve as the necessary mediator of blessing, so that both great powers now will serve YHWH and will be blessed by him (Isa. 19:23–25;[107] cf. 27:13; Ps. 68:32). Here Amos (Amos 9:7), Ezekiel (Ezek. 3:6b; 16:52ff.), and especially Deutero-Isaiah had provided preparatory work. According to Isa. 66:21, YHWH shall take priests and levites even from the nations. Yes, even Philistines, people of Tyre, and Africans will say that they are born of Zion, the mother of the nations (Psalm 87). YHWH the king (Isa. 24:21–23) will set the table for a festive meal for the nations on Zion (Isa. 25:6) which will surpass as well as expand the earlier meal of the covenant for Israel on Sinai (Exod. 24:10f.),[108] and he shall destroy the "shroud" that covers the nations (Isa. 25:7). Moreover, the disparity about the nations that exists within the Old Testament can already be made clear by the contrasts offered by Jer. 48:46f. and 49:5f., 38f. Indeed, placed immediately after Isa. 25:6–8 is the passage of Isa. 25:9–12 (v. 10!), which, with an entirely different intention, declares that Moab is strewn like straw in a dung pit. Or, following Zeph. 3:8 which speaks of YHWH pouring out his wrath over the nations, Zeph. 3:9f., inserted later, speaks of the nations offering their prayers to YHWH who shall give them "pure lips."[109]

Thus the nations shall inquire about salvation and its signs (1 Kings 8:41ff.; Isa. 11:10; 49:6f.; and 55:5) and shall turn away from their false and impotent idols to worship the one true God (Jer. 16:19–21; cf. Zeph. 2:11). There shall be people who will be able to join the people of God and to experience their salvation (Isa. 56:1–8) who had formerly not been allowed to join the congregation (Deut. 23:2–9). It is only here that one is able to experience that YHWH is "with" his people and how he is "with" them. One desires to be with this people in order to be with YHWH (Zech. 8:20–23; cf. 2:15).

Furthermore, this participation of the nations in the community of God's people and in their salvation consequently not only is made possible by YHWH but at the same time is thought to be mediated by Israel and its destiny as well as by Jerusalem and its Zion (cf. also Isa. 66:8bff.; 18ff.; 35:8–10). This mediation occurs because this nation is YHWH's witness to the world, both in terms of what it is and what it experiences, including what it suffers. God's history with Israel, in which his work is actualized, is directed toward the world that is to recognize him. This occurs both on soteriological and doxological grounds. YHWH wills to save, continues to save, and also is glorified before the world. Within the Old Testament, it is Deutero-Isaiah who scales the heights of these declarations.[110] According to Isa. 51:4f., even YHWH himself imparts the תּוֹרָה = tôrâ ("law") and מִשְׁפָּט = mišpāṭ ("justice") to the nations.

However, in this connection, which is analogous to the "blessing for the nations" of the Yahwist[111] or to the "kingdom of priests" in Exod. 19:6,[112] there is no active mission work, carried out by either Israel or the Servant of God[113] to the nations,[114] that comes under consideration. Rather, the things that are considered include Israel's existence and destiny, YHWH's sovereignty over his Zion, the light that radiates from there and moves outward to the nations, and the drawing of the nations into this event wrought on Israel's behalf, an event which they see and by which they come to know YHWH (cf. Isa. 60:1–3).[115] This is the missionary work that widens the effect, divinely willed, of God's action on behalf of Israel[116] (cf. Isa. 55:5; Pss. 102:16, 23; and 126:2b.). The Book of Jonah is also misunderstood, if one interprets it as a call to undertake a mission to the heathen. Much more, it has to do with Israel's not standing as a barrier between YHWH and the nations, due to its proud and egotistical certainty in its own salvation. Further, YHWH's compassion toward the heathen (cf. Exod. 34:6 in Jonah 4:2) is not to be indignantly contested or undervalued. The only possible discussion of an active missionary involvement in the Old Testament occurs in Isa. 66:19, and even the phenomenon of the "proselyte" (naturally a term not actually used) is not very frequently encountered in the Old Testament.[117]

These statements about the possible salvation also of the nations may not, however, as so often happens, be so set apart that they are understood to express, so to speak, the final and definitive word from the Old Testament in this matter. By contrast, there are also statements that continue unto the conclusion of the Old Testament (Isaiah 24–27; Zechariah 14; and Daniel) that speak about the judgment or even the annihilation these nations shall experience. Light and shadows are both cast upon the nations, as upon Israel itself, according to the Old Testament,[118] and elected Israel was not finally able to come to a full expression of universal salvation.[119] Following immediately the positive word of YHWH in Isa. 51:4–6 in which his light goes forth to the nations is the statement in vv. 7f. that speaks of the threat of their being devoured. Israel does not fundamentally abandon its particularity even in apocalyptic.[120]

YHWH's salvation was and is first of all earmarked for Israel. And when there was talk also of salvation for the nations and of their praising of YHWH (cf. also Pss. 22:28f.; 47:8–10; 97:1; 98:4, 9; 99:1f.; 102:23; 117; 145:13; and 150:6), then Israel and its Zion can serve as the mediator of this salvation, as these texts at the same time show. One cannot imagine Israel not in this picture, for YHWH himself has placed it there for the realization of his plan for salvation (cf. Exod. 19:5f.; Zech. 8:23; Pss. 47:10; 97:8; 98:3; 99:2; 102:22; and 145:10). "Salvation is from the Jews" (John 4:22). The call to worship, "Praise YHWH, all peoples, praise him all nations" (Psalm 117), and the hope expressed by Psalm 100[121] ("Make a joyful noise to YHWH all the world") present a grand vision that is to be attained. However, the Old Testament was not positively clear about the way to this hope and how it was to be realized.

15.7 The Servant of God

Within the literary context of the so-called Deutero-Isaiah (Isaiah 40–55),[122] whose proclamation is of prominent significance for the question about the nations and their salvation within the Old Testament, are found the so-called Songs of the Servant of God (Isa. 42:1–4; 49:1–6; 50:4–9; 52:13–53:12).[123] These texts represent the high point of the Old Testament statements that deal with the relationship of Israel to the nations.

The statements about the suffering of the prophet Jeremiah and the symbolic experiences of Ezekiel prepare us for what Deutero-Isaiah says about the servant of God. While the summary definition of these texts as "songs" does not reveal their distinctive character but rather much more blurs it, they still follow one another in a clear sequence and point to a close (probably even biographical) connection. In addition, these songs are clearly tied to the rest of the message of Deutero-Isaiah. These songs in Isaiah 40–55 clearly intend that both an individual and the people of Israel are to be designated as the "servant of YHWH" (cf., e.g., Isa. 41:8–16; 43:10; and 44:1–5, 21f.).[124] This dual identity of the "servant of YHWH" is even taken into the second servant song, probably as an addition (Isa. 49:3). If one asks who then may be meant by the individual servant of God, then the so-called autobiographical explanation, which was already familiar in Acts 8:34, suggests itself as the most plausible one over against the collective, the messianic, and the royal-ideological interpretations. For Deutero-Isaiah, the "king" is YHWH himself (Isa. 52:7), the "messiah" is Cyrus (Isa. 45:1), and the covenant of David is valid now for the nation as a whole and no longer for only a Davidic descendant or the dynasty (Isa. 55:3). Further, the servant has a mission to Israel (Isa. 42:3; 49:5f.) and is clearly described as a figure of the present. Nevertheless, one is compelled to consider the fact that in these texts the prophet is described as having a prominent function, with a certain accumulation of offices and tasks.

The first three songs show the work of the servant, from his introduction and installation (Isa. 42:1–4), to his mandate and the more precise description of his mission (Isa. 49:1–6), to his lament over his office and his suffering (Isa. 50:4–9). The fourth song, which is closely connected to the three preceding ones, however, probably was formulated in the student circles of the prophet.[125] In its middle section (Isa. 53:1–10a) and the words of a number of people, or of one who speaks for them, contained there, the song looks back at the work of the servant. These people admit that they were disappointed in the person, significance, and work of the servant who in the meantime had died and presumably was even murdered. They admit that they did not recognize in him the work of YHWH. In the speeches of God (Isa. 52:13–15; 53:10b–12) that frame the middle section, there is a look into the future, and YHWH transmits in these speeches the new lense through which to see the servant and provides the meaning of his destiny, especially his suffering and dying, which was previously not known.

Accordingly, while the servant had a mission to Israel (Isa. 42:3; 49:5f.), he also and especially exerted a positive influence on the nations (Isa. 42:3f.; 49:1,

6). He carried YHWH's מִשְׁפָּט = *mišpāṭ* ("justice") to them, which means here God's salvific will and his positive decision on their behalf.[126] The servant *was not to be* a light to the nations, and this is not mentioned as his mission, but rather he *is* this light; that is, his influence consists in the fact (Isa. 49:6; cf. 42:6) that "light," that is, salvation, is to be transmitted to the nations. His death then may have even a positive significance for those who now in thanksgiving revise their earlier view of the servant (Isa. 53:4f.). Indeed, this death possesses an atoning significance (Isa. 53:10: אָשָׁם = *'āšām*[127]) as a guilt offering for the "many" that includes also those people who do not belong either to the "we" of the middle section of the fourth song or to Israel itself (Isa. 53:11f.).[128] In this way a meaning for suffering is attempted, suffering in which YHWH is not absent but rather is present and works through it to bring about salvation. Meaning was also given to the suffering of the servant of God, both Israel and the prophet, whose true significance was not recognized at the time.[129] It is YHWH himself who opens the eyes to see this and promises through the work of this servant a consequence that will go beyond Israel itself.[130] Indeed, YHWH's "plan" (Isa. 53:10b) does not run its full course with his activity of salvation for Israel. Thus these sentences from Deutero-Isaiah, and in particular the Servant Songs, formulate the high points of the declarations of the Old Testament about the nations.

15.8 The Openness of the Old Testament

Directly in the relationship of Israel and YHWH with the nations and their salvation, the phenomenon appears that must yet be mentioned at the conclusion of this effort to set forth a description of Old Testament theology, namely, the openness of the Old Testament.[131] How YHWH in the final analysis will regard the nations is not clearly answered in the Old Testament. However, this indicates at the same time that "openness" is a decisive characteristic of the Old Testament image of God. One is perhaps to remain open even to an additional witness to this God,[132] open to his new coming that goes beyond his coming in the cult or his activity during the return home from exile, and open to his final, complete, and salvific sovereignty over all nations and over his world. God for the sake of his love (cf. only Hos. 11:8f.; Isa. 54:7f., 10) does not fail because of the sin of Israel, and he does not allow Israel to fail during its Old Testament journey. Also, the eschatologization of much theological language is not identical to Israel's failures in this world.[133] Rather, faith here is known in its essence also as hope, as the waiting for God and his new activity, and in the end as the final establishment of his sovereignty. Indeed, God acts in history, yet his mystery is not removed by this activity.[134] Even this remains open to his final coming which will fully reveal who he is. The Old Testament provides information about the God who elects, who speaks and acts in word and in history, and who accompanies his people in these ways. The Old Testament tells of this speaking and acting God who promises that which is new, or has already proclaimed his threats. As a result, he is the object of lament and the subject of praise; he is answered in thanksgiving, and he is praised in hope. And all this transpires, even though one continued to experience the incalculable character of God, something that the history of Old Testament wisdom's conception of order demonstrates. The "openness of the Old Testament" does not directly imply or even mean only an openness to the New Testament. Only a Christian theologian is able to speak of the Old Testament's openness to the New Testament. Such a theologian comes to the Old Testament by way of the New Testament, using it as the basis to approach the Old Testament critically and questioningly.

The Old Testament proves its continuing worth above all in the fact that here the fundamental structures of faith, basic structures of divine activity, human wonderment, and the believing response of both a community and the individuals who comprise it, may be recognized. This is especially clear, for example, in the attribution of history, word, and religious language. God's activity could be experienced, believed, and witnessed as activity that is historical, that elects, and thereby at the same time that obligates. This activity was not in principle only an activity that occurred once and for all; rather, it continued to occur ever again (the ancestors, kingship, Zion, and the priests), so that one remained open to new experiences with this God and was able to incorporate the new within the fundamental structure of the old, thus enriching and expanding it. Furthermore, history came to be experienced and explained as a unity directed toward a goal. Eschatology developed as the result of the experience of history. Yet all of this yielded only a cautious and reticent discourse about God himself and his "characteristics." YHWH is a God who wills to have and thus provides personal community with human beings who are seen in their totality. Thus he wishes to know a community formed by law and justice and he wants to strengthen, cleanse, and sanctify it by means of its cultic activity. One's faith in him should have more of his impress and should have more vitality when one is bound to him, is responsible before him, and exists in the community elected by him. This world, including joy in this life and rejoicing over its presence, is important to this faith. YHWH thus continues ever to encounter one as the electing and yet at the same time demanding God. He comes as both a threatening and a promising God ever anew to his people, to individual worshipers as well as to the nations. God is not to be limited to what has gone before, nor is he to be spoken of primarily or exclusively in terms of the past, for he is the God of yesterday, today, and tomorrow.

Thus faith in YHWH could be described as the binding, sustaining, and enduring element in Israel's history, during both its small and especially its great disruptions, as, for instance, the conquest or, above all, the exile. The discovery and the development of these fundamental structures of Old Testament faith, however, cannot remain only historically oriented and purely descriptive. Old Testament theology shall have to join in the endeavor within Christian theology to produce a "biblical theology," which perhaps likewise is to search for the common fundamental structures of its witnesses as well as for its structural analogies, in order for the Christian faith to receive and keep its significance. The question concerning the one, the divided, or even the two "peoples of God" will continue to keep alive the question about Israel as the people of God and the other nations.

Consequently, the employment of the Old Testament in the New Testament will have to be taken up at least in the (Christian) effort to write a "biblical theology,"[135] if not in the attempt to produce a "theology of the Old Testament."[136] This effort at writing an Old Testament theology has by necessity carried out and set forth an orientation that looks back at the world of the Old Testament. This will see to it that the important message of the Old Testament will not be treated in too cursory a fashion.

ABBREVIATIONS

A more complete list of abbreviations
will be found on pages 264–268 in Volume I.

AMZ	*Allgemeine Missionszeitschrift*
ANEP	J. B. Pritchard, ed., *The Ancient Near East in Pictures* (1969)
ArztChr	*Arzt und Christ*
ATSAT	Arbeiten zu Text und Sprache im Alten Testament
BET	Beiträge zur biblischen Exegese und Theologie
BiLi	*Bibel und Liturgie*
BThBull	*Biblical Theology Bulletin*
BSt	Biblische Studien
CC	Continental Commentaries
Conc (D)	*Concilium* (German edition)
DBS	*Dictionnaire de la Bible, Supplément*
Diak	*Diakonia*
fzb	Forschung zur Bibel
IKaZ	*Internationale katholische Zeitschrift*
JLH	*Jahrbuch für Liturgie und Hymnologie*
JNES	*Journal of Near Eastern Studies*
Jud	*Judaica*
KAT	Kommentar zum Alten Testament
MDOG	*Mitteilungen der Deutschen Orientgesellschaft*
OTS	*Oudtestamentische Studiën*
QD	Quaestiones Disputatae
RevSR	*Revue des sciences religieuses*
SEÅ	*Svensk exegetisk årsbok*
StNT	Studien zum Neuen Testament
SThU	*Schweizerische theologische Umschau*
ThBeitr	*Theologische Beiträge*
ThEx	Theologische Existenz heute
WA	Weimar Ausgabe (Weimar edition of Luther's *Works*)
ZAH	*Zeitschrift für Althebräistik*
ZBK AT	*Zürcher Bibelkommentar, Altes Testament*
ZEE	*Zeitschrift für evangelische Ethik*

NOTES

Chapter 6. The Narratives about the Ancestors

1. [Part Three.] For the theological significance of the land, see Vol. I, pp. 117–128. For the question of the so-called conquest, i.e., the settlement of various groups in different ways and in several infiltrations, see the descriptions of the histories of Israel (H. Donner; A. H. J. Gunneweg; and that of S. Herrmann, *A History of Israel in Old Testament Times,* rev. ed., Philadelphia, 1981); and the literature cited in Vol. I, p. 306 n. 570.

2. [Part Three.] For the problem of the "Canaanites," see Vol. I, p. 342 n. 668, as well as below, pp. 8–9, and the index.

3. Above all, see K. Galling, *Die Erwählungstraditionen Israels,* 1928 (BZAW 48), 27–56; A. Alt, *Der Gott der Väter,* 1929 (=*KS* 1, 1ff.); V. Maag, "Der Hirte Israels," *SThU* 28, 1958, 2–28 (=*Kultur, Kulturkontakt und Religion,* 1980, 111ff.); C. Westermann, "Arten der Erzählung in der Genesis," TB 24, 1964, 9–91 (=*Die Verheissungen an die Väter,* 1976, 9ff.); H. Weidmann, *Die Patriarchen und ihre Religion im Licht der Forschung seit J. Wellhausen,* 1968 (FRLANT 94); H. D. Preuss, ". . . ich will mit dir sein!" *ZAW* 80, 1968, 139–173; R. E. Clements, "אברהם," *ThWAT* 1, cols. 53–62; J. Scharbert, "Patriarchentradition und Patriarchenreligion," *VuF* 19/2, 1974, 2–22; C. Westermann, *Genesis 12–36: A Commentary,* Minneapolis, 1985 (CC); idem, *Die Verheissungen an die Väter,* 1976 (FRLANT 116); S. Terrien, *The Elusive Presence,* New York, 1978, 63ff.; R. Martin-Achard, "Abraham. I: A. T.," *TRE* 1, 364–372; E. Blum, *Die Komposition der Vätergeschichte,* 1984 (WMANT 57); H.-J. Zobel, "יעקֹ(ו)ב," *ja'ăqō(ô)b," ThWAT* 3, cols. 752–777; R. Albertz, "Isaak. I: A. T.," *TRE* 16, 292–296; H.-J. Zobel, "Jakob/Jakobsegen. I. A. T.," *TRE* 16, 461–466; W. Thiel, "Geschichtliche und soziale Probleme der Erzväter-Überlieferungen," *Theologische Versuche* 14, 1985, 11–27; M. Köchert, *Vätergott und Väterverheissungen,* 1988 (FRLANT 142); H. Cazelles, "Der persönliche Gott Abrahams und der Gott des Volkes Israel," in R. Mosis and L. Ruppert, eds., *Der Weg zum Menschen,* FS A. Deissler, 1989, 46–61; M. Görg, ed., *Die Väter Israels,* FS J. Scharbert, 1989; P. Weimar, "Abraham," *NBL* 1, cols. 14–21; K. Berge, *Die Zeit des Jahwisten,* 1990 (BZAW 186). Cf. also G. von Rad, *Old Testament Theology,* vol. 1: *The Theology of Israel's Historical Traditions,* New York, 1985, 165–187; A. Deissler, *Die Grundbotschaft des Alten Testaments: Ein theologischer Durchblick,* 1972, 61ff.; W. Zimmerli, *Old Testament Theology in Outline,* Atlanta, 1978, 18–21.

4. Similarly, cf. in this regard the "court style," psalms, the legend of the primeval flood, wisdom literature, etc.

5. Cf. Vol. I, pp. 52–53.

6. For the history of interpretation, cf. C. Westermann, *Genesis 12–36;* and M. Köchert, *Vätergott und Väterverheissungen,* 13ff.

7. For this, see W. Schatz, *Genesis 14: Eine Untersuchung,* 1972. Cf. also C. Westermann, *Genesis 12–36,* 182–208; and E. Blum *Die Komposition der Vätergeschichte,* 462ff. n. 5.

8. For the critical scrutiny of the texts that are often called upon in this regard, see W. Thiel,

"Geschichtliche und soziale Probleme, as well as J. H. Walton, *Ancient Israelite Literature in Its Cultural Context,* Grand Rapids, 1989, 49–58.

9. For this, see J. Scharbert, "Patriarchentradition"; C. Westermann, *Genesis 12–36,* 67–70. He presents here a table that points to a latitude of dating the ancestors, ranging from 2200 B.C.E. to 1200 B.C.E.! A concisely stated view of this matter is found in E. Blum, *Die Komposition der Vätergeschichte,* 491f.

10. However, even E. Blum (*Die Komposition der Vätergeschichte,* 504), who is rather critical in this regard, comes to the conclusion: "It appears to me for several reasons . . . to be most probable that a historical recollection of the origins of Israel in the nonsettlement groups has made an impact on this stream of the tradition." Cf. also the still more critical position of M. Köchert, *Vätergott und Väterverheissungen.*

11. Cf. C. Westermann, *Genesis 12–36,* 84–86.

12. See below, pp. 5–9.

13. The personal names of the Abram genealogy in Gen. 11:27ff. (also vv. 22ff.), e.g., are found also as place-names in this area (cf. *ThWAT* 1, col. 365; and S. Herrmann, *Geschichte Israels,* 2d ed., 1980, 66ff.).

14. Cf. W. Thiel, *Die soziale Entwicklung Israels in vorstaatlicher Zeit,* 2d ed., 1985, 31ff.

15. Cf. M. Köchert, *Vätergott und Väterverheissungen,* 115ff.

16. In this passage, how is Jacob's living in tents related to his being a "wholesome man" (איש תם = *'îš tām*)?

17. Forty-five times in Genesis 12–25 the root הלך = *hlk* ("go, walk") occurs. Cf. H. Gross, "*hālak* in den Abraham-Geschichten," in FS J. Scharbert, 73–82.

18. The various listings of possessions "presuppose not nomadic but rather settled associations" (W. Thiel, *Die soziale Entwicklung Israels in vorstaatlicher Zeit,* 32).

19. Cf. Vol. I, p. 122; and below, pp. 14–15.

20. A critique of the theses of a pre-Israelite traditions history of the ancestral traditions is found in E. Blum, *Die Komposition der Vätergeschichte,* 491ff.

21. Thus, e.g., M. Noth and G. von Rad.

22. Cf. the certainly critical examination of this thesis by M. Köchert, *Vätergott und Väterverheissungen,* passim. A counter critique has been offered by L. Schmidt, "Ein radikale Kritik an der Hypothese von Vätergott und Väterverheissungen," *ThR* 54, 1989, 415–421.

23. A. Alt, *Der Gott der Väter* (=*KS* 1, 66).

24. Cf., however, the reflections of H.-P. Müller ("Gott und die Götter in den Anfängen der biblischen Religion: Zur Vorgeschichte des Monotheismus," in O. Keel, ed., *Monotheismus im Alten Israel und seiner Umwelt,* 1980, 99–142, esp. 120ff.). For a critique, see esp. M. Köckert, *Vätergott und Väterverheissungen,* 92ff.

25. However, the problem of the "Fear of Isaac" is certainly not so quickly solved, according to the view of M. Köckert (*Vätergott und Väterverheissungen,* 63ff.) who follows K. Koch (in R. Albertz et al., eds., *Schöpfung und Befreiung,* FS C. Westermann, 1989, 107–115). According to Köckert , פחד = *pahad* should mean "loins, genitals," a view that fails for the simple fact that, since Abraham is already dead, one could hardly swear by reference to this reproductive power (Gen. 31:53b). Furthermore, in the analogous scenes in Gen. 24:2f. and 47:29 any mention of פחד = *pahad* is missing.

26. Thus W. H. Schmidt, *Alttestamentlicher Glaube,* 6th ed., 27.

27. Gen. 24:12, 27, 42, 48; 26:24; and 28:13. The last passage probably belongs to J. Also see the summaries of Exod. 3:13ff.; 6:3; and Josh. 24:15ff. Consequently, most of these are in secondary connections and compositions.

28. Cf. K. Koch, "Die Götter, denen die Väter dienten," in *Studien zur alttestamentlichen und altorientalischen Religionsgeschichte,* 1988, 9–31, esp. 14f.

29. Gen. 31:5, 29, 42; 46:3; cf. 32:10; 46:1; 49:25; 50:17; Exod. 15:2; and 18:4.

30. Cf. E. Blum, *Die Komposition der Vätergeschichte,* 499f. (lit.); K. Koch, "Die Götter, denen die Väter dienten," 18ff.; and H.-P. Müller, "Gott und die Götter in den Anfängen der biblischen Religion," 115f.

31. Cf. W. H. Schmidt, BK II/1, 147ff.

32. Cf. also R. Rendtorff, *ThLZ* 88, 1963, col. 740 (=*TB* 57, 127). "The God of their ancestor" in Gen. 31:53 is here clearly a harmonizing addition.

33. Especially in V. Maag, "Der Hirte Israels," 2–28 (=*Kultur, Kulturkontakt und Religion*, 1980, 111ff.).
34. K. Koch, "Die Götter, denen die Väter dienten," 31.
35. For E. Blum (*Die Komposition der Vätergeschichte*, 495ff.), this acceptance of a nomadic ancestral religion is now altogether a problem.
36. V. Maag, "Der Hirte Israels," 9f., 14f. Cf. V. Maag, "Das Gottesverständnis des Alten Testaments," *NThT* 21, 1966/1967, 162–207 (=*Kultur, Kulturkontakt und Religion*, 256ff.), there 165ff. and 260ff. Critical of this is M. Köckert, *Vätergott und Väterverheissungen*, 248ff.
37. Cf. K. Berge, *Die Zeit des Jahwisten*, 11–76.
38. Cf. also Vol. I, pp. 149–151; and E. Otto, "El," *NBL* 1, cols. 507f.
39. W. H. Schmidt, *Alttestamentlicher Glaube*, 6th ed., 25.
40. According to O. Eissfeldt (*KS* V, 1973, 50–62), the Canaanite El was actually the one who promised descendants and the possession of the land to the ancestors.
41. J. C. de Moor (*The Rise of Yahwism*, 1990 [BETL 91], 229–234 assumes as much. His efforts at dating (Late Bronze Age) in combination with the Ugaritic texts are not able to convince. He also sees, nevertheless, the deity El as the "God of the ancestors."
42. Cf. R. Albertz, *Persönliche Frömmigkeit und offizielle Religion*, 1978, 88–91.
43. That the combination with YHWH (Gen. 28:17 + 19) is an artificial, secondary formation is seen already in the name "Beth-El," which contains *no* theophoric element that derives from the name YHWH. For this, see V. Maag, "Der hieros logos von Bethel," in *Kultur, Kulturkontakt und Religion*, 29ff.
44. E. Blum (*Die Komposition der Vätergeschichte*, 186–190) directs critical queries at these passages and their interpretation.
45. In P, the appellation continues on to Exod. 6:3 (Gen. 17:1; 28:3f.; 35:9–12; 48:3f.; Exod. 6:3; and Gen. 43:14 R^P?). According to Num. 24:4, 16f. (J), this designation of God occurs in a text that likewise is ancient. For this, see K. Koch, in R. Albertz et al., eds., *Schöpfung und Befreiung,* FS C. Westermann, 1989, 25ff.; *Šaddaj*, 118–152 (originally—without appendixes—in *VT* 26, 1976, 299–332).
46. Cf. H.-J. Zobel, "עֶלְיוֹן, *ʿaeljôn*," *ThWAT* 6, cols. 131–151. H. Niehr (*Der höchste Gott*, 1990 [BZAW 190], 61–68) sees things differently. His statement that "in the meantime only a post-exilic dating of these texts" may be allowed (p. 65) is not at all convincing.
47. According to H.-P. Müller ("Gott und die Götter," 115), this was an ancient Bedouin El, "who among the so-called father gods has been freed to shape its own individual identity while related to various communities."
48. "The Bible witnesses to a process of the continuing knowledge of God" (K. Koch, in R. Albertz et al., eds., *Schöpfung und Befreiung*, 1989, 31). Cf. also H.-J. Zobel, "Der frühe Jahwe-Glaube in der Spannung von Wüste und Kulturland," *ZAW* 101, 1989, 342–365, esp. 349ff.
49. Cf. Vol. I, pp. 59 and 78, and the index for this.
50. *TUAT* I/6, 544ff. (line 27).
51. Cf. by contrast the later expression, "YHWH, the God of Israel," in Josh. 8:30, etc.
52. Thus with H. Mölle, *Der sogenannte Landtag zu Sichem*, 1980 (fzb 42). Cf. also V. Maag, "Sichembund und Vätergötter," VT Suppl 16, 1967, 205–218 (=*Kultur, Kulturkontakt und Religion*, 300ff.). Cf. Vol. I, p. 75.
53. H.-P. Müller, "Gott und die Götter," 127.
54. "Between the semi-nomadic religion and the agricultural religion of Canaan stood Yahwistic faith as the third element" (H.-J. Zobel, "Der frühe Jahwe-Glaube in der Spannung von Wüste und Kulturland," 343). For the connections and contrasts between YHWH, El, and Baal, see the well-summarized and instructive essay by T. N. D. Mettinger, "The Elusive Essence," in E. Blum et al., eds., *Die Hebräische Bibel und ihre zweifache Nachgeschichte*, FS R. Rendtorff, 1990, 393–417.
55. Thus M. Köckert, *Vätergott und Väterheissungen*, passim. Cf. L. Schmidt, "Eine radikale Kritik an der Hypothese von Vätergott und Väterverheissungen," 415–421. See also Vol. I, p. 150.
56. For this, see also H. Vorländer, *Mein Gott*, 1975 (AOAT 23); and H. Cazelles, "Der persönliche Gott Abrahams und der Gott des Volkes Israel," 46–61. Cf. also E. Zenger, "Jahwe und die Götter," *ThPh* 43, 1968, 338–359 (esp. 352f.; cited also by J. Schreiner, "Das Gebet

Jakobs," in FS J. Scharbert, 1989, 297): "The 'God of the ancestor' in Genesis is the protector and sustainer of a clan of shepherds. The details of the life of this clan, begetting and birth, marriage and death, the struggle for herds, rivalries of women and concubines, problems of succession, the battle with other groups for wells, and much more that is found in the legends of the ancestors are all the things to which this God of the ancestor attends. This God has no direct connection to the cosmos, to the agricultural land, to a temple, or to a palace. His sphere is the family in the wider sense: human beings and herds. He rules over the concrete human life. His utterance occurs by verbal inspiration of the head of the tribe, by promise and command. He travels with his worshipers and is always with them wherever they are and in whatever they do. Therefore there is no specialized cult with those who specialize in cultic service. The fundamental attitude toward him is obedience and trust." For such deities of ancestors and clans, see also Chr. Sigrist and R. Neu, eds., *Ethnologische Texte zum Alten Testament*, 1, 1989, 171ff.

57. M. Köckert is critical of this in his *Vätergott und Väterverheissungen*, 177f.
58. In the promise of the land to the ancestors, the predicate "land flowing with milk and honey" never once appears. Cf. also Vol. I, p. 120.
59. Thus M. Köckert, *Vätergott und Väterverheissungen*, 323, as his summation.
60. "No other farmer's culture of the ancient Near East has narrative traditions that are handed down from the pre-sedentary period; in sociological as well as in religiohistorical detail, the narrative of the ancestors contains a fullness of characteristics that cannot be explained as a mere retrojection of later circumstances but instead speaks precisely against this" (H.-P. Müller, "Gott und die Götter," 126, esp. 114ff., which itemize the El deities in the narratives of the ancestors).
61. V. Maag, "Der Hirte Israels," 22.
62. V. Maag, "Malkût JHWH," VT Suppl 7, 1959, 129–153, esp. 140 (=*Kultur, Kulturkontakt und Religion*, 145ff., esp. 156).
63. Ibid., 153 (=169).
64. In regard to this source, we largely follow H. Seebass, "Jahwist," *TRE* 16, 441–451 (esp. 444 for a textual inventory in the ancestral stories).
65. In regard to this source, see once more H. Seebass, "Elohist," *TRE* 9, 520–524.
66. Traditiohistorically speaking, it is probably the case that originally there was mentioned only *one* element in the promise. However, it is difficult to decide between the promise of the land and the promise of offspring because of the necessary connection between the two.
67. For this, see J. Emerton, "The Origin of the Promises to the Patriarchs in the Older Sources of the Book of Genesis," *VT* 32, 1982, 14–32.
68. Cf. also pp. 112f.
69. In Gen. 26:3–5, at least v. 5 probably exhibits language that is Deuteronomistically influenced.
70. Cf. Gen. 22:18 (secondary). For blessing as a mission, see H. W. Wolff, "Das Kerygma des Jahwisten," *EvTh* 24, 1964, 73–98 (TB 22, 2d ed., 1973, 345ff.). For a different view, see L. Schmidt, "Israel ein Segen für die Völker?" *ThViat* 12, 1975, 135–151, which is followed here.
71. Cf. also Vol. I, pp. 180f.
72. Thus, e.g., with H. Seebass, "Jahwist"; L. Schmidt, "Israel ein Segen für die Völker?" W. H. Schmidt, "Ein Theologe in salomonischer Zeit? Plädoyer für den Jahwisten," *BZ* NF 25, 1981, 82–102; and K. Berge, *Die Zeit des Jahwisten*.
73. K. Berge, *Die Zeit des Jahwisten*, 229ff., 273ff.
74. Gen. 12:7; 13:14f., 17; 15:7–21; 17:8; 24:7; 26:3, 4; 28:4, 13; 35:12; and 48:4. Of those which belong to P are Gen. 17:8; 35:12; and 48:4. The promise of the land (to the ancestors) outside of Genesis includes Exod. 13:5, 11; 32:13; 33:1; Num. 11:12; 14:16, 23; 32:11; Deut. (here as an "oath" to the ancestors or rather to them and their successors) 1:8, 35; 6:10, 18f., 23; 7:8, 12f.; etc. For Deuteronomy, cf. H. D. Preuss, *Deuteronomium*, 1982 (EdF 164), 186f.; and esp. Th. Römer, *Israels Väter*, 1990 (OBO 99). Concerning this, see below. For the theme "land," see also Vol. I, pp. 117ff.
75. Thus with H. Seebass, "Gehörten Verheissungen zum ältesten Bestand der Väter-Erzählungen?" *Bibl* 64, 1983, 189–210. J. Scharbert ("Die Landverheissung als 'Urgestein' der Patriarchen-Tradition," in A. Caquot et al., eds., *Mélanges bibliques et orientaux*, FS M. M. Del-

cor, 1985 [AOAT 215], 359–368) also includes Gen. 13:14f. as part of the "primeval bedrock" of the patriarchal tradition, but not Gen. 12:7.

76. R. Rendtorff, e.g., runs into the danger of such a view (*Das Überlieferungsgeschichtliche Problem des Pentateuch*, 1976 [BZAW 147], 37ff.).

77. Cf. Vol. I, pp. 66f.

78. Cf. (with additional attempts at establishing reasons) G. E. Mendenhall, "The Nature and Purpose of the Abraham Narratives," in P. D. Miller, Jr., et al., eds., *Ancient Israelite Religion, FS* F. M. Cross, Philadelphia, 1987, 337–356.

79. For this, see A. R. Müller, "Die Mehrungsverheissung und ihre vielfältige Formulierung," in *FS* J. Scharbert, 1989, 259–266; and E. Blum, *ThWAT* 7, cols. 300–313.

80. Among these, Gen. 18:1–16a is the oldest text. Cf. also Gen. 17:15f., 19, 21: P.

81. "Great nation": Gen. 12:2; 18:18; 21:13, 18; and 46:3. Numerous offspring (cf. also *ThWAT* 2, cols. 672–679): Gen. 13:16; 15:5; 16:10; 17:5, 6, 20; 18:18; 26:24; 28:3, 14; 32:13; 35:11; 47:27; 48:4, 16, 19. As an oath of YHWH with a pointing to the number of the stars: Gen. 22:16f.; 26:3f. (both passages point to obedience); and Exod. 32:13. Gen. 22:15–18 is clearly secondary, v. 5 in 26:3–5 is at least Deuteronomistically influenced, and both texts stand in close relationship.

82. In regard to the overall explanation of the composition criticism and historical reception of the promises by M. Köckert (*Vätergott und Väterverheissungen*, passim), cf. the critique by L. Schmidt, "Eine radikale Kritik an der Hypothese von Vätergott und Väterverheissungen," *ThR* 54, 1989, 415–421.

83. Cf. H. D. Preuss, ". . . ich will mit dir sein!" *ZAW* 80, 1968, 139–173 (see also *ThWAT* 1, cols. 485–500); M. Görg, *ThG* 70, 1980, 214–240; and R. Winling, *RevSR* 51, 1977, 89–139.

84. Is this source introduced with Gen. 15:1*, 3, 4? For the Elohist, see H. W. Wolff, "Zur Thematik der elohistischen Fragmente im Pentateuch," *EvTh* 29, 1969, 59–72 (=*TB* 22, 2d ed., 1973, 402ff.). Then see H. Seebass, "Elohist," *TRE* 9, 520–524.

85. Cf. the formula of the word event in Gen. 15:1 that is found especially in prophetic texts. Genesis 15 as a whole is a later chapter that consists of numerous literary strata. Cf. J. Ha, *Genesis 15*, 1989 (BZAW 181), esp. 197: "a theological compendium of Pentateuchal history." Also cf. H. Mölle, *Genesis 15: Eine Erzählung von den Anfängen Israels*, 1988 (fzb 62); E. Haag, "Die Abrahamtradition in Gen 15," in *FS* J. Scharbert, 1989, 83–106; and below, n. 96.

86. For this, see W. Richter, "Das Gelübde als theologische Rahmung der Jakobüberlieferungen," *BZ* NF 11, 1967, 21–52.

87. See J. Scharbert, *Solidarität in Segen und Fluch im Alten Testament und in seiner Umwelt*, 1: *Väterfluch und Vätersegen*, 1958 (BBB 14). For this solidarity, see also Vol. I, pp. 60–64.

88. Cf. H. D. Preuss, *Deuteronomium*, 184.

89. For a critique, see M. Köckert, *Vätergott und Väterverheissungen*, 177ff.

90. Cf. H.-J. Zobel, *ThWAT* 3, cols. 758f., 762f.

91. Passages in H.-J. Zobel, *ThWAT* 3, cols. 771f.

92. E. Blum, *Die Komposition der Vätergeschichte*, 505.

93. Cf. R. Smend, *Elemente alttestamentlichen Geschichtsdenkens*, 1968 (ThSt 95), = *Die Mitte des Alten Testaments,*, 1986, 160ff.

94. For this, see N. Lohfink, "Die Priesterschrift und die Geschichte," VT Suppl 29, 1978, 189–225 (=*Studien zum Pentateuch*, 1988 [SBAB 4], 213ff.; esp. 222f. n. 29 for the listing of the priestly texts that is followed here). For the texts of P, see also E. Blum, *Die Komposition der Vätergeschichte*, 420ff., who views P as a redactional stratum, not as a "source" in and of itself. For the lack of the blessing of increase for the land animals (in opposition to fish and fowl; Gen. 1:22), cf. Vol. I, pp. 180f.

95. See also Vol. I, pp. 121–122.

96. There is no question that Gen. 15:7ff. contains in essence an older narrative about this "covenant." Although J. C. de Moor (*The Rise of Yahwism*, 255f.) seeks to point out Ugaritic parallels to the "covenant" in the ancestral narratives, it still is to be noted that the corresponding term in the Ugaritic texts is missing. For the ritual in Gen. 15:19ff. that contains a potential self-cursing, cf. the parallel in *KAI* 222 A 40. For Genesis 15 as a whole, cf. the literature mentioned above in n. 85. In addition, see E. Blum, *Die Komposition der*

Vätergeschichte, 362ff.; and M. Köckert, *Vätergott und Väterverheissungen*, 204ff. Further, see below, p. 15 and pp. 160f.

97. Cf. Vol. I, p. 65.

98. W. Zimmerli, "Sinaibund und Abrahambund," in *Gottes Offenbarung*, 2d ed., 1969 (TB 19), 205–216; see p. 214 for the following citation.

99. Cf. H.-J. Zobel, *ThWAT* 3, col. 772, who argues that this name "obviously has been preferred, because it does not stand in danger of being politically misunderstood (ibid., 773) as the "(house) of Israel" could be (ibid., cols. 771f., the passages).

100. Chr. Jeremias, "Die Erzväter in der Verkündigung der Propheten," in H. Donner et al., eds., *Beiträge zur alttestamentlichen Theologie*, FS W. Zimmerli, 1977, 206–222; J. Jeremias, "Jakob im Amosbuch," in FS J. Scharbert, 1989, 139–154; and H.-J. Zobel, *ThWAT* 3, cols. 770–773.

101. This critically alludes to Gen. 25:23, 26, 28–34; 27:36; and 32:2, 23ff. See F. Diedrich, *Die Anspielungen auf die Jakob-Tradition in Hosea 12, 1–13,3*, 1977 (fbz 27); H.-D. Neef, *Die Heilstraditionen Israels in der Verkündigung des Propheten Hosea*, 1987 (BZAW 169), 15ff.; and D. R. Daniels, *Hosea and Salvation History*, 1990 (BZAW 191), 33ff.

102. For the "ancestors" in the Deuteronomistically edited Book of Jeremiah, cf. Th. Römer, *Israels Väter*, 1990 (OBO 99), 395ff.; for Ezekiel, ibid., 491f.

103. See K. Baltzer, "Schriftauslegung bei Deuterojesaja? Jes. 43,22–28 als Beispiel," in FS J. Scharbert, 1989, 11–16; and Th. Römer, *Israels Väter*, 535ff.

104. Cf. the "high places of Isaac" (Amos 7:9) and the "house of Isaac" (Amos 7:16), then the references to the city and the sanctuary of Beersheba (Amos 5:5; 8:14), "the milieu of which is connected with the Isaac traditions" (Chr. Jeremias, "Die Erzväter in der Verkündigung der Propheten," 207 n. 3 with literature; cf. also R. Albertz, *TRE* 16, 296). The function of the mentioning of Isaac in these texts, moreover, is not clearly established.

105. Ezek. 28:25; 37:25 refer to Jacob and to the gift of the land (cf., however, 33:24). Isa. 41:8f.; 43:1; 51:2; [cf., however, 63:16]; Jer. 33:25f.; Ezek. 20:5, 42; 28:25; 36:28; 37:25; 39:25; 47:14; Obadiah 10; Micah 7:18ff.; Isa. 14:1; 29:22; and Mal. 1:2. Then also Neh. 9:6, 23; and Ps. 105:7ff., 42–45. Cf. also Amos 3:13; 9:8 (secondary). For the theme of increase in the prophets, cf. E. Blum, *ThWAT* 7, cols. 310–313.

106. For a more detailed analysis, see below, pp. 160f. For "covenant," cf. Vol. I, pp. 84f.

107. See H. D. Preuss, *Deuteronomium*, 186f. (lit.); above all, see Th. Römer, *Israels Väter*.

108. Deut. 1:8, 35; 6:10, 18f., 23; 7:8, 13; 8:1; 9:5; 10:11; 11:9, 21; 19:8; 26:3, 15; 27:3; 28:11; 30:20; 31:7, 20, 21; and 34:4: thus in Deuteronomy only in the chapters providing the framework and in the late text of 19:8. Elsewhere, see Josh. 1:6; 5:6; 21:43f.; and Judg. 2:1; cf. also Jer. 11:5 and 32:22. For additional texts in the Book of Jeremiah that mention the ancestors, cf. Th. Römer, *Israels Väter*.

109. See also Th. Römer, *Israels Väter*.

110. Thus in Deut. 1:8; 6:10; 30:20; cf. 9:27; 34:4.

111. 1 Kings 11:6, 33; 15:11; 2 Kings 3:2; 14:3; 16:2; 1 Kings 22:54; 2 Kings 14:3; 15:3, 9, 34; 18:3; 21:20; 23:32, 37; and 24:9.

112. To this, cf. Vol. I, pp. 208ff.

113. Cf. also Th. Römer, *Israels Väter*, 344f.

114. For the "ancestors" in the psalms, cf. Th. Römer, *Israels Väter*, 521ff. For Psalm 105, cf. N. Füglister, "Psalm 105 und die Väterverheissung," in FS J. Scharbert, 1989, 41–59.

115. Ps. 14:7 par.; 20:2; 24:6; 46:8, 12; 75:10; 76:7; 78:5; 21, 71; 81:2, 5; 84:9; 94:7; 114:1; 135:4; and 147:19. Cf. H.-J. Zobel, *ThWAT* 3, cols. 773–775.

116. Cf. below, chapter 8 (pp. 39ff.).

117. Cf. K. Baltzer, "Jerusalem in den Erzväter-Geschichten der Genesis?" in E. Blum et al., eds., *Die Hebräische Bibel*, 3–12.

118. For the problem of "Israel and the nations," cf. below, chapter 15 (pp. 284ff.).

119. For Psalm 47, cf. E. Zenger, "Der Gott Abrahams und die Völker," in FS J. Scharbert, 1989, 413–430. According to Zenger, v. 10 belongs to a postexilic or exilic redaction of the psalms.

120. For Gen. 18:16 (23)ff., cf. J. Krašovec and R. Kilian, in FS J. Scharbert, 1989, 169–182 and 160f.

121. For the role of the promise of a son in the Ugaritic Dan'el text, cf. K. Koch, "Die Sohnesver-

heissung an den ugaritischen Daniel," *ZA* NF 24, 1967, 211–221 (=*Studien zur alttesta-mentlichen und altorientalischen Religionsgeschichte*, 1988, 106ff. with supplements).

122. To this, cf. Vol. I, pp. 37, 190, 214, 330.

123. Cf., e.g., Prov. 1:8, 10, 15; 2:1; 3:1, 11, 12, 21; 4:1, 3, 10, 20; 5:1, 17, 20; 6:1, 3, 20; 7:1, 24; 10:1; 15:5, 20; 17:6, 21, 25; 19:13, 18, 26, 27; 20:20; 23:15, 19, 22, 26; 24:13, 21; 27:11; 29:3; and 30:11, 17. Cf. also Job 8:8; 15:10, 18; and 31:18. Somewhat differently nuanced is Prov. 22:28 (cf. Deut. 19:14; 27:17).

124. Cf. D. Wittmann, "Israels Gotteserfahrung auf dem Wege," *PTh* 78, 1989, 247–257.

Chapter 7. Kingship and Messianic Hope

1. For this, see, above all, A. Alt, "Das Königtum in den Reichen Israel und Juda," *VT* 1, 1951, 2–22 (=idem, *KS* 2, 1953, 116ff.); J. Scharbert, *Heilsmittler im Alten Testament und im Alten Orient*, 1964; J. A. Soggin, *Das Königtum in Israel*, 1967 (BZAW 104); idem, "מלך *melek* König," *THAT* 1, cols. 908–920; idem, "Der Beitrag des Königtums zur israelitischen Religion," *VT* Suppl 23, 1972, 9–26; T. Veijola, *Die ewige Dynastie*, Helsinki, 1975; T. N. D. Mettinger, *King and Messiah*, Lund, 1976; T. Veijola, *Das Königtum in der Beurteilung der deuteronomistischen Historiographie*, Helsinki, 1977; F. Crüsemann, *Widerstand gegen das Königtum*, 1978 (WMANT 49); K. H. Whitelam, *The Just King*, 1979 (JSOT Suppl 12); A. H. J. Gunneweg and W. Schmithals, *Herrschaft*, 1980; K. Seybold et al., "מלך/מלך *melek/ mālak*," *ThWAT* 4, cols. 926–957 (lit.); L. Schmidt, "Königtum. II: A. T.," *TRE* 19, 327–330; and K. W. Whitelam, "Israelite Kingship," in R. E. Clements, ed., *The World of Ancient Israel*, Cambridge, 1989, 119–139.

2. On this, also see R. de Vaux, *Das Alte Testament und seine Lebensordnungen* 1, 2d ed., 1964, 163ff.; and J. J. M. Roberts, "In Defense of the Monarchy: The Contribution of Israelite Kingship to Biblical Theology," in P. D. Miller, Jr., et al., eds., *Ancient Israelite Religion,* FS F. M. Cross, Philadelphia, 1987, 377–396.

3. Deut. 17:15; 1 Kings 8:16; 11:34; 1 Chron. 28:4; 2 Chron. 6:6; Pss. 78:70; 89:4; in reference to Solomon, cf. also 1 Chron. 28:5f.; 29:1.

4. E.-J. Waschke, "Das Verhältnis alttestamentlicher Überlieferungen im Schnittpunkt der Dynastiezusage und die Dynastiezusage im Spiegel alttestamentlicher Überlieferungen," *ZAW* 99, 1987, 157–179.

5. Cf. B. S. Childs, *Old Testament Theology in a Canonical Context,* Philadelphia, 1985, 112ff.; W. Zimmerli, *Old Testament Theology in Outline,* Atlanta, 1978, 83–86; from the commentaries, see, above all, J. A. Soggin, *Judges,* 1981 (OTL); in addition, esp. U. Becker, *Richterzeit und Königtum,* 1990 (BZAW 192); there also are more refined literary, critical differentiations within the texts that are under consideration here in a more general way (e.g., Judges 1 or 2:11–19; par.).

6. Cf. M. Noth, "The Background of Judges 17–18," in B. W. Anderson and W. Harrelson, eds., *Israel's Prophetic Heritage,* FS J. Muilenburg, New York, 1962, 65–85; and H. D. Preuss, *Verspottung fremder Religionen im Alten Testament,* 1971 (BWANT 92), 60ff. (lit.).

7. Cf. H. W. Jüngling, *Richter 19—Ein Plädoyer für das Königtum,* 1981 (An Bib 84).

8. Cf. below, pp. 23, 26f. Because U. Becker (*Richterzeit und Königtum*) largely leaves out of consideration the Deuteronomistic view of kingship in Samuel and Kings and tends to view Judges 19–21 as post-Deuteronomistic, he is able to discover only criticisms of the monarchy in the Deuteronomistic texts.

9. Judg. 10:1–5; 12:7–15. Cf. among others W. Richter, "Zu den 'Richtern Israels,' " *ZAW* 77, 1965, 40–72; A. J. Hauser, "The 'Minor Judges'—A Re-evaluation," *JBL* 94, 1975, 190–200; J. A. Soggin, "Das Amt der 'Kleinen Richter' in Israel," *VT* 30, 1980, 245–248; E. Th. Mullen, *CBQ* 44, 1982, 185–201; U. Becker (*Richterzeit und Königtum*), 223f. For the title "judge," cf. H. Niehr, *Herrschen und Richten: Die Wurzel špṭ im Alten Orient und im Alten Testament,* 1986 (fzb 54).

10. For the Samson stories, which in addition portray Samson as a "Nazarite," cf. also below, p. 191.

11. Cf. Vol. I, pp. 160–163.
12. Judg. 3:7–11, 12–15a, 30; 4:1–3, 23f.; 5:31b; 6:1, 6b; 8:28; 10:6f., 10a; 11:33b; 13:1; 15:20; and 16:31b.
13. Cf. Vol. I, p. 161.
14. This is not the place to engage in a debate about the literary, historical location of this text; cf. U. Becker, *Richterzeit und Königtum*, 174ff., 190ff.
15. See the following part of this section (pp. 21–24).
16. Thus according to K. Seybold, *ThWAT* 4, col. 935; the more frequent words are יהוה = YHWH; אלהים = *'ĕlōhîm*; and בֵּן = *bēn* ("son"). Cf. also *THAT* 2, col. 532.
17. For the social-historical and other continuing questions in this connection, see J. J. M. Roberts, "In Defense of the Monarchy," 387ff.; and I. Finkelstein, "The Emergence of the Monarchy in Israel," *JSOT* 44, 1989, 43–74.
18. Cf. by contrast, e.g., the so-called Sumerian King List: *RGT*, 2d ed., 113f.; *TUAT* I/4, 328–337; for this, also see *WdM* I, 92f.
19. Thus, according to the Babylonian tablet VAT 17019 (BE 13383), edited by W. R. Mayer ("Ein Mythos von der Erschaffung des Menschen und des Königs," *Or* 56, 1987, 55–68) and commented on by H.-P. Müller ("Eine neue babylonische Menschenschöpfungserzählung im Licht keilschriftlicher und biblischer Parallelen — Wirklichkeitsauffassung im Mythos," *Or* 58, 1989, 61–85).
20. Cf. also H.-W. Jüngling, *Richter 19 — Ein Plädoyer für das Königtum*.
21. For this, see G. von Rad, *Old Testament Theology*, vol. 1: *The Theology of Israel's Historical Traditions*, New York, 1985, 325–327; and esp. W. Dietrich, *David, Saul und die Propheten*, 1987 (BWANT 122), who has attempted to uncover various narrative and editorial strata.
22. For these problems, see L. Schmidt, "König und Charisma im Alten Testament," *KuD* 28, 1982, 73–87.
23. The combination of anointing and the receiving of the Spirit is found again in Isa. 61:1.
24. For the anointing of kings, see R. de Vaux, *Ancient Israel*, vol. 1: *Social Institutions*, New York, 1961, 103 (the anointing of priests first occurs in the postexilic period); and E. Kutsch, *Salbung als Rechtsakt im Alten Testament und im Alten Orient*, 1963 (BZAW 87). See pp. 52ff. for the anointing of the king in Judah and Israel. In the other countries of the ancient Near East, the anointing of the king is clearly expressed only among the Hittites. *EA* 51, lines 6ff., mentions the anointing of a Syrian king *by* the pharaoh. Egypt was aware of the anointing of high officials by the king, but, by contrast, the anointing of the king during his enthronement is not clearly attested (cf. E. Kutsch, *Salbung als Rechtsakt*, 34ff.).
25. For this historical work see Vol. I, pp. 188f., 216f.
26. For this, see esp. T. Veijola, *Das Königtum in der Beurteilung der deuteronomistischen Historiographie*, 1977. According to H. J. Boecker (*Die Beurteilung der Anfänge des Königtums in den deuteronomistischen Abschnitten des 1. Samuelbuches*, 1969 [WMANT 31]), only certain aspects (imperialistic, theological) of the monarchy are seen here in a critical light. Critical for the distribution of the various evaluations of the monarchy by the different Deuteronomistic strata is the study of U. Becker, "Der innere Widerspruch der deuteronomistischen Beurteilung des Königtums (am Beispiel von 1 Sam 8)," in M. Oeming and A. Graupner, eds., *Altes Testament und christliche Verkündigung*, FS A. H. J. Gunneweg, 1987, 246–270; cf. for this subject also J. J. M. Roberts ("In Defense of the Monarchy") and N. Lohfink ("Der Begriff des Gottesreichs vom Alten Testament her gesehen," in J. Schreiner, ed., *Unterwegs zur Kirche*, 1987, 58f. n. 60) with differentiations drawn between a text "friendly to kingship" from the time of Josiah (Deuteronomistic History I) and an expanded rendition from the exilic period that is "critical of kingship" (Deuteronomistic History II).
27. For this, see Vol. I, pp. 152–159.
28. Here the word משל = *mšl* ("ruler"), not מלך = *melek* ("king"), is used.
29. Saul-Samuel (1 Samuel 13 + 15); David-Nathan (2 Samuel 12); Ahab-Elia (1 Kings 17–19; 21). Cf. Ahaz-Isaiah (Isaiah 7); and Jeremiah-Zedekiah (Jeremiah 26; 34; 36; 38).
30. Cf. Vol. I, pp. 128–138.
31. For this, see H. Donner, *Die Verwerfung des Königs Saul*, 1983; F. Foresti, *The Rejection of Saul in the Perspective of the Deuteronomistic School*, Rome, 1984; and U. Berges, *Die Verwerfung Sauls. Eine thematische Untersuchung*, 1989 (fzb 61).

32. H. Donner (*Die Verwerfung des Königs Saul*, 252f.) thinks of the priesthood of Nob in this regard because of 1 Sam. 21:2–10 and 22:6–23. It appears to me that a pro-Davidic attitude of the Deuteronomistic narrator is more probable.
33. Cf. p. 28 for this.
34. The notice in 2 Sam. 8:18b, according to which the sons of David were priests, is both unclear and obscure. Since this text had a strange feel about it, the Chronicler altered it (1 Chron. 18:17).
35. K. Koch, *Das Wesen altägyptischer Religion im Spiegel ägyptologischer Forschung*, 1989, 12. Koch speaks there (pp. 11–13) of the "sacral absolutism" of the pharaoh. For the theological evaluation of the king in ancient Egypt, cf., e.g., the texts in *RGT*, 2d ed., 53–56; H. Bonnet, *Reallexikon der ägyptischen Religionsgeschichte*, 2d ed., 1971, 380–388; and J. Assmann, *Ma'at: Gerechtigkeit und Unsterblichkeit im Alten Ägypten*, 1990 (see there the appendix).
36. Texts of this ritual are now found in *TUAT* II/2, 212–227; a song for the sacred marriage may be found in *TUAT* II/5, 659–673.
37. For the place of the king in Mesopotamia, see *RLA* VI, 140–173.
38. The "sacrifices of the king" are mentioned in 2 Sam. 6:17; 24:25; 1 Kings 8:5; 9:25; 10:5; 12:33; and 2 Kings 16:15; cf. Ezekiel 45f. which has the analogous term נשׂיא = *nāśî'* ("prince"). 2 Chron. 8:12ff. elaborates on 1 Kings 9:25; cf. 2 Chronicles 35 with 2 Kings 23:21–24 for the passover of Josiah. Is this relatively infrequent mention of the priestly activities of the kings the result of a later removal of such statements? Cf. 2 Sam. 8:18 with 1 Chron. 18:17; see also 2 Chron. 26:16–20 and below, n. 40. For the problem of the king and the cult, see R. de Vaux, *Ancient Israel*, 1:113–114.
39. According to Ezek. 45:13–46:15, the נשׂיא = *nāśî'* ("prince") has complete authority to carry out a precisely regulated sacrifice; however, it is probably intentional that he is not named "king."
40. Cf. to this J. P. Weinberg, "Der König im Weltbild des Chronisten," *VT* 39, 1989, 415–437; there see 428f.
41. Cf. W. Eichrodt, *Theology of the Old Testament*, vol. 1 (OTL), Philadelphia, 1961, 441.
42. C. below, pp. 257–259.
43. Cf. Vol. I, pp. 43f., 45, 122, 211, 215, 236–239.
44. For David, see L. A. Sinclair, "David. I: A. T.," *TRE* 8, 378–384 (lit.); W. Dietrich, "David in Überlieferung und Geschichte, *VuF* 22/1, 1977, 44–64; and T. Veijola, *David*, 1990.
45. According to this, see, above all, T. Veijola, *Die ewige Dynastie*; W. Dietrich, *David, Saul und die Propheten*; and J. H. Grønbaek, *Die Geschichte vom Aufstieg Davids*, Copenhagen, 1971.
46. See L. Schmidt, *Menschlicher Erfolg und Jahwes Initiative*, 1970 (WMANT 38).
47. Cf. above, pp. 21f.
48. For this, see Vol. I, pp. 253–258.
49. Cf. below, pp. 39–51.
50. For this, now see E.-J. Waschke, "Das Verhältnis alttestamentlicher Überlieferungen," 157–179 (lit.).
51. Vv. 11b + 16(b)? Vv. 12, 13b? Or even two older oracles: Vv. 1a, 2, 3, 4, 5a*, and vv. 8a*, 9a, 12, 14, 15, 17 (thus T. Veijola; however, his literary-critical work carries little conviction; cf. E.-J. Waschke, "Das Verhältnis alttestamentlicher Überlieferungen," 162, n. 23). Rather, vv. 1b, 11, 13, 16 are to be seen as resulting from later editing. The promise to the physical son of David is especially to be contrasted with the promise of the continuation of the dynasty. For 2 Kings 8:19, see below.
52. G. von Rad, *Theology*, 1:311: "highly creative in the tradition."
53. See below, pp. 39f. For this subject, see also T. Veijola, *Die ewige Dynastie*.
54. Thus E.-J. Waschke, "Das Verhältnis alttestamentlicher Überlieferungen," 167.
55. For this, see, above all, G. von Rad, *Theology*, 1:311–316; E. Würthwein, *Die Erzählung von der Thronfolge Davids—theologische oder politische Geschichtsschreibung?* 1974 (ThSt 115); and H. Schnabl, *Die "Thronfolgeerzählung David's,"* 1988.
56. For Num. 24:15–19 and its relationship to David, cf. K. Seybold, "Das Herrscherbild des Bileamorakels," *ThZ* 29, 1973, 1–19 (cf. also in U. Struppe, ed., *Studien zum Messiasbild im*

Alten Testament, 1989 [SBAB 6], 89ff.); and H.-J. Zobel, "Bileam-Lieder und Bileam-Erzäh-
lung," in E. Blum et al., eds., *Die Hebräische Bibel und ihre zweifache Nachgeschichte,* FS
R. Rendtorff, 1990, 141–154.

57. See pp. 32f.
58. Cf. below, pp. 35–38 and 275f.
59. See F. Crüsemann, *Widerstand gegen das Königtum;* W. H. Schmidt, "Kritik am Königtum,"
    in H. W. Wolff, ed., *Probleme biblischer Theologie,* FS G. von Rad, 1971, 440–461; and N.
    Lohfink, "Der Begriff des Gottesreichs vom Alten Testament her gesehen," 33–86; there,
    above all, 57ff.
60. N. Lohfink, "Der Begriff des Gottesreichs vom Alten Testament her gesehen," 58.
61. Cf. the placement of ruler and king next to each other in Gen. 37:8.
62. Cf. Vol. I, pp. 152f., 155f.
63. For Isaiah, cf. N. Lohfink, "Der Begriff des Gottesreichs vom Alten Testament her gesehen," 60ff.
64. Cf. pp. 35–37.
65. For this, see H. D. Preuss, *Deuteronomium,* 1982 (EdF 164), 136ff. in connection with N. Loh-
    fink (there p. 232, no. 522).
66. Cf. L. Perlitt, "Ein einzig Volk von Brüdern," in D. Luhrmann and G. Strecker, eds., *Kirche,*
    FS G. Bornkamm, 1980, 27–52.
67. 1 Kings 1:48; 2:4, 24, 33, 45; 5:19; 8:24ff.; 9:5; 11:11ff.; 34, 36, 39; 13:2; 15:4; 2 Kings 8:19;
    18:3; 19:34; 20:5; and 21:7ff. For this, see I. A. Provan, *Hezekiah and the Books of Kings,*
    1988 (BZAW 172), 91ff. Cf. also below, n. 72.
68. See E. Zenger, "Die deuteronomistische Interpretation der Rehabilitierung Jojachins," *BZ* NF
    12, 1968, 16–30.
69. See J. Debus, *Die Sünde Jerobeams,* 1967 (FRLANT 93).
70. Cf. the passages in n. 67 above.
71. Here there may have been a characteristic Deuteronomistic hand at work. Cf. also 1 Kings
    6:12.
72. For the textual and translation problems in 2 Kings 8:19, the theological interpretation, and
    the related questions of Deuteronomistic theology that open up in this connection, see the im-
    portant contribution of N. Lohfink, "Welches Orakel gab den Davididen Dauer?" U. Struppe,
    ed., *Studien zum Messiasbild,* 127–154. According to Lohfink, the promise of Nathan as a
    promise of eternal sovereignty has lost its historical power with the death of Solomon and the
    division of the empire (according to the understanding of Deuteronomy 1). 1 Kings 11:36 is
    then a new promise (ibid., 149ff.).
73. Thus also in P: Num. 1:16; 2:3ff.; 16:2; etc. However, this term is not used exclusively (cf.
    Gen. 17:6; 35:11).
74. Cf. Vol. I, pp. 186f.
75. 2 Samuel 7 seeks rather to combine effectively both of these covenants. For the covenant of
    David, see also pp. 31f.
76. Cf. how Jerusalem/Zion/Temple are analogously regarded. See chapter 8.
77. Cf. the following sect. 8 (pp. 41–51).
78. See, above all, G. Widengren, *Sakrales Königtum im Alten Testament und im Judentum,* 1955;
    K. H. Bernhardt, *Das Problem der altorientalischen Königsideologie im Alten Testament,* 1961
    (VT Suppl 8); H. Frankfort, *Kingship and the Gods,* 6th ed., Chicago and London, 1969; C.
    Westermann, "Das sakrale Königtum in seinen Erscheinungsformen und seiner Geschichte,"
    TB 55, 1974, 291–308; and J. H. Eaton, *Kingship and the Psalms,* 2d ed., London, 1986.
79. An overview of this is found in H. H. Schrey, "Die alttestamentliche Forschung der sogenann-
    ten Uppsala-Schule," *ThZ* 7, 1951, 321–341. Also see G. Widengren, *Sakrales Königtum im
    Alten Testament und im Judentum;* C. Westermann, *Das sakrale Königtum;* and in brief K.
    Seybold, *ThWAT* 4, cols. 946f. Further, see J. H. Hayes and F. C. Prussner, *Old Testament
    Theology: Its History and Development,* London, 1985, 166ff.
80. Cf., however, Vol. I, p. 157.
81. For this, cf. p. 230.
82. Cf. W. von Soden, "Königtum, sakrales," *RGG,* 3d ed., III, cols. 1712–1714; R. de Vaux, *An-
    cient Israel,* 1:111–113; and H. Ringgren, *ThWAT* 4, cols. 930–933. For the monarchy in
    Ugarit, cf. O. Loretz, *Ugarit und die Bibel,* 1990, 204–206 (the king, e.g., as the "son of El").

For the ancient Near Eastern monarchy in general, see W. Fauth, "Diener der Götter—Liebling der Götter: Der Altorientalische Herrscher als Schützling höherer Mächte," *Saec.* 39, 1988, 217–246. For Gudea as "son" of the deity, see *RGT*, 2d ed., 137.

83. Cf. above, n. 38.
84. See B. Janowski, "Das Königtum Gottes in den Psalmen: Bemerkungen zu einem neuen Gesamtentwurf," *ZThK* 86, 1989, 389–454;. See there pp. 424–433 with the list of additional, important literature (W. von Soden; P. Welten) and also the question of the actualization in Israel's cult brought about by the cultic drama. Cf. n. 80.
85. For the theological understanding of the Old Testament cult, see chapter 13, pp. 209ff.
86. See p. 33.
87. Cf. below, p. 116; and for this subject, among others, see W. H. Schmidt, *Alttestamentlicher Glaube*, 6th ed., 225ff.
88. Thus, e.g., the so-called KRT-Text (KTU 1.14–16).
89. Recent surveys of the Ugaritic texts and Ugaritic religion include H. Gese, M. Höfner, and K. Rudolph, *Die Religionen Altsyriens, Altarabiens und der Mandäer*, 1970. See there H. Gese, 1–232. Also see D. Kinet, *Ugarit und die Bibel*, 1981 (SBS 104); and O. Loretz, *Ugarit und die Bibel*.
90. For a different, recent view, see J. H. Eaton, *Kingship and the Psalms*. For a critique, see esp. M. Noth, "Gott, König, Volk im Alten Testament," *ZThK* 47, 1950, 157–191 (= TB 6, 3d ed., 1966, 188ff.).
91. Cf. above, pp. 26–29.
92. Cf. pp. 26 and 21–22.
93. For this, see H.-D. Hoffmann, *Reform und Reformen: Untersuchungen zu einem Grundthema der deuteronomistischen Geschichtsschreibung*, 1980 (AThANT 66); his thesis of an almost single authorship of the Deuteronomistic History is certainly to be criticized.
94. Cf. also E.-J. Waschke, "Das Verhältnis alttestamentlicher Überlieferungen," 178f.
95. For this topic, see M. Weinfeld, *ThWAT* 1, cols. 799–801; and W. Eichrodt, *Theology*, 1:44.
96. Cf. Vol. I, pp. 156f.
97. See F. C. Fensham, "Widow, Orphan, and the Poor in Ancient Near Eastern Legal and Wisdom Literature," *JNES* 21, 1962, 129–139; M. Schwantes, *Das Recht der Armen*, 1977; and W. Thiel, *Die soziale Entwicklung Israels in vorstaatlicher Zeit*, 2d ed., 1985 (see the index; above all, pp. 75, 153f.). For the place of Deuteronomy, see N. Lohfink, "Das deuteronomische Gesetz in der Endgestalt—Entwurf einer Gesellschaft ohne marginale Gruppen," *BN* 51, 1990, 25–40.
98. Cf. pp. 45f.
99. Taking the designation of this category of psalms in a narrow sense. In a broader sense, one should add Psalms 18; 20; 21; 101; 132; as well as Psalms 89 (vv. 20ff., 47–52) and 144:1–11.
100. In addition to the commentaries, see above all for the royal psalms G. von Rad, *Old Testament Theology*, vol. 2: *The Theology of Israel's Prophetic Tradition*, New York, 1965, 319–324; O. Loretz, *Die Königspsalmen*, 1988 (UBL 6); and S. Wagner, "Das Reich des Messias: Zur Theologie der alttestamentlichen Königspsalmen," *ThLZ* 109, 1984, cols. 865–874.
101. For the rites of coronation, see R. de Vaux, *Ancient Israel*, 1:109–113; G. von Rad, "Das judäische Königsritual," *ThLZ* 72, 1947, cols. 211–216 (=TB 8, 3d ed., 1965, 205ff.). For the "protocol," see H.-J. Kraus, BK XV/1, 5th ed., 150f.
102. Cf. above, p. 25.
103. Mesopotamia and Egypt were not familiar with the anointing of the king. In addition, the belief that the king was the bearer of the spirit of the deity while known in Israel was unknown in Israel's religious environment (2 Sam. 16:13; 23:1f.; and Isa. 11:1ff.; this is the case for David and for his ruling descendants; cf. pp. 21 and 25).
104. G. von Rad, *Theology*, 1:321.
105. 2 Samuel 7:14 "linguistically is oriented toward the covenant formula": E.-J. Waschke, "Das Verhältnis alttestamentlicher Überlieferungen," 167.
106. For this expression, see above, pp. 27–28, and Vol. I, index.

107. Cf. the commentaries on Psalm 2; and W. Thiel, "Der Weltherrschaftsanspruch des judäischen Königs nach Psalm 2," *Theologische Versuche* 3, 1971, 53–63.
108. The expression "court language" was introduced by H. Gressmann, *Der Messias*, 1929 (FRLANT 43) [passim; see index]; cf. also H. Gressmann, *Der Ursprung der israelitisch-jüdischen Eschatologie*, 1905 (FRLANT 6), 250ff.
109. A small selection of such texts in *RGT*, 2d ed., 53–56, 131f., 137, 248ff.; *TUAT* II/5, 673ff., 726f.
110. Thus G. von Rad, *Theology*, 1:322.
111. Thus S. Wagner, "Das Reich des Messias," col. 868.
112. G. von Rad, *Theology*, 1:323.
113. For these, see pp. 34ff.
114. "One may hardly go beyond what texts such as Isa. 9:5f.; 11:1–5; Micah 5:1–3; and Jer. 23:5 themselves say about this point, for this was at the same time both the expression and the claim of each king of Jerusalem" (E.-J. Waschke, "Das Verhältnis alttestamentlicher Überlieferungen," 176).
115. See J. Becker, "Die kollektive Deutung der Königspsalmen," *ThPh* 52, 1977, 561–578.
116. Thus with O. H. Steck, *Friedensvorstellungen im alten Jerusalem*, 1972 (ThSt 111), 19f. For YHWH as king, see Vol. I, pp. 152–159.
117. Cf. J. Weinberg, "Der König im Weltbild des Chronisten," 415–437; esp. 436ff.
118. N. Lohfink, "Welches Orakel gab den Davididen Dauer?" and U. Struppe, *Studien zum Messiasbild* 127–154, esp. 141 (138ff. for the Chronicler).
119. For the assessment of the monarchy in the postexilic period, cf. also J. Maier, *Zwischen den Testamenten*, 1990, (NEB AT, Supplement, vol. 3) 237f.
120. See also Vol. I, pp. 160–163.
121. See E. Rohland, *Die Bedeutung der Erwählungstraditionen Israels für die Eschatologie der alttestamentlichen Propheten*, diss., Heidelberg, 1956; G. Fohrer, *Messiasfrage und Bibelverständnis*, 1957; S. Mowinckel, *He That Cometh*, 2d ed., Oxford, 1959; H. W. Wolff, *Frieden ohne Ende*, 1962 (BSt 35); S. Herrmann, *Die prophetischen Heilserwartungen im Alten Testament*, 1965 (BWANT 85); M. Rehm, *Der königliche Messias*, 1968; W. H. Schmidt, "Die Ohnmacht des Messias," *KuD* 15, 1969, 18–34 (also in U. Struppe, ed., *Studien zum Messiasbild*; U. Kellermann, *Messias und Gesetz*, 1971 (BSt 61); K. Seybold, *Das davidische Königtum im Zeugnis der Propheten*, 1972 (FRLANT 107); J. Becker, *Messiaserwartung im Alten Testament*, 1977 (SBS 83); H. Cazelles, *Alttestamentliche Christologie*, 1983; H. Strauss, *Messianisch ohne Messias*, 1984; K.-D. Schunck, "Die Attribute des eschatologischen Messias," *ThLZ* 111, 1986, cols. 641–652; E.-J. Waschke, "Die Frage nach dem Messias im Alten Testament als Problem alttestamentlicher Theologie," *ThLZ* 113, 1988, cols. 321–332; cf. E.-J. Waschke, *ThLZ* 112, 1987, cols. 78f.; R. E. Clements, "The Messianic Hope in the Old Testament," *JSOT* 43, 1989, 3–19; and U. Struppe, ed., *Studien zum Messiasbild*. Cf. also G. von Rad, *Theology*, 2:169–175; and W. H. Schmidt, *Alttestamentlicher Glaube*, 6th ed., 231ff.
122. For the scholarship on this, see, e.g., R. E. Clements, "The Messianic Hope in the Old Testament."
123. Cf. pp. 256–259.
124. The LXX interprets these texts as messianic.
125. Cf. G. von Rad, *Theology*, 1:339, for the Deuteronomistic History.
126. See above, pp. 27–28.
127. See above, pp. 32–33, and the assessments of G. von Rad (*Theology*, 1:30, 323).
128. See above, pp. 33–34.
129. For this problem, cf. H.-P. Müller, *Ursprünge und Strukturen alttestamentlicher Eschatologie*, 1969 (BZAW 109).
130. Cf. above, pp. 27f., and below, pp. 274–277.
131. For Jer. 23:5f., cf. also H.-J. Hermisson, in E. Blum et al., eds., *Die Hebräische Bible*, FS R. Rendtorff, 1990, 278, 284f., and 290f. For righteousness as salvation, cf. Vol. I, pp. 171–179.
132. For the tensions in the relationship of messiah, law, and divine sovereignty and the different

lines of attribution which may be traced out for each of these entities, see U. Kellermann, *Messias und Gesetz*.

133. The participle הנפלת (*hannōpelet* = "falling") must not be translated as referring to the past!
134. From the comprehensive literature on this text, I shall mention only from the recent period H. Irsigler, "Zeichen und Bezeichnetes in Jes 7:1–17," *BN* 29, 1985, 75–114 (lit.). Also found in U. Struppe, ed., *Studien zum Messiasbild*, 155–197.
135. For the "messianic" texts in Isaiah, see A. Laato, *Who Is Immanuel?* Åbo, 1988.
136. Thus with K.-D. Schunck, "Der fünfte Thronname des Messias (Jes. ix 5–6)," *VT* 23, 1973, 108–110 (cf. his essay in *ThLZ* 111, 1986, cols. 644–650).
137. For the frequently encountered view that Isa. 9:1–6 is an addition, see the methodological, critical reflections of N. Lohfink in *Unterwegs zur Kirche*, 65, 83.
138. Cf. H.-J. Hermisson, "Zukunftserwartung und Gegenwartskritik in der Verkündigung Jesajas," *EvTh* 33, 1973, 58–61.
139. Even if one takes this only out of Micah 1–3!
140. For "branch" (צמח = *semah*), cf. Zech. 3:8; 6:12.
141. Ezekiel 34 and 37:15ff. certainly are present in a later redaction.
142. See above, pp. 31–32.
143. For these songs, see pp. 303–305.
144. For this idea, see pp. 253f.
145. For this problem, see U. Kellermann, *Messias und Gesetz*, 57ff.; also see 91f. for the two messiahs in the texts of Qumran. For Haggai and Zechariah, cf. also K. Seybold, "Die Königserwartung bei den Propheten Haggai und Sacharja," *Jud* 28, 1972, 69–78 (also in U. Struppe, ed., *Studien zum Messiasbild*, 243–252).
146. For the historical development of the Old Testament's witness to the messiah, cf. H. Gese, "Der Messias," in *Zur biblischen Theologie*, 3d ed., 1989, 128–151.
147. For this, see above, pp. 33f.
148. "4QpsDanA = 4Q 246 and *Ethiopic Enoch* 45–47 interpret this in a messianic fashion. For this topic, see K. Koch et al., *Das Buch Daniel*, 1980 (EdF 144), 216ff.; and H. Haag, "בן־אדם," *ThWAT* 1, cols. 682–689.
149. For this, see E. Kutsch, *Salbung als Rechtsakt*, 1963 (BZAW 87).
150. E.-J. Waschke, "Die Frage nach dem Messias," col. 325.
151. Cf. also Dan. 9:25ff. where the anointed one and the prince most likely refer to the high priest Joshua; cf. the commentaries.
152. See esp. W. H. Schmidt, "Die Ohnmacht des Messias."
153. See J. Becker, *Die Messiaserwartung im Alten Testament*, 63ff., who is somewhat too confident in his discovery of such transformations, especially in the texts of Isaiah.
154. Cf. the reflections of G. Fohrer, *Grundstrukturen*, 17ff.; E.-J. Washcke, "Die Frage nach dem Messias," cols. 328ff.; and also H. D. Preuss, *Das Alte Testament in christlicher Predigt*, 1984. Also see the comprehensive contribution by E. Zenger, "Jesus von Nazaret und die messianischen Hoffnungen des alttestamentlichen Israel," in U. Struppe, ed., *Studien zum Messiasbild*, 23–66. In addition, see the introduction by Struppe (pp. 7–21). Cf. also Vol. I and the "fundamental structures" in the index.

Chapter 8. The Temple and the City of God (the So-called Zion Tradition)

1. See M. Schmidt, *Prophet und Tempel*, 1948; H. Schmid, "Jahweh und die Kulttraditionen von Jerusalem," *ZAW* 67, 1955, 168–197; G. Fohrer, "Zion-Jerusalem im Alten Testament," in *Studien zur alttestamentlichen Theologie und Geschichte*, 1969 (BZAW 115), 195–241 (cf. *ThWNT* 7, 291ff.); J. Schreiner, *Sion-Jerusalem, Jahwes Königssitz*, 1963 (StNT 7); H. Gese, "Der Davidsbund und die Zionserwählung," *ZThK* 61, 1964, 1–26 (= *Vom Sinai zum Zion*, 3d ed., 1990, 113ff.); R. E. Clements, *God and Temple*, Oxford, 1965; G. Wanke, *Die Zionstheologie der Korachiten*, 1966 (BZAW 97); Th. A. Busink, *Der Tempel von Jerusalem*, vol. 1, 1970; vol. 2, 1980; F. Stolz, *Strukturen und Figuren im Kult von Jerusalem*, 1970 (BZAW 118); J. Jeremias, "Lade und Zion," in H. W. Wolff, ed., *Probleme biblischer Theologie*, FS

G. von Rad, 1971, 183–198 (= *Das Königtum Gottes in den Psalmen,* 1987 [FRLANT 141], 167ff.); O. H. Steck, *Friedensvorstellungen im alten Jerusalem,* 1972 (ThSt 111); V. Fritz, *Tempel und Zelt,* 1977 (WMANT 47); H.-J. Kraus, *Theologie der Psalmen,* 1979 (BK XV/3), 88–103; E. Otto, *Jerusalem—die Geschichte der Heiligen Stadt,* 1980 (cf. also idem, "Kultus und Ethos in Jerusalemer Theologie," *ZAW* 98, 1986, 161–179); B. C. Ollenburger, *The City of the Great King,* Sheffield, 1987 (JSOT Suppl 41); E. Otto, "צִיּוֹן *ṣijjôn*," *ThWAT* 6, cols. 994–1028 (lit.); O. H. Steck, "Zion als Gelände und Gestalt," *ZThK* 86, 1989, 261–281; B. Janowski, "Das Königtum Gottes in den Psalmen: Bemerkungen zu einem neuen Gesamtentwurf," *ZThK* 86, 1989, 389–454, esp. 428ff.; cf. also G. von Rad, *Old Testament Theology,* vol. 2: *The Theology of Israel's Prophetic Traditions,* New York, 1985, 61–62; and W. H. Schmidt, *Alttestamentlicher Glaube,* 6th ed., 249–262.

2. The age of Psalm 68 is debated. It is more than doubtful, in my view, that the psalm already would have originated in the thirteenth century B.C.E. However, see the opinion of J. C. de Moor, *The Rise of Yahwism,* 1990 (BETL 91) [see there the index]; cf. also Vol. I, p. 280. This thesis is connected to his other wide-reaching views about early Yahwism.

3. Cf. below, pp. 44f., and, moreover, Vol. I, p. 32.

4. Enuma eliš VI, 38ff.: *AOT,* 2d ed., 122f.; *ANET,* 2d and 3d eds., 68f.

5. 2 Sam. 10:12; Pss. 46:5; 48:2f., 9; 87:3; 101:8; Isa. 60:14; and 1 Chron. 19:13; cf. Tob. 13:10.

6. Isa. 48:2; 52:1; Neh. 11:1; and Dan. 9:24. Cf. Isa. 64:9 and Obadiah 17.

7. 2 Sam. 5:7, 9; 6:10; 1 Kings 2:10; 3:1; 8:1; 9:24; 11:27; 1 Chron. 11:5, 7; Isa. 22:9; etc.

8. Pss. 3:5; 48:2; 87:1 plural; Joel 2:1; 4:17; Isa. 27:13; 56:7; 65:11, 25; 66:20; Zech. 8:3; and Dan. 9:16.

9. Cf. the song of praise directed toward the city of Arbela: *TUAT* II/5, 768–770.

10. See J. Schreiner, *Sion-Jerusalem,* 219ff.

11. For this motif, see F. Stolz, *Strukturen und Figuren,* 72ff.; and H.-M. Lutz, *Jahweh, Jerusalem und die Völker,* 1968 (WMANT 27). The assault of the nations is a postexilic motif complex for E. Otto, *ThWAT* 6, col. 1023; cf. also G. Wanke, *Die Zionstheologie der Korachiten.*

12. This "Zion torah" has great significance in the traditiohistorical views of H. Gese and P. Stuhlmacher. Cf. H. Gese, "Das Gesetz," in *Zur biblischen Theologie,* 3d ed., 1989, 55–84; P. Stuhlmacher, "Das Gebet als Thema biblischer Theologie," in *Versöhnung, Gesetz und Gerechtigkeit,* 1981, 136–165. Cf. Vol. I, p. 92.

13. Enuma eliš VI, 38ff.; *AOT,* 2d ed., 122; *ANET,* 2d and 3d eds., 68. For the temple precinct of Babylon with the ziggurat Etemenanki and the low-lying temple of Esagila, cf. also H. Klengel, ed., *Kulturgeschichte des alten Vorderasien,* 1989, 404ff.

14. See V. Fritz, *Tempel und Zelt,* 16–19.

15. For the "Angel of Yahweh," see Vol. I, pp. 165–166.

16. The contrasting account in Judg. 1:8 "perhaps originated from an incorrect interpretation of the conclusion of 1:7 and thus does not correspond to the facts" (G. Fohrer, "Zion-Jerusalem im Alten Testament," 207 n. 65).

17. For the ark, see Vol. I, pp. 253–254. For the cherubim throne, see Vol. I, pp. 256f.

18. Or only against a certain interpretation of this temple?

19. See G. von Rad, *Old Testament Theology,* vol. 1: *The Theology of Israel's Historical Tradition,* New York, 1985, 61–62; and esp. J. Schreiner, *Sion-Jerusalem,* 80ff.

20. See W. H. Schmidt, *Königtum Gottes in Ugarit und Israel,* 2d ed., 1966 (BZAW 80), 68ff. Cf. the text in *RGT,* 2d ed., 215–220.

21. A brief overview is found in V. Fritz, *Tempel und Zelt,* 37ff., esp. 41ff. in particular the temple of Arad. Also see M. Görg, "Arad," *NBL* 1, cols. 145ff. Rich in materials is the volume H. Weippert, *Palästina in vorhellenistischer Zeit,* 1988 (Handbuch der Archäologie 2/1), esp. 620ff. Unfortunately there is no index to these materials. There is an excursus concerning Jerusalem, the temple building, and so forth (pp. 449–476).

22. Jebusites are mentioned as the pre-Israelite inhabitants of the city-state of Jerusalem in Josh. 15:8, 63; 18:28; Judg. 1:21; 19:10; 2 Sam. 5:6, 8; and 24:18.

23. See F. Stolz, *Strukturen und Figuren,* esp. 149ff.; and O. H. Steck, *Friedensvorstellungen,* 9ff. M. Tsevat debates this, "ירושלם *jerûšālem/jerûšālajim,*" *ThWAT* 3, cols. 930–939, esp. 932f.

24. See J. A. Emerton, ed., *Studies in the Pentateuch,* VT Suppl 41, 1990, 45–71.

25. "This shows that Israel, already embodied in the patriarchs, was knowingly obligated to the precursor of David as well as Jerusalem and its cult" (J. Jeremias, "Lade und Zion," 185). Cf. H.-J. Zobel, "עֶלְיוֹן *'aeljôn*," *ThWAT* 6, cols. 131–151. For Gen. 14:18ff., cf. also above, pp. 17f; for the blessing of Melchizedek, see Vol. I, p. 175. For a different view, see H. Niehr, *Der höchste Gott*, 1990 (BZAW 190), who says that "for religio-historical and literary-historical reasons . . . it is no longer correct to maintain the identification of YHWH with El (p. 10). Also see there on pp. 167ff. the "Jerusalem tradition of the cult." If in respect to the conquest, the oppression in Egypt is spoken of as a whole as "the Old Testament's reconstructions of history" (p. 188) and as a construct that has nothing to do with the real course of Israel's religious history (p. 188), then the certainty with which this judgment is rendered is astonishing. Indeed, if true, Hosea would be cast aside with one wave of the hand (p. 186).

26. Did this occur during the time of David or for the first time in the postexilic period? Cf. K. Baltzer, "Jerusalem in den Erzvätergeschichten der Genesis?" in E. Blum et al., eds., *Die Hebräische Bibel und ihre zweifache Nachgeschichte*, FS R. Rendtorff, 1990, 3–12; and above, p. 16.

27. For this, cf. Vol. I, pp. 173f.

28. Isa. 1:26; 60:17; 62:1; Joel 2:23f.; Zech. 8:3; Pss. 72:3; and 85:9ff. In addition, see F. Stolz, *Strukturen und Figuren*, 181ff., 216, 218f.; and O. H. Steck, *Friedensvorstellungen*, 26f.

29. For this possible influence, see Vol. I, p. 230.

30. See E. Lipiński, "צָפוֹן *ṣapôn*," *ThWAT* 6, cols. 1093–1102. For Zaphon as Baal's "holy mountain" and "mountain of my possession," see *KTU* 1.3:III, 29f. Cf. *RGT*, 2d ed., 216f., 218, 227.

31. Concerning the temple, see, e.g., *RGT*, 2d ed., 130f.; *TUAT* II/5, 686–688; and A. Falkenstein and W. von Soden, *Sumerische und akkadische Hymnen und Gebete*, 1953, 131ff. When a temple was repaired (or built), one used for this, according to the account of repairs set forth in *TUAT* II/4, 490–493, asphalt and pitch (cf. Gen. 11:3) and caused its pinnacle "once again to rival heaven" (Gen. 11:4). For the assessment of the temple in Israel's cultural environment, see M. V. Fox, ed., *Temple in Society*, Winona Lake, Ind., 1988.

32. For the kingship of YHWH, see Vol. I, pp. 152–159.

33. "The military deity, YHWH, who came out of the wilderness, has been put together with the militant god, Baal, who is the lord of Zaphon" (H. Spieckermann, *Heilsgegenwart*, 1989 [FRLANT 148], 194).

34. Less so Baal; cf. Vol. I, pp. 155f.

35. For the temple building, see J. Schreiner, *Sion-Jerusalem*, 137ff.; Th. A. Busink, *Der Tempel von Jerusalem*; and H. Weippert, *Palästina in vorhellenistischer Zeit*.

36. A Jebusite prehistory even for the temple is assumed by K. Rupprecht, *Der Tempel von Jerusalem*, 1976 (BZAW 144). Cf. also M. J. Mulder, *OTS* 25, 1989, 49–62.

37. See Th. A. Busink, *Der Tempel von Jerusalem*; and H. Weippert, *Palästina in vorhellenistischer Zeit*. Further, see V. Fritz, *Tempel und Zelt*, 13ff.; A. Kuschke, "Tempel," *BRL*, 2d ed., 1977, 333–342. Cf. also the outline of "Temple D" in Ebla: H. Klengel, ed., *Kulturgeschichte des alten Vorderasien*, 1989, 224f.

38. For the problem of the "dwelling" of YHWH, see Vol. I, pp. 250–253.

39. Cf. Exod. 23:19; 34:26; Deut. 23:19; 1 Kings 8:27, 29; Isa. 56:5, 7; 66:20; Jer. 7:2; Pss. 5:8; 23:6; and 66:13. The "House of YHWH," mentioned in the reconstructed inscription on the ivory pomegranate that came into the possession of the Israel Museum in Jerusalem, was probably the (Solomonic) temple. Cf. N. Avigad, "The Inscribed Pomegranate from the 'House of the Lord,' " *BA* 53, 1990 (Nr. 3), 157–166.

40. Cf. above, p. 324 n. 17.

41. For the "countenance" of YHWH, see Vol. I, pp. 163–165.

42. R. de Vaux, *Ancient Israel*, vol. 2: *Religious Institutions*, New York, 1961, 327–328.

43. H. Spieckermann, *Heilsgegenwart*, 108; esp. 96ff. dealing in detail with Exodus 15 under the theme "Exodus and Temple Mount," and 88ff. for salvation history and temple cult.

44. See S. Schroer, *In Israel gab es Bilder*, 1987 (OBO 74), 46ff.; and Th. A. Busink, *Der Tempel von Jerusalem*, 1:162ff.

45. B. Janowski, "Das Königtum Gottes," 417f. Also see idem, "Tempel und Schöpfung," *JBTh* 5, 1990, 37–69. In the latter article, he explores the temple symbolism and theology of Israel

as well as their (transformed) incorporation into the creation and sanctuary theology in the Priestly source.

46. R. de Vaux, *Ancient Israel*, 2:312. An attempt at the reconstruction of the text is made by R. C. Scott, "The Pillars Jachin and Boaz," *JBL* 58, 1959, 143–149.

47. For their significance, cf. also E. Würthwein, ATD 11/1, 89ff.

48. According to J. Jeremias ("Lade und Zion," 197), the complete Zion tradition in its oldest form represented "nothing more for Israel at that time than a contemporary exegesis of the ark and its tradition carried out with the help of Canaanite motifs." Critical of this view is H. Spieckermann, *Heilsgegenwart*, 95f., etc.; and B. Janowski, "Das Königtum Gottes," 429f. (with notes), and further literature. Completely different is the view of H. Niehr, *Der höchste Gott.*

49. Cf. also H. Gese, "Der Davidsbund und die Zionserwählung."

50. From the beginning, this significance was probably not as great for Jerusalem as has often been assumed. Thus H. Spieckermann, *Heilsgegenwart*, 95f., etc.; and B. Janowski, "Das Königtum Gottes," 429f.

51. Cf. *TGI*, 2d ed., nr. 39. In addition, J. Schreiner, *Sion-Jerusalem*, 236ff.; and R. Liwak, "Die Rettung Jerusalems im Jahr 701 v. Chr.," *ZThK* 83, 1986, 137–166.

52. These texts may be sought among the following: Isa. 1:4–9; 10:5–15, 27b-32; 22:1–14; 28:23–29; 29:15f.; 30:1–5, 6f.; 31:1–3, 4–9; and 32:9–14.

53. E.g., Isa. 1:21–26; 7:1ff.; 14:24–27; 28:16f.; 29:1–7; and 31:1–9. According to R. Kilian (*Jesaja 1–39*, 1983 [EdF 200], 40–97; similarly also E. Otto, *ThWAT* 6, cols. 1012ff.), none of these texts belongs to Isaiah. Rather, they contain the words of later, mostly postexilic poets and redactors. Cf. also O. Kaiser, *Isaiah 1–12: A Commentary,* 2d ed., London; Philadelphia, 1983 (OTL); and idem, *Isaiah 13–39: A Commentary,* 2d ed., London; Philadelphia, 1980 (OTL) and *TRE* 16, 636–658. Kilian also considers the Zion psalms to be postexilic. For a different view, see esp. G. von Rad, *Theology* 2:155–159; J. Schreiner, *Sion-Jerusalem*, 243ff.; and H. Wildberger, *Isaiah 1–12,* Minneapolis, 1991 (CC). Here, one shall have to make some precise differentiations. This is true also with respect to the combinations of Zion, remnant, Immanuel, the messiah, cornerstone, and so forth, which B. G. Webb carries out in the Book of Isaiah as a whole ("Zion in Transformation," in D. Clines et al., eds., *The Bible in Three Dimensions*, 1990 [JSOT Suppl 87], 65–84).

54. Thus, e.g., Isa. 8:9ff.; 14:28–32; 17:12–14; 29:8; and 30:27–33.

55. According to E. Otto (*ThLZ* 113, 1988, col. 736), Zion theology, moreover, represented a "counterpunch . . . thrown against the experiences with the superior powers of Babylonia and Persia in the exilic and postexilic periods."

56. Cf. already Vol. I, pp. 170f., and above, p. 39.

57. Cf. T. N. D. Mettinger, *The Dethronement of Sebaoth*, Lund, 1982 (CB OT 18), 38–79.

58. Deut. 12:5, 11, 14, 18, 21, 26; 14:23–25; 15:20; 16:2, 6, 7, 11, 15, 16; 17:8, 10; 18:6; 23:17; 26:2; 31:11; Josh. 9:27; 1 Kings 8:16, 44; 11:13, 32, 36; 14:21; and 2 Kings 21:7; 23:27; cf. 2 Chron. 6:5, 6, 34, 38; 7:12, 16; 12:13; 33:7; and Neh. 1:9.

59. Cf. B. Janowski, " 'Ich will in eurer Mitte wohnen,' " *JBTh* 2, 1987,177ff., 186f. (lit.).

60. Pss. 76:68; 132:13; Zech. 1:17; 2:16; 3:2; 2 Chron. 6:5, 6, 34, 38; 7:12, 16; 12:13; 33:7; and Neh. 1:9.

61. Cf. H. D. Preuss, *Deuteronomium*, 1982 (EdF 164), 1–19.

62. In Qoh. 1:1 the "King of *Jerusalem*" is only part of the "fiction" beginning with the superscription. For this, see R. Lux, "Ich, Kohelet, bin König . . .": Die Fiktion als Schlüssel zur Wirklichkeit in Kohelet 1,12 - 2,26," *EvTh* 50, 1990, 331–342.

63. Cf. H.-J. Kraus, *Theology of the Psalms,* (CC) Minneapolis, 1986, 78–83; and H. Spieckermann, *Heilsgegenwart.*

64. It is the heavenly throne, and less so the ark, that is seen in close association with the temple. Cf. Ps. 68:19 and the study of B. Janowski, "Das Königtum Gottes," 428–446.

65. Cf. also Vol. I, pp. 158f.

66. H. Spieckermann (*Heilsgegenwart*, 73–86) believes he can make a more distinct differentiation and that he can point to a development.

67. For YHWH as king, see Vol. I, pp. 152–159.

68. For this, see Vol. I, pp. 167–170.

69. For the theology of the cult and the temple in the Priestly document, see V. Fritz, *Tempel und*

Zelt, passim; and B. Janowski, " 'Ich will in eurer Mitte wohnen,' " 165–193. See also the previous note.

70. Cf. Isa. 1:21; 3:1–9, 16f.; 22:14; 29:1–7; 32:14; Micah 1:5; 3:1f., 9–12 = cited in Jer. 26:18; Zeph. 1:12; Hab. 2:12; Jer. 4:6; 5:1; 6:6f.; 7:1ff.; 9:18; 13:22, 26; 14:16; 32:3; 34:2, 22; Ezek. 16; 22:19–21; and 24:9–13. Cf. also E. Otto, "עיר *'îr,*" *ThWAT* 6, cols. 56–74, esp. 70f.

71. For the theology of the exile, see L. Perlitt, "Anklage und Freispruch Gottes," *ZThK* 69, 1972, 290–303.

72. The exile was therefore "not the place of complete abandonment by God," since probably there were forms of worship there that emerged from "necessity." See W. Zimmerli, *Ezekiel: A Commentary on the Book of the Prophet Ezekiel,* vol. 1 (Hermeneia), Philadelphia, 1979–1983, 261–262.

73. See B. Janowski, " 'Ich will in eurer Mitte wohnen' "; and Vol. I, pp. 167f., for the "glory of YHWH."

74. For P and Ezekiel, see also T. N. D. Mettinger, *The Dethronement of Sebaoth,* 80–115; also see above, p. XX.

75. For the priestly אהל מעד (*'ōhel mō'ēd,* "tent of meeting"), cf. Vol. I, pp. 254–256.

76. In addition to the commentaries and the literature mentioned there, cf. R. de Vaux, *Ancient Israel,* 2:322–323.

77. Cf. Vol. I, p. 122. For this feature of Deutero-Isaiah, cf. H. D. Preuss, *Deuterojesaja: Eine Einführung in seine Botschaft,* 1976, 45f.

78. Cf. below, p. 329 n. 99.

79. That not everyone was resigned to this form of existence can be seen in the Books of Chronicles with the restoration of war, conquest, and fortresses.

80. G. von Rad, *Theology,* 2:292: "now comprised only as a city."

81. Or is "this people" the Jewish community itself? Thus K. Koch, "Haggais unreines Volk," *ZAW* 79, 1967, 52–66 (=*Spuren des hebräischen Denkens,* 1991, 206ff.).

82. Cf. above, pp. 39–40. Additional comments about the role of Zion in Isaiah 40–66 are found in O. H. Steck, *Bereitete Heimkehr,* 1985 (SBS 121); and "Tritojesaja im Jesajabuch," in J. Vermeylen, ed., *The Book of Isaiah,* 1989 (BETL 81), 361–406 (lit.).

83. See K. Seybold, *Die Wallfahrtspsalmen,* 1978 (BThSt 3). For the postexilic meaning and significance of the temple, cf. also J. Maier, *Zwischen den Testamenten,* 1990 (NEB AT, Supplement, vol. 3), 196ff.

84. Cf. V. Fritz, *Tempel und Zelt,* esp. 147ff.; M. Kartveit, *Motive und Schichten der Landtheologie in I Chronik 1–9,* Stockholm, 1989 (CB OT 28); and M. Oeming, *Das wahre Israel,* 1990 (BWANT 128).

85. Cf. above, n. 82.

86. For an additional history of Jerusalem, see E. Otto, *Jerusalem,* 127ff., 174ff. Also see the article "Jerusalem" (different authors) in *TRE* 16, 590–635.

87. Cf. immediately following pp. 49f.

88. Cf. Vol. I, pp. 253f.

89. "Yahweh, the deity who came from the wilderness, or from Egypt (Hos. 12:10; and 13:4) or from Sinai (Deut. 33:2; Judg. 5:5; and Ps. 68:9), took upon himself a twofold assignment in the promised land. On the one hand, he develops from a tribal deity into a deity of a nation: Jahweh, the God of Israel—Israel, the people of Yahweh. On the other hand, he was transformed from a deity without a fixed dwelling place into a royal deity enthroned over the cherubim in the Canaanite temples of the land of Canaan before finally being established as a temple deity in his own Jerusalem temple after an initial Canaanite apprenticeship. The Zadokite priests made rich usage of the Canaanite religious heritage that has been entrusted to them: Yahweh, King of the pantheon—Yahweh, my King and my God" (H. Spieckermann, *Heilsgegenwart,* 284).

90. Cf., e.g., *RGT,* 2d ed., 130f., 136f.; or also *TUAT* II/5, 768–770 (Song of Praise to the City of Arbela).

91. See E. Otto, "Kultus und Ethos in Jerusalemer Theologie," *ZAW* 98, 1986, 161, 179.

92. For these, cf. Vol. I, pp. 152ff.

93. Cf. Gen. 2:10–14 and El's dwelling place "at the source of the streams" on the cosmic mountain (*KTU* 1.2: III, 4f.; 1.3:V, 6f.; 1.4:IV, 21f.; 1.6:I, 33f.; and 1.17:VI, 47f.). In addition, see J. Jeremias, "Lade und Zion," 192f.; and O. Loretz, *Ugarit und die Bibel,* 1990, 66f.

94. Cf. below, n. 105.
95. Thus, esp. H.-J. Kraus, *Gottesdienst in Israel*, 2d ed., 1962, 215ff.
96. O. H. Steck ("Zion als Gelände und Gestalt," *ZThK* 86, 1989, 266f.) gives consideration to a "Yahweh—Zion—Festival" for which he enlists Psalms 24; 47; and 93; as well as Psalms 46 and 48.
97. "The enemy may perhaps have designated the songs according to an external characteristic in contrast to the Israelite who designated them according to their inner nature" (H. Spieckermann, *Heilsgegenwart*, 118). However, is the term "Song of Zion" only an "external" characteristic?
98. Cf. above, pp. 44f.
99. Isa. 40:9–11; 49:14–17; 51:3, 9–11, 17–23; 52:1–3, 7–10, 11–12; 54; etc. Cf. above, pp. 46f.; and J. Marböck, "Exodus zum Zion," in J. Zmijewski, ed., *Die Alttestamentliche Botschaft als Wegweisung*, FS H. Reinelt, 1990, 163–179.
100. On account of Zech. 8:4, 20, עוֹד = *'ôd* is hardly to be understood as "continue"; cf. Vol. I, p. 35.
101. Cf. also below, pp. 298f. For the place of Isaiah 35, especially its views of the temple and the presence of YHWH, in the history of Israelite faith, cf. O. H. Steck, *Bereitete Heimkehr*, 1985 (SBS 121), 48f. n. 19.
102. Cf. already above, p. 47.
103. Cf. below, pp. 284–307.
104. Cf. below, pp. 27 + 91.
105. See O. H. Steck, *Friedensvorstellungen*, 25ff.; and Vol. I, pp. 137f.
106. J. Schreiner, *Sion-Jerusalem*, 155.
107. O. H. Steck, "Zion als Gelände und Gestalt," 267.
108. 2 Kings 19:21 par.; Isa. 1:8; 10:32; 16:1; 22:4; 52:2; 62:11; Jer. 4:30f.; 6:2, 23; Ezek. 16:44; Micah 1:13; 4:8, 10; Zeph. 3:14; Zech. 2:14; 9:9; Lam. 2:1, 13, 15, 18; 4:22; etc. Additional passages are found in E. Otto, *ThWAT* 6, cols. 1010f.
109. So with O. H. Steck, "Zion als Gelände und Gestalt," 272–278.
110. H. Spieckermann, *Heilsgegenwart*, 292.

Chapter 9. Priests and Levites

1. See W. Graf Baudissin, *Die Geschichte des alttestamentlichen Priesterthums*, 1899 (reprinted 1967); H.-J. Kraus, *Gottesdienst in Israel*, 2d ed., 1962, 113ff.; R. de Vaux, *Ancient Israel*, vol. 2: *Religious Institutions*, New York, 1961, 345–357; A. H. J. Gunneweg, *Leviten und Priester*, 1965 (FRLANT 89); A. Cody, *A History of Old Testament Priesthood*, Rome, 1969 (AnBib 35); A. Deissler, "Das Priestertum im Alten Testament," *Der priesterliche Dienst* 1, 1970, 9–80; H. Valentin, *Aaron*, 1978 (OBO 18); W. Dommershausen (and others), "כהן *kohen*," *ThWAT* 4, cols. 62–79 (lit.); D. Kellermann, "לוי *lewî*," *ThWAT* 4, cols. 499–521 (lit.); and H. Schulz, *Leviten im vorstaatlichen Israel und im Mittleren Osten*, 1987. Also cf. W. Eichrodt, *Theology of the Old Testament*, vol. 1 (OTL), Philadelphia, 1961, 392–436; G. von Rad, *Old Testament Theology*, vol. 1: *The Theology of Israel's Historical Tradition*, New York, 1985, 241–250; W. Zimmerli, *Old Testament Theology in Outline*, Atlanta, 1978, 92–99; A. Deissler, *Grundbotschaft*, 127ff.; B. S. Childs, *Old Testament Theology in a Canonical Context*, Philadelphia, 1985; and A. Bertholet, *Biblische Theologie des Alten Testaments* 2, 1911, 9–23.
2. See Vol. I, pp. 29 + 35f.
3. For the Hebrew כֹּהֵן = *kōhēn* (priest), cf. the Arabic *kahin* ("seer, soothsayer") and the Ugaritic *kahinu* for a cultic official.
4. Cf. above, pp. 7f.
5. Cf. p. 42.
6. According to A. H. J. Gunneweg, *Leviten und Priester*, 109ff, this is a text that has been redacted several times and actualized in different ways.
7. For this, cf. Vol. I, pp. 253–254.

8. Cf. A. van den Born, "Ephod," *BL*, 2d ed., cols. 402f.; I. Friedrich, *Ephod und Choschen*, 1968; and M. Görg, "Efod," *NBL* 1, cols. 472f. For the tradition strand of the "Ephod as an image" (Judg. 8:27; 17:5; etc.), cf. S. Schroer, *In Israel gab es Bilder*, 1987 (OBO 74), 136ff.

9. See H. Madl, "Die Gottesbefragung mit dem verb שאל," in H.-J. Fabry, ed., *Bausteine biblischer Theologie, FS G. J. Botterweck*, 1977 (BBB 50), 37–70. The oracle lots, Urim and Thummim, also belong to these settings (Deut. 33:8; 1 Sam. 28:6; and Lev. 8:8), although no one knew how to handle them in the the postexilic period (Ezra 2:63; and Neh. 7:65). Cf. below, p. 65.

10. Cf. L. A. Snijders, *ThWAT* 4, cols. 881–884.

11. Cf. the "holy" in Exod. 29:44 and the whole of Exodus 29 and Leviticus 8.

12. Cf. also Ezek. 44:4–20, 22–31.

13. Cf. Vol. I, pp. 131–132.

14. Cf. above, n. 6.

15. 2 Samuel 8:17 has a corrupted text. For Zadok, cf. in addition 2 Sam. 17:15; 20:25; 1 Kings 1:8, 32, 34; and 2:35. Also cf. above, p. 42.

16. Thus with W. H. Schmidt, BK II/1, 205. For Aaron, cf. also R. de Vaux, *Ancient Israel*, 2:294–297; H. Schmid, *Die Gestalt des Mose*, 1986 (EdF 237), 88–93; and M. Görg, "Aaron," *NBL* 1, cols. 1f.

17. The source analysis of this verse is unclear.

18. H. Valentin, *Aaron*, 165ff.

19. According to H. Valentin (*Aaron*, 196f.), Exod. 17:8ff. is the oldest text. This book, important for getting through the material, delights too much in hypotheses. For another view of Exod. 17:10b, 12, cf., e.g., E. Zenger, *Israel am Sinai*, 1982, 76ff.

20. For Exodus 32 and the ancient source that is probably contained in it, cf. also Vol. I, pp. 109–110.

21. See H. D. Preuss, *Verspottung fremder Religionen im Alten Testament*, 1971 (BWANT 92), 53ff.; and F. Kohata, *Jahwist und Priesterschrift in Exodus 3–14*, 1986 (BZAW 166), 219ff.

22. For the relationship between the Aaronides, Zadokites, and Levites, cf. also J. A. Emerton, ed., *Studies in the Pentateuch*, VT Suppl 41, 1990, 149–159.

23. Cf. p. 318 n. 38. That David's sons were supposed to be priests is mentioned only in 2 Sam. 8:18 and here in an unclear note. Cf. p. 319 n. 34. For the problem of 1 Samuel 13 in the context of the theme of the "rejection" of Saul, cf. above, p. 23, with p. 318 n. 31.

24. Cf., e.g., 1 Kings 3:4, 15 Solomon (before the building of the temple). A similar act of Ahaz (2 Kings 16:12ff.) is already looked at critically. At the same time the altar mentioned in this passage was constructed under foreign influence.

25. Cf. above, p. 23.

26. Cf. above, pp. 42–43.

27. Cf. above, pp. 23–24 + 41–42.

28. For the cultic expression "to draw near or to bring near" (קרב = *qārab*), cf. J. Kühlewein, *THAT* 2, cols. 678f.; and R. Gane and J. Milgrom, *ThWAT* 7, cols. 150, 152–156.

29. Cf. pp. 44f., and H. D. Preuss, *Deuteronomium*, 1982 (EdF 164), 1–19 (lit.).

30. For the Levites, cf. pp. 58–62.

31. For a more complete analysis, cf. R. de Vaux, *Ancient Israel*, 2:397–403.

32. For anointing, cf. R. de Vaux, *Das Alten Testament und seine Lebensordnungen* 1, 2d ed., 1964, 169ff.; and E. Kutsch, *Salbung als Rechtsakt im Alten Testament und im Alten Orient*, 1963 (BZAW 87).

33. This is probably a later redactional insertion in Num. 35:25ff.

34. Cf. n. 32.

35. Cf. W. Paschen, *Rein und Unrein*, 1970 (StANT 24); D. P. Wright, *The Disposals of Impurity*, Atlanta, Ga., 1987; and below, pp. 62f. For the dietary laws, cf. also E. Firmage, "The Biblical Dietary Laws and the Concept of Holiness," VT Suppl 41, 1990, 177–208.

36. For atonement and the blood ritual, cf. pp. 233f. + 243.

37. Cf. the arrangment of the priests in 1 Chron. 24:3–19.

38. See, e.g., R. de Vaux, *Ancient Israel*, 2:394–397; and A. H. J. Gunneweg, *Geschichte Israels*, 6th ed., 1989, 160ff.

39. Cf. the genealogies in 1 Chron. 5:27ff.; and 6:34–38.

40. Thus R. de Vaux, *Ancient Israel*, 2:394–397, with a reference to Num. 3:1–3; and Lev. 10:1ff. Cf. p. 329 n. 22.
41. Cf. p. 60.
42. The assignment to different sources is unclear.
43. Cf. H. Schmid, *Die Gestalt des Mose*, 1986 (EdF 237), 88ff.
44. Cf. H. Schmid, *Mose: Überlieferung und Geschichte*, 1968 (BZAW 110), 81ff.
45. F. Ahuis (*Autorität im Umbruch*, 1983) looks for possible backgrounds to Numbers 16–17.
46. Elsewhere, the covenant of salt is referred only to the house of David in 2 Chron. 13:5 and to YHWH and the people in Lev. 2:13. "The fundamental concept here is that through the common eating of salt a 'covenant' relationship between the partners is brought about" (M. Noth, *Numbers* [OTL], Philadelphia, 1968, 137). "Salt" accordingly stands naturally as a symbol for continuation, for "binding obligations emerge out of the hospitality shown to a guest within the context of the community of a meal" (H. Eising, *ThWAT* 4, col. 913).
47. Cf. below, chapter 13.
48. Cf. above, pp. 54f.
49. Cf. D. Kellermann, *ThWAT* 4, cols. 503ff. See also H. Schmid, *Die Gestalt des Mose*, 52.
50. Thus H. Schulz, *Leviten im vorstaatlichen Israel und im Mittleren Osten*.
51. Thus with H.-J. Zobel, *Stammesspruch und Geschichte*, 1965 (BZAW 95), 69.
52. For these texts, cf. D. Kellermann, *ThWAT* 4, cols. 503 + 509.
53. Thus with H.-J. Zobel, *Stammesspruch und Geschichte*, 65. Differently, e.g., H. Donner, *Geschichte Israels* 1, 1984, 130f.
54. Also in Exod. 15:22ff., Exod. 15:22b (25b?) takes aim at Levi.
55. Cf. Vol. I, pp. 70f. and 73–75. In addition, cf. above, p. 32.
56. Cf. above, p. 58.
57. See H. Utzschneider, *Künder oder Schreiber?* 1989, 64ff.
58. See D. Kellermann, *ThWAT* 4, cols. 519f.
59. Deut. 12:12, 18f.; 14:27, 29; 16:11, 14; 18:6f.; and 26:11ff.
60. For the ark, cf. Vol. I, pp. 253–254.
61. Cf. Vol. I, p. 126.
62. Deut. 17:9, 18; 18:1; 21:5; 24:8; 27:9; 31:9.
63. For this problem, cf. H. Schmid, *Die Gestalt des Mose*, 66–69.
64. 2 Kings 23:9 says nothing at all about this but rather refers to the priests of high places. It is probable that at least not all of these priests were identical to country levites.
65. Thus, e.g., G. von Rad, H. W. Wolff, and O. H. Steck.
66. Thus G. von Rad, *Theology*, 1:71–77. Critical of this view is, e.g., D. Mathias, " 'Levitische Predigt' und Deuteronomismus," *ZAW* 96, 1984, 23–49.
67. Thus with A. H. J. Gunneweg, *Leviten und Priester*, 37ff., 44ff., and 78ff. For Deut. 33:8–11, see also D. Kellermann, *ThWAT* 4, cols. 509f.
68. For a more detailed treatment of Numbers 16–17, see F. Ahuis, *Autorität im Umbruch*, 1983.
69. Cf. the passages cited on pp. 60–61.
70. Cf. the Books of Chronicles; see below.
71. Cf. the firstborn in Exod. 13:11–15.
72. D. Kellermann, *ThWAT* 4, col. 519.
73. See D. Kellermann, *ThWAT* 4, cols. 510ff.
74. An exact differentiation of literary sources, additions, basic stratum, etc., is here resisted. Cf. for this the commentaries and especially "Zusätzen kultischer Prägung in der Chronik," in Th. Willi, *Die Chronik als Auslegung*, 1972 (FRLANT 106), 194–204. For the position and role of the levites in the Books of Chronicles, cf. G. von Rad, *Das Geschichtsbild des chronistischen Werkes*, 1930 (BWANT 4/3), 80f., 88–119; and M. Oeming, *Das wahre Israel*, 1990 (BWANT 128), 142ff.
75. Cf. the additions 1 Sam. 6:15; 2 Sam. 15:24; and 1 Kings 8:4.
76. For the ark in the Books of Chronicles, cf. 1 Chron. 6:16; 13–17; 22:19; 28:2, 18; 2 Chron. 1:4; 5; 6:11, 41; 8:11; and 35:3. For this topic, see G. von Rad, *Das Geschichtsbild des chronistischen Werkes*, 98ff.
77. In the Chronicler, יהוה מִשְׁכַּן (*miškan yahweh* = the "dwelling of YHWH") and the אהל מועד (*'ōhel mô'ēd* = "tent of meeting") are designations that are very close to each other; cf. 1

Chron. 23:26 with 23:32. For "tent" in these connections, cf. also K. Koch, *ThWAT* 1, cols. 138ff.; and D. Kellermann, "מִשְׁכָּן *miškan*," *ThWAT* 5, cols. 62–69, esp. 66ff.

78. Some texts (a particular stratum?) in the Books of Chronicles speak about a service of the levites at the אֹהֶל מוֹעֵד ('*ōhel mô'ēd* = "tent of meeting"). Cf. 1 Chron. 23:26, 32; 1 Chron. 9:19f.; and 2 Chron. 24:6.

79. For the levites as cult singers, see G. von Rad, *Das Geschichtsbild des chronistischen Werkes*, 102ff. In the texts brought under consideration he discovers two different strata.

80. Generally according to their service and their division: 1 Chron. 9:17–34; and 23:3–32.

81. Or is this only the holy of holies (Lev. 10:18)?

82. Cf. J. Hausmann, "Gottesdienst als Gotteslob," in H. Wagner, ed., *Spiritualität*, 1987, 83–92.

83. Cf. 1 Chron. 5:12f., 18; 15:3; and 2 Chron. 22:10ff. For the shewbread, compare 2 Chron. 13:11 and Lev. 24:8 to 1 Chron. 9:32.

84. For the "spirit of YHWH," cf. Vol. I, pp. 160–163.

85. For the discussion concerning the levitical cities, see M. Oeming, *Das wahre Israel*, 153–157.

86. For sacrifices, cf. pp. 238–245.

87. See G. Liedke and C. Petersen, "הוֹרָה," *THAT* 2, cols. 1032–1043.

88. Cf. above, p. 329 n. 9.

89. For this text, see D. R. Hildebrand, "Temple Ritual," *VT* 39, 1989, 154–168; and above, p. 327, n. 81.

90. Cf. p. 329 n. 35.

91. Cf. Vol. I, pp. 240–241.

92. Cf. also P. J. Budd, "Priestly Instruction in Pre-exilic Israel," *VT* 23, 1973, 1–14.

93. Cf. pp. 87f.

94. See (including the literature) H. D. Preuss, *Deuterojesaja: Eine Einführung in seine Botschaft*, 1976, 71ff.; and O. Fuchs, *Die Klage als Gebet*, 1982, 314ff.

95. For these, see R. Rendtorff, *Die Gesetze in der Priesterschrift*, 2d ed., 1963, 74ff.; G. von Rad, *Theology*, 1:262; and H. Ringgren, *ThWAT* 2, cols. 365f.

96. According to B. Janowski (*Sühne als Heilsgeschehen*, 1982 [WMANT 55], 222), this is only a "neutral determination . . . that serves to provide each sacrifice, described according to its individual ritual records in what has preceded, with the correct designation."

97. Thus, according to G. von Rad, "Die Anrechnung des Glaubens zur Gerechtigkeit," TB 8, 3d ed., 1965, 130–135. M. Oeming, "Ist Genesis 15 ein Beleg für die Anrechnung des Glaubens zur Gerechtigkeit?" *ZAW* 95, 1983, 182–197, is critical of this view. According to him, Abram reckons to YHWH. Cf., however, also the colloquial use in 2 Sam. 19:20; and R. Mosis, " 'Glauben' und 'Gerechtigkeit'—zu Gen. 15, 6," in FS J. Scharbert, 1989, 225–257.

98. Cf. pp. 160–163.

99. See K. Koch, "Tempeleinlassliturgien und Dekaloge," in H. W. Wolff, ed., *Probleme biblischer Theologie*, FS G. von Rad, 1971, 45–60; S. Ö. Steingrimsson, *Tor der Gerechtigkeit*, 1984 (ATSAT 22); and E. Otto, "Kultus und Ethos in Jerusalemer Theologie," *ZAW* 98, 1986, 161–179. J. Assmann has pointed to Egyptian parallels, *Ma'at: Gerechtigkeit und Unsterblichkeit im Alten Ägypten*, 1990, 141–149.

100. Would these have been the doors leading to the inner court of the temple, and not the outer gates? Thus with good reasons, W. Beyerlin, *Weisheitlich-kultische Heilsordnung: Studien zum 15. Psalm*, 1985 (BThSt 9), 94–97.

101. E. Otto, "Kultus und Ethos," 167.

102. Cf. p. 87.

103. E. Otto, "Kultus und Ethos," 164.

104. Cf. below, chapter 12.

105. Cf. F.-L. Hossfeld, "Nachlese zu neueren Studien der Einzugsliturgie von Psalm 15," in J. Zmijewski, ed., *Die Alttestamentliche Botschaft als Wegweisung*, FS H. Reinelt, 1990, 135–156.

106. Cf. the critical queries of B. Janowski, "Das Königtum Gottes in den Psalmen: Bemerkungen zu einem neuen Gesamtentwurf," *ZThK* 86, 1989, 436 n. 191. For Psalm 24, also cf. H. Strauss, *Gott preisen heisst vor ihm leben*, 1988 (BThSt 12), 70–79. See his comment on p.

75: "The decisive purpose of the testimony of entrance liturgies is to emphasize that Israel, in its efforts to live in conformity with the requirements of the Torah for both its cultic ritual and its ethical behavior in secular life, can be assured (once again) of encountering in YHWH's sanctuary the complete presence of the כבוד (=*kābôd*; "glory") of its God from of old."

107. Cf. Num. 10:2, 8–10; 1 Chron. 13:8; 15:24, 28; 16:6, 42; 2 Chron. 5:12f.; 7:6; 13:14; 29:26–28; Ezra 3:10; and Neh. 12:35, 41.

108. For blessing, see Vol. I, pp. 179–183.

109. For the so-called "Aaronide blessing" in Num. 6:24–26, cf. esp. K. Seybold, *Der aaronitische Segen: Studien zu Numeri 6/22–27,* 1977; M. Riebel, "Der Herr segne und behüte dich. . . . Überlegungen zum Segen anhand Num 6,24–26," *BiLi* 58, 1985, 229–236; and R. Wonneberger, "Der Segen als liturgischer Sprechakt," in K. Oehler, ed., *Zeichen und Realität* 2, 1984, 1069–1079. For the small silver plate found in the Valley of Hinnom that has a text that at least is partially close to Num. 6:24–26, cf., e.g., R. Riesner, *ThBeitr* 18, 1987, 104–108; M. C. A. Korpel, "The Poetic Structure of the Priestly Blessing," *JSOT* 45, 1989, 3–13; and now *TUAT* II/6, 929.

110. Cf. W. Beyerlin, *Die Rettung der Bedrängten in den Feindpsalmen der Einzelnen auf institutionelle Zusammenhänge untersucht,* 1970 (FRLANT 99).

111. *Textes Ougaritiques* 2, Paris, 1989. Cf. in addition *TUAT* II/2 + 3, 1987/1988 for texts from other regions.

112. For these texts, cf. K. Koch, "Alttestamentliche und altorientalische Rituale," in E. Blum et al., eds., *Die Hebräische Bibel und ihre zweifache Nachgeschichte,* FS R. Rendtorff, 1990, 75–85; R. Rendtorff, *Die Gesetze in der Priesterschrift,* 2d ed.; and idem, *Leviticus* (BK III/1 = 2), 1985 + 1990.

113. Cf. 1 Sam. 2:13; Jer. 2:8; and Hos. 4:6.

114. For this, see B. Janowski, *Sühne als Heilsgeschehen,* 222ff., etc.

115. For "expiation," cf. below, pp. 233f. + 242f.

116. Cf. above, p. 53.

117. א and ת = crooked and straight? no and yes? = ארר = *'rr* ("cursed") and תמם = *tmm* ("innocent"). Cf. also H. H. Rowley, *Faith,* 28f.

118. W. Dommershausen, *ThWAT* 4, col. 73.

119. Cf. below, chapter 13, for the theological understanding of the Old Testament cult.

120. For the priestly portrayal of history, cf. N. Lohfink, "Die Priesterschrift und die Geschichte," VT Suppl 29, 1978, 189–225 (=*Studien zum Pentateuch,* 1988 [SBAB 4], 213ff.); and V. Fritz, "Das Geschichtsverständnis der Priesterschrift," *ZThK* 84, 1987, 426–439.

121. Cf. O. Plöger, *Theokratie und Eschatologie,* 3d ed., 1968 (WMANT 2).

122. See Vol. I, pp. 157ff.

123. Cf., e.g., the Egyptian ritual of Apophis (J. Assmann, *Ma'at: Gerechtigkeit und Unsterblichkeit im Alten Ägypten,* 185f.).

124. "Cultus" is associated with "to cultivate." An Egyptian temple ritual having to do with "caring" for idols may be found in *TUAT* II/3, 1988, 391ff.

125. Th. C. Vriezen, *An Outline of Old Testament Theology,* Oxford, 1958, 265.

126. Ibid., 265.

127. Thus with W. Eichrodt, *Theology,* 1:436. Cf. H. Spieckermann, *Heilsgegenwart,* 222: "Temple theology is . . . not eschatologically oriented." This is certainly not true in general for the Old Testament cult, as, e.g., the YHWH enthronement psalms demonstrate (cf. Vol. I, p. 158, with 320 n. 163).

Chapter 10. The Prophets

1. See the selected literature: H. W. Wolff, "Hauptprobleme alttestamentlicher Prophetie," *EvTh* 15, 1955, 116–168 (=TB 22, 206ff.; also see TB 76, 1987, for additional essays on prophecy); G. Fohrer (a series of reviews of prophetic scholarship), *ThR* 19, 1951; 20, 1952; 28, 1962; 40, 1975; 41, 1976; 45, 1980; and 47, 1982; A. Heschel, *The Prophets,* New York, 1962; J.

Lindblom, *Prophecy in Ancient Israel,* Oxford, 1962; W. Zimmerli, *Das Gesetz und die Propheten,* 1963; O. Kaiser, "Wort des Propheten und Wort Gottes," in E. Würthwein and O. Kaiser, eds., *Tradition und Situation: Studien zur alttestamentlichen Prophetie,* FS A. Weiser, 1963, 75–92; C. Westermann, *Grundformen prophetischer Rede* (1960), 5th ed., 1978; J. Scharbert, *Die Propheten Israels bis 700 v. Chr.,* 1965; idem, *Die Propheten Israels um 600 v. Chr.,* 1967; S. Herrmann, *Die prophetischen Heilserwartungen im Alten Testament,* 1965 (BWANT 85); G. Fohrer, *Studien zur alttestamentlichen Prophetie (1949–1965),* 1967 (BZAW 99); idem, *Die symbolischen Handlungen der Propheten,* 2d ed., 1968 (AThANT 54); M.-L. Henry, *Prophet und Tradition,* 1969 (BZAW 116); W. H. Schmidt, *Zukunftsgewissheit und Gegenwartskritik: Grundzüge prophetischer Verkündigung,* 1973 (BSt 64); S. Herrmann, *Ursprung und Funktion der Prophetie im alten Israel,* 1976; O. Keel, "Rechttun oder Annahme des drohenden Gerichts?" *BZ* NF 21, 1977, 200–218; J. Jeremias, "נביא *nābî'* Prophet," *THAT* 2, cols. 7–26; K. Koch, *The Prophets,* 2 vols., Philadelphia, 1983–1984; idem, in R. Coggins et al., eds., *Israel's Prophetic Tradition,* Cambridge, 1982; FS P. Ackroyd, Cambridge, 1982; E. Osswald, "Aspekte neuerer Prophetenforschung," *ThLZ* 109, 1984, cols. 641–650; G. Wallis, ed., *Vom Bileam bis Jesaja,* 1984; G. Wallis, ed.; *Zwischen Gericht und Heil,* 1987; J. L. Mays and P. J. Achtemeier, *Interpreting the Prophets,* Philadelphia, 1987; E. Beaucamp, *Les prophètes d'Israel,* Paris, 1987; H.-P. Müller, "נביא *nābî'*," *ThWAT* 5, cols. 140–163; and J. F. A. Sawyer, *Prophecy and the Prophets in the Old Testament,* Oxford, 1987. Cf. also: W. Eichrodt, *Theology of the Old Testament,* vol. 1 (OTL), Philadelphia, 1961, 303–391; G. von Rad, *Old Testament Theology,* vol. 2: *The Theology of Israel's Prophetic Tradition,* New York, 1965 passim; G. Fohrer, *Grundstrukturen,* 71ff.; A. Deissler, *Grundbotschaft,* 97ff.; B. S. Childs, *Old Testament Theology in a Canonical Context,* Philadelphia, 1985, 122ff.; W. H. Schmidt, *Alttestamentlicher Glaube,* 6th ed., 262ff.; P. van Imschoot, *Theology of the Old Testament* 1, 1965, 148ff.; J. L. McKenzie, *A Theology of the Old Testament,* 1974, 85ff.; and S. Terrien, *The Elusive Presence,* New York, 1978, 227ff.

2. This chapter can only set forth the important characteristics of the phenomenon of "prophecy" and of "prophetic writings." Any discussion of particular problems cannot be undertaken. The "introductions" to the Old Testament, especially those of O. Kaiser (5th ed., 1984; and R. Smend, 4th ed., 1990), should be consulted for literary and redactional analyses of these books.

3. Cf. J. Vollmer, *Geschichtliche Rückblicke und Motive in der Prophetie des Amos, Hosea und Jesaja,* 1971 (BZAW 119), 28ff.

4. Cf. F. Diedrich, *Die Anspielungen auf die Jakob-Tradition in Hosea 12, 1–13,3,* 1977 (fzb 27); H.-D. Neef, *Die Heilstraditionen Israels in der Verkündigung des Propheten Hosea,* 1987 (BZAW 169), 15ff.; D. R. Daniels, *Hosea and Salvation History,* 1990 (BZAW 191); and J. Vollmer, *Geschichtliche Rückblicke und Motive in der Prophetie des Amos, Hosea und Jesaja,* 105ff.

5. Cf. Vol. I, pp. 64ff.

6. See below, pp. 91f. + 265–267.

7. See pp. 74f.

8. Thus with J. Jeremias, *THAT* 2, col. 8.

9. Niphal and hithpael for "to be beside oneself."

10. Cf. Vol. I, pp. 195–200, 208–219.

11. Cf. H. W. Wolff, "Das Geschichtsverständnis der alttestamentlichen Prophetie," *EvTh* 20, 1960, 218–235 (=TB 22, 2d ed., 1973, 289ff.). Also H. W. Wolff, "Die eigentliche Botschaft der klassischen Propheten," in H. Donner et al., eds., *Beitrage zur alttestamentlichen Theologie,* FS W. Zimmerli, 1977, 547–557 (=TB 76, 1987, 39ff.).

12. Thus, e.g., M. Buber and G. Fohrer.

13. Thus W. H. Schmidt, *Zukunftsgewissheit und Gegenswartskritik.*

14. "*The menacing irruption of a divine reality unperceived by their contemporaries*—it is this, to put it in the most general terms, which is the decisively new factor in the phenomenon of classical prophecy" (W. Eichrodt, *Theology,* 1:344).

15. Thus K. Koch (and collaborators), *Amos,* 1976 (AOT 30), 158f.

16. See H. Krämer, R. Rendtorff, R. Meyer, and G. Friedrich, *ThWNT* 6, 781–863.

17. See J. Jeremias, *THAT* 2, cols. 7–26; and H.-P. Müller, *ThWAT* 5, cols. 140–163 (see n. 1, pp. 332–333.
18. *AOT*, 2d ed., 71ff.; *ANET*, 2d + 3d eds., 25–29; and *TGI*, 2d ed., 41ff.
19. Differently J. Becker, "Historischer Prophetismus und biblisches Prophetenbild," in J. Zmijewski, ed., *Die Alttestamentliche Botschaft als Wegweisung*, FS H. Reinelt, 1990, 11-23.
20. For overviews, see F. Nötscher, "Prophetie im Umkreis des alten Israel," *BZ* NF 10, 1966, 161–197; and L. Wächter, in *Von Bileam bis Jesaja*, 9–31 (lit.). For Akkadian prophets, see esp. R. Borger, *BibOr* 28, 1971, 3–24; and H. Hunger and E. Kaufmann, *JAOS* 95, 1975, 371–375. For translated texts, see *RGT*, 2d ed., 142ff.; and *TUAT* II/1, 56ff. Cf. also J. H. Walton, *Ancient Israelite Literature in Its Cultural Context*, Grand Rapids, 1989, 201–227.
21. See F. Ellermeier, *Prophetie in Mari und Israel*, 1968; K. Koch, *UF* 4, 1972, 53–78; E. Noort, *Untersuchungen zum Gottesbescheid in Mari*, 1977 (AOAT 202); and A. Schmitt, *Prophetischer Gottesbescheid in Mari und Israel*, 1982 (BWANT 114). A selection of texts is also found in *TUAT* II/1, 83–93.
22. Cf. below, p. 77.
23. *KAI* nr. 202A; *TUAT* I/6, 626ff.; and *RGT*, 2d ed., 247–250. See H.-J. Zobel, "Das Gebet um Abwendung der Not," *VT* 21, 1971, 91–99.
24. Cf. *TUAT* II/1, 102ff. See S. Herrmann, in *Congress Volume: Bonn, 1962*, VT Suppl 9, 1963, 47–65.
25. Thus, esp. B. Duhm, *Theologie der Propheten*, 1875; and idem, *Israels Propheten*, 1916.
26. For this, see H. J. Stoebe, KAT VIII/1, 202f.
27. נבא (*nb'*) hithpael.
28. See W. Eichrodt, *Theology*, 1:301–303. However, he distinguishes here between Yahwistic and degenerate nebiism.
29. Cf. O. H. Steck, *Israel und das gewaltsame Geschick der Propheten*, 1967 (WMANT 23). See Steck's index.
30. For Genesis 15, cf. the literature cited on p. 315 n. 85.
31. As the "seer of the gods," Balaam is now found in the inscription of Deir 'Alla (ca. 700 B.C.E.?): *TUAT* II/1, 138ff. Cf. also Vol. I, pp. 59–60.
32. נביאה (*nĕbî'â* = "woman prophet" or "woman prophetess"?).
33. For the beginnings of prophecy in Israel, cf. H.-J. Zobel, in *Von Bileam bis Jesaja*, 32ff.
34. This narrative has played a role in the discussion of an appropriate Old Testament hermeneutic. Cf. H. D. Preuss, *Das Alte Testament in christlicher Predigt*, 1984, 91 (lit.); A. H. J. Gunneweg, "Die Prophetenlegende I Reg 13—Missdeutung, Umdeutung, Bedeutung," in V. Fritz et al., eds., *Prophet und Prophetenbuch*, FS O. Kaiser, 1989 (BZAW 185), 73–81.
35. See E. Haller, *Charisma und Ekstasis*, 1960 (ThEx 82); and S. J. de Vries, *Prophet against Prophet*, Grand Rapids, 1978.
36. Cf. below, pp. 82–86.
37. Cf. Vol. I, pp. 218f. 1 Chron. 16:22; 29:29; 2 Chron. 12:5–8; 15:1–7, 8; 16:7–10; 19:2f.; 20:20, 37; 21:12 (letter of Elijah!); 28:9–11; and 36:12, 16.
38. See, above all, G. Fohrer, *Elia*, 2d ed., 1968 (AThANT 53); O. H. Steck, *Überlieferung und Zeitgeschichte in den Elia-Erzählungen*, 1968 (WMANT 26); L. Bronner, *The Stories of Elijah and Elisha*, Leiden, 1968; and G. Hentschel, *Die Elijaerzählung*, 1977. Cf. also G. von Rad, *Old Testament Theology*, 2:14–25; K. Koch, *The Prophets*, 1:32–35; H. Seebass, "Elia. I: A. T.," *TRE* 9, 498–502 (lit.); P. Weimar, "Elija," *NBL* 1, cols. 516–520; and A. J. Hauser and R. Gregory, *From Carmel to Horeb*, 1990 (JSOT Suppl 85). Cf. also Vol. I, pp. 105f. + 113.
39. For the different forms of prophetic narratives, cf. K. Koch, *Was ist Formgeschichte?* 3d ed., 1974, 225ff., 246ff.; and A. Rofé, *The Prophetical Stories*, Jerusalem, 1982 (1988).
40. Cf. for 1 Kings 18:21–39, e.g., E. Würthwein, "Zur Opferprobe Elias I Reg 18,21–39," in V. Fritz et al., eds., *Prophet*, FS O. Kaiser, 1989 (BZAW 185), 277–284.
41. See R. Bohlen, *Der Fall Nabot*, 1978 (TThSt 35).
42. 1 Kings 17:24; 20:28; 2 Kings 1:9ff.; 4:7ff.; 5:8; 6:6ff.; 7:2, 17–19; and 8:2ff.
43. See esp. H.-C. Schmitt, *Elisa*, 1972; H. Schweizer, *Elischa in den Kriegen*, 1974 (StANT 37); and H.-J. Stipp, *Elischa—Propheten—Gottesmänner*, 1987 (ATSAT 24). Cf. G. von Rad,

Theology, 2:25–32; H. Seebass, "Elisa," *TRE* 9, 506–509; and H.-J. Stipp, "Elischa," *NBL* 1, cols. 522f.

44. Secondarily transferred to Elijah in 2 Kings 2:12.
45. Cf. Vol. I, p. 124.
46. Cf. W. Thiel, "Sprachliche und thematische Gemeinsamkeiten nordisraelitischer Propheten-Überlieferungen," in J. Zmijewski, ed., *Die alttestamentliche Botschaft als Wegweisung,* FS H. Reinelt, 1990, 359–376.
47. Thus R. Rendtorff, "Erwägungen zur Frühgeschichte des Prophetentums in Israel," *ZThK* 59, 1962, 145–167 (=TB 57, 1975, 220ff.).
48. See W. Richter, *Die sogenannten vorprophetischen Berufungsberichte,* 1970 (FRLANT 101).
49. Cf., e.g., the contributions of V. Fritz, E. S. Gerstenberger, J. Jeremias, and L. Perlitt (in V. Fritz et al., eds., *Prophet und Prophetenbuch,* FS O. Kaiser, although they come to rather different conclusions.
50. Cf. also G. von Rad, *Theology,* 2:52–53.
51. The "Spirit of YHWH/God" in this sense is missing in Amos, Hosea, Isaiah, Micah, and Jeremiah. In Micah 3:8 the mention of the "Spirit of YHWH" is an addition, while Hos. 9:7 ("the man of the spirit is mad") perhaps makes clear the reasons that led to the "silence about the Spirit." The discussion of the "Spirit" occurs in older prophecy (Elijah, Elisha) and then again in Ezekiel, Deutero-Isaiah, and later. Cf. J. Scharbert, "Der 'Geist' und die Schriftpropheten," in R. Mosis and L. Ruppert, eds., *Der Weg zum Menschen,* FS A. Deissler, 1989, 82–97. For this topic, cf. Vol. I, pp. 160f.
52. Thus with G. von Rad, *Theology,* 2:87–88, which follows L. Köhler here. Cf. to what follows also Vol. I, pp. 195ff., something that is intentionally taken up here once again.
53. See O. Grether, *Name und Wort Gottes im Alten Testament,* 1934 (BZAW 64); G. von Rad, *Theology,* 2:90–98. W. H. Schmidt, *Alttestamentlicher Glaube,* 6th ed., 296ff.; and idem, "דבר *dābar,*" *ThWAT* 2, cols. 89–133 (lit.).
54. Exception: Ezekiel? All prophets, moreover, were seen in this way by H. Gunkel and G. Hölscher. According to them, the prophets spoke while in ecstasy. A helpful analysis of these questions is found in F. Maass, "Zur psychologischen Sonderung der Ekstase," *WZ,* Leipzig 3, 1953/1954 (Gesellsch.-Sprachwiss. Reihe), 297–301. Cf. also G. Dautzenberg, "Ekstase," *NBL* 1, cols. 506f.
55. See R. Kiliam, "Die prophetische Berufungsberichte," in *Theologie im Wandel,* 1967, 356–376; B. Vieweger, *Die Spezifik der Berufungsberichte Jeremias und Ezechiels,* 1986; and S. Breton, *Vocación y Misión,* Rome, 1987 (AnBib 111).
56. J. Lindblom, "Einige Grundfragen der alttestamentlichen Wissenschaft," in W. Baumgartner et al., eds., *Festschrift Alfred Bertholet zum 80. Geburtstag,* 1950, 325–337, esp. 327.
57. In speaking of this, K. Koch (*The Prophets,* 1:40) remarks that a "stimulus for profounder vision" was evoked.
58. For this, see L. Rost, *Studien zum Alten Testament,* 1974 (BWANT 101), 39ff.
59. Cf. also D. U. Rottzoll, *VT* 39, 1989, 323–340, for this formula which can be regarded in many texts as a formula of legitimation.
60. In contrast to this, K. Baltzer (*Die Biographie der Propheten,* 1975) wishes to understand them as the "viziers" of God, i.e., of King YHWH. The "thus said YHWH" would be then more of a formula of proclamation than a messenger formula.
61. Cf. also H. W. Wolff, "Zur Gotteserfahrung der Propheten," TB 76, 1987, 25–38.
62. Cf. G. von Rad, *Theology,* 2:177.
63. See O. Kaiser, "Word of the Prophet and Word of God." Cf. also G. Fohrer, *ThLZ* 83, 1958, cols. 243ff., with J. Hempel; and B. Lang, *Wie wird man Prophet in Israel?* 1980, 11ff., 31ff. The stages of inspiration include first perception, then attainment followed by the breakthrough, the phase of prophetic activity, and then the taking over of the "role" (including the role of God). Also see A. Stiglmair, " '. . . So spricht Jahwe . . .' — Prophetenwort als Wort Gottes," in J. Zmijewski, ed., *Die Alttestamentliche Botschaft als Wegweisung,* FS H. Reinelt, 1990, 345–357. G. von Rad (Theology, 2:132) notes that the contribution of observant thinking should not be undervalued.
64. "Jahweh's new word for Israel which he allowed the prophet to read off from the horizon of world-history" (G. von Rad, *Theology,* 2:130).

65. "Israel's prophets were the heralds of a future springing from a simple responsibility on the part of their audience on the one hand and a simple divine ground of reality on the other. As such, they tower above all comparable figures of ancient times" (K. Koch, *The Prophets*, 1:7).
66. Cf. already H. Schultz, *Alttestamentliche Theologie*, 5th ed., 1896, 202: "The prophets read the will of God in the flaming scripture of world history."
67. Cf. once more H. W. Wolff, "Die eigentliche Botschaft der klassischen Propheten."
68. Cf. below, pp. 81–87.
69. See W. Dietrich, *Prophetie und Geschichte*, 1972 (FRLANT 108).
70. C. Kuhl (*Israels Propheten*, 1956, 7), by contrast, speaks of the writing prophets as "forth-tellers."
71. G. von Rad (*Theology*, 2:53) speaks of "the incredible variety of forms they used in their preaching, ranging over the whole field of expression then available."
72. Cf. above, p. 63.
73. For this, see Chr. Hardmeier, *Texttheorie und biblische Exegese*, 1978.
74. See R. Bach, *Die Aufforderungen zur Flucht und zum Kampf im alttestamentlichen Prophetenspruch*, 1962 (WMANT 9).
75. This formula is found 435 times in the Old Testament. For the secular origin and use of this formula, cf., e.g., Gen. 32:4–6; Exod. 4:21–33; and 2 Kings 18:28f. Among the writing prophets, the formula is not present in Hosea, Joel, Jonah, and Zephaniah. For this formula, see C. Westermann, *Grundformen prophetischer Rede,* 5th ed., 1978, 70ff., 135; H. Niehr, "Botenformel/Botenspruch," *NBL* 1, cols. 318f.; and above, nn. 59–60, as well as p. 69.
76. Cf. J. T. Greene, *The Role of the Messenger and Message in the Ancient Near East*, Atlanta, Ga., 1989.
77. For the prophets as messengers, see, e.g., Isa. 6:8; Jer. 49:14; Nahum 2:1, 14; Isa. 42:19; 44:26; Hag. 1:13; Mal. 2:7; and 3:1.
78. For this, cf. C. Westermann, *Basic Forms of Prophetic Speech*, Louisville, Ky., 1991, 188–189.
79. See P. K. D. Neumann, *Hört das Wort Jahwäs: Ein Beitrag zur Komposition alttestamentlicher Schriften*, 1975.
80. For this, see C. Westermann, *Basic Forms*; and J. Barton, "Begründungsversuche der prophetischen Unheilsankündigung im Alten Testament," *EvTh* 47, 1987, 427–435. For individual prophets, cf. below, pp. 87ff.
81. For the precise structure of these words, cf. K. Koch et al., *Amos*, 1976 (AOAT 30), 287ff.
82. For the oracles against the nations, cf. also pp. 284–307. K. Koch (*Amos*, 252) has shaped a "generic paradigm" for these oracles against the nations.
83. An original connection between the announcement of disaster and the demonstration of guilt is contested by K.-F. Pohlmann in regard to the early texts of Jeremiah (*Die Ferne Gottes*, 1989, BZAW 179, 193ff.). This connection may have existed for the first time in the exilic and postexilic texts (ibid., 208f.). The portrait of YHWH presented here for both the history (ibid., 202f., 209ff.) and the situation of Israel appears in this regard to be the actual, critical point of concern. Cf. Vol. I, pp. 78ff.; and also J. Conrad, in *Zwischen Gericht und Heil*, 91ff.
84. Cf. also L. Markert, *Struktur und Bezeichnung des Scheltworts*, 1977 (BZAW 140); and B. Lang, "Drohwort," *NBL* 1, cols. 450–452.
85. Cf. O. Keel, "Rechttun oder Annahme des drohenden Gerichts?"
86. Thus H. W. Wolff, in H. Donner et al., eds., *Beiträge zur Alttestamentlichen Theologie, FS W. Zimmerli*, 1977, 553.
87. Cf. also below, pp. 271f.
88. Thus G. Warmuth, *Das Mahnwort*, 1976.
89. Thus with K. A. Tångberg, *Die prophetische Mahnrede*, 1987 (FRLANT 143). Cf. also J. Jeremias, "Tod und Leben in Am 5:1–17," in R. Mosis and L. Ruppert, eds., *Der Weg zum Menschen, FS* A. Deissler, 1989, 134–152.
90. With C. Westermann, *Prophetic Oracles of Salvation in the Old Testament,* Louisville, 1991.
91. Cf. pp. 274–277 for this topic.
92. Cf. above, p. 63.
93. Cf. pp. 299f.
94. For the "generic paradigm" of general textual forms, cf. K. Koch et al., *Amos*, 1976.

95. See p. 355 n. 55, and the literature listed there. In addition, see W. Zimmerli, *Ezekiel: A Commentary on the Book of the Prophet Ezekiel,* vol. 1 (Hermeneia), Philadelphia, 1979–1983, 97–100 ("The Form Criticism and Tradition-History of the Prophetic Call Narratives").

96. Thus F. Horst, "Die Visionsschilderungen der alttestamentlichen Propheten," *EvTh* 20, 1960, 193–205.

97. See K. Koch, "Vom profetischen zum apokalyptischen Visionsbericht," in D. Hellholm, ed., *Apocalypticism in the Mediterranean World and the Near East,* 2d ed., Tübingen, 1989, 413–446.

98. Thus with H.-G. Schöttler, *Gott inmitten seines Volkes,* 1987 (TThSt 43), 204–206.

99. See G. Fohrer, "Die Gattung der Berichte über symbolische Handlungen der Propheten," *ZAW* 64, 1952, 101–120 (=BZAW 99, 92ff.).

100. *ThR* NF 20, 1952, 203.

101. Cf. Vol. I, p. 26, and once again the contributions of V. Fritz, E. S. Gerstenberger, and L. Perlitt in V. Fritz et al., eds., *Prophet und Prophetenbuch,* FS O. Kaiser, 1989 (BZAW 185). Also see R. E. Clements, "The Prophet and His Editors," in D. J. A. Clines et al., eds., *The Bible in Three Dimensions,* JSOT Suppl 87, 1990, 203–220.

102. "From the prophets' angle of vision, all of their words are the 'word of God,' which in the sincerity of their faith proceed to be proclaimed unconditionally. Indeed, it is in their role as a *nābî'* that they select the corresponding form of speech. Their words are stamped by their own way of life or way of faith and by the tradition of faith that is entrusted to them (A. Stiglmair, "Prophetenwort als Wort Gottes," in J. Zmijewski, ed., *Die Alttestamentliche Botschaft als Wegweisung,* FS H. Reinelt, 1990, 345–357, esp. p. 350.

103. Cf. the so-called *perfectum propheticum (GK,* 28th ed., p. 323).

104. Cf. H. W. Wolff, "Das Geschichtsverständnis der alttestamentlichen Prophetie," *EvTh* 20, 1960, 218–235 (=TB 22, 2d ed., 289ff.), and Vol. I, pp. 195f. and 215ff.

105. Cf. pp. 253–283.

106. See H.-J. Kraus, *Prophetie und Politik,* 1952 (ThEx 36); E. Jenni, *Die politischen Voraussagen der Propheten,* 1956 (AThANT 29); W. Dietrich, *Jesaja und die Politik,* 1976; and J. Goff, *Prophetie und Politik in Israel und im alten Ägypten,* 1986. For the proximity of people and community, see Vol. I, pp. 50–64.

107. Cf., e.g., Isaiah 20 (Isaiah goes about "naked"); Jeremiah 13; 16; 19; 24; 27–28; and 32 (girdle, prohibition against marriage, jar, two baskets of figs, wooden and iron yokes, and the purchase of a field); Ezekiel 3; 4; 5; 12; 24; and 37:15ff. (a prophet struck dumb, a brick, unclean bread and lying on the side, shaving and dividing the hair, baggage of the exiles, prohibition against mourning, and the two sticks); Zech. 3:8–10; 6:9–14; and 11:4–16.

108. Thus with G. Fohrer, *Die symbolischen Handlungen der Propheten.* Cf. also B. Lang, "Ein—Mann—Strassentheater" (= *Wie wird man Prophet in Israel?* 1980, 29).

109. For the oracles of the prophets against the foreign nations, cf. pp. 287f.

110. Cf. also below, pp. 267–271.

111. Is the Northern Kingdom alone intended here, so that the Southern Kingdom, Judah, is not affected at all? If so, then the catastrophe that is so often found in this text would not be so radical. Cf. K.-F. Pohlmann, *Die Ferne Gottes,* 204ff.

112. Cf. Jer. 6:30; 7:29; 12:7f.; 14:19ff.; cf. Deut. 8:19f.; Lam. 2:7; and 3:45. Also see Lev. 26:44; 1 Sam. 12:22; Jer. 31:35–37; Psalms 89; and 94:14. Taken together, these are texts that originate in the vicinity of the exile and often belong to Deuteronomistic redactions or Deuteronomistic passages. Cf. further, pp. 265–267.

113. Cf. pp. 274f.

114. For the motifs in the words of salvation, cf. C. Westermann, *Prophetic Oracles.*

115. Cf. above, pp. 34–38.

116. See the following selection: G. Quell, *Wahre und falsche Propheten,* 1952; E. Osswald, *Falsche Prophetie im Alten Testament,* 1962; J. L. Crenshaw, *Prophetic Conflict,* 1971 (BZAW 124); F. L. Hossfeld and I. Meyer, *Prophet gegen Prophet,* 1973; G. Münderlein, *Kriterien wahrer und falscher Prophetie,* 1974; R. P. Carroll, *When Prophecy Failed,* London, 1979; Chr. Schneider, *Krisis des Glaubens,* 1988; and G. T. Sheppard, "True and False Prophecy within Scripture," in G. M. Tucker et al., eds., *Canon, Theology, and Old Testament Interpretation,* Philadelphia, 1988, 262–282. Cf. also, B. S. Childs, *Theology,* 133f.

117. See A. R. Johnson, *The Cultic Prophet in Ancient Israel*, 2d ed., Cardiff, 1962; A. Haldar, *Associations of Cult Prophets among the Ancient Semites*, Uppsala, 1945; and R. de Vaux, *Ancient Israel*, 2:384–386.
118. Thus, above all, H. Graf Reventlow in his earlier works on these prophets.
119. Cf. the introductions to the Old Testament.
120. See M. Noth, "Amt und Berufung im Alten Testament," in his TB 6, 3d ed., 1966, 309–333.
121. Cf. above, p. 334 n. 34.
122. Cf. the literature cited in n. 35, p. 334.
123. For the stratigraphy of 1 Kings 22, cf. Chr. Schneider, *Krisis des Glaubens*, 24ff.
124. Cf. above, p. 76.
125. Jer. 4:9f.; 5:12–14, 30f.; 6:9–15; 14:10–18; 23:9–32; 27:9ff.; 28; 29; 32:32; and 37:19. In addition, see H.-J. Kraus, *Prophetie in der Krisis*, 1964 (BSt 43); and I. Meyer, *Jeremia und die falschen Propheten*, 1977 (OBO 13). I. Meyer (ibid.) and F. L. Hossfeld and I. Meyer, *Prophet gegen Prophet,* 57ff., set forth a chronological arrangement of the stratigraphy of these texts. Cf. also Chr. Schneider, *Krisis des Glaubens,* 36ff.; and S. Herrmann, *Jeremia*, 1990 (EdF 271), 140–145, 198f.
126. The following passages belong to the Deuteronomistic redaction of the Book of Jeremiah: Jer. 14:13–16; 23:17, 32; 26*; 27:9f., 14f., 16–18; 28:14*, 16bβ; 29:8f., 15, 21–23*, 24–32*; 32:32; and 37:19. Cf. Chr. Schneider, *Krisis des Glaubens*, 68ff.
127. Cf. also Ezek. 22:23–31.
128. For efforts to provide a more precise definition of this group, cf. J. L. Crenshaw, *Prophetic Conflict*, 5–22.
129. F. L. Hossfeld and I. Meyer, *Prophet gegen Prophet*, 11.
130. For the problem of the fulfillment of prophetic pronouncements, cf. the good reflections already set forth by H. Schultz, *Alttestamentliche Theologie*, 5th ed., 1896, 203–208. Then see E. Jenni, *Die politischen Voraussagen der Propheten*, 1956 (AThANT 29).
131. G. Quell, *Wahre und falsche Propheten*, 1952, 192ff. "There is no longer a problem, at the most a challenge."
132. Thus, e.g., J. L. Crenshaw, *Prophetic Conflict*; and F. L. Hossfeld and I. Meyer, *Prophet gegen Prophet.*
133. Thus with J. Jeremias, "Die Vollmacht des Propheten im Alten Testament," *EvTh* 31, 1971, 305–322, esp. 320.
134. Chr. Schneider (*Krisis des Glaubens*, 81ff.) speaks of the false prophets' distorted process for knowing God and of the disturbance in their relationship with God, where YHWH's involvement had abated. "According to all of this, the materialization of false prophecy proceeds from an impaired relationship with God that effectuates a narrowing and hardening of the attitude of faith. In connection with this, there was a disturbance in the prophetic process of knowing that affected the prophetic message and led to a calming view of the present situation by the prophets in question" (p. 85).
135. Cf. F. Stolz, "Der Streit um die Wirklichkeit in der Südreichsprophetie des 8. Jahrhunderts," *WuD* NF 12, 1973, 9–30; there pp. 28f.
136. Cf. above, pp. 76 + 83f.
137. The prophets are treated by von Rad primarily under this point of view (actualization or new interpretation of tradition) (*Theology*). Cf. the critical overview of E. Osswald, *ThLZ* 109, 1984, cols. 641ff., esp. 643ff. See further for this topic G. Fohrer, "Tradition und Interpretation im Alten Testament," *ZAW* 73, 1961, 1–30 (=BZAW 115, 54ff.); J. Vollmer, *Geschichtliche Rückblicke und Motive in der Prophetie des Amos, Hosea und Jesaja*, 1971 (BZAW 119); M.-L. Henry, *Prophet und Tradition*, 1969 (BZAW 116); W. Zimmerli, "Die kritische Infragestellung der Tradition durch die Prophetie," in O. H. Steck, ed., *Zu Tradition und Theologie im Alten Testament*, 1978 (BThSt 2), 57–86.
138. For these, see also E. Osswald, in *Von Bileam bis Jesaja*, 84ff.; and W. Zimmerli, "Das Gottesrecht bei den Propheten Amos, Hosea und Jesaja," in R. Albertz et al., eds., *Schöpfung und Befreiung*, FS C. Westermann, 1980, 216–235.
139. Cf. L. Markert, "Amos/Amosbuch," *TRE* 2, 471–487 (lit.); and H. Weippert, "Amos/Amosbuch," *NBL* 1, cols. 92–95.

140. Amos 2:10f. originates from the Deuteronomistic redaction of the Book of Amos. Cf. W. H. Schmidt, "Die Deuteronomistische Redaktion des Amosbuches," *ZAW* 77, 1965, 178–183.
141. For קֵץ (*qēṣ* = "end"), cf. Sh. Talmon, *ThWAT* 7, cols. 84–92.
142. Amos 2:6–13; 3:9–11; 4:1–3; 5:7–10, 11f., 21–27; 6:1–6, 8, 11, 12–14; 8:4–7; and 9:7f. For the social criticism located in the various redactional strata of the Book of Amos and for their social-historical background, cf. G. Fleischer, *Von Menschenverkäufern, Baschankühen und Rechtsverkehrern*, 1989 (BBB 74).
143. Amos 4:4f.; 5:21–27; cf. 2:8; and 5:4–6:14f.
144. G. Fleischer, *Von Menschenverkäufern, Baschankühen und Rechtsverkehrern*, 344, 420.
145. Cf. also Hos. 7:1; 10:4; 12:8f.; Isa. 1:10–17, 23; 2:7; 3:13–15; 5:8f., 11f., 20–23; 10:1f.; Micah 1:10–16; 2:1–5, 6–10; 3:1–4, 5–7, 9–12; and 6:9–16. For this, see H. Donner, "Die soziale Botschaft der Propheten im Lichte der Gesellschaftsordnung in Israel," *OrAnt* 2, 1963, 229–245; G. Wanke, "Zu Grundlage und Absicht prophetischer Sozialkritik," *KuD* 18, 1972, 2–17; M. Fendler, "Die Sozialkritik des Amos," *EvTh* 33, 1973, 32–53; M. Schwantes, *Das Recht der Armen*, 1977; W. Schottroff, "Der Prophet Amos: Versuch der Würdigung seines Auftretens unter sozialgeschichtlichem Aspekt," in W. Schottroff and W. Stegemann, eds., *Der Gott der kleinen Leute* (vol. 1: AT), 1979, 39–66. See further, G. Fleischer, *Von Menschenverkäufern, Baschankühen und Rechtsverkehrern*.
146. Cf. Amos 2:8; 4:4f.; 5:4–6, 14f., 21–27; Hos. 2:15; 4:4ff.; 5:1ff.; 6:6; 8; 9:1–7; 10:1–2; Micah 1:2–7; 3:9–12; 5:12f.; 6:6–8; Isa. 1:10–17; 29:1; Jer. 6:16–21; 7; 14:11f.; Mal. 1:10; and Isa. 66:1–4. In addition, see p. 63.
147. Cf. pp. 272–274. For this, also see K. Koch, *The Prophets*, 1:159–163; and H. D. Preuss, *Jahweglaube und Zukunftserwartung*, 1968 (BWANT 87), 170ff.
148. Cf. above, p. 76.
149. See also K. Koch, *The Prophets*, 1:44.
150. Cf. above, p. 36.
151. For Hosea, see J. Jeremias, "Hosea/Hoseabuch," *TRE* 15, 586–598 (lit.); and 72 n. 4 for literature on Hosea.
152. Hos. 2:4–15; 4; 5:1–7; 8:1–14; 9:10–12; 10:5ff.; 12:12ff.; and 13:1–3.
153. Hos. 1:4; 3:4; 5:1; 7:3–7; 8:4, 10; 9:15–17; 10:3f., 7, 15b; and 13:9–11.
154. Hos. 2:5, 15f.; 4:6, 10; 5:1, 7; 6:7; 8:14; 9:10–17; 10:1f.; 11:1–9; and 13:5–8.
155. Cf. still Jer. 9:3; and Ezek. 33:24. For the absence of the tradition of the ancestors in the pre-exilic prophets and for literature on Hosea 12, see above, pp. 14f. and n. 151.
156. Should these passages be removed on account of the "covenant phobia" of German-speaking Old Testament scholars (thus K. Koch, *The Prophets,* 1:90)? At least in Hos. 8:1, I see no basis for this. Moreover, Hos. 6:7 has a background different from that of the covenant with YHWH. Cf. Vol. I, pp. 84–87.
157. Hos. 2:4, 7; 3:3; 4:10, 12ff., 18; 5:3f.; and 9:1.
158. Hos. 3:5 and 14:2 are secondary.
159. See O. Kaiser, "Jesaja/Jesajabuch," *TRE* 16, 636–658 (lit.). His literary-critical as well as redactional theses, to be sure, are not followed here. Cf. rather W. H. Schmidt, "Die Einheit der Verkündigung Jesajas," *EvTh* 37, 1977, 260–272.
160. For "justice and righteousness," cf. K. Koch, *The Prophets* 1:56–62.
161. For the (four) periods of his activity and the texts assigned to each of these, cf. the suggestion of G. Fohrer, *Der Prophet Jesaja*, vol. 1, 1967, 5–10; after that, see also K. Koch, *The Prophets*, 1:107.
162. Cf. Vol. I, pp. 240f. For Zion in Isaiah, cf. above, pp. 44f.
163. For the theme of "obstinacy" (6:9f.), cf. G. von Rad, *Theology*, 2:147–151; K. Koch, *The Prophets,* 1:108–113; O. H. Steck, *EvTh* 33, 1973, 77–90; R. Kilian, *Jesaja 1–39*, 1983 (EdF 200), 112ff.; and Vol. I, p. 107. One cannot point to Deuteronomistic influence in Isaiah 6 (thus O. Kaiser, *Isaiah 1–12: A Commentary*, 2d ed. (OTL), Philadelphia, 1983, 117–133). Cf. L. Perlitt, "Jesaja und die Deuteronomisten," in FS O. Kaiser, 1989 (BZAW 185), 133–149.
164. See J. Hausmann, *Israels Rest*, 1987 (BWANT 124); and below, pp. 271f.
165. W. Werner sees things differently (*Studien zur alttestamentlichen Vorstellung vom Plan Jahwes*, 1988 [BZAW 173]). Cf. Vol. I, pp. 207f + 212.

166. Cf. above, pp. 36f.; and also K. Koch, *The Prophets*, 1:132–140. Cf. the reflections of N. Lo-
    hfink on Isa. 9:1–6 and the location of this passage in the "memoir" of Isaiah (6:1–9:6) in J.
    Schreiner, ed., *Unterwegs zur Kirche*, 1987, 65 n. 83: "The prophet does not even consider
    the possibility that Yahweh's power over history will end when what now claims to repre-
    sent alone his kingship upon the earth comes to an end. . . . Nor does he even mention the
    possibility that when the present system is destroyed in judgment, Yahweh also may come
    to an end."
167. W. H. Schmidt, *EvTh* 37, 1977, 272.
168. See H. W. Wolff, *Micah: A Commentary*, Minneapolis, 1990 (CC); and K. Koch, *The
    Prophets*, 1:94–105.
169. Cf. M. Klopfenstein, "Das Gesetz bei den Propheten," in *Mitte der Schrift*? 1987, 283–297.
170. Cf., however, Isa. 1:10, 16f.; Hos. 4:1f., 6; Jer. 2:8; 7:5; and 22:15f.
171. See K. Seybold, *Profane Prophetie: Studien zum Buch Nahum*, 1989 (SBS 135).
172. See E. Otto, "Habakuk/Habakukbuch," *TRE* 14, 300–306 (lit.).
173. Thus, e.g., by E. Otto, ibid. For Hab. 2:4, see below, p. 363 n. 477.
174. Cf. K. Seybold, *Satirische Prophetie: Studien zum Buch Zefanja*, 1985 (SBS 120). The texts
    are given on pp. 109ff. They are "satirical," e.g., on account of certain images (1:8f.; and
    2:1f.) or comparisons (1:11f.; 2:5f.; and 2:13f.).
175. See K. Seybold, *Satirische Prophetie*, 83ff.
176. See S. Herrmann, "Jeremia/Jeremiabuch," *TRE* 16, 568–586 (lit.); W. Thiel, in *Zwischen
    Gericht und Heil*, 35ff.; and S. Herrmann, *Jeremiah*, 1990 (EdF 271).
177. For his four periods of activity and the assignment of texts to each of these, cf. K. Koch, *The
    Prophets*, 2:16; and S. Herrmann, *Jeremiah*, 27ff.
178. Jer. 11:18–12:6; 15:10–21; 17:14–18; 18:18–23; and 20:7–18. For the laments of God and
    of Jeremiah (Jer. 4:19–22; 6:10; 8:18–23; etc.; then see the confessions) as well as those of
    humans generally (cf. Jer. 14:1–15:4; and 31:18–20) in the Book of Jeremiah, cf. D. H. Bak,
    Klagender Gott - Klagende Menschen, 1990 (BZAW 193).
179. See also G. von Rad, *Theology*, 2:209–210.
180. See N. Kilpp, *Niederreissen und aufbauen*, 1990 (BThSt 13), 21–41; see there pp. 42–67 for
    Jeremiah 29 and pp. 68–85 for Jeremiah 32.
181. See W. Beyerlin, *Reflexe der Amosvisionen im Jeremiabuch*, 1989 (OBO 93).
182. For a different assessment of Jeremiah 32, see G. Wanke, "Jeremias Ackerkauf: Heil im
    Gericht?" in V. Fritz et al., eds., *Prophet*, FS O. Kaiser, 1989 (BZAW 185), 265–276. Ac-
    cording to Wanke, Jer. 32:6–14 (v. 15 is Deuteronomistic) deals with the following: "Even
    as the field, which is purchased by the prophet and kept safe by the deed of purchase stored
    in an earthenware vessel for a long period of time, remains withheld from his use, so in the
    future the land shall remain withheld from the disposition of the user" (p. 271). The text,
    however, does not permit one to recognize such a relationship between the action and the
    symbolized event. Even if v. 15 (correctly) is seen as Deuteronomistic, v. 14 says nothing
    about what Wanke finds here.
183. For this, see esp. W. Thiel, *Die deuteronomistische Redaktion von Jeremia 1–25*, 1973
    (WMANT 41); and idem, *Die deuteronomistische Redaktion von Jeremia 26–45*, 1981
    (WMANT 52).
184. Cf. below, pp. 265–267.
185. See T. Odashima, *Heilsworte im Jeremiabuch*, 1989 (BWANT 125); and S. Herrmann, *Jer-
    emiah*, 119ff.
186. See S. Herrmann, BK XII/1, 69ff., and N. Kilpp, *Niederreissen und aufbauen*.
187. See H. W. Wolff, BK XIV/3, 1977 (cf. his essay in *EvTh* 37, 1977, 273–284 = TB 76, 1987,
    109ff.); and J. Wehrle, *Prophetie und Textanalyse*, 1987.
188. For this, see W. Zimmerli, "Ezechiel/Ezechielbuch," *TRE* 10, 766–781 (lit.); J. Reindl, in
    Zwischen Gericht und Heil, 58ff.; B. Lang, *Ezechiel*, 1981 (EdF 153); *NBL* 1, cols. 649–652;
    J. Lust, ed., *Ezekiel and His Book*, 1986 (BETL 74); and R. M. Hals, *Ezekiel*, 1989 (FOTL
    19).
189. For this, see Vol. I, pp. 167–170. For the "word of proof" (cf. n. 193), cf. Vol. I, pp.
    205ff.
190. See O. Keel, *Jahwe-Visionen und Siegelkunst*, 1977 (SBS 84/85).

191. For these, see Th. Krüger, *Geschichtskonzepte im Ezechielbuch*, 1989 (BZAW 180).
192. His assessment of the commandments of YHWH ("which were not good"; Ezek. 20:25f.) is unique within the Old Testament, especially if what is meant is not limited only to the following verse that mentions the birth of the firstborn. Cf. Vol. I, p. 298 n. 390.
193. Thus, at least 54 times in Ezekiel. See above, n. 189; and W. Zimmerli, BK XIII/1, 55*ff.
194. W. Zimmerli, *Ezekiel*, 1:36–41.
195. Cf. below, pp. 277ff.
196. For this text, see D. Michel, "Deuterojesaja," *TRE* 8, 510–530 (lit.); *NBL* 1, cols. 410–413 (lit.). It is also clear that more recent scholarly studies do not see chaps. 40–55 of Isaiah entirely as a unit and do not believe that one is able to attribute these chapters to a single prophet. An assessment of the differences in the texts in Isaiah 40–55 (along with Isaiah 35 and 56–66) has been carried out in the works of O. H. Steck. For a different view that still regards chaps. 40–48 as "uniform," see H. D. Preuss, *Deuterojesaja: Eine Einführung in seine Botschaft*, 1976.
197. Cf. Vol. I, pp. 234f.
198. Cf. Vol. I, pp. 176f.
199. For the so-called servant songs, see below, pp. 303–305.
200. Is this actually only a "rhetorical point"? Thus G. von Rad, *Theology*, 2:244, n. 16.
201. Cf. above, p. 32.
202. See H. W. Wolff, *Haggai: A Commentary*, Minneapolis, 1988 (CC), and BK XIV/6, 1986.
203. Cf. p. 47.
204. For this book, see the more recent commentaries of D. L. Petersen, *Haggai and Zechariah 1–8: A Commentary*, OTL, Philadelphia, 1984; C. L. and E. M. Meyers, *Haggai, Zechariah 1–8: A New Translation with Introduction and Commentary*, New York, 1987 (AB); A. Deissler, NEB, 1988; and R. Hanhart, BK XIV/7, 1990ff. Further, see H.-G. Schöttler, *Gott inmitten seines Volkes*, 1987 (TThSt 43).
205. See S. Sekine, *Die tritojesajanische Sammlung (Jes 56–66) redationsgeschichtlich untersucht*, 1989 (BZAW 175); and K. Koenen, *Ethik und Eschatologie im Tritojesajabuch*, 1990 (WMANT 62).
206. See esp. O. H. Steck, "Tritojesaja im Jesajabuch," in J. Vermeylen, ed., *The Book of Isaiah*, Louvain, 1989, 361–406.
207. For him, see W. Rudolph, KAT XIII/4, 1976; A. Renker, *Die Tora bei Maleachi*, 1979; and A. Deissler, NEB, 1988.
208. Cf. Th. Lescow, "Dialogische Strukturen in den Streitreden des Buches Maleachi," *ZAW* 102, 1990, 194–212.
209. See H. Utzschneider, *Künder oder Schreiber?* 1989.
210. Cf. also P. R. House, *The Unity of the Twelve*, 1990 (JSOT Suppl 97).
211. See H.-J. Zobel, "Jona/Jonabuch," *TRE* 17, 229–234 (lit.).
212. It is a matter of debate as to whether the psalm in Jonah 2:3–10, which Jonah prays while in the belly of the fish, is original to the book.
213. For YHWH's "repentance" and Exod. 34:6f., see Vol. I, pp. 246 + 241f.
214. Cf. pp. 293 + 302 and, if possible, K.-P. Hertzsch, *Der ganze Fisch war voll Gesang* (many issues and editions).
215. Or only the end of the false prophets? Cf. above, p. 83f.
216. Cf. H.-P. Müller, *ThWAT* 5, cols. 162f.
217. Cf. below, pp. 277ff.

Chapter 11. The Israelite and His Relationship to God (Anthropology)

1. [Part Four.] Cf. Vol. I, pp. 208ff. + 226ff.
2. For Old Testament anthropology in general, see J. Hempel, *Gott und Mensch im Alten Testament*, 2d ed., 1936 (BWANT 38); W. Eichrodt, *Das Menschenverständnis des Alten Testaments*, 1947 (AThANT 4); W. Zimmerli, *Das Menschenbild des Alten Testaments*, 1949 (ThEx NF 14); L. Köhler, *Der hebräische Mensch*, 1953; G. Pidoux, *L'homme dans l'Ancien*

Testament, Neuchâtel and Paris, 1953; R. Patai, *Sitte und Sippe in Bibel und Orient,* 1962; W. Zimmerli, *Was ist der Mensch?* 1964; R. de Vaux, *Ancient Israel,* vol. 1: *Social Institutions,* New York, 1961; F. J. Stendebach, *Der Mensch . . . wie ihn Israel vor 3000 Jahren sah,* 1972; H. W. Wolff, *Anthropology of the Old Testament,* Philadelphia, 1974; H. Seebass, "Über den Beitrag des Alten Testaments zu einer theologischen Anthropologie," *KuD* 22, 1976, 41–63; R. Lauha, *Psychophysischer Sprachgebrauch im Alten Testament,* Helsinki, 1983; E.-J. Waschke, *Untersuchungen zum Menschenbild der Urgeschichte,* 1984; and J. W. Rogerson, *Anthropology and the Old Testament,* Sheffield, 1984. Cf. also L. Köhler, *Theologie,* 74ff.; E. Jacob, *Theologie,* 122–147; G. von Rad, *Old Testament Theology,* vol. 2: *The Theology of Israel's Prophetic Tradition,* New York, 1965, 347–349; W. Zimmerli, *Old Testament Theology in Outline,* Atlanta, 1978, 32–37; and C. Westermann, *Elements of Old Testament Theology,* Atlanta, 1982, 85–117.

3. For the following, cf. esp. the works of L. Köhler, R. Patai, and R. de Vaux mentioned above in n. 2.

4. Cf. M. Augustin, *Der schöne Mensch im Alten Testament und im hellenistischen Judentum,* 1983.

5. For the passages, images, and metaphors of Canticles, cf. esp. the commentary by O. Keel, *ZBK AT* 18, 1986.

6. Cf. L. Köhler, *Der hebräische Mensch,* 101ff.

7. Cf. H. W. Wolff, *Anthropology of the Old Testament,* 119–121.

8. Cf. the commentaries as well as the calculations made by J. W. Walton (*Ancient Israelite Literature in Its Cultural Context,* Grand Rapids, 1989, 127–131).

9. For the ages, life expectancy, and quality of life of the elderly according to the Old Testament, cf. F. L. Hossfeld, "Graue Panther im Alten Testament? Das Alter in der Bibel," *ArztChr* 36, 1990, 1–11. Cf. below, p. 343 n. 42.

10. Cf. the summary in L. Köhler, *Der hebräische Mensch,* 30ff.

11. Cf. the Egyptian Akhenaton hymn: AOT, 2d ed., 16; *RGT,* 2d ed., 45.

12. Cf. the overview in R. Patai, *Sitte und Sippe,* 206f.

13. Cf. L. Köhler, *Der hebräische Mensch,* 51–55; R. de Vaux, *Ancient Israel,* 1:43–46; and M. Noth, *Die israelitischen Personennamen im Rahmen der gemeinsemitischen Namengebung,* 1928 (BWANT 46) (and the reprint).

14. For the problem of "schools" in ancient Israel, cf. H. D. Preuss, *Einführung in die alttestamentliche Weisheitsliteratur,* 1987, 45f. (lit.); and D. W. Jamieson-Drake, *Scribes and Schools in Monarchic Judah,* 1991 (JSOT Suppl 109).

15. Cf. Vol. I, pp. 213, 232.

16. Cf. H. W. Wolff, *Anthropology of the Old Testament,* 143–148; K. Seybold and U. Müller, *Krankheit und Heilung,* 1978; and J. Scharbert, "Krankheit. II: A. T.," *TRE* 19, 680–683.

17. For the definition of leprosy, or Hansen's disease, cf. L. Köhler, *Der hebräische Mensch,* 42ff.

18. Luther's translation of Sir. 38:15 is not appropriate for the intended meaning.

19. See N. Lohfink, "'Ich bin Jahwe, dein Arzt' (Exod. 15:26)," in *"Ich will euer Gott werden": Beispiele biblischen Redens von Gott,* 1981 (SBS 100), 11–73.

20. Cf. also the theme "Suffering" below, (pp. 141–146).

21. Cf. for Mesopotamia the numerous references found under "Krankheiten" in *RLA* VI, 223. For the laments, see A. Falkenstein and W. von Soden, *Sumerische und akkadische Hymnen und Gebete,* 1953; M.-J. Seux, *Hymnes et Prières aux Dieux de Babylonie et d'Assyrie,* Paris, 1976; W. Mayer, *Untersuchungen zur Formensprache der babylonischen "Gebetsbeschwörungen,"* Rome, 1976, 67ff., 111ff., etc.; and H. W. F. Saggs, *Mesopotamien,* 1966, 445ff., 672ff. For Egypt, see *LÄ* III, cols. 757–764, under "Krankheit, Krankheitsabwehr, Krankheitsbeschreibung und -darstellung" (lit.).

22. Judg. 14:5f.; 1 Sam. 17:34–36; 2 Sam. 23:20; 1 Kings. 18:46; and 22:34f.: "A people does not simply know about such matters; rather, it experiences them; a nation does not simply tell about such matters; rather, it expresses its delight in them" (L. Köhler, *Der hebräische Mensch,* 18).

23. Cf. below, pp. 237f.

24. Cf. E. Kutsch, "חתן *htn,*" ThWAT 3, cols. 288–296. In the Old Testament, the verb "to circumcise" is מול (= *mûl*). Cf., however, Exod. 4:24–26 which brings together circumcision and

the "bloody bridegroom." For this passage, see E. Blum, et al., eds., *Die Hebräische Bibel und ihre zweifache Nachgeschichte,* FS R. Rendtorff, 1990, 41–54.

25. Cf. (in addition to the appropriate articles in *THAT* and *ThWAT*) H.-P. Stähli, *Knabe-Jüngling-Knecht: Untersuchungen zum Begriff* נער *im Alten Testament,* 1978 (BET 7).

26. As Lev. 27:1–8 shows, the different stages of life are "valued" at different financial levels.

27. Cf. R. Patai, *Sitte und Sippe,* 17f. For the dominating role of the father in the Israelite family, see also H.-F. Richter, *Geschlechtlichkeit, Ehe und Familie im Alten Testament und seiner Umwelt,* 1978 (BET 10), 119ff.; and then esp. L. Perlitt, "Der Vater im Alten Testament," in H. Tellenbach, ed., *Das Vaterbild in Mythos und Geschichte,* 1976, 50–101 (there are essays in this volume by other authors that also deal with the portrait of the father in ancient Egypt, ancient Greece, and the New Testament). In addition, see P. A. H. de Boer, *Fatherhood and Motherhood in Israelite and Judean Piety,* Leiden, 1974.

28. In Gen. 2:24, the opposite is not presupposed. Cf., e.g., C. Westermann, *Genesis 1–11: A Commentary,* CC, Minneapolis, 1984, 233–234, for this passage.

29. For the organization of the nation, cf. Josh. 7:14; and Vol. I, p. 62.

30. Cf. H. F. Richter, *Geschlechtlichkeit, Ehe und Familie im Alten Testament und seiner Umwelt;* and H. W. Wolff, *Anthropologie des Alten Testaments,* 243ff.; and B. Lang, "Ehe (AT)," *NBL* 1, cols. 475–478. For marriage in the cultural environment of Israel at the time, cf. V. Korošec et al. "Ehe," *RLA* II, 281–299; S. Allam, "Ehe," *LÄ* I, cols. 1162–1181; H. Klengel, *Kulturgeschichte des alten Vorderasien,* 1989 (see the subject index). See also below, nn. 40 and 54.

31. We are not instructed about the more precise background of homosexual intercourse between men that is prohibited in the Holiness Code (Lev. 18:22; and 20:13) and mentioned possibly in 2 Sam. 1:26 (or is the latter only a reference to brotherly love?). A lesbian relationship between women is not mentioned in the Old Testament, probably since it was of no interest to males. However, the proposal that this has to do (only) with a demarcation from pagan customs (Gen. 19:4–8; and Judg. 19:22–26) or cultic acts has no evidence. David and Jonathan, whose love toward each other is mentioned (1 Sam. 18:1; 19:1; and 2 Sam. 1:26), had, nevertheless, their interests in women and children. In addition, as is so often the case, one has to distinguish in this matter between stipulations of laws from a later period and (earlier) customs. For this topic, cf. R. Patai, *Sitte und Sippe,* 182ff. For the cultural environment of Israel at that time, cf. the appropriate articles in *RLA* and *LÄ.*

32. For Deut. 22:13–21, C. Locher, *Die Ehre einer Frau in Israel,* 1986 (OBO 70).

33. Only kings could support more wives. David is said to have had ten wives (2 Sam. 20:3) and Abijah fourteen. Solomon is said to have had a thousand, not including many foreign women (1 Kings 11:1–8), who are mentioned more as a warning of the consequences: they seduced him into forsaking YHWH. Deuteronomy (17:17) warns against this practice of a king having many wives.

34. L. Köhler, *Der hebräische Mensch,* 81.

35. Cf. H.-F. Richter, *Geschlechtlichkeit, Ehe und Familie im Alten Testament und seiner Umwelt,* 75ff.

36. Cf. also Gen. 28:28f. and (more removed) Ruth 3f. For this topic, see H.-F. Richter, *Geschlechtlichkeit, Ehe und Familie im Alten Testament und seiner Umwelt,* 86ff.

37. Cf. below, pp. 199f.

38. Thus, e.g., according to the Mesopotamian Atrahasis epic (cf. W. von Soden, *MDOG* 111, 1979, 1–33). For this, see R. Albertz, "Die Kulturarbeit im Atraḫasīs-Epos im Vergleich zur biblischen Urgeschichte," in R. Albertz et al., eds., *Schöpfung und Befreiung,* FS C. Westermann, 1980, 38–57. Cf. also Vol. I, p. 231, and the text VAT 17019 (BE 13383) from Babylon, line 29: "[The forced] labor to the gods he commanded be imposed upon him."

39. Cf. below, pp. 254–257.

40. Is it the case that the wife, in contrast to the maid and slave (in Exod. 20:10; and Deut. 5:14), is not mentioned, because it was understood that she would also work on the Sabbath, e.g., she must take care of the family? See below, p. 108.

41. Cf. Vol. I, pp. 187f.

42. Cf. R. Z. Dulin, *A Crown of Glory: A Biblical View of Aging,* New York, 1988. Cf. further above, p. 342 n. 9.

43. Cf. David, 1 Kings 1:1–4; Isaac, Gen. 27:21; and Jacob, Gen. 48:10, etc.
44. In Gen. 19:31 this idiom is used to refer to sexual intercourse.
45. Cf. H. D. Preuss, "Bibelarbeit über Psalm 39," in P. Godzik and Jeziorowski, *Von der Begleitung Sterbender*, 1989, 101–116 (there 101–103).
46. For the view and evaluation of death, see below, pp. 149–150.
47. Cf. H. Jahnow, *Das hebräische Leichenlied*, 1923 (BZAW 36), 2–57; R. Patai, *Sitte und Sippe*, 260ff.; R. de Vaux, *Ancient Israel*, 1:56–61; E. Kutsch, "'Trauerbräuche' und 'Selbstminderungsriten'" im Alten Testament," in K. Lüthi, E. Kutsch, and W. Dantine, *Drei Wiener Antrittsreden*, 1965 (ThSt 78), 23–42 (=BZAW 168, 1986, 78ff.); Th. J. Lewis, *Cults of the Dead in Ancient Israel and Ugarit*, Atlanta, Ga., 1989 (HSM 39); and B. Lorenz, "Bestattung und Totenkult im Alten Testament," *ZRGG* 42, 1990, 21–31. See also P. Heinisch, *Die Trauergebräuche bei den Israeliten* 1931; W. Eichrodt, *Theology of the Old Testament*, vol. 2 (OTL), Philadelphia, 1967, 212–223; and for the cult of the dead and the cult of impending death, along with their various materials, K. Spronk, *Beatific Afterlife in Ancient Israel and in the Ancient Near East*, 1986 (AOAT 219). Cf. also Vol. I, pp. 262–263.
48. "The beloved deceased person, once dead, is a member of another world, i.e., the kingdom of the dead, and therefore is something frightful. The dead person, then, is to be avoided, for he or she is 'impure.' It is on this basis that the mourning rites and customs concerning the dead are to be explained in their essential nature. They have to do with protection and separation from the dead" (L. Köhler, *Der hebräische Mensch*, 100).
49. Cf. Th. J. Lewis, *Cults of the Dead in Ancient Israel and Ugarit;* and O. Loretz, *Ugarit und die Bibel*, 1990, 125ff.
50. Lev. 11:32–35; 19:27f., 31; 20:6, 27; 21:5; Num. 5:2, 19:11; Deut. 14:1; 18:11; and Ezek. 44:25.
51. Gen. 15:15; 25:8; 47:30; 1 Kings 13:22; 2 Kings 22:20; etc. (cf. *ThWAT* 1, col. 10).
52. 1 Kings 13:22; 14:11; 16:4; 21:24; 2 Kings 9:10; Jer. 7:33; 8:1f.; 9:21; 14:16; 22:19; 25:33; Ezek. 29:5; and Ps. 79:2f.
53. Cf. Vol. 1, pp. 262–263.
54. From the extensive literature that deals with these questions, one may only mention M. Löhr, *Die Stellung des Weibes zu Jahwe-Religion und Kult*, 1908; G. Beer, *Die soziale und religiöse Stellung der Frau im israelitischen Altertum*, 1919; H. J. Boecker, *Frau und Mann*, 1977; J. H. Ottwell, *And Sarah Laughed: The Status of Woman in the Old Testament*, Philadelphia, 1977; F. Crüsemann and H. Thyen, *Als Mann und Frau geschaffen*, 1978; M. de Merode-de Croy, *Die Rolle der Frau im Alten Testament, Conc* (D) 16, 1980 (4), 270–275; E. S. Gerstenberger and W. Schrage, *Frau und Mann*, 1980; M. S. Heister, *Frauen in der biblischen Glaubensgeschichte*, 1981; E. S. Gerstenberger, "Herrschen oder Lieben: Zum Verhältnis der Geschlechter im Alten Testament," in J. Jeremias and L. Perlitt, eds., *Die Botschaft und die Boten*, FS H. W. Wolff, 1981, 335–347; J. Ebach, "Frau. II: A. T.," *TRE* 11, 422–424 (lit.); A. Brenner, *The Israelite Woman*, Sheffield, 1985; G. I. Emmerson, "Woman in Ancient Israel," in R. E. Clements, ed., *The World of Ancient Israel*, Cambridge, 1989, 371–394; and K. Engelken, *Frauen im Alten Israel*, 1990 (BWANT 130). Cf. also B. S. Childs, *Old Testament Theology in a Canonical Context*, Philadelphia, 1985.
55. See H. Kosmala, *ThWAT* 1, col. 909; H. Donner, in R. von Kienle et al., eds., *Festschrift Johannes Friedrich zum 65. Geburtstag*, 1959, 105–145; and G. I. Emmerson, "Woman in Ancient Israel," 373ff.
56. The citation is from L. Köhler, *Der hebräische Mensch*, 72.
57. The two much-contested texts of Exod. 38:8 and 1 Sam. 2:22, which mention female cult personnel, do not support what one often reads out of them. 1 Sam. 2:22 mentions women at the sanctuary in order to elucidate the sin that happened there. Exod. 38:8 may be an adaptation of this text although without having recognized the critical undertone that resides there. Cf. for this topic P. Bird, "The Place of Woman in the Israelite Cultus," in P. D. Miller, Jr., et al., eds., *Ancient Israelite Religion*, FS F. M. Cross, Philadelphia, 1987, 397–419. As a consequence of their monthly "impurity" and the impurity associated with giving birth to a child, the Old Testament excludes women from the priesthood. Cf. above, p. 52.
58. Cf. the descriptions of the "good" male and the warnings concerning the "evil" woman (Prov.

11:16, 22; 14:1; 21:9, 19; 25:24; 27:15f.; Qoh. 7:26; cf. Sir. 9:3; 25:17ff.; 26:5ff.; and 42:6) or the counsel about the necessity of the woman's subjection to the man (Sir. 9:2).

59. When women rule, this brings about disorder and is a sign of disaster: Isa. 3:12.

60. For the concubine (פילנש/פלנש = *pîlegeš/pilegeš*), see K. Engelken, *Frauen im Alten Israel*, 74ff.

61. Cf. above, p. 343 n. 40.

62. For adultery, see Vol. I, pp. 32, 57, 104.

63. Cf. the representations in A. Parrot, *Der Tempel von Jerusalem, Golgatha und das Heilige Grab*, 1956, 70; *BHHW* III, cols. 1945f.; and L. D. Sporty, "The Location of the Holy House of Herod's Temple," *BA* 54, 1991 (1), 30. Already similar to the intentions of the Books of Chronicles; see M. Oeming, *Das wahre Israel*, 1990 (BWANT 128), 209.

64. Cf. F. Crüsemann, *Als Mann und Frau geschaffen*, 34ff.

65. Cf. C. Locher, *Die Ehre einer Frau in Israel*.

66. Cf. above, p. 103 with 343 n. 66. Then see R. Neu, "Patrilokalität und Patrilinearität in Israel," *BZ* NF 34, 1990, 222–223 (the Old Testament leaves no traces of an original matriarchy). For the position of the woman and for the view of marriage in Israel's cultural environment, cf. also H.-F. Richter, *Geschlechtlichkeit, Ehe und Familie im Alten Testament und seiner Umwelt*, 149ff.; and H. Klengel, *Kulturgeschichte des alten Vorderasien*, 1989 (see the index).

67. E. S. Gerstenberger traces this development and its ancient seeds in J. Jeremias and L. Perlitt, eds., *Die Botschaft und die Boten*, FS H. W. Wolff ("Herrschen oder Lieben").

68. Cf. the following: C. Westermann, "אדם *'ādām* Mensch," *THAT* 1, cols. 41–57; F. Maass, "אדם." *ThWAT* 1, cols. 81–94; and W. H. Schmidt, "Anthropologische Begriffe im Alten Testament," *EvTh* 24, 1964, 374–388. In addition, see pp. 341–342 n. 2, for other literature, especially the books of H. W. Wolff and R. Lauha. For articles on other important terms, see the following: H. Bratsiotis, "בשׂר," *ThWAT* 1, cols. 850–867; G. Gerleman, "בשׂר *bāśār* Fleisch," *THAT* 1, cols. 376–379; G. Gerleman, "דם *dām* Blut," *THAT* 1, cols. 448–451; B. Kedar-Kopfstein, "דם *dām*," *ThWAT* 2, cols. 248–266; F. Stolz, "לב *lēb* Herz," *THAT* 1, cols. 861–867; and H.-J. Fabry, "לב *lēb*," *THWAT* 4, cols. 413–451. For כבד = *kbd* ("liver"), see P. Stenmans, *ThWAT* 4, col. 22; D. Kellermann, "כליות *kĕlājôt*," *ThWAT* 4, cols. 185–192; C. Westermann, "נפשׁ *naefaeš* Seele," *THAT* 2, cols. 71–96; H. Seebass, "נפשׁ *naepaeš*," *ThWAT* 5, cols. 531–555; H. Lamberti-Zielinski, "נשׁמה *nĕšāmāh*," *ThWAT* 5, cols. 669–673; R. Albertz and C. Westermann, "רוח *rûaḥ* Geist," *THAT* 2, cols. 726–753; and S. Tengström and H.-J. Fabry, "רוח *rûaḥ*," *ThWAT* 7, cols. 385–425. Then see J. Scharbert, *Fleisch, Geist und Seele im Pentateuch*, 2d ed., 1967 (SBS 19). See in addition the commentaries on Genesis 1–3; Psalms 8 and 104; etc., as well as E. Sellin, *Theologie*, 2d ed., 57–65; and W. Eichrodt, *Theology*, 2:118–150.

69. For the parallels in Israel's cultural environment at that time, cf. C. Westermann, *Genesis 1:11*, for both commentary and examples; and *RGT*, 2d ed., 81, 87.

70. Cf. K. Berge, *Die Zeit des Jahwisten*, 1990 (BZAW 186), 69ff.

71. The goddess Nammu and the goddess Mami formed (*formatio*) humans from the clay (*RGT*, 2d ed., 102f.; W. von Soden, *ZA* 68, 1978, 65; lines 192ff.: Atraḥasis Epic), or Enki dug a hole in the ground with a hoe (*emersio*) [*RGT*, 2d ed., 101f.] and so forth. Cf. also, e.g., S. N. Kramer, *Sumerian Mythology*, 2d ed., 1961 (Harper Torchbooks), 51–53, 69–71. M. Eliade, ed., *Quellen des alten Orients*, 1: *Die Schöpfungsmythen*, 1964 (and many others); G. Pettinato, *Das altorientalische Menschenbild und die sumerischen und akkadischen Schöpfungsmythen*, 1971 (for this, see H. M. Kümmel, *WO* 7[1], 1973, 25–38).

72. Gen. 6:3, 12; Isa. 31:3; 40:6; Jer. 17:5; Pss. 56:5; 78:39; 109:24; Job 10:4; 34:15; and 2 Chron. 32:8. Given a positive meaning only in Ezek. 11:19 and 36:26. Together with נפשׁ = *nepeš* ("soul, breath, life, being," etc.), it can designate the entire human person (Isa. 10:18; Pss. 16:9; 63:2; and 84:3), as does the term עצם = *'eṣem* ("bones") (Job 2:5).

73. The passages that Bratsiotis (*ThWAT* 1, col. 863) enlists to prove this idea do not support his argument.

74. Thus the human being (also the animal as well) is more an "animated body" than a "living soul" (H. H. Rowley, *Faith*, 74, 79). For the gift of breath, cf. also *RGT*, 2d ed., 72. For Gen. 2:7, cf. also below, p. 350 n. 178.

75. See, however, P. Heinisch, *Theologie des Alten Testaments*, 1940, 130f., 133, 135f. ("Unsterblichkeit der Seele"). Cf. for the later period, however, Wisd. 2:22f.; 3:13; 4:10–5:23; and 8:19f.
76. This contrasts with the ancient Egyptian understandings of anthropology (*ka, ba,* and *akh*): cf. e.g., the illustrations in K. Koch, *Das Wesen altägyptischer Religion im Spiegel ägyptologischer Forschung*, 1989, 54; and *WdM* I, 342f., 370–372 for the *ba* and *ka*. See further H. P. Hasenfratz, "Zur 'Seelenvorstellung' der alten Ägypter," *ZRGG* 42, 1990, 193–216.
77. For the "spirit of YHWH," cf. Vol. I, pp. 160–163.
78. For this problem, cf. J. Finkenzeller, "Die 'Seele' des Menschen im Verständnis von Theologie und Philosophie," in W. Baier et al., eds., *Weisheit Gottes, Weisheit der Welt*, FS J. Kard. Ratzinger, 1987, vol. 1, 277–291.
79. Cf. the numerous passages in *ThWAT* 5, col. 550.
80. Exod. 23:12; 31:17; and 2 Sam. 16:14.
81. Cf. H. Seebass, *ThWAT* 5, cols. 543–545.
82. Cf. W. H. Schmidt, *EvTh* 24, 1964, 381: "The human being is an individual to the extent that he strives after something."
83. Cf. the passages in *THAT* 2, cols. 90. In addition, see H. W. Wolff, *Anthropology of the Old Testament*, 10–25.
84. Exod. 21:23f.; Deut. 12:23; Judg. 5:18; 1 Sam. 25:29; 2 Sam. 23:17; 1 Kings 19:3; 2 Kings 7:7; Jer. 17:21; Job 2:4; etc.; cf. "to strive after life" (1 Sam. 20:1; 22:23; etc.).
85. Cf. the passages in *ThWAT* 5, col. 550.
86. Cf. below, pp. 242f. + 251f.
87. See H. Brunner, *Das hörende Herz*, 1988 (OBO 80), 3–41. Cf., e. g., *RGT*, 2d ed., 76, 87.
88. Num. 32:7, 9; Deut. 1:28; 15:10; Josh. 7:5; Judg. 19:6, 9; 1 Sam. 1:8; Pss. 25:17; 84:3; 105:3; Prov. 17:22; Cant. 3:11; Qoh. 5:19; etc.
89. Cf. Exod. 7:22; 28:3; Deut. 6:6; 8:5; 1 Sam. 27:1; Ezek. 3:10; Job 12:3; Prov. 2:10; 15:14; 16:23; 18:15; Qoh. 7:21; etc.
90. 1 Kings 8:39; Pss. 17:3; 33:15; 44:22; 105:25; 139:23; Prov. 15:11; 16:19; 19:21; 20:5; and 21:1.
91. Cf. below, pp. 128 + 138.
92. Cf. the passages in *ThWAT* 4, cols. 441f.
93. Cf. yet heart and soul (Ps. 13:3); heart and spirit (Exod. 35:21; Deut. 2:30; Josh. 2:11; 5:1; etc.); and heart and flesh (Pss. 63:2 and 84:3).
94. W. H. Schmidt, *EvTh* 24, 1964, 387.
95. See J. J. Stamm, *Die Gottebenbildlichkeit des Menschen*, 1959 (ThSt 54); H. Wildberger, "Das Abbild Gottes," *TThZ* 21, 1965, 245–259, 481–501 (=TB 66, 1979, 110ff.); O. Loretz, *Die Gottebenbildlichkeit des Menschen*, 1967; L. Scheffczyk, *Der Mensch als Bild Gottes*, 1969 (WdF 124); H. D. Preuss, "דמות/דמה *dāmāh/děmût*," *ThWAT* 2, cols. 266–277; H. Wildberger, "צלם *ṣaelaem* Abbild," *THAT* 2, cols. 556–563; J. Ebach, "Die Erschaffung des Menschen als Bild Gottes," *WuP* 66, 1977, 198–214; W. Gross, "Die Gottebenbildlichkeit des Menschen im Kontext der Priesterschrift," *ThQ* 161, 1981, 244–264; F. J. Stendebach, "צלם *ṣaelaem*," *ThWAT* 6, cols. 1046–1055 (lit.); G. A. Jónsson, *The Image of God*, Lund, 1988 (CB OT 26) [especially for form criticism]; and J. Scharbert, "Der Mensch als Ebenbild Gottes in der neueren Auslegung von Gen 1,26," in W. Baier et al., eds., *Weisheit Gottes, Weisheit der Welt*, FS J. Kard. Ratzinger, 1987, vol. 1, 241–258 (lit.).
96. Cf. Vol. I, pp. 256–258.
97. For these different prepositions, cf. W. H. Schmidt, *Die Schöpfungsgeschichte der Priesterschrift*, 2d ed., 1967 (WMANT 17), 133.
98. That צלם (= *ṣelem;* "image") designates more the external form and דמות (= *děmût;* "likeness") more the contents of the image is supported by the discovery in 1979 of a statue originating in the ninth century B.C.E. at Tell Fecheriye that has a Neo-Assyrian and Aramaic inscription. For the transliteration and translation of this, see Chr. Dohmen, *BN* 22, 1983, 91–106; and J. Naveh, in P. D. Miller, Jr., et al., eds., *Ancient Israelite Religion*, 101–113; see also *TUAT* I/6, 634–637.
99. For the plural suffix, cf. C. Westermann, *Genesis 1:11*, 145–147.

100. Cf. also J. A. Soggin, "'Imago Dei'—Neue Überlegungen zu Genesis 1,26f.," in M. Oeming and A. Graupner, eds., *Altes Testament und christliche Verkündigung,* FS A. H. J. Gunneweg, 1987, 385–389.

101. The works of N. Lohfink (*Unsere grossen Wörter,* 1977, 156–171) and K. Koch ("Gestaltet die Erde, doch heget das Leben!" in H.-G. Geyer et al., eds., *"Wenn nicht jetzt, wann dann?"* FS H.-J. Kraus, 1983, 23–36) have helped with the correct translation and interpretation of these verbs. Cf. N. Lohfink, "Die Priesterschrift und die Geschichte," VT Suppl 29, 1978, 189–225 [esp. 219–221] (= SBAB 4, 1988, 213ff.); and E. Zenger, *Gottes Bogen in den Wolken: Untersuchungen zu Komposition und Theologie der priesterschriftlichen Urgeschichte,* 1983 (SBS 112), 90ff. Similarly, H.-J. Zobel, "רדה *rādāh*," *ThWAT* 7, cols. 351–358 (a responsible, positive, godlike activity that is understood as a blessing and that contributes to the maintenance and continuance of creation). More skeptical is J. Scharbert in W. Baier et al., eds., *Weisheit Gottes, Weisheit der Welt,* FS J. Kard. Ratzinger 1, 1987, 241–258 (see above, n. 95). Cf. Vol. I, p. 233.

102. "P^g is not aware of any dynamic history that ever moves beyond itself and aims toward an unrealized eschaton, once Israel stepped across the Jordan" (N. Lohfink, SBAB 4, 249).

103. Cf. below, pp. 235–238.

104. "Semantically "to make holy" certainly means "to separate out," and yet for what end and purpose? P^g provides the answer to this in its history of the Sinai. The *meaning* and *purpose* of creation, which God has fully equipped once for all as a 'house of life' (Gen. 2:2), are first unfolded in Israel. For it is Israel who discovers and posits the theological secret of the seven days of creation: creation is intended to be a "house of life" inhabited by a people, yes even all of humanity, in whose midst the creator God himself is present. The 'door' to this reality is the seventh day" (E. Zenger, *Gottes Bogen in den Wolken,* 101).

105. Cf. W. Zimmerli, "Der Mensch im Rahmen der Natur nach den Aussagen des ersten biblischen Schöpfungsberichtes," *ZThK* 76, 1979, 139–158.

106. Cf. the references in the works by H. Wildberger ("צלם *ṣaelaem* Abbild") and F. J. Stendenbach ("צלם *ṣaelaem*"). For Egypt (*twt* = image; cf. Thutankamon; in addition also *hnty*), cf. E. Hornung, in O. Loretz (*Die Gottebenbildlichkeit des Menschen,* 123ff.) and M. Görg, "Das Menschenbild der Priesterschrift," *BiKi* 42, 1987, 26 (see below, n. 111); and B. Ockinga, *Die Gottebenbildlichkeit im Alten Ägypten und im Alten Testament,* 1984 (Ockinga [p. 145] opposes the thesis of a "democratization" of previously existing titles of rank).

107. Cf. the "Instruction for Merikare," line 132 or sec. 46 (W. Helck, *Die Lehre für König Merikare,* 1977, 85, and *RGT,* 2d ed., 72): humans as the images of God.

108. Cf. Vol. I, p. 228.

109. Cf. Vol. I, pp. 244–246.

110. SBAB 4, 245.

111. Cf. once again the previously mentioned works of N. Lohfink and E. Zenger in n. 101. Then, M. Görg, "Das Menschenbild der Priesterschrift," 21–29.

112. M. Görg, "Das Menschenbild der Priesterschrift," 25.

113. Cf. above, p. 112.

114. M. Görg ("Das Menschenbild der Priesterschrift," 23) wishes to see the flood and the ark as metaphors reflecting the events of the exilic situation of the contemporaries of P^g.

115. Cf. above, pp. 13f.

116. Cf. below, pp. 237f.

117. See W. Gross, "Jakob, der Mann des Segens: Zu Traditionsgeschichte und Theologie der priesterschriftlichen Jakobsüberlieferungen," *Bibl* 49, 1968, 321–344.

118. "If the way of the true Israel is elucidated by the characteristics of Noah for moving into and through the catastrophe of the exile, the pattern of Abraham can become the symbolic transparency for seeing the way out of the exile for Israel's future oriented toward the cult" (M. Görg, "Das Menschenbild der Priesterschrift," 24).

119. Cf. Vol. I, pp. 253–254.

120. W. Zimmerli, *Das Menschenbild des Alten Testaments,* 14.

121. M. Görg, "Das Menschenbild der Priesterschrift," 29.

122. E. Zenger, *Gottes Bogen in den Wolken,* 165.

123. E.-J. Waschke, *Untersuchungen zum Menschenbild der Urgeschichte,* 49.
124. Ibid, 179. Cf, as a whole, pp. 179ff.
125. Cf. also H.-F. Richter, "Zur Urgeschichte des Jahwisten," *BN* 34, 1986, 39–57 (sees J as containing several strata); and F. J. Stendebach, "Das Menschenbild des Jahwisten," *BiKi* 42, 1987, 15–20.
126. Thus, e.g., L. Schmidt, W. H. Schmidt, H. Seebass, and now K. Berge, *Die Zeit des Jahwisten,* 1990 (BZAW 186).
127. L. Schmidt, "Überlegungen zum Jahwisten," *EvTh* 37, 1977, 230–247; see p. 241.
128. For biological elements of anthropology and the anthropological terms, cf. above, pp. 97–114.
129. The view that Gen. 2:16f. does not mean physical death but rather spiritual death, which places humans outside the community of life with God (thus, e.g., O. Procksch, *Theologie,* 495), cannot be supported.
130. J. M. Kennedy "Peasants in Revolt," (JSOT 47, 1990, 3–14) finds in Genesis 2–3 intimations of a failed farmer's revolt against royal social and economic interests.
131. One may compare this with the reasons for the coming of the deluge in the flood narratives in the ancient Near Eastern environment of Israel or the divine decisions and measures taken to annihilate or reduce the human race. Examples are found in J. Bottéro and S. N. Kramer, *Lorsque les dieux faisaient l'homme,* Paris, 1989, 548–601; *RGT,* 2d ed., 35–38 (Re is old and has become impotent; the noise of humans (rebellion?) disturbs the gods (*RGT,* 2d ed., 115f.; W. von Soden, *ZA* 68, 1978, 73f.). The version of the flood found on Tablet 11 of the Gilgamesh Epic provides no reason at all (lines 14ff.; cf. *RGT,* 2d ed., 119). Cf. also R. Oberforcher, *Die Flutprologe als Kompositionsschlüssel der biblischen Urgeschichte,* 1981.
132. Whether Gen. 6:1–4 aims in this direction is uncertain, as is the assignment of this section to J.
133. W. Zimmerli, *Das Menschenbild des Alten Testaments,* 12.
134. Does Gen. 16:1–6 narrate a "fall" of Abram and Sarai? Thus W. Berg, *BN* 19, 1982, 7–14.
135. Cf. the fine reflections of E.-J. Waschke (*Untersuchungen zum Menschenbild der Urgeschichte,* 145ff.) about the joining together of both "sources" in the primeval history.
136. Cf. Vol. I, pp. 188f., 216f.
137. Cf. below, pp. 185f., 188–193; and Vol. I, pp. 80–95.
138. Cf. above, pp. 67–96.
139. Cf. below, pp. 188 + 287f.
140. Cf. Vol. I, pp. 161f.
141. Cf. below, pp. 245–250, for the theme of "prayer." Cf. further H.-J. Kraus, *Theology of the Psalms,* Minneapolis, 1986 (CC); and H. Goeke, "Die Anthropologie der individuellen Klagelieder," *BiLe* 14, 1973, 13–29, 112–137.
142. The questions concerning the dating of individual psalms are not very decisive for the following investigation. Moreover, that the psalms should exist for us, on the one hand, as prayers from a more familial cult carried out in local sanctuaries and, on the other hand, as components of the late-postexilic worship of God in the synagogue, while the preexilic temple cult should have been widely inaccessible and limited to a "royal" cult of the orthodox community, cannot in my opinion be demonstrated. However, see E. S. Gerstenberger, *Psalms,* Part 1 [Pss 1–60], Grand Rapids, 1988 (FOTL 14). For the theme "creation and salvation," see Vol. I, pp. 235–239.
143. For the problem of the "enemy," adversary, and opponent of the psalmist in the Psalter, cf., e.g., Psalms 5; 7; 9; 13; 17; 22; 36; 57; etc. See, e.g., O. Keel, *Feinde und Gottesleugner,* 1968 (SBM 7); L. Ruppert, *Der leidende Gerechte und seine Feinde,* 1973; and H.-J. Kraus, *Theology,* 125–136.
144. By what means this would be experienced and how it would work out requires a new investigation.
145. Cf., e. g., Psalms 3; 4; 6; 10; 13; etc.
146. The biblical references are numerous: Pss. 9:19; 10:2, 9; 14:6; 18:28; 40:18; 41:2; 68:11; 69:33; 70:6; 72:2, 4, 13; 74:19; 82:3f.; 86:1; 109:22; 147:6; 149:4; etc. Cf. H.-J. Kraus, *Theology,* 150–154.
147. Twenty-seven occurrences are found in the Psalter: Pss. 27:9; 31:17; 35:27; 69:18; 86:2, 4, 16; 89:51; 102:15, 29; 109:28; and 143:2, 12. In addition to these, there are fourteen occur-

rences in Psalm 119 where עֶבֶד = *'ebed* ("servant") readily designates, then, the pious person who is faithful to the law.

148. Cf. below, pp. 141–146.
149. Cf. below, pp. 260f.
150. These also need a thoroughgoing investigation. Cf. the only previous study by J. Köberle, "Die Motive des Glaubens an die Gebetserhörung im Alten Testament," in FS der Universität Erlangen für Prinzregent Luitpold von Bayern, 1901, 3–30.
151. Cf., e.g., Pss. 3:4ff.; 4:2ff.; 6:10; 9:8ff.; 11; 18:8ff.; 22:5; 26:8; 27:4ff.; 34; 42:2f.; 43:3f.; 46; 48; 50; 52:10f.; 59:6; 63:3ff.; 65:2f., 5ff.; etc.
152. Cf. Vol. I, pp. 171–179.
153. Pss. 3:8; 5:3; 7:2, 4; 13:4; 18:3, 7, 29f.; 22:2, 11; 25:2; 31:15; 35:23f.; 38:16, 22; 40:6, 18; 42:6f., 12; 43:4f.; 59:2, 11, 18; 63:2; 68:25; 69:4; 71:4, 12, and 22; 84:4, 11; 86:2, 12; 89:27; 94:22; 102:25; 109:26; 118:28; 119:115; 140:7; 143:10; 145:1; and 146:2. See O. Eissfeldt, " 'Mein Gott' im Alten Testament," *ZAW* 61, 1945–1948, 3–16 (= *KS* 3, 1966, 35ff.). For "my king," cf. Vol. I, pp. 155f.
154. Pss. 5:10f.; 7:15; 17:11; 25:19; 28:3; 35:4, 16, 19f.; 36:3, 5; 38:13; 40:15; 41:8; 52:4; 54:7; 55:16; 56:6f.; 63:10; 64:7; 69:5; 70:3; 71:10, 13; 86:14, 17; 94:23; 109:3, 5; and 140:3, 5.
155. A more precise investigation of sapiential anthropology does not exist. See some of the related comments in H. W. Wolff, *Anthropology of the Old Testament,* 206–213. See also below, pp. 265–267, for the ethos of wisdom.
156. For the role of the cult in wisdom literature, cf. pp. 250f.
157. Cf. below, p. 190.
158. Prov. 10:16 "sin" as the opposition of "life" (also text-critically debated). In 24:9, חַטָּאת = *ḥṭ't* also means simply "mistake"; in 29:16, פֶּשַׁע = *pš'* stands for "crime." For Prov. 20:9, see below.
159. But probably in the eyes of YHWH or the king? Cf. v. 8 in this regard. Cf. also the previous note.
160. Cf. H. D. Preuss, *Einführung in die alttestamentliche Weisheitsliteratur,* 1987, 34ff. and 36ff.
161. For the "fear of YHWH," see below, pp. 157f.
162. There is behavior that demonstrates that one fears YHWH, and, just the opposite, there is behavior that "slanders" YHWH (חָרַף = *ḥāraf*).
163. Prov. 10:1, 8, 14; 12:15f.; 13:16, 20; 14:1, 3, 8, 15f., 18, 24, 33; 15:2, 5, 7, 14, 20f.; 16:22; 17:16, 24, 28; 21:11; 22:3; 26:12; etc.
164. Prov. 4:18f.; 10:3, 6f., 13f., 16, 20, 23–25, 28–32; 11:5f., 8, 10f., 18, 21, 23, 31; 12:3, 5–7, 10, 12, 21, 26; 13:5f., 9, 21, 25; 14:11, 32; 15:6, 8f., 28; 17:15; 21:12, 15, 18, 29; 25:26; 29:6, 16, 27; etc.
165. Cf. Vol. I, pp. 184–194. Cf., e.g., Prov. 10:3, 6f., 9, 10f., 15f., 30; 11:3, 5f., 17, 18, 21, 31; 12:7, 21; 13:25; 14:11, 32; 15:6, 29; 16:3, 5; etc.
166. Prov. 3:7; 26:5, 12, 16; and 28:11.
167. Thus R. Lux, " 'Die ungepredigte Bibel' : Überlegungen zum theologischen Ort der Weisheit in der christlichen Verkündigung," *PTh* 79, 1990, 524–544, esp. 539.
168. Ibid., pp. 538–539.
169. Cf. below, pp. 203–207.
170. Prov. 3:16, 18; 4:4, 10, 13, 22f.; 5:5f., 11f.; 6:23; 8:35; 9:11, 18; 10:2, 27; 11:4, 19; 12:28; 13:14; 14:27; 15:24; 16:17, 22; 18:21; 19:8, 16, 23; and 24:14.
171. Prov. 10:8, 11, 13f., 18–21, 31f.; 11:9; 12:6, 13f., 17–19; 13:2f., 13; 14:3; 15:1f., 4, 7, 23; 16:1, 13, 20, 23–24; 17:4, 7, 20, 27f.; 18:4, 6–8, 20f.; 19:5, 9; 21:23; 22:11, 14; 24:26; 25:11f., 15; 26:4f., 23–25; 27:2; 31:8f.; etc. Cf. W. Bühlmann, *Vom rechten Reden und Schweigen,* 1976 (OBO 12).
172. Cf. above, pp. 111f.
173. Cf. R. Lux, " 'Ich, Kohelet, bin König. . . .' Die Fiktion als Schlüssel zur Wirklichkeit in Kohelet 1,12–2,26," *EvTh* 50, 1990, 331–342, esp. 338. Cf., e.g., Qoh. 1:13, 16f.; 2:1, 3, 10, 15, 20, and 23 ("Die Fiktion als Sprache des Herzens," in R. Lux, "Ich, Kohelet, bin König . . . ," 338ff.).
174. Prov. 4:4, 21, 23; 6:18, 21; 7:3, 25; 14:33; 15:7, 14, 28; 16:1, 5, 9; 17:20; 18:12, 15; 19:21; 20:5; 22:1, 15, 17; 27:19; 28:14, 26; etc.

175. Cf. *LÄ* II, col. 1168; and III, 249f.
176. Prov. 4:25; 6:13, 17; 10:10; 16:30; 17:24; 20:12; 21:4; 22:9; 23:5, 26, 29, 33; 25:7; 27:20; 28:27; 30:13, 17; etc.
177. The idiom stands close to similar Egyptian formulae or even is identical with them. Cf. H. Brunner, *Das hörende Herz,* 1988 (OBO 80), 3–41. This is generally the Egyptian view of the heart.
178. Prov. 20:27, which speaks of the breath or spirit (נשׁמה = *nišmâ*) of humanity as a lamp of YHWH (נר = *nēr*), perhaps has a corrupted text. Or is "spirit" to be understood here as a penetrating thought or as the function of the conscience? K. Koch explains Prov. 20:27 by reference to Gen. 2:7 according to which נשׁמה = *nĕšāmâ* designates breath that enables humans to speak (*BN* 48, 1989, 50–60 = "Spuren des hebräischen Denkens," [*Gesammelte Aufsätze* I] 1991, 238ff.). [The references to this important collection of essays could not be further worked into chapters 6–10 of the present volume.]
179. Prov. 3:13; 6:12; 8:34; 12:3, 25, 27; 15:20; 16:27f.; 18:16; 19:3, 22; 20:25; 21:16; 24:1f.; 26:18f.; 27:19f.; 28:23; 29:23, 27; etc.
180. For this, cf. H.-P. Müller, *Das Hiobproblem,* 1978 (EdF 84); H. D. Preuss, *Einführung in die alttestamentliche Weisheitsliteratur,* 1987, 69–113; and J. Ebach, "Hiob/Hiobbuch," *TRE* 15, 360–380 (lit.).
181. From the Book of Job the reader of the Old Testament can learn a great deal about how the Old Testament persons themselves envisioned the kingdom and the destiny of the dead. Cf. Vol. I, pp. 261–263.
182. Cf. also H.-P. Müller, "Gottes Antwort an Ijob und das Recht religiöser Wahrheit," *BZ* NF 32, 1988, 210–231; and W. Strolz, "Schöpfungsweisheit im Buch Ijob," *Diak.* 21, 1990, 314–322. Cf. also Vol. I, p. 229.
183. Cf. Deutero-Isaiah and Israel's ancient Near Eastern environment; see Vol. I, pp. 168, 205, 229, and 241.
184. "It is not the individual self but rather the limited human being, as long as he breathes, who discovers the multivarious nature of what already exists and continues to exist *within* the created world" (W. Strolz, "Schöpfungsweisheit im Buch Ijob," 319).
185. And indeed daughters with the beautiful names of Jemimah, Keziah, and Keren-happuch (Job 42:14).
186. "The conclusion of the Book does not narrate the victory of what was the correct teaching but rather the life of the one who is restored" (J. Ebach, *TRE* 15, 370).
187. For this book, see D. Michel, *Qohelet,* 1988 (EdF 258); and idem, *Untersuchungen zur Eigenart des Buches Qohelet,* 1989 (BZAW 183).
188. Sixteen times in Qoheleth.
189. Cf. above, p. 349 n. 173 (R. Lux) and the connection of heart and tongue according to Egyptian texts: *RGT,* 2d ed., 32, 82.
190. Translation of the German translation by D. Michel.
191. Thus with D. Michel, *Qohelet,* 132.
192. D. Michel (*Qohelet,* 152f.) has shown that the evil word about women in Qoh. 7:26 (cf. also v. 28) is to be understood as a citation that is taken up by Qoheleth in the context of Qoh. 7:25–29 and offers a critical comment.
193. In Qoh. 11:9c another orthodox addition registers a word that indicates that this admonition to enjoy life goes too far.
194. For חלק = *ḥēleq* ("portion") in Qoheleth, cf. D. Michel, *Untersuchungen zur Eigenart des Buches Qohelet,* 118–125.
195. Cf. below, p. 153.
196. The meaning of this verse is debated. I follow D. Michel, *Qohelet,* 147f., or idem, *Untersuchungen zur Eigenart des Buches Qohelet,* 138ff.
197. It is not possible to translate the last sentence of Qoh. 7:18, "Whoever fears God shall behave in the right way in every case" (N. Lohfink, NEB), for this would interpret this text as having to do with a false decision. The text rather is an addition that still wishes to rescue something from what was said.
198. Qoh. 12:8, 9–11, and 12–14 are different editorial additions. Only 12:8 could be a frame that conforms to what precedes as well as to Qoheleth's own spirit.

199. Translation by D. Michel.
200. Cf. Qoheleth's portrayal of humanity also in H. D. Preuss, *Einführung in die alttesta-mentliche Weisheitsliteratur,* 1987, 131–133 (lit).
201. W. Zimmerli (*Das Menschenbild des Alten Testaments,* 4) speaks of a "series of character-istic constants." That here the idea of "basic structures" is not completely identical with what G. Fohrer (*Theologische Grundstrukturen des Alten Testaments,* 1972) has expressed may be clear (cf. Vol. I, p. 24). For Fohrer, cf. also H. Seebass, *KuD* 22, 1976, 54–62.
202. Cf. also W. H. Schmidt, " 'Was ist der Mensch?' " *BiKi* 42, 1987, 12–15 (cf. his *Glaube und Lernen* 4, 1989, 111–129).
203. H. Seebass, *KuD* 22, 1976, 43.
204. "The Old Testament person lives by a call" (W. Zimmerli, *Das Menschenbild des Alten Testaments,* 15; cf. also 9).
205. See L. Perlitt, "Wovon der Mensch lebt (Dtn 8,3b)," in J. Jeremias and L. Perlitt, eds., *Die Botschaft und die Boten,* FS H. W. Wolff, 1981, 403–426.
206. Cf. H. W. Wolff, *Anthropology of the Old Testament,* 74–79; and J. Arambarri, *Der Wort-stamm "hören" im Alten Testament,* 1990 (SBB 20). Cf. further, pp. 154ff.
207. Cf. above, pp. 21–22; and Vol. I, pp. 342–343 n. 677.
208. For the forms of the Old Testament understanding of the relationship to God, including, e.g., faith, the fear of YHWH, and the knowledge of YHWH, see below, pp. 153ff.
209. Cf. also H. Seidel, *Das Erlebnis der Einsamkeit im Alten Testament,* 1969.
210. The Old Testament often speaks of *joy* as the fundamental emotion of human beings. Cf., e.g., H. Schultz, *Alttestamentliche Theologie,* 5th ed., 1896, 368: "The principal character of the religious mood of pious Israelites is not the feeling of fear and uncertainty but rather the full, joyful consciousness of the grace and the delight of God." See further W. Eichrodt, *Das Menschenverständnis des Alten Testaments,* 33; and L. Köhler, *Theologie,* 4th ed., 138f. A comprehensive investigation of this topic is yet to be done.
211. Here one can only point out the significance of Old Testament personal names for the Old Testament view of humanity.
212. For the Old Testament statements about human sin and guilt as well as atonement and for-giveness, see pp. 170ff.
213. Cf. p. 259.
214. For the fundamental experiences and feelings of the Old Testament human being (the rela-tionship to God in terms of dependence, responsibility, culpability, and security) which also are to be joined together with hope, cf. F. Maass, *ThWAT* 1, cols. 91–94; cf. also idem, *Was ist Christentum?* 1978, 20ff.
215. The dead in Sheol are not able to speak anymore but rather are able only to chirp (Isa. 8:19; and 29:4; צפף = *ṣpp*). The "stillness of the dead" rules there (cf. Vol. I, p. 262), something that is as terrible for the Orientals as a "hellish noise" is for us. For the value of language in the thinking of ancient Egypt, cf. J. Assmann, *Ma'at: Gerechtigkeit und Unsterblichkeit im Alten Ägypten,* 1990, 69–85 etc. What J. G. Herder thinks he must say in regard to conver-sational style is certainly true for many modern theologians: "It appears they have made themselves known with language, but not from the heart" (*Vom Geist der Ebräischen Poe-sie* I, 1782 [cited according to the Stuttgart edition, 1827], 16).
216. Cf. the following selection of writings on this topic: G. Gerleman, "Struktur und Eigenart der hebräischen Sprache," *SEÅ* 22/23, 1957/1958, 252–264; Th. Boman, *Das hebräische Denken im Vergleich mit dem griechischen,* 5th ed., 1968; J. Barr, *The Seman-tics of Biblical Language,* London, 1961; G. Gerleman, "Bemerkungen zum alttesta-mentlichen Sprachstil," in *Studia biblica et semitica,* FS Th. C. Vriezen, Wageningen, 1966, 108–114; L. Alonso Schökel, *Sprache Gottes und der Menschen,* 1968; W. Zimmerli, "Die Weisung des Alten Testaments zum Geschäft der Sprache," TB 19, 2d ed., 1969, 277–299; K. Koch, "Gibt es ein hebräisches Denken?" *PBl* 108, 1968, 258–276 (=*Spuren des he-bräischen Denkens* [*Gesammelte Aufsätze* I], 1991, 3ff.); idem, *Was ist Formgeschichte?* 3rd ed., 1974 (333ff.); cf. K. Koch, *The Growth of the Biblical Tradition,* New York, 1969; W. de Pater, *Theologische Sprachlogik,* 1971; W. von Soden, *Sprache, Denken und Be-griffsbildung im Alten Orient,* 1974; J. F. A. Sawyer, *Semantics in Biblical Research,* Lon-don, 1972; A. Jepsen " 'Hebräisch'—die Sprache Jahwes?" in H. Donner et al., eds.,

Beiträge zur alttestamentlichen Theologie, FS W. Zimmerli, 1977, 196–205; B. Kedar, *Biblische Semantik,* 1981; M. Silva, *Biblical Words and Their Meaning,* Grand Rapids, 1983 (however, especially for the New Testament); D. Michel, "Hebräisch. I: A. T.," *TRE* 14, 505–510 (lit.); R. Albertz, "Die Frage des Ursprungs der Sprache im Alten Testament," in J. Gessinger and W. von Rahden, eds., *Theorien vom Ursprung der Sprache,* 2, 1989, 1–18 [for Genesis 2–3 and 11]; K. Koch, "Die hebräische Sprache zwischen Polytheismus und Monotheismus," in *Spuren [Gesammelte Aufsätze* I; see above], 25–64; cf. also G. von Rad, *Theology* 2:357–362; and H. Graf Reventlow, *Hauptprobleme,* 130f. (lit.), for "Hebrew thought."

217. More skeptical, however, also more differentiated (e.g., between Jewish and Israelite), is the work of E. A. Knauf, "War 'Biblisch-Hebräisch' " eine Sprache?" *ZAH* 3, 1990, 11–23. Cf., however, also K. Koch (*Spuren,* 36 n. 45): "The language of Canaan spoken in the South is indeed not identical with . . . Ugaritic. Even less so is the Hebrew of the Masoretes with the spoken Northern Hebrew or Jewish Hebrew of the preexilic period. Nevertheless, one can rely on a fundamental similarity of the structures of meaning."

218. This is analogously true of YHWH's names (cf. Vol. I, p. 140).

219. "Those who are not able to speak with each other are also those who are not able to have feelings for each other, to interact with each other, and to believe each other" (L. Köhler, *Theologie,* 4th ed., 116). Does Zeph. 3:9 promise the abolishing of separate languages? Cf. also the Sumerian text in *RGT,* 2d ed., 112f. For a study that is more comprehensive in its treatment of the text than it is the subject, see Chr. Uehlinger, *Weltreich und "eine Rede": Eine neue Deutung der sogenannten Turmbauerzählung (Gen 11, 1–9),* 1990 (OBO 101).

220. Ezra 4:8–6:18; 7:12–26; Dan. 2:4b–7:28; Jer. 10:11; and two words in Gen. 31:47 are in so-called biblical Aramaic.

221. For this, see the investigation by Y. Kutscher, *History of the Hebrew Language,* Jerusalem and Leiden, 1982. Cf. now also the short study in B. K. Waltke and M. O'Connor, *An Introduction to Biblical Hebrew Syntax,* Winona Lake, Ind., 1990, 3–15.

222. Extrabiblical evidence for "old Hebrew" includes, e.g., the ostraca of Arad, Lachish, and Samaria, the farmer's calendar of Gezer, the Siloam inscription, and the temple jars.

223. Cf. Vol. I, pp. 45f. and 69f., and for the topic also L. Ruppert, "Glaubensaussagen Israels im Wandel," in *Sprache und Erfahrung als Problem der Theologie,* 1978, 93–107.

224. Differently A. Jepsen, " 'Hebräisch'—die Sprache Jahwes?" 196–205. He argues that the tribes freed from Egypt already spoke Hebrew. Thus there was no change in language. Cf. also W. Weinberg, "Language Consciousness in the Old Testament," *ZAW* 92, 1980, 185–204.

225. Other accents (a special quality of the *veritas hebraica*) in H. Hempelmann, "Veritas Hebraica als Grundlage christlicher Theologie," in K. Haacker and H. Hempelmann, *Hebraica Veritas,* 1989, 39–78 (H. Hempelmann).

226. K. Koch, *Was ist Formgeschichte?* 3d ed., 333. Cf. K. Koch, *Biblical Tradition.*

227. Cf. Vol. I, pp. 229–232, for the verbs used in speaking about "revelation."

228. See W. de Pater, *Theologische Sprachlogik.* Cf. in addition (from the abundance of literature on this theme): P. Ricoeur and E. Jüngel, *Metaphor,* 1974; Th. Michels and A. Paus, eds., *Sprache und Sprachverständnis in religiöser Rede,* 1973; I. U. Dalferth, *Religiöse Rede von Gott,* 1981; and M. Kaempfert, ed., *Probleme der religiösen Sprache,* 1983 (WdF 442).

229. This change in language is certainly debated as well. Cf. R. Degen, "Zur neueren hebräistischen Forschung," *WO* 6, 1971, 47–79, esp. 58f.

230. Are such already intended in Neh. 8:7f.?

231. For this as a whole, along with the peculiar syntax of Hebrew, see the works mentioned in n. 221 above.

232. Additional examples are found in G. Gerleman, in *Studia biblica et semitica,* FS Th. C. Vriezen, 110f.

233. Cf. G. von Rad, *Old Testament Theology,* vol. 1: *The Theology of Israel's Historical Traditions,* New York, 1965, 431, n. 32.

234. See above, pp. 111f.

235. W. Zimmerli, "Die Weisung des Alten Testaments zum Geschäft der Sprache," 295. Cf. J. G. Herder, *Vom Geist der Ebräischen Poesie* 1, p. 20: "Now for the Hebrews nearly everything is the verb: i.e., everything lives and acts."

236. Cf. Vol. I, pp. 156f.; and also W. Gross, *Die Pendenskonstruktion im Biblischen Hebräisch,* 1987.

237. The sequence of words (subject- predicate, or reversed) and the different uses of the copula ן = w as a copulative or consecutive ן produce additional differentiations. Cf. for the Hebrew system of tenses also A. Jepsen, " 'Hebräisch'—die Sprache Jahwes?" 203ff.; and J. G. Herder, *Vom Geist der Ebräischen Poesie* 1, p. 19: "How restless and uncertain are the times of their verbs" (at the objection of his dialogue partner).

238. Cf. already Vol. I, pp. 220f.

239. "It (Hebrew) has many ways of expressing a command or a wish: imperative of the second person, jussive, voluntative, cohortative, imperfect, infinitive absolute, elliptical conditional sentences, and interrogative sentences introduced with מי = *mî* or מי יתן = *mî yittēn*" (G. Gerleman, *SEÅ* 22/23, 257).

240. This brief summary is dependent on H. Irsigler, *Einführung in das Biblische Hebräisch* 1, 1978 (ATSAT 9), 23. Cf. also F. Diedrich, *Die Anspielungen auf die Jakob-Tradition in Hosea 12,1–13,3,* 1977 (fzb 27), 225–230.

241. For the elucidation of these findings, significant are the works of O. Rössler. A categorization with additional literature is found in B. Janowski, *Sühne als Heilsgeschehen,* 1982 (WMANT 55), 333.

242. A classification of the grammatical functions of the verb is found in H. Irsigler, *Einführung in das Biblische Hebräisch* 1, 79f.

243. Cf. for the last-mentioned, grammatical phenomena: D. Michel, *Grundlegung einer hebräischen Syntax* 1, 1977. For אלהים = *'ĕlōhîm,* see Vol. I, p. 147.

244. First efforts: B. Kedar, *Biblische Semantik.* Important also is H. Schweizer's *Metaphorische Grammatik,* 1981 (ATSAT 15), 80ff.

245. Thus with Th. C. Vriezen, *An Outline of Old Testament Theology,* Oxford, 1958, 224–227; and K. Koch, *Was ist Formgeschichte?* 3d ed., 326; cf. K. Koch, *The Growth of Biblical Tradition.* Further, "As the ancient Near Eastern mythological decoration (e.g., on the king's bed at Ugarit, *ANEP,* 817f.) allows one to assume, *miṭṭā* is not simply regarded as an item of daily use, i.e., a bed, but also as an 'animated' entity" (K. Koch, *Was ist Formgeschichte?* 3d ed., 312). Cf. K. Koch, *The Growth of Biblical Tradition,* and idem, *Spuren,* 54, for the royal throne which is summoned to descend into the underworld in the Ugaritic Text *KTU* 1.161:20–22.

246. Cf. for these two ideas K. Engelken, *Frauen im Alten Israel,* 1990 (BWANT 130).

247. Cf. U. Winter, *Frau und Göttin,* 1983 (OBO 53), 235–238; and *KTU* 1.24:7, where there is also a discussion of the birth of a son by a "young woman" (*gmlt*).

248. Cf. even in the New Testament: Matt. 8:12; 9:15; 13:38; 23:15; and Acts 13:10.

249. Cf. H. Haag, *ThWAT* 1, cols. 672–682.

250. Cf. Vol. I, pp. 171–179; and below, pp. 167–170. Further now, see K. Koch, *Spuren,* 45–50. P. 64: "Hebrew thinking is Canaanite thinking under the impress of a new experience of God."

251. In spite of the objections of R. Bartelmus (*HYH: Bedeutung und Funktion eines hebräischen "Allerweltswortes,"* 1982 [ATSAT 17], this is to be held fast. Moreover, the all too important theological consequences which both C. H. Ratschow and Th. Boman have drawn from this (cf. also M. Kartagener, "Zur Struktur der hebräischen Sprache," *StGen* 15, 1962, 31–39, esp. 35f., 38) are to be reduced. For שפט = *špṭ,* cf. H. Niehr, *Herrschen und Richten,* 1986 (fzb 54).

252. Cf. W. von Soden, *Sprache, Denken und Begriffsbildung im Alten Orient,* 39; and *WO* 4, 1967, 38–47.

253. In my opinion it is not a question of "attesting to the word of God in its own linguistic form within the structures of this world." Thus H. Hempelmann, "Veritas Hebraica als Grundlage christlicher Theologie," 68.

254. Cf. Vol. I, pp. 195–200; and above, pp. 73–76.

255. H.-R. Müller-Schwefe (*Die Sprache und das Wort,* 1961, esp. sec. 10, 150ff.: "Sprache und Wort im Alten Testament") speaks also about the Old Testament's "active word."

256. Cf. E. Balla, "Das Problem des Leides in der Geschichte der israelitisch-jüdischen Religion," *Gunkel-Eucharisterion* 1, 1923, 214–260; H. Schmidt, *Gott und das Leid im Alten Testa-*

ment, 1926; J. J. Stamm, *Das Leiden des Unschuldigen in Babylon und Israel,* 1946 (AThANT 10); J. Scharbert, *Der Schmerz im Alten Testament,* 1955 (BBB 8); E. S. Gerstenberger and W. Schrage, *Leiden,* 1977; K. Seybold and U. Müller, *Krankheit und Heilung,* 1978; D. J. Simundson, *Faith under Fire: Biblical Interpretations of Suffering,* Minneapolis, 1980; O. Kaiser, *Der Mensch unter dem Schicksal,* 1985 (BZAW 161); H. D. Preuss, "Die Frage nach dem Leid des Menschen—Ein Versuch biblischer Theologie," in M. Oeming and A. Graupner, ed., *Altes Testament und christliche Verkündigung,* FS A. H. J. Gunneweg, 1987, 52–80 (lit.) [what follows is largely in connection with this essay]; and H. Haag, "Vom Sinn des Leidens im Alten Testament," *IKaZ* 17, 1988, 481–494.

257. The passages continue to serve only as examples. For additional ones, see E. Balla, "Das Problem des Leides"; and E. S. Gerstenberger and W. Schrage, *Leiden.*

258. Cf. K. Seybold, *Das Gebet des Kranken im Alten Testament,* 1973 (BWANT 99); and above, p. 102.

259. K. Seybold, *Krankheit und Heilung,* 78.

260. Cf. the listing of the horrors of war in E. S. Gerstenberger, *Leiden,* 49–53.

261. Cf. L. Ruppert, *Der leidende Gerechte,* 1972 (fzb 5); idem, *Der leidende Gerechte und seine Feinde,* 1973; and idem, *Jesus als der leidende Gerechte?* 1972 (SBS 59).

262. Cf. the passages in E. S. Gerstenberger, *Leiden,* 70ff.

263. Cf. the large number of texts in E. Balla, "Das Problem des Leides," 222ff. (nn.).

264. Cf. G. Fohrer, "Kurzer Bericht über das Problem des Leides," in *Glaube und Welt im Alten Testament,* 1948, 92ff.

265. Cf. Vol. I, pp. 258f. Names: Lev. 16:8ff.; Isa. 34:14; and Prov. 30:15. E. S. Gerstenberger (*Leiden,* 54ff.) finds as a consequence of drawing on additional texts that are supposed to speak of demons a broad basis for this view.

266. Cf. J. J. Stamm, *Das Leiden des Unschuldigen,* 9ff.; and J. Hempel, *Heilung als Symbol und Wirklichkeit,* 2d ed., 1965, 260ff.

267. Cf. W. Westendorf, "Krankheit," *LÄ* III, cols. 757–759; and idem, "Schmerz," *LÄ* V, cols. 662f.

268. According to the point of view provided by the Old Testament narrator (1 Sam. 6:9), even the Philistines cannot disregard this.

269. "In the Old Testament sphere overall this means . . . that to speak of human fate is to speak of humans under Yahweh" (O. Kaiser, *Der Mensch unter dem Schicksal,* 76). Cf. Vol. I, pp. 106–107.

270. In addition to the large group of texts mentioned, cf. esp. Genesis 21: Hagar; Gen. 42:21f.; 44:16; 45:5ff.: Joseph; Job 5:18; 9:23; and Ps. 88:17f.

271. Against H. Vorländer, in B. Lang, ed., *Der einzige Gott,* 1981, 87 + 99.

272. Cf. also Exod. 34:6f.; Deut. 32:6; 1 Sam. 2:6f.; 2 Sam. 7:14; Isa. 63:16–19; and Ps. 103:8f.

273. For this, see Vol. I, pp. 184–194.

274. Joseph story; Jacob narratives in their final redaction ("from deceiver to one who fights with God"); then Deut. 4:30; 8:2, 5; 2 Sam. 7:14; Isa. 43:24; Jer. 31:18; and Hos. 2:8–19. Cf. Isa. 30:20; 2 Chron. 32:31; in the Book of Job the speeches of Elihu, Job 32–37 (33:14ff.!) and the "acceptance" of chastisement, Job 5:17–27; 22:1–30; 33:15–30; 36:7–12; postexilic psalms: 94:12 (?); 118:18; and 119:71; further, see Prov. 3:11f.

275. Jer.11:18–12:6; 15:10–21; 17:(12?) 14–18; 18:18–23; and 20:7–18. The extent of the literature that addresses this subject prohibits a full listing here. One should see the commentaries and introductions to the Old Testament. It appears to me, with all due acknowledgment of the Deuteronomistic and other redactions, that one is able to recognize also in these confessions indeed an autobiographical reference to Jeremiah. This does not exclude a later typical, exemplary understanding and use (cf. above, p. 91).

276. Cf. F. Ahuis, *Der klagende Gerichtsprophet,* 1982.

277. Cf. below, pp. 303–305.

278. Cf. below, p. 247f.

279. See L. Ruppert, *Der leidende Gerechte;* idem, *Der leidende Gerechte und seine Feinde;* and idem, *Jesus als der leidende Gerechte?* 1972 (SBS 59). Although it is not to be discussed here, one should note that Ruppert also takes up the continuing development of this motif in early Jewish writings and the question of the exaltation of this suffering righteous person.

280. See E. S. Gerstenberger, *Leiden,* 79–83.
281. Deut. 4:30, 40; Josh. 1:1–9; 23:2–16; 24; Judg. 2:6–3:9; 1 Sam. 12:9–11; 1 Kings 8:31ff.; 11:9–12; 2 Kings 17:7–23; 18:7; and 22:18ff.
282. E. S. Gerstenberger, *Leiden,* 83.
283. N. Lohfink has shown this: " 'Ich bin Jahwe, dein Arzt' (Ex 15,26)," in *"Ich will euer Gott werden,"* 1981 (SBS 100), 11–73.
284. Cf. also J. Scharbert, *Der Schmerz im Alten Testament,* 216ff. ("Der Schmerz Jahwes"); and T. Fretheim, *The Suffering of God,* Philadelphia, 1984.
285. For the expressions of suffering in the Book of Jeremiah, which have been and continue to be much discussed, cf. the citations of literature in M. Oeming and A. Graupner, ed., *Altes Testament und christliche Verkündigung,* FS A. H. J. Gunneweg, 61 n. 17.
286. There is to this point only G. von Rad, *Theology,* 1:402–404. A comprehensive work on this theme is still lacking.
287. Cf. above, p. 62f.
288. G. von Rad, *Theology* 1:405–407, sees its differently. Cf. below, p. 150.
289. For the hope of resurrection, cf. below, pp. 150–153.
290. Cf. below, pp. 255ff.
291. Cf. below, pp. 245–250.
292. Pss. 22:2; 42:10; 43:2; 44:10, 24f.; 74:1, 11; 79:10; 80:13; 88:15; 115:2; Lam. 5:20; Jer. 14:19; etc. The questioning word למה = *lāmâ* ("why") asks not only for the reason but also for the purpose and intention ("for what reason").
293. Pss. 6:4; 10:1, 13; 13:2; 22:2; 42:10; 43:2; 88:14f.; and 94:3.
294. Pss. 6:2; 10:1, 13; 17:13; and 26:2–11: punishment. Pss. 32:3–5; 38:4f., 19; and 39:12: chastisement (etc.).
295. Cf. L. Perlitt, "Anklage und Freispruch Gottes," *ZThK* 69, 1972, 290–303. For the problem of the exile, cf. also D. L. Smith, *The Religion of the Landless: The Social Context of the Babylonian Exile,* Bloomington, Ind., 1989.
296. For Lamentations (in addition to the commentaries), cf. R. Brandscheidt, *Gotteszorn und Menschenleid,* 1983 (TThSt 41); and C. Westermann, *Die Klagelieder: Forschungsgeschichte und Auslegung,* 1990.
297. In Isa. 65:11, however, there are still mentioned two deities of fate.
298. For the problem of pain in the Book of Job, cf. E. Kutsch, "Hiob: leidender Gerechter — leidender Mensch," *KuD* 19, 1973, 197–214 (= BZAW 168, 1986, 290ff.); O. Kaiser, "Leid und Gott: Ein Beitrag zur Theologie des Buches Hiob," in U. Fabricius and R. Volp, eds., *Sichtbare Kirche,* FS H. Laag, 1973, 13–21 (= BZAW 161, 1985, 54ff.); J. Lévèque, "Le sens de la souffrance d'après le livre de Job," *RTL* 6, 1975, 438–445; E. Ruprecht, "Leiden und Gerechtigkeit bei Hiob," *ZThK* 73, 1976, 424–445; W. Berg, "Gott und der Gerechte in der Rahmenerzählung des Buches Hiob," *MThZ* 32, 1981, 206–221. Cf. also D. J. Simundson, *Faith under Fire,* 81ff.
299. For the evaluation of pain as education in the speeches of Elihu (Job 32–37), see above, p. 354 n. 274, and the additional texts of Job that are cited there.
300. To these, now cf. also the brief notices from an open evening with K. Barth in *Glauben und Lernen* 3, 1988, 7f.; and above, pp. 103f.
301. Cf. L. Perlitt, "Die Verborgenheit Gottes," in H. W. Wolff, ed., *Probleme biblischer Theologie,* FS G. von Rad, 1971, 367–382; and S. E. Balentine, *The Hidden God,* Oxford, 1983.
302. So with M. Sion, cited by J. Lévèque, *Job et son Dieu* 2, Paris, 1970, 532 n. 3. However, cf. also G. von Rad in *Führung zum Christentum durch das Alte Testament,* 1934, 65; and in general, O. Kaiser, *Ideologie und Glaube,* 1984.
303. Cf. above, pp. 101f. and pp. 140f.
304. For the view and value of life in general, cf. L. Dürr, *Die Wertung des Lebens im Alten Testament und im antiken Orient,* 1926; G. Gerleman, "חיה *ḥjh* leben," *THAT* 1, cols. 549–557; H. Ringgren, "חיה *ḥājāh* und Deriv.," *ThWAT* 2, cols. 874–898; and R. Martin-Achard, *La mort en face,* Geneva, 1988, 9–36. For the view and evaluation of life in cultures of ancient Israel's contemporary world, cf. L. Dürr and H. Ringgren.
305. The statement that plants or animals "live," with חיה = *ḥāyâ* ("to live") as a verb, is found nowhere in the Old Testament (Hos. 14:8 has a corrupted text). In regard to the adjective חי

= ḥāy ("alive, living"), however, this is very different for animals. This adjective, however, does not modify plants. Cf. above, pp. 139–140.

306. Gen. 45:27; Num. 21:8f.; Josh. 5:8; Judg. 15:19; 2 Kings 1:2; 8:8–10, 14; and 20:1, 7 par.
307. And elsewhere in Deuteronomy: 4:1; 5:33; 6:2; 8:1, 3; 11:8f., 21; 16:20; 22:7; and 25:15.
308. Cf. G. von Rad, " 'Gerechtigkeit' und 'Leben' in der Kultsprache der Psalmen," in W. Baumgartner et al., eds., *Festschrift Alfred Bertholet zum 80.* 1950, 418–437 (= TB 8, 3d ed., 1965, 225ff.).
309. Prov. 3:1f., 22; 4:4, 10, 13, 22f.; 6:23; 7:2; 8:35; 9:6, 11; 10:17; and 15:24. Cf. the contrastive statements about the path to death in Prov. 2:19; 5:6; 8:36; 15:10; and 19:16.
310. Cf. also Ps. 133:3; Jer. 2:13; 17:13; then cf. above, pp. 62f., and below, pp. 251f.
311. Cf. W. Zimmerli, " 'Leben' und 'Tod' im Buche des Propheten Ezechiel," *ThZ* 13, 1957, 494–508 (= TB 19, 2d ed., 1969, 178ff.).
312. Gen. 42:2; 43:8; 47:19; Deut. 33:6; 2 Kings 18:32; Ezek. 18:21, 28; 33:15; Pss. 89:49; and 118:17; cf. conversely 2 Kings 20:1 (= Isa. 38:1). Cf. also the substantives in Deut. 30:19; 2 Sam. 15:21; Jer. 8:3; 21:8; Jonah 4:3, 8; Prov. 8:35f.; 18:21; and the adjectives in Num. 17:13; 1 Kings 3:22, 26; 21:15; Isa. 8:19; Ruth 2:20; and Qoh. 9:5.
313. Cf. G. Quell, *Die Auffassung des Todes in Israel,* 1925, reprint 1967; Chr. Barth, *Die Errettung vom Tode in den individuellen Klage- und Dankliedern des Alten Testaments,* 1947, 2d ed. (with two appendixes, a bibliography, and indexes newly edited by B. Janowski), 1987; L. Wächter, *Der Tod im Alten Testament,* 1967; E. Jüngel, *Tod,* 1971; U. Kellermann, "Überwindung des Todesgeschicks in der alttestamentlichen Frömmigkeit vor und neben dem Auferstehungsglauben," *ZThK* 73, 1976, 259–282; H. Gese, "Der Tod im Alten Testament," in H. Gese, ed., *Zur biblischen Theologie,* 1977, 3d ed., 1989, 31–54; O. Knoch, "Wirst du an den Toten Wunder wirken?" 1977; O. Kaiser and E. Lohse, *Tod und Leben,* 1977; K.-J. Illman, *Old Testament Formulas about Death,* Åbo, 1979; G. Gerleman, "שְׁאוֹל *šĕ'ôl* Totenreich," *THAT* 2, cols. 837–841; L. Perlitt, "Der Tod im Alten Testament," *PTh* 70, 1981, 391–405; H. Ringgren, K.-J. Illman, and H.-J. Fabry, "מוּת *mût* und Deriv.," *ThWAT* 4, cols. 763–787; M. Krieg, *Todesbilder im Alten Testament,* 1988 (AThANT 73); R. Martin-Achard, *La mort en face,* Geneva, 1988; Chr. Dohmen, *Schöpfung und Tod,* 1989 (SBB 17); M. A. Knibb, "Life and Death in the Old Testament," in R. E. Clements, ed., *The World of Ancient Israel,* Cambridge, 1989, 395–415; and W. Berg, "Jenseitsvorstellungen im Alten Testament mit Hinweisen auf das frühe Judentum," in A. Gerhards, ed., *Die grössere Hoffnung der Christen,* 1990 (QD 127), 28–58. Cf. further the literature in Vol. I, pp. 261–263 (on the kingdom of the dead), as well as p. 283 n. 47, and p. 295 n. 332 on the rites of mourning. In addition, see H. H. Rowley, *Faith,* 150ff.; H. Ringgren, *Israelite Religion,* Philadelphia, 1966; H. W. Wolff, *Anthropology of the Old Testament,* 99–118; and several contributions in J. H. Marks and R. M. Good, eds., *Love and Death in the Ancient Near East,* FS M. H. Pope, Guilford, Conn. 1987.
314. Cf. Vol. I, pp. 261–263.
315. Cf. further Isa. 38:18; Pss. 49:15; 55:16; 89:49; Prov. 5:5; and 7:27. שְׁאוֹל = *šĕ'ôl* (Sheol) can stand for מָוֶת = *māwet* and vice versa: Hos. 13:14; Isa. 28:15, 18; Pss. 6:6; 18:6; 22:16; etc.
316. Cf. the texts listed in nn. 306 and 307 above.
317. Chr. Barth, *Die Errettung vom Tode,* 152.
318. For the metaphors and images used for the world of the dead, cf. M. Krieg, *Todesbilder im Alten Testament,* 142ff.; and O. Keel, *Die Welt der altorientalischen Bildsymbolik und das Alten Testament,* 2d ed., 1977, 53ff.
319. *ThWAT* 4, col. 766. A more precise integration into ancient Near Eastern thinking (the conquest of chaos by cosmos; the creative role of sunlight in this connection; the help of God "in the morning," etc.) and additional texts are found in B. Janowski, *Rettungsgewissheit und Epiphanie des Heils* 1, 1989, 65ff., 178f.
320. Cf. Chr. Hardmeier, " 'Denn im Tod ist kein Gedenken an dich . . .' (Psalm 6,6): Der Tod des Menschen—Gottes Tod?" *EvTh* 48, 1988, 292–311.
321. For this psalm, cf. H. D. Preuss, "Psalm 88 als Beispiel alttestamentlichen Redens vom Tod," in A. Strobel, ed., *Der Tod—ungelöstes Rätsel oder überwundener Feind?* 1974, 63–79.
322. Luther's translation, "Come again, human children," is indeed beautiful, although it con-

sciously carries a Christian concept in the Old Testament. Literally, "return back = to the dust" is meant.

323. Cf. above, pp. 109f.

324. Cf. L. Wächter, *Der Tod im Alten Testament,* 1967, 198ff. Cf., however, the isolated case of Num. 27:3.

325. For the interpretation of Genesis 2–3 under the viewpoint of death and dying and at the same time the investigation of the stratification and origin of the final text, cf. Chr. Dohmen, *Schöpfung und Tod.* Cf. also O. Kaiser, *Tod und Leben,* 16ff.

326. Jer. 20:6; 22:11f., 26; 42:16f.; Ezek. 12:13; 17:16; and Amos 7:17.

327. Cf. the texts mentioned above in n. 309.

328. "We ought not to understand 'desacralization' in a modern and therefore false way. Rather, this has to do with the 'exclusion of the power of death that exists independent of God' " (H. Gese, *Zur biblischen Theologie,* 3d., ed., 1989, 39–40).

329. Cf. G. von Rad, *Theologie* 1, 5th ed., 399–403; also idem, *Theologie* 2, 4th ed., 361ff.

330. Lev. 21:1–5; Num. 6:6f.; 19:14–16; and Deut. 14:1.

331. According to 1 Sam. 28:13, the "witch of Endor" saw a "god" ascend.

332. Cf. above, p. 344 nn. 47–48 and p. 356 n. 313, as well as n. 335 below. Also see H. Jahnow, *Das hebräische Leichenlied,* 1923 (BZAW 36), 2–57; R. de Vaux, *Das Alten Testament und seine Lebensordnungen* 1, 2d ed., 1964, 99–107; and E. Kutsch, " 'Trauerbräuche' und 'Selbstminderungsriten' im. Alten Testament," in K. Lüthi, E. Kutsch, and W. Dantine, *Drei Wiener Antrittsreden,* 1965 (ThSt 78), 23–42 (= BZAW 168, 1986, 78ff.). Cf. also the material in K. Spronk, *Beatific Afterlife in Ancient Israel and in the Ancient Near East,* 1986 (AOAT 219). See the following passages: Gen. 37:34; Lev. 10:6; 19:27f.; 21:5, 10; Deut. 14:1; 2 Sam. 1:11ff.; 3:31; 1 Kings 21:17ff.; Isa. 15:2; 22:12; Jer. 4:8; 16:5ff.; 48:36ff.; Ezek. 24:17, 22f.; 27:30f.; Amos 8:10; Dan. 10:3, 12; etc.

333. For the areas of rites of mourning, burial, death, "caring for the dead," the relationship of the dead to YHWH, cf. now also E. Zenger, "Das alttestamentliche Israel und seine Toten," in K. Richter, ed., *Der Umgang mit den Toten,* 1990 (QD 123), 132–152.

334. Cf. P. Torge, *Seelenglaube und Unsterblichkeitshoffnung im Alten Testament,* 1909, 58ff.

335. Cf. Th. J. Lewis, *Cults of the Dead in Ancient Israel and Ugarit,* Atlanta, G., 1989; and O. Loretz, *Ugarit und die Bibel,* 1990, 125ff.

336. Lev. 11:32–35; 19:27f., 31; 20:6, 27; 21:5; Num. 5:2; 19:11; Deut. 14:1; 18:11; and Ezek. 44:25.

337. Cf. *ThWAT* 4, col. 767. Textual references are in Chr. Barth, *Die Errettung vom Tode,* 78.

338. Cf. esp. the lament of Gilgamesh over his dead friend Enkidu and the negative answer that Gilgamesh receives from the ale-wife: "Gilgamesh Epic," Table X, II/1ff.; Table X, III/1ff.; and then the description of the kingdom of the dead: Table XII. Cf. R. Stola, "Zu Jenseitsvorstellungen im Alten Mesopotamien," *Kairos* NF 14, 1972, 258–272. Also cf. M. Hutter, *Altorientalische Vorstellungen von der Unterwelt,* 1985 (OBO 63).

339. Cf. the descriptions in the Egyptian literature of the dead and future life. This literature in its important parts is easily accessible: E. Hornung, *Das Totenbuch der Ägypter,* 1979; idem, *Ägyptische Unterweltsbücher,* 2d ed., 1984. For the theology and the descriptions of the journey of the sun, cf. B. Janowski, *Rettungsgewissheit und Epiphanie des Heils* 1, 135ff.

340. Cf. For this and other things, cf. C. E. Sander-Hansen, *Der Begriff des Todes bei den Ägyptern,* Copenhagen, 1942; H. Kees, *Totenglauben und Jenseitsvorstellungen der alten Ägypter,* 3d ed., 1977; H. Altenmüller, *Grab und Totenreich der alten Ägypter,* 1976; and A. J. Spencer, *Death in Ancient Egypt,* 1982 (Penguin Books).

341. Cf. A. Schmitt, *Entrückung—Aufnahme—Himmelfahrt,* 1973 (fzb 10); idem, "Zum Thema 'Entrückung' im Alten Testament," *BZ* NF 26, 1982, 34–49.

342. Thus with A. Schmitt, *BZ* NF 26, 1982, 44–49, who points to the other texts in the Elijah and Elias cycle that deal with this theme (1 Kings 17:17–24; 2 Kings 1:1–18; 4:8–37; 8:7–15; and 13:20f.).

343. Part b of Ps. 49:16 begins with מִיַּד = *miyyad.*

344. G. von Rad, *Theology,* 1:406; H. Gese, *Zur biblischen Theologie,* 3d ed., 45f.; and O. Kaiser, *Tod und Leben,* 70f., find "translation" also in Pss. 49:16 and 73:24. For a different view,

see, e.g., U. Kellermann, "Überwindung des Todesgeschicks in der alttestamentlichen Frömmigkeit vor und neben dem Auferstehungsglauben," 276f.

345. Cf. the passages in chap. 1–2 of the description by A. Schmitt along with his essay. These
are found in n. 341 above. For Adapa, cf. also WdM I, 39.

346. Cf. R. Martin-Achard, *De la mort à la résurrection d'après l'Ancien Testament, Neuchâtel
and Paris, 1956; F. Nötscher, Altorientalischer und alttestamentlicher Auferstehungsglaube,*
1926; reprint with an addendum by J. Scharbert, 1970; U. Wilckens, *Auferstehung,* 1970; K.
Spronk, *Beatific Afterlife in Ancient Israel and in the Ancient Near East,* 1986 (AOAT 219);
W. Dietrich, "Leben beiderseits der Todesgrenze," *PTh* 76, 1987, 154–171; A. Rebic, "Der
Glaube an die Auferstehung im Alten Testament," *IKaZ* 19, 1990, 4–12. Cf. also W.
Eichrodt, *Theology,* 2:496–529.

347. Cf. also Isa. 26:19 with the reviving dew mentioned there as well as the discussion by O.
Loretz, *Ugarit und die Bibel,* 1990, 162f.

348. Cf. above, p. 110.

349. Cf. W. H. Schmidt, "Baals Tod und Auferstehung," *ZRGG* 15, 1963, 1–13; and O. Loretz,
Ugarit und die Bibel, 1990, 73–78, 113.

350. Cf. Vol. I, pp. 160–163.

351. The following see the matter differently: E. Haag ("Ez 37 und der Glaube an die Auferstehung der Toten," *TThZ* 82, 1973, 78–92), who sees this text as already dealing with resurrection; and R. Bartelmus ("Ez 37,1–14, die Verbform *wĕqatal* und die Anfänge der Aufer-
stehungshoffnung," *ZAW* 97, 1985, 366–389) who finds in Ezek. 37:7a, 8b-10a an
interpolation from the Maccabean period. While Ezekiel himself reckons only with the restitution of the people, the editor hopes for a real resurrection of Jewish comrades who had
fallen in the Maccabean wars.

352. The different view of Th. Mende (" 'Ich weiss, dass mein Erlöser lebt' [Ijob 19,25]," *TThZ*
99, 1990, 15–35) appears not to be justified for reasons of problematic literary-critical differentiation.

353. Cf. H. D. Preuss, " 'Auferstehung' in Texten alttestamentlicher Apokalyptik (Jes. 26,7–19;
Dan 12,1–4)," in U. Gerber and E. Güttgemanns, ed, *"Linguistische" Theologie,* 1972,
101–133.

354. W. Dietrich, "Leben beiderseits der Todesgrenze," 162.

355. To this understanding of the background, cf. also M. Hengel, *Judentum und Hellenismus,* 2d
ed., 1973, 357ff.

356. Cf. F. J. Helfmeyer, " 'Deine Toten—meine Leichen': Heilszusage und Annahme in Jes
26,19," in H.-J. Fabry, ed., *Bausteine biblischer Theologie,* FS G. J. Botterweck, 1977 (BBB
50), 245–258.

357. Cf. above, pp. 147f.

358. Cf. the commentary on this text in H. Wildberger, BK X/2. Different is the view of G. Quell,
Die Auffassung des Todes, 42.

359. O. Kaiser points also to the texts from *Ethiopian Enoch* (chaps. 22 and 24–27) which were
found in Cave 4 in Qumran and thus may be even older than Daniel 12.

360. See U. Kellermann, *Auferstanden in den Himmel,* 1979 (SBS 95).

361. Cf. K. Schubert, "Die Entwicklung der Auferstehungslehre von der nachexilischen bis zur
frührabbinischen Zeit," *BZ* NF 6, 1962, 177–214.

362. Cf. also O. Kaiser, *Tod und Leben,* 8ff.; and U. Kellermann, *ZThK* 73, 1976, 278ff. Cf., e.g.,
Wisd. 4:20–5:23; and above, pp. 109f.

363. Cf. F. König, *Zarathrustras Jenseitsvorstellungen und das Alte Testament,* 1964.

364. J. Hempel, *Gott und Mensch im Alten Testament,* 2d ed., 1936 (BWANT 38), passim (cf.
likewise p. 3 for the thesis).

365. G. Fohrer, *Grundstrukturen,* 102ff., 110ff.

366. According to C. Westermann *Genesis 1–11,* 414, the word is even "in process from a more
specific to a more general meaning."

367. For the "fear of YHWH," mentioned in Josh. 24:14, cf. below, pp. 155ff.

368. "*Šm'* appears to be a key word for the Deuteronomic and Deuteronomistic school and their
descendants": H. Schult, *THAT* 2, col. 975 (in the article "שמע *šm'* hören," *THAT* 2, cols.
974–982). At this point this school is also rather close to sapiential thinking in which hear-

ing also plays a significant role. Certainly, there is in wisdom literature the emphasis on listening to the counsel of the sage. See above, pp. 112f., for the "hearing heart." Cf. further J. Arambarri, *Der Wortstamm "hören" im Alten Testament*, 1990 (SBB 20). He remarks that this is "an expression of the correct, religious, basic attitude before God (which has become a formal utterance in Deuteronomic and Deuteronomistic theology)" (p. 111).

369. Cf. also Exod. 23:21 and J. S. Schreiner, "Hören auf Gott und sein Wort in der Sicht des Deuteronomiums," *Miscellanea Erfordiana*, 1962, 27–47; A. K. Fenz, *Auf Jahwes Stimme hören*, 1964; H. D. Preuss, *Deuteronomium*, 1982, 198f. (with additional literature); and J. Arambarri, *Der Wortstamm "hören" im Alten Testament*, 33–123.

370. Cf. to this text, Vol. I, pp. 64–66, 70.

371. For the other verbs of obedience readily used in Deuteronomic/Deuteronomistic texts (keep/maintain; to travel in YHWH's paths; to stray [neither right nor left] from his paths; to follow him; and others), cf. the list under the superscription "Law and Obedience," in H. D. Preuss, *Deuteronomium*, 194ff.

372. Cf. J. P. Floss, *Jahwe dienen—Göttern dienen*, 1975 (BBB 45); and I. Riesener, *Der Stamm* עבד *im Alten Testament*, 1979 (BZAW 149).

373. Deut. 4:28; 5:7; 6:14; 7:4, 16, 25; 8:19; 11:16, 28; 12:2–4, 30, 31; 13:3, 7, 8, 14; 17:3, 18, 20; 20:18; 28:14, 36, 64; 29:17, 25; 30:17; and 31:16, 20; cf. Exod. 20:3; 23:13; and 34:14 (sg.).

374. Deut. 6:13; 10:12, 20; 13:5; Josh. 24:14; and 1 Sam. 12:14, 24.

375. Cf. E. Jenni, "אהב *'hb* lieben," *THAT* 1, cols. 60–73; and G. Wallis, "אהב und Deriv.," *ThWAT* 1, cols. 105–128.

376. Deut. 10:12; 11:13; and Josh. 22:5; אהב = *'āhab* occurs by itself in Deut. 6:5; 7:9; 11:1, 22; 13:4; 19:9; and 30:6, 16, 20. For the possible background of Deuteronomic/Deuteronomistic discourse about "love" (the language of diplomats of the ancient Near East to characterize sincere loyality toward the covenant partner?), cf. W. L. Moran, "The Ancient Near Eastern Background of the Love of God in Deuteronomy," *CBQ* 25, 1963, 77–87; and the additional literature provided by H. D. Preuss, *Deuteronomium*, 198.

377. The (exilic) commandment of the love of neighbor in Lev. 19:18 (34) stands rather isolated within the Old Testament. This does not mean the neighbor in general but rather people who are one's fellow citizens. The commandment seeks to shape programmatically the cohesion of the late exilic community and their future life in Israel. Cf. H.-P. Mathys, *Liebe deinen Nächsten wie dich selbst*, 1986 (OBO 71); and below, p. 190.

378. However, it is not only that they are to love YHWH. Cf. the connection of the love of YHWH and his chosen in Deut. 4:37; 7:7f., 13; and 10:15. In addition, cf. Vol. I, pp. 33f.

379. Cf. in addition to Exod. 20:6 and Deut. 5:10 also Deut. 6:5; 10:12; 11:1, 13, 22; 13:4; 19:9; and 30:6, 16, 20; then see Josh. 22:5; 23:11; and 1 Kings 3:3: Deuteronomistic.

380. For the cultic expression "Be glad before YHWH," see below, pp. 225f.

381. Ps. 119:47f., 97, 113, 119, 127, 140, 159, 163, 165, and 167.

382. For the passages in the Psalter that mention the love for worship and the temple (Pss. 26:8; 27:4; and 122:6; cf. Isa. 66:10; and Lam. 1:2), cf. G. Wallis, *ThWAT* 1, cols. 126f.

383. Deut. 13:5; 1 Kings 14:8; 18:21; 2 Kings 23:3; Jer. 2:2; Hos. 11:10; and 2 Chron. 34:31.

384. See F. J. Helfmeyer, *Die Nachfolge Gottes im Alten Testament*, 1968 (BBB 29); the passages are found on pp. 130ff. The focus also here is on the Deuteronomic/Deuteronomistic literature.

385. Cf. W. Schottroff, "שׁכח *škḥ* vergessen," *THAT* 2, cols. 898–904. The essay by H. D. Preuss, "שׁכח *šākah*," appears in *ThWAT* 7. See also the passages listed there.

386. See H.-P. Stähli, "עזב," *THAT* 2, cols. 249–252; and E. S. Gerstenberger, "עזב *'āzab*," *ThWAT* 5, cols. 1200–1208. See the other passages listed there.

387. Cf. S. Plath, *Furcht Gottes: Der Begriff* ירא *im Alten Testament*, 1963; J. Becker, *Gottesfurcht im Alten Testament*, 1965 (AnBib 25); L. Derousseaux, *La crainte de Dieu dans l'Ancien Testament*, Paris, 1970; H.-P. Stähli, "ירא *jr'* fürchten," *THAT* 1, cols. 765–778; and H. F. Fuhs, "ירא *jāre'* und Deriv.," *ThWAT* 3, cols. 869–893.

388. It is lacking entirely, e.g., in Ezekiel and in the Priestly source.

389. For the formula, "Do not fear!" (אל תירא = *'al tîrā'*), cf. above, p. 63; and *THAT* 1, cols. 771–773 as well as *ThWAT* 3, cols. 883–885.

390. *THAT* 1, col. 766.
391. Deut. 4:10; 5:29; 6:2, 13, 24; 8:6; 10:12, 20; 13:5; 14:23; 17:19; 28:58; 31:12, 13; (25:18 with אלהים = '*ĕlōhîm*); Josh. 4:24; 24:14; (Judg. 6:10); 1 Sam. 12:14, 18, 24; 2 Sam. 6:9; 1 Kings 8:40, 43 2 Chron. 6:31, 33); 18:3, 12; 2 Kings 4:1; and 17:7, 25, 28, 32–39, 41; here in verbal forms, often with ל = *lĕ* with the infinitive construct and YHWH as the object. Often the suffix pronoun is attached to God: "your" (sg. and pl.) and "our." Cf. also J. P. Floss, *Jahwe dienen—Göttern dienen*, 84ff.
392. Deut. 4:10; 6:13; 10:12; 13:5; 14:23; 17:19; Josh. 24:14; 1 Sam. 12:14; and 2 Kings 17:28, 32–39; cf. Jer. 32:39f. in a Deuteronomistically formed promise.
393. Deut. 5:29; 6:24; 8:6; and 13:5.
394. Cf. also Exod. 15:14–16; Deut. 26:8; 1 Sam. 4:7f.; Jer. 32:21; and Micah 7:15–17.
395. Deut. 31:12f.; Josh. 4:24; 1 Sam. 12:24; 1 Kings 8:40, 43; and 2 Kings 17:25, 32–39. Cf. Isa. 25:3; 41:5; Jer. 10:7; Hab. 3:2 (?); Zech. 9:5; and Pss. 65:9; and 76:9.
396. Deut. 4:10; 31:12f.; and 2 Kings 17:28; cf. Josh. 4:24; 1 Sam. 12:24; 2 Chron. 26:5; and Isa. 29:13: To fear YHWH only according to human commandments which one teaches.
397. The fear of God occurs only in Pss. 55:20 and 66:16, texts that belong to the so-called Elohistic Psalter. Apart from that, the fear of YHWH occurs as a noun only in Pss. 34:12 and 111:10.
398. Altogether, just under 80 passages. Adjectives: Pss. 15:4; 22:24; 115:11, 13; 118:4; and 135:20; cf. Mal. 3:16, 20. With suffixes ("him, your"): Pss. 22:26; 25:14; 31:20; 33:18; 34:8, 10; 60:6; 85:10; 103:11, 13, 17; 111:5; 119:74, 79; and 147:11.
399. Pss. 19:8ff.; 25:12; 34:12; 112:1; 119:63, 79; and 128:1.
400. Pss. 33:8; 64:10; (65:9); 67:8; (76); and 102:16; cf. 2:11.
401. Pss. 5:8; 40:4; 52:8; 76; and 130:4.
402. This has been argued from time to time on the basis of Pss. 115:11, 13; 118:4; and 135:20; but this is hardly correct.
403. Pss. 135:20; cf. Pss. 15:4; 22:24, 26; 34:8, 10; 25:12, 14; 31:20; 60:11; 85:10; 86:11; 103:11, 13, 17; 111:5; 118:4; 145:19; and 147:11.
404. The passages are Prov. 1:7, 29; 2:5; 3:7; 8:13; and 9:10. In the congested verse of 8:13, the "fear of the Lord" may be a gloss, while the phrase may well be an addition in 7:1 LXX that presents a different concept of the fear of YHWH. Then see 10:27; 14:2, 26, 27; 15:16, 33; 16:6; 19:23; 22:4; 23:17; 24:21f.; 28:14; and 31:30.
405. The phrase "fear of God" is not found in Proverbs.
406. The exception is Qoh. 8:12b.
407. "In order to" with ל = *lĕ* in synthetic *parallelismus membrorum*.
408. Cf. further Pss. 34:8, 10, 12; and 111:10. Also see Pss. 33:18; 112:1ff., 7f.; 119:38; 128:1–4; Isa. 11:2; and 33:6.
409. G. Vanoni attempts in thirty-six pages devoted to Prov. 15:16 (BN 35, 1986, 73ff.) to demonstrate that wisdom also leads to the center of Yahwistic faith. However, he has very little to say about the important fear of YHWH which is found in the text (pp. 83f.), and describes it as "the correct social behavior that grows out of the recognition of the social order of YHWH" (p. 84). Unfortunately he does not say where he discovers this content in Proverbs. F. J. Steiert also sets forth his views on the fear of YHWH in the proverbs (*Die Weisheit— Ein Fremdkörper im Alten Testament?* 1990, 117–120). He raises the criticism that I overlook the "religious aspect" of this (p. 118), something that is simply unfounded. For his part, when he takes into consideration Micah 6:8 (p. 119) to elucidate the contents of the fear of YHWH in Proverbs, then this procedure is not only questionable but also semantically impossible, for the expression "the fear of YHWH" is not used there at all.
410. Prov. 8:13; 14:2; 15:16; 16:6; and 23:17f.
411. Cf. Vol. I, pp. 184–194.
412. Cf. n. 387 above for the work mentioned by L. Derousseaux.
413. Cf. J. Becker, *Gottesfurcht*, 190.
414. Cf. E. Pfeiffer, "Die Gottesfurcht im Buche Kohelet," in H. G. Reventlow, ed., *Gottes Wort und Gottes Land*, FS H. W. Hertzberg, 1965, 133–158.
415. Qoh. 3:14; 5:6; 7:18; 8:12b (2), 13; and 12:13. Qoh. 9:2 and 12:5 do not belong here.

416. "Whoever fears God shall escape everything": יצא = *yāṣā'* ("escape") with the accusative is seldom found.

417. "Fear God and keep his commandments": addition of the so-called second epilogist as סוף דבר הכל = *sôp dābār hakkōl* ("end of the matter, the all"); cf. to the spirit expressing itself here: Deut. 13:5; 17:19; 28:58; 31:12f.; Lev. 19:32; 25:17, 36, 43; also Mal. 3:5 imbued with this content.

418. It is only here that the term occurs in the plural in wisdom literature.

419. ירא אלהים = *yĕrē' 'ĕlōhîm* ("fear of God"): adjective, Job 1:1, 8; 2:3; verb, Job 1:9; יראת שדי = *yir'at šadday* ("fear of Shaddai"): Job 6:14; יראת אדני = *yir'at 'ădōnay* ("fear of Adonay"): Job 28:28, an addition at the end of the chapter. Cf. Prov. 1:7; and 9:10.

420. Here יראה = *yirâ* ("fear") invariably stands as an absolute.

421. Gen. 20:11; 22:12; 42:18; Exod. 1:17, 21; and 18:21. Cf. also H. W. Wolff, "Zur Thematik der elohistischen Fragmente im Pentateuch," *EvTh* 29, 1969, 59–72 (= TB 22, 2d ed., 1973, 402ff.).

422. G. von Rad, *Genesis: A Commentary,* rev. ed. (OTL), Philadelphia, 1972, 229, Gen. 20:11.

423. H. W. Wolff, TB 22, 2d ed., 408.

424. Ibid., 409.

425. Ibid., 411.

426. Ibid., 417.

427. For the thesis of L. Derousseaux, *La crainte de Dieu dans l'Ancien Testament,* 149ff., that the discussion of the fear of God had its origin in Northern Israelite traditions, these passages (together with Hos. 10:3 and the Elohist) are hardly sufficient.

428. For נורא = *nôrā'* ("wonderment") as a predicate of God (over 30 times), cf. e.g. Exod. 15:11; Deut. 7:21; 10:17; etc., especially in the Zion and YHWH Melek psalms (Pss. 47:3; 76:8, 13; 96:4; and 99:3). For these, see H.-P. Stähli, *THAT* 1, cols. 769f.; and H. F. Fuhs, *ThWAT* 3, cols. 879f.

429. Cf. G. Ebeling, "Jesus und Glaube," *ZThK* 55, 1958, 64–110 (= *Wort und Glaube* 1, 1960, 203ff; hereafter cited); E. Pfeiffer, "Glaube im Alten Testament," *ZAW* 71, 1959, 151–164; H. Wildberger, "'Glauben,' Erwägungen zu האמין," in *Hebräische Wortforschung,* FS W. Baumgartner, 1967 (VT Suppl 16), 1967, 372–386 (= TB 66, 1979, 146ff.; hereafter cited); R. Smend, "Zur Geschichte von האמין," in *Hebräische Wortforschung,* FS W. Baumgartner, 1967 (VT Suppl 16), 284–290 (= *Die Mitte des Alten Testament* [*Gesammelte Studien* 1] 1986, 118ff.; hereafter cited); H. Wildberger, "'Glauben' im Alten Testament," *ZThK* 65, 1968, 129–159 (= TB 66, 1979, 161ff.; hereafter cited); H. Wildberger, "אמן *'mn* fest, sicher," *THAT* 1, cols. 177–209; A. Jepsen, "אמן und Deriv.," *ThWAT* I, cols. 313–348; H.-J. Hermisson and E. Lohse, *Glauben,* 1978; K. Haacker, "Glaube. II/2: A. T.," *TRE* 13, 279–289 (lit.); and G. Wallis, "Alttestamentliche Voraussetzungen einer biblischen Theologie, geprüft am Glaubensbegriff," *ThLZ* 113, 1988, cols. 1–13. Cf. also J. Barr, *Semantics,* 161–205; C. Westermann, *Theology,* 68–72; and K. Koch, *Spuren des hebräischen Denkens,* 1991, 12.

430. Cf. אמן = *'āman* niphal in Deut. 7:9: the "loyal" God (cf. Isa. 49:7).

431. For Hab. 2:4, cf. below, n. 477.

432. We are not going to treat here "faith" between human beings (e.g., Gen. 45:26; 1 Kings 10:7; and Prov. 14:15). Cf. *THAT* and *ThWAT* above.

433. Cf. the overview in A. Jepsen, *ThWAT* 1, col. 322.

434. G. Ebeling, "Jesus und Glaube," 210.

435. Cf. Vol. I, pp. 27–39.

436. Cf. H.-J. Hermisson and E. Lohse, *Glauben,* 9ff.

437. The building report from J has now fallen out in favor of the Priestly text.

438. Cf. also K. Jaroš, "Abraham, Vater des Glaubens, Glaube als Vertrauen," *BiLi* 49, 1976, 5–14.

439. There is no debate over the originality of this text, since it circumvents the presently existing, overall context.

440. V. Maag has sought to connect "faith" in a still stronger way with the ancestral stories in that he has pointed to the nomadic form of these groups' existence that is described there. In these

stories, faith and trust in God belong to a relationship with God in which people are on their journey, following the leadership of the deity; cf. *Kultur, Kulturkontakt und Religion,* 1980, 131f., 266.

441. Cf. above, pp. 315f., nn. 85 + 96.
442. Cf. H. H. Schmid, "Gerechtigkeit und Glaube," *EvTh* 40, 1980, 396–420.
443. For "righteousness," cf. below, pp. 167–170.
444. M. Oeming questions the earlier criticism dealing with "Abram reckoning something to YHWH" and proposes his own answer ("Ist Genesis 15,6 ein Beleg für die Anrechnung des Glaubens zur Gerechtigkeit?" *ZAW* 95, 1983, 182–197). Much to the point is the work of K. Haacker, *TRE* 13, 383 (he does not directly accept M. Oeming's view). See, however, R. W. L. Moberly, "Abraham's righteousness (Genesis XV 6)," VT Suppl 41, 1990, 103–130.
445. The feminine צדקה = *sĕdāqâ* ("righteousness, salvific deed") is a *nomen unitatis* and thus cannot as a result be related to Abram's continuing attitude of faith. Rather, the term refers to the promise of YHWH, characterized as a salvific deed (so with R. Mosis, " 'Glauben' und 'Gerechtigkeit' — zu Gen 15,6," 246–253).
446. R. Mosis, " 'Glauben' und 'Gerechtigkeit' — zu Gen 15,6," 246–253.
447. Cf. K. Haacker, *TRE* 13, 283: durative-iterative aspect. Also see his essay in K. Haacker and H. Hempelmann, *Hebraica Veritas,* 29f. (behavior of continuation, fundamental habit; v. 6 therefore is also well understandable as a transition to Gen. 15:7ff.). Also see R. Mosis, " 'Glauben' und 'Gerechtigkeit' — zu Gen 15,6," 235, 243: stative-durative description of a condition. Mosis also shows how and why the LXX transformed the LXX Gen. 15:6 into a passive and introduced in v. 6a Αβρα(α)μ = *abr(a)am* (pp. 254–257).
448. For this passage, cf. also B. Johnson, *ThWAT* 6, col. 913, with additional literature. Also see R. Mosis, " 'Glauben' und 'Gerechtigkeit' — zum Gen 15,6," 249ff.
449. Cf. M. Oeming, *ZAW* 95, 1983, 193ff.; K. Seybold, *ThWAT* 3, cols. 253ff.; and above, pp. 63–64.
450. G. von Rad, "Die Anrechnung des Glaubens zur Gerechtigkeit," *ThLZ* 76, 1951, cols. 129–132 (= TB 8, 3d ed., 1965, 130ff.). In addition, the noncultic usage of the verb predominates.
451. Cf. also Pss. 27:13; 116:10; Job 29:24; and 39:24. For Judg. 11:20 and Hab. 1:5, cf. H. Wildberger, *Erwägungen,* 374f.; and A. Jepsen, *ThWAT* 1, col. 325.
452. Cf. also Gen. 45:26; Exod. 4:5; 1 Kings 10:7; and Jer. 40:14.
453. G. Ebeling, "Jesus und Glaube," 218.
454. Cf. below, pp. 259ff.
455. H.-J. Hermisson and E. Lohse, *Glauben,* 25.
456. To this text and its division into sources, cf. Vol. I, p. 40.
457. Here secondary.
458. Are there here later additions that point to theological reflection?
459. The distinction between the two aspects proposed by M. Buber (*Zwei Glaubensweisen,* 1950 = *Werke* 1, 651ff.) appears to me not to be sustainable in regard to the Old Testament facts, as one can construe no contrast between ל האמין = *h'myn l* and כי האמין = *h'myn ky* (e.g. in Exod. 4:1 + 5).
460. Cf. H. Gross, "Der Glaube an Mose nach Exodus (4.14.19)," in H. J. Stoebe et al., eds., *Wort, Gebot, Glaube,* FS W. Eichrodt, 1970 (AThANT 59), 57–65.
461. Cf. the event and its interpretation, Vol. I, pp. 40–46.
462. One should not deny a certain proximity of these statements to Deuteronomistic linguistic usage. However, should one actually speak here of an already fully developed Deuteronomistic movement that deals with the phenomenon of "not believing"?
463. "Faith comes to expression [in the Old Testament] where it loses its matter-of-factness" (C. Westermann, *Theology,* 72).
464. Cf. Vol. I, pp. 79–80.
465. Cf. also H.-C. Schmitt, "Redaktion des Pentateuch," *VT* 32, 1982, 179 + 183f.
466. Cf. the overview by H.-C. Schmitt, "Redaktion des Pentateuch," 177.
467. Cf. thus also R. Smend, "Zur Geschichte von האמין."
468. In reference to the theme of faith within the theology of the Pentateuch, H.-C. Schmitt ("Redaktion des Pentateuch," 170–189) prefers to speak of a "redaction of the Pentateuch in the spirit of prophecy."
469. However, thus Chr. Hardmeier, *WuD* 15, 1979, 33–54.

470. The inclusion of this Isaianic text in 2 Chron. 20:20 is modified by additions.
471. Somewhat differently nuanced in H. Wildberger, TB 66, 151: "However, 'faith' in Isaiah, in order to say it sharply, is not faith in God and also not faith in the prophetic word. Rather, emerging from the knowledge of God and his promises (2 Sam. 7:16), it is an attitude of firmness, confidence, and trust with respect to the threatening nature of the concrete situation." Faith is to be shown here "existentially as an attitude toward life that maintains confidence" (p. 152); cf. Wildberger, TB 66, 164.
472. For the problems of dating and source analysis in 2 Samuel 7, cf. above, pp. 25f.
473. This view was maintained by G. von Rad, *Holy War in Ancient Israel*, Grand Rapids, 1991 (and later editions) (AThANT 20), who speaks of a clear, sharply defined stream of tradition and not only of a relationship of dependency based on the history of ideas (e.g., H. Wildberger, Exod. 14:13, 31) (p. 58).
474. H. Wildberger, TB 66, 169; and *THAT* 1, col. 190.
475. One has in fact not said "amen" to it; cf., however, Pss. 41:14; 72:19; 89:53; 106:48; Neh. 8:6; etc., i.e., one has not allowed oneself to enter into the message in an approving, obedient, and trusting way.
476. Cf. below, pp. 304f.
477. That Hab. 2:4, which is so important a witness to the righteousness brought about by faith (Rom. 1:17; and Gal. 3:11), must be excluded here from the Old Testament witness to faith is due, on the one hand, to the fact that the substantive אמונה = *'ĕmûnâ* ("faith"), not, however, the verb אמן = *'mn* ("to believe"), is used there. On the other hand, in Habakkuk one is to think of the word in terms of "loyalty, trustworthiness," or something similar, rather than faith. For this passage, cf. the overview by K. Haacker, *TRE* 13, 287f.
478. Cf. E. S. Gerstenberger, "בטח *bṭh* vertrauen," *THAT* 1, cols. 300–305; and A. Jepsen, "בטח und Deriv.," *ThWAT* 1, cols. 608–615.
479. E.g., Gen. 34:25; Judg. 8:11; 18:7ff.; Isa. 31:1; Jer. 5:17; 17:5; Ezek. 38:10f.; Pss. 44:7; 49:7; 52:9; 118:8f.; Job 8:14; 18:14; and Prov. 11:28. Cf. *ThWAT* 1, cols. 611ff. with additional passages.
480. A. Jepsen, *ThWAT* 1, col. 613.
481. Ibid., col. 615.
482. Cf. B. Beck, "Kontextanalysen zum Verb בטח," in H.-J. Fabry, ed., *Bausteine biblischer Theologie*, FS G. J. Botterweck, 1977 (BBB 50), 71–97.
483. Pss. 13:6; 25:2; 26:1; 28:7; 31:7, 15; 52:10; 55:24; 56:4, 5, 12; 71:5; 86:2; and 143:8.
484. Lev. 25:18f.; 26:5; Deut. 12:10; 33:12, 28; Isa. 14:30; 32:17f.; Jer. 23:6; 32:37; 33:16; Ezek. 28:26; 34:25, 27f.; 38:8, 14; 39:26; and Zech. 14:11.
485. Cf. Vol. I, pp. 184–194.
486. Cf. E. S. Gerstenberger, *THAT* 1, col. 303.
487. Cf. E. S. Gerstenberger, "חסה *ḥsh* sich bergen," *THAT* 1, cols. 621–623; and J. Gamberoni, "חסה *ḥāsāh* und Deriv.," *ThWAT* 3, cols. 71–83.
488. "Altogether 37 of 58 passages [of the verb as well as the noun] in Psalms": E. S. Gerstenberger, *THAT* 1, col. 622.
489. Pss. 7:2; 17:7; 25:20; 31:2; 57:2; 61:4f.; 71:1; 141:8; 142:6; and 144:2; cf. Jer. 17:17.
490. Pss. 5:12; 31:20; 64:11; 71:7; and 94:22.
491. Isa. 4:6; 14:32; 25:4; 28:16, 17; 57:13; Joel 4:16; and Zeph. 3:12.
492. Pss. 7:2; 11:1; 16:1; 25:20; 31:2; 57:2; 71:1; and 141:8. "In him" (Pss. 18:3; and 144:2).
493. Pss. 2:12; 5:12; 17:7; 18:31; 31:20; and 34:23.
494. The "capacity for salvation" is attested here to Abraham (according to K. Koch, *THAT* 2, col. 522).
495. For the "*righteousness of YHWH*," cf. Vol. I, pp. 171–179; for righteousness as behavior between humans, see also below, pp. 193f.
496. Cf. K. Koch, "צדק *ṣdq* gemeinschaftstreu/heilvoll sein," *THAT* 2, cols. 507–530; B. Johnson, "צדק und Deriv.," *ThWAT* 6, cols. 898–924 (lit.); J. Scharbert, "Gerechtigkeit. I: A. T.," *TRE* 12, 404–411 (lit.); W. Dietrich, "Der rote Faden im Alten Testament," *EvTh* 49, 1989, 232–250; A. Rebić, "Der Gerechtigkeitsbegriff im Alten Testament," *IKaZ* 19, 1990, 390–396; cf. also G. von Rad, *Theology*, 1:370–383; and H. Graf Reventlow, *Rechtfertigung im Horizont des Alten Testaments*, 1971, 105ff.

497. Cf. K. Whitelam, *The Just King,* 1979 (JSOT Suppl 12).
498. Later texts.
499. K. Koch, *Spuren des hebräischen Denkens,* 1991, 110.
500. 2 Samuel 8:15; Isa. 1:21; 5:7, 16; 9:6; 16:5; Jer. 3:11; 9:23; 22:3; Ezek. 16:51f.; 18:5, 19, 21, 27; 33:13, 16, 19; 45:9; Amos 5:7, 24; 6:12; and Zeph. 2:3; cf., however, also Pss. 1:5; 37:30; and 119:121.
501. 1 Sam. 26:23; 1 Kings 3:6; Isa. 1:26; 11:5; Hos. 2:21f.; Ps. 85:11f.; and 89:15. Connected with "blessing": Ps. 24:4f. For the linguistic field of צדקה/צדק = *ṣdq/ṣdqh,* cf. *ThWAT* 6, cols. 905–909.
502. Cf. Vol. I, pp. 184–194 for the "relationship between deed and consequence"; and K. Koch, *THAT* 2, cols. 516f.
503. Cf. Vol. I, p. 178.
504. For "righteousness" in the Psalter, cf. also H. Graf Reventlow, *Rechtfertigung im Horizont des Alten Testaments,* 66ff.
505. Additional examples for the action of a צדיק = *ṣaddîq* ("righteous one") are found in such texts as Pss. 1:5; 37:30; Prov. 10:11, 20f., 31f.; 12:26; 13:5; 21:26; and 29:7.
506. Cf. G. Braulik, "Gesetz als Evangelium," *ZThK* 79, 1982, 127–160 (= SBAB 2, 1988, 123ff.; esp. 144ff. for the passage).
507. Therefore, a צדיק = *ṣdyq* ("righteous one") is here not made out of a רשע = *rš* ("guilty/evil person"). In addition, the language is neither forensic nor efficacious. Neither is the discussion one about the compassion of God. As far as that goes, the approximation to the justification of the sinner is not so apparent as G. Braulik ("Gesetz als Evangelium," 149ff.) and N. Lohfink (cited by Braulik, 145 n. 66) think. Cf. also K. Koch, *THAT* 2, col. 520: "The bestowing of a *rāšā'* with *ṣĕdāqâ,* therefore the 'justification of the godless,' is unthinkable not only in the Psalter but also in the entire Old Testament." Cf., however, below p. 184.
508. Cf. B. Johnson, *ThWAT* 6, cols. 919–921.
509. Prov. 2:20; 3:33; and 4:18; cf. Ps. 34:22. Cf. also below, pp. 203–207.
510. Cf. Vol. I, pp. 184–194.
511. Cf. W. Schottroff, "ידע *jd'* erkennen," *THAT* 1, cols. 682–701 (lit.); J. Bergmann and G. J. Botterweck, "ידע *jāda'* und Deriv.," *ThWAT* 3, cols. 479–512 (lit.). Cf. also Th. C. Vriezen, *Theology,* 139–143.
512. Hos. 2:22; 4:1, 6; 5:4; 6:3, 6; 8:2; 13:14; Jer. 2:8; 4:22; 5:4f.; 9:2, 5; and 22:16.
513. Cf. also Isa. 11:2; 33:6; and Jer. 31:34.
514. Deut. 4:39; 7:9; 8:5; and 9:3, 6.
515. For the so-called formula of recognition ("you shall know that I am YHWH," and similar expressions), cf. Vol. I, pp. 204ff.
516. Cf. P. D. Miller, Jr., *Sin and Judgment in the Prophets,* 1982 (SBL MS 27).
517. Cf. J. Köberle, *Sünde und Gnade im religiösen Leben des Volkes Israel bis auf Christum,* 1905; R. Knierim, *Die Hauptbegriffe für Sünde im Alten Testament,* 1965; J. Scharbert, *Prolegomena eines Alttestamentlers zur Erbsündenlehre,* 1968; K. Koch, ed., *Um das Prinzip der Vergeltung in Religion und Recht des Alten Testaments,* 1972 (WdF 125); R. Koch, *Il peccato nel Vecchio Testamento,* Turin, 1973; K.-D. Schunck, "Die Korrelation von Sünde und Gericht im Alten Testament," in *Theologie im Kontext von Kirche und Gesellschaft,* 1987, 70–78 (= *Altes Testament und heiliges Land, Gesammelte Studien* 1, 1989, 229ff.); E. Kutsch "Das posse non peccare und verwandte Formulierungen als Aussagen biblischer Theologie," *ZThK* 84, 1987, 267–278; cf. also E. Sellin, *Theologie,* 2d ed., 69–74; W. Eichrodt, *Theology,* 2:380–495; L. Köhler, *Theologie,* 4th ed., 157–171; G. von Rad, *Theology,* 1:262–277; W. Zimmerli, *Theology,* 167–170; C. Westermann, *Theology,* 118–138; R. Knierim, "חטא *ht'* sich verfehlen," *THAT* 1, cols. 541–549; "עון *'awōn* Verkehrtheit," *THAT* 2, cols. 243–249; "פשע *paeša'* Verbrechen," *THAT* 2, cols. 488–495; K. Koch, "חטא *ḥāṭā'* und Deriv.," *ThWAT* 2, cols. 857–870; "עון *'āwon* und Deriv.," *ThWAT* 5, cols. 1160–1177; and H. Seebass, "פשע *pāša'* und Deriv.," *ThWAT* 6, cols. 791–810. Cf. also N. Lohfink, *Unsere grossen Wörter,* 1977 (etc.), 209ff.
518. Cf. also A. H. J. Gunneweg, "Schuld ohne Vergebung?" *EvTh* 36, 1976, 2–14 (= *Sola Scriptura,* 1983, 116ff.); and O. H. Steck, *Die Paradieserzählung,* 1970 (BSt 60).
519. For the view of human beings in the Yahwist as a whole, cf. above, pp. 119–121.

520. That the woman is here the "dialogue partner" of the serpent and was the first one seduced who in turn involved the man primarily has its basis probably in the ancient, originally mythological contrast between the woman and the phallic symbol (the serpent). This motif was altered and overlaid with other materials, although its fundamental structure was nonetheless retained. It may seem remarkable to us today that women appear in such a shocking way. To reinterpret this makes little sense. The Old Testament simply takes part here in the patriarchal and androcentric worldview and understanding of society at the time. That the woman has to suffer more than the man and that she will be ruled by him (Gen. 3:16ff.) are seen as the purpose of this narrative, at least as concerns the woman. However, while this is seen as the diminishment of life by the narrator, he does not give his approval and does not now propose this element as the purpose of the story. The narrator, "on the basis of what he knew about this area, regarded this matter for what it was, and that was it was terrible. He attributed blame for what happened to the humans and did not place the blame on the will of God. Theologically seen, one can neither construct order from punishment nor can one see in negative things the good will of God. One is no more able to make the subjection of the woman to the man into a modern commandment than one can the sentence of the man to have to work the stony land of Palestine by the sweat of his brow and to be afraid of snakes" (F. Crüsemann, *Als Mann und Frau geschaffen*, 67). Important for Genesis 3 is the fact that it here involves a common, fundamental, human event, that sin also disturbs and destroys human community. For this topic, see F. Crüsemann and H. Thyen, *Als Mann und Frau geschaffen*, 1978, esp. 17–20, 52–68. Then see naturally the numerous commentaries and monographs on Genesis 2–3, the most important of which are cited and listed by Crüsemann. Supplementing this is, e.g., H. Kuhlmann, "Freispruch für Eva?!" *BThZ* 7, 1990, 36–50. To be especially pointed out is the interpretation of O. H. Steck, *Die Paradieserzählung*, 1970 (BSt 60). For the woman, cf. also above, pp. 107–109.

521. The first different view is found in *4 Ezra* 7:118: "Ah, Adam, what have you done! When you sinned, your fall came upon not only you but also upon us, your descendants."

522. When Old Testament texts say that someone already is born in sin or even already may be "desired"(= conceived) in sin (Ps. 51:7; cf. Job 15:14) what is meant may be explained by the analogous statement that no pure person can come from impure persons (Job 4:17; 14:4; and 25:4). This expression is then an expression of experience, not a dogmatic assertion (cf. 1 Kings 8:46; Pss. 14:3; 130:3; 143:2; and even Gen. 6:5 and 8:21: J). The worshiper or the one reflecting over humanity sees himself or herself from his or her inception and in essence as a sinner. The first text to see this differently is Sir. 25:24.

523. Cf. J. Scharbert, *Prolegomena eines Alttestamentlers zur Erbsündenlehre*.

524. R. Rothe, *Theologische Ethik* 3, 2d ed., 1870, 1–107 (here time and again).

525. Cf. L. Rost, "Die Schuld der Väter," in Paul Althaus, ed., *Solange es "heute" heisst*, FS R. Hermann, 1957, 229–233 (= *Studien zum Alten Testament*, 1974 [BWANT 101], 66ff.); and J. Scharbert, "Unsere Sünden und die Sünden unserer Väter," *BZ* NF 2, 1958, 14–26.

526. According to the Babylonian perspective, sin entered the world through the gods (cf. the so-called "Babylonian Theodicy," lines 276ff. = *ANET*, 3d ed., 604). In addition, humans have within themselves the blood of the evil god Kingu (Enuma eliš VI, 31ff.: *RGT*, 2d ed., 110).

527. Cf. Deut. 15:9; and 22:26.

528. See the bases for the primeval flood given above, p. 120.

529. A. H. J. Gunneweg ("Schuld ohne Vergebung?") compares in an instructive way the contrast between the new entrance of God in Genesis 12 and Genesis 2–11 with the contrast between Rom. 3:21 and Rom. 1:18–3:20. A different emphasis is set forth by J. J. Scullion, "What of Original Sin? The Covergence of Genesis 1–11 and Romans 5:12," in R. Albertz et al., eds., *Schöpfung und Befreiung*, FS C. Westermann, 1989, 25–36. Cf. also E. Haag, "Die Ursünde und das Erbe der Gewalt im Licht der biblischen Urgeschichte," *TThZ* 98, 1989, 21–38.

530. Cf. above, pp. 114–117; and N. Lohfink, *Unsere grossen Wörter*.

531. Cf. R. Smend, "'Das Ende ist gekommen': Ein Amoswort in der Priesterschrift," in J. Jeremias and L. Perlitt, eds., *Die Botschaft und die Boten*, FS H. W. Wolff, 1981, 67–72.

532. Cf. G. Gerleman, "Schuld und Sühne: Erwägungen zu 2 Sam 12," in J. Zmijewski, ed., *Die Alttestamentliche Botschaft als Wegweisung*, FS W. Zimmerli, 1977, 132–139; and G. Hentschel, "Der Auftritt des Natan (2 Sam 12,1–5a)," in FS H. Reinelt, 1990, 117–133.

533. As is well known, the Books of Chronicles omit this narrative about the sinful David.
534. Cf. Vol. I, pp. 79–80.
535. E.-J. Waschke, "Schuld und Schuldbewältigung nach dem prophetischen Zeugnis des Alten Testaments," *ThLZ* 115, 1990, cols. 1–10; esp. 6.
536. Cf. R. Knierim, *Hauptbegriffe,* 13 n. 1. Also to be mentioned would be, e.g., עזב = '*zb* ("abandon"); שכח = *škh* ("forget"); זנה = *znh* ("to be a prostitute"); מאס = *m's* and נאץ = *n's* ("to despise"); נדד = *ndd* and סור = *sûr* ("yield"); בגד = *bgd* ("to behave disloyally"); and הלך אחרי = *hlk 'hry* ("to follow after," e.g., "strange gods").
537. Cf. the conjunction of the terms in Exod. 34:7; Lev. 16:21; Num. 14:18; Isa. 59:12; Jer. 33:8; Ezek. 21:29; Micah 7:18f.; Pss. 32:1, 5; 51:3–7; 59:4; Job 7:20f.; 13:23; and Dan. 9:24. See R. Knierim, *Hauptbegriffe,* 229ff. (for "the sum of all transgressions against God," p. 237). It is obvious that something can be said about the meaning of "sin" in the Old Testament, not only by means of an analysis of the term, but also by paying attention to the particular context, the genre of each text, etc. However, this cannot take place here, so that the articles in *THAT* and *ThWAT* as well as Knierim's study must be consulted. Then one can determine where the precise differences are. The following description is based largely on these studies.
538. Cf. R. Knierim, *Hauptbegriffe,* 60ff.
539. According to R. Knierim, *THAT* 1, col. 544: 30 times (cf. his *Hauptbegriffe,* 20ff.), e.g., Josh. 7:20; 1 Sam. 15:24; 2 Sam. 12:13; 19:21; 24:10; Pss. 41:5; and 51:6.
540. R. Knierim, *THAT* 1, col. 544; and idem *Hauptbegriffe,* 28ff. Examples include Num. 14:40; 21:7; Judg. 10:10, 15; 1 Sam. 7:6; 12:10; 1 Kings 8:47; Jer. 3:25; 8:14; 14:7, 20; Dan. 9:5ff.; and Neh. 1:6.
541. Cf. Exod. 32:30f.; Num. 32:23; Deut. 9:16, 18; Jer. 40:3; and Hos. 10:9: Deuteronomic/Deuteronomistic or prophetic. Then see Gen. 40:1; 1 Sam. 19:4; etc. (cf. R. Knierim, *Hauptbegriffe,* 38ff., 42f.).
542. Gen. 20:9; 26:10; Num. 27:3; Deut. 19:15; 24:16; 2 Sam. 24:17; 1 Kings 13:34; 2 Kings 14:16; Hos. 8:5; 14:1; Pss. 38:4; 51:7; and Dan. 9:16. Cf. R. Knierim, *Hauptbegriffe,* 73ff.
543. To this text, cf. also R. Knierim, *Hauptbegriffe,* 104ff.; and L. Schmidt, "De Deo," 1976 (BZAW 143), 131ff.
544. For this topic, cf. also R. Knierim, *Hauptbegriffe,* 97ff. See there (p. 108) the expression "something new."
545. Cf. the passages in *ThWAT* 2, col. 862; and below, pp. 178–179.
546. Isa. 5:18f.; 30:1; Jer. 3:25; 5:25; 13:9; 14:7, 20; 16:10f., 18; 17:1, 3; 40:3; Ezek. 16:51f.; Hos. 10:8f.; Micah 1:13; and 3:8.
547. K. Koch, *ThWAT* 2, col. 864. Passages include Deut. 15:9; 21:22; 23:22; 24:15f.; 2 Kings 14:6 = 2 Chron. 25:4; Lev. 19:17; 20:20; 22:9; Num. 9:13; 18:22, 32; and 27:3. Cf. Ezek. 18:4, 20; and 23:49.
548. Cf. below, p. 243.
549. K. Koch, *ThWAT* 2, col. 867.
550. Cf. below, p. 194.
551. K. Koch, *ThWAT* 2, col. 868. Cf. Num. 28:15, 22, 30; 29:5, 16, 19, 25; and Ezek. 45:18–25. Leviticus 16 is the high point. Cf. below, p. 183.
552. Cf. also R. Knierim, *Hauptbegriffe,* 185ff.
553. The Old Testament is familiar with a sin that is "unintentional," that occurred by mistake (בשגגה = *bišgāgâ*). Atonement was possible for this sin (Lev. 4:2, 22, 27; 5:15; 22:14; Num. 15:27–29) was impossible, for such a sin required banishment and the sentence of death (Num. 15:30; cf. 18:22). Cf. P. Heinisch, *Theologie des Alten Testaments,* 1940, 222f. However, even unwitting mistakes were still "sins": Gen. 20:9; Num. 22:34; Leviticus 4–5; Pss. 38:4, 19; and 41:5; cf. Ps. 19:13.
554. Cf., e.g., Gen. 44:16; Num. 14:19; Josh. 22:20; 1 Sam. 25:24; 2 Sam. 3:8; Isa. 22:14; and Jer. 11:10. Cf., however, the restrictions in R. Knierim, *THAT* 2, cols. 245f.; and idem, *Hauptbegriffe,* 239ff.
555. Cf. Gen. 4:13; 44:16; 1 Sam. 25:24; 2 Sam. 14:9; and 2 Kings 7:9 in the confession of guilt.
556. Gen. 4:13; 15:16; 19:15; Deut. 19:15; 1 Kings 17:18; 2 Kings 7:9; Isa. 5:18; 30:13; 64:6; Jer. 13:22; Ezek. 18:30; 44:12; Hos. 5:5; Pss. 25:11; 32:2, 5; and Job 31:11, 28.
557. Lev. 16:22; 22:16; 26:39f.; Isa. 14:21; 53:5, 11; Jer. 11:10; 14:20; Ezek. 4:4ff.; 18:17, 19f.;

Lam. 5:7; Dan. 9:16; and Neh. 9:2 as examples. A different view is stressed in Jer. 31:29f.; and Ezek. 18:2ff.; cf. Gen. 18:24f. and Num. 16:22.

558. Exod. 20:5; 34:7; Lev. 26:40; Num. 14:18; Josh. 7; 2 Sam. 21:1; 24:12–17; 1 Kings 14:10; and 2 Kings 23:26.

559. Isa. 1:4; 5:18; 22:14; 30:13; 59:2; Jer. 2:22; 5:25; 11:10; 13:22; 14:10; 30:14f.; Ezek. 4:17; 9:9; 14:10; Hos. 4:8; 5:5; 7:1; 8:13; 9:7, 9; 12:9; 13:12; 14:2; Amos 3:2; etc. Cf. R. Knierim, *Hauptbegriffe*, 200ff., 211ff., and 215f.

560. Pss. 31:11; 32:5; 36:3; 38:5, 19; 40:13; 49:6; 51:4, 7; 59:4f.; 65:4; 85:3; 89:32f.; 90:8; 106:43; 107:17; 109:14; 130:3; Dan. 9:13; and Ezra 9:6, 13a.

561. Cf. also Lev. 16:21; 26:40ff.; Isa. 53:5f.; 64:5; as well as the passages in the prior note. See R. Knierim, *Hauptbegriffe*, 208ff.

562. Cf. Gen. 31:36; Exod. 22:8; 1 Sam. 24:10–14; Amos 1:3, 6, 9, 11, 13; 2:1, 4, 6; and Prov. 28:24. Cf. also R. Knierim, *Hauptbegriffe*, 113ff., 126ff., and 160 ff.

563. Here in part with the use of the verbs: Isa. 1:2; 43:27; 50:1; 66:24; Jer. 2:8, 29; 5:6; 33:8; Ezek. 2:3; 14:11; 37:23; 39:24; Zeph. 3:11; and Micah 1:5.

564. R. Knierim, *THAT* 2, col. 494.

565. Pss. 32:5; 39:9; 51:3, 5; Ezek. 33:10; etc. in confessions. Cf. R. Knierim, *Hauptbegriffe*, 125ff., 133ff. (there for the suffix third person and with כֹל = *kōl*).

566. Cf. R. Knierim, *THAT* 2, col. 494.

567. Cf. H. J. Stoebe, "רעע *rʻ*" schlecht sein," *THAT* 2, cols. 794–803.

568. Cf. טוֹב = *ṭôb* is translated as both "good" and "beautiful."

569. Gen. 38:7, 10; Num. 22:34; 32:13; Deut. 4:25; 9:18; 17:2; 31:29; Judg. 2:11; 3:7, 12; 4:1; 6:1; 10:6; 13:1; 1 Sam. 15:19; 2 Sam. 12:9; 1 Kings 11:6; and 14:22; then an additional twenty times in the Books of Kings as well as in the parallel passages in the Books of Chronicles. Outside the historical books, see Jer. 7:30; 18:10; 32:30; 52:2; Isa. 59:15; 65:12; 66:4; Ps. 51:6; and Prov. 24:18.

570. Deut. 13:2–6; 17:2–7; 19:16–19; 21:18–21; 22:13–21; 23–27; and 24:7 (cf. also 19:11–13; 21:2–9 as variations?). For this textual group, cf. H. D. Preuss, *Deuteronomium*, 1982 (EdF 164), 119f. (lit.).

571. Cf. V. Maag "Unsühnbare Schuld," *Kairos* NF 2, 1966, 90–106 (= *Kultur, Kulturkontakt und Religion,* 1980, 234ff.), for the connection of the death penalty with "unpardonable guilt," for this exists wherever world order (as social, cultic order, etc.) is destroyed by a deed so that the evildoer must be eradicated and handed over to the "un-world."

572. Cf. Vol. I, p. 200.

573. Cf. also E. S. Gerstenberger and W. Schrage, *Leiden,* 1977, 62f.

574. Cf. above, pp. 141f.

575. Cf. Vol. I, pp. 184–194.

576. Cf. also A. Gamper, *Gott as Richter in Mesopotamien und im Alten Testament,* 1966, where especially the prayer's pleas, "Judge me with = Create for me justice," is investigated.

577. Jer. 18:23; Pss. 69:28; 109:14; Neh. 3:37: עָוֹן = *ʻāwôn.* Cf. Exod. 23:21; Josh. 24:19; and Amos 5:12 with פֶּשַׁע = *pešaʻ.*

578. Exod. 10:17; 32:30; 34:9; Lev. 4:20, 26, 31, 35, etc.; 1 Sam. 15:25; 1 Kings 8:34, 36, 50; Jer. 31:34; 36:3; Ezek. 37:23f.; Pss. 25:18; and 32:1, 5. Cf. also R. Knierim, *Hauptbegriffe,* 91ff.

579. Exod. 34:7, 9; Num. 14:18f.; 2 Sam. 19:20; 24:10; Isa. 6:7; 40:2; 64:6, 8; Jer. 14:7; 31:34; 33:8; 36:3; 50:20; Ezek. 36:33; Hos. 14:3; Micah 7:18f.; Zech. 3:4, 9; Pss. 25:11; 32:2; 51:4, 11; 78:38; 79:8; 103:3, 10; 130:8; Ezra 9:7, 13; etc. Cf. R. Knierim, *Hauptbegriffe,* 224ff.

580. Gen. 50:17; Exod. 34:7; Lev. 16:16; Num. 14:18; 1 Sam. 25:28; 1 Kings 8:50; Isa. 43:25; 44:22; Micah 7:18; Pss. 25:7; 32:1; and 51:3. Cf. R. Knierim, *Hauptbegriffe,* 114ff.

581. Cf. below, pp. 270f.

582. Cf. J. J. Stamm, *Erlösung und Vergeben im Alten Testament,* 1940; K. Koch, "Sühne und Sündenvergebung um die Wende von der exilischen zur nachexilischen Zeit," *EvTh* 26, 1966, 217–239 (*Spuren des hebräischen Denkens,* 1991, 184ff.); H. Thyen, *Studien zur Sündenvergebung im Neuen Testament und seinen alttestamentlichen und jüdischen Voraussetzungen,* 1970 (FRLANT 96); H. Graf Reventlow, *Rechtfertigung im Horizont des Alten Testaments,* 1971; C. Göbel, " 'Denn bei dir ist die Vergebung . . . ,' " *Theologische Versuche* 8, 1977, 21–33. See in addition E. Sellin, *Theologie,* 2d ed., 107–116; W. Eichrodt,

Theology, 2:443–483; and L. Köhler, *Theologie,* 4th ed., 202–209. Also see H. Gese, "Die Sühne," in *Zur biblischen Theologie* (1977), 3d ed., 1989, 85–109; A. Schenker, *Versöhnung und Sühne,* 1981; B. Janowski, *Sühne als Heilsgeschehen,* 1982 (WMANT 55); M. Kiuchi, *The Purification Offering in the Priestly Literature,* 1987 (JSOT Suppl 56); F. Maass, "כפר *kpr* pi. sühnen," *THAT* 1, cols. 842–857; and B. Lang, "כפר *kíppaer* und Deriv.," *ThWAT* 4, cols. 303–318. Also see J. J. Stamm, "גאל *g'l* erlösen," *THAT* 1, cols. 383–394; H. Ringgren, "גאל und Deriv.," *ThWAT* 1, cols. 884–890; H. J. Stoebe, "חנן *ḥnn* gnädig sein," *THAT* 1, cols. 587–597; D. N. Freedman, J. Lundbom, and H.=J. Fabry, "חנן *ḥānan* und Deriv.," *ThWAT* 3, cols. 23–40; F. Stolz, "נשא *nś'* aufheben, tragen," *THAT* 2, cols. 109–117; D. N. Freedman, B. E. Willoughby, and H.-J. Fabry, "נשא *nāśā'* und Deriv.," *ThWAT* 5, cols. 626–643; J. J. Stamm, "סלח *salaḥ* "vergeben," *THAT* 2, cols. 150–160; J. Hausmann, "סלח *salaḥ* und Deriv.," *ThWAT* 5, cols. 859–867; J. J. Stamm, "פדה *pdh* auslösen, befreien," *THAT* 2, cols. 389–406; and H. Cazelles, "פדה *padah* und Deriv.," *ThWAT* 6, cols. 514–522.

583. Cf. above, p. 175; and Vol. I, pp. 243–244. There one will also find the divine predicates that are used here, with חנן = *ḥnn,* רחם = *rḥm,* etc.

584. Cf. W. Zimmerli, "Die Eigenart der prophetischen Rede des Ezechiel," *ZAW* 66, 1954, 1–26 (= TB 19, 2d ed., 1969, 148ff., hereafter cited; esp. 157–161 for נשא עון = *nś' 'wn*).

585. According to Jer. 44:22, even YHWH could not and desired not to bear any more the abomination of Israel.

586. To bear one's own חטא/עון = *'āwôn/ḥēṭ'* ("offense, guilt," "sin"), see Gen. 4:13; Exod. 28:43; Lev. 5:1, 17; 7:18; 17:16; 19:8, 17; 20:17, 19f.; 22:9; 24:15; Num. 5:31; 9:13; 14:34; 18:22f., 32; Ezek. 14:10; 16:58; 23:35, 49; 44:10, 12, chiefly in texts from P and Ezekiel. To bear the עון = *'āwôn* ("offense, guilt"), etc., of another, see Exod. 28:38; 34:7; Lev. 10:17; 16:22; 22:16; Num. 14:18, 33; 18:1; 30:16; Isa. 33:24; 53:12; Ezek. 4:4, 5, 6; 18:19f.; Hos. 14:3; Micah 7:18; Pss. 32:5; and 85:3. Cf. 2 Kings 18:14; and Micah 7:9. Cf. also R. Knierim, *Hauptbegriffe,* 50–54, 114–119, 193, 202–204, 217–222, and 226.

587. In the context of intercession (Abraham: Gen. 18:23ff.; and 20:7; Moses: Exod. 32:11–13; 33:12–16; 34:9; Num. 11:2; Deut. 3:24f.; 9:26–29; and Ps. 106:23; Samuel: 1 Sam. 7:9; and 12:16–19, 23; Solomon: 1 Kings 8:23–61; Elijah: 1 Kings 17:20; Elisha: 2 Kings 4:33; Jeremiah: Jer. 27:18; 37:3; and 42:2–4 [forbidden: Jer. 7:16; and 11:14; cf. 15:1]; Ezekiel: Ezek. 13:4f.; and 22:30; Amos: Amos 7:2, 5; cf. also Ps. 99:6–8; Lot: Gen. 19:18–22; and Job 42:8f.), a term for "forgiveness" emerges in Gen. 18:24, 26 [נשא = *nś,* "to carry, take away"]; Exod. 32:30 [כפר = *kpr,* "to atone, cover"]; Exod. 32:32 [נשא = *nś',* "to carry, take away"]; 1 Kings 8:30, 39, 50 (סלח = *slḥ,* "forgive"]; and Amos 7:2 [סלח = *slḥ,* "forgive"]). Intercession, while having to do with forgiveness, is not limited to or often connected with it. The connection with forgiveness, with the exception of Amos 7:2, occurs only in (exilic and) postexilic texts. In addition, this forgiveness pertains only to forgiveness for the nation, never for an individual. Accordingly, the situation is problably that of a people who, in view of the punishment of the exile, have become aware of their sins. This provided the background for these intercessions for forgiveness which were articulated as a necessity.

588. Cf. below, pp. 233f.

589. With the derivations from חטא = *ḥṭ'* ("sin") in Gen. 50:17; Exod. 10:17; 32:32; 1 Sam. 15:25; and Ps. 25:18 (cf. Josh. 24:19); with פשע = *peša'* ("crime") as a petition in Gen. 50:17; and 1 Sam. 25:28; and in 1 Kings 8:50; Pss. 25:7; and 51:3 with another verb. As a petition with עון = *'āwôn* ("transgression, guilt") in Gen. 4:13 and Hos. 14:3 (with other verbs in Exod. 34:9; Num. 14:19; 2 Sam. 19:20; 24:10; Pss. 25:11; 51:4, 11; 79:8; and 1 Chron. 21:8).

590. In doxologies the verb is used with פשע = *peša'* ("crime") in Exod. 34:7; Num. 14:18; Micah 7:18; and Ps. 32:1; and with עון = *'āwôn* ("transgression, guilt") in Micah 7:18; Pss. 32:2; 78:38; 85:3; 103:3, 10; and Ezra 9:13. Cf. Exod. 34:7; and Num. 14:18 as a divine self-predication.

591. Cf. J. Hausmann, *Der Rest Israels,* 1987 (BWANT 124), 170ff.; and below, pp. 271f.

592. In respect to the petition, this was not different in Israel's ancient Near Eastern environment. Cf., e.g., the examples of so-called penitential psalms, laments, and prayers of entreaties in A. Falkenstein and W. von Soden, *Sumerische und akkadische Hymnen und Gebete,* 1953, 225ff., 263ff.; and *TUAT* II/5, 1989. For the religious classification of forgiveness there (also in regard to sin), cf. M. Jastrow, *Die Religion Babyloniens und Assyriens,* 2/1, 1912, 1–137;

and H. Vorländer, *Mein Gott,* 1975 (AOAT 23), 99, 102–107. Also see J. Assmann, *Ägyptische Hymnen und Gebete,* 1975, 349ff. For the religious classification of sin there, see M. H. van Voss, "Sünde und Schuld (Sündenbekenntnis)," *LÄ* VI, cols. 108–110. Cf., e.g., also: "He who would be without sin against his god, is it not the one who always gives attention to the law? Human beings, as many as there are, are full of sin!" (*TUAT* II/5, 779 [Mesopotamia]).

593. That David (in 2 Samuel 12–13) spoke only a simple "I have sinned" was too little for later theologians. There must be added an expressive and more complete petition for forgiveness: Psalm 51 (cf. there vv. 1f.).

594. There with a verbal adjective in the *qaṭṭāl*-form. For this, see B. Kedar, *Biblische Semantik,* 1982, 107f.: "The *qattal*-form underscores that what is described is a divine attribute and not only a way of behaving."

595. Cf. already in n. 587 above.

596. See G. Hentschel, NEB 2 Könige, 1985, 24: This is an addition from a postexilic redactor. "Naaman wrestles now with a problem of later proselytes: how may one reconcile the confession in monotheism with the professional responsibilities of a high state official?"

597. J. Hausmann, *ThWAT* 5, col. 866. For the "go in peace" and the different prepositions ל and ב used with this expression, cf. E. Jenni, *ZAH* 1, 1988, 2–8 (as is the case here in 2 Kings 5:19, ל has to do more with a general, prospective condition of well-being, while ב points to the present, particular situation at the moment of departing).

598. Cf. Lev. 4:20, 26, 31, 35; 5:10, 13, 16, 18, and 26. Then also Lev. 19:22; and Num. 15:25, 28.

599. For these types of sacrifices, see below, p. 243.

600. Cf. above, 553.

601. "The priest effectuates atonement for him/her/them, and he/she/they shall be forgiven." For this formula, see B. Janowski, *Sühne als Heilsgeschehen,* 1982 (WMANT 55), 250ff.

602. B. Janowski, *Sühne als Heilsgeschehen,* 359. "Atonement is therefore no act of 'self-redemption' (or even of the appeasement and assuagement of God), but rather atonement is both the reality made possible by God in the cultic event and that nullification of the connection between sin and disaster which benefits human beings." For "atonement," cf. below, pp. 233f.

603. See (besides the works of H. Gese and A. Schenker mentioned above in n. 582) esp. B. Janowski, *Sühne als Heilsgeschehen.* Cf. there the index, p. 392. See under "כפר-נסלח-Formel" and esp. 249ff.

604. Cf. J. J. Stamm, *Erlösen und Vergeben im Alten Testament,* 1940, 70ff.

605. Cf. ibid, 78ff.; and H. J. Stoebe, "רפא *rp'* heilen," *THAT* 2, cols. 803–809. For Jer. 3:21–4:2, cf. R. Mosis, "Umkehr und Vergebung—Eine Auslegung von Jer 3,21–4,2," *TThZ* 98, 1989, 39–60.

606. Cf. H. J. Stoebe, "חנן *ḥnn* gnädig sein," *THAT* 1, cols. 587–597; D. N. Freedman, J. Lundbom, and H.-J. Fabry, "חנן *ḥānan*," *THWAT* 3, cols. 23–40 and Vol. I, p. 278.

607. Pss. 4:2; 6:3; 9:14; 25:16; 26:11; 27:7; 30:11; 31:10; 41:5, 11; 51:3f.; 56:2; 86:3, 16; and 119:29, 58, 132.

608. Cf. J. J. Stamm, "פדה *pdh* auslösen, befreien," *THAT* 2, cols. 389–406; and H. Cazelles, "פדה *pādāh* und Deriv.," *ThWAT* 6, cols. 514–522.

609. Deut. 7:8; 9:26; 13:6; 15:15; 21:8; and 24:18; cf. 2 Sam. 7:23 (= 1 Chron. 17:21); Micah 6:4; Pss. 78:42; 111:9; and Neh. 1:10.

610. Thus with G. von Rad, *Theology,* 1:177. Cf. Vol. I, p. 47. Also see there for the formulae "with a strong hand and an outstretched arm" (p. 47) and "from the house of slaves" (p. 43).

611. Cf. also the overview in J. J. Stamm, *THAT* 2, col. 398.

612. Thus in the so-called Elohistic Psalter (Psalms 42–83) probably for "YHWH."

613. Cf. J. J. Stamm, "גאל *g'l* erlösen," *THAT* 1, cols. 383–394; and H. Ringgren, "גאל," *ThWAT* 1, cols. 884–890.

614. Israel's ancient Near Eastern environment is also aware of this institution (cf. J. J. Stamm, *THAT* 1, cols. 385f.). In Israel, the important bond to YHWH is also active in shaping and reshaping religious and social life (cf. Lev. 25:23f., 42 regarding land and slave).

615. Cf. again the assortment in J. J. Stamm, *THAT* 1, col. 388.

616. Isa. 43:1; 44:22f.; 48:20; and 52:3, 9. For גאל = *gō'ēl* ("redeemer") as a predicate of YHWH, cf. Isa. 41:14; 43:14; 44:6, 24; 47:4; 48:17; 49:7, 26; and 54:5, 8.
617. J. J. Stamm, *THAT* 1, col. 391.
618. One cannot say (e.g., on account of Amos 7:2; Jer. 5:1; and 2 Samuel 12 and 14) that forgiveness plays "no role" in the preexilic period (thus K. Koch, "Sühne und Sünden Vergebung um die Wende von der exilischen zur nachexilischen Zeit,"*EvTh* 26, 1966, 218–219). Even in Isa. 6:7, the issue is one of an act of forgiveness. With the use of another verb, YHWH's reaction is described as remorse about an intended action in Amos 7:3. Since this text deals only with the reprieve from a sentence, this means that the passage is consciously silent about any forgiveness that has taken place (!). All of this, however, says nothing against the use of the term "forgive" in v. 2. By contrast, the term "sin" is fully limited to the postexilic period.
619. "The reference to the deity who removes sin points to the greatest progress in the understanding of God which extended past the prophets to become a part of the exilic and postexilic periods" (K. Koch, "Sühne und Sünden," 223).
620. Cf. Vol. I, pp. 162f.
621. Cf. especially what already has been stated about the "righteousness of YHWH" in Vol. I, pp. 176–177.
622. Cf. (besides H. Graf Reventlow, *Rechtfertigung im Horizont des Alten Testaments*): H. H. Schmid, "Rechtfertigung als Schöpfungsgeschehen," in J. Friedrich, et al., eds., *Rechtfertigung,* FS E. Käsemann, 1976, 403–414; W. Zimmerli, "Alttestamentliche Prophetie und Apokalyptik auf dem Wege zur 'Rechtfertigung des Gottlosen,' " in FS E. Käsemann, 1976, 575–592; H. Gross, " 'Rechtfertigung' nach dem Alten Testament," in P.-G. Müller and W. Stenger, eds., *Kontinuität und Einheit,* FS F. Mussner, 1981, 17–29; and W. H. Schmidt, " 'Rechtfertigung des Gottlosen' in der Botschaft der Propheten," in J. Jeremias and L. Perlitt, eds., *Die Botschaft und die Boten,* FS H. W. Wolff, 1981, 157–168. Over against these see Koch, *THAT* II, col. 520: "A gift of *ṣedāqā* to one who is a *rāšā',* and thus the 'justification of the godless,' is unthinkable not only in the Psalter but also in the entire Old Testament." This may be so (cf. 1 Kings 8:32; or Deut. 25:1); however, the Old Testament expresses this state of affairs differently from the way Paul understands it.

Chapter 12. The Life of the Elect (Foundational Questions for Ethics and Ethos)

1. See E. Jacob, "Les bases théologiques de l'éthique de l'Ancien Testament," VT Suppl 7, 1960, 39–51; F. Horst, *Gottes Recht,* 1961 (TB 12); W. Schweitzer, "Glaube und Ethos im Neuen and Alten Testaments," *ZEE* 5, 1961, 129–149; J. Hempel, *Das Ethos des Alten Testaments,* 2d ed., 1964 (BZAW 67); M. A. Klopfenstein, *Die Lüge nach dem Alten Testaments,* 1964; J. L'Hour, *Die Ethik der Bundestradition im Alten Testament,* 1967 (SBS 14); H. van Oyen, *Ethik des Alten Testaments,* 1967; C. F. Whitley, *The Genius of Ancient Israel,* Amsterdam 1969 (86ff.); I. Soisalon-Soisinen, "Das ethische Moment in der frühisraelitischen Religion," *ZEE* 13, 1969, 146–153; J. L. Crenshaw and J. T. Willis, eds., *Essays in Old Testament Ethics* (J. P. Hyatt in Memoriam), New York, 1974; G. Wallis, "Natur und Ethos: Erwägungen zur Ethik des Alten Testaments," *Theolische Versuche* 7, 1976, 41–60; M. Gilbert, J. L'Hour, and J. Scharbert, *Morale et Ancien Testament,* Louvain, 1976; J. Barton, "Understanding Old Testament Ethics," *JSOT* 9, 1978, 44–64; J. A. Fischer, "Ethics and Wisdom," *CBQ* 40, 1978, 293–310; E. W. Davies, *Prophecy and Ethics,* 1981 (JSOT Suppl 16); W. H. Schmidt, "Aspekte alttestamentliche Ethik," in J. Moltmann, ed., *Nachfolge und Bergpredigt,* 1981, 12–36; E. Würthwein and O. Merk, *Verantwortung,* 1982; Chr. J. H. Wright, *Living as the People of God: The Relevance of Old Testament Ethics,* Leicester, 1983; W. C. Kaiser, Jr., *Toward Old Testament Ethics,* Grand Rapids, 1983; R. Smend, "Ethik. III: A. T.," *TRE* 10, 423–435 (lit.); E. Otto, "Sozial- und rechtshistorische Aspekte in der Ausdifferenzierung eines altisraelitischen Ethos aus dem Recht," in *Osnabrücker Hochschulschriften* (FB III), 9, 1987, 135–161; A. Soete, *Ethos der Rettung–Ethos der Gerechtigkeit,* 1987; R. R. Wilson, "Approaches to O. T. Ethics," in G. M. Tucker, et al., eds., *Canon, Theology, and Old Testament Interpreta-*

tion, FS B. S. Childs, Philadelphia, 1988, 62–74; and E. Otto, "Ethik (AT)," *NBL* 1, cols. 608–610 + 613. Cf. also P. Heinisch, *Theologie des Alten Testaments,* 1940, 152–189; O. Procksch, *Theologie,* 677–699; W. Eichrodt, *Theology of the Old Testament,* vol. 2 (OTL), Philadelphia, 1967, 316–322; H. H. Rowley, *Faith,* 2d ed., 124ff.; Th. C. Vriezen, *An Outline of Old Testament Theology,* Oxford, 1958, 315–342; W. Zimmerli, *Old Testament Theology in Outline,* Atlanta, 1978, 133–141; and W. H. Schmidt, *Alttestamentliche Glaube,* 6th ed., 109ff. For the history of criticism, see E. Otto, *VuF* 36, 1991 (1), 3–37 (lit.).

2. Cf. Vol. I, p. 19.
3. W. Schottroff, *VuF* 19/2, 1974, 48.
4. For this problematic issue, cf. J. Barton, "Understanding Old Testament Ethics," *JSOT* 9, 1978, 44ff.
5. H. J. Boecker, *Recht und Gesetz im Alten Testament und im Alten Orient,* 2d ed., 1984, 117.
6. Cf. below, pp. 203–207.
7. Th. C. Vriezen, *Die Erwählung Israels nach dem Alten Testament,* 1953 (AThANT 24), 34.
8. A. Soete, *Ethos der Rettung,* 80.
9. There is a certainly very wonderful Jewish legend according to which the Israelites, when they were allowed to break camp at Sinai, did so quickly and traveled as far as possible (Num. 10:33: they set out immediately three days journey in a procession). They had no desire for any more laws! Thus, L. Ginsberg, *The Legends of the Jews* 3, Philadelphia, 1910 (and reprint), 242.
10. A. Soete, *Ethos der Rettung,* 114.
11. J. L'Hour, *Die Ethik der Bundestradition,* 32ff.
12. For the relationship of the individual and the community, see Vol. I, pp. 60–64.
13. Cf. below, pp. 189ff.
14. Cf. above, pp. 167–170; and Vol. I, pp. 171–179.
15. Cf. above, p. 168.
16. Cf. above, pp. 153ff.
17. Cf. more precisely below, pp. 203–207.
18. "This happens in an obvious way; reflection over the origin and character of this basic knowledge, perhaps in the sense of later theories of natural law, is foreign to the texts" (R. Smend, *TRE* 10, 427).
19. Cf., however, also below, pp. 287f.
20. Th. C. Vriezen, *Theology,* 315.
21. See J. Schreiner, "Gastfreundschaft im Zeugnis der Bibel," *TThZ* 89, 1980, 50–60; and H.-W. Jüngling, *Richter 19—Ein Plädoyer für das Königtum,* 1981 (AnBib 84), 172ff., 294ff.
22. According to S. Nyström, *Beduinentum und Jahwismus,* Lund, 1946, 24–40, the law of hospitality and blood vengeance are residues of bedouin life in Israel.
23. Cf. E. Merz, *Die Blutrache bei den Israeliten,* 1916 (BWAT 20); R. de Vaux, *Ancient Israel,* vol. 1: *Social Institutions,* New York, 10–12; H. J. Boecker, *Recht und Gesetz im Alten Testament und im Alten Orient,* 2d ed., 1984 (see the index).
24. Cf. Gen. 9:6; Exod. 21:12, 23; Lev. 24:17–21; Num. 35:16–33; and Deut. 19:11–13 Examples: Gen. 27:45; 42:22; Judg. 8:18–21; 9:23f.; 2 Sam. 1:16; 2:22f.; 3:27, 30; 4:11; 14:7, 11; 2 Kings 14:5; and 2 Chron. 24:25..
25. Deut. 17:12; 19:13; and 22:21f.; cf. Judg. 20:13. Also see Deut. 13:6; 17:7; 19:19f.; 21:9, 21; 22:21, 24; 24:7; Josh. 7:12f.; and Micah 5:12f. "The ethic of the Old Testament gained its dynamic from Yahweh's power of integration, for he was the one God of Israel, who, contrary to the modern social process, always placed additional spheres of life under the order of his divine will. Ever more consistently, Yahweh was conceived as the ground of possibility for an ethic whose basic values were communal faithfulness (*ṣedāqâ*) and solidarity (*ḥesed*)" (E. Otto, *NBL* 1, col. 610).
26. Cf. Vol. I, pp. 81 + 89.
27. Thus with J. Hempel, *Das Ethos des Alten Testaments,* 2d ed., 29. Cf. E. Jacob, "Les bases théologiques de l'éthique de l'Ancien Testament," 42: "The separation founded on election."
28. Prov. 3:32; 6:16; 11:1, 20; 12:22; 15:8, 9, 26; 16:5; 17:15; 20:10, 23; 21:27; and 28:9. Cf. also Ps. 5:7; Isa. 1:13; Lev. 18:22–30; and 20:13. What was an "abomination" for an Egyptian is mentioned in Gen. 43:32; 46:34; and Exod. 8:22.

29. Deut. 7:25f.; 12:31; 13:15; 14:3; 17:1, 4; 18:9, 12; 20:18; 22:5; 23:18f.; 25:16; 27:15; and 32:16. For the texts in Deuteronomy, cf. H. D. Preuss, *Deuteronomium,* 1982 (EdF 164), 34, 38, 89, 114f., 118f., and 181 (lit.). Also see Preuss, "תועבה *tōʿēbah,*" in *ThWAT;* and E. S. Gerstenberger, *THAT* 2, cols. 1051–1055.

30. For this commandment, cf. H.-P. Mathys, *Liebe deinen Nächsten wie dich selbst,* 1986 (OBO 71). Concerning the twofold commandment of love (p. 154), he writes: "The summary of the twofold commandment of love is set forth in the Old Testament in Deut. 6:5 and Lev. 19:18. This twofold commandment exhibits the same structure as the Decalogue: in its first part the behavior toward God is dominant (with the stress on the demand for the exclusive love of God), while in the second the conduct is directed toward the neighbor, without bringing the two explicitly together in an inner relationship." For the "neighbor" as the tribal relatives and members of the nation, the friend (Job 16:20; 19:21; and 32:3: the friends of Job), the neighbor, and the beloved (and fellow human beings in general?), cf. D. Kellermann, "רע *rēaʿ,*" *ThWAT* 7, cols. 545–555. Cf. above, p. 343 n. 37.

31. "Formulations of judgment of legal proceedings that have occurred" (H. J. Boecker, *Recht und Gesetz im Alten Testament und im Alten Orient,* 133). Cf. E. Otto, *Osnabrücker Hochschulschriften,* 138 (lit.), and Vol. I, p. 82.

32. Cf. below, pp. 235–238.

33. Cf., e.g., the prophets and Deuteronomy against folk piety; YHWH in the Book of Proverbs or YHWH in the Priestly source; etc.

34. Cf. above, p. 87.

35. Cf. J. Pons, *L'oppression dans l'Ancien Testament,* Paris, 1981.

36. Cf. W. Schottroff, "Der Prophet Amos: Versuch der Würdigung seines Auftretens unter sozialgeschichtlichem Aspekt," in W. Schottroff and W. Stegemann, *Der Gott der kleinen Leute* 1 (AT), 1979, 39–66.

37. By a segmentary society is understood here an "acephalous (i.e., not politically organized through a central authority) society that has a political organization which is mediated through groups that politically were of equal rank, homogeneous, and subdivided into several or many levels." Thus Chr. Sigrist, *Regulierte Anarchie,* 1979, 30. This means that this society consists of a chain of equal and coexisting entities (mostly clans) among whom genealogical self-definitions are of significance and group solidarity is constitutive. One recognizes in this type of society a developed consciousness of relational associations and of a particular position among the genealogies that have common ancestors, while territorial groups are often congruent with genealogical connections. This society had a developed sense of "we" and lived "especially out of a considerably deep-seated need for equality." The combination of this segmentary form of society with the monotheistic worship of the God YHWH may be "without analogy." The last citations are taken from N. Lohfink, "Die segmentären Gesellschaften Afrikas als neue Analogie für das vorstaatliche Israel," *BiKi,* 1983 (2), 55–58, esp. 57–58. Also my portrayal here is dependent on this essay. For this subject, cf. also H.-W. Jüngling, "Die egalitäre Gesellschaft der Stämme Israels," *BiKi,* 1983 (2), 59–64; and Vol. I, pp. 57–59. Whether with that all arguments for a (modified) kind of "amphictyony" are dismissed is another question.

38. According to N.-P. Lemche (*Early Israel,* 1985, VT Suppl 37), the ethical dimension of Yahwistic religion was its own special feature, and this is especially in contrast to Canaanite religion. However, if this was so, YHWH must have assumed a role that was fundamentally different from the other gods, for they "represent no uniform understanding of being and do not allow the opening up of a self-contained, main horizon of meaning. Whoever wants to derive from the gods of myth claims placed on humanity is involved, corresponding to the nature of the gods, in contradictions, in adverse moral systems, and in arbitary features" (A. Soete, *Ethos der Rettung,* 55). Thus, in the ancient Near East, the law was anchored more in the monarchy than in the gods. For the "Canaanites," cf. also Vol. I, p. 231 n. 668.

39. Nazirite vows could be made both for a period of time and forever. For what was to be renounced, cf. Judg. 13:5, 14. This institution was later expanded and regulated as an institution in Num. 6:1–21. Cf. G. Mayer, *ThWAT* 5, cols. 329–334 (lit.).

40. Here דרך יהוה = *derek yahweh* ("way of YHWH") stands beside משפט אלהים = *mišpaṭ ʾĕlōhîm* ("justice of Elohim").

41. Cf. E. Jacob, "Marcher avec Dieu" (VT Suppl 7, 42; cf. *Theologie,* 142). See in addition K. Koch et al., "דרך *derek,*" *ThWAT* 2, cols. 288–312.
42. F. J. Helfmeyer, *Die Nachfolge Gottes im Alten Testament,* 1968 (BBB 29); cf. above, pp. 154f.
43. Cf. Vol. I, pp. 125–127.
44. Is this different in Old Testament wisdom literature? Cf., e.g., Prov. 22:2; and below, pp. XXXf.
45. Cf. F. Horst, "Naturrecht und Altes Testament," *EvTh* 10, 1950/1951, 253–273 (=TB 12, 235ff.).
46. Cf. above, pp. 167–170; and Vol. I, pp. 184–194.
47. Cf. above, pp. 114–117.
48. Deut. 1:16; 3:20; 10:9; 15:2, 7, 11, 12; 17:15, 20; 18:7, 15; etc. Cf. Also Lev. 19:17; 25:25, 35f., 39, 47. In addition, see L. Perlitt, "Ein einzig Volk von Brüdern," in D. Luhrmann and G. Strecker, eds., *Kirche,* FS G. Bornkamm, 1980, 27–52.
49. Cf. above, p. 60. N. Lohfink wishes to see Deuteronomy as a "draft of a society without marginal groups" (*BN* 51, 1990, 25–40).
50. See below, p. 199 n. 110; cf., however, Jer. 22:15f.; and Ps. 72:1–4.
51. Exod. 23:6, 11; Deut. 15:1–11; 24:14; and Lev. 25:36f. Cf. among the prophets the frequent reflection on the poor and wretched, אביון, דל, עני/ו = *'ny/w, dl, 'bywn:* Amos 2:6f.; 4:1; 5:11f.; and 8:4, 6; cf. Isa. 10:2; 11:4; Jer. 5:28f.; Ezek. 18:12; etc. See also M. Schwantes, *Das Recht der Armen,* 1977 (BET 4).
52. See W. Schottroff, "Arbeit und sozialer Konflikt im nachexilischen Juda," in L. Schottroff and W. Schottroff, eds., *Mitarbeiter der Schöpfung,* 1983, 104–108, esp. 114ff.
53. Exod. 22:24; Lev. 25:35–38; Deut. 23:20f.; Ezek. 18:8, 13, 17; 22:12; and Ps. 15:5. Cf., however, Prov. 28:8. For this topic, see also R. Kessler, "Das hebräische Schuldenwesen," *WuD* NF 20, 1989, 181–195. This is different in regard to the foreigner (Deut. 23:20f.) who, especially as a merchant, was customarily charged interest, and particularly high interest at that (cf. below, pp. 295f.).
54. Cf., e.g., the passages mentioned above in nn. 51 and 53 and in addition also Lev. 19:35f.; Deut. 16:18–20; 19:14; 24:7, 14; and 25:13–16.
55. L. Perlitt, "Ein einzig Volk von Brüdern," 41; Perlitt, however, has probably overlooked the fact that the famous lament text, which is associated with Deut. 24:14f. and is found on the ostracon of Metzad Hashavyahu in lines 10f., speaks also of "brothers" (or are physical brothers meant?); cf. in addition F. Crüsemann, "'. . . damit er dich segne in allem Tun deiner Hand' (Deut. 14:29)," *Mitarbeiter der Schöpfung,* 72–103, esp. 75 = 79.
56. H. van Oyen, *Ethik des Alten Testaments,* 45.
57. Cf. J. Hempel, *Das Ethos des Alten Testaments,* 2d ed., 89ff.
58. Cf. Vol. I, pp. 226–227.
59. For the prophetic social criticism, see above, p. 87 and esp. K. Koch, "Die Entstehung der sozialen Kritik der Profeten," in H. W. Wolff, ed., *Probleme biblischer Theologie,* FS G. von Rad, 1971, 236–257 (= *Spuren des hebräischen Denkens,* 1991, 146ff.).
60. See J. Hempel, *Das Ethos des Alten Testaments,* 2d ed., 32ff.
61. Cf., however, the ethos of wisdom literature; see below, pp. 203–207.
62. For the "properties of moral action" (as, e.g., both reward and punishment), cf. W. Eichrodt, *Theology* 2:349–364.
63. Cf. above, pp. 182 + 208.
64. "Also the requirement, including its legal formulations, still needed no direct religious legitimation. Rather, kinship relationships that had their foundation in Yahweh produced this legitimation" (E. Otto, *NBL* 1, col. 608).
65. E. Otto, ibid.
66. See B. Johnson, "משפט *mišpaṭ,*" *ThWAT* 5, cols. 93–107; and H. Ringgren and B. Johnson, "צדק *ṣādaq* und Deriv.," *ThWAT* 6, cols. 898–924.
67. For Zeph. 1:11, 18; 2:3; and 3:11f. cf. also G. Gorgulho, "Zefanja und die historische Bedeutung der Armen," *EvTh* 51, 1991, 81–92.
68. See H.-J. Zobel, "חסד *hesed,*" *ThWAT* 3, cols. 48–71; cf. also E. Kellenberger, *häsäd wä'ämät als Ausdruck einer Glaubenserfahrung,* 1982 (AThANT 69); and above, p. 168.

69. Cf. Vol. I, pp. 50–52.
70. Cf. Vol. I, pp. 100–104.
71. For this chapter, cf. A. Soete, *Ethos der Rettung,* 153ff.; and above, pp. 167–170, for "righteousness."
72. Cf. the literature cited on p. 372 n. 30. L. Mathys (*Liebe deinen Nächsten wie dich selbst,* 79) remarks about Leviticus 19 as a whole: "Leviticus 19 sets forth the program of the late-exilic community; the chapter contains all that was fundamentally envisioned for this community's common life in the Diaspora and its future life in Israel."
73. Thus with H. Ringgren, *Israelite Religion,* Philadelphia, 1966, 134.
74. See below, pp. 203–207.
75. See H. D. Preuss, *Freiheit, Gleichheit, Brüderlichkeit,* 1990 (lit.).
76. K. Koch, *ZEE* 5, 1961, 78 (= *Spuren,* 114).
77. See H. Rücker, *Die Begründungen der Weisungen Jahwes im Pentateuch,* 1973; and R. Sonsino, *Motive Clauses in Hebrew Law,* Ann Arbor, Mich., 1980.
78. M. A. Klopfenstein, *Die Lüge nach dem Alten Testament,* 1964.
79. Ibid., 321f.
80. Ibid., 353. Cf. J. Hempel, *Das Ethos des Alten Testaments,* 2d ed., 35ff. For further thinking about general theological consequences, cf. D. Bonhoeffer, "Was heisst: 'Die Wahrheit sagen,'" in *Ethik* (ed. E. Bethge), n.d., 283ff.; and W. Zimmerli, *Theology,* 139–140.
81. Cf. Vol. I, pp. 60f.
82. See H.-J. Fabry, "לֵב/לֵבָב *leb/lebāb,*" *ThWAT* 4, cols. 413–451, esp. 438ff. Cf. above, pp. 112f.
83. Cf. R. Smend, *TRE* 10, 430.
84. See H.-W. Jüngling, *ThPh* 59, 1984, 1–38; and F. Crüsemann, "'Auge um Auge . . . ' (Ex. 21, 24f.)," *EvTh* 47, 1987, 411–426.
85. "Later additions?" See the following note.
86. Exod. 22:20b is redacted by Deuteronomistic editors, as also was Exod. 22:23; and 23:9b, 13. For a now more precise study of the Covenant Code, see L. Schwienhorst-Schönberger, *Das Bundesbuch (Exod. 20:22–23:33),* 1990 (BZAW 188). Cf. to these social-ethical spheres also Exod. 22:20ff.; 23:6–11; Lev. 19:10, 13, 33ff.; 23:22; 25:25ff., 39ff.; Deut. 24:10ff., 17–20; 27:19; and then Isa 1:17, 21–23; Jer. 5:28; 7:6; 21:12; 22:3, 16f.; Ezek. 18:5ff.; 22:7; Hos. 5:11; Amos 5:7, 10–12; Micah 2:2; Zech. 7:10; and Mal. 3:5.
87. E. Otto, *Wandel der Rechtsbegründungen in der Gesellschaftsgeschichte des antiken Israel,* 1988, 75.
88. See the previous note: the law of regulating conflict; casuistic law with sanctions; law protecting the rights of the weak, families, and clans; institutions of judgment that are local and beyond; etc.
89. E. Otto, *Wandel der Rechtsbegründungen,* 69.
90. Ibid., 72. Cf. E. Otto, "Sozial- und rechtshistorische Aspekte," 146f.
91. Cf. the literature mentioned in n. 77 above.
92. Cf. again the literature mentioned in n. 77 above.
93. Cf. pp. 209–252.
94. Cf. K. Koch, "Wesen und Ursprung der 'Gemeinschaftstreue' im Israel der Königszeit," *ZEE* 5, 1961, 72–90 (= *Spuren des hebräischen Denkens,* 1991, 107ff., esp. 119ff.).
95. Cf. Vol. I, pp. 161f.
96. Cf. Vol. I, pp. 79–80; cf. also H.-J. Zobel, "Die Zeit der Wüstenwanderung Israels im Lichte prophetischer Texte," *VT* 41, 1991, 192–202.
97. Cf. R. Smend, *TRE* 10, 431–434.
98. Cf. further, pp. 153ff.
99. Cf. above, p. 87.
100. J. Halbe, *Das Privilegrecht Jahwes* Ex 34, 10–26, 1975 (FRLANT 114).
101. F. Crüsemann (*Bewahrung der Freiheit,* 1983) unfortunately does not allow one exactly to know whether he is thinking of the Decalogue in Exodus 20 or in Deuteronomy 5 in his social-historical interpretation of the Decalogue. Further, the Decalogue of Deuteronomy 5 is not a product of the Deuteronomic period (between Hosea and Deuteronomy) or school but rather is a Deuteronomistic text. For this and the following, cf. Vol. I, pp. 107–109.
102. For marriage, see above, pp. 103f.

103. See F. Horst, "Das Eigentum nach dem Alten Testament," in TB 12, 1961, 203–221; for the possession of the land, see Vol. I, pp. 125–127.
104. Cf. F. Horst, "Der Diebstahl im Alten Testament," in TB 12, 1961, 167–175.
105. Cf. above, pp. 87 + 191. Exploitation, ownership by accumulation of the land, charging of interest, venality, and debt slavery are the most frequently criticized ways of conduct: Exod. 22:24; Deut. 23:20f.; Lev. 25:35–37; Ps. 15:5; Amos 2:7f.; 3:10; 4:1; 5:7–11; 6:1–6; 8:4–6; Isa. 1:21, 26; 5:8–10; Micah 2:1–5; etc. For venality, see also below, p. 203.
106. See H.-J. Fabry, "Noch ein Dekalog! Die Thora des lebendigen Gottes in ihrer Wirkungsgeschichte: Ein Versuch zu Deuteronomium 27," in M. Bohnke and H. Heinz, eds., *Im Gespräch mit dem dreieinen Gott,* FS W. Breuning, 1985, 75–96.
107. For Leviticus 18, cf. F. J. Stendebach, "Überlegungen zum Ethos des Alten Testaments," *Kairos* NF 18, 1976, 273–281: culturally and socially conditioned rules, which originated out of the community's ethical instinct for self-preservation, seek to protect the social, fundamental unity of the extended family from biological degeneration and inner discord" (p. 277). Then there are editions where the situation of the extended family is given up and the Decalogue mainly becomes law against sexual offenses in defending against Canaanite practice (p. 279).
108. E. Otto, *Körperverletzungen in den Keilschriftrechten und im Alten Testament,* 1991 (AOAT 226).
109. See above, p. 192.
110. *TUAT* I/1 (1982), 40 + 76. For this subject, see J. Hempel, *Das Ethos des Alten Testaments,* 2d ed., 28; and J. N. Fensham, "Wisdom, Orphan and the Poor in Ancient Near Eastern Legal and Wisdom Literature," *JNES* 21, 1962, 129–139.
111. See W. Dietrich, *Israel und Kanaan. Vom Ringen zweier Gesellschaftssysteme,* 1979 (SBS 94); cf., however, above in n. 107.
112. See H. D. Preuss, "Arbeit. I: A. T.," *TRE* 3, 613–618; W. Schottroff, "Arbeit," *NBL* 1, cols. 151–154; and V. Hirth, "Die Arbeit als ursprüngliche und bleibende Aufgabe des Menschen," *BZ* NF 33, 1989, 210–221 (lit.). Here he adjusts the exaggerated theses on the topic by J. Kegler, F. Crüsemann, and F. Kiss. Also see V. Hirth, "Der Wandel des Arbeitsverständnisses in Altisrael beim Übergang zur Königszeit," *BN* 55, 1990, 9–13. See also above, pp. 104f.
113. As F. Crüsemann critically advised, we consequently cannot come closer to amplify the "reality of the world of labor," because of the brevity of the Old Testament statements about the topic. Thus we know only very little about this reality (in L. and W. Schottroff, *Mitarbeiter der Schöpfung,* 72).
114. Cf. above, p. 191.
115. For this, cf. above, p. 87.
116. Thus, e.g., according to the Mesopotamian Epic of Atraḫasis (cf. W. von Soden, *MDOG* 111, 1979, 1–33). For this, see G. Pettinato, *Das altorientalische Menschenbild und die sumerischen und akkadischen Schöpfungsmythen,* 1971 (see H. Kümmel, *WO* 7, 1973, 25–38); R. Albertz, "Die Kulturarbeit im Atraḫasīs-Epos im Vergleich zur biblischen Urgeschichte," in R. Albertz et al., eds., *Schöpfung und Befreiung,* FS C. Westermann, 1980, 38–57. Cf. also V. Hirth, *BZ* NF 33, 1989, 215, as well as Vol. I, pp. 226 + 239f.; and the text VAT 17019 (BE 13383) from Babylon, line 29: "He commanded the (forced) labor of the gods to be placed upon them"; the text is published by W. R. Mayer, "Ein Mythos von der Erschaffung des Menschen," *Or* 56, 1987, 55–68; the intepretation by comparison to the Old Testament has been made by H.-P. Müller, "Eine neue babylonische Menschenschöpfungserzählung," *Or* 58, 1989, 61–85.
117. See *TRE* 3, 614f.
118. That the "tabernacle" was artistically produced by human handicraft according to its heavenly primeval pattern (Exod. 25:9, 40) has nothing to do with the question here under discussion.
119. Prov. 6:6–11; 10:4ff.; 11:16; 12:11–17, 24, 27; 13:4; 14:23; 15:19; 18:9; 19:15, 24; 20:4, 13; 21:25; 22:13; 24:30–34; and 26:13–16.
120. Cf. V. Hirth, *BZ* NF 33, 1989, 221.
121. Cf. *TRE* 3, 615f.
122. Cf. below, pp. 235–238.

123. For the omission of the wife in the Sabbath commandment, see above, p. 343 n. 40, and p. 108.
124. Cf. above, p. 105, with 343 nn. 39–40.
125. See L. Köhler, *Theologie*, 4th ed., 143–145; M.-L. Henry, *Das Tier im religiösen Bewusstsein des alttestamentlichen Menschen*, 1958; W. Pangritz, *Das Tier in der Bibel*, 1963; J. Hempel, "Gott, Mensch und Tier im Alten Testament," in J. Hempel, ed., *Apoxysmata*, 1961 (BZAW 81), 198–229; O. Keel, "Tiere als Gefährten und Feinde des Menschen," *Heiliges Land* 7, 1979, 51–59; 8, 1980, 19–26; R. Bartelmus, "Die Tierwelt in der Bibel," *BN* 37, 1987, 11–37; and H. Kirchhoff, *Sympathie für die Kreatur*, 1987.
126. Gen. 1:20, 30; 2:19 (addition?); 9:10, 12, 15f.; Lev. 11:10, 46; Ezek. 47:9; similarly Ps. 104:30. Cf. above, p. 111–112.
127. Cf., e.g., the text "Enki and Ninḫursa(n)g(a)," in *ANET*, 2nd and 3d eds., 37–41 (esp. 38), and the textual excerpt in *RGT*, 2d ed., 110f.
128. Thus, however, G. von Rad, *Genesis: A Commentary*, rev. ed. [OTL], Philadelphia, 1972, 60, for this passage.
129. Thus with N. Lohfink; E. Zenger; and K. Koch. Cf. above, p. 115, with 347 n. 101.
130. See O. Keel, *Das Böcklein in der Milch seiner Mutter und Verwandtes—Im Lichte eines altorientalischen Bildmotivs*, 1980 (OBO 33); M. Haran, *ThZ* 41, 1985, 135–159; B. Janowski, *ZDPV* 102, 1986, 184–189 (see the additional literature there); and E. A. Knauf, *Bibl* 69, 1988, 153–169. The Urgaritic text *KTU* 1.23:14 does not provide an exact, extra-Israelite text for this custom.
131. Cf. Vol. I, pp. 125f.
132. M.-L. Henry, *Das Tier im religiösen Bewusstsein des alttestamentlichen Menschen*, 27.
133. See below, pp. 238–245.
134. Gilgamesh's friend Enkidu dwelt among the animals before he knew a woman, and for this reason the animals withdrew from him (Table 1), e.g., AOT, 2d ed., 152f.; *ANET*, 2d and 3d eds., 73ff.
135. See Vol. I, p. 249.
136. Cf. J. Jeremias, "Ich bin wie ein Löwe für Efraim," in *"Ich will euer Gott werden,"* 1981 (SBS 100), 75–95.
137. See H. D. Preuss, *Verspottung fremder Religionen im Alten Testament*, 1971 (BWANT 92), 108–110. See here also the possible "model," Akhenaton's hymn to the sun, although it certainly does not offer this figure of speech. For a different view of this, see C. Uehlinger, "Leviathan," *Bibl* 71, 1990, 499–526.
138. L. Köhler, *Theologie*, 4th ed., 145.
139. A small selection of views for this includes: the "creation of the wife as a punishment" takes place on account of the man's rejection of the animals as the helper in Gen. 2:4bff. (thus J. Hempel, "Gott, Mensch und Tier im *Alten Testament*," 207f.). Differently E. König (*Die Genesis*, 2d and 3d eds., 1925, 218): "Walking upright, a soulful glance, and a sparkling laugh" are lacking in animals.
140. For the Old Testament dietary laws, cf. finally E. Firmage, "The Biblical Dietary Laws and the Concept of Holiness," VT Suppl 41, 1990, 177–208. For "clean and unclean," cf. above, p. 57.
141. For the peace with animals, see H. Gross, *Die Idee des ewigen und allgemeinen Weltfriedens im Alten Orient und im Alten Testament*, 1956 (TThSt 7), 83ff.
142. For these comparisons between humans and the animal world, not to be discussed here, cf. W. Pangritz, *Das Tier in der Bibel*, 95ff.
143. Cf. in general as well as for the problem of professional wisdom and professional ethics: H. D. Preuss, *Einführung in die alttestamentliche Weisheitsliteratur*, 1987, e.g., 36ff. Since a great deal is discussed there, here only a little will be briefly described. In addition, see above, p. 169 for the righteous and the wicked, p. 199 for the industrious and the lazy, and p. 113 for the evaluation of speech in Proverbs.
144. Cf. D. Kellermann, *ThWAT* 7, col. 551 (see above, p. 372 n. 30); and above, pp. 126–129.
145. See also J. Barton, "Understanding Old Testament Ethics," 52ff.
146. For example, אַל = 'l ("not") plus the jussive instead of לֹא = l' ("no") with the imperfect; or Prov. 3:27–30 where one may not, in regard to the content, contrast each of the concluding

clauses of the verses to its preceding context. For this topic, cf. J. A. Fischer, "Ethics and Wisdom," *CBQ* 40, 1978, 293–310; and J. Bright, "The Apodictic Prohibition: Some Observations," *JBL* 92, 1973, 185–204.
147. Prov. 14:5, 25; 15:27; 17:15, 26; 18:5; 19:28; 21:15; 22:22; 24:23ff.; 25:18; 28:21; 29:7; and 31:5, 8f.; cf., however, 17:8; 19:6; and 21:14 where the sage, employing his own "measures," can also speak differently.
148. Cf. H. D. Preuss, *Deuteronomium*, 86ff. (lit.).
149. Cf. also Vol. I, pp. 184–194, for the relationship between deed and result.
150. See J. Halbe, "'Altorientalisches Weltordnungsdenken' und alttestamentliche Theologie," *ZThK* 76, 1979, 381–418. Cf. A. Soete, *Ethos der Rettung*, 246: "Therefore, this is a matter of the human as the realization of divine order."
151. For the ethos of wisdom, see J. Fichtner, *Die altorientalische Weisheit in ihrer israelitisch-jüdischen Ausprägung*, 1933 (BZAW 62), 12ff.; J. W. Gaspar, *Social Ideas in the Wisdom Literature of the Old Testament*, Washington, D. C. 1947; C. Westermann, *Roots of Wisdom*, Louisville, Ky., 1995; and B. Lang, "Weisheit als Ethos," *RHS* 33, 1990, 281–288. Moreover, I can judge only in a critical fashion the attempt by F.-J. Steiert to interpret the sapiential ethos in combination with other Old Testament texts (*Die Weisheit Israels—Ein Fremdkörper im Alten Testament?* 1990). Further, see H. van Oyen, *Ethik des Alten Testaments*, 141ff.; W. Zimmerli, *Theologie*, 6th ed., 136ff.; and A. Soete, *Ethos der Rettung*, 204ff. One must also point to the important book by J. Assmann that incorporates, yet also modifies and corrects, much of what is represented here in overarching correlations of understanding, *Ma'at: Gerechtigkeit und Unsterblichkeit im Alten Ägypten*, 1990, esp. 60ff. (sins against Ma'at; active and communicative solidarity; etc.).
152. The entire book of 4 Maccabees is later devoted to this theme.
153. Prov. 10:20; 11:13; 12:19; 13:3; 15:2, 23, 26, 30; 16:24; 20:15; 24:26; 25:9, 11, 15; 26:20–28; etc. See W. Bühlmann, *Vom rechten Reden und Schweigen*, 1976 (OBO 12); and also, in addition, J. Assmann, *Ma'at*, 69ff., etc. In Proverbs, statements are made about the power of language that are almost nowhere else made in the Old Testament.
154. Cf., e.g., Prov. 11:2; 16:18; 18:12; and 21:4 regarding pride; 12:8, 15; 13:10, 16; and 14:6f. concerning intelligence; 13:12 concerning hope; and 14:13, 29f.; 15:13, 15, 18; 17:22; 18:14; and 25:28 regarding emotions. Cf. also 11:17.
155. Prov. 2:16ff.; 5:3ff.; 6:24ff.; 7:5ff.; 22:14; 29:3; 30:20 (cf. p. 295); Joseph in Genesis 39 and Job 31:9f.
156. For how the legal texts and the prophets see this question, see p. 199. That in the Book of Proverbs the topics of poverty and wealth receive other emphases may only be indicated here (cf., e.g., Prov. 10:15 [18:11!]; 11:4; 18:23; 22:2, 7; 28:11, 22; etc.).
157. Prov. 3:27f.; 11:17, 24; 14:21, 31; 18:16; 19:17; 21:10; 22:9, 16; 23:10f.; 28:3, 27; 29:14; 30:14; etc. For the positive evaluation of the charging of interest (Prov. 28:8), cf. above, p. 192.
158. Cf. above, p. 200.
159. J. Fichtner, *Die altorientalische Weisheit in ihrer israelitisch-jüdischen Ausprägung*, 24.
160. Prov. 10:3, 16, 24, 30; 11:2, 3f., 6, 17f., 23, 31; 12:2, 14, 21, 28; 13:25; 14:27; 15:9, 24f.; 16:5, 7, 18; 17:13, 20; 18:10, 11, 16; 19:4, 5, 7, 23; 20:13, 17, 24; 21:18, 20f., 31; 22:4, 8f.; 26:27; etc. See H. D. Preuss, *Einführung in die alttestamentliche Weisheitsliteratur*, 50ff. ("JHWH in der älteren Weisheit"). Cf. Vol. I, pp. 184–194.
161. Prov. 10:29; 11:1; 15:3, 11; 16:11; 21:1–3, 30; and 22:19, 23. Also 23:11?
162. Prov. 6:30f.; 10:2; 16:8; 21:6; and 28:16, 22.
163. Prov. 11:1; 16:11; 20:10, 23; cf. Hos. 12:8; Amos 8:5; Micah 6:10f. Cf. the ancient Near Eastern comparative material in J. Fichtner, *Die altorientalische Weisheit in ihrer israelitisch-jüdischen Ausprägung*, 25ff.
164. Cf. above, p. 190. Cf., e.g., Exod. 23:1–3, 8; Deut. 1:17; 16:18f.; 27:25; Lev. 19:15, 35; then also Isa. 1:15–17, 23; 5:7, 23; Jer. 5:28; Amos 5:7, 10–12; Micah 3:1; Zeph. 3:1ff.; etc.
165. Cf. above, pp. 157ff.
166. For the role of the cult in Old Testament wisdom literature, cf. below, pp. 250f.
167. For the "pleasing" acts (often in antithesis to "abomination"), cf. Prov. 11:1, 20; 12:2, 22; 15:8; 16:7; and 18:22. For "abomination/loathing," cf. above, p. 189 and n. 28.

168. See H. D. Preuss, *Einführung in die alttestamentliche Weisheitsliteratur*, 56f., with an indication of similar statements in texts of Israel's cultural environment.
169. Cf. H. Brunner, *Altägyptische Weisheit*, 1988, 115, 201, 245, 246, 266, 467; and see the article "הוֹעֵבָה" = *tô'ēbâ* ("abomination"; appears in *ThWAT*).
170. Cf. above, p. 272 n. 29.
171. Thus, however, P. J. Nel, *The Structure and Ethos of the Wisdom Admonitions in Proverbs*, 1982 (BZAW 158). Cf. also R. Lux, "Die ungepredigte Bibel," 535f.
172. See H. D. Preuss, *Einführung in die alttestamentliche Weisheitsliteratur*, 114ff. (lit.); and D. Michel, *Qohelet*, Sheffield, 1988, 22ff.
173. Because Qoheleth often inquired about "profit" (יִתְרוֹן = *yitrôn*), one should not conclude that he was a businessman or at the least had a mercenary spirit. Cf. G. Ogden, *Qoheleth*, Sheffield, 1987, 22ff.
174. Qoh. 1:16–18; 2:4–11, 18, 23, 24f.; 3:13, 22; 4:4–12, 13–16; 5:2, 11, 17f.; 6:7–9, 11f.; 7:15–17; 8:15, 16f.; 9:9, 11; and 10:3, 18.
175. Cf., however, above, n. 192.
176. Qoh. 5:9ff.; 6:7ff.; 7:15; 8:5–14; and 9:2f., 11.
177. Qoh. 2:24; 3:12f.; 5:17f.; 8:15; 9:17f.; and 11:9f.
178. See H. D. Preuss, *Einführung in die alttestamentliche Weisheitsliteratur*, 69ff. (lit.); and J. Ebach, "Hiob/Hiobbuch," *TRE* 15, 360–380 (lit.).
179. See G. Fohrer, "The Righteous Man in Job 31," in *Essays in Old Testament Ethics*, 1–22; and E. Osswald, "Hiob 31 im Rahmen der alttestamentlichen Ethik," *Theologische Versuche* 2, 1970, 9–26.
180. Cf. Vol. I, pp. 184–194.
181. Prov. 16:1, 9, 33; 19:14, 21; 20:24; 21:1f., 30f.; and 25:2.
182. See H. D. Preuss, *Einführung in die alttestamentliche Weisheitsliteratur*, 137ff. (lit.).
183. See W. Eichrodt, *Theology*, 2:322–325; Th C. Vriezen, *Theology*, 336–342; and W. C. Kaiser, Jr., *Toward Old Testament Ethics*, 34ff.
184. See I. Cardellini, *Die biblischen "Sklaven"—Gesetze im Lichte des keilschriftlichen Sklavenrechts*, 1981 (BBB 55); and G. Kehrer, *"Vor Gott sind alle gleich,"* 1983 (see here the contributions of B. Lang and H. G. Kippenberg). Cf. also F. Crüsemann, "'Auge um Auge,' " *EvTh* 47, 1987, 419–422.
185. Female slaves are mentioned in Exod. 21:7, 20, 26f., 32; 23:12; Lev. 25:44; Deut. 15:12, 17; 21:10–14; Jer. 34:9ff.; 2 Chron. 28:10; and Neh. 7:67; special regulations are established for this in Exod. 21:4, 7–11.
186. That עִבְרִי = *'ibrî* (Heb.) once had meant a social status and did not refer to an ethnic origin is unimportant for our situation.
187. Slavery due to indebtedness is mentioned in Exod. 21:2–6, 7–11; 22:1f.; Lev. 25:39–55; Deut. 15:1f., 12–18; and 1 Sam. 25:10.
188. For Nehemiah 5, see K. Baltzer, in P. D. Miller, Jr., et al., *Ancient Israelite Religion*, FS F. M. Cross, Philadelphia 1987, 477–485.
189. Cf. pp. 107–109 and 344 n. 54, for the literature mentioned there.
190. The suspicion arises that in the statements of as well as about the woman in Prov. 31:10ff. it is the man who is describing the woman in terms of how he would have liked to see her.
191. For the Decalogue, cf. Vol. I, pp. 100–104.
192. Cf., however, the desecration of the messengers of David by the Ammonites and the following reaction to it according to 2 Samuel 10.
193. Cf. above, pp. 188 + 196.
194. See Vol. I, pp. 136–137.
195. Cf. above, p. 372 n. 30.

Chapter 13. The Worship of Israel (Cult)

1. S. Mowinckel, *Religion und Kultus*, 1953; R. Rendtorff, "Der Kultus im alten Israel," *JLH* 2, 1956, 1–12 (= TB 57, 1975, 89ff.); E. L. Ehrlich, *Kultsymbolik im Alten Testament und im nachbiblischen Judentum*, 1959; H.-J. Kraus, *Gottesdienst in Israel*, 2d ed., 1962; idem, "Gottesdienst im alten und im neuen Bund," *EvTh* 25, 1965, 171–206 (= *Biblisch-theologi-*

sche Aufsätze, 1972, 195ff.); H.-J. Hermisson, *Sprache und Ritus im alttestamentlichen Kult,* 1965 (WMANT 19); R. de Vaux, *Ancient Israel,* vol. 2: *Religious Institutions,* New York, 1961; H. H. Rowley, *Worship in Ancient Israel,* London, 1967; B. A. Levine, *In the Presence of the Lord,* Leiden, 1974; E. Otto and T. Schramm, *Fest und Freude,* 1977; J. Jeremias, *Theophanie,* 2d ed., 1977 (WMANT 10); M. Haran, *Temples and Temple Service in Ancient Israel,* Oxford, 1978; S. Terrien, *The Elusive Presence,* New York, 1978, 9ff.; F.-E. Wilms, *Freude vor Gott: Kult und Fest in Israel,* 1981; B. Diebner, "Gottesdienst. II: A. T.," *TRE* 14, 5–28 (lit.); idem, *Freude am Gottesdienst,* in J. Schreiner, ed., *Freude am Gottesdienst,* FS J. G. Plöger, 1983; J. Milgrom, *Studies in Cultic Theology and Terminology,* Leiden, 1983; and P. J. Budd, "Holiness and Cult," in R. E. Clements, ed., *The World of Ancient Israel,* Cambridge, 1989, 275–298. See further M. Eichrodt, *Theology of the Old Testament,* vol. 1 (OTL), Philadelphia, 1961, 98–177; L. Köhler, *Theologie,* 4th ed., 171ff.; Th. C. Vriezen, *An Outline of Old Testament Theology,* Oxford, 1958, 21–28, 276–314; W. Zimmerli, *Old Testament Theology in Outline,* Atlanta, 1978, 125–133; C. Westermann, *Elements of Old Testament Theology,* Atlanta, 174–216; J. L. McKenzie, *A Theology of the Old Testament,* Garden City, N.Y., 1974, 37ff.; and B. S. Childs, *Old Testament Theology in a Canonical Context,* Philadelphia, 1985.

2. For the form-critical situation regarding the "cult in the Old Testament," cf. the succinct study by B. Diebner, *TRE* 14, 16–21.

3. According to J. L. McKenzie (*A Theology of the Old Testament,* 32), the cultus was the most normal and most frequent form of the Israelites' experience of God.

4. For the election of Jerusalem, Zion, and the temple, cf. chapter 8 (pp. 39–51).

5. Cf. below, pp. 225–235.

6. Cf. already, pp. 189 + 206.

7. Cf. W. Zimmerli, *Theology,* 130–131; and above, p. 202. Also see J. Maier, *Zwischen den Testamenten,* 1990 (NEB AT, Supplement, vol. 3), 221ff.

8. Num. 16:5ff.; 17:20; Deut. 18:5; 21:5; 1 Sam. 2:28; Ps. 105:26; 1 Chron. 15:2; and 2 Chron. 29:11. Cf. chapter 9 (p. 52).

9. Cf. above, n. 4.

10. Cf. Vol. I, pp. 254–256.

11. Cf. Vol. I, pp. 65 + 255.

12. Cf. above, pp. 62–65.

13. Cf. above, pp. 64 + 197.

14. L. Köhler, *Theologie,* 4th ed., 171(ff.).

15. J. Wellhausen, *Israelitische und jüdische Geschichte,* 9th ed., 1958, 17; cf. his remark in *Grundrisse zum Alten Testament,* 1965 (TB 27), 77: "The cult is the general point of departure for religion even for the Israelites. This feature does not separate them from pagans but rather unites them with them."

16. Cf. above, pp. 63 + 87–88.

17. Cf. Isa. 1:10–17; Jer. 7:1ff., 21ff.; Hos. 6:6; Amos 4:4f.; 5:21–27; and Micah 6:6–8; then see also Pss. 50:7–15; 51:18f.; etc.

18. Vol. I, pp. 104ff.

19. W. Zimmerli's (*Theology,* 125–133) treatment of the cultus under the heading "Liturgical and Ritual Commandments" is too one-sided. However, it is important that for the average Israelite, in contrast to the Egyptian, the temple cultus was accessible. Consequently, the Israelite was not limited to encountering the deity when its divine image was moved outside the temple. Cf. J. Assmann, *Ägyptische Hymnen und Gebete,* 1975, 11ff., etc. The differently oriented interpretation of a (primarily only royal) temple cult of the preexilic period by E. S. Gerstenberger (*Psalms* I, Grand Rapids, 1988 [FOTL 14]) in my view is unfounded.

20. Cf. G. von Rad, *Old Testament Theology,* vol. 1: *The Theology of Israel's Historical Traditions,* New York, 1985, 242–243, and the New Testament's words of the eucharistic meal.

21. Exod. 12:11, 14, 27, 48; 13:6; 16:23, 25; 31:15; 32:5; Lev. 23:5f., 41; 25:2, 4; Deut. 15:2; etc.; cf. also Exod. 5:1. For "to serve him/me," see already Exod. 3:18; 7:16, 26; 8:16; and 9:1, 13.

22. In Israel's ancient Near Eastern environment, it could be stated differently. Cf., e.g., Enuma eliš VI, 8, 34f. (AOT, 2d ed., 121f.; and *ANET,* 2d and 3d eds., 68); and H. Bonnet, *Reallexikon der ägyptischen Religionsgeschichte,* 2d ed., 1971, 405–411, "Kult/Kultbild."

23. Exod. 12:25f.; 13:5; 30:16; Num. 4:47; 8:11; Josh. 22:27; 2 Chron. 35:10, 16; etc.
24. Cf. H. Ringgren, *ThWAT* 5, cols. 1010–1012. The verb עבד (*'bd;* "to labor, work, serve") can stand also for the worship of the deity as well as for human labor, and so forth.
25. Cf., however, e.g., W. Herrmann, *Der Verkehr des Christen mit Gott,* (1886), 7th ed., 1921. There is no mention of the cult in this book.
26. Thus (with and after V. Grønbech) esp. J. Pedersen, *Israel—Its Life and Culture,* I/II, 1926, 99f.
27. Thus, e.g., S. Mowinckel, *Religion und Kultus,* 1953, 73ff.
28. Thus A. Weiser, *Glaube und Geschichte im Alten Testament,* 1961, 303ff. ("Zur Frage nach den Beziehungen der Psalmen zum Kult").
29. Thus C. Westermann, *Das Loben Gottes in den Psalmen,* 1954 (etc.), 65ff.
30. Cf., e.g., W. Beyerlin, *Herkunft und Geschichte der ältesten Sinaitraditionen,* 1961.
31. Cf., however, Vol. I, pp. 253–254.
32. With R. Gyllenberg, "Kultus und Offenbarung," in FS S. Mowinckel, Oslo, 1955, 72–84.
33. Cf. Vol. I, pp. 208ff. + 226ff.
34. "The event of salvation does not primarily obtain through ritual enactment its actuality and significance for the future, but rather possessed these elements from the beginning for this expression of faith:" W. H. Schmidt, "Wort und Ritus," *PTh* 74, 1985, 68–83, esp. 81, and there in opposition to E. Otto and T. Schramm, *Fest und Freude,* 1977, 17.
35. Cf. "Word," Vol. I, pp. 195–200.
36. Cf. Vol. I, pp. 65–67.
37. Isa. 30:27ff.; Joel 2:10f.; Micah 1:3ff.; Habakkuk 3; Pss. 18:8–16; 77:17–20; and Job 38:1f.
38. Cf. below, pp. 224ff.
39. Cf. the stimulating and rich volume by H. Spieckermann, *Heilsgegenwart: Eine Theologie der Psalmen,* 1989 (FRLANT 148).
40. Cf. Vol. I, pp. 235f.
41. R. Rendtorff, "Kult, Mythos und Geschichte im Alten Israel," in E. Blum et al., eds., *Die Hebräische Bibel und ihre zweifache Nachgeschichte,* FS H. Rendtorff, 1958, 121–129, esp. 128 (= TB 57, 110ff., esp. 117).
42. Cf. below, pp. 231–233.
43. Differently E. Otto and T. Schramm, *Fest und Freude,* 17f., 25, 29, 31, 33–35, 61ff., etc. Cf. E. Otto, *TRE* 11, 96–106. At this point one might again raise the question (as was raised before in connection with history, Vol. I, pp. 219f. and will be raised in the discussion of eschatology, chapter 14, pp. 272f.; cf. pp. 138–139.) concerning the Israelite understanding of time for which a fundamental and comprehensive investigation continues to be lacking.
44. See M. Noth, "Die Vergegenwärtigung des Alten Testaments in der Verkündigung," *EvTh* 12, 1952/1953, 6–17 (-*Probleme alttestamentlicher Hermeneutik,* ed. C. Westermann, 2d ed., 1963 [TB 11], 54ff.).
45. Cf. Vol. I, pp. 45 + 198; and above, p. 101f.
46. Exod. 10:2; 12:26f.; 13:8, 14–16; Deut. 4:9f.; 6:7–20; 11:19ff.; 32:7; and Josh. 4:6f., 21–24. For this topic, cf. also Judg. 6:33; Pss. 44:2; 48:13–15; and 78:3f.
47. Cf. Vol. I, p. 45.
48. Cf. above, pp. 23f.
49. Cf. also H.-J. Kraus, *Theology of the Psalms* (CC), Minneapolis, 1986, 101–106 ("Theology of Worship").
50. Cf. below, pp. 245–250.
51. Lev. 20:8; 21:8, 15; 22:9; etc. Cf. Exod. 31:13.
52. However, L. Köhler, *Theologie,* 4th ed., 171.
53. For this topic, cf. G. Fohrer, *History of Israelite Religion,* Nashville, 1972, and the sections especially that deal with questions about the cultus.
54. Many things from earlier sections (e.g., 3. Sinai/Moses; 6. Ancestors; 7. Kinship; 8. Zion/Jerusalem; 9. Priests/Levites) must once more be mentioned, since the synopses that are sought here will not allow one to avoid some repetition.
55. Cf. below, pp. 235–238.
56. Cf. below, pp. 240f.
57. Cf. the sacrifice of the Babylonian primordial flood hero Utnapishtim or before that of the

Sumerian Ziusudra: *RGT,* 2d ed., 115, 122. Cf. there also the "odor of appeasement" (Gen. 8:21). To this term, cf. T. Kronholm, "רוח *rwḥ*," *ThWAT* 7, cols. 382–385, esp. 385. Cf. further below, p. 389 n. 285.

58. An intentional inconsistency is found in Exodus 12, the Passover.
59. Cf. above, pp. 7f.
60. See R. de Vaux, *Ancient Israel,* 2:289–294.
61. Apart from these passages in the ancestral narratives, the sanctuary of Mamre is nowhere else mentioned in the Old Testament.
62. Cf. above, pp. 41ff.
63. Cf. above, pp. 7f.
64. Cf. Vol. I, p. 70, in regard to Exod. 24:11.
65. What these Teraphim were (even gods of healing?) and what they looked like is not to be discussed here (cf. also Judg. 17:5; 18:14, 17ff.; and 1 Sam. 19:13ff.). See S. Schroer, *In Israel gab es Bilder,* 1987 (OBO 74), 136ff.
66. Gen. 31:34: Rachel had placed the "household god" under the saddle of her camel and then sat upon it even though she was in "the way of women" (v. 35). For this topic, cf. H. D. Preuss, *Verspottung fremder Religionen im Alten Testament,* 1971 (BWANT 92), 56ff.
67. Cf. the references to bibliography on pp. 315–316 nn. 85 + 96.
68. Possibly with expansions in Genesis 17 from the postexilic period.
69. Cf. Vol. I, p. 100.
70. L. Rost, *Das kleine Credo,* 1965, 101ff. Rost also was responsible for the long-standing and much appropriated thesis that Leviticus 16 with its "goat for Azazel" was the ritual for just the reverse, i.e., the changing of pastureland in order to return again to the wilderness. Cf. below, pp. 233f.
71. For the wider Old Testament history of Passover, cf. below, pp. 228f.
72. Cf., however, below, p. 228.
73. Cf. Vol. I, pp. 61, 69, 143, and 281. See there pp. 139–144, 95–100, and 40–46 also for "YHWH," for the figure of Moses, as well as for the exodus from Egypt.
74. For the Sinai covenant, Sinai tradition, and Sinai texts, Exodus 19; 20; 24; and 34, cf. Vol. I, pp. 64–76.
75. Is the blood of circumcision meant here?
76. See W. H. Schmidt, "Wort und Ritus," *PTh* 74, 1985, 68–78, esp. 72ff.; and Vol. I, p. 70, for the text, the rite, and their meaning.
77. Differently, H. Gese, "Die Sühne," in *Zur biblischen Theologie,* 3d ed., 1989, 85–106, esp. 98f. and 123.
78. For this passage, cf. L. Perlitt, *Bundestheologie im Alten Testament,* 1969 (WMANT 36), 190ff.
79. Cf. Vol. I, pp. 77–84; and the work by L. Perlitt (cf. the previous note).
80. Cf. Vol. I, p. 78.
81. Cf., e.g., H. Schmid, *Mose: Überlieferung und Geschichte,* 1968 (BZAW 110), 81ff.
82. For the "ark," cf. Vol. I, pp. 253–254.
83. For the "tent (of meeting)," cf. Vol. I, pp. 254–256.
84. Cf. Vol. I, p. 255.
85. For this, see, e.g., K. Jaroš, *Die Stellung des Elohisten zur kanaanäischen Religion,* 1974 (OBO 4), 272ff.; and M. Rose, *Deuteronomist und Jahwist,* 1981 (AThANT 67), 301ff.
86. Cf. S. Schroer, *In Israel gab es Bilder,* 1987 (OBO 74), 104–115.
87. For these problems, cf. Vol. I, pp. 104–117. For the Sabbath, cf. below, pp. 235–238.
88. See above, n. 82.
89. Judg. 20:1, 3; 21:1, 5, 8; 1 Sam. 7:5ff.; 10:17; Josh. 9:3; 10:1ff.; 18:25; Judg. 6:11, 24; 8:27, 32; 9:5; Josh. 19:47; and Judg. 18:29; etc.
90. Cf. R. de Vaux, *Ancient Israel,* 2:302–311; and H.-J. Kraus, *Gottesdienst in Israel,* 2d ed., 1962, 160ff.
91. Cf. Vol. I, pp. 57–59.
92. Judg. 6:25–32; 13:15–23; 1 Sam. 1:3, 21; 2:12ff.; 6:14; 7:9f., 16f.; 9:12f.; and 10:8.
93. For the priests, cf. above, pp. 89ff.
94. Cf. below, pp. 224–235.

95. See J. Gray, *The Legacy of Canaan,* 2d ed., 1965 (VT Suppl 5), 192ff.; D. Kinet, *Ugarit,* 1981 (SBS 104), 144ff.; and O. Loretz, *Ugarit und die Bibel,* 1990, 121f. For the prohibition against boiling a kid in its mother's milk, cf. above, p. 376 n. 130.
96. Cf. below, pp. 238–245.
97. Cf. Vol. I, pp. 111f.
98. Cf. above, pp. 23f.
99. For this, see Vol. I, pp. 253–254.
100. Cf. chapter 8 (pp. 39ff.) and Vol. I, pp. 173f., regarding the "Righteousness of YHWH."
101. Cf. chapter 7 (pp. 19ff.).
102. Cf. above, p. 45.
103. Cf. above, pp. 32f.
104. See Vol. I, pp. 152–159.
105. Cf. Vol. I, pp. 145f.
106. For this problem, cf. the instructive overview by W. Dietrich, *Israel und Kanaan,* 1979 (SBS 94). Cf. in addition Vol. I, p. 342 n. 668.
107. Cf. also Jeremiah 44; Ezekiel 8 + 23; and 2 Kings 16:7ff.
108. See below as well as H.-D. Hoffmann, *Reform und Reformen,* 1980 (AThANT 66).
109. Cf. above, p. 191, for them and for the Nazirites.
110. See above, pp. 53 + 65.
111. Vol. I, pp. 165–166.
112. For the more exact problem of the temple building as well as its outfitting, significance, and history, see pp. 42ff. It was important that, in contrast to the other cultures in Israel's contemporary world, Old Testament worship was not supported by its own landownership, since it depended, not on such possessions, but rather on gifts from the Israelites. Cf. F. Crüsemann, "Religiöse Abgaben und ihre Kritik im Alten Testament," in W. Lienemann, ed., *Die Finanzen der Kirche,* 1989, 485–524.
113. Cf. 1 Kings 14:16; 15:34; 16:2, 19, 26, 31; 22:53; 2 Kings 3:3; 10:29, 31; 13:2, 6, 11 etc., on through 2 Kings. See J. Debus, *Die Sünde Jeroboams,* 1967 (FRLANT 93).
114. For the latter, see 1 Kings 12:32; 13:33; 15:14; 22:44; 2 Kings 12:4; 14:4; 15:4, 35; and 17:32.
115. See K.-D. Schunck, "במה," *ThWAT* 1, cols. 662–667; P. Welten, "Kulthöhe," *BRL,* 2d ed., 194f.; and I. W. Provan, *Hezekiah and the Books of Kings,* 1988 (BZAW 172), 57ff., for the theme of במה = *bāmâ* ("high place") in the Books of Kings.
116. See J. Gamberoni, "מצבה *maṣṣebâh,*" *ThWAT* 4, cols. 1064–1074; and Vol. I, p. 110.
117. See J. C. de Moor, "אשרה," *ThWAT* 1, cols. 473–481; S. M. Olyan, *Asherah and the Cult of Yahweh in Israel,* Atlanta, Ga., 1988; and K. Koch, *Aschera als Himmelskönigin in Jerusalem, UF* 20, 1988, 97–120. Cf. also Vol. I, pp. 110f. See also Judg. 6:26; 1 Kings 14:23; and 2 Kings 17:10.
118. Cf. also Hos. 4:13; 10:1–8; "under every green tree": Deut. 12:2; 1 Kings 14:23; 2 Kings 16:4; 17:32; Jer. 2:20, etc.
119. Cf. S. Schroer, *In Israel gab es Bilder.*
120. Although their translation and interpretation are debated (cf. only S. Mittmann, *ZDPV* 97, 1981, 139–152), these texts are found, e.g., in K. A. D. Smelik, *Historische Dokumente aus dem alten Israel,* 1987, 138f., 141ff.; and *TUAT* II/4, 1988, 556ff., 561ff. Cf. Vol. I, pp. 110 + 141f.
121. K. Koch, *UF* 20, 1988, 99.
122. YHWH occurs here in the abbreviated form of the name. Cf. Vol. I, p. 140.
123. The texts in *ANET,* 2d and 3d eds., 491.
124. See H. Spieckermann, *Juda unter Assur in der Sargonidenzeit,* 1982 (FRLANT 129), 170ff.; and M. Hutter, *Hiskija, König von Juda,* 1982.
125. See N. Lohfink, "Zur neueren Diskussion über 2 Kön 22–23," in N. Lohfink, ed., *Das Deuteronomium,* Louvain, 1985 (BETL 68), 24–28 (cf. also Lohfink's essay in P. D. Miller, Jr., et al., eds., *Ancient Israelite Religion,* FS F. M. Cross, Philadelphia, 1987, 459–475); K. Koch, *UF* 20, 1988 (102–107); K. Višaticki, *Die Reform des Josija und die religiöse Heterodoxie in Israel,* 1987; and H. Spieckermann, *Juda unter Assur in der Sargonidenzeit.*
126. Cf. H.-D. Hoffmann (see above, n. 108).

127. Cf. H. D. Preuss, *Deuteronomium.*
128. For the Asherahs and maṣṣebôt, cf. Vol. I, pp. 110f.; and the literature cited above in nn. 116–117.
129. See W. Roth, "Deuteronomistisches Geschichtswerk/Deuteronomistische Schule," *TRE* 8, 543–552 (lit.). In addition to the articles in *TRE,* cf. for the corpora of texts mentioned in the following discussion the so-called "Introductions in the Old Testament," especially the ones by O. Kaiser and R. Smend. See further, Vol. I, pp. 188f. and 199f., as well as the index.
130. Cf. below, p. 228.
131. Cf. Vol. I, pp. 180f. and 229, as well as above, p. 45.
132. L. Auerbach, "Die Babylonische Datierung," *VT* 2, 1952, 334–342; "Der Wachsel des Jahres-Anfangs," *VT* 9, 1959, 113–121; and "Die Umschaltung," *VT* 10, 1960, 69f.; and H.-J. Kraus, *Gottesdienst in Israel,* 2d ed., 1962, 59–61.
133. Cf. 1 Kings 8:23ff. Deuteronomistic: temple as the place of prayer, but YHWH hears in heaven (see Vol. I, pp. 250–253).
134. For his message, cf. above, pp. 93f.
135. Vol. I, pp. 167–170.
136. Both groups of text are not uniform, however.
137. See E. Zenger, *Gottes Bogen in den Wolken,* 1983 (SBS 112). For Genesis 23 (land where the ancestors are buried), cf. Vol. I, p. 122.
138. See above, p. 15.
139. See H. D. Preuss, "Heiligkeitsgesetz," *TRE* 14, 713–718 (lit.).
140. For these texts: H. Utzschneider, *Das Heiligtum und das Gesetz: Studien zur Bedeutung der sinaitischen Heiligtumstexte (Ex 25–40; Lev 8–9),* 1988 (OBO 77). Utzschneider also certainly sees here many texts from the later, postexilic period.
141. See below, pp. 226 + 230 + 233.
142. For the sacrifices, cf. above, p. 180, and below, pp. 233f. + 242f.
143. Cf. also below, pp. 241f.
144. Cf. above, p. 62.
145. 1 Chron. 15:16ff.; 29:20; 2 Chron. 5:12f.; 20:21, 26, 28; 23:13; and 29:27.
146. Cf. the descriptions of the "history of Israel."
147. Cf. also Deut. 27:3f., 12ff. along with the Chronicler's reinterpetation of the localization of blessing and cursing on Gerizim and/or Ebal. See the commentaries for this.
148. See J. Hausmann, *Israels Rest,* 1987 (BWANT 124), 5ff.
149. Cf. also (besides the literature cited on pp. 378–379 n. 1): R. Martin-Achard, *Essai biblique sur les fêtes d'Israel,* Geneva, 1974; G. Sauer, "Israels Feste und ihr Verhältnis zum Jahweglauben," in G. Braulik et al., eds., *Studien zum Pentateuch,* FS W. Kornfeld, 1977, 135–141; E. Otto, "Feste und Feiertage. II: A. T.," *TRE* 10, 96–106; D. Michel, "Fest (AT)," *NBL* 1, cols. 666–668; and P. Weimar, "Kult und Fest: Aspekte eines Kultverständnisses im Pentateuch," in K. Richter, ed., *Liturgie – ein vergessenes Thema der Theologie?* 1986 (QD 107), 65–83. Also see B. Kedar-Kopfstein, "גח *ḥag,*" *ThWAT* 2, cols. 730–744; O. Procksch, *Theologie,* 543–551; and W. H. Schmidt, *Alttestamentlicher Glaube,* 6th ed., 142ff.
150. Num. 10:10; 28:14; 2 Kings 4:23; Isa. 1:13f.; Lev. 16:29; Judg. 20:26; 1 Kings 21:9; 2 Kings 4:23; Joel 1:14; Ps. 81:4; etc.
151. Cf. above, pp. 223f., for these two festivals.
152. Isa. 1:14; 30:29; Jer. 9:16ff.; 14:12f.; 33:11; 36:6; Amos 4:4f.; 5:21; Micah 1:8; 6:7; etc.
153. Cf. W. H. Schmidt, BK II/1, 251–253.
154. Or is the statement, "You were brought out of Egypt at this time" (v. 15), an addition?
155. Cf. Vol. I, p. 126.
156. See J. Halbe, *Das Privilegrecht Jahwes,* 1975 (FRLANT 114), 170ff.
157. The oldest Passover text is probably Exod. 12:21–23 (see below).
158. Cf. Vol. I, pp. 40ff.
159. See G. Braulik, "Die Freude des Festes," in his *Studien zur Theologie des Deuteronomiums,* 1988 (SBAB 2), 161–218.
160. Is the participation of the married woman obviously understood? Cf. 1 Sam. 1:3f. For the expression "before YHWH," cf. R. Sollamo, *SEÅ* 50, 1985, 21–32; and M. D. Fowler, *ZAW* 99, 1987, 384–390, who see differently the closeness of this formula to worship.

161. Cf., e.g., K. Elliger, HAT I/4, 1966, for this passage.
162. Cf. above, p. 221 and n. 132.
163. Cf. *TRE* under the appropriate heading.
164. There it could have been, at the most, "straw mats."
165. Cf. below, p. 243.
166. J. Wellhausen (*Prolegomena zur Geschichte Israels,* 4th ed., 1895, 82ff.) preferred to speak here of the "denaturalization" (p. 90) as well as the historicization of religion.
167. See D. Kellermann, "מצה = *maṣṣah,*" *ThWAT* 4, cols. 1074–1081 (lit.).
168. Differingly, J. Halbe, "Erwägungen zu Ursprung und Wesen des Massotfestes," *ZAW* 87, 1975, 324–346.
169. M. Noth, *Exodus: A Commentary* (OTL), Philadelphia, 1962, 95 (the "12:8" refers to Exod. 12:8).
170. See esp. E. Otto, "פסח *pasaḥ*/פסח *paesaḥ,*" *ThWAT* 6, cols. 659–682 (lit.). Then also B. Janowski, "Azazel—biblisches Gegenstück zum ägyptischen Seth?" in E. Blum et al., eds., *Die Hebräische Bibel,* FS R. Rendtorff, 1990, 97–110 (esp. 100f.); and R. Kaschani, "Das jüdische Pesach und seine Ursprünge in der Sicht israelischer Forscher", in *Der Freund Israels* 153, 1990 (2), 4–9.
171. Moreover, he stands in some degree of tension to the YHWH who also smites; cf., e.g., J. Schreiner, "Exodus 12, 21–23 und das israelitische Pascha," in G. Braulik et al., eds., *Studien zum Pentateuch,* FS W. Kornfeld, 1977, 69–90 (= *Segen für die Völker,* 1987, 38ff.).
172. For the later components, see below.
173. Thus for a long time, scholarship was in agreement with L. Rost, *Das kleine Credo,* 101–112. According to him, the festival has to do with a ritual of nomadic shepherds of small cattle and sheep and their change of pasture during the New Year into the settled country, after the harvest began and the harvested fields became available to the herds for grazing. The ritual of Azazel may have been the counterpart to the fall entrance into the region of the steppes in search of pastureland. The aim of this apotropaic ritual that was analogous in a way to magic was to protect through this practice the herd and its owners. The author must certainly admit that the thesis of his teacher concerning the Passover about a *pre*-Israelite stage of the ritual continues to possess some probability. For example, "house" could easily have replaced "tent" later on. Cf. D. Michel, *NBL* 1, cols. 667f., and the "before the contact with Canaan" in B. Janowski, *UF* 12, 1980, 250. For Azazel and Leviticus 16, see below, pp. 252f.
174. See J. Schreiner, "Exodus 12, 21–23 und das israelitische Pascha," in G. Braulik et al., eds., *Studien zum Pentateuch,* FS W. Kornfeld, 1977, 69–90 (and his *Segen für die Völker,* 1987, 38ff.). His application of the JE text to the Assyrian threat (with reference to 2 Kings 23:21–23: according to Schreiner there was no festival prior to Josiah) cannot be demonstrated.
175. Thus B. Janowski, *UF* 12, 1980, 250f. For זבח = *zebaḥ,* see below, p. 239.
176. Cf. the overview of E. Otto, *TRE* 11, 97–99; and *ThWAT* 6, cols. 669–674; and for these texts also M. Köckert, "Leben in Gottes Gegenwart: Zum Verständnis des Gesetzes in der priesterschriftlichen Literatur," *JBTh* 4, 1989, 29–61 (esp. 44–51 and 49–51, which deal with the reemphasis within the P section by means of later additions).
177. Were these adjustments made in connection with the situation of the exile, when the temple was destroyed? Cf. M. Köckert, "Leben in Gottes Gegenwart," 29–61 (esp. 47); and also J. Schreiner, "Exodus 12, 21–23 und das israelitische Pascha," 89.
178. Cf. p. 166.
179. See R. Schmitt, *Exodus und Passah,* 2d ed., 1982 (OBO 7).
180. For this, see also P. Laaf, in H.-J. Fabry, ed., *Bausteine biblischer Theologie,* FS G. J. Botterweck, 1977 (BBB 50), 169–183.
181. Cf. E. Otto, *TRE* 11, 100.
182. See E. Kutsch, *Das Herbstfest in Israel,* diss., Mainz, 1955 (cf. *ThLZ* 81, 1956, cols. 493–495); T. Kronholm, "סכך *sākak* und Deriv.," *ThWAT* 5, cols. 838–856; and S. Springer, *Neuinterpretation im Alten Testament,* 1979 (SBB), 13–108.
183. Lev. 23:39; Judg. 21:19; Ezek. 45:25; Hos. 9:5; cf. 1 Kings 8:2, 65; 12:32; etc.
184. See below, pp. 233f.
185. Cf. esp. H. Cazelles, "Nouvel an (Fête du)," DBS 6, Paris, 1960, cols. 555–645 (there also

cols. 622ff. for the history of scholarship). See the articles appearing in *TRE,* including the literature listed there. Further, see K. van der Toorn in the Louvain Congress volume (VT Suppl 43).

186. Cf. above, p. 383 n. 132.
187. Cf. O. Loretz, *Ugarit und die Bibel,* 1990 (also see Ugarit in the index).
188. Cf. the rituals for the *akitu* festival in *TUAT* II/2, 212ff.
189. Cf. pp. 231–233.
190. Does the original form of Psalm 8 belong here? Cf. Vol. I, p. 228.
191. Thus esp. A. Weiser, *The Psalms: A Commentary* (OTL), Philadelphia, 1962, for his interpretation of the psalms. However, also G. von Rad, *Das formgeschichtliche Problem des Hexateuch,* 1938 (BWANT 4/26) [cf. TB 8, 9ff.]; and R. Rendtorff, TB 57, 1975, 95f., 106. For a criticism of this, see E. Kutsch, *Verheissung und Gesetz,* 1973 (BZAW 131), 153ff. Cf. also Vol. I, pp. 68 + 84f.
192. This is also the case in regard to the "tent festival of Beersheba" that H.-J. Kraus has discovered (*Gottesdienst in Israel,* 2d ed., 1962, 82, 155ff.).
193. For "YHWH as king," see Vol. I, pp. 152–159. There (pp. 316f. n. 98) one finds literature for the YHWH enthronement psalms and for a festival of enthronement.
194. Altogether S. Mowinckel pointed to 46 psalms that he related to the theme of the festival of YHWH's enthronement. Cf. *Psalmenstudien* 2, 1922 (new printing 1961).
195. Thus also in Ugarit. Cf. O. Loretz, *Ugarit und die Bibel,* 1990 (see the index, esp. 96ff.).
196. While today the temporary loss of the sovereignty of Marduk is (correctly) denied, this idea was considered to be out of the question for Yahwistic faith. Still, the kind of kingship represented by Baal's rule, which was temporarily lost in a repeated struggle, does not remain out of consideration. Adherents of this view continue in spite of the important expressions on the topic by P. Welten ("Königsherrschaft Jahwes und Thronbesteigung: Bemerkungen unerledigten Fragen," *VT* 32, 1982, 297–310); and B. Janowski ("Das Königtum Gottes in den Psalmen: Bemerkungen zu einem neuen Gesamtentwurf," *ZThK* 86, 1989, 389–454 [lit.!], esp. 425ff.).
197. Thus with E. Otto, *BN* 42, 1988, 100.
198. Cf. B. Janowski, "Das Königtum Gottes in den Psalmen," 430ff.
199. However, see H.-J. Kraus, *Gottesdienst in Israel,* 2d ed., 1962, 242ff.; W. Vischer, *Die Immanuel-Botschaft im Rahmen des königlichen Zionfestes,* 1955 (ThSt 45).
200. See B. Janowski, "Das Königtum Gottes in den Psalmen," 428ff.
201. E. Otto, *BN* 42, 95.
202. B. Janowski, "Das Königtum Gottes in den Psalmen," 417f.
203. Ibid., 407.
204. Ibid., 415. Thus there is already here a connection of the sovereignty of God and teaching (and not for the first time in the proclamation of Jesus).
205. Ibid., 433.
206. Ibid., 445.
207. Cf. the commentaries: e.g., M. Noth, *Leviticus: A Commentary* (OTL), rev. ed., Philadelphia, 1977; and K. Elliger, HAT I/4.
208. Thus there is, e.g., already in v. 29a a final note; between v. 2 and v. 3 there is no clear connection; vv. 6 + 11; 9b + 15, and 4 + 32 point to duplications and tensions; and so forth.
209. See B. Janowski, *Sühne als Heilsgeschehen,* 1982 (WMANT 55); N. Kiuchi, *The Purification Offering in the Priestly Literature,* 1987 (JSOT Suppl 56), 87ff.; and F. H. Gorman, *The Ideology of Ritual,* 1990 (JSOT Suppl 91), 61ff., 181ff.
210. Cf. Lev. 14:2b–8, 48–53; and Zech. 5:5–11. For the surrounding cultures, cf. the particulars in B. Janowski, *Sühne als Heilsgeschehen,* 210f. = nn. 137 and 211ff.; e.g., the Hittite text in *TUAT* II/2, 285–288; and O. Loretz, *Ugarit und die Bibel,* 1990, 115–221.
211. For the differentiation between the lifting up of both hands and only one, cf. D. P. Wright, J. Milgrom, and H.-J. Fabry, "סמך *sāmak,*" *ThWAT* 5, cols. 880–889, esp. 884ff.
212. For the distinction between a small (for the sacrifice by an individual) and great (for the sacrifice by the community or by the high priest as their cultic representative) blood rite, see B. Janowski, *Sühne als Heilsgeschehen,* 222ff., etc.: [the small blood rite: "some of the blood of the animal offered as a sin sacrifice on the horns of the altar of burnt sacrifice standing in

the forecourt of the precinct of the sanctuary . . . , the residual blood poured out on its foundation . . . , where it can run off in a drain (cf. Ezek. 43:13); the large blood ritual: with "the application of blood . . . on the curtains . . . before the holy of holies (sprinkling seven times . . . with the finger) as well as on the incense altar standing in front" (p. 223); the remainder of the blood is poured out on the base of the altar of burnt sacrifice]. For the significance of the blood in these connections, cf. the article, "דם" = *dām* in *THAT* and *ThWAT* as well as F. H. Gorman, *The Ideology of Ritual*, 181ff. See below, p. 388 n. 264.

213. See B. Janowski, *Sühne als Heilsgeschehen*, 271ff.

214. According to L. Rost, *Das kleine Credo*, 107f. (and above, p. 378 n. 173 for the Passover lamb): a sacrifice of pacification for the lord of the wilderness, a wilderness demon, during the change of pasture by small cattle nomads in the wilderness regions, i.e., winter quarters. Differently now B. Janowski, "Azazel—biblisches Gegenstück zum ägyptischen Seth?" in E. Blum et al., eds., *Die Hebräische Bibel*, FS R. Rendtorff, 1990, 97–110.

215. Cf. also O. Loretz, *Leberschau, Sündenbock, Asasel in Ugarit und Israel*, 1985 (UBL 3); A. Schenker, *Versöhnung und Sühne*, 1981 (there pp. 111ff. on Leviticus 16). For the far-reaching questions (in connection, e.g., with the theses of R. Girard), cf. among others R. Schwager, *Brauchen wir einen Sündenbock?* 1978.

216. Cf. H. Gese, "Die Sühne," in *Zur biblische Theologie*, 3d ed., 1989, 85–106; and esp. B. Janowski, *Sühne als Heilsgeschehen;* esp. 198ff. for Leviticus 16. For the theme "atonement," cf. also above, p. 180.

217. Cf. above, pp. 210 + 214; and Vol. I, p. 10.

218. For the problem of the translation and identification, cf., e.g., M. Zohary, *Pflanzen der Bibel*, 1983, 96f. Additional literature is present in A. van der Wal, *Planten uit de Bijbel*, Amsterdam, 1982, 40–42.

219. Cf., e.g., A. Falkenstein and W. von Soden, *Sumerische und akkadische Hymnen und Gebete*, 1953, 306. Rituals of purification are found in *TUAT* II/2, 169–175. Also see R. Gieshammer, "Reinheit, kultische," *LÄ* V, cols. 212ff., along with additional key terms of reference.

220. Cf. Vol. I, p. 257.

221. Cf. for this problem W. Zwickel, *Räucherkult und Räuchergeräte*, 1990 (OBO 97), 188f., 195.

222. For this passage, cf. B. Janowski, *Sühne als Heilsgeschehen*, 123–129. Exhaustive and with other nuances is the study by V. (A.) Hurovitz, "Isaiah's Impure Lips and Their Purification in Light of Akkadian Sources," *HUCA* 60, 1989, 39–89.

223. See E. Jenni, *Die theologische Begründung des Sabbatgebotes im Alten Testament*, 1956 (ThSt 46); N. E. A. Andreasen, *The Old Testament Sabbath*, Missoula, Mont., 1972; N. Lohfink, *Unsere grossen Wörter*, 1977 (and other editions), 190–208; K. A. Strand, ed., *The Sabbath in Scripture and History*, Washington, D.C., 1982; F. Crüsemann, *Bewahrung der Freiheit: Das Thema des Dekalogs in socialgeschichtlicher Perspektive*, 1983, 53–58, esp. 58: "The required rest is the reverse of slave labor" (thus with reference to the "house of slaves" in the prologue of the Decalogue in Deut. 5:6; and Exod. 20:2); G. Robinson, *The Origin and Development of the Old Testament Sabbath*, Frankfurt am Main and Bern 1988 (cf. ZAW 92, 1980, 32–42); R. Bartelmus, "Mk 2,27 und die ältesten Fassungen des Arbeitsruhegebotes im Alten Testament: Biblisch-theologische Beobachtungen zur Sabbatfrage," *BN* 41, 1988, 41–64; M. Köckert, "Leben in Gottes Gegenwart, 29–61 (esp. 51–56 for the Sabbath in P); E. Spier, *Der Sabbat*, 1989; M. Köckert, "Das Gebot des siebten Tages," in FS J. Henkys, 1989, 170–186; and J. Scharbert, "Biblischer Sabbat und modernes Wochenende," in J. Zmijewski, ed., *Die Alttestamentliche Botschaft*, FS H. Reinelt, 1990, 285–306. Cf. also W. H. Schmidt, *Alttestamentlicher Glaube*, 6th ed., 105ff.

224. Cf. Gen. 8:22; Josh. 5:12; Isa. 14:4; 24:8; 33:8; etc.

225. For the general problems of the Decalogue, see Vol. I, pp. 100–104.

226. Of course in Exod. 20:11 the verb נוח = *nwḥ* ("to rest"), along with the divine name YHWH, is used for this rest, while the divine appellation אלהים = *'lhym* and the verb שבת = *šbt* ("to rest") are found in Gen. 2:3.

227. Cf. Vol. I, pp. 65f.

228. Accordingly one has concluded that the Sabbath originally may have been the day of the full

moon (thus, e.g., A. Lemaire, "Le Sabbat à l'époque royale israélite," *RB* 80, 1973, 161–185). Cf., however, by contrast E. Kutsch, "Der Sabbat—ursprünglich Vollmondtag?" *Kleine Schriften zum Alten Testament,* 1986 (BZAW 168), 71–77; Kutsch's criticism strikes in the end also at T. Veijola who likewise sees in the Sabbath in preexilic times the day of the full moon, while he considers the actual Sabbath as a day of rest and so forth to have originated for the first time in the postexilic period ("Die Propheten und das Alter des Sabbatgebots," in V. Fritz et al., eds., *Prophet und Prophetenbuch,* FS O. Kaiser, 1989 [BZAW 185], 246–264). To go along with this (hardly apt) derivation, one often finds that it is connected with the Akkadian *šapattu/šabattu* which can designate the day of the full moon (15th day of the month) (*AHw* III, 1172a). For the problematic nature of the Sabbath and the day of the full moon, cf. also E. Otto, *TRE* 11, 103.

229. External to the Old Testament but internal to Israel is the testimony concerning the Sabbath offered perhaps by line 7 in the petition of a harvester in Metzad Ḥašavyahu dating from the time around 600 B.C.E.

230. Thus with F. Crüsemann, *Bewahrung der Freiheit;* cf. also V. Hirth, *BN* NF 23, 1989, 216.

231. See, e.g., H.-J. Kraus, *Gottesdienst in Israel,* 2d ed., 1962, 57f., 104f.

232. Cf. further the Qumran texts, apocalyptic (Apocalypse of John!), rabbinic texts, etc.

233. Cf. H.-J. Kraus, *Gottesdienst in Israel;* and A. S. Kapelrud, "The Number Seven in Ugaritic Texts," *VT* 18, 1968, 494–499.

234. Thus R. de Vaux, *Ancient Israel,* 2:480.

235. The Sinai covenant shows through only here in P which does not mention it anywhere else. For this topic, cf. Vol. I, p. 386. For the problems of this passage, see M. Köckert, *JBTh* 4, 1989, 53–56.

236. Cf. also N. Negretti, *Il Settimo Giorno,* Rome, 1973.

237. Cf. as a contrast, e.g., the Epic of Atraḫasis, according to which humanity was created in order to free the gods from labor (there Tablet I, 1ff., 37ff., 149ff., and 240ff.). The German translation is made by W. von Soden, *ZA* 68, 1978, 50–94.

238. Cf. above, pp. 114–117.

239. "The liberating power of Yahweh breaks through here in exemplary and remarkable fashion to those who do not otherwise participate in it" (F. Crüsemann, *Bewahrung der Freiheit: Das Thema des Dekalogs in sozialgeschichtlicher Perspektive,* 1983, 58). For the absence of the married woman in this enumeration, cf. p. 108.

240. M. Köckert, *JBTh* 4, 1989, 52; however, a presentation that is probably too one-sided.

241. Ibid., 56.

242. See E. Ruprecht, "Stellung und Bedeutung der Erzählung vom Mannawunder (Ex 16) im Aufbau der Priesterschrift," *ZAW* 86, 1974, 269–307.

243. See M. Köckert, *JBTh* 4, 1989, 51ff.

244. For the so-called "Sabbath year," cf. Vol. I, pp. 126f.

245. See W. H. Schmidt, BK II/1, 228f., and the additional bibliography there. Also see W. Kornfeld, "Beschneidung," *NBL* 1, cols. 276–279; M. Köckert, *JBTh* 4, 1989, 33–44; and above, pp. 102–103.

246. Cf. above, p. 13.

247. Deut. 10:16; 30:6; Jer. 4:4; 6:10; 9:24f.; and Lev. 26:41; cf. also Lev. 19:23–25. See H.-J. Fabry, *ThWAT* 4, cols. 446f.

248. Cf. the literature cited on p. 329 n. 35; p. 386 nn. 219 and 222, as well as the article מהור *ṭhwr* ("clean") and ממא = *ṭm'* ("unclean") in *THAT* and *ThWAT.* Further, see D. P. Wright, *The Disposal of Impurity,* Atlanta, Ga., 1987 (SBL Diss. Ser. 101). Then see the overview by P. van Imschoot, *BL,* 2d ed., 1467–1470; and W. Eichrodt, *Theology,* 1:133–137.

249. Cf. above, p. 202.

250. For the source analysis of these complex chapters, see K. Elliger, HAT I/4, 1966, 140ff.

251. See R. de Vaux, *Les sacrifices de l'Ancien Testament,* Paris, 1964; R. Rendtorff, *Studien zur Geschichte des Opfers im Alten Israel,* 1967 (WMANT 24); and G. A. Anderson, *Sacrifices and Offerings in Ancient Israel,* Atlanta, Ga., 1987. Cf. further A. Bertholet, *Biblische Theologie des Alten Testaments* 2, 1911, 29–40, 48–50 (with the reckoning of the number of sacrificed animals); W. Eichrodt, *Theology,* 1:141–172; L. Köhler, *Theologie,* 4th ed., 172f.; G. von Rad, *Theology,* 1:250–262; and W. H. Schmidt, *Alttestamentlicher Glaube,* 6th ed., 152ff.

252. The sacrificial lists include the following terms, among others: *kll, dbḥ, šlmm, mnḥ,* and *šrp* (see, e.g., *KTU* 1.27; 31; 39–41). Blood, however, more than likely had no special cultic significance. Cf. J. Gray, *The Legacy of Canaan,* 2d ed., 1965 (VT Suppl 5), 195ff.; D. Kinet, *Ugarit,* 1981 (SBS 104), 144ff.; and O. Loretz, *Ugarit und die Bibel,* 1990, 121f.

253. Cf. G. van der Leeuw, *Phänomenologie der Religion,* 4th ed., 1977, 393ff.; and G. Widengren, *Religionsphänomenologie,* 1969, 280ff.

254. For the texts in Leviticus 1–5, 6–7, cf. the commentaries (M. Noth, *Levicticus;* K. Elliger, HAT I/4; and R. Rendtorff, BK III); R. Rendtorff, *Studien zur Geschichte des Opfers im Alten Israel;* and B. Janowski, *Sühne als Heilsgeschehen,* see the index.

255. For the locations of these texts, cf. above, pp. 64f.

256. What was the character of the sacrifice of Noah, e.g., after the primeval flood (Gen. 8:20), or what was the occasion and background of the sacrifices of Cain and Abel (Gen. 4:3f.)?

257. Cf. the תּוֹדָה (= *tôdâ,* "thanksgiving") sacrifice: Amos 4:5; Jer. 17:26; cf. Lev. 7:13, 15.

258. תָּמִיד = *tāmîd* ("continual, regular"): Exod. 29:38–42; and Num. 28:1–8.

259. Cf. above, pp. 62f.

260. Cf. Lev. 1:3f.; 7:18; and 17:4. "To credit," however, occurs only in Lev. 7:18 and 17:4; cf. above, pp. 161f. Cf. also the use of these terms in the (prophetic) polemic against the cult (cf. above, pp. 63 and 87: 1 Sam. 15:22f.; Isa. 1:11ff.; Hos. 6:6; Mal. 1:10ff.; 2:13; Pss. 40:7–9; and 51:8, 18. For the topic, see R. Rendtorff, *Studien zur Geschichte des Opfers im Alten Israel,* 253ff.; as well as H. M. Barstad, "רצה/רצוֹן *rāṣāh/rāṣôn,*" *ThWAT* 7, cols. 640ff.

261. Cf. above, pp. 63f.

262. See also B. Lang, "זבח/זבח *zābaḥ/zaebaḥ,*" *ThWAT* 2, cols. 509–531; and R. Rendtorff, BK III, 115–136.

263. Only זבח = *zebaḥ* ("sacrifice," "communion sacrifice") is encountered in the stories of the ancestors, with the exception of Genesis 22 (עוֹלָה = *'ôlâ;* "burnt offering").

264. In Deut. 32:17, 38 the root זבח = *zebaḥ* ("sacrifice") was also used for a sacrifice to foreign gods.

265. See B. Kedar-Kopfstein, "דם *dām,*" *ThWAT* 2, cols. 248–266; esp. 260ff. G. Andre, "זרק *zāraq,*" *ThWAT* 2, cols. 686–689; esp. 687; B. Janowski, *Sühne als Heilsgeschehen,* 222ff. and index; J. Wehrle, "Blut," *NBL* 1, cols. 306–308. In addition, cf. above, pp. 252–253 n. 212, for the blood ritual.

266. Cf. G. Gerleman, *THAT* 2, cols. 931f.

267. Exod. 29:27f. and Num. 10:10 are later additions.

268. Cf. only Deut. 27:1–8; 1 Sam. 10:8; 2 Sam. 24:25; 1 Kings 3:15; 2 Kings 16:13; etc.

269. Cf. R. Schmid, *Das Bundesopfer in Israel,* 1964 (StANT IX); W. Eisenbeis, *Die Wurzel* שלם *im Alten Testament,* 1969 (BZAW 113), 222–296; here one finds a discussion of every occurrence. Also cf. R. Rendtorff, BK III, 81–136.

270. R. Rendtorff (*Studien zur Geschichte des Opfers im Alten Israel,* 123ff.) denies this; cf. also B. Janowski, "Erwägungen zur Vorgeschichte des israelitischen ŠᵉLAMÎM-Opfers," *UF* 12, 1980, 231–259 (lit.).

271. B. Janowski, "Erwägungen zur Vorgeschichte des israelitischen ŠᵉLAMÎM-Opfers"; and G. A. Anderson, *Sacrifices and Offerings in Ancient Israel,* 36ff.

272. Cf. W. Eisenbeis, *Die Wurzel* שלם *im Alten Testament,* 244ff.

273. Cf. B. Janowski, *UF* 12, 1980, 257f.

274. Cf. only the famous sacrifice of the respective primeval heroes at the end of the flood and the reaction of the gods that then followed. See, e.g., *RGT,* 2d ed., 115 and 122 (Gilgamesh Epic, Tablet XI, lines 159f.).

275. Cf. Vol. I, pp. 163–165.

276. See also D. Kellermann, "עלה/עוֹלָה *'olāh/'ôlāh,*" *ThWAT* 6, cols. 105–124; R. Rendtorff, BK III, 15–80; and P. Weimar, "Brandopfer," *NBL* 1, cols. 321–323.

277. For the religiohistorical dissemination of the burning of sacrifices (e.g., not evidenced in Mesopotamia, Egypt, and Hatti, but only among certain groups of West Semites), cf. L. Rost, "Erwägungen zum israelitischen Brandopfer," in W. F. Albright et al., eds., *Von Ugarit nach Qumran,* FS O. Eissfeldt, 1958 (BZAW 77), 177–183 (= *Das kleine Credo,* 1965, 112ff.); and idem, *Studien zum Opfer im Alten Israel,* 1981 (BWANT 113), 11ff.

278. In addition to Gen. 8:21 (added?) and 1 Sam. 26:19, the expression occurs three times in Ex-

odus, 17 times in Leviticus, 18 times in Numbers, and 4 times in Ezekiel. See B. Janowski, *Sühne als Heilsgeschehen,* 217f. n. 176; and above, pp. 380–381 n. 57.

279. For these occasions, see R. Rendtorff, *Studien zur Geschichte des Opfers im Alten Israel,* 74–89. For the royal sacrifice, see N. Poulssen, *König und Tempel im Glaubenszeugnis des Alten Testaments,* 1967 (SBM 3); and above, p. 319 n. 38.

280. See H.-J. Fabry, "סמך *sāmak," ThWAT* 5, cols. 880–889; and R. Rendtorff, BK III, 32–34.

281. Cf. above, nn. 213 and 264.

282. In Judg. 11:31 and 2 Kings 3:27, עולה = *'ôlâ* is used to refer to human sacrifice (cf. Gen. 22:2).

283. See H.-J. Fabry and W. Weinfeld, "מנחה *minḥāh," ThWAT* 4, cols. 987–1001; and R. Rendtorff, BK III, 81–114.

284. Gen. 32:14; Judg. 3:15; and 1 Sam. 10:27.

285. For the production of incense, see the prescription in Exod. 30:34–38; and for the topic, D. Kellermann, *ThWAT* 4, col. 457.

286. Lev. 2:2, 9, 16; 6:8; and 24:7. See H. Eising, *ThWAT* 2, cols. 589–591. The translation is debated (fragrance sacrifice? commemorative sacrifice?).

287. See Chr. Dohmen, *ThWAT* 5, cols. 490–492.

288. Cf. above, n. 264.

289. Cf. Leviticus 16 and above, pp. 233f. For the topic, see the comprehensive study by B. Janowski, *Sühne als Heilsgeschehen.*

290. The number of the possible preexilic texts for the atoning, cultic actions between God and humans is small (e.g., Isa. 6:7?). Cf. B. Janowski, *Sühne als Heilsgeschehen,* 103–181 (summary: 175–181), for the passages outside the Priestly document.

291. See K. Koch, "חטא = *ḥāṭā' und Deriv.," ThWAT* 2, cols. 857–870; N. Kiuchi, *The Purification Offering in the Priestly Literature,* 21ff., 39ff.; and R. Rendtorff, BK III, 137ff.

292. See K. Kellermann, "אשם," *ThWAT* 1, cols. 463–472.

293. K. Koch, "חטא *ḥāṭā' und Deriv.," ThWAT* 2, cols. 866, 869, disputes this "translation" and thinks more in terms of the transfer of the חטאה (=*ḥaṭṭā't*) sphere by means of the representative death of an animal (p. 869).

294. See R. Rendtorff, *Studien zur Geschichte des Opfers im Alten Testament,* 200ff. Cf. R. de Vaux, *Ancient Israel,* 2:420–422; and above, p. 366 n. 553.

295. Cf. D. Kellermann, "אשם," 469: the offering of confession for every situation of gross negligence and finally the guilt offering in severe cases. R. Rendtorff, *Studien zur Geschichte des Opfers im Alten Testament,* 207–211, differentiates between sanctuary (חטאת = *ḥṭ't;* "sin offering") and the individual (אשם = *'šm;* "guilt offering"), at least in respect to the original use. For Lev. 14:13ff. and Num. 6:12 this distinction already has become difficult to make.

296. Heb. סלח = *slḥ* ("to forgive"); Lev. 4:20, 26, 31, 35; 5:10, 13, 16, 18, and 26. Cf. J. Hausmann, *ThWAT* 5, cols. 861f.; for this topic, cf. above, pp. 180f.

297. See H.-P. Müller, "מלך *molek," ThWAT* 4, cols. 957–968 (here: מלך = *mlk* as a sacrificial term); G. Heider, *The Cult of Molek,* 1985 (JSOT Suppl 34); here מלך = *mlk* is a deity). Agreeing with Heider are J. Lust, *EThL* 63, 1987; 361–366; and J. Day, *Molech: A God of Human Sacrifice in the Old Testament,* Cambridge et al., 1989. Cf. also WdM I, 299ff.; and *TUAT* II/4, 606–620 (Punic inscriptions for the MLK sacrifice).

298. H.-P. Müller, "מלך *molek,"* 967.

299. Cf. W. Eichrodt, *Theology,* 1:148–151; and R. Golling, *Zeugnisse von Menschenopfern im Alten Testament,* diss., Berlin (East), 1975 (see *ThLZ* 102, 1977, cols. 147–150).

300. Cf. W. Eichrodt, *Theology,* 1:152–154.

301. Cf. above, pp. 16 and 42.

302. For the problem of the king's title (1 Sam. 8:15, 17), cf. F. Crüsemann, in L. and W. Schottroff, eds., *Mitarbeiter der Schöpfung,* 1983, 90f.

303. Cf. Exod. 22:28b; the human firstborn was then redeemed: Exod. 13:2, 15; 34:20; and Num. 18:15; cf. also Neh. 10:37.

304. For this "creedal text," cf. Vol. I (also see its biblical index).

305. Cf. above, p. 242 (with n. 285); and R. E. Clements, "קטר *qṭr und Deriv.," ThWAT* 7, cols. 10–18 (see also the passages there).

306. See W. Zwickel, *Räucherkult und Räuchergeräte,* 1990 (OBO 97).

307. Thus with R. de Vaux, *Ancient Israel*, 2:451.
308. To be discussed in the ensuing section.
309. The numerous sacrifices perhaps cause one to ask here about the attitude of Old Testament humans toward animals. Cf. above, pp. 200–203.
310. See C. Westermann, *Praise and Lament in the Psalms*, Atlanta, 1981; E. S. Gerstenberger, *Der bittende Mensch*, 1980 (WMANT 51); R. Albertz, "Gebet. II: A. T.," *TRE* 12, 1984, 34–42; H. Graf Reventlow, *Gebet im Alten Testament*, 1986; and R. E. Clements, *The Prayers of the Bible*, London, 1986. Also see W. Eichrodt, *Theology* 1:172–176; P. Heinisch, *Theologie des Alten Testaments*, 1940, 204–212; G. von Rad, *Theology*, 1:355–370; W. Zimmerli, *Theology*, 148–155; and C. Westermann, *Theology*, 153–156.
311. Cf. also E. S. Gerstenberger, "עתר *'ātar*," *ThWAT* 6, cols. 489–491; and פלל *pll* und Deriv.," ibid., cols. 606–617. עתר *'tr* ("to make supplication") occurs, e.g., in Judg. 13:8; Job 33:26; Ezra 8:23; 2 Chron. 33:13, 19; פלל = *pll* hithpael ("to pray"; see also H.-P. Stähli, "פלל = *pll* beten," *THAT* 2, cols. 427–432) occurs, e.g., in 1 Sam. 2:1; 2 Sam. 7:27; 1 Kings 8:28f.; Dan. 9:20; and Ezra 10:1. It is striking that here פלל = *pll* hithpael ("to pray") can also be used for prayer to foreign gods (Isa. 16:12; 44:17; and 45:20). For קרא *qr'* ("to call"), cf. likewise *THAT* 2 and *ThWAT* 7.
312. Especially by E. S. Gerstenberger, *Der bittende Mensch*.
313. Thus R. Albertz, *TRE* 12, 35.
314. Even if probably not in the crass form presented by E. S. Gerstenberger (see his works on the Psalter cited below, n. 333; and p. 348 n. 142).
315. Ibid., 134.
316. R. Albertz correctly points to the significance of personal names, which can be small prayers in the form of names consisting of verbal clauses and expressions of thanks (*TRE* 12, 38).
317. E. S. Gerstenberger, *ThWAT* 6, col. 609.
318. See J. Schreiner, "Das Gebet Jakobs (Gen 32:10–13)," in FS J. Scharbert, 1989, 287–303.
319. Cf. Vol. I, pp. 189 + 216; above, pp. 21f.; and below, n. 324 and pp. 263f.
320. Cf. also B. Hornig, *Das Prosagebet der nachexilischen Zeit*, diss. theol., Leipzig, 1957 (Cf. *ThLZ* 83, 1958, cols. 644–646); and M. Greenberg, *Biblical Prose Prayer*, Berkeley, 1983.
321. See E. Aurelius, *Der Fürbitter Israels*, 1988 (CB OT 27).
322. Exod. 8:4–9, 24–27; 9:27–33; and 10:16–19.
323. Exod. 32:11ff., 30ff.; 33:12f.; 34:9; Num. 11:2, 11–15; 12:13; 14:13ff.; and 21:7ff.
324. "To cry" to the Lord (צעק = *ṣ'q*/זעק = *z'q*) has especially the promise of a positive reaction from YHWH according to Deuteronomistic texts. Cf. only Judg. 3:9, 15; 4:3; 6:6f.; 10:10, 12, 14; 1 Sam. 7:8; 12:10; etc. Cf. also Exod. 2:23f. P; 3:7, 9 JE; and Deut. 26:7 Deuteronomistic.
325. Jer. 11:18–12:6; 15:10–21; 17:14–18; 18:18–23; and 20:7–18. Cf. above, p. 91.
326. Cf. R. Albertz, "עתר," *'tr* beten," *THAT* 2, cols. 385f.; cf. pp. 178 + 244f.
327. See O. Plöger, "Reden und Gebete im deuteronomistischen und chronistischen Geschichtswerk," *Aus Spätzeit des Alten Testaments*, 1971, 50–66.
328. For the last-mentioned text, cf. J. Hausmann, "Gottesdienst als Gotteslob," in H. Wagner, ed., *Spiritualität*, 1987, 83–92.
329. Standing, which is seldom, is mentioned in 1 Sam. 1:9, 26; 1 Kings 8:22; and Jer. 18:20; kneeling is mentioned in 1 Kings 8:54; Isa. 44:17; Ps. 95:6; Ezra 10:1; and Dan. 6:11; and falling down on the ground is found in 2 Sam. 7:18; Isa. 45:14; etc. Cf. also *ThWAT* 2, cols. 789ff.
330. Cf. O. Keel, *Die Welt der altorientalischen Bildsymbolik und das Alte Testament: Am Beispiel der Psalmen*, 2d ed., 1977, 287ff.
331. See H. D. Preuss, "צום *ṣûm*," *ThWAT* 6, cols. 959–963; Th. Podella, *Ṣôm-Fasten: Kollektive Trauer um den verborgenen Gott im Alten Testament*, 1989 (AOAT 224).
332. Cf. L. Perlitt, "Die Verborgenheit Gottes," in H. W. Wolff, ed., *Probleme biblischer Theologie*, FS G. von Rad, 1971, 367–382; and Th. Podella (see the previous footnote).
333. Cf., above all, H.-J. Kraus, BK XV, 1–3, 5th ed., 1978; H. Seidel, *Auf den Spuren der Beter*, 1980; K. Seybold, *Die Psalmen: Eine Einführung*, 1986 (2d ed., 1991); E. S. Gerstenberger, *Psalms*, Part 1, with an Introduction to Cultic Poetry, Grand Rapids, 1988 (FOTL 14) [cf. above, p. 348 n. 142, + above, n. 314]; and H. Spieckermann, *Heilsgegenwart: Eine The-*

ologie der Psalmen, 1989 (FRLANT 148). Cf. the literature listed in n. 310, p. 390. See further chapter 8 for the psalms of Zion; chapter 7 for the royal psalms; Vol. I, pp. 153ff., for the YHWH enthronement hymns; and pp. 231–233 for the "enthronement festival." Also see Vol. I, pp. 227ff., for the creation psalms; and pp. 64ff. above for the "liturgies." Cf. also above, pp. 123–126.

334. Cf. H. Spieckermann, *Heilsgegenwart,* 285.

335. Cf. also H. D. Preuss, "Erfahrungen im betenden Umgang mit Psalmen," in H. D. Preuss, ed., *Erfahrung—Glaube—Theologie,* 1983, 43–64.

336. And not all the psalms that are collected in the Psalter are legitimate prayers, but also include reflections, instructive poems, liturgies, etc.

337. This is often somewhat different in the postexilic prayers where the address of God is expanded through the adding of hymnic elements. One obviously does not dare to do more in confronting God immediately and directly with one's concerns. Cf. Isa. 63:7ff.; Neh. 9:5ff.; 2 Chron. 20:5ff. Also see for these R. Albertz, *TRE* 12, 39. Cf., however, 2 Chron. 14:10.

338. Cf. the "my God," "my help," "my savior," "my shepherd," and "our God," the "shepherd of Israel," etc. For this, see H. Spieckermann, *Heilsgegenwart,* 276–279; see there also the passages cited. Further, see A. Aejmelaeus, "The Traditional Prayer in the Psalms," *BZAW* 167, 1986, 1–117.

339. This is found in the lament of the individual as well as the communal lament and elsewhere: Pss. 6:4; 10:1; 13:2; 22:12, 20; 27:9; 35:22; 42:3; 69:18; 74:10; 80:5; 90:13; 94:3, 8; and 119:82, 84. Cf. to the concealment of the divine face Vol. I, pp. 164–165. For the significance of the lament in the Book of Jeremiah, cf. above, pp. 91f.

340. AOT, 2d ed., 261f.; cf. Vol. I, p. 140.

341. Pss. 23:3; 25:11; 31:4; 79:9; and 109:21. Cf. Vol. I, p. 151.

342. Cf. Pss. 10:1; 22:2, 12, 20; 35:22; 38:22; and 71:12. Also 27:9; 30:8; 55:2; 69:18; 89:47; 102:3; 104:29; and 143:7. See also J. Ebach, " 'Herr, warum handelst du böse an diesem Volk?' " *Conc*(D) 26, 1990, 430–436.

343. That the judgment of the gods against a city was also known in Israel's ancient Near Eastern environment, along with the lament over this destruction that was, e.g., to move the gods to return to their abandoned city, is shown, e.g., in the Mesopotamian laments over Ur, Uruk, Nippur, and Eridu. Also known there are the "laments over the remote deity." Cf. p. 390 nn. 330–332 for the literature mentioned there; and J. Krecher, "Klagelied," *RLA* VI, 1–6, as well as J. H. Walton, *Ancient Israelite Literature in Its Cultural Context,* Grand Rapids, 1989, 160–163.

344. Cf. Vol. I, p. 155.

345. Cf. Vol. I, pp. 174f.

346. Cf., e.g., Pss. 9:10; 12:6; 14:6; 18:28; 35:10; 116:6; 140:13; 146:7; and 149:4.

347. Cf. Vol. I, pp. 261f., and above, p. 141ff.

348. See F. Ahuis, *Der klagende Gerichtsprophet,* 1982.

349. See esp. O. Keel, *Feinde und Gottesleugner,* 1969 (SBM 7). See also p. 348 n. 143.

350. K. Koch, *Was ist Formgeschichte?* 3d ed., 1974, 200. Cf. K. Koch, *The Growth of the Biblical Tradition,* New York, 1969, 163.

351. Cf. H. Graf Reventlow, *Gebet,* 172. In order to gain a look into the prayers of the cultures surrounding Israel, the following selections of texts (in translation) are offered: A. Falkenstein and W. von Soden, *Sumerische und Akkadische Hymnen und Gebete,* 1953; M. J. Seux, *Hymnes et prières aux Dieux de Babylonie et d'Assyrie,* Paris, 1976; J. Assmann, *Ägyptische Hymnen und Gebete,* 1975; R. Lebrun, *Hymnes et prières Hittites,* Louvain-La-Neuve 1980; *TUAT* II/5, 1989 [texts from the Mesopotamian region]; *TUAT* II/6, 1991 [Hittite, Ugaritic, and Egyptian texts]. See also J. H. Walton, *Ancient Israelite Literature in Its Cultural Context,* 135–168.

352. See previously only J. Köberle, "Die Motive des Glaubens an die Gebetserhörung im Alten Testament," in FS der Universität Erlangen für Prinzregent Luitpold von Bayern, 1901, 3–30. Cf. above, pp. 125–126.

353. See M. Möller, "Gebet und Kerygma in den Psalmen," *Theologische Versuche* 3, 1971, 11–29.

354. Cf. *TRE* 12, 302–304, esp. 303.

355. For a comprehensive study of this problem, see L. G. Perdue, *Wisdom and Cult*, Missoula, Mont., 1977 (also includes a look at the ancient Near Eastern cultures surrounding ancient Israel). J. Fichtner takes a brief look also at this theme (*Die altorientalische Weisheit in ihrer israelitisch-jüdischen Ausprägung*, 1933 [BZAW 62], 36ff.).

356. Cf. above, p. 258. See H. D. Preuss, *Einführung in die alttestamentliche Weisheitsliteratur*, 1987 (passim).

357. J. Fichtner, *Die altorientalische Weisheit in ihrer israelitisch-jüdischen Ausprägung*, 36.

358. Ibid., 43ff.; and H. D. Preuss, *Einführung in die alttestamentliche Weisheitsliteratur*, 138–147 (lit.).

359. Cf. W. Beyerlin, *Weisheitlich kultische Heilsordnung: Studien zum 15. Psalm*, 1985 (BThSt 9).

360. For this pair of ideas, cf. V. Vajta, *Die Theologie des Gottesdienstes bei Luther*, 1952.

361. See W. H. Schmidt, "Wort und Ritus," *PTh* 74, 1985, 68–83.

362. See above, pp. 67f. and 87ff.

363. Cf. for the cultus in Ugarit, e.g., O. Loretz, *Ugarit und die Bibel*, 1990, 95ff.; for the cultus in ancient Egypt, H. Bonnet, *Reallexikon der ägyptischen Religionsgeschichte*, 2d ed., 1971, 405–410; and for the cultus in ancient Mesopotamia, H. W. F. Saggs, *Mesopotamien*, 1966, 445ff.

364. Cf. G. von Rad, " 'Gerechtigkeit' und 'Leben' in der Kultsprache der Psalmen," in W. Baumgartner et al., eds., *Festschrift Alfred Bertholet zum 80. Geburtstag*, FS A. Bertholet, 1950, 418–437 (= TB 8, 3d ed., 1965, 225ff.).

365. Pss. 24:5; 36:11; 85:11ff.; 99:4; 118:19; 119:40; 143:11; and 145:7.

366. Cf. also above, pp. 197f., for ethics and ethos.

Chapter 14. The Future of the People of God (Expectations concerning the Future, Eschatology, Apocalyptic)

1. Selected literature includes H. Gressmann, *Der Ursprung der israelitisch-jüdischen Eschatologie*, 1905; S. Mowinckel, *Psalmenstudien*, 2: *Das Thronbesteigungsfest Jahwäs und der Ursprung der Eschatologie*, Kristiania (Oslo), 1922 (reprint: Amsterdam, 1961); H. Gressmann, *Der Messias*, 1929; E. Rohland, *Die Bedeutung der Erwählungstraditionen Israels für die Eschatologie der alttestamentlichen Propheten*, diss., Heidelberg, 1956; S. Mowinckel, *He That Cometh*, 2d ed., Oxford, 1959; O. Plöger, *Theokratie und Eschatologie*, (1959), 3d ed., 1968 (WMANT 2); S. Herrmann, *Die prophetischen Heilserwartungen im Alten Testament*, 1965 (BWANT 85); H.-J. Kraus, "Die ausgebliebene Endtheophanie," *ZAW* 78, 1966, 317–332 (= *Biblisch-theologische Aufsätze*, 1972, 134ff.); H. D. Preuss, *Jahweglaube und Zukunftserwartung*, 1968 (BWANT 87) [lit.]; W. Zimmerli, *Der Mensch und seine Hoffnung im Alten Testament*, 1968; H.-P. Müller, *Ursprünge und Strukturen alttestamentlichen Eschatologie*, 1969 (BZAW 109); F. Hecht, *Eschatologie und Ritus bei den Reformpropheten*, 1971; H. D. Preuss, "בוא," *ThWAT* 1, cols. 536–568; H. D. Preuss, ed., *Eschatologie im Alten Testament*, 1978 (WdF 480) [lit.]; J. Gray, *The Biblical Doctrine of the Reign of God*, Edinburgh, 1979; R. Smend, "Eschatologie. II: Altes Testament," *TRE* 10, 256–264 (lit.); W. H. Schmidt and J. Becker, *Zukunft und Hoffnung*, 1981; W. Werner, *Eschatologische Texte in Jesaja 1–39*, 1982 (fzb 46); idem, *Hermeneutik eschatologischer biblischer Texte*, Greifswald, 1983; D. E. Gowan, *Eschatology in the Old Testament*, Philadelphia, 1986, 1–31; J. Schreiner, "Eschatologie im Alten Testament," *Handbuch der Dogmengeschichte*, 4, Fasc. 7a, 1986; and G. Wanke, "Eschatologie (AT)," *NBL* 1, cols. 588–591 + 94 (lit.). Cf. also H. H. Rowley, *Faith*, 177ff.; and G. von Rad, *Old Testament Theology*, vol. 2: *The Theology of Israel's Prophetic Traditions*, New York, 1965, 112–125.

2. Cf. the different contributions and the introduction in the collection of essays, H. D. Preuss, ed., *Eschatologie im Alten Testament*. K. Koch (in J. Rohls and G. Wenz, eds., *Vernunft des Glaubens*, FS W. Pannenberg, 1988, 275, cf. 280) now understands the term "eschatology" as "the expectation of an age that in its structure and in its divine-human relationship contrasts with all previously experienced periods."

3. See chapter 10 above, pp. 67–96.
4. Cf. only R. Smend, *TRE* 10, 256f.
5. See below, pp. 255 + 274f.
6. Cf. above, pp. 37 + 93f.
7. Cf. above, pp. 80f.
8. Cf. above, pp. 26, 32f., 35.
9. Th. C. Vriezen, *An Outline of Old Testament Theology,* Oxford, 1958, 367 (cf. his essay in VT Suppl 1, 1953, 225f.).
10. Or must one point already to Hosea? Thus R. Kilian, "Überlegungen zur alttestamentlichen Eschatologie," in R. Kilian et al., eds., *Eschatologie, FS* E. Neuhäusler, 1981, 23–39, esp. 37 ("faded away unnoticed"). For this topic, cf. also D. Kinet, "Eschatologische Perspektiven im Hoseabuch," in ibid., 41–57.
11. R. Kilian, "Überlegungen zur alttestamentlichen Eschatologie," 32.
12. Cf. below, pp. 258ff.
13. Cf. also H. D. Preuss, "Eschatologie. 1. Im A. T.," *EKL,* 3d ed., vol. 1, cols. 1109–1111.
14. H. P. Müller, *Ursprünge und Strukturen,* 15ff., 129ff., and 173ff. (something too schematic?).
15. For the festival of enthronement, cf. Vol. I, pp. 157f.; and above, pp. 231–233.
16. Cf. also W. Werner, *Eschatologische Texte,* 12–16. Then see W. H. Schmidt, " 'Denk nicht mehr an das Frühere!' Eschatologische Erwartung—Aspekte des Alten Testaments," in *Glaube und Lernen* 4, 1989, 17–32; esp. 20f. for the prophetic-eschatological expectation that goes beyond the present conditions or even reaches beyond its possibilities: this expectation handles a future toward which God himself directly or indirectly shall lead; this future is thought of as imminent; it concerns the entire nation, and proceeds toward a universal horizon; it is no longer possible that this eschatology is either a continuation or maintenance of the given situation; where salvation is expected after judgment, this is to be final, lasting, and irreversible.
17. G. Wanke, "Eschatologie im Alten Testament," in ed. H. D. Preuss, ed., 352ff.
18. H. Gunkel, *Schöpfung und Chaos in Urzeit und Endzeit,* (1895), 2d ed., 1921: an ancient Near Eastern (esp. Babylonian) scheme of primeval time and end time.
19. H. Gressmann, *Der Ursprung der israelitisch-jüdischen Eschatologie:* a large complex of conceptualization from the prehistorical period, esp. of Babylonian origin; the influence of extra-Israelite conceptions of catastrophes.
20. Cf., e.g., E. Hornung, *Einführung in die Ägyptologie,* 1967, 111f., 117; J. Assmann, in B. Hellholm, ed., *Apocalypticism in the Mediterranean World and the Near East,* 2d ed., Tübingen, 1989, 345–377; and J. Assmann, *Ma'at: Gerechtigkeit und Unsterblichkeit im Alten Ägypten,* 1990, 58ff.; etc. Then see the references in W. H. Schmidt, *Glaube und Lernen* 4, 1989, 23, nn. 30 + 31.
21. *ΒΑΣΙΛΕΙΑ ΤΟΥ ΘΕΟΥ,* 1926.
22. See p. 278 n. 1.
23. Cf. also above, pp. 231–233.
24. G. Fohrer, "Die Struktur der alttestamentlichen Eschatologie," *ThLZ* 85, 1960, cols 401–420 (=BZAW 99, 1967,32–58; also in H. D. Preuss, ed., *Eschatologie im Alten Testament,* 147ff.).
25. "If G. Fohrer means that the proclamation of the final salvation in the future immobilizes human beings, then he contradicts with this view the experiences of those who believe in God and hope in him": G. Hentschel, "Alttestamentliche Eschatologie—ein Irrweg?" in J. Bernard, ed., *Heil in Zeit und Endzeit,* 1982, 46–58, esp. 53.
26. E. Sellin, *Die israelitisch-jüdische Heilandswartung,* 1909; idem, *Der alttestamentliche Prophetismus,* 1912, 103ff. (hope in a new theophany at Sinai).
27. L. Dürr, *Ursprung und Ausbau der israelitisch-jüdischen Heilandswartung,* 1925 (faith in YHWH as the helper of Israel).
28. O. Procksch, *Theologie,* 582 (Israel's faith in God holds to the future), however, without developing this more exactly. Cf. also R. Kilian, "Überlegungen zur alttestamentlichen Eschatologie."
29. Cf. to the following: H. D. Preuss, *Jahweglaube und Zukunftserwartung.*
30. Cf. Vol. I, pp. 141f. In what follows, cross-references are more seldom given, because, e.g.,

the corresponding chapters (as, e.g., in regard to the ancestral stories: chapter 6 etc.) can easily be found.

31. Cf. Vol. I, pp. 206–208.
32. Cf. even G. Fohrer, *ThZ* 26, 1970, 6: "Hope is provided . . . by community with God." For the connection of election and eschatology, cf. also K. Schubert, "Die jüdisch-christliche Oekumene—Reflexionen zu Grundfragen des christlich-jüdischen Dialogs," *Kairos* NF 22, 1980, 1–33.
33. H. H. Rowley, *Faith,* 177.
34. Above all, G. Fohrer, "Die Struktur der alttestamentlichen Eschatologie."
35. V. Maag, "Eschatologie als Funktion des Geschichtserlebnisses," *Saec.* 12, 1961, 123–130 (= *Kultur, Kulturkontakt und Religion,* 1980, 170ff.).
36. Cf. Vol. I, pp. 40–41.
37. Cf. R. Kilian, *Überlegungen zur alttestamentlichen Eschatologie,* 32.
38. Cf. Vol. I, pp. 207–208 and 212, and the literature listed there.
39. G. Fohrer, "Die Struktur. . . . ," in *Eschatologie im Alten Testament,* 171ff. Similarly already J. Hempel and G. Schneider (cf. H. D. Preuss, *Jahweglaube und Zukunftserwartung,* 78 n. 34); and also R. Kilian, *Überlegungen zur alttestamentlichen Eschatologie.*
40. H. Gross, *Der Idee des ewigen und allgemeinen Weltfriedens im Alten Orient und im Alten Testament,* 1956 (TThSt 7), 77 nn. 31 and 80, and n. 37.
41. G. von Rad, *Theology,* 2:99–125 (in dependence on E. Rohland; see above, n. 1).
42. For Gen. 6:13, cf. R. Smend, " 'Das Ende is gekommen': Ein Amoswort in der Priesterschrift," J. Jeremias and L. Perlitt, eds., *Die Botschaft und die Boten,* FS H. W. Wolff, 1981, 67–72; cf. above, p. 173.
43. Cf. also above, pp. 236f.
44. Cf. Vol. I, pp. 250 + 252.
45. Thus according to the Sumerian text, *RGT,* 2d ed., 110f.
46. Cf. H. D. Preuss, *Jahweglaube und Zukunftserwartung,* 1976, 108f.
47. H. D. Preuss, *Jahweglaube und Zukunftserwartung,* 214. Cf. also D. Kinet, "Eschatologische Perspektiven im Hoseabuch," 41: "Hosea's characteristic image of God is constitutive for his unusual perspective about the future" (cf. only Hos. 11:1–11).
48. W. Zimmerli, *Der Mensch und seine Hoffnung.*
49. C. Westermann, "Das Hoffen im Alten Testament," *ThViat* 4, 1952, 19–70 (= TB 24, 1964, 219ff.). See also W. Zimmerli, *Der Mensch und seine Hoffnung,* 8ff.
50. Cf. the corresponding articles in *THAT* and *ThWAT.*
51. See W. Zimmerli, *Der Mensch und seine Hoffnung,* 19ff.
52. So with W. Zimmerli, *Der Mensch und seine Hoffnung,* 37.
53. See Vol. I, pp. 184–194.
54. Prov. 10:2; 11:4, 19; 12:28; 13:14; 14:27; 15:24; 18:21; and 23:14.
55. Prov. 10:28; 11:23; 24:19f.; 26:12; and 29:20.
56. W. Zimmerli, *Der Mensch und seine Hoffnung,* 23ff.; C. Westermann, "Das Hoffen im Alten Testament," 228ff.; and H. D. Preuss, *Einführung in die alttestamentliche Weisheitsliteratur,* 1987, 98 (lit.).
57. See W. Zimmerli, *Der Mensch und seine Hoffnung,* 27ff.
58. Qoh. 2:12–17; 3:19–22; 6:6, 12; 7:1; 8:8; 9:4–6; 11:8; and 12:7.
59. For this topic, cf. D. Michel, *Untersuchungen zur Eigenart des Buches Qohelet,* 1989 (BZAW 183), esp. 116–125: "Qoheleth's polemic against the theologumenon of the overcoming of the destiny of death in Qoh. 3:19–22 and his conception of חלק = *ḥeleq* ("portion") of humanity."
60. See W. Zimmerli, *Der Mensch und seine Hoffnung,* 33ff.; and H. D. Preuss, *Jahweglaube und Zukunftserwartung,* 102–108.
61. Thus C. Westermann, TB 24, 220.
62. Jer. 14:8; cf. 17:13; and 50:7. Then see also Ps. 71:5: "my hope." Cf. Pss. 25:5, 21; 31:15; 38:16; 39:8; and 69:4.
63. Pss. 13:6; 31:15, 25; 33:20–22; 40:5; 84:13; 86:2; etc.; cf. also 7:2; 11:1; 16:1; etc.
64. Pss. 6:5; 11:7; 25:6; 31:2; etc.; and other similar expressions.
65. Pss. 5:12; 13:6; and 33:18; then also 25:6f.; 42:7; 45:18; etc.

66. Pss. 27:14; 37:5, 7; 42/43; 62:2, 6; and 131. Then see Psalm 73.
67. Lam. 3:25f.; Pss. 25:3; 33:18; 37:9; 40:5; 69:7; 146:5; and Isa. 49:23; cf. Pss. 130:7 ("Israel hopes in the Lord!"); and 131:3.
68. Cf. Pss. 25:3, 5, 21; 33:20ff.; Isa. 25:9; and 33:2.
69. Overall one may point here only to (without differentiations in literary strata and so forth) Ezekiel; Deutero-Isaiah; and the Holiness Code. Cf. also the "night visions" of Zechariah as a blueprint for the new community.
70. Cf. also above, pp. 245–250, for this prayer.
71. See W. Zimmerli, *Der Mensch und seine Hoffnung,* 49ff. For the condition of the text of J, cf. H. Seebass, *TRE* 16, 441–451, esp. 443–445. For the dating, cf. Vol. I, p. 41.
72. For the curse, see also Gen. 12:3b, 27, 29c; Num. 24:9c.; Deut. 27:15–26; and 28:16–19.
73. For the Priestly narrator in general, see W. Zimmerli, *Der Mensch und seine Hoffnung,* 66ff. Also see N. Lohfink, "Die Priesterschrift und die Geschichte," VT Suppl 29, 1978, 189–225 (SBAB 4, 1988, 213ff.). For P, cf. further Vol. I, pp. 217f. and 232f.
74. Cf. above, pp. 235–238 + 259.
75. For the covenant of Noah, cf. also Vol. I, pp. 72–74, 233. For the covenant of Abraham, see above, pp. 13f.
76. Cf. above, p. 222.
77. Cf. Vol. I, pp. 118f. and 121.
78. For the Deuteronomistic History, cf. Vol. I, pp. 188f. and 216f. Also cf. above, p. 154.
79. Cf. H. D. Preuss, *Deuteronomium,* 20ff., 75ff.; W. Zimmerli, *Theologie,* 6th ed., 156–159; and idem, *Der Mensch und seine Hoffnung,* 91ff.
80. Cf. Vol. I, pp. 73f.
81. Deut. 26:7; Josh. 24:7; Judg. 3:9, 15; 4:3; 6:6f.; 10:10, 12; 1 Sam. 9:16; and 12:8, 10. U. Becker (*Richterzeit und Königtum,* 1990 [BZAW 192], 78f.) attaches too little significance to this זעק = z'q ("to cry out").
82. Cf., e.g., 1 Kings 15:4f.; and above, pp. 27–28.
83. See E. Zenger, *BZ* NF 12, 1968, 16–30 (cf. above, p. 320 n. 68).
84. See H. D. Preuss, *Deuteronomium,* 24, 193, etc.
85. Cf. Vol. I, p. 119, for this and for the "oath" to the ancestors.
86. Deut. 3:20; 12:9; 25:19; 28:65; Josh. 1:13, 15; 21:43ff.; 22:4; 23:1; Judg. 3:30; 8:28; 1 Kings 5:18; and 8:56. See H. D. Preuss, *Deuteronomium,* 194; and *ThWAT* 5, cols. 297–307. Further, see G. Braulik, "Zur deuteronomistischen Konzeption von Freiheit und Frieden," VT Suppl 36, 1985, 29–39 (= SBAB 2, 1988, 219ff.).
87. See H. D. Preuss, *Deuteronomium,* 165–169, along with additional literature.
88. Cf. below, pp. 264–267.
89. This psalm is similar to Deuteronomy 32 and presupposes the writing of the Deuteronomistic History. Cf. T. Veijola, *Verheissung in der Krise,* Helsinki, 1982, 50ff.
90. This involves, above all, murmuring about creaturely necessities (water and nourishment: Exod. 15:22–25a; 17:1–7 and Num. 21:1–3; Exodus 16 and Numbers 11); the threat of enemies (Exod. 17:8–13, 15f.; scouts: Numbers 13–14); and murmuring on account of the position of Moses (Num. 12:1–16; Numbers 16). Cf. Vol. I, pp. 79–80.
91. See Vol. I, p. 293 n. 293, and the literature listed there. Cf. also H.-J. Zobel, "Die Zeit der Wüstewanderung Israels," VT 41, 1991, 201f.
92. W. Zimmerli, *Theology,* 176.
93. Cf. Vol. I, p. 78; and above, p. 178.
94. Whether a report of war with the Amalekites in 1 Samuel 15 belonged to the older textual stratum (as W. Dietrich argues; see the following note) is questionable due to Deut. 25:17–19 (Dtr.).
95. Cf. above, p. 24, and the literature mentioned in n. 31. Further, see W. Dietrich, *David, Saul, und die Propheten,* 1987 (BWANT 122), 10ff.
96. Cf. Deut. 20:1–9 to 1 Sam. 13:2ff. and Deut. 20:10–18 to 1 Samuel 15.
97. 2 Kings 23:27; Hos. 4:6; 9:17; Jer. 6:30; 7:29; 12:7f.; 23:33, 39; and 33:24. Cf. also Ps. 78:67f. For the theological meaning of the exile, cf. also D. L. Smith, *The Religion of the Landless,* Bloomington, Ind., 1989.
98. Cf. Th. C. Vriezen, *Die Erwählung Israels nach dem Alten Testament,* 1953 (AThANT 24), 99f.

99. That an allusion to 1 Samuel 15 exists here (and in Hos. 6:6; see J. Jeremias, *TRE* 15, 587) is unlikely.
100. See H. Ringgren, "Einige Schilderungen des göttlichen Zorns," in FS A. Weiser, 1963, 107–113; J. Bergman and E. Johnson, "אַנף," *ThWAT* 1, cols. 376–389 (other verbs for this subject are also found here along with additional passages to the ones mentioned here); and C. Westermann, "Boten des Zorns: Der Begriff des Zornes Gottes in der Prophetie," J. Jeremias and L. Perlitt, eds., *Die Botschaft und die Boten*, FS H. W. Wolff, 1981, 147–156.
101. The idea that the secondary addition of the formula of jealousy (DtrN, the stratum of Deuteronomic law) to the deed and consequence relationship may have introduced the concept of "unjustified divine judgment" (thus U. Becker, *Richterzeit und Königtum*, p. 75) completely misjudges the situation.
102. Pss. 44:10, 24; 60:3, 12; 74:1; 77:8, 10; 79:5f., 8; 80:5; 89:39, 47; etc. Cf. Lam. 1:12; 2:1ff.; 4:11; etc.
103. Cf. Vol. I, p. 164.
104. Deut. 31:17f.; 32:20; Micah 3:4; etc.
105. Pss. 44:25; and 89:47.
106. See L. Perlitt, "Die Verborgenheit Gottes," in FS G. von Rad, 1971, 367–382. Cf. also סתר = *str* ("to hide") in *THAT* and *ThWAT*.
107. Cf. C. Westermann, "Boten des Zorns," 151. He writes: "The wrath of God is limited; it has both a beginning and an end" (this is said even in regard to the prophecy of judgment).
108. See K. Seybold, "Gericht Gottes. I: A. T.," *TRE* 12, 460–466 (lit.). Further, see W. Eichrodt, *Theology of the Old Testament*, vol. 1 (OTL), Philadelphia, 1961, 457–471; L. Köhler, *Theologie*, 4th ed., 209ff.; W. Zimmerli, *Theology*, 183–200. Cf. to the following also chapter 10 (The Prophets) above and then esp. pp. 87–96.
109. Cf. also H. D. Preuss, *Jahweglaube und Zukunftserwartung*, 154–204. However, there are several texts (e.g., concerning the idea of the "remnant") that, in terms of literary and/or redaction criticism, are judged differently than my present assessment.
110. Amos 2:13; 4:3; 5:27; 6:7, 9f.; and 7:1, 4, 9, 11–17.
111. Cf. Vol. I, p. 142.
112. Hos. 1:5; 2:11ff.; 4:3f.; 5:7, 12, 14; 7:12, 15, 16; 8:3, 13; 9:3; 10:6, 14f.; 11:5f.; 12:10; 13:7ff.; 14:1; etc.
113. "Here the love of God, with all its passion, breaks through in all its illogicality (or, more accurately, its own peculiar logic)" W. Zimmerli, *Theology*, 190.
114. Cf. Vol. I, pp. 240f.
115. For the judgment also against Assyria, cf. below, p. 288.
116. Jer. 1:13ff.; 4:5–31; 5:15–17; 6:1–8, 22–26; 8:16f.; 10:22; 13:20; and 25:9.
117. E. Noort, "JHWH und das Böse," *OTS* 23, 1984, 120–136, esp. 131. Cf. also Chr. Dohmen, *ThWAT* 7, cols. 607–609.
118. Cf. above, pp. 77f.
119. Cf. Vol. I, p. 137.
120. For this problem, cf. the important essay by O. Keel, "Rechttun oder Annahme des drohenden Gerichts?" *BZ* NF 21, 1977, 200–218. Cf. also L. Markert and G. Wanke, "Die Propheteninterpretation: Anfragen und Überlegungen," *KuD* 22, 1976, 191–220.
121. Cf. W. Zimmerli, *Das Gesetz und die Propheten*, 1963, 105; and idem, *Theology*, 186, 192–193.
122. O. Keel, "Rechttun oder Annahme des drohenden Gerichts?" 202.
123. Ibid., 210.
124. Ezek. 37:1–14 (cf. there v. 11). Then see Amos 4:3; 5:5, 27; 6:7; 7:17; and 9:1–4, 8a.
125. Cf. already above, p. 78. Also see the literature there (nn. 88f.).
126. Cf. yet Amos 5:4–6, 14f.; Hos. 5:15; 6:6; 12:3–7; 14:2, 5; Isa. 1:16f., 18ff.; 7:4–9; 28:16f.; 30:15; and 31:6. G. Sauer contests the existence of "repentance" in Isaiah (H. J. Stoebe et al., eds., *Wort, Gebot, Glaube*, FS W. Eichrodt, 1970, 277–295). However, in this regard, one shall have to pay attention not only to the word but also to the function of prophetic preaching. Subsequently, cf. also H. W. Hoffmann, *Die Intention der Verkündigung Jesajas*, 1974 (BZAW 136). See further, Micah 6:6–8; Zeph. 2:1–3; Ezek. 3:17b, 21; Jer. 3:6ff., 12f., 14f.; 4:1f., 3f., 14; 6:8; 13:15–17; 18:11; 21:11b-12; and 25:5. Moreover, in the Book of Je-

remiah the theme of "repentance" appears predominantly pre-Deuteronomistic (see T. Odashima, *Heilsworte im Jeremiabuch*, 1989 [BWANT 125]) and Deuteronomistic texts. Accordingly, "repentance" was a prophetic demand that was not heeded (Jer. 18:12; 25:4) yet continues to be a demand that stands as a new proposition before the people of YHWH (e.g., Jer. 25:4ff.; 26:2ff.; 31:5ff.; 36:3, 7; etc.).

127. Thus G. von Rad, *Theology*, 2:115. Here occurs the famous sentence: "To my mind, it is far more important to realise that there is this break which goes so deep that the new state beyond it cannot be understood as the continuation of what went before." Cf. also W. Eichrodt, *Theology*, 1:385: "The certainty that history will be finally broken off and abolished in a new age."

128. See O. Kaiser, *Einleitung in das Alte Testament*, 5th ed., 1984, 307f.; etc.

129. Cf. the similarity in the conception of the remnant; see sec. 8, which immediately follows.

130. Thus with R. Smend, *TRE* 10, 263. For the theme of "resurrection," cf. above, pp. 151–153.

131. See J. Hausmann, *Israels Rest*, 1987 (BWANT 124).

132. Ibid., 215.

133. For the "war of the brothers" articulated in these texts, cf. K. Koenen, *Ethik und Eschatologie im Tritojesajabuch*, 1990 (WMANT 62), 157–208.

134. See E. Jenni, "יוֹם *jōm* Tag," *THAT* 1, cols. 723–726 (see the additional literature cited here). Cf. further G. Eggebrecht, "Die früheste Bedeutung und der Ursprung der Konzeption vom 'Tage Jahwes,' " *Theologische Versuche* 13, 1983, 41–56. For the Day of YHWH as the "Day of Wrath," see H. Spieckermann, "Dies Irae," *VT* 39, 1989, 194–208. Cf. also G. von Rad, *Theology*, 2:119–125.

135. The text in Micah 7:4 is unclear.

136. Cf. below, p. XXX.

137. Isa. 13:6; Ezek. 7:7; Joel 1:15; 2:1; 4:14; and Zeph. 1:7, 14.

138. Cf. H. D. Preuss, *Jahweglaube und Zukunftserwartung*, 174–176 along with its literature.

139. See H. Seebass, "אַחֲרִית," *ThWAT* 1, cols. 224–228.

140. See M. Wagner, "קֵץ *qēṣ* Ende," *THAT* 2, cols. 659–663; and S. Talmon, "קֵץ *qēṣ*," *ThWAT* 7, cols. 84–92.

141. See R. Smend, " 'Das Ende is gekommen': Ein Amoswort in der Priesterschrift," in J. Jeremias and L. Perlitt, eds., *Die Botschaft und die Boten*, FS H. W. Wolff, 1981, 67–72.

142. See also W. Eichrodt, *Theology*, 1:472–511.

143. Hos. 2:4a; 4:4–11; 5:5, 12, 14; 6:1–6; 8:3, 7; 9:10–17; and 13:1–14:1.

144. Hos. 3:5; 5:15; 10:10; 13:12–14; and 14:2f.

145. For the possible stages in a "history of the theology" of the statements of hope and texts about repentance in the Book of Hosea, cf. J. Jeremias, "Zur Eschatologie des Hoseabuches," in J. Jeremias and L. Perlitt, eds., *Die Botschaft und die Boten*, FS H. W. Wolff, 1981, 217–234.

146. Cf. above, p. 120.

147. Cf. Isa. 28:5f. For the conception of the remnant in Isaiah 1–39, see p. 271.

148. For Micah 5:1–4a, see above, p. 37.

149. Nevertheless, the verse does not belong to the "legitimate" texts in the Book of Jeremiah; cf. S. Herrmann, BK XII, 67–72. Cf., however, for the entire problem N. Kilpp, *Niederreissen und aufbauen*, 1990 (BThSt 13); and S. Herrmann, *Jeremia: Der Prophet und das Buch*, 1990 (EdF 271).

150. Pre-Deuteronomistic (however, not Jeremianic; why not exactly?) words of salvation are found in the Book of Jeremiah by T. Odashima, *Heilsworte im Jeremiabuch*. These are found, e.g., in Jer. 2:2–3:4, 3:12f*, 21–25; and 10:19f. For chapter 32, cf. also p. 92 and Vol. I, p. 121.

151. Thus with N. Kilpp, *Niederreissen und aufbauen*, 179, 182.

152. See C. Westermann, *Prophetic Oracles of Salvation in the Old Testament*, Louisville, Ky., 1991 with differentiations made according to writings or corpora of texts, contents, chronological arrangement, salvation for Israel or disaster for the nations, pledge of salvation, promise of salvation, description of salvation, and many others factors.

153. See H. D. Preuss, *Deuterojesaja;* and W. Grimm and K. Dittert, *Deuterojesaja: Das Trostbuch Gottes*, 1990. D. Michel presents another viewpoint ("Deuterojesaja," *TRE* 8, 510–530;

lit.). A better differentiation is offered by H.-J. Hermisson, "Einheit und Komplexität Deuterojesajas," in J. Vermeylen, ed., *The Book of Isaiah,* Louvain 1989 (BETL 81), 287–312. For Deutero-Isaiah's words of salvation, see also C. Westermann, *Prophetic Oracles,* 39–66; and W. Zimmerli, *Theology,* 215–227.

154. Cf. Vol. I, pp. 136f.
155. Isa. 40:3–5, 9–11; 41:17–20; 43:16–21; 48:20f.; 49:14–17, 18ff.; 51:3, 9–15; and 52:1–2, 7–10, 11f. Cf. Vol. I, pp. 43f. and 156.
156. Isa. 44:1–6; 45:14–17, 18–25; 41:17–20; 45:1–7; and 49:24–27.
157. H. D. Preuss, *Deuterojesaja,* 31. For the message of the postexilic prophets, see above, pp. 94–96, and below, p. 292.
158. For the role of Cyrus and for the covenant of David in Deutero-Isaiah, cf. above, p. 37; for the "Servant of God," cf. below, pp. 303–305; for creation theology, cf. Vol. I, pp. 234f.; and for the kingship of YHWH, cf. Vol. I, pp. 156f.
159. See above, pp. 34ff.
160. See also H.-P. Müller, *Ursprünge und Strukturen,* 173ff.
161. See above, pp. 44f., and the index.
162. See R. Mosis, "Die Wiederherstellung Israels," in R. Mosis and L. Ruppert, eds., *Der Weg Zum Menschen,* FS A. Deissler, 1989, 110–113.
163. And Psalm 51 changes this promise into a prayer for individuals; cf. W. H. Schmidt, " 'Denkt nicht mehr an das Frühere!' Eschatologische Erwartung—Aspekte des Alten Testaments," in *Glaube und Lernen* 4, 1989, 17–32, esp. 17–19.
164. See also H.-J. Kraus, "Schöpfung und Weltvollendung," *EvTh* 24, 1964, 462–485 (= *Biblisch-theologische Aufsätze,* 1972, 151ff.).
165. Cf. Vol. I, pp. 160f.
166. Jer. 31:31–34; Ezek. 36:24–28 (cf. vv. 16–23 as a contrast); Isa. 42:1–4; 49:6; 51:1–8; then also Isa. 2:2–4 and Micah 4:1–5.
167. Cf. Vol. I, pp. 236.
168. See H. D. Preuss, *Jahweglaube und Zukunftserwartung,* 61 + 141 (with the passages and literature).
169. W. H. Schmidt, *Glaube und Lernen* 4, 1989, 27. Cf. also H. D. Preuss, *EKL,* 3d. ed., vol. 1, col. 1110: "The goal of the journey of God is the establishment of his full sovereignty, and it is not humanity alone that solves its own problems as well as those of the world."
170. Cf. again C. Westermann, *Prophetic Oracles.*
171. Cf. above, pp. 65f.
172. See F. Hecht, *Eschatologie und Ritus bei den Reformpropheten.*
173. Cf. above, p. 397 n. 128.
174. G. von Rad, *Theology,* 2:301–308.
175. For wisdom, such a theme occurs first in the early Jewish wisdom books of Jesus ben Sirach and, above all, the Wisdom of Solomon.
176. "In this thinking beyond the deliverance of Israel, which is to be announced immediately, to what is to happen next, an apocalyptic course is proclaimed. . . . What is proclaimed is the program of a predetermined course for the future established by a mysterious, transcendent act of God in which humanity itself plays no active role" (W. Zimmerli, *Der Mensch und seine Hoffnung,* 153).
177. See J. Becker, *Israel deutet seine Psalmen,* 1966 (SBS 18), 49ff., 45ff.
178. Thus H. Gese, "Anfang und Ende der Apokalyptik, dargestellt am Sacharjabuch," *ZThK* 70, 1973, 20–49 (= *Vom Sinai zum Zion,* 3d ed., 1990, 202ff.).
179. Cf. I. Willi-Plein, *Prophetie am Ende,* 1974 (BBB 42).
180. D. E. Gowan esp. stresses the significance of Zion in the Old Testament eschatology (*Eschatology in the Old Testament*).
181. Cf. in addition to the commentary by H. W. Wolff (BK XIV/2, 1969, 3d. ed., 1985) esp. H. P. Müller, "Prophetie und Apokalyptik bei Joel," *ThViat* 10, 1965/1966, 231–252; and S. Bergler, *Joel als Schriftinterpret,* 1988.
182. Cf. above, pp. 271–274.
183. In addition to the commentaries, see esp. M.-L. Henry, *Glaubenskrise und Glaubensbe-*

währung in den Dichtungen der Jesajaapokalypse, 1967 (BWANT 86); and W. R. Millar, *Isaiah 24–27 and the Origin of Apocalyptic,* Missoula, Mont., 1976.

184. Cf. above, pp. 151–153, for the theme "resurrection."

185. See H. D. Preuss, " 'Auferstehung' in Texten alttestamentlicher Apokalyptik," in U. Gerber and E. Güttgemanns, eds., *"Linguistische" Theologie,* 1972, 101–133.

186. See H. H. Rowley, *Apokalyptik,* 3d ed., 1965; J. M. Schmidt, *Die jüdische Apokalyptik,* (1969), 2d ed., 1976; P. von der Osten-Sacken, *Die Apokalyptik in ihrem Verhältnis zu Prophetie und Weisheit,* 1969 (ThEx 157); J. Schreiner, *Alttestamentlich-jüdische Apokalyptik,* 1969; K. Koch, *Ratlos vor der Apokalyptik,* 1970; H. D. Preuss, "Texte aus dem Danielbuch (mit Einführung in die alttestamentliche Apokalyptik)," in *Calwer Predigthilfen,* 6, 1971, 213–315; W. Schmithals, *Die Apokalyptik,* 1973; P. D. Hanson, *The Dawn of Apocalyptic,* Philadelphia, 1975; I. Willi-Plein, "Das Geheimnis der Apokalyptik," *VT* 27, 1977, 62–81; *Apocalypses et théologie de l'espérance,* Paris 1977; D. S. Russell, *Apocalyptic, Ancient and Modern,* London, 1978; J. Lebram and K. Müller, "Apokalyptik/Apokalypsen. II: AT und III: Die frühjüdische Apokalyptik: Anfänge und Merkmale," *TRE* 3, 192–202 + 202–251 (lit.); J. Coppens, *La relève apocalyptique du messianisme royale,* 2 vols., Louvain, 1979 +1983 (BETL 50, 61); K. Koch and J. M. Schmidt, eds., *Apokalyptik,* 1982 (WdF 365) (lit.); P. D. Hanson, ed., *Visionaries and Their Apocalypses,* London 1983; J. J. Collins, "The Place of Apocalypticism in the Religion of Israel," in P. D. Miller, Jr., et al., eds., *Ancient Israelite Religion,* FS F. M. Cross, Philadelphia, 1987, 539–558; D. Hellholm, ed., *Apocalypticism in the Mediterranean World and the Near East,* 2d ed., Tübingen, 1989; P. R. Davies, "The Social World of Apocalyptic Writings," in R. E. Clements, ed., *The World of Ancient Israel,* Cambridge, 1989, 251–271; K. Müller, "Apokalyptik," *NBL* 1, cols. 124–132; cf. also C. Westermann, *Theology,* 149–152; W. H. Schmidt, *Alttestamentlicher Glaube,* 6th ed., 324ff.; and the thematic volume, J. J. Collins, ed., *Apocalypse: The Morphology of a Genre, Semeia* 14, 1979.

187. In addition to the commentaries, cf., above all, K. Koch (and collaborator), *Das Buch Daniel,* 1980 (EdF 144); J. Lebram, "Daniel/Danielbuch," *TRE* 8, 325–349 (lit.); J. J. Collins, *Daniel with an Introduction to Apocalyptic Literature,* Grand Rapids, 1984 (FOTL 20); and E. Haag, " 'Daniel' und 'Daniel(Buch),' " *NBL* 1, cols. 383–387.

188. Since we are limiting our study to the Old Testament canon, the development of the Enoch literature, so important for early Jewish apocalyptic, but not present in the Old Testament, will not be examined. However, see below, n. 189.

189. J. J. Collins, ed., "Introduction: Towards the Morphology of a Genre," *Semeia* 14, 1979, 9.

190. See K. Koch, "Vom profetischen zum apokalyptischen Visionsbericht," in D. Hellholm, ed., *Apocalypticism,* 413–446.

191. For "vision," cf. also K. Berger, *Hermeneutik des Neuen Testaments,* 1988, 391–394. See also pp. 412ff. for apocalyptic metaphorical language and other matters. Also see H. S. Kvanvig, "The Relevance of the Biblical Visions of the End Time," *HorBibTheol* 11 (1), 1989, 35–58.

192. Both terms are used by and in I. Willi-Plein, "Das Geheimnis der Apokalyptik."

193. Cf. E. Osswald, "Zum Problem der vaticinia ex eventu," *ZAW* 75, 1963, 27–44.

194. Cf., e.g., F. König, *Zarathustras Jenseitsvorstellungen und das Alte Testament,* 1964; O. Kaiser and E. Lohse, *Tod und Leben,* 1977, 76f.; and J. Maier, *Zwischen den Testamenten* (NEB AT, Supplement, vol. 3), 1990, 31–34, 122–125.

195. Cf. K. Müller, *TRE* 3, 212f.; and O. Kaiser and E. Lohse, *Tod und Leben,* 71ff.

196. So with H.-P. Müller, "Mantische Weisheit und Apokalyptik," *VT* Suppl 22, 1972, 268–293.

197. Cf. the works by P. von der Osten-Sacken, H. D. Preuss, and K. Koch mentioned above in n. 186.

198. See K. Koch, "Spätisraelitisches Geschichtsdenken am Beispiel des Buches Daniel," *HZ* 193, 1961, 1–32 (= *Apokalyptik,* 276ff.).

199. *KTU* 1.17–19. See K. Kinet, *Ugarit,* 1981 (SBS 104), 118–126; and B. Margalit, *The Ugaritic Poem of AQHT,* 1989 (BZAW 182).

200. Thus, e.g., now *4 Ezra* 7:50.

201. For the theme of "resurrection," cf. above, pp. 151–153.

202. Cf. Vol. I, p. 224.
203. Cf. Vol. I, pp. 158f.
204. In my opinion, the major question in the Book of Daniel and in apocalyptic as a whole is not "What is God doing in the end time?" (so W. H. Schmidt, *Alttestamentlicher Glaube*, 6th ed., 326).
205. Cf. above, p. 137.

Chapter 15. The Chosen People of God and the Nations

1. See A. Bertholet, *Die Stellung der Israeliten und der Juden zu den Fremden*, 1896; H. Gross, *Weltherrschaft als religiöse Idee im Alten Testament*, 1953 (BBB 6); F. M. Th. de Liagre-Böhl, "Missions und Erwählungsgedanke in Alt-Israel," in his *Opera Minora*, Groningen and Djakarta, 1953, 81–100; J. Hempel, "Die Wurzeln des Missionswillens im Glauben des Alten Testaments," *ZAW* 66, 1954, 244–272; R. Martin-Achard, *Israël et les nations*, Neuchâtel and Paris, 1959; A. Rétif and P. Lamarche, *Das Heil der Völker*, 1960; P. Altmann, *Erwählungstheologie und Universalismus im Alten Testament*, 1964 (BZAW 92); N. K. Gottwald, *All the Kingdoms of the Earth*, New York, 1964; H.-M. Lutz, *Jahwe, Jerusalem und die Völker*, 1968 (WMANT 27); J. Schreiner, "Berufung und Erwählung Israels zum Heil der Völker," *BuL* 9, 1968, 94–114; H. Schmidt, *Israel, Zion und die Völker*, diss., Zurich, 1966 (Marburg, 1968); L. Perlitt, "Israel und die Völker," in G. Liedke, ed., *Studien zur Friedensforschung* 9, 1972, 17–64; G. Liedke, "Israels als Segen für die Völker," in ibid., 65–74; P. E. Dion, *Dieu universel et peuple élu*, Paris, 1975; F. Huber, *Jahwe, Juda und die anderen Völker beim Propheten Jesaja*, 1976 (BZAW 137); W. Gross, "YHWH und die Religionen der Nicht-Israeliten," *ThQ* 169, 1989, 34–44; and B. Malchow, "Causes of Tolerance and Intolerance toward Gentiles in the First Testament," *BThBull* 20, 1990 (1), 3–9. Cf. also Th. C. Vriezen, *An Outline of Old Testament Theology*, Oxford, 1958, 227–231; and W. H. Schmidt, *Alttestamentlicher Glaube*, 6th ed., 319ff.
2. Th. C. Vriezen, *Theology*, 76: "For instance, the truth of Israel's election is an untruth if it is rationally understood to mean that *for that reason* God has rejected the nations of the world, that *for that reason* Israel is of more importance to God than those other nations, for Israel was only elected in order to serve God in the task of leading those other nations to God."
3. H. H. Rowley, *The Biblical Doctrine of Election*, 2d ed., London, 1964, 45.
4. Cf. Vol. I, pp. 40–49.
5. Each of these two sources has a different purpose that certainly stands behind these differently accentuated statements.
6. Cf. above, chapter 8 (pp. 39–51).
7. For this topic, cf. W. Dietrich, *Israel und Kanaan*, 1979 (SBS 94). For the prohibition against making covenants with the nations and their gods (Exod. 23:32; 34:12f.; Deut. 7:2; and Judg. 2:2), see esp. E. Schwarz, *Identität durch Abgrenzung*, 1982, 41ff.; and J. Halbe, *Das Privilegrecht Jahwes Ex 34:10–26*, 1975 (FRLANT 114).
8. Cf. above, pp. 49f. For similar ideas in Israel's Near Eastern environment, cf. H. Schmidt, *Israel, Zion und die Völker*, 412ff.
9. Vol. I, pp. 155ff.
10. Cf. above, pp. 87–92.
11. Cf. below, pp. 291f.
12. O. Oeming, *Das wahre Israel*, 1990 (BWANT 128), 91.
13. With the LXX and 4QDtn one is to read here "sons of the gods" instead of the "sons of Israel." See R. Meyer, "Die Bedeutung von Dtn 32:8f., 43 (4Q) für die Auslegung des Moseliedes," in A. Kuschke, ed., *Verbannung und Heimkehr*, FS W. Rudolph, 1961, 197–209.
14. Cf. below, pp. 303–305.
15. Cf. Vol. I, pp. 104–107, and pp. 111–117.
16. Cf. sec. 2, immediately following.
17. Cf. Th. C. Vriezen, *Die Erwählung Israels nach dem Alten Testament*, 1953 (AThANT 24), 34.
18. Cf. Vol. I, pp. 59f.
19. Cf. above, chapter 7 (pp. 19–38).

20. For the following section, cf. esp. P. E. Dion, *Dieu universel et peuple élu,* 21–140.
21. See the more detailed discussion in L. Perlitt, "Israel und die Völker," 19ff.
22. Cf. Vol. I, p. 281 n. 3.
23. See J. Schreiner, "Segen für die Völker in der Verheissung an die Väter," *BZ* NF 6, 1962, 1–31; and idem, *Segen für die Völker,* 1987, 196ff.
24. Cf. above, p. 11, with n. 70. Differently, G. Liedke, *Israel als Segen für die Völker,* 67ff.
25. See F. Kohata, *Jahwist und Priesterschrift in Exodus 3–14,* 1986 (BZAW 166), 175, 188.
26. Cf. ibid., 189.
27. Cf. Vol. I, p. 42.
28. Also cf. K. Jaroš, *Die Stellung des Elohisten zur kanaanäischen Religion,* 1974 (OBO 4).
29. See O. Bächli, "Zur Aufnahme von Fremden in die altisraelitische Kultgemeinde," in H. J. Stoebe et al., eds., *Wort, Gebot, Glaube,* FS W. Eichrodt, 1970 (AThANT 59), 21–26.
30. Cf. only C. Westermann, *Genesis 12–36: A Commentary* (CC), Minneapolis, 1985, 541–542, for this passage.
31. From the extensive literature on this topic, see particularly J. Barton, *Amos's Oracles against the Nations,* Cambridge, 1980. Cf. also B. Gosse, *Isaie 13,1–14,23,* 1988 (OBO 78).
32. Cf. L. Perlitt, "Israel und die Völker," 59f.
33. The oracles against Tyre (Amos 1:9ff.), Edom (1:11f.), and Judah (2:4f.) are mostly and correctly seen as secondary.
34. Micah 4:1–5 is secondary.
35. Cf. H. W. Wolff, BK XIV/4, 14f.
36. F. Huber, *Jahwe, Juda und die anderen Völker beim Propheten Jesaja;* J. Høgenhaven, *Gott und Volk bei Jesaja,* 1988, 114–168; G. I. Davies, "The Destiny of the Nations in the Book of Isaiah," in J. Vermeylen, ed., *The Book of Isaiah,* Louvain, 1989 (BETL 81), 93–120.
37. Cf. to Isaiah also above, pp. 44f., for the "Zion tradition."
38. Cf. above, pp. 278f.
39. Cf. also below, pp. 298f.
40. See B. Gosse, *Isaie 13,1–14:23.*
41. Cf. also the brief description of the messages of individual prophets in chapter 10 (above, pp. 87–96).
42. See G. Schmitt, *Du sollst keinen Frieden schliessen mit den Bewohnern des Landes,* 1970 (BWANT 91).
43. Cf. Vol. I, pp. 136–137.
44. Cf. H. Klein, "Die Aufnahme Fremder in die Gemeinde des Alten und Neuen Bundes," *ThBeitr* 12, 1981, 21–42, esp. 27f.
45. See H. D. Preuss, *Deuteronomium,* 142f. with literature.
46. Cf. above, n. 13.
47. Cf. V. Hirth, "Der Dienst fremder Götter als Gericht Jahwes," *BN* 45, 1988, 40f.
48. Cf. 2 Kings 18:34f.; Jer. 2:28; Micah 7:10; and Ps. 115:2. Then see Exod. 32:12; Deut. 9:26–28; 28:37; 1 Kings 9:7; Jer. 24:9; 25:9; 29:18; Ezek. 22:4; 23:32; 36:4; Pss. 44:14; 79:4; 89:42; and 2 Chron. 7:20.
49. See Vol. I, p. 124.
50. Cf. above, pp. 179f.
51. Cf. S. Herrmann, BK XII, 59, who remarks about this issue that "it is difficult to move beyond matters of opinion"; and ibid., pp. 60f.: "The validity of his words should reach beyond Judah and be of exemplary significance for the nations."
52. For the relationship of Israel/Judah and Edom, cf. H.-J. Fabry, in F.-L. Hossfeld, ed., *Vom Sinai zum Horeb,* 1989, 67–72.
53. Ezek. 17:22–24; 29:6; 36:23, 36; 37:28; 38:16; and 39:7, 23; cf. 21:10 ("all flesh"). Cf. Vol. I, pp. 205–207.
54. Ezek. 20:9, 14, 22, 44; 28:22; and 39:7, 13.
55. In Exod. 6:7; 16:6, 12; and 29:46 (P) with Israel as the knowing subject, i.e., the one who is to know YHWH.
56. J. Schreiner, "Berufung und Erwählung Israels zum Heil der Völker," 102.
57. Isa. 41:17–20; 45:4–6; and 49:26; cf. 45:14–17, 18–25.
58. Cf. Vol. I, p. 34.

59. See A. Wilson, *The Nations in Deutero-Isaiah*, Lewiston, N.Y., and Queenston, Ontario, 1986.
60. Cf. P. E. Dion, *Dieu universel et peuple élu*, 55f.; and H. D. Preuss, *Verspottung fremder Religionen im Alten Testament*, 1971 (BWANT 92), passim.
61. Cf. E. Zenger, "Der Gott Abrahams und die Völker: Beobachtungen zu Psalm 47," in FS J. Scharbert, 1989, 413–430. His findings are largely followed here.
62. Cf. Vol. I, pp. 155f.
63. "Whether Ps. 47:10a intends to say something that extends beyond the relationship of the people of God to the nations (or whether this redactional addition had seen here a theological problem) is an open question. If one considers the fact that even texts such as Isa. 60:3ff.; 66:23; Zech. 14:16; Ps. 102:23; etc., keep the nations and Israel separate, although they make the nations clearly into worshipers of YHWH, the answer appears to me to be negative" (E. Zenger, "Der Gott Abrahams und die Völker,"429).
64. For more precise details, see O. H. Steck, "Tritojesaja im Jesajabuch," in J. Vermeylen, ed., *The Book of Isaiah*, Louvain,1989 (BETL 81), 361–406, esp. 386ff.
65. See H. Utzschneider, *Künder oder Schreiber?* 1989, 84ff.
66. Does this actually have to do with a "breathtaking diminishment of Jerusalem's claim of cultic privilege, i.e., esp. made by its priests"? (thus, H. Utzschneider, ibid., 57).
67. See M. Oeming, *Das wahre Israel*.
68. For this process as a whole, see E. Schwarz, *Identität durch Abgrenzung*, 1982.
69. Cf. the elegant study by J. Jeremias, *Die Reue Gottes*, 1975 (BSt 65); and Vol. I, pp. 244–246.
70. This is the only place in the Old Testament where Exod. 34:6 (par.) is associated with pagans. Cf. to this formula also Vol. I, pp. 241–243; and H. Spieckermann, "'Barmherzig und gnädig ist der Herr'," *ZAW* 102, 1990, 1–18. He states in regard to the Book of Jonah: "The little prophetic book is an outstanding affirmation and application of the formula of grace" (p. 16).
71. This literature does not approach existence on the basis of Israelite faith and identity even when using the language of the "fear of God"! For this, cf. above, pp. 157f.
72. In Job 12:9, there probably exists a scribal error. Cf. Vol. I, p. 140.
73. Cf. G. Fohrer, KAT XVI, 117f.
74. J. Wellhausen, *Israelitische und jüdische Geschichte*, 9th ed., 1958, 24: "The military camp, the cradle of the nation, was also the oldest sanctuary. There Israel was, and there Yahweh was." For this topic, see Vol. I, pp. 128–138.
75. Cf. pp. 300–303.
76. Cf. B. Lang, "נכר *nkr*," *ThWAT* 5, cols. 454–462; L. A. Snijders, "זור/זר *zur/zar*," *ThWAT* 2, cols. 556–564; P. Welten, "Zur Frage nach dem Fremden im Alten Testament," FS R. Mayer, 1986, 130–138; L. Schwienhorst-Schönberger, "'... denn Fremde seid ihr gewesen im Lande Ägypten,'" *BiLi* 63, 1990, 108–117.
77. Thus B. Lang, "נכר *nkr*," *ThWAT* 5, col. 459.
78. P. Welten, "Zur Frage nach dem Fremden im Alten Testament," 133.
79. B. Lang, "נכר *nkr*," *ThWAT* 5, col. 457.
80. See D. Kellermann, "גור und Deriv.," *ThWAT* 1, cols. 979–991; there esp. cols. 989f. for תושׁב, "a sojourner," who is often mentioned alongside the stranger and is difficult to distinguish from him (see below). Cf. also, L. Schwienhorst-Schönberger, "'... denn Fremde seid ihr gewesen im Lande Ägypten.'"
81. Exod. 22:20; 23:9; Lev. 19:10, 33; 23:22; Deut. 14:29; 24:17, 19–21; 26:13; 27:19; Jer. 7:6; Ezek. 22:7; Zech. 7:10; Mal. 3:5; etc. However, "Out of the many stipulations for protection of the widows and the orphans in the ancient Near Eastern legal collections, there is not a single known passage where this protection may be applied to strangers. Such stipulations for protection appear to represent a unique feature of Israel" (P. Welten, "Zur Frage nach dem Fremden im Alten Testament," with reference to Th. Krapf, "Traditionsgeschichtliches," *VT* 34, 1984, 87–91).
82. Lev. 19:34; Deut. 10:19; cf. 23:8 (in Edom); 26:5 (verb); Ps. 105:23; Isa. 52:4; 1 Chron. 16:19; cf. Acts 13:17; Eph. 2:19; and also Gen. 15:13.

83. With Heb. עֶבֶד = *'ebed* ("slave"): Deut. 5:15; 15:15; 16:12; and 24:18, 22. Compare also 7:18; 16:3; 24:9; and 25:17. Thus, this is a common theme in Deuteronomic and Deuteronomistic literature. Israel's "act of remembering" is provoked by the historical references back to the period in Egypt and the liberation that brought the slaves out from there. For these arguments, cf. L. Schwienhorst-Schönberger, *Das Bundesbuch (Ex 20,22–23,33)*, 1990 (BZAW 188), 338–357, 386f.
84. Cf. Vol. I, pp. 38 + 44.
85. Thus F. A. Spina, "Israelites as *gērîm* 'Sojourners,' in Social and Historical Context," in C. L. Meyers and M. O'Connor, eds., *The Word of the Lord Shall Go Forth*, FS D. N. Freedman, Winona Lake, Ind., 1983, 322–335, esp. 322f. (in combination with *'apiru*).
86. Thus P. Welten, "Zur Frage nach dem Fremden im Alten Testament," 136.
87. D. Kellermann, *ThWAT* 1, col. 991.
88. This term is found 13 times in the Old Testament.
89. Gen. 23:4; Exod. 12:45; Lev. 22:10; 25:6, 23, 35, 40, 45, 47[2]; and Num. 35:15.
90. K. Elliger, HAT I/4, 293f.; cf. D. Kellermann, *ThWAT* 1, col. 990.
91. Cf. Vol. I, pp. 132 + 136–137. Whether the oracles against the foreign nations were components of the Old Testament cultus (Nahum against Assyria?) is debated.
92. See P. Höffken, *Untersuchungen zu den Begründungselementen der Völkerorakel des Alten Testaments*, diss., Bonn, 1977; and B. Malchow, "Causes of Tolerance and Intolerance toward Gentiles in the First Testament," 3f.
93. Cf. chapter 8 (pp. 41–51).
94. Cf. also Vol. I, pp. 136–137.
95. Cf. K. Seybold, *TRE* 12, 463, for this topic.
96. For a more detailed view of Isaiah 35, see O. H. Steck, *Bereitete Heimkehr*, 1985 (SBS 121), 42f. and also 49ff.
97. Cf., e.g., Isa. 10:24–27; 14:24–27; 17:12–14; 49:23, 26; Joel 2:18–20; and Zech. 9:1–8. See C. Westermann, *Prophetic Oracles of Salvation in the Old Testament*, Louisville, Ky., 1991, 195–203.
98. Cf. Vol. I, pp. 136f.
99. Ezek. 29:6; 36:23, 36; 38:16; 39:23; cf. Josh. 4:24; and 1 Kings 8:60. For this topic, cf. W. Zimmerli, TB 51, 203, and above, p. 291.
100. Cf. above, p. 290.
101. Cf. above, pp. 47f.
102. According to Isa. 42:24b, Israel does *not* do either of these!
103. For Isaiah 60, cf. B. Langer, *Gott als "Licht" in Israel und Mesopotamien*, 1989 (ÖBS 7); and below n. 115.
104. Isa. 2:2–4; 11:10; 18:7; 27:13; Micah 4:1–5; Jer. 3:17; 16:19 (cf. Isa. 45:14f.; 49:22f.); Pss. 46:10; and 76:4; cf. also Hos. 1:5; 2:20; Micah 5:9–13; Zech. 9:10; etc. For this topic, see also R. Bach, "'. . . der Bogen zerbricht, Spiesse zerschlägt und Wagen mit Feuer verbrennt,'" in H. Wolff, ed., *Probleme biblischer Theologie*, FS G. von Rad, 1971, 13–26.
105. Cf. Vol. I, pp. 152–159.
106. Isa. 56:6f.; cf. 45:23; 60:1–14; 66:18f., 23; Zech. 14:16f.; 1 Kings 8:41ff.; and 2 Chron. 6:32f.
107. For the difficult efforts at identification (Assyria = Persian? Both powers = the Diadochi? etc.) as well as the question about the unity of the text, cf. the commentaries. For the theological upshot of this issue, cf. H. Wildberger, BK X/2, 746.
108. For Exodus 24, cf. Vol. I, p. XX. For this topic, see H. Wildberger, "Das Freudenmahl auf dem Zion," *ThZ* 33, 1977, 373–383 (= TB 66, 1979, 274ff.).
109. For Zeph. 3:9f., cf. O. H. Steck, *BZ* NF 34, 1990, 90–95.
110. Isa. 40:5; 41:4f., 20; 43:8–13; 44:5, 6–8 (the blessing of the ancestors from Gen. 12:3 is echoed here); 45:3, 20–24; 49:22f., 26; and 55:4f.; cf. Ezek. 21:4, 10, "all flesh"; Isa. 19:16–25. For the last-mentioned text: J. Schreiner, *Segen für die Völker*, 215ff.; P. E. Dion, *Dieu universel et peuple élu*, 107ff.; and B. Renaud, "Das Verhalten Israels den Völkern gegenüber als prophetische Kritik," *Conc* (D) 24, 1988, 455–461, esp. 459f. (also for Isaiah 19).

111. Cf. above, p. 11.
112. Cf. Vol. I, pp. 66f.
113. See pp. 303–305, immediately following.
114. For a different view, see esp. P. Volz, KAT IX/2, 1932. Then see F. M. Th. de Liagre-Böhl, *Opera Minora,* 95f.; and esp. E. Sellin, "Der Missionsgedanke im Alten Testament," *AMZ,* 1925, 33–45, 66–72; cf. also P. Altmann, *Erwählungstheologie und Universalismus,* 26: "Israel's commission is a mission to the world." However, in agreement with my argument, see W. Zimmerli, *EvTh* 22, 1962, 26f.: "In Deutero-Isaiah, however, the recognition breaks through in a complete way that in the renewed act of forgiveness for Israel this people shall become a witness to the great acts of YHWH before the eyes of the nations. They will be a witness to YHWH's mighty acts, not through intentional missions and proclamation but rather through their experience of YHWH's forgiveness. This forgiveness of Israel must be spoken about in the world of the nations."
115. "Mission therefore inaugurates the final period in preparing the way for the sole worship of Yahweh in the world": J. Hempel, "Die Wurzeln des Missionwillens," *ZAW* 66, 1954, 263; cf. esp. 270. For Isaiah 60 (1–3), cf. above, n. 104; and O. H. Steck, "*Lumen Gentium*— Exegetische Bemerkungen zum Grundsinn von Jesaja 60,1–3," in W. Baier et al., eds., *Weisheit Gottes, Weisheit der Welt,* FS J. Kard. Ratzinger, vol. 2, 1987, 1279–1294.
116. Cf. W. Zimmerli, "Der Wahrheitserweis Jahwes nach der Botschaft der beiden Exilspropheten," in E. Würthwein and O. Kaiser, eds., *Tradition und Situation,* FS A. Weiser, 1963, 133–151 (= TB 51, 1974, 192ff.).
117. 1 Kings 8:41–43; Isa. 56:1–8; then esp. in the Books of Chronicles in regard to members of the former Northern Kingdom: 2 Chron. 15:1–15; 19:4; and 28:9–15. 2 Chron. 15:1–7 is often seen as an example of a postexilic synagogue sermon.
118. Th. C. Vriezen, *Theology,* 354.
119. Therefore the following thesis, e.g., is overstated and too one-sided: "The universal dominion of God's interest in history is as precisely proclaimed in the canonical Old Testament as it is later in the New Testament, in spite of the Old Testament's clear emphasis on the special election of Israel. This is at least the case at the end of the Old Testament period in which the New Testament itself is indeed situated" (N. Lohfink, "Die Sorge Gottes um die rechte Gesellschaft—Eine gemeinsame Perspektive von Altem und Neuem Testament," in M. Klopfenstein et al, eds., *Mitte der Schrift?* 1987, 357–384, esp. 374). The "universal dimension of God's interest in history" is not at all clear everywhere in the Old Testament. Indeed, this theme is by no means attested as it is in the New Testament. This assessment is not intended to be a value judgment but rather wishes to establish the facts clearly. The texts consulted time and again (and also by N. Lohfink, ibid., 376f.) that speak of the nations' pilgrimage to Zion are only two or three among many; many more passages (Joel 4; Zechariah 14; etc.) stand in opposition to them.
120. Cf. K. Berger, *Hermeneutik des Neuen Testaments,* 1988, 140 (here he makes a critical separation between W. Pannenberg and himself).
121. Cf. N. Lohfink, "Die Universalisierung der 'Bundesformel' in Ps 100,3," *ThPh* 65, 1990, 172–183.
122. The possible stratification of this text will not be examined here. Cf. above, pp. 93f.
123. See H. D. Preuss, *Deuterojesaja: Eine Einführung in seine Botschaft,* 1976, 92ff.; and esp. H. Haag, *Der Gottesknecht bei Deuterojesaja,* 1985 (EdF 233) [lit.]. Cf. also Zimmerli, *Old Testament Theology in Outline,* Atlanta, 1978, 221–224.
124. Cf. H.-J. Hermisson, "Israel und der Gottesknecht bei Deuterojesaja," *ZThK* 79, 1982, 1–24.
125. Cf. esp.: E. Kutsch, *Sein Leiden und Tod—unser Heil,* 1967 (BSt 52); and O. H. Steck, "Aspeckte des Gottesknechts in Jes 52,13 - 53,12," *ZAW* 97, 1985, 36–58.
126. Thus with J. Jeremias, "מַשְׁפָּט im ersten Gottesknechtlied," *VT* 22, 1972, 31–42.
127. Cf. above, p. 243.
128. The explanation of the "many" is certainly debated. Cf., e.g., H.-J. Hermisson, *ZThK* 79, 1982, 16–24 (Israel, the congregation). However, he also says in his essay in FS H. W. Wolff, 1981, 285–287, esp. p. 287: "Because Israel returns to Yahweh through the servant, Yahweh's plan is successful through him, for the nations then come to salvation" (cf. *ZThK* 79,

1982, 24). Even more plain is the statement by O. H. Steck, "Aspekte des Gottesknechtes in Jes 52, 13—53, 12," *ZAW* 97, 1985, 40: "Israel is meant."
129. Cf. above, pp. 141–146.
130. Whether Isaiah 53 produces an aftermath in Zech. 12:9ff. is debated. In any case, the designation of the "many" has become important, moreover, for the Qumran community. The expression was already significant in Dan. 12:2f., and later perhaps in Mark 10:45 and the words of institution for the Eucharist.
131. Thus with W. Zimmerli, *Theology*, 238–240. Cf. also G. von Rad, *Old Testament Theology*, vol. 2: *The Theology of Israel's Prophetic Tradition*, New York, 1965, 357–387; and E. Zenger, *BiLi* 63, 1990 (3), 134f.
132. Cf. H. D. Preuss, *Das Alte Testament in christlicher Predigt*, 1984, 22ff., for the relationship of the New and Old Testaments, and esp. 29ff.
133. For such theses in the work of E. Hirsch and R. Bultmann, cf. H. D. Preuss, ibid., chap. 5; also see this chapter on the whole for what follows.
134. Cf. W. Zimmerli, *EvTh* 22, 1962, 28.
135. Cf. only John 15:16 or Romans 9–11.
136. Thus, e.g., already Jepsen (see Vol. I, p. 271 n. 24) and others (cf. Vol. I, p. 12).

ENGLISH TRANSLATIONS OF SELECTED GERMAN AND FRENCH BOOKS

Boman, Thorlief. *Das hebräische Denken im Vergleich mit dem griechischen* (1952); ET, *Hebrew Thought Compared with Greek*, trans. Jules L. Moreau (New York, 1970).

Bottéro, Jean, *Mésopotamie* (1987); ET, *Mesopotamia: Writing, Reasoning, and the Gods*, trans. Zainab Bahrani and Marc Van De Mieroop (Chicago, 1992).

Botterweck, G. Johannes, and Helmer Ringgren, eds. *Theologisches Wörterbuch zum Alten Testament* (1973–); ET, *Theological Dictionary of the Old Testament*, trans. John T. Willis (Grand Rapids, 1974–).

Buber, Martin. *Königtum Gottes* (3d newly rev. ed., 1956); ET, *Kingship of God*, trans. Richard Scheimann (3d newly enlarged ed., London, 1967).

Eichrodt, Walther. *Theologie des Alten Testaments 1. Gott und Volk* (8th ed., 1968); ET, *Theology of the Old Testament 1*, trans. J. A. Baker (OTL, Philadelphia, 1961; based on Eichrodt's 6th ed., 1959).

———. *Theologie des Alten Testaments 2 and 3. Gott und Welt/Gott und Mensch* (7th ed., 1974); ET, *Theology of the Old Testament 2*, trans. J. A. Baker (OTL, Philadelphia, 1967; based on Eichrodt's 5th ed., 1964).

Fohrer, Georg. *Geschichte der israelitischen Religion* (1969); ET, *History of Israelite Religion*, trans. David C. Green (Nashville, 1972).

Gerstenberger, Eberhard, and Wolfgang Schrage. *Leiden* (1977); ET, *Suffering*, trans. John E. Steely (Nashville, 1980).

Gunneweg, A. H. J. *Vom Verstehen des Alten Testaments: Eine Hermeneutik* (2d rev. ed., 1988); ET, *Understanding the Old Testament*, trans. John Bowden (Philadelphia, 1978). Based on the first German edition, 1977.

Gurney, O. R., Die Hethiter (1969), German trans. of *The Hittites* (London, 1952).

Herrmann, Siegfried. *Zeit und Geschichte* (1977); ET, Time and History, trans. James L. Blevines (Nashville, 1981).

Jacob, Edmond. *Théologie de l'Ancien Testament* (rev. ed., 1968); German trans. *Grundfragen alttestamentlicher Theologie* (1970). ET, *Theology of the Old Testament,* trans. Arthur W. Heathcote and Philip A. Allcock (London, 1958), based on the first French edition published in 1955.

Kittel, Rudolf. *Die Religion des Volkes Israel* (2d rev. ed, 1929); ET, *The Religion of the People of Israel,* trans. R. Caryl Micklem (New York, 1925).

Koch, Klaus. *Die Profeten* (2d ed., 1987); ET, *The Prophets,* 1 and 2, trans. by Margaret Kohl (Philadelphia, 1984). Based on the first German edition, 1978.

Köhler, Ludwig. *Theologie des Alten Testaments* (4th ed., 1966); ET, *Old Testament Theology,* trans. A. S. Todd (London and Philadelphia, 1957). English translation based on German first edition (1953).

Miskotte, K. H., *Wenn die Götter schweigen* (1963); ET, *When the Gods Are Silent,* trans. and intro. John W. Doberstein (London, 1967). English translation based on the Dutch original, *Als de goden zwijgen: over de zin van het Oude Testament* (1956).

Morenz, Siegfried. *Ägyptischen Religion* (1960); ET, *Egyptian Religion,* trans. Ann E. Keep (Ithaca, N.Y., 1973).

Rad, Gerhard von. *Theologie des Alten Testaments, 1: Die Theologie der geschichtlichen Überlieferungen* (5th ed., 1966); ET, *Theology of the Old Testament, 1: Theology of Israel's Historical Traditions,* trans. D. M. G. Stalker (New York, 1962; based von Rad's 2d ed., 1957).

————. *Theologie des Alten Testaments 2. Die Theologie der prophetischen Überlieferungen,* (4th ed., 1965); ET, *Theology of the Old Testament 2. The Theology of Israel's Prophetic Traditions,* trans. D. M. G. Stalker (New York, 1965). Based on von Rad's first edition.

Saggs, H. W. F. *Mesopotamien* (1966). German translation of *The Greatness That Was Babylon: A Survey of the Ancient Civilization of the Tigris-Euphrates Valley* (London, 1962); fully revised English version published in 1988.

Schmidt, W. H. *Alttestamentlicher Glaube in seiner Geschichte* (6th ed., 1987); ET, *The Faith of the Old Testament: A History,* trans. John Sturdy (Philadelphia). Based on the 4th German edition, 1982.

Smend, Rudolf. *Jahwekrieg und Stämmebund* (2d ed., 1966); ET, *Yahweh War and Tribal Confederation. Reflections upon Israel's Earliest History,* trans. Max Gray Rogers (Nashville, 1970).

Vaux, Roland de. *Das Alte Testament und seine Lebensordnungen* 1 and 2 (2d ed., 1964). Based on the French first edition, *Les Institutions de l'Ancien Israel* (1961); ET, *Ancient Israel: Its Religious and Social Institutions,* trans. John McHugh (London, 1961).

Vriezen, Th. C., *Theologie des Alten Testaments in Grundzügen* (1956). *An Outline of Old Testament Theology,* trans. by S. Neuijen (Newton, Mass., 1962). Based on the second Dutch edition, *Hoofdlijnen der Theologie van het Oude Testament* (1954).

Wellhausen, Julius. *Prolegomena zur Geschichte Israels* (9th. ed., 1958); ET, *Prolegomena to the History of Ancient Israel,* trans. J. Sutherland Black and Allan Menzies (Gloucester, Mass., 1973).

Westermann, Claus. *Der Segen in der Bibel und im Handeln der Kirche* (1968); ET, *Blessing in the Bible and the Life of the Church,* trans. Keith R. Crim (Philadelphia, 1978).

————. *Theologie des Alten Testaments in Grundzügen* (2d ed., 1985); ET, *Elements of Old Testament Theology,* trans. D. W. Stott (Atlanta, 1982). Based on the first German edition, 1978.

Wolff, H. W. *Anthropologie des Alten Testaments* (3d ed., 1977); ET, *Anthropology of the Old Testament,* trans. Margaret Kohl (Philadelphia, 1974). Based on the first German edition (1973).

Zimmerli, Walther. *Grundriss der alttestamentlichen Theologie* (6th ed., 1989); ET, *Old Testament Theology in Outline,* trans. D. E. Green (Atlanta, 1978; based on Zimmerli's 1975 revision of the first edition).

INDEX OF HEBREW WORDS

Volume I

Volume II

Index of Hebrew Words

SELECT INDEX OF BIBLICAL CITATIONS

(Old Testament books are listed in the order of the Hebrew Bible.)

INDEX OF SUBJECTS

When a subject cannot be found on the referenced page,
it may be found in one of the endnotes for that page.